IDEAS ACROSS TIME

Classic and Contemporary Readings for Composition

Igor Webb
Adelphi University

Boston Burr Ridge, IL Dubuque, IA New York
San Francisco St. Louis Bangkok Bogotá Caracas Kuala Lumpur
Lisbon London Madrid Mexico City Milan Montreal New Delhi
Santiago Seoul Singapore Sydney Taipei Toronto

Published by McGraw-Hill, an imprint of The McGraw-Hill Companies, Inc., 1221 Avenue of the Americas, New York, NY 10020.

This book is printed on acid-free paper.

2 3 4 5 6 7 8 9 0 FGR/FGR 0 9 8 7

ISBN-13: 978-0-07-288261-2
MHID: 0-07-288261-1

Editor-in-chief/Vice president: *Emily Barrosse*
Publisher: *Lisa Moore*
Sponsoring editor: *Christopher Bennem*
Director of development: *Carla Samodulski*
Development editor: *Bennett Morrison*
Editorial coordinator: *Jesse Hassenger*
Marketing manager: *Tamara Wederbrand*
Media producer: *Christie Ling*
Production editor: *Mel Valentín*
Design manager: *Cassandra Chu*
Text designer: *Glenda King*
Cover designer: *Cassandra Chu*
Photo research coordinator: *Natalia Peschiera*
Photo researcher: *Jennifer Blankenship*
Art editor: *Robin Mouat*
Production Supervisor: *Randy Hurst*
Composition: *ICC Macmillan Inc.*
Printer: *Quebecor World, Fairfield*

Cover (clockwise from top left): Library of Congress, Library of Congress, © Jon Hrusa/epa/Corbis, Library of Congress, Library of Congress, © Stephanie Pilick/dpa/Corbis

Credits: The credits section for this book begins on page 720 and is considered an extension of the copyright page.

Library of Congress Cataloging-in-Publication Data

Ideas across time: classic and contemporary readings for composition / [compiled by] Igor Webb
p. cm.
Includes index.
ISBN-13: 978-0-07-288261-2
ISBN-10: 0-07-288261-1
1. College readers. I. Webb, Igor
PE1417 .I34 2007
808/.0427 22 2006047028

www.mhhe.com

Table of Contents

Preface

Ideas Across Time aims to support students' exploration of their lives and of the world around them by explicitly linking everyday experience in the United States today with writing by major thinkers, past and present. Each chapter illuminates how we got here from there, making reading more meaningful and writing better informed. Each chapter treats a different significant aspect of life today, such as identity, democracy, science, or art, establishing a reasonably coherent narrative of the development of today's institutions, knowledge, beliefs, ideologies, and practices.

In each chapter, the readings begin with a Keynote essay, usually right out of the morning newspaper, intended to emphasize the immediacy and broad implications of the subject. These contemporary selections are followed by a chronological sequence of essays that trace the historical development of the idea under discussion. Although a number of the pieces that follow the Keynote selection are from classical Greece or Rome, for the most part these essays date back to around two hundred years ago and proceed chronologically to the present. Each chapter, moreover, not only begins but also ends with a contemporary essay, allowing students to reexamine our present-day slant on the subject at hand after having had the chance to explore key texts from the past. Most chapters also include literary works and visual material that can deepen understanding and stimulate writing.

Each essay is supported by a complete apparatus—a series of questions about content, rhetoric, and connections among ideas intended to help focus reading and to encourage reflective writing. The book's Introduction offers a helpful prospectus to college-level reading; and a guide to writing is found in the Appendix. Although each selection is meant mainly to be read for itself, the apparatus in each case leads to further exploration of a topic or an author and, in conjunction with the website, can be a good starting point for an essay or research paper. Each chapter opens with a general introductory essay, aimed to orient students to the intellectual terrain of the chapter; and each selection opens with a headnote providing useful information about the writer or artist of the selection to follow.

As a venture into the major questions of our time, *Ideas Across Time* contains essays and visual material that can be at once unsettling and exhilarating. Carefully read and thoughtfully explored, the combination of provocative contemporary readings and generative readings from the past found in this book provides not only a broad and strong foundation for liberal studies but also an authentic encounter with knowledge and its transformative power.

Supplements

Reading selections are supported online at the *Ideas Across Time* Online Learning Center, which has been designed to be integral to the text. On the website, you will find connections to further readings or to the complete online texts of works that *Ideas Across Time* has excerpted, as well as links to contextual information. The website enables students to probe every issue in depth. It also features instructional writing content powered by Catalyst, McGraw-Hill's premier online learning tool.

Acknowledgments

This book would never have seen the light of day without the encouragement and counsel of my friend and colleague Harvey Wiener, whose long devotion to enlarging students' ambitions in their reading and writing has been an enormous resource in bringing *Ideas Across Time* to fruition.

I have been extremely fortunate to work with a gifted and wise group of editors at McGraw-Hill, including Lisa Moore, Alexis Walker, Bennett Morrison, Victoria Fullard, Jesse Hassenger, Christopher Bennem, Thomas L. Briggs, and Mel Valentin. I owe them each a great debt. I am also grateful to colleagues across the country who generously offered their expertise to improving earlier versions of *Ideas Across Time:*

Patrick Amelotte, Casper College
Michael Austin, Shepherd College
Jeffrey Cain, Sacred Heart University
Sarah Dangelantonio, Franklin Pierce College
Frances Davidson, Mercer County Community College
Monika Giacoppe, Ramapo College of New Jersey
Gary Grassinger, Community College of Allegheny County
Elizabeth Hanson, University of North Florida
William Hearell, Stephen F. Austin State University
John Hodgson, Cameron University
Anita Aukee Johnson, Monterey Peninsula College

Lynn Koller, Embry-Riddle Aeronautical University
David McCracken, Coker College
Mark Montgomery, Cayuga Community College
David Salomon, Black Hills State University
Sylvia Shurbutt, Shepherd University
Judy Sieg, Spartanburg Technical College
Meryl Siegal, Laney College
Helen Szymanski, College of DuPage
Martha Terrill, Arkansas College
Justin Williamson, Pearl River College
Carol Silverberg, Hartwick College
Joy Eichner Lynch, Contra Costa College

Ideas Across Time grew out of the foundation course of the Core Curriculum adopted in the late 1980s at Adelphi University, which is still being taught today by the Adelphi Honors College. The original course, called "The Modern Condition," was developed by talented administrators in the University Provost's Office and by several faculty committees. It would be impossible to acknowledge the contributions of all the people involved, but I do want in particular to thank Joyce Jesionowski, Beverly Lawn, Peter Costello, Eugene Roth, Bernard Avishai, Susan Weisser, Alan Sadovnik, and Larry Sullivan. I also owe special thanks to the dean and the associate dean of the Honors College at Adelphi, Richard Garner, Diane Della Croce, and Ann Craig for research assistance.

I have, finally, been especially lucky to have been able to teach "The Modern Condition" class on which this text is based to many generations of Honors College students, whose wit, intelligence, and curiosity have inspired so many choices that have helped shape this book. Thank you!

Igor Webb
Adelphi University

Introduction

Today, many centuries after the invention of writing, the familiar appearance of words in print can make us forget that a book or an essay in a magazine—a "text"—is *someone's* writing. What appears printed on the page is not a disembodied assemblage of marks and lines but rather the voice of an absent person—angry, lyrical, analytical, contemplative, informative, funny, and so on. Reading attentively begins, then, by listening for the voice of the writer. The writer is a person not unlike you, a person whose published essay, story, history, or novel began in the same way as your writing in college: as an idea that needs to be put into words. The writers anthologized in this book each began with a blank page, with ideas that were not fully formed, with information not yet put into clear order.

The writers in this book—along with the painters, designers, and photographers—are not only good communicators, though. They are also formidable creative thinkers, and what these writers and artists have expressed has been essential in the making of our world. How we look at the universe and ourselves, and how we order our lives together, has changed over time because of the ideas of these writers. These ideas invite careful attention, therefore, not only because they can be subtle or difficult but because they bear directly on each of our lives. Understanding and appreciating these ideas is an inescapable part of understanding ourselves.

A new idea, however, may be an uncomfortable thing to encounter. For this reason, the selections in this book need to be read sensitively. The philosopher Friedrich Nietzsche (1844–1900), one of the most radical of the modern philosophers, took the bold step of offering his readers advice about how they should read *him*. What he said remains worth considering. He urged his readers "to read slowly, deeply, looking cautiously before and aft, with reservations, with doors left open, with delicate eyes and fingers. . . ."

This is good advice. Nietzsche wanted to foster a receptive attitude in his readers. He hoped for readers who, when they encountered a live thought, something that knocked them for a loop or made them gasp for breath, were willing to be receptive. To engage genuinely with something new and live requires a willingness to be open to unfamiliar or even hostile points of view, analyses, arguments, or philosophies. As active learners, we pick up a book or an essay not to reinforce knowledge or values, but to learn something new and appreciate a different way of looking at things.

THE DISCIPLINE OF READING

Of course, you already have experience reading and writing; now, though, you're writing in a new context and for a new audience. College writing, writing with ideas, demands that you display a greater sophistication and rigor, a higher standard of performance, and a deeper seriousness than may have been demanded of you before.

We can begin to look at the discipline of reading from the vantage of these higher expectations.

Approaching the Text

The selections in this book were each written (or made) not for experts but for the general reader, a curious, educated, alert citizen of the world. They were written for *you*. They *assume* you will give them a sympathetic listen. The authors of these pieces take it for granted that you will be familiar with the words and images they use, with their rhetorical ploys, and with their allusions. They assume you are prepared to understand, if not necessarily to agree with, what they have to say.

The organization of this book will help you meet the expectations of these writers and artists. Each chapter opens with an overview of the ideas and the chief concerns addressed in the chapter. These introductory passages sketch a history of the chapter's theme and orient you to the intellectual terrain of the chapter. In addition to these chapter introductions, you will find headnotes introducing each selection. These headnotes contain biographical and other important information about the writer or artist. You will also find suggestions following each selection about where to find out more about the topic, writer, or artist.

The Practical Skills of Reading

Chief among the practical skills and habits that every able reader employs are annotation, various forms of what might be called "word searches," and directed questioning.

Annotation

Annotation is literally your own running commentary on what you are reading, conducted right there on the page. This commentary should be directed partly to understanding the material and partly to forming responses and fashioning analyses. It involves underlining important words, phrases, or sentences. You want to underline, for example, the writer's main ideas and the chief statements, examples, and illustrations that the writer uses to support these main ideas. Also underline parts of the writing that puzzle, enrage, or amuse you. In the margin, write thumbnail summaries of key points, establishing a ready outline of the piece for later reference, say, at the point when you sit down to write a paper about the selection. Most importantly, jot down questions or ideas that the writing provokes in you. Because annotation is an active process, it is better done with a pen or pencil than a highlighter. A highlighter can be used to identify key passages or words, but it is cumbersome for writing down questions or ideas. Your possible reluctance to write in a book has to give way to a different engagement with the printed page, an engagement that takes the form of a dialogue between you and the writer.

Word Searches

An important part of this dialogue has to do with words themselves. No piece of writing can be well understood if you are unfamiliar with key words in the text. As a general rule, however, looking up every word you are not absolutely confident about is probably not necessary. Most of us build up our vocabulary by exposure to words over time—by repeatedly finding them in print or hearing them in use. If you come across a word that is familiar but that you cannot define, you may find it helpful to use the surrounding words to provide you with the word's meaning. On the other hand, a wholly unfamiliar word is probably a word from a specialized vocabulary or a word outside the usual contexts of your reading. It is a word, therefore, whose meaning you can master only by using a dictionary.

In addition to underlining words whose meanings you don't know, highlight or underline words that are especially important to the writer. What words does the writer use to convey a central idea or *thesis?* What words express the writer's attitude toward the essay's subject? What words appear two or three or more times? By annotating this way, you will have an easily accessible record of the writer's main ideas and the language in which the writer communicates these ideas.

Directed Questioning

Your annotation, finally, should be a record of your questions and observations. An able reader is alert to suggestions, implications, and also confusions and contradictions in a piece of writing. A powerful piece of writing naturally triggers responses in the reader, not just at the conclusion of the essay or the climax of a story but at each step of the way. In addition, we invariably read for a purpose. That purpose may be simple and direct—the reading is an assignment for a class—or it may be subtle and personal—the reading promises to clarify a religious or ethical matter that has been troubling you. The purpose for which you are reading provides a focus and direction to your reading and a motivation for your specific questions. If, for example, you are reading a general account of the procedures involved in stem cell research in preparation for your essay on the morality of stem cell research, your focus will be on those parts of your reading that bear most on the question of morality. You may have practical questions and questions about the biology of stem cells, but since your paper is going to be about the morality of stem cell research, your questions ought to be directed to that goal. Your purpose will guide your reading as well as your annotation.

It is nevertheless the case that there are some general questions that you will want to bear in mind no matter what you are reading. Here are the main ones:

1. How does the writer define the subject of the selection? (What is the essay about?)
2. What is the writer trying to say?
3. How does the writer get the job done? (How is the essay developed and organized? Is the writing clear? Are you following the argument or just stumbling along?)
4. How does the writer's diction (word choice) express key ideas and attitudes?
5. What evidence does the writer use to support the essay's main ideas? How effective is that evidence?
6. What points/sentences do you find most persuasive? Pleasing? Memorable?
7. What points/sentences puzzle you?
8. What points/sentences do you find least persuasive? Displeasing? Irritating?
9. What questions does the selection raise?
10. What ideas does the writing provoke?

Keep these questions in mind when you read and annotate each selection.

A SAMPLE ANNOTATION

Here's how annotation looks in practice. The following passage is Abraham Lincoln's famous address, delivered on November 19, 1863, at the dedication of the Soldiers' Cemetery on the grounds of the Battle of Gettysburg in Pennsylvania. A turning point in the Civil War, Gettysburg claimed more than 7,000 Union and Confederate lives over three days of battle (June 1–3, 1863); overall Gettysburg casualties rose to more than 45,000. Lincoln's address, a mere 272 words, took less than two minutes to deliver and wasn't even heard by most of those present. Many who did hear it didn't like it. But subsequent generations have recognized it as a majestic piece of oratory that transformed the meaning of the Constitution. For most of the century and a half since this speech was first delivered, schoolchildren across the nation have been required to memorize and often recite its words.

patrimony birth

why not "eighty"? the frame

> Four score and seven years ago our fathers brought forth on this continent, a new nation, conceived in liberty, and dedicated to the proposition that all men are created equal. "liberty for all"?! true?

new nation's principles

> Now we are engaged in a great civil war, testing whether that nation, or any nation so conceived and so dedicated, can long endure. We are met on a great battlefield of that war. We have come to dedicate a portion of that field, as a final resting place for those who here gave their lives that the nation might live. It is altogether fitting and proper that we should do this.

now: civil war can the nation endure

rising emphasis

alliteration

> But, in a larger sense, we cannot dedicate—we cannot consecrate—we cannot hallow—this ground. The brave men, living and dead, who struggled here, have consecrated it, far above our poor power to add or detract. The world will little note, nor long remember what we say here, but it can never forget what they did here. It is for us the living, rather, to be dedicated here to the unfinished work which they who fought here have thus far so nobly advanced. It is rather for us to be here dedicated to the great task remaining before us—that from these honored dead we take increased devotion—that we here highly resolve that these dead shall not have died in vain—that this nation, under God, shall have a new birth of freedom—and that the government of the people, by the people, for the people, shall not perish from the earth.

dedication to principles but work unfinished

pledge of allegiance

repetition parallelism of opening

shall not perish

This annotation offers you a *sample* of what any annotation might look like. No two readers are likely to underline exactly the same things or ask exactly the same questions. Nonetheless, every annotation will aim to achieve similar goals: to identify the main ideas, to isolate the main points of contention, and to ask the central questions.

The annotations in this case—underlinings and jotted comments or questions—are of three kinds: annotations that isolate the main ideas, queries ("Is this true?"), and observations ("patrimony"). The comments in the right-hand margin provide a bare outline of the essay:

new nation's principles
can that nation endure?
dedication to principles but work unfinished
shall not perish

This outline allows you to take in the whole essay at a glance. The underlinings on the page flesh out this bare outline. They isolate main ideas, key words, and suggestive ideas, providing at greater length and in the precise words of the writer those points established in the outline. Lincoln brilliantly captures the new ground he wants the nation to stand on by claiming that he is staking his position on the originating ideas of the republic. He invokes "our fathers." But was the Constitution in fact dedicated to the idea that all men are created equal ("and does the word 'men' include women?")? The jottings in the margins record various responses to the reading, such as questions ("is this true?"), suggestive ideas ("liberty for all?!"), or rhetorical observations ("repetition," "parallelism"). The Gettysburg Address is an eloquent document. As such, it invites far more attention to its rhetoric than might be the case in other essays. The annotations point to the essay's word choice, repeated antitheses (oppositions and contrasts), imagery (such as its use of images of birth), alliteration ("poor power"), repetition, parallelism, use of tricolons (division of a main idea into three harmonious parts, as in "of . . . by . . . for the people"), and so on. Emotion and thought, rhetoric and meaning powerfully reinforce each other in this historic piece of writing.

READING A PAINTING OR A PHOTOGRAPH

Reading and writing about works of art require some additional comments. Obviously, you can't approach a painting as if it were an essay about the economy. A painting is a work of art. We know that even a portrait—a painting that explicitly aims to represent what a person actually looks like—is artificial and can never be an exact mirror. Indeed, we do not want it to be a mirror. When we look at another person, we see not only his or her physical characteristics but also inner qualities that we expect the artist to convey through means such as color, light, and pose. Even a photograph, an exact image recorded by a machine, has a similar purpose and method. One of the century's great photographers, Robert Doisneau, said, "Photography is a false witness, a lie." How can a photograph "lie"? In a number of ways. The photo might be purposely composed to portray something in a certain way and so fail to show what "actually happened." Moreover, many photos, like paintings, are "composed." They are put together for aesthetic effect, with conscious attention to light, patterns, lines, and the innumerable other features of visual communication. Even a documentary photograph—say, a photograph of an accident—is shaped by the photographer in a way similar to how a painter composes a portrait or a landscape. Writers also "compose" their essays and bring an inevitable bias that critical readers can and should consider. But does this amount to "a lie"? Perhaps it is a lie if you think a photo is a document—that is, an objective, unmediated, unedited glimpse of a moment in time. If you discover that a document has been invented or altered in some way you may well conclude that it lies. But if you think a photo is a work of art, by its nature related to its subject in complex ways, and of course liable to many interpretations, then you may well see a photo's "false witness" as revealing a deeper-than-documentary truth.

With these thoughts in mind, here are some questions to help you read a painting or photograph:

1. *What are the main features of the composition of the work?* Composition is about drawing the viewer's (reader's) eye to the overall purpose of the work, something the artist achieves by the arrangement of the work's parts and

their relation to one another. So you want to look at light and shade, color, line, and pattern, and, in general, at how the work achieves symmetry (or insists on asymmetry).

2. *How big is the work?* A small painting—24 by 24 *inches,* say—needs to be looked at differently than one that is 24 by 24 *feet.* Consider if the artist is making a small, significant point, or is depecting a grand, sweeping event. (In reproductions, like those in a book, look for indications of the size of the work.)
3. *Is the work composed to convey emotion?* Or a statable argument ("police are brutal")? Or a symbolic reflection? What elements of the composition convey the emotion, argument, or symbolism?
4. *How does the composition balance representational and abstract elements?* Why has the artist chosen the specific formal elements of the work?
5. *What is missing from the image?* Remember: what is not shown is often as powerful as what is.

READING LITERATURE

Like painting and photography, literature is a special case and so should be approached with special consideration. One thing that makes literature a special case is that it's often fiction, something made up but conveyed in such a way as to make it look as it if it were real. To make a story seem natural and authentic a writer relies on form and other conventions of literature.

In reading a story, therefore, here are some questions to keep in mind:

1. *Who is telling the story, and why?* The "I" of an essay usually represents the writer. But the "I" of a story is a creation, a character, or maybe just a voice. Why has the writer chosen to have *this* person tell the story?
2. *What is the tone of the narration?* Does it sound as if we should believe everything the narrator says, or is the narrator not to be trusted? Holden Caulfield, the narrator of *The Catcher in the Rye,* is an example of an unreliable narrator whose version of events should not be taken at face value. Alternately, a child narrator may not grasp events as an adult might and, therefore, offers a skewed recounting.
3. *What are the main facts?* Where and when is the story happening? What do the main facts imply? What happens? Is what happens a matter of action? Recollection? Impression? Reflection?
4. *What is the theme or controlling purpose of the story?* Do you have the sense that some idea about life is being conveyed? If so, how is this idea communicated to the reader? By means of what happens (plot)? By a contrast between events and their retelling to the reader? By means of tone?

These questions may apply also to poetry, but poetry is a special case within a special case. What distinguishes poetry from prose is its compression. The dominant modern form for poems is the lyric, and in this short form everything counts in an exaggerated way—every word, every line break, every change of pace or tone. This can seem like a secret code that needs deciphering. Often it can seem that everything in the poem has to "stand for" something else. To help you approach poems with confidence, here are some useful questions to guide your reading:

1. *What are the obvious features of the poem?* How does it look on the page? Does it have a rhyme scheme? Are the lines more or less the same length? Can you determine why the poet has chosen to end lines the way he or she does? Does the poem have stanzas? Is each stanza composed of the same number of lines? When reading the poem out loud, do you notice any particular rhythm or other kinds of sound patterns?
2. *Is there a discernible personality communicated by the poem?* Poems don't usually have narrators, but poets often assume a "voice" or "persona" for their poems. What are the characteristics of the poet's voice? Do you believe the voice in the poem is the writer's? If so, what makes you think so? If not, why not?
3. *What's striking, if anything, about the poet's diction?* What are the main devices the poet employs—such as imagery, repetition, symbolism, and metaphor?
4. *Is there a story?* Or is the poem about an impression or an event that sparks reflection? What happens between the beginning of the poem and the end? What's the theme, and how is the theme conveyed to the reader?

These introductory remarks are intended to serve as a brief, and hopefully useful, introduction to the discipline of reading at the college level. In the Appendix, you will find a similar introduction to college writing. For the present, it is time to move beyond introduction and to begin your reading and writing. Taken as whole, the readings and visual selections in this book offer a fascinating and fairly thorough view of many of the urgent issues in our lives today. See what *you* think.

chapter 1

American Identity

The soldier, adventurer, poet, and courtier Sir Walter Ralegh (1552–1618) wrote the first history in English while imprisoned on trumped-up charges of treason in the infamous Tower of London. Ten years after being jailed—by James, successor to the great Queen Elizabeth (of whom Ralegh had been a favorite)—Ralegh published his ambitious and groundbreaking (and unfinished) *The History of the World* (1614). The work is an especially apt place to begin a discussion of changing American identity because it is one of the best examples we have of the Elizabethan worldview, that is, of the understanding of human events held in common by the explorers, colonists, and rulers who established the "New World." In 1584, Ralegh landed on the southeast coast of the present United States. He named the place "Virginia" after his virgin queen, paving the way for the English colonization both of the Jamestown settlement (1607) and of the Massachusetts Bay Colony by the Puritans (1620–1643).

Ralegh's *History* was especially popular among the Puritans. It naturally appealed to them that he saw the record of human affairs as a revelation of God's will—in the language of the time, as "providential." His history opens with a long account of Creation, contrasting the universal chaos that preceded God's Creation with the order and plan that followed it. The theme of Ralegh's whole unfinished book, from the moment of Creation to the development of English history, is of the underlying divine order unfolding below the chaos and disorder of so much misguided human activity.

This is, then, the founding myth of American history. The Puritans embraced the vision of their settlement in the New World as an enterprise in accord with Providence, and so too did the plantation owners of Virginia. The old Europe, tyrannical and corrupt, would send its chosen to the New World, soon creating what Hector St. John de Crevecoeur, in his widely read *Letters from an American Farmer* (1782—see pp. 22–27), styled "the most perfect society now existing in the world." At the heart of this new society was a "new man," said Crevecoeur, "the American," an unprecedented figure on the stage of history, for in the United States "individuals of all nations are melted into a new race of men."

George Washington, ever the truth-teller, said Crevecoeur's book was too flattering, and it's not hard to see why. But whatever qualifications Crevecoeur's thesis may require—and he provided some himself (see pp. 22–27)—it's important to pause and fully to register the fact that it gave memorable expression to a powerful and hugely attractive new reality, compressed into that mesmerizing phrase "the American Dream." The tyranny and corruption of the Old World could be redeemed by the self-sufficiency and equality of the New. In particular, the frozen identities of the Old World, the world of closed communities, of ranks and classes and servitude for the masses, could be actively and positively recast in the amazing melting pot of the new egalitarian society, producing a brand-new, unfettered identity, forward looking, free—the American.

An important qualification of Crevecoeur's romance of the American and of his picture of America as melting pot was the presence of injustice and corruption in America itself. Not all the nations feeding populations into the New World were melted into the melting pot—in particular, not the African slaves. And, to complicate matters further, there were the nations already present on the continent, nations of Native Americans whose systematic extermination the European colonists justified by reference to God's providential plan. Finally, the passage from the Old World to the New was rarely as exuberant as Crevecoeur claimed. Immigrants could easily feel that they were neither Europeans nor Americans and that their hyphenated condition as, say, Irish-Americans was stubbornly irresolvable.

These keynotes of early American society echo down to our own day. The mobility of the modern world has made possible, or made necessary, vast migrations of people, some seeking new lives, some fleeing old lives. In the opening selection of this chapter, "Changing America," Joel L. Swerdlow examines the impact on American identity of the vast influx of peoples in recent decades. He tells this story by focusing on the students in one American high school, a school that symbolizes a whole national history. Located, appropriately, in Virginia, where Europeans first settled North America, and named after a fabled Confederate cavalry commander, J. E. B. Stuart, the school today is a breathtaking mix, with half its students coming—either as first- or second-generation immigrants—from over seventy countries.

In their reflections on identity, these students illustrate both the continuing divides in American society and the persistent allure of the notion of change and its invitation continually to reinvent the self. Half a century ago, the writer James Baldwin, whose father had been born a slave, confronted the peculiar American denial both of present social reality and of history. Baldwin, born a free man, still found it necessary to travel to Europe in the middle of the twentieth century to flee the "fury of the color problem." But then he was surprised to discover in Paris that he was "as American as any Texas GI." Why? Because he had been bred in a society, that uniquely *American* society, "in which nothing is fixed and in which the individual must fight for his identity."

Writing in 1985, the novelist Mary Gordon says the constant quest for identity is peculiarly American, "a somewhat tiresome but always self-absorbing process of national definition." Not only is the American's personal identity self-consciously bound up with national identity, but, as Gordon tells it, the standard symbols of national identity—Plymouth Rock, Valley Forge—may well not speak to the actual experience of individuals. For her, the touchstone of American identity is Ellis Island, which she visits to pay homage to the ghosts of her ancestors, immigrants from Europe. Judith Ortiz Cofer, a native of Puerto Rico whose father joined the U.S. Navy and moved his family to Paterson, New Jersey, further develops this theme. She chooses a powerful image for the title of her evocative memoir, "Silent Dancing." The image comes from a home movie of a party at her family's house in Paterson when she was a girl. The movie is in color—but it is silent. In looking back to that time in her quest to clarify identity, Cofer finds colorful dancing but a tantalizing silence. What the memory means is left ambiguous, left for the reader to sort out.

This chapter includes an excerpt from Walt Whitman's epic poem about America, "Song of Myself." Whitman, as close as anyone can come to being our national poet, celebrates the diversity and vivacity of the American common people in supple, distinctly American English, writing in long lines without rhyme and meter. The poem cuts American literature loose from its European forebears, announcing not only a new national identity but a new artistic form to express it.

KEYNOTE

Changing America (2001)

Joel L. Swerdlow

Joel L. Swerdlow is a senior editor of the National Geographic Society. He is author of *Nature's Medicine: Plants That Heal* (2000) and, with Jan C. Scruggs, of *To Heal a Nation: The Vietnam Veterans Memorial* (1985). Swerdlow has also edited *Presidential Debates: 1988 and Beyond* (1987) and *Media Technology and the Vote: A Source Book* (1988). His writing has appeared in *Harper's, Rolling Stone, The Wilson Quarterly*, and *The Washington Post*. "Changing America" first appeared in the September 2001 *National Geographic*.

J. E. B. Stuart High School opened in Falls Church, Virginia, in 1959. At that time the school, named for a famous Confederate cavalry commander in the American Civil War, possessed a student body of 1,616—virtually all Anglo-American. Change came slowly, accelerating during the mid-1990s,

An influx of immigrants, especially Asian and Hispanic, is changing the face of the United States—and the prom scene for students at J. E. B. Stuart High School.

when immigration to the United States—legal and illegal—reached today's near-record level of a million people a year. According to the 2000 census, 10 percent of America's 281 million residents were born in other countries, the highest percentage since 1930 and the largest number in U.S. history. Before 1965 more than three-quarters of all immigrants to the U.S. came from Europe, owing largely to quotas that favored northern Europeans. In 1965 Congress removed those quotas, and since then more than 60 percent of immigrants have come from Asia, Africa, the Caribbean, the Middle East, and Latin America. Says Kenneth Prewitt, former director of the U.S. Census Bureau, "We're on our way to becoming the first country in history that is literally made up of every part of the world."

Immigration patterns worldwide show a flow of people from poor countries to those with stronger economies, especially to industrialized countries with aging workforces. The influx is changing the makeup of populations in Britain, now 7 percent foreign-born, and France, also 7 percent. Immigrants now constitute nearly 10 percent of Germany's population, and 17 percent of residents in Canada are non-Canadian. In many ways J. E. B. Stuart mirrors this immigration revolution. Half of its 1,400 students were born in 70 countries.

In "Combating Intolerance," an elective course for juniors and seniors at Stuart, class discussions cover such topics as hate crimes, Ku Klux Klan violence, and why "No Irish Need Apply" appeared on job posters in cities where

Irish immigrants looked for work in the 19th century. The morning I sit in, one of the students remarks: "America is a country of immigrants but also a country that sometimes hates immigrants."

"So why would anyone want to immigrate to the U.S.?" I ask, wondering if the students can reconcile this country's ideals with its shortcomings.

5 Hands go up. "It's a country that gives people a chance to escape," a boy from Eritrea says. "People have a natural right to life, liberty, and the pursuit of happiness," declares a girl from Nicaragua. More hands wave. "What makes America special is that things are more 'wishable,' more likely to happen here," says a boy from Vietnam. "It's the tolerance," adds one voice. And then another: "The best way for us to learn tolerance is just seeing people of other cultures every day here." Heads nod in agreement.

They seem a little smug to me. "What's it like in this school for kids who don't speak English?" I ask. The class on intolerance is silent. "Do you ever do anything with them?" Someone in the back makes a comment, and the last row laughs.

Students in this class reflect a wide range of colors and cultures, but all speak English fluently and with no accent. Earlier that morning I'd eaten in the cafeteria and had heard many students who could not answer even simple questions from the people at the cash registers.

In 1990 some 32 million U.S. residents spoke a language other than English at home, and more than 7 million lived in households with no fluent English speaker over 14 years old. When language data from the 2000 census become available next year, the number of households with little or no English is sure to be much larger.

A basic command of English is a requirement for U.S. citizenship. Many argue that it also constitutes a foundation for economic self-sufficiency.

10 For the students who arrive at J. E. B. Stuart speaking no English, life can be tough. Two volunteers from "Combating Intolerance" escort me to a nearby corridor where English as a Second Language (ESL) is taught. "I *never* come here," says one. He was born in Pakistan but learned English when he came to the U.S. at age ten. "Yeah," adds the other boy, born in the U.S. but whose parents are Middle Eastern. "I haven't been here in *years*."

Ruth DeJong's ESL class emphasizes experiential learning. Students color pictures of objects in books to show that they understand words she is using. They get up and stand next to the window when she says "window." They write the new words and use them in sentences. As DeJong helps them pronounce words, her enthusiasm makes the students laugh. "Is anybody in here handsome?" she asks. A student raises his hand. "Yes," he says haltingly, "I am handsome."

DeJong's classroom is filled with teenagers, but the props make it look like a room for first or second graders. Stuffed animals lie on a sofa. Wall charts show pronouns, colors, parts of the human body. Everything—"window," "blinds," "pencil sharpener"—has a label. Among the books on the shelves are *What the Dinosaurs Saw, Morris the Moose,* and *Who Sees You at the Zoo?* Along with them are dictionaries: Italian, Korean, Persian, Russian, Turkish, French, Hindi, Spanish, Portuguese, Vietnamese, Swahili, Serbo-Croatian.

DeJong, who has taught ESL for 20 years, says, "About a fifth of the students now are nonliterate in their native language. That makes it much more difficult for them to learn English." A child's age of arrival in the U.S., she explains, is crucial. Young children have little difficulty with English, learning it in elementary school at the same time they learn to read. For many of the students in her class, who are beginning English and only starting to read at ages 14 to 17, it is much harder.

"Let's do some reading now," DeJong says, passing out a booklet written by local teachers. It contains reading and vocabulary lessons based on fictional students. "Many students are at school," reads one student. "They are talking and laughing. They are not talking to Ali. He is sad and afraid."

15 Slowly and softly, DeJong calls on everyone, even those who never raise their hands. She is both gentle and persistent. If they don't learn to speak and read English now, she knows, they won't stay in school—no matter how intelligent they are.

One-fifth of the full-time jobs in the U.S. pay eight dollars an hour or less. Filling most of these jobs are the 40 percent of the workforce who have no education beyond high school. Similar figures characterize most industrialized countries. For immigrants with poor language skills and little money, entering a technology-driven job market is increasingly difficult.

J. E. B. Stuart's computer labs are furnished with up-to-date equipment. The teachers are patient, and students still struggling with English participate here along with everyone else, learning to use word-processing software and to cruise the Internet. I find Mel Riddile, the high school's principal, standing in the hall outside one of the labs, greeting each passing student by name.

"Maybe the key to success lies in computers," I suggest. Riddile disagrees. "Computers are important," he says, "but not as important as literacy. The kids have to be able to read or they can't even use computers," Riddile continues. "Here we spell hope 'r-e-a-d.' We make them 'haves' by teaching them to read. It's no guarantee, but it's essential."

Riddile shows me how reading programs permeate the school's curriculum. Students who need extra help attend a reading laboratory, but even in science and mathematics a systematic effort is made to teach reading. In the school's library, students seem to feel no social stigma as they select the easiest books.

20 Emphasizing that more than half of his students qualify for free or reduced-price meals in the cafeteria, Riddile describes efforts to keep them in school: 6 a.m. automated wake-up calls help, as do special counselors who speak foreign languages. But some still drop out, he says, because they either need to work or become too discouraged. Parents, unfamiliar with the inner workings of an American high school and sometimes illiterate in their own language, are ill-equipped to help their children succeed. "We're the best hope these kids have," says Riddile.

In the end Riddile is upbeat. Students who attend Stuart enjoy a special advantage, he says. "Going to school here makes them better prepared for the world. They're living in the workplace of the 21st century."

A visit to the counselors' offices offers further perspective on the workplace of the 21st century. "Immigrants often do the work no one else wants to do," says one of the counselors, referring to child care, housekeeping, and restaurant work. There is no shortage of such jobs in Fairfax County, Virginia, the jurisdiction that operates J. E. B. Stuart—where the median household income is $80,000 a year. "But students don't want these types of jobs. Their parents do this kind of work out of necessity, but most of the students hope to do something more professional."

"How many go on to college?" I ask.

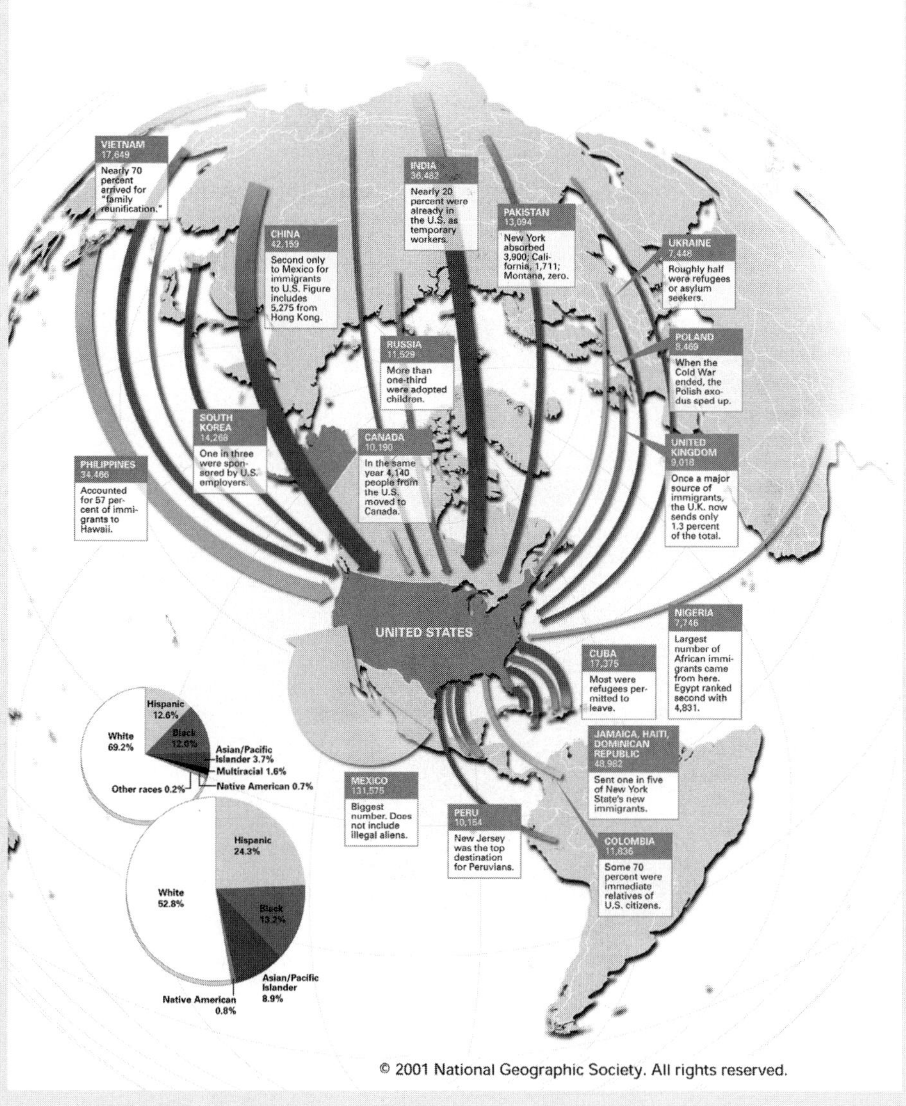

"About 59 percent of the student body as a whole goes on to four-year colleges and 21 percent to two-year schools," another counselor replies. "But the numbers are much lower for foreign-born students. The big economic jump may be made by their children. Remember that many of the kids here have already passed through a great filter. They have a much better chance of making it than do lots who don't get here. It's relative. For them, to have a job and a home and enough money to feed a family can be a very big accomplishment."

"Too many very capable students simply do not think of themselves as college material," says Mark Rogers, coordinator of J. E. B. Stuart's International Baccalaureate (or IB, for short) program, a rigorous precollege curriculum for juniors and seniors. The work required is significant: For every course, a student can count on at least one hour of homework every night.

Some 250 students (about 20 percent of the student body) take at least one IB course, although the program is open to all upper-classmen. Most of the students in the IB classes I visited were nonimmigrant whites. Rogers says teachers try to recruit a broader range of students by persuading them to take special preparatory courses in the ninth and tenth grades. But the work is especially difficult for immigrant students because courses require fluency in English.

One pattern is clear: The longer immigrant families have been in the U.S.—and the longer they have spoken English—the more likely their children are to

Pausing to pray during a private girls-only ice skating party, members of a Muslim youth group maintain their modesty. "Wearing the head scarf is a big challenge," says Fatima Abdallah, the group's 22-year-old coordinator. "People call us terrorists or foreigners. But most of us grew up here and are part of this society."

take IB courses. They are following the same pattern that has characterized most assimilation in the U.S.

Statistics about literacy and language and college prospects aside, what about being a teenager at J. E. B. Stuart—an immigrant teenager *or* an American teenager in this small-scale melting pot? A teenager with black skin or white skin, brown, yellow, or red skin—a teenager who speaks English or Spanish or Chinese or Hindi?

"I don't want to be white," says a white student from Poland. I'm in the library with a cross section of students who volunteered to speak with me.

30 Others agree with the Polish-born youth, but I'm confused. They explain. To call someone "white" is an insult, as are synonymous terms like Wonder bread. "I don't consider myself white," says a young woman from Russia. She has white skin. "Whites act white and do white stuff."

"What's 'white stuff'?" I ask.

"White kids act different. They hang out differently. Whites are privileged. They're smart, do homework on time, run the student government, participate in plays and musicals, sell stuff, have parents who are involved in the school."

"When you go to apply for a job," says one boy, "you have to act white."

"What do you do on weekends?" I ask. They all answer: Eat at a diner, talk, chill, watch television, go to an outlet mall, be with a boyfriend while he gets his car inspected, talk on the telephone, go to a movie.

35 "Sounds like what a white person would do," I say. Several students shake their heads, amazed at my inability to understand.

Most white students remain silent during these discussions. "I won't apologize for being white," says one.

I end up wondering if these kids aren't just struggling with an age-old adolescent dilemma: wanting to achieve versus wanting to be "cool." If achievement—or at least too much achievement—is unfashionable and achievement, as they have defined it, is "white," then "white" is not cool.

Whether they want to end up "white" or not, the kids here know they're in a blender: People of different colors and textures go in, and a mixture that appears homogeneous comes out. Everyone has a backpack. Most boys wear jeans and T-shirts; many girls wear short skirts or tight pants, showing a bit of bare midriff. Boys and girls wear earrings and talk about the same music.

But running beneath the sameness in fashion and attitude is a current of ethnic soul—a diversity that many of the students cling to even as they conform. They may sense that they are losing their family stories in the blender. Students here come from places where there's war, civil unrest, or extreme poverty. Some have horrible memories; a few have seen family killed. Most of them, though, have asked their parents very little about their decisions to immigrate. "My parents don't talk much about it," one explains. Another girl says, "I'm Malaysian, but one set of my grandparents was from Thailand. I don't know anything beyond that."

40 The students' ethnic awareness coupled with the sense of losing their ethnic identity creates a subtle tension, even in the relatively benign atmosphere of

the high school. "Hey, Italian!" evokes a response of "Hey, mulatto!" Pakistani girls are teased about wearing pajamas to school.

"I'm forgetting Arabic," says one student. "I can feel it fading away, being sucked away from me."

"It's part of becoming an American," says a friend.

This pattern persists even in the Hispanic community, which now constitutes more than 12 percent of U.S. residents. Roughly half of second-generation Hispanics assimilate so completely that they don't learn Spanish.

"We feel better with our own people," explains one student when I ask about apparently segregated groups in the cafeteria, which has a distinct geography that all the students can readily map out. Groups that sit together include Pakistani, Spanish-speakers, Moroccan, freshmen, cheerleaders, slackers, and nerds. Blacks who have recently arrived from Africa do not sit with the black Americans. Some tables are frequented by students who live in the same apartment building.

45 Despite such boundaries, most tables appear just plain mixed. At what looks like a typical table I pass out a piece of paper and ask everyone to write down his or her ethnic background. The results: "half Greek, half Middle Eastern," "Greek," "Saudi Arabian," "Bolivian," "African American," "Hispanic," "white (American)," "Russian," "African," "Pakistani," "confused," "mixed—black with?"

Lunch in the cafeteria seems dominated by interaction between two groups that transcend ethnic differences: boys and girls. Hand-holding, hugging, and occasional kissing have been very much in evidence throughout the school. Even some of the Muslim girls, who wear clothes that cover their entire bodies, have magazine pictures of muscular black men wearing only bikini briefs taped up inside their lockers.

What do these teenagers think of the cultural rules their parents try to enforce? A Sikh student says he finally talked his father into letting him cut his hair. Some of the Muslim girls argue with their parents about what kinds of dresses they can wear. One girl says that her mother told her she would have to marry an Asian man, and another girl insists that people must marry for love. A third girl reports that her mother says that people marry people, not cultures.

But most Stuart students are too young to be thinking of marriage. Conversations, especially among the boys, quickly turn to cars. "A car means freedom," one says. "You can go anywhere—your car is your life." A friend, who is saving his minimum-wage earnings for a car, says, "I know this girl farther out in Virginia I want to visit. With a car we could go to the shore or to New York. Doesn't everyone want to get away?"

At 2:05 p.m. the school day ends, and a rush to buses and cars begins. Some students get rides with parents or friends. Music blares from radios, kids sit on the grass, shouting, laughing, and flirting.

50 I go for ice cream with several boys, most from the football team. It's a typical J. E. B. Stuart group: an African American, an Afghan Italian, a Cambodian, and a Palestinian. They're talking about rap music when two girls walk in. One of the boys goes over to talk to them. When he returns, the others tease him. He defends himself: "I just asked if they'd like to chill together sometime."

As one chapter ends for graduating senior Truc Nguyen and her classmates at Stuart High, another one commences. "The great social adventure of America is no longer the conquest of the wilderness but the absorption of fifty different peoples," observed journalist Walter Lippmann in 1913. Today the adventure continues.

These are normal American teenagers, I think, wondering how I'll get them to discuss immigration issues. Then I realize that they've already taught me the most important lesson. Young people whose backgrounds span the spectrum of human cultures are becoming "normal American teenagers," and in the process they will change America. We may not know yet what the change will mean, but the kids themselves know they are at the heart of something significant. As one boy, speaking simply and confidently, told me: "We make America more interesting."

LEADING QUESTIONS

"I suppose," writes Mary Gordon (see her essay "The Ghosts of Ellis Island," pp. 37–42), "it is part of being an American to be engaged in a somewhat tiresome but always self-absorbing process of national definition." Swerdlow's story about J. E. B. Stuart High School seems to illustrate this observation: the idea of a "changing America" occurs in the bright light, as it were, of that torch on the Statue of Liberty, which long ago defined America as always in process. And long before that, at the very moment of the American Revolution, the Loyalist Hector de Crevecoeur (pp. 22–27) declared America to be a "melting pot" of nations.

Why does the concern with identity form such a large part of the American story? What is the relation between personal and national identity? Is the immigrant experience the definitive American experience? Or is being an American about the permanence of change, and if this is so, is America in this way the first modern nation? The European nations, and even more the ancient civilizations in India, China, and Africa, looked to the past for their identities: the national character was a matter of a fixed history. If what defines America is change, and therefore choice, are we necessarily an unstable society? Are we comfortable with continuous change, or does the constant redefinition of the nation make us uneasy both as individuals and as a society?

How do the essays in this chapter answer these questions?

LEARNING MORE

1. What exactly *was* the "2000 census"? What sort of information does it contain?
2. What is the median household income for your community?
3. What were the immigration quotas imposed by the federal government for the period between 1945 and 1965? How and why were these changed?

QUESTIONING THE TEXT

1. In what ways is J. E. B. Stuart High School a mirror of worldwide immigration patterns?
2. What positive reasons for being in the United States do the students at J. E. B. Stuart High School offer? Is there anything about being in the United States that they find negative?
3. What is the attitude of the students whom the writer interviews toward those who know little or no English?
4. What is the importance of English to U.S. citizenship?
5. What is the median household income of Fairfax County? Does this figure suggest an affluent middle class or a lower-income community?
6. Who takes IB classes at the school?
7. Why is being white not cool?
8. How do these students relate to the culture of their parents?
9. What "most important lesson" have these students taught the writer?

ANALYZING THE WRITER'S CRAFT

1. How does the opening paragraph effectively set the stage for the rest of the essay?
2. The writer chooses to include himself as an actor in his essay (for example, "The morning I sit in . . .," par. 3). What are the advantages and disadvantages of this rhetorical choice?

3. How does the writer let quotations do the work of laying out both the facts and the issues in this essay? Discuss two or three examples.
4. What does the writer imply by the last sentence of par. 6? Why does he not comment more directly?
5. How do the sources of the writer's statistics make his essay more authoritative?
6. Should the writer have cited sources for the second sentence of par. 9? Why or why not?
7. What does the writer mean by "increasingly difficult" at the close of par. 16?
8. What does it mean that more than half of the school's students qualify for free or reduced-price meals in the cafeteria (par. 20)? Why does the writer not refer to this fact earlier?
9. In what ways does the writer probe the experience of students at the school beyond issues of literacy and class? Do you find these reflections to be fair? Persuasive? Adequate? Explain.
10. Is the essay's conclusion effective? Why or why not?

MAKING CONNECTIONS

1. Swerdlow's picture of the students at J. E. B. Stuart is a familiar one in American history, the picture of a dynamic mixture of peoples. In what ways does his picture reflect or qualify the version of American identity we find in Crevecoeur (pp. 22–27), Gordon (pp. 37–42), or Ortiz Cofer (pp. 45–52)?
2. In *The Communist Manifesto* (see Chapter 4, pp. 264–273), Karl Marx and Friedrich Engels argue that industrial capital acts as a kind of enormous economic magnet, drawing to it not only raw material but also individuals from every corner of the globe. In what ways does Marx and Engels's analysis provide an illuminating background to Swerdlow's story? What do you think the students in J. E. B. Stuart High School would think of Marx and Engels's vision of "universal interdependence of nations"?
3. Walt Whitman "celebrates" the diversity of America (pp. 55–59). How do you imagine the students in J. E. B. Stuart High School would respond to his enthusiastic embrace of all kinds of people and all kinds of vocations in the United States?
4. Is there a religious dimension to American diversity? Is faith an essential feature of being an American (regardless of what that faith may be)? Or is separation of church and state what distinguishes us? How do the essays in Chapter 2, "Belief," help answer these questions?

FORMULATING IDEAS FOR WRITING

1. Swerdlow uses the following quotation from Woodrow Wilson (written in 1913) as an epigraph for his essay: "The great melting-pot of America, the place where we are all made Americans of, is the public school, where men

of every race, and of every origin, and of every station of life send their children, or ought to send their children, and where, being mixed together, they are all infused with the American spirit and developed into the American man and the American woman." Discuss with reference to J. E. B. Stuart and, if you like, your own high school.

2. Interview an immigrant who came to the United States some time ago—perhaps your grandmother—and a recent immigrant, and write an essay reflecting on the similarities and differences between their experiences.
3. After doing some research, write an essay discussing attitudes toward the place of English in U.S. primary and secondary education.
4. Write an essay exploring Richard Rodriguez's notion of "brown" (see Chapter 6, pp. 542–549) with reference to J. E. B. Stuart High School.

Letters from an American Farmer (1782)

Hector St. John de Crevecoeur

It is somehow fitting that the most influential Revolution-era portrait of that new phenomenon in world history, "the American"—*Letters from an American Farmer* (1782)—should have been published in England by a Frenchman unsympathetic to the American Revolution. Born Michel-Guillaume-Jean de Crevecoeur in Normandy in 1735, Crevecoeur did not arrive in New York until 1759, changing his name to Hector St. John. But his work as a surveyor and trader with Native American tribes took him to all corners of the colonies, and in 1769 he settled with his new wife on a farm in Orange County, New York. A Loyalist, Crevecoeur returned to London in 1780, soon thereafter publishing *Letters*, which was an immediate international success. Between 1783 and 1785, Crevecoeur served as an extremely well-liked French consul to New York, New Jersey, and Connecticut. But he settled permanently in France after 1785, living the last twenty years of his life in the Normandy where he had been born. The selections from *Letters* that follow include Crevecoeur's enormously influential, original, and justly famous answer to what has become a perennial question, "What is an American?" as well as his stricken account of that "strange order of things" whereby the gaiety and riches of "Charles-Town" in what is today South Carolina derive from the "wretchedness" of slavery.

I wish I could be acquainted with the feelings and thoughts which must agitate the heart and present themselves to the mind of an enlightened Englishman, when he first lands on this continent. He must greatly rejoice that he lived at a time to see this fair country discovered and settled; he must necessarily feel a share of national pride, when he views the chain of settlements which embellishes these extended shores. When he says to himself, this is the work of my countrymen, who, when convulsed by factions,[1] afflicted by a variety of miseries and wants, restless and impatient, took refuge here. They brought along with them their national genius,[2] to which they principally owe what liberty they enjoy, and what substance they possess. Here he sees the industry of his native country displayed in a new manner, and traces in their works the embryos of all the arts, sciences, and ingenuity which flourish in Europe. Here he beholds fair cities, substantial villages, extensive fields, an immense country filled with decent houses, good roads, orchards, meadows, and bridges, where an hundred years ago all was wild, woody, and uncultivated! What a train of pleasing ideas this fair spectacle must suggest; it is a prospect which must inspire a good citizen with the most heartfelt pleasure. The difficulty consists in the manner of viewing so extensive a scene. He is arrived on a new continent; a modern society offers itself to his contemplation, different from what he had hitherto seen. It is not composed, as in Europe, of great lords who possess everything, and of a herd of people who have nothing. Here are no aristocratical families, no courts, no kings, no bishops, no ecclesiastical[3] dominion, no invisible power giving to a few a very visible one; no great manufacturers employing thousands, no great refinements of luxury. The rich and the poor are not so far removed from each other as they are in Europe. Some few towns excepted, we are all tillers of the earth, from Nova Scotia to West Florida. We are a people of cultivators, scattered over an immense territory, communicating with each other by means of good roads and navigable rivers, united by the silken bands of mild government, all respecting the laws, without dreading their power, because they are equitable. We are all animated with the spirit of an industry which is unfettered and unrestrained, because each person works for himself. If he travels through our rural districts he views not the hostile castle, and the haughty mansion, contrasted with the clay-built hut and miserable cabin, where cattle and men help to keep each other warm, and dwell in meanness, smoke, and indigence.[4] A pleasing uniformity of decent competence appears throughout our habitations. The meanest of our log-houses is a dry and comfortable habitation. Lawyer or merchant are the fairest titles our towns afford; that of a farmer is the only appellation of the rural inhabitants of our country. It must take some time ere he can reconcile himself to our dictionary, which is but short in words of dignity, and names of honor. There, on a Sunday, he sees a congregation of respectable farmers and their wives, all clad in neat homespun,[5] well mounted, or riding in their own humble wagons. There is not among them an esquire, saving the unlettered magistrate. There he sees a parson as simple as his flock, a farmer who does not riot on the labor of others. We

---

[1] factions: partisan disputes.

[2] genius: national character.

[3] ecclesiastical: religious, clerical.

[4] indigence: poverty.

[5] homespun: plain, homely material.

have no princes, for whom we toil, starve, and bleed; we are the most perfect society now existing in the world. Here man is free as he ought to be; nor is this pleasing equality so transitory as many others are. Many ages will not see the shores of our great lakes replenished with inland nations, nor the unknown bounds of North America entirely peopled. Who can tell how far it extends? Who can tell the millions of men whom it will feed and contain? for no European foot has as yet traveled half the extent of this mighty continent!

The next wish of this traveler will be to know whence came all these people? They are a mixture of English, Scotch, Irish, French, Dutch, Germans and Swedes. From this promiscuous breed, that race now called Americans have arisen. The eastern provinces[6] must indeed be excepted, as being the unmixed descendants of Englishmen. I have heard many wish that they had been more intermixed also: for my part, I am no wisher, and think it much better as it has happened. They exhibit a most conspicuous figure in this great and variegated picture; they too enter for a great share in the pleasing perspective displayed in these thirteen provinces. I know it is fashionable to reflect on them, but respect them for what they have done; for the accuracy and wisdom with which they have settled their territory; for the decency of their manners; for their early love of letters; their ancient college,[7] the first in this hemisphere; for their industry, which to me who am but a farmer is the criterion of everything. There never was a people, situated as they are, who with so ungrateful a soil have done more in so short a time. Do you think that the monarchical ingredients which are more prevalent in other governments have purged them from all foul stains? Their histories assert the contrary.

In this great American asylum, the poor of Europe have by some means met together, and in consequence of various causes; to what purpose should they ask one another what countrymen they are? Alas, two thirds of them had no country. Can a wretch who wanders about, who works and starves, whose life is a continual scene of sore affliction or pinching penury,[8] can that man call England or any other kingdom his country? A country that had no bread for him, whose fields procured him no harvest, who met with nothing but the frowns of the rich, the severity of the laws, with jails and punishments; who owned not a single foot of the extensive surface of this planet? No! Urged by a variety of motives, here they came. Everything has tended to regenerate them; new laws, a new mode of living, a new social system; here they are become men: in Europe they were as so many useless plants, wanting vegetative mold and refreshing showers; they withered, and were mowed down by want, hunger, and war; but now by the power of transplantation, like all other plants they have taken root and flourished! Formerly they were not numbered in any civil lists[9] of their country, except in those of the poor; here they rank as citizens. By what invisible power has this surprising metamorphosis been performed? By that of the

[6] eastern provinces: New England.
[7] ancient college: Harvard, founded in 1636.
[8] penury: poverty.
[9] civil lists: rolls of honors.

laws and that of their industry. The laws, the indulgent laws, protect them as they arrive, stamping on them the symbol of adoption; they receive ample rewards for their labors; these accumulated rewards procure them lands; those lands confer on them the title of freemen, and to that title every benefit is affixed which men can possibly require. This is the great operation daily performed by our laws. From whence proceed these laws? From our government. Whence the government? It is derived from the original genius and strong desire of the people ratified and confirmed by the crown. This is the great chain which links us all, this is the picture which every province exhibits, Nova Scotia excepted. There the crown has done all, either there were no people who had genius, or it was not much attended to: the consequence is that the province is very thinly inhabited indeed; the power of the crown in conjunction with the mosquitoes has prevented men from settling there. Yet some parts of it flourished once, and it contained a mild, harmless set of people. But for the fault of a few leaders, the whole were banished. The greatest political error the crown ever committed in America was to cut off men from a country which wanted nothing but men!

What attachment can a poor European emigrant have for a country where he had nothing? The knowledge of the language, the love of a few kindred as poor as himself, were the only cords that tied him: his country is now that which gives him land, bread, protection, and consequence: *Ubi panis ibi patria*[10] is the motto of all emigrants. What then is the American, this new man? He is either a European, or the descendant of a European, hence that strange mixture of blood, which you will find in no other country. I could point out to you a family whose grandfather was an Englishman, whose wife was Dutch, whose son married a French woman, and whose present four sons have now four wives of different nations. *He* is an American, who, leaving behind him all his ancient prejudices and manners, receives new ones from the new mode of life he has embraced, the new government he obeys, and the new rank he holds. He becomes an American by being received in the broad lap of our great *Alma Mater.* Here individuals of all nations are melted into a new race of men, whose labors and posterity will one day cause great changes in the world. Americans are the western pilgrims, who are carrying along with them that great mass of arts, sciences, vigor, and industry which began long since in the east; they will finish the great circle. The Americans were once scattered all over Europe; here they are incorporated into one of the finest systems of population which has ever appeared, and which will hereafter become distinct by the power of the different climates they inhabit. The American ought therefore to love this country much better than that wherein either he or his forefathers were born. Here the rewards of his industry follow with equal steps the progress of his labor; his labor is founded on the basis of nature, *self-interest;* can it want a stronger allurement? Wives and children, who before in vain demanded of him a morsel of bread, now, fat and frolicsome, gladly help their father to clear those fields whence exuberant crops are to arise to feed and to clothe them all; without any part being

---

[10] *Ubi panis . . . :* Latin for "Where there's bread, there's one's country."

claimed, either by a despotic prince, a rich abbot, or a mighty lord. Here religion demands but little of him; a small voluntary salary to the minister, and gratitude to God; can he refuse these? The American is a new man, who acts upon new principles; he must therefore entertain new ideas, and form new opinions. From involuntary idleness, servile dependence, penury, and useless labor, he has passed to toils of a very different nature, rewarded by ample subsistence. —This is an American. . . .

5 Everywhere one part of the human species are taught the art of shedding the blood of the other; of setting fire to their dwellings; of leveling the works of their industry: half of the existence of nations regularly employed in destroying other nations. What little political felicity is to be met with here and there, has cost oceans of blood to purchase; as if good was never to be the portion of unhappy man. Republics, kingdoms, monarchies, founded either on fraud or successful violence, increase by pursuing the steps of the same policy, until they are destroyed in their turn, either by the influence of their own crimes, or by more successful but equally criminal enemies.

If from this general review of human nature, we descend to the examination of what is called civilized society; there the combination of every natural and artificial want, makes us pay very dear for what little share of political felicity we enjoy. It is a strange heterogeneous assemblage of vices and virtues, and of a variety of other principles, forever at war, forever jarring, forever producing some dangerous, some distressing extreme. Where do you conceive then that nature intended we should be happy? Would you prefer the state of men in the woods, to that of men in a more improved situation? Evil preponderates in both; in the first they often eat each other for want of food, and in the other they often starve each other for want of room. For my part, I think the vices and miseries to be found in the latter, exceed those of the former; in which real evil is more scarce, more supportable, and less enormous. Yet we wish to see the earth peopled; to accomplish the happiness of kingdoms, which is said to consist in numbers. Gracious God! to what end is the introduction of so many beings into a mode of existence in which they must grope amidst as many errors, commit as many crimes, and meet with as many diseases, wants, and sufferings!

The following scene will I hope account for these melancholy reflections, and apologize for the gloomy thoughts with which I have filled this letter: my mind is, and always has been, oppressed since I became a witness to it. I was not long since invited to dine with a planter who lived three miles from ———, where he then resided. In order to avoid the heat of the sun, I resolved to go on foot, sheltered in a small path, leading through a pleasant wood. I was leisurely traveling along, attentively examining some peculiar plants which I had collected, when all at once I felt the air strongly agitated; though the day was perfectly calm and sultry. I immediately cast my eyes toward the cleared ground, from which I was but at a small distance, in order to see whether it was not occasioned by a sudden shower; when at that instant a sound resembling a deep rough voice, uttered, as I thought, a few inarticulate monosyllables. Alarmed and surprised, I precipitately looked all round, when I perceived at about six rods distance something resembling a cage, suspended to the limbs of a tree; all the branches of which appeared covered with large birds of prey, fluttering about, and anxiously endeavoring to perch on the cage. Actuated by an involuntary motion of my hands, more than by any design of my mind, I fired at them; they all flew to a short distance, with a most hideous noise: when, horrid to think and painful to repeat, I perceived a Negro, suspended in the cage, and left there to expire! I shudder when I recollect that the birds had already picked out his eyes, his cheek bones were bare; his arms had been attacked in several places, and his body seemed covered with a multitude of wounds. From the edges of the hollow sockets and from the lacerations with which he was disfigured, the blood slowly dropped, and tinged the ground beneath. No sooner were the birds flown, than swarms of insects covered the whole body of this unfortunate wretch, eager to feed on his mangled flesh and to drink his blood. I found myself suddenly arrested by the power of affright and terror; my nerves were convulsed; I trembled, I stood motionless, involuntarily contemplating the fate of this Negro, in all its dismal latitude. The living specter, though deprived of his eyes, could still distinctly hear, and in his uncouth dialect begged me to give him some water to allay his thirst. Humanity herself would have recoiled back with horror; she would have balanced whether to lessen such reliefless distress, or mercifully with one blow to end this dreadful scene of agonizing torture! Had I had a ball in my gun, I certainly should have dispatched him; but finding myself unable to perform so kind an office, I sought, though trembling, to relieve him as well as I could. A shell ready fixed to a pole, which had been used by some Negroes, presented itself to me; filled it with water, and with trembling hands I guided it to the quivering lips of the wretched sufferer. Urged by the irresistible power of thirst, he endeavored to meet it, as he instinctively guessed its approach by the noise it made in passing through the bars of the cage. "Tankè, you whitè man, tankè you, putè somè poison and givè me." "How long have you been hanging there?" I asked him. "Two days, and me no die; the birds, the birds; aaah me!" Oppressed with the reflections which this shocking spectacle afforded me, I mustered strength enough to walk away, and soon reached the house at which I intended to dine. There I heard that the reason for this slave being thus punished was on account of his having killed the overseer of the plantation. They told me that the laws of self-preservation rendered such executions necessary; and supported the doctrine of slavery with the arguments generally made use of to justify the practice; with the repetition of which I shall not trouble you at present.

Adieu.

LEARNING MORE

How did slavery get established in the Carolinas? What were the main elements of the economy of that region? What was the impact of the abolition of slavery on the Carolinas?

QUESTIONING THE TEXT

1. What connections does Crevecoeur establish between England and America?
2. What are the main contrasts that Crevecoeur draws between Europe and America?
3. What do you think is Crevecoeur's notion of freedom?
4. Why does Crevecoeur call America an "asylum" (par. 3)? What do you think he means when he says that in America the European immigrants "are become men" (par. 3)?
5. How does Crevecoeur portray government in America?
6. What is your response to his assertion that "we are the most perfect society now existing in the world"? Does Crevecoeur adequately support this claim, or is he overstating his case? What do you think made George Washington say that Crevecoeur had painted too "flattering" a picture of life in America?
7. Crevecoeur says that *Ubi panis, ibi patria* (Where there's bread, that's where my country is) is the motto of all emigrants (par. 4). Does Crevecoeur believe, then, that it is only material well-being that binds the new Americans to their new nation?
8. In your own words, summarize Crevecoeur's answer to his question: What is the American?
9. What is Crevecoeur's view of slavery?
10. How does slavery affect Crevecoeur's outlook on the human species? On America?

ANALYZING THE WRITER'S CRAFT

1. In his long first paragraph, Crevecoeur displays considerable rhetorical skill both in advancing his argument and in painting his portrait of the new nation. Discuss, for example, his use of repetition (of, say, "must," "because," "immense," and "pleasing"). Or examine his metaphors ("silken bands of mild government"). Finally, discuss his use of comparisons and contrasts.
2. Discuss the impact of Crevecoeur's many questions in par. 3.
3. How does Crevecoeur go about defining an American (par. 4)? What sort of supporting evidence does he use?
4. What are the main elements of Crevecoeur's comparison between Charles-Town and Lima on the one hand, and the West Indies on the other? What is the purpose of these comparisons and contrasts?
5. How does Crevecoeur establish compassion for the slaves? What audience do you think Crevecoeur had in mind for these passages? Explain.
6. Is Crevecoeur's final paragraph necessary to his argument? Why or why not.

MAKING CONNECTIONS

1. Compare and contrast Crevecoeur's, Alexis de Tocqueville's (Chapter 6, pp. 458–460), and Richard Rodriguez's (Chapter 6, pp. 542–549) attitudes toward the notion of America as a "melting pot."
2. How is what James Baldwin (pp. 29–35) discovers about being an American the same as or different from what Crevecoeur says his English visitor would discover?
3. What do you think Mike Lefevre (Chapter 4, pp. 300–307) would say to Crevecoeur, and vice versa?
4. Compare and contrast Crevecoeur's account of American life and Daniel J. Boorstin's (Chapter 5, pp. 390–402).

FORMULATING IDEAS FOR WRITING

1. Using Crevecoeur's essay as a model, write your own essay in answer to the question, What is an American?
2. Many years have passed since Crevecoeur wrote his account of the United States. Write an essay that makes note of changes in American life from then to now but aims mainly to assess whether Crevecoeur's view could be seen as still pertinent and illuminating, or as historically interesting but no longer applicable.
3. Imagine Crevecoeur descending from heaven to present-day South Carolina. You are assigned by the local newspaper to interview him. What would you ask? How might he respond?
4. Is Crevecoeur's account too idealistic, painting less a picture of reality than a picture of something that Crevecoeur would like to see in the new nation? Write an essay that answers this question by comparing *Letters* with Tocqueville's observations in *Democracy in America* (see Chapter 6, pp. 458–460).

The Discovery of What It Means to Be an American (1959)

James Baldwin

James Baldwin (1924–1987) holds a unique place in American culture of the second half of the twentieth century. In distinctively stirring and often painfully evocative prose, he waged a kind of verbal holy war against the entrenched forces of denial and vengeance in American society, meaning in black as well as in white America. He wanted simply to be a writer, to be acknowledged as no more and no less than a man in thrall to the artist's vocation—but nothing in his life or his times allowed him a designation as plain as that. Homosexual, black, in his own eyes small and frail and ugly, Baldwin more than any other figure of the age expressed the intractable "twoness," to use W. E. B. Du Bois' coinage (Chapter 6, pp. 472–479), of so much of American life. Perhaps the power, the vaulting music, the intensity of feeling and the clarity of thought of Baldwin's prose derived from the fact that what he wrote about was a matter of life and death for him personally as much as, if not more than, a matter of grave importance for the nation.

His battle against denial and vengeance began at home. Born the illegitimate first child of Emma Berdis Jones on August 2, 1924, in Harlem, Baldwin grew up in a bitter embrace with the man his mother married when James was three years old, whose name became his name, and whom Baldwin believed to be his real father. (He did not learn otherwise until he was in his teens.) David Baldwin, the son of a slave, was a lay preacher whose religious passion was fed by the fierce expectation that God would avenge the primal injustice of slavery by smiting white America. After their marriage, Emma Jones had eight children with David Baldwin, all of whom James had to care for under what he felt to be the hard, cruel gaze of his stepfather. Nevertheless, at fourteen, Baldwin experienced a religious conversion, and he preached in his stepfather's church until, at age seventeen, he lost his faith. The cadences of the preacher's calling and of the Bible can be heard in everything Baldwin ever wrote.

Shortly after graduating from high school in 1943, Baldwin met Richard Wright, for him at the time "the greatest black writer in the world." In 1948, fleeing American racism and homophobia, Baldwin followed Wright to Paris. There, Baldwin became part of an illustrious intellectual circle in postwar France, including some of the world's major writers and thinkers, such as Jean-Paul Sartre, Simone de Beauvoir, and Jean Genet. In this selection, originally published in *The New York Times Book Review* while he was in Paris, Baldwin muses on what it means to be an American.

In 1957, Baldwin saw a photo of white Americans in Charlotte-Mecklenburg, North Carolina, spitting on Dorothy Counts as she and three other African-American children tried to integrate an all-white school. He returned to the United States and immediately became one of the central figures in the civil rights movement. His enormously influential essays on race and identity were collected in *Notes of a Native Son* (1955), *Nobody Knows My Name* (1962), and *The Fire Next Time* (1963). Among his other notable works of literature are the novels *Giovanni's Room* (1956) and *Another Country* (1962) and the play *Blues for Mister Charlie* (1964). In these works, Baldwin delved into the fret and danger of what he saw as our riven life in America, split into hostile opposites—black and white, gay and straight, female and male. Throughout, he stuck to his message that the greatest danger to self and to society is the corrosive burn of hatred. Baldwin died on November 30, 1987, in St. Paul de Vence on the French Riviera.

"It is a complex fate to be an American," Henry James[1] observed, and the principal discovery an American writer makes in Europe is just how complex this fate is. America's history, her aspirations, her peculiar triumphs, her even more peculiar defeats, and her position in the world—yesterday and today—are all so profoundly and stubbornly unique that the very word "America" remains a new, almost completely undefined and extremely controversial proper noun. No one in the world seems to know exactly what it describes, not even we motley[2] millions who call ourselves Americans.

I left America because I doubted my ability to survive the fury of the color problem here. (Sometimes I still do.) I wanted to prevent myself from becoming *merely* a Negro; or, even, merely a Negro writer. I wanted to find out in what way the *specialness* of my experience could be made to connect me with other people instead of dividing me from them. (I was as isolated from Negroes as I was from whites, which is what happens when a Negro begins, at bottom, to believe what white people say about him.)

In my necessity to find the terms on which my experience could be related to that of others, Negroes and whites, writers and non-writers, I proved, to my astonishment, to be as American as any Texas GI. And I found my experience was shared by every American writer I knew in Paris. Like me, they had been divorced from their origins, and it turned out to make very little difference that the origins of white Americans were European and mine were African—they were no more at home in Europe than I was.

The fact that I was the son of a slave and they were the sons of free men meant less, by the time we confronted each other on European soil, than the fact that we were both searching for our separate identities. When we had found these, we seemed to be saying, why, then, we would no longer need to cling to the shame and bitterness which had divided us so long.

5 It became terribly clear in Europe, as it never had been here, that we knew more about each other than any European ever could. And it also became clear that, no matter where our fathers had been born, or what they had endured, the fact of Europe had formed us both, was part of our identity and part of our inheritance.

I had been in Paris a couple of years before any of this became clear to me. When it did, I, like many a writer before me upon the discovery that his props have all been knocked out from under him, suffered a species of breakdown and was carried off to the mountains of Switzerland. There, in that absolutely alabaster[3] landscape, armed with two Bessie Smith[4] records and a typewriter, I began to try to recreate the life that I had first known as a child and from which I had spent so many years in flight.

---

[1] Henry James: major American novelist (1843–1916), many of whose books explored American identity in the context of Europe.

[2] motley: diversified; multicolored.

[3] alabaster: translucently white.

[4] Bessie Smith: a great jazz singer (1895–1937) tragically killed in a car accident.

It was Bessie Smith, through her tone and her cadence, who helped me to dig back to the way I myself must have spoken when I was a pickaninny,[5] and to remember the things I had heard and seen and felt. I had buried them very deep. I had never listened to Bessie Smith in America (in the same way that, for years, I would not touch watermelon), but in Europe she helped to reconcile me to being a "nigger."

I do not think that I could have made this reconciliation here. Once I was able to accept my role—as distinguished, I must say, from my "place"—in the extraordinary drama which is America, I was released from the illusion that I hated America.

The story of what can happen to an American Negro writer in Europe simply illustrates, in some relief, what can happen to any American writer there. It is not meant, of course, to imply that it happens to them all, for Europe can be very crippling, too; and, anyway, a writer, when he has made his first breakthrough, has simply won a crucial skirmish in a dangerous, unending, and unpredictable battle. Still, the breakthrough is important, and the point is that an American writer, in order to achieve it, very often has to leave this country.

10 The American writer, in Europe, is released, first of all, from the necessity of apologizing for himself. It is not until he *is* released from the habit of flexing his muscles and proving that he is just a "regular guy" that he realizes how crippling this habit has been. It is not necessary for him, there, to pretend to be something he is not, for the artist does not encounter in Europe the same suspicion he encounters here. Whatever the Europeans may actually think of artists, they have killed enough of them off by now to know that they are as real—and as persistent—as rain, snow, taxes, or businessmen.

Of course, the reason for Europe's comparative clarity concerning the different functions of men in society is that European society has always been divided into classes in a way that American society never has been. A European writer considers himself to be part of an old and honorable tradition—of intellectual activity, of letters—and his choice of a vocation does not cause him any uneasy wonder as to whether or not it will cost him all his friends. But this tradition does not exist in America.

On the contrary, we have a very deep-seated distrust of real intellectual effort (probably because we suspect that it will destroy, as I hope it does, that myth of America to which we cling so desperately). An American writer fights his way to one of the lowest rungs on the American social ladder by means of pure bullheadedness and an indescribable series of odd jobs. He probably *has* been a "regular fellow" for much of his adult life, and it is not easy for him to step out of that lukewarm bath.

We must, however, consider a rather serious paradox: though American society is more mobile than Europe's, it is easier to cut across social and occupational lines there than it is here. This has something to do, I think, with the problem of status in American life. Where everyone has status, it is also perfectly

---

[5] pickanniny: term used for a black child, now considered derogatory.

possible, after all, that no one has. It seems inevitable, in any case, that a man may become uneasy as to just what his status is.

But Europeans have lived with the idea of status for a long time. A man can be as proud of being a good waiter as of being a good actor, and, in neither case, feel threatened. And this means that the actor and the waiter can have a freer and more genuinely friendly relationship in Europe than they are likely to have here. The waiter does not feel, with obscure resentment, that the actor has "made it," and the actor is not tormented by the fear that he may find himself, tomorrow, once again a waiter.

15 This lack of what may roughly be called social paranoia causes the American writer in Europe to feel—almost certainly for the first time in his life—that he can reach out to everyone, that he is accessible to everyone and open to everything. This is an extraordinary feeling. He feels, so to speak, his own weight, his own value.

It is as though he suddenly came out of a dark tunnel and found himself beneath the open sky. And, in fact, in Paris, I began to see the sky for what seemed to be the first time. It was borne in on me—and it did not make me feel melancholy—that this sky had been there before I was born and would be there when I was dead. And it was up to me, therefore, to make of my brief opportunity the most that could be made.

I was born in New York, but have lived only in pockets of it. In Paris, I lived in all parts of the city—on the Right Bank and the Left, among the bourgeoisie and among *les misérables*, and knew all kinds of people, from pimps and prostitutes in Pigalle to Egyptian bankers in Neuilly. This may sound extremely unprincipled or even obscurely immoral: I found it healthy. I love to talk to people, all kinds of people, and almost everyone, as I hope we still know, loves a man who loves to listen.

This perpetual dealing with people very different from myself caused a shattering in me of preconceptions I scarcely knew I held. The writer is meeting in Europe people who are not American, whose sense of reality is entirely different from his own. They may love or hate or admire or fear or envy this country—they see it, in any case, from another point of view, and this forces the writer to reconsider many things he had always taken for granted. This reassessment, which can be very painful, is also very valuable.

This freedom, like all freedom, has its dangers and its responsibilities. One day it begins to be borne in on the writer, and with great force, that he is living in Europe as an American. If he were living there as a European, he would be living on a different and far less attractive continent.

20 This crucial day may be the day on which an Algerian taxi-driver tells him how it feels to be an Algerian in Paris. It may be the day on which he passes a café terrace and catches a glimpse of the tense, intelligent, and troubled face of Albert Camus.[6] Or it may be the day on which someone asks him to explain Little Rock and he begins to feel that it would be simpler—and, corny as the

[6] Albert Camus: Nobel Prize–winning French novelist (1913–1960), associated with existentialism.

words may sound, more honorable—to *go* to Little Rock than sit in Europe, on an American passport, trying to explain it.

This is a personal day, a terrible day, the day to which his entire sojourn has been tending. It is the day he realizes that there are no untroubled countries in this fearfully troubled world; that if he has been preparing himself for anything in Europe, he has been preparing himself—for America. In short, the freedom that the American writer finds in Europe brings him, full circle, back to himself, with the responsibility for his development where it always was: in his own hands.

Even the most incorrigible maverick has to be born somewhere. He may leave the group that produced him—he may be forced to—but nothing will efface his origins, the marks of which he carries with him everywhere. I think it is important to know this and even find it a matter for rejoicing, as the strongest people do, regardless of their station. On this acceptance, literally, the life of a writer depends.

The charge has often been made against American writers that they do not describe society, and have no interest in it. They only describe individuals in opposition to it, or isolated from it. Of course, what the American writer is describing is his own situation. But what is *Anna Karenina*[7] describing if not the tragic fate of the isolated individual, at odds with her time and place?

The real difference is that Tolstoy was describing an old and dense society in which everything seemed—to the people in it, though not to Tolstoy—to be fixed forever. And the book is a masterpiece because Tolstoy was able to fathom, and make us see, the hidden laws which really governed this society and made Anna's doom inevitable.

25 American writers do not have a fixed society to describe. The only society they know is one in which nothing is fixed and in which the individual must fight for his identity. This is a rich confusion, indeed, and it creates for the American writer unprecedented opportunities.

That the tensions of American life, as well as the possibilities, are tremendous is certainly not even a question. But these are dealt with in contemporary literature mainly compulsively; that is, the book is more likely to be a symptom of our tension than an examination of it. The time has come, God knows, for us to examine ourselves, but we can do this only if we are willing to free ourselves of the myth of America and try to find out what is really happening here.

Every society is really governed by hidden laws, by unspoken but profound assumptions on the part of the people, and ours is no exception. It is up to the American writer to find out what these laws and assumptions are. In a society much given to smashing taboos without thereby managing to be liberated from them, it will be no easy matter.

It is no wonder, in the meantime, that the American writer keeps running off to Europe. He needs sustenance for his journey and the best models he

[7] *Anna Karenina:* Published 1875–1877, this is one of the great Russian novels, by Leo Tolstoy (1828–1910). It chronicles the illicit love affair of Anna Karenina who, in her despair at finding a way forward, commits suicide at the novel's end.

can find. Europe has what we do not have yet, a sense of the mysterious and inexorable[8] limits of life, a sense, in a word, of tragedy. And we have what they sorely need: a new sense of life's possibilities.

In this endeavor to wed the vision of the Old World with that of the New, it is the writer, not the statesman, who is our strongest arm. Though we do not wholly believe it yet, the interior life is a real life, and the intangible dreams of people have a tangible effect on the world.

LEARNING MORE

Baldwin relies significantly on his few references, each of which carries within it a whole world of meanings. It seems important to have more than just a casual acquaintance with the following (see the *Ideas Across Time* website to get started).

1. The role of Henry James as a particular kind of expatriate American writer
2. The songs of Bessie Smith, and the fate of Bessie Smith as it sheds light on race relations in the United States
3. The philosophical outlook of Albert Camus
4. Little Rock as a symbol of the civil rights movement
5. The import of Leo Tolstoy's *Anna Karenina*

QUESTIONING THE TEXT

1. In his opening paragraph, what does Baldwin indicate is "complex" about the fate of being an American?
2. Why did Baldwin leave America for Europe?
3. What did American writers encountering one another abroad discover that, according to Baldwin, they could not discover at home?
4. What part did Bessie Smith play in Baldwin's recovery from his breakdown?
5. What makes it possible for the American writer abroad to stop "apologizing for himself" (par. 10)?
6. In what way is the stratification of European society a good thing for the American writer abroad?
7. How would the American writer's experience of Europe be different if he were living there as a European?
8. What, for Baldwin, distinguishes American society from European society?
9. What do you think Baldwin means when he says that Americans are "much given to smashing taboos without thereby managing to be liberated from them"?
10. What qualities of the Old and New Worlds would Baldwin like to combine?

[8] inexorable: unyielding; inevitable; incapable of being moved.

11. At the beginning of his essay, Baldwin says he wanted to find what "could be made to connect me with other people instead of dividing me from them" (par. 2). What did he find to connect him with others?
12. Having finished Baldwin's essay, what do you think are, for him, the main things that make all Americans—regardless of status or race—American? Do you agree?

ANALYZING THE WRITER'S CRAFT

1. One characteristic feature of Baldwin's style is his use of multiple modifiers, as in *"a new, almost completely undefined and extremely controversial* proper noun" (par. 1). Quote two or three examples of this feature of Baldwin's writing, and discuss its rhetorical effects with respect to argument and persuasion.
2. How is Baldwin's opening quotation a point of reference for each part of his essay?
3. Baldwin's way of developing an argument is characteristically organic; that is, one point seems to grow from the previous point rather than to have been planned or outlined as a sequence beforehand. The process of writing seems to be literally a process of thinking, too. For example, although the essay begins as a study of the American abroad, it soon is strictly about the American writer abroad. How, then, does Baldwin maintain coherence in his essay? What are the advantages of his organic mode of developing ideas? Are there any disadvantages?
4. At two points in his essay, Baldwin makes a transition by use of extra white space, as if to mark the end of one section and the beginning of another (between pars. 7 and 8, and between pars. 19 and 20). Why do you think Baldwin chose to exaggerate these particular transitions? Are there other transitions in his essay that you found to be especially emphatic? Especially effective?
5. What do Baldwin's allusions (for example to Henry James or Bessie Smith) add to his argument? Can you think of references he might have used instead? How do his allusions affect the tone of his essay, or color his argument?
6. Discuss how Baldwin uses comparison and contrast to develop his essay.
7. Is his conclusion effective? Explain.

MAKING CONNECTIONS

1. How do you think Baldwin might react to Crevecoeur's definition of an American (pp. 22–27)? To what extent would he agree? To what extent would he disagree? What might he add?
2. After reading Richard Rodriguez (pp. 542–549), would Baldwin embrace the concept of "brown"?
3. Consider whether this essay would be better placed in Chapter 7, "Art"?

FORMULATING IDEAS FOR WRITING

1. Discuss Baldwin's essay from the point of view of struggling with deep-seated preconceptions. (What preconceptions did Baldwin discover in his own view of himself and of America? Did he succeed in overcoming his preconceptions?)
2. If you have had the opportunity to spend some time abroad, compare and contrast American culture with another culture you know. What did you learn about yourself from being abroad?
3. Write an essay that explores/amplifies/questions Baldwin's understanding of what it means to be an American.
4. Write an essay that explores/amplifies/questions Baldwin's view that Americans "have a very deep-seated distrust of real intellectual effort" (par. 12).

The Ghosts of Ellis Island (1985)

Mary Gordon

Mary Catherine Gordon, one of the most forceful voices in American writing of the post–World War II generation, was born into a working-class family in Far Rockaway, New York, on December 8, 1949. Her family circumstances embodied some of the abiding themes of American life, such as the story of arrival and assimilation in New York and worship within the Catholic Church. (Her family, Gordon says, "took deep pleasure in the liturgical world of the Church.") Gordon's father died when she was seven, and she was raised by her alcoholic mother and Irish grandmother. In the memoir of her father, *The Shadow Man: A Daughter's Search for Her Father* (1996), Gordon recounts her discoveries, several decades after his death, that her father, a writer of Catholic devotional poetry, was an often virulently anti-Semitic Jew and an immigrant who had denied his immigrant past.

These diverse forces in her background naturally find their way into her work, which explores the abiding story of the experience of immigrant generations in the New World with an intensity, assurance, and moral seriousness rooted both in her personal history and in the time she came of age, the Sixties. Her concerns can be seen as traditional but cast in the sensibility of a contemporary American feminist. Gordon, for example, addresses issues of faith and meaning in contemporary secular culture, of finding one's roots within grim family or social circumstances, and of women's still-difficult search for full self-realization. Commenting on her role as the McIntosh Professor of English at

Barnard College, that is, on being a woman teaching in a women's college, Gordon has remarked: "I can deliberately attend to the needs of the female voice, which I think is unattended to in most co-ed institutions."

Gordon is the author of six highly regarded novels, as well as a book of essays and collections of stories. Her novels include the best-seller *Final Payments* (1978), *The Company of Women* (1981), *Spending* (1998), and most recently *Pearl* (2005). Her essays were collected in *Good Boys and Dead Girls, and Other Essays* (1991). A graduate of Barnard (1971), Gordon received an M.A. from Syracuse University in 1973. She is the recipient of a Guggenheim Fellowship and of the Lila Acheson Wallace–Reader's Digest Writer's Award. Gordon, the mother of two adult children, lives in New York.

In the essay that follows, "The Ghosts of Ellis Island," originally published in *The New York Times* in 1985, Gordon explains why for her the usual "shrines of America's past greatness," such as Gettysburg and Mount Vernon, have always seemed merely abstractions. *Her* America begins in Ellis Island.

I once sat in a hotel in Bloomsbury[1] trying to have breakfast alone. A Russian with a habit of compulsively licking his lips asked if he could join me. I was afraid to say no; I thought it might be bad for détente. He explained to me that he was a linguist, and that he always liked to talk to Americans to see if he could make any connection between their speech and their ethnic background. When I told him about my mixed ancestry—my mother is Irish and Italian, my father a Lithuanian Jew—he began jumping up and down in his seat, rubbing his hands together, and licking his lips even more frantically:

"Ah," he said, "so you are really somebody who comes from what is called the boiling pot of America." Yes, I told him, yes I was, but I quickly rose to leave. I thought it would be too hard to explain to him the relation of the boiling potters to the main course, and I wanted to get to the British Museum. I told him that the only thing I could think of that united people whose backgrounds, histories, and points of view were utterly diverse was that their people had landed at a place called Ellis Island.

I didn't tell him that Ellis Island was the only American landmark I'd ever visited. How could I describe to him the estrangement I'd always felt from the kind of traveler who visits shrines to America's past greatness, those rebuilt forts with muskets behind glass and sabers mounted on the walls and gift shops selling maple sugar candy in the shape of Indian headdresses, those reconstructed villages with tables set for fifty and the Paul Revere silver gleaming? All that Americana—Plymouth Rock, Gettysburg, Mount Vernon, Valley Forge—it all inhabits for me a zone of blurred abstraction with far less hold on my imagination than the Bastille or Hampton Court.[2] I suppose I've always

[1] Bloomsbury: once a London neighborhood, near the British Museum and the University of London. Made famous as a literary center by Virginia Woolf, who lived there with her siblings and held Thursday evening gatherings that included T. S. Eliot, E. M. Forster, and John Maynard Keynes, among other leading intellectuals.

[2] Hampton Court: once the main palace of the British royalty just outside London.

known that my uninterest in it contains a large component of the willed: I am American, and those places purport to be my history. But they are not mine.

Ellis Island is, though; it's the one place I can be sure my people are connected to. And so I made a journey there to find my history, like any Rotarian traveling in his Winnebago to Antietam[3] to find his. I had become part of that humbling democracy of people looking in some site for a past that has grown unreal. The monument I traveled to was not, however, a tribute to some old glory. The minute I set foot upon the island I could feel all that it stood for: insecurity, obedience, anxiety, dehumanization, the terrified and careful deference of the displaced. I hadn't traveled to the Battery and boarded a ferry across from the Statue of Liberty to raise flags or breathe a richer, more triumphant air. I wanted to do homage to the ghosts.

5 I felt them everywhere, from the moment I disembarked and saw the building with its high-minded brick, its hopeful little lawn, its ornamental cornices. The place was derelict when I arrived; it had not functioned for more than thirty years—almost as long as the time it had operated at full capacity as a major immigration center. I was surprised to learn what a small part of history Ellis Island had occupied. The main building was constructed in 1892, then rebuilt between 1898 and 1900 after a fire. Most of the immigrants who arrived during the latter half of the nineteenth century, mainly northern and western Europeans, landed not at Ellis Island but on the western tip of the Battery at Castle Garden, which had opened as a receiving center for immigrants in 1855.

By the 1880s the facilities at Castle Garden had grown scandalously inadequate. Officials looked for an island on which to build a new immigration center because they thought that on an island immigrants could be more easily protected from swindlers and quickly transported to railroad terminals in New Jersey. Bedloe's Island was considered, but New Yorkers were aghast at the idea of a "Babel" ruining their beautiful new treasure, "Liberty Enlightening the World." The statue's sculptor, Frédéric Auguste Bartholdi, reacted to the prospect of immigrants landing near his masterpiece in horror; he called it a "monstrous plan." So much for Emma Lazarus.[4]

Ellis Island was finally chosen because the citizens of New Jersey petitioned the federal government to remove from the island an old naval powder magazine that they thought dangerously close to the Jersey shore. The explosives were removed; no one wanted the island for anything. It was the perfect place to build an immigration center.

---

[3] Antietam: The 1862 battle that changed the course of the Civil War, the bloodiest battle in U.S. history (23,000 soldiers were killed or wounded, nine times more than on D-Day in World War II). A major defeat for the South, this victory enabled Lincoln's Emancipation Proclamation.

[4] Emma Lazarus: American poet (1849–1887) who wrote the sonnet ("The New Colossus") that is inscribed at the base of the Statue of Liberty:

> Give me your tired, your poor,
> Your huddled masses, yearning to breathe free,
> The wretched refuse of your [the world's] teeming shore.
> Send these, the homeless, temptest-tost to me,
> I lift my land beside the golden door!

I thought about the island's history as I walked into the building and made my way to the room that was the center in my imagination of the Ellis Island experience: the Great Hall. It had been made real for me in the stark, accusing photographs of Louis Hine[5] and others who took those pictures to make a point. It was in the Great Hall that everyone had waited—waiting, always, the great vocation of the dispossessed. The room was empty, except for me and a handful of other visitors and the park ranger who showed us around. I felt myself grow insignificant in that room, with its huge semicircular windows, its air, even in dereliction, of solid and official probity.

I walked in the deathlike expansiveness of the room's disuse and tried to think of what it might have been like, filled and swarming. More than sixteen million immigrants came through that room; approximately 250,000 were rejected. Not really a large proportion, but the implications for the rejected were dreadful. For some, there was nothing to go back to, or there was certain death; for others, who left as adventurers, to return would be to adopt in local memory the fool's role, and the failure's. No wonder that the island's history includes reports of three thousand suicides.

10 Sometimes immigrants could pass through Ellis Island in mere hours, though for some the process took days. The particulars of the experience in the Great Hall were often influenced by the political events and attitudes on the mainland. In the 1890s and the first years of the new century, when cheap labor was needed, the newly built receiving center took in its immigrants with comparatively little question. But as the century progressed, the economy worsened, eugenics became both scientifically respectable and popular, and World War I made American xenophobia[6] seem rooted in fact.

Immigration acts were passed; newcomers had to prove, besides moral correctness and financial solvency, their ability to read. Quota laws came into effect, limiting the number of immigrants from southern and eastern Europe to less than 14 percent of the total quota. Intelligence tests were biased against all non-English-speaking persons and medical examinations became increasingly strict, until the machinery of immigration nearly collapsed under its own weight. The Second Quota Law of 1924 provided that all immigrants be inspected and issued visas at American consular offices in Europe, rendering the center almost obsolete.

On the day of my visit, my mind fastened upon the medical inspections, which had always seemed to me most emblematic of the ignominy and terror the immigrants endured. The medical inspectors, sometimes dressed in uniforms like soldiers, were particularly obsessed with a disease of the eyes called trachoma, which they checked for by flipping back the immigrants' top eyelids

[5] Louis Hine: "The Father of American Documentary Photography," Hine (1874–1940) documented the human face of the American story in famous photos of Ellis Island, of children laboring in factories, and in world-renowned images of men building the Empire State Building in New York City.

[6] xenophobia: fear and hatred of foreigners.

with a hook used for buttoning gloves—a method that sometimes resulted in the transmission of the disease to healthy people. Mothers feared that if their children cried too much, their red eyes would be mistaken for a symptom of the disease and the whole family would be sent home. Those immigrants suspected of some physical disability had initials chalked on their coats. I remembered the photographs I'd seen of people standing, dumbstruck and innocent as cattle, with their manifest numbers hung around their necks and initials marked in chalk upon their coats: "E" for eye trouble, "K" for hernia, "L" for lameness, "X" for mental defects, "H" for heart disease.

I thought of my grandparents as I stood in the room; my seventeen-year-old grandmother, coming alone from Ireland in 1896, vouched for by a stranger who had found her a place as a domestic servant to some Irish who had done well. I tried to imagine the assault it all must have been for her; I've been to her hometown, a collection of farms with a main street—smaller than the athletic field of my local public school. She must have watched the New York skyline as the first- and second-class passengers were whisked off the gangplank with the most cursory of inspections while she was made to board a ferry to the new immigration center.

What could she have made of it—this buff-painted wooden structure with its towers and its blue slate roof, a place *Harper's Weekly* described as "a latter-day watering place hotel"? It would have been the first time she'd have heard people speaking something other than English. She would have mingled with people carrying baskets on their heads and eating foods unlike any she had ever seen—dark-eyed people, like the Sicilian she would marry ten years later, who came over with his family, responsible even then for his mother and sister. I don't know what they thought, my grandparents, for they were not expansive people, nor romantic; they didn't like to think of what they called "the hard times," and their trip across the ocean was the single adventurous act of lives devoted after landing to security, respectability, and fitting in.

15 What is the potency of Ellis Island for someone like me—an American, obviously, but one who has always felt that the country really belonged to the early settlers, that, as J. F. Powers wrote in "Morte D'Urban," it had been "handed down to them by the Pilgrims, George Washington and others, and that they were taking a risk in letting you live in it."[7] I have never been the victim of overt discrimination; nothing I have wanted has been denied me because of the accidents of blood. But I suppose it is part of being an American to be engaged in a somewhat tiresome but always self-absorbing process of national definition. And in this process, I have found in traveling to Ellis Island an important piece of evidence that could remind me I was right to feel my differentness. Something had happened to my people on that island, a result of the eternal wrongheadedness of American protectionism and the predictabilities of simple greed. I came to the island, too, so I could tell the ghosts that I was one of them, and that I honored them—their stoicism, and their innocence, the fear that turned them inward, and their pride. I wanted to tell them that I liked them better than the Americans who made them pass through the Great Hall and stole their names and chalked their weaknesses in public on their clothing. And to tell the ghosts what I have always thought: that American history was a very classy party that was not much fun until they arrived, brought the good food, turned up the music, and taught everyone to dance.

LEARNING MORE

When Mary Gordon visited Ellis Island in 1985, it was still largely abandoned, but in September 1990, after an extensive restoration, the main building was reopened as a museum dedicated to the history of immigration. Furthermore, you can now search for information about your family's arrival at Ellis Island on line. For links to Ellis Island history see the *Ideas Across Time* website.

QUESTIONING THE TEXT

1. How does the Russian linguist's (par. 1) interest in American speech trigger Gordon's reflections on American identity?

[7] J. F. Powers: Powers (1917–1999) was the best-known American Catholic writer, often writing stories about priests and the Church, of the twentieth century.

2. What prompted Gordon to visit Ellis Island and not the usual "shrines" (par. 3) of American history?
3. What does Gordon learn about why Ellis Island was established? What ironies does she discover in its establishment?
4. Does Gordon view the historical record of American policies toward immigrants that Ellis Island represents as admirable? Shameful? Or . . . ?
5. Why does Gordon think of the medical inspections (par. 12) as "most emblematic" of Ellis Island?
6. How does the "adventure" (par. 14) of the ocean crossing contrast with the life of Gordon's grandparents once they arrived? Why do you think Gordon draws attention to this contrast?
7. How is Gordon like the "ghosts" of Ellis Island? What identity as an American does she want to claim?

ANALYZING THE WRITER'S CRAFT

1. What is the thesis of Gordon's essay? Where is it stated?
2. Gordon employs many comparisons and contrasts to build her essay. Choose two or three that you find especially effective, and explain their importance.
3. What is the effect of opening the essay in London, and specifically in Bloomsbury? Is Gordon's use of the Russian linguist useful for introducing the themes of her essay?
4. What's Gordon's point in quoting the Russian's malapropism—"boiling pot" instead of "melting pot"? Is she being fair or unfair? Funny or nasty?
5. Gordon divides her essay into two parts, pars. 1–7 and pars. 8–15. What distinguishes these two sections of her essay? How else might she have moved from her first section to the rest of her essay?
6. How does Gordon evoke the "ghosts" of Ellis Island?
7. What sort of picture of arrival at Ellis Island emerges from Gordon's account? Is her version of events fair? How could you check? What is the relation between Gordon's account of arrival at Ellis Island and the conclusion of her essay?

MAKING CONNECTIONS

1. How does Gordon's view of American identity compare with that of Crevecoeur (pp. 22–27)?
2. James Baldwin (pp. 29–35) had to go abroad to embrace his identity as an American. Do you think that what happened to Baldwin in Paris also happened to Gordon in London? Explain.
3. Chapter 4, "Economic Life," contains several personal accounts of work life (see Louisa May Alcott, pp. 275–286, and Barbara Ehrenreich, pp. 316–319).

What do you imagine Gordon's response to these accounts would be? Would she identify with these writers or find herself estranged from them? Explain.

4. Alexis de Tocqueville (Chapter 6, pp. 458–462) argued in the early nineteenth century that the outstanding feature of American life was our belief in equality. He saw both good and bad things in this quality of American society. Do you find any evidence in Gordon's essay of her views on equality? Explain. Read Tocqueville's essay and consider whether Gordon might or might not agree with his analysis.

FORMULATING IDEAS FOR WRITING

1. If your family came to the United States through Ellis Island, write a brief history of their experiences. Use the Ellis Island website to trace this history, keeping in mind the historical points Gordon makes about Ellis Island. What stands out in your family's lore about the experience of arrival in America?
2. Gordon speaks of "the eternal wrongheadedness of American protectionism and the predictabilities of simple greed" (par. 15). Explain what you think she means by these phrases? What evidence does she provide to support these judgments of American behavior? How are protectionism and greed central to the "self-absorbing process national definition"?
3. For a long period of its history, the United States received immigrants without much question or scrutiny. People simply arrived—no formal permission was required. Ellis Island was established as a screening center at the very close of the nineteenth century—people still arrived without prior permission but had to be cleared for entry upon arrival. Then in 1924, the system changed, and potential immigrants had to be issued visas at American offices abroad in order to enter the United States. Write an essay that explores the pluses and minuses of these three systems; conclude by making a case for the one system of these three that you believe is (or was) the best.
4. Clearly, with the exception of Native Americans, the United States is a nation of immigrants. Yet from the nineteenth century right down to today, U.S. citizens have sharply disagreed about what should be the nation's policy toward immigration. Some Americans in the past have been strongly opposed to allowing any new immigrants into the country, and some American today favor severe restrictions on immigration. At first blush, it seems odd that citizens of a nation of immigrants should be hostile to immigration. What, then, is the rationale offered by those who oppose most new immigration? Write an essay that first explains, and then agrees or disagrees, with the argument that the American national interest is best served by severe restrictions on new immigration.

Silent Dancing (1990)

Judith Ortiz Cofer

Judith Ortiz Cofer, one of the leading voices of the Latina literature that emerged in 1980s and 1990s, was born in 1952 in Hormigueros, Puerto Rico. Her father joined the U.S. Navy shortly before Ortiz Cofer's birth; when he was stationed on a ship assigned to the Brooklyn Naval Yard, the family moved to Paterson, New Jersey. Ortiz Cofer was three years old. Her twenty-year-old mother found the move unsettling, and during the times when her father's ship went on missions abroad, the family returned to her grandmother's house in Hormigueros. This constant back-and-forth between languages and cultures gave dynamic form to Ortiz Cofer's childhood and is the central experience she has explored in various genres throughout her writing career. She has credited her grandmother with teaching her that storytelling is "a form of empowerment . . . the women in my family were passing on power from one generation to another through fables and stories." Much of Ortiz Cofer's work shows the strong imprint of an oral tradition.

In 1967, Ortiz Cofer moved with her family to Augusta, Georgia. She received her B.A. in English from Augusta College and an M.A. from Florida Atlantic University. In 1984, she began teaching at the University of Georgia in Athens, where she is today Franklin Professor of English and Creative Writing.

Ortiz Cofer has produced work in a great variety of genres, including poetry, the short story, memoir, children's and young adult literature, the essay, and the novel; and, as in this selection, she is fond of mixing genres. Although the richness of texture as well as the profound tensions of biculturalism characterize all of Ortiz Cofer's writing, she has emphasized her role as a writer of creative work, insisting on the power of free expression and remaining aloof from the Puerto Rican literary world of New York. Her essays question the limited expectations sometimes imposed on writers identified with ethnic minorities to create works of sociology or reportage rather than art. Instead, her storytelling reverberates with symbols and images, exploring the interior of experience and accepting as essentially human the irresolvable ambiguities of modern life.

Ortiz Cofer began her career writing poetry but gained international prominence with her first novel, *The Line of the Sun* (1989), a landmark in Puerto Rican literature. Nominated for a Pulitzer Prize, *The Line of the Sun* is the first novel ever published by the University of Georgia Press and is also the first novel written about the Puerto Rican diaspora that the University of Puerto Rico Press translated into Spanish. *An Island like You: Stories of the Barrio* (1996) was named Best Book of the Year by the American Library Association. Ortiz Cofer's persistent exploration of the roles of women in Latin culture is evident in her most recent works—*The Year of Revolution* (1998), *Sleeping with One Eye Open: Women Writers and the Art of Survival* (1999), and *Woman in Front of the Sun: On Becoming a Writer* (2000). The present selection comes from *Silent Dancing: A Partial Remembrance of a Puerto Rican Childhood* (1990).

We have a home movie of this party. Several times my mother and I have watched it together, and I have asked questions about the silent revelers coming in and out of focus. It is grainy and of short duration, but it's a great visual aid to my memory of life at that time. And it is in color—the only complete scene in color I can recall from those years.

We lived in Puerto Rico until my brother was born in 1954. Soon after, because of economic pressures on our growing family, my father joined the United States Navy. He was assigned to duty on a ship in Brooklyn Yard—a place of cement and steel that was to be his home base in the States until his retirement more than twenty years later. He left the Island first, alone, going to New York City and tracking down his uncle who lived with his family across the Hudson River in Paterson, New Jersey. There my father found a tiny apartment in a huge tenement that had once housed Jewish families but was just being taken over and transformed by Puerto Ricans, overflowing from New York City. In 1955 he sent for us. My mother was only twenty years old, I was not quite three, and my brother was a toddler when we arrived at *El Building*, as the place had been christened by its newest residents.

My memories of life in Paterson during those first few years are all in shades of gray. Maybe I was too young to absorb vivid colors and details, or to discriminate between the slate blue of the winter sky and the darker hues of the snow-bearing clouds, but that single color washes over the whole period. The building we lived in was gray, as were the streets, filled with slush the first few months of my life there. The coat my father had bought for me was similar in color and too big; it sat heavily on my thin frame.

I do remember the way the heater pipes banged and rattled, startling all of us out of sleep until we got so used to the sound that we automatically shut it out or raised our voices above the racket. The hiss from the valve punctuated my sleep (which has always been fitful) like a nonhuman presence in the room—a dragon sleeping at the entrance of my childhood. But the pipes were also a connection to all the other lives being lived around us. Having come from a house designed for a single family back in Puerto Rico—my mother's extended-family home—it was curious to know that strangers lived under our floor and above our heads, and that the heater pipe went through everyone's apartments. (My first spanking in Paterson came as a result of playing tunes on the pipes in my room to see if there would be an answer.) My mother was as new to this concept of beehive life as I was, but she had been given strict orders by my father to keep the doors locked, the noise down, ourselves to ourselves.

5 It seems that Father had learned some painful lessons about prejudice while searching for an apartment in Paterson. Not until years later did I hear how much resistance he had encountered with landlords who were panicking at the influx of Latinos into a neighborhood that had been Jewish for a couple of generations. It made no difference that it was the American phenomenon of ethnic turnover which was changing the urban core of Paterson, and that the human flood could not be held back with an accusing finger.

"You Cuban?" one man had asked my father, pointing at his name tag on the Navy uniform—even though my father had the fair skin and light-brown hair of his northern Spanish background, and the name Ortiz is as common in Puerto Rico as Johnson is in the United States.

"No," my father had answered, looking past the finger into his adversary's angry eyes. "I'm Puerto Rican."

"Same shit." And the door closed.

My father could have passed as European, but we couldn't. My brother and I both have our mother's black hair and olive skin, and so we lived in El Building and visited our great-uncle and his fair children on the next block. It was their private joke that they were the German branch of the family. Not many years later that area too would be mainly Puerto Rican. It was as if the heart of the city map were being gradually colored brown—*café con leche*[1] brown. Our color.

10 *The movie opens with a sweep of the living room. It is "typical" immigrant Puerto Rican decor for the time: The sofa and chairs are square and hard-looking, upholstered in bright colors (blue and yellow in this instance), and covered with the transparent plastic that furniture salesmen then were so adept at convincing women to buy. The linoleum on the floor is light blue; if it had been subjected to spike heels (as it was in most places), there were dime-sized indentations all over it that cannot be seen in this movie. The room is full of people dressed up: dark suits for the men, red dresses for the women. When I have asked my mother why most of the women are in red that night, she has shrugged, "I don't remember. Just a coincidence." She doesn't have my obsession for assigning symbolism to everything.*

The three women in red sitting on the couch are my mother, my eighteen-year-old cousin, and her brother's girlfriend. The novia *is just up from the Island, which is apparent in her body language. She sits up formally, her dress pulled over her knees. She is a pretty girl, but her posture makes her look insecure, lost in her full-skirted dress, which she has carefully tucked around her to make room for my gorgeous cousin, her future sister-in-law. My cousin has grown up in Paterson and is in her last year of high school. She doesn't have a trace of what Puerto Ricans call* la mancha *(literally, the stain: the mark of the new immigrant—something about the posture, the voice, or the humble demeanor that makes it obvious to everyone the person has just arrived on the mainland). My cousin is wearing a tight, sequined, cocktail dress. Her brown hair has been lightened with peroxide around the bangs, and she is holding a cigarette expertly between her fingers, bringing it up to her mouth in a sensuous arc of her arm*

---

[1] *café con leche:* coffee with milk.

as she talks animatedly. My mother, who has come up to sit between the two women, both only a few years younger than herself, is somewhere between the poles they represent in our culture.

It became my father's obsession to get out of the barrio, and thus we were never permitted to form bonds with the place or with the people who lived there. Yet El Building was a comfort to my mother, who never got over yearning for *la isla.* She felt surrounded by her language: The walls were thin, and voices speaking and arguing in Spanish could be heard all day. *Salsas* blasted out of radios, turned on early in the morning and left on for company. Women seemed to cook rice and beans perpetually—the strong aroma of boiling red kidney beans permeated the hallways.

Though Father preferred that we do our grocery shopping at the supermarket when he came home on weekend leaves, my mother insisted that she could cook only with products whose labels she could read. Consequently, during the week I accompanied her and my little brother to *La Bodega*—a hole-in-the-wall grocery store across the street from El Building. There we squeezed down three narrow aisles jammed with various products. Goya's and Libby's—those were the trademarks that were trusted by *her mamá*, so my mother bought many cans of Goya beans, soups, and condiments, as well as little cans of Libby's fruit juices for us. And she also bought Colgate toothpaste and Palmolive soap. (The final *e* is pronounced in both these products in Spanish, so for many years I believed that they were manufactured on the Island. I remember my surprise at first hearing a commercial on television in which Colgate rhymed with "ate.") We always lingered at La Bodega, for it was there that Mother breathed best, taking in the familiar aromas of the foods she knew from Mamá's kitchen. It was also there that she got to speak to the other women of El Building without violating outright Father's dictates against fraternizing with our neighbors.

Yet Father did his best to make our "assimilation" painless. I can still see him carrying a real Christmas tree up several flights of stairs to our apartment, leaving a trail of aromatic pine. He carried it formally, as if it were a flag in a parade. We were the only ones in El Building that I knew of who got presents on both Christmas day and *dia de Reyes,* the day when the Three Kings brought gifts to Christ and to Hispanic children.

15 Our supreme luxury in El Building was having our own television set. It must have been a result of Father's guilt feelings over the isolation he had imposed on us, but we were among the first in the barrio to have one. My brother quickly became an avid watcher of Captain Kangaroo and Jungle Jim, while I loved all the series showing families. By the time I started first grade, I could have drawn a map of Middle America as exemplified by the lives of characters in "Father Knows Best," "The Donna Reed Show," "Leave It to Beaver," "My Three Sons," and (my favorite) "Bachelor Father," where John Forsythe treated his adopted teenage daughter like a princess because he was rich and had a Chinese houseboy to do everything for him. In truth, compared to our neighbors in El Building, *we* were rich. My father's Navy check provided us with

financial security and a standard of life that the factory workers envied. The only thing his money could not buy us was a place to live away from the barrio—his greatest wish, Mother's greatest fear.

In the home movie the men are shown next, sitting around a card table set up in one corner of the living room, playing dominoes. The clack of the ivory pieces was a familiar sound. I heard it in many houses on the Island and in many apartments in Paterson. In "Leave It to Beaver," the Cleavers played bridge in every other episode; in my childhood, the men started every social occasion with a hotly debated round of dominoes. The women would sit around and watch, but they never participated in the games.

Here and there you can see a small child. Children were always brought to parties and, whenever they got sleepy, were put to bed in the host's bedroom. Babysitting was a concept unrecognized by the Puerto Rican women I knew: A responsible mother did not leave her children with any stranger. And in a culture where children are not considered intrusive, there was no need to leave the children at home. We went where our mother went.

Of my preschool years I have only impressions: the sharp bite of the wind in December as we walked with our parents toward the brightly lit stores downtown; how I felt like a stuffed doll in my heavy coat, boots, and mittens; how good it was to walk into the five-and-dime and sit at the counter drinking hot chocolate. On Saturdays our whole family would walk downtown to shop at the big department stores on Broadway. Mother bought all our clothes at Penney's and Sears, and she liked to buy her dresses at the women's specialty shops like Lerner's and Diana's. At some point we'd go into Woolworth's and sit at the soda fountain to eat.

We never ran into other Latinos at these stores or when eating out, and it became clear to me only years later that the women from El Building shopped mainly in other places—stores owned by other Puerto Ricans or by Jewish merchants who had philosophically accepted our presence in the city and decided to make us their good customers, if not real neighbors and friends. These establishments were located not downtown but in the blocks around our street, and they were referred to generically as *La Tienda, El Bazar, La Bodega, La Botánica.* Everyone knew what was meant. These were the stores where your face did not turn a clerk to stone, where your money was as green as anyone else's.

20 One New Year's Eve we were dressed up like child models in the Sears catalogue: my brother in a miniature man's suit and bow tie, and I in black patent-leather shoes and a frilly dress with several layers of crinoline underneath. My mother wore a bright red dress that night, I remember, and spike heels; her long black hair hung to her waist. Father, who usually wore his Navy uniform during his short visits home, had put on a dark civilian suit for the occasion: We had been invited to his uncle's house for a big celebration. Everyone was excited because my mother's brother Hernan—a bachelor who could indulge himself with luxuries—had bought a home movie camera, which he would be trying out that night.

Even the home movie cannot fill in the sensory details such a gathering left imprinted in a child's brain. The thick sweetness of women's perfumes mixing with the ever-present smells of food cooking in the kitchen: meat and plantain *pasteles,* as well as the ubiquitous rice dish made special with pigeon peas—*gandules*—and seasoned with precious *sofrito*[2] sent up from the Island by somebody's mother or smuggled in by a recent traveler. *Sofrito* was one of the items that women hoarded, since it was hardly ever in stock at La Bodega. It was the flavor of Puerto Rico.

The men drank Palo Viejo rum, and some of the younger ones got weepy. The first time I saw a grown man cry was at a New Year's Eve party: He had been reminded of his mother by the smells in the kitchen. But what I remember most were the boiled *pasteles*—plantain or yucca rectangles stuffed with corned beef or other meats, olives, and many other savory ingredients, all wrapped in banana leaves. Everybody had to fish one out with a fork. There was always a "trick" pastel—one without stuffing—and whoever got that one was the "New Year's Fool."

There was also the music. Long-playing albums were treated like precious china in these homes. Mexican recordings were popular, but the songs that brought tears to my mother's eyes were sung by the melancholy Daniel Santos, whose life as a drug addict was the stuff of legend. Felipe Rodríguez was a particular favorite of couples, since he sang about faithless women and brokenhearted men. There is a snatch of one lyric that has stuck in my mind like a needle on a worn groove: *De piedra ha de ser mi cama, de piedra la cabezera . . . la mujer que a mi me quiera . . . ha de quererme de veras. Ay, Ay, Ay, corazón, porque no amas.*[3] . . . I must have heard it a thousand times since the idea of a bed made of stone, and its connection to love, first troubled me with its disturbing images.

The five-minute home movie ends with people dancing in a circle—the creative filmmaker must have set it up, so that all of them could file past him. It is both comical and sad to watch silent dancing. Since there is no justification for the absurd movements that music provides for some of us, people appear frantic, their faces embarrassingly intense. It's as if you were watching sex. Yet for years I've had dreams in the form of this home movie. In a recurring scene, familiar faces push themselves forward into my mind's eyes, plastering their features into distorted close-ups. And I'm asking them: "Who, is *she?* Who is the old woman I don't recognize? Is she an aunt? Somebody's wife? Tell me who she is."

> "See the beauty mark on her cheek as big as a hill on the lunar landscape of her face—well, that runs in the family. The women on your father's side of the family wrinkle early; it's the price they pay for that fair skin. The young girl with the green stain on her wedding dress is *La Novia*—just up from the Island. See, she lowers her eyes when she approaches the camera, as she's supposed to. Decent girls never look at you directly in the face. *Humilde,* humble, a girl should express humility in all her actions. She will make a good wife for your cousin. He should consider himself lucky to have met her only weeks after she arrived here. If he marries her quickly, she will make him a good Puerto Rican–style wife; but if he waits too long, she will be corrupted by the city—just like your cousin there."

---

[2] *sofrito:* a distinctive Puerto Rican cooking base.

[3] *De piedra . . . amas:* "My bed will be made of stone, stone also my pillow, the woman who dares love me, will have to love me for real. Ay, Ay, Ay, my heart, why aren't you able to love. . . ."

"She means me. I do what I want. This is not some primitive island I live on. Do they expect me to wear a black mantilla on my head and go to mass every day? Not me. I'm an American woman, and I will do as I please. I can type faster than anyone in my senior class at Central High, and I'm going to be a secretary to a lawyer when I graduate. I can pass for an American girl anywhere—I've tried it. At least for Italian, anyway—I never speak Spanish in public. I hate these parties, but I wanted the dress. I look better than any of these *humildes* here. My life is going to be different. I have an American boyfriend. He is older and has a car. My parents don't know it, but I sneak out of the house late at night sometimes to be with him. If I marry him, even my name will be American. I hate rice and beans—that's what makes these women fat."

"Your *prima*[4] is pregnant by that man she's been sneaking around with. Would I lie to you? I'm your *Tía Política*,[5] your great-uncle's common-law wife—the one he abandoned on the Island to go marry your cousin's mother. *I* was not invited to this party, of course, but I came anyway. I came to tell you that story about your cousin that you've always wanted to hear. Do you remember the comment your mother made to a neighbor that has always haunted you? The only thing you heard was your cousin's name, and then you saw your mother pick up your doll from the couch and say: 'It was as big as this doll when they flushed it down the toilet.' This image has bothered you for years, hasn't it? You had nightmares about babies being flushed down the toilet, and you wondered why anyone would do such a horrible thing. You didn't dare ask your mother about it. She would only tell you that you had not heard her right, and yell at you for listening to adult conversations. But later, when you were old enough to know about abortions, you suspected.

"I am here to tell you that you were right. Your cousin was growing an *Americanito* in her belly when this movie was made. Soon after she put something long and pointy into her pretty self, thinking maybe she could get rid of the problem before breakfast and still make it to her first class at the high school. Well, *Niña*,[6] her screams could be heard downtown. Your aunt, her mamá, who had been a midwife on the Island, managed to pull the little thing out. Yes, they probably flushed it down the toilet. What else could they do with it—give it a Christian burial in a little white casket with blue bows and ribbons? Nobody wanted that baby—least of all the father, a teacher at her school with a house in West Paterson that he was filling with real children, and a wife who was a natural blonde.

"Girl, the scandal sent your uncle back to the bottle. And guess where your cousin ended up? Irony of ironies. She was sent to a village in Puerto Rico to live with a relative on her mother's side: a place so far away from civilization that you have to ride a mule to reach it. A real change in scenery. She found a man there—women like that cannot live without male company—but believe me, the men in Puerto Rico know how to put a saddle on a woman like her. *La Gringa*,[7] they call her. Ha, ha, ha. *La Gringa* is what she always wanted to be. . . ."

---

[4] *prima:* female cousin.

[5] *Tía Política:* aunt by marriage.

[6] *niña:* girl.

[7] *La Gringa:* "Gringo" or "gringa" is used, insultingly, to designate a white North American. Here it is used to ridicule a Puerto Rican girl who hopes to mimic a blonde American.

The old woman's mouth becomes a cavernous black hole I fall into. And as I fall, I can feel the reverberations of her laughter. I hear the echoes of her last mocking words: *La Gringa, La Gringa!* And the conga line keeps moving silently past me. There is no music in my dream for the dancers.

25 When Odysseus visits Hades to see the spirit of his mother, he makes an offering of sacrificial blood, but since all the souls crave an audience with the living, he has to listen to many of them before he can ask questions. I, too, have to hear the dead and the forgotten speak in my dream. Those who are still part of my life remain silent, going around and around in their dance. The others keep pressing their faces forward to say things about the past.

My father's uncle is last in line. He is dying of alcoholism, shrunken and shriveled like a monkey, his face a mass of wrinkles and broken arteries. As he comes closer I realize that in his features I can see my whole family. If you were to stretch that rubbery flesh, you could find my father's face, and deep within *that* face—my own. I don't want to look into those eyes ringed in purple. In a few years he will retreat into silence, and take a long, long time to die. *Move back. Tio,* I tell him. *I don't want to hear what you have to say. Give the dancers room to move. Soon it will be midnight. Who is the New Year's Fool this time?*

LEARNING MORE

The number of immigrants to the United States from Latin America mushroomed following the Second World War. Perhaps as a consequence, the distinct heritage, customs, and experiences of people from different Latin American nations can get mixed together into a single storyline by the mainstream culture. But as Ortiz Cofer's work shows, in this case as in all others, the truth is in the details. To find out more about the history of Puerto Rico, and about Puerto Rican migration to the mainland, see the *Ideas Across Time* website.

QUESTIONING THE TEXT

1. This essay opens with a description, in italics, of a silent home movie, a movie, as we learn later, of a party held in the Ortiz home in Paterson. More about this movie, again in sections printed in italics, appears in the essay. How does this movie trigger Ortiz Cofer's writing? What function does the description of this movie serve in the essay? What information does this movie convey that the rest of the essay doesn't?
2. Write two brief paragraphs giving the main details—of biography and of personality—we need to know about Ortiz Cofer's father and mother.
3. What were the ambitions for his children of Ortiz Cofer's father? Of her mother? Did Ortiz Cofer have these same ambitions for herself? Were the children able to fulfill the ambitions of their parents?
4. What distinguished the culture the Ortiz family brought with it from Puerto Rico from the mainstream culture of Paterson? Cite two examples of the differences Ortiz points out. Are there similarities, too? If so, what are they?

5. What distinguished the Ortiz family from others in *El Building?* What is Ortiz Cofer's attitude toward these differences?
6. How did the television shows Ortiz Cofer watched as a girl affect her experience as an immigrant in America?
7. Finally, the home movie is inadequate—it "cannot fill the sensory details" of the party. What is it, then, that's missing? How important is what's missing? Explain.
8. In retrospect, Ortiz Cofer attaches symbolic importance to the fact that all the women at the party wore red. What does the color red symbolize for her? Explain. What do you think is the function, and importance, in the essay of the "New Year's Fool"?
9. How do the differences of culture color the closing paragraphs of the essay, especially the facts and judgments presented in quotation marks?
10. How do you interpret the conclusion of the essay—the sentences in italics with which the essay closes? Is there an answer to the question, Who is the New Year's Fool this time? Why or why not?
11. Ortiz Cofer writes about the party in the movie long after it first occurred. How is the contrast between the mature Judith and the young Judith conveyed? How does the writing of this essay help the mature Judith understand the past?
12. How is "Silent Dancing" an appropriate title for this essay?

ANALYZING THE WRITER'S CRAFT

1. This essay does not work the way less personal and more argumentative or analytical essays work. It is mainly narrative in form, a meditative memoir. But that's not to say that it does not contain argument and analysis. Is there something like a thesis in this essay? If so, what is it—and what evidence in the essay would you use to support your presentation of a thesis? If not, what is the point of the essay—and what evidence in the essay supports your idea of its main point?
2. Discuss the way in which Ortiz Cofer uses different voices in this essay—for example, the voice that speaks in italics, the voices in quotation marks at the close of the essay, the voices in Spanish, and the implicit voices of the father and the mother.
3. What is the effect of the Spanish words in this essay? Are there any words you cannot understand? Does Ortiz Cofer expect all her readers to understand all her Spanish words and phrases? Explain. How would you explain the reason for using words in an essay that many readers might not understand?
4. What audience might Ortiz Cofer have in mind for this essay? Explain.
5. This essay employs a great many contrasts and comparisons—the comparison/contrast between the father and the mother, for example, or the comparison/contrast between the supermarket and the *bodegas*, and so forth. Choose two especially evocative comparisons and contrasts, and show how they convey the main themes of the essay.

6. The child's experience is sensuous in ways that can be muted in adulthood. How does Ortiz Cofer convey the richness of the sensuous experience of her childhood? What details are especially effective in conveying her childhood experiences of sights, sounds, tastes, and smells?
7. "It is both comical and sad to watch silent dancing" (par. 24). How is it comical? How sad? How does this trenchant observation serve as a transition, or introduction, to the questions later in the paragraph, as well as to the new and surprising voices that appear in quotation marks?
8. Who are the speakers quoted in par. 24?
9. What new information do these speakers bring to the essay? How does what these speakers have to say change the focus and effect of the essay?
10. What does the allusion to Odysseus tell us about the writer? What is the effect of this allusion?
11. Does Ortiz Cofer identify with her assimilated cousin, *La Gringa?* Explain.
12. Why do you think Ortiz Cofer saves her father's uncle for last? Why is he so difficult for her to deal with?

MAKING CONNECTIONS

1. Compare and contrast what "the immigrant experience" means to Mary Gordon (pp. 37–42) and to Ortiz Cofer. To what extent are the similarities and differences in their views of this experience reflected in the form of their essays, that is, in how they choose to explore and to convey that experience? Explain.
2. Ortiz Cofer is sometimes identified as a feminist. See the essays by Simone de Beauvoir, Betty Friedan, and bell hooks in Chapter 6 (pp. 481–494, 496–509, and 528–539, respectively), and consider how what they see as feminism illuminates or diverges from Ortiz Cofer's point of view.
3. Ortiz Cofer identifies her family as "colored brown" (par. 9). Is her idea of brown the same as or different from that of Richard Rodriguez (Chapter 6, pp. 542–549)?
4. N. Scott Momaday's "The Arrowmaker" (Chapter 7, pp. 612–618) is about what he sees as the central oral story of his Native American culture. Do you find Momaday's explanation of oral culture helpful in rereading Ortiz Cofer's essay? Or vice versa? Explain.

FORMULATING IDEAS FOR WRITING

1. Every writer's personal history provides the ground for the themes or images or dilemmas of his or her work, whether directly, or obliquely, or indirectly. But the ethnic writer—a troublesome category in itself—can be seen both by his or her community and by the larger community as being responsible for a kind of sociology or for conveying sociological truths rather than for creating art and promoting the far less circumscribed truths of art.

The writer can be viewed as a spokesperson for her or his community rather than as an independent creative artist. Write an essay that explores these dilemmas of ethnic writing. Does the ethnic writer have a special responsibility to her or his community? Should art always be first and foremost art, a free expression without any social obligations? Or do those who tap the rich culture of their origins for their writing also assume a debt to that culture, an implicit obligation to use their voices in order to advance the well-being of their ethnic group?

2. Explore the pros and cons of using languages other than English in American writing. Does using Spanish or, say, Vietnamese terms or sentences in an English essay offer outsiders a form of entry into the minority culture, or does it exclude most readers from that culture? Are essays or stories about the immigrant experience of Puerto Ricans by definition aimed mainly at Puerto Ricans and intended for Puerto Ricans? Or, while the integrity of these essays and stories may depend on their accuracy of detail, is the truth of these stories notable only if they speak to us all as Americans, or indeed as human beings living in a particular time and place?
3. Write about an event in your childhood that conveys the different ambitions your father and your mother had for you at that time.
4. Write an analysis of Ortiz Cofer's essay that focuses on gender roles and gender relations. What distinguishes the men and the women in this essay? How is the experience of biculturalism borne more heavily by the women than by the men? Although the essay focuses more on the women than the men, at its conclusion the writer sees her father's face in the shriveled face of his uncle, and sees her face in her father's face. The concluding image of the story is of her uncle's face, and the concluding words are her reaction to that face and the emotions and ideas it arouses in her. Explain the essay's ending from the vantage point of gender.

Song of Myself (1855)

Walt Whitman

The most American of American poets, Walt (born Walter) Whitman (1819–1892) gave birth almost single-handedly to a modern and distinctly American idiom. His masterwork *Leaves of Grass*, published anonymously by the poet himself in 1855 and revised continually until its final publication in the "death bed" edition of 1892, fashioned a new language and a free form to exhibit the great themes of American life, which for Whitman were private and public, personal and political. He was the bard of egalitarian democracy and the champion of an extravagant individualism. "Song of Myself," the longest poem in the original *Leaves of Grass,* invents an "I" that wantonly conflates individual identity and more or less everything else. When Whitman says he sings of himself, he sings equally of the nation's masses, singly and collectively—freeman and slave, male and female, sane and insane, immigrant and Native American, and so forth. Moreover, his singing is not the rule-bound verse in specialized language of Europe but the plain diction of common people displayed in long, sinuous lines without rhyme or obvious meter. The self-proclaimed wild spirit of American possibility, of political and psychic freedom, Whitman showed the writers who followed him—which is to say, all the writers of the next century—how to work in what came, appropriately, to be called "free verse."

Whitman grew up in a humble but politically radical family on Long Island, one of eight children. For the most part, he was self-taught, and he never really had a trade or profession. He worked as teacher, journalist, carpenter, and clerk—but he worked at none of these for very long, or with much attention. Rather, he did nothing, strolled in the cities, wrote his poems. He never made much money, and he lived all his life in exceptionally modest circumstances. But this wandering and apparently aimless existence fed Whitman's grand, immensely ambitious program to create a poetic persona that could call forth the visionary potential of radical democracy and embrace and celebrate the vivacity of common life.

In the late 1850s, Whitman composed a series of twelve poems, "Live Oak, with Moss," that tell of a homosexual love affair. He never published these during his lifetime, and was frequently in trouble even for obliquely homosexual passages in *Leaves of Grass*. Although he did not feel it was possible to publish openly homoerotic work, Whitman nevertheless stressed the beauties and energies, and the holiness, of sex in his poetry, and at this distance of time, his sexual meanings are robust and playful in a distinctly contemporary way.

During the Civil War, Whitman lived in Washington and devoted himself tirelessly to nursing the wounded, to the detriment of his own health. He captured the grandeur and tragedy of those years in his elegy for Lincoln, "When Lilacs Last in the Dooryard Bloom'd." In 1873, he suffered a stroke, from which he never fully recovered. After living for a time at his brother George's house in Camden, New Jersey, he finally settled into a home of his own in Camden, earning a living by occasional publication. But he also began to earn the admiration of literary celebrities such as the British Poet Laureate Alfred, Lord Tennyson, and gathered around him a group of American disciples. He died in Camden on March 26, 1892.

The lines that follow are from "Song of Myself" in the 1855 edition of *Leaves of Grass.*

The pure contralto sings in the organloft,
The carpenter dresses his plank. . . . the tongue of his foreplane whistles its
    wild ascending lisp,
The married and unmarried children ride home to their thanksgiving
    dinner,

The pilot seizes the king-pin, he heaves down with a strong arm,
The mate stands braced in the whaleboat, lance and harpoon are ready,
The duck-shooter-walks by silent and cautious stretches,
The deacons are ordained with crossed hands at the altar,
The spinning-girl retreats and advances to the hum of the big wheel,
The farmer stops by the bars[1] of a Sunday and looks at the oats and rye,
The lunatic is carried at last to the asylum a confirmed case,
He will never sleep any more as he did in the cot in his mother's bedroom;
The jour printer[2] with gray head and gaunt jaws works at his case,
He turns his quid of tobacco, his eyes get blurred with the manuscript;
The malformed limbs are tied to the anatomist's table,
What is removed drops horribly in a pail;
The quadroon girl is sold at the stand. . . . the drunkard nods by the barroom stove,
The machinist rolls up his sleeves. . . . the policeman travels his beat. . . . the gate-keeper marks who pass,
The young fellow drives the express-wagon. . . . I love him though I do not know him?
The half-breed straps on his light boots to compete in the race,
The western turkey-shooting draws old and young. . . . some lean on their rifles, some sit on logs,
Out from the crowd steps the marksman and takes his position and levels his piece;
The groups of newly-come immigrants cover the wharf or levee,
The woollypates hoe in the sugarfield, the overseer views them from his saddle;
The bugle calls in the ballroom; the gentlemen run for their partners, the dancers bow to each other;
The youth lies awake in the cedar-roofed garret and harks to the musical rain,
The Wolverine[3] sets traps on the creek that helps fill the Huron,
The reformer ascends the platform, he spouts with his mouth and nose,
The company returns from its excursion, the darkey brings up the rear and bears the well-riddled target,
The squaw wrapt in her yellow-hemmed cloth is offering moccasins and beadbags for sale,
The connoisseur peers along the exhibition-gallery with halfshut eyes bent sideways,
The deckhands make fast the steamboat, the plank is thrown for the shoregoing passengers,
The young sister holds out the skein, the elder sister winds it off in a ball and stops now and then for the knots,

[1] bars: fence rails.
[2] jour printer: journeyman printer.
[3] Wolverine: refers to persons living in Michigan.

The one-year wife is recovering and happy, a week ago she bore her first child,
The cleanhaired Yankee girl works with her sewing-machine or in the factory or mill,
The nine months' gone is in the parturition chamber, her faintness and pains are advancing;
The pavingman leans on his two handed rammer—the reporter's lead flies swiftly over the notebook—the signpainter is lettering with red and gold,
The canal-boy trots on the towpath—the bookkeeper counts at his desk—the shoemaker waxes his thread,
The conductor beats time for the band and all the performers follow him,
The child is baptised—the convert is making the first professions,
The regatta is spread on the bay. . . . how the white sails sparkle!
The drover watches his drove, he sings out to them that would stray,
The pedlar sweats with his pack on his back—the purchaser higgles about the odd cent,
The camera and plate are prepared, the lady must sit for her daguerreotype,
The bride unrumples her white dress, the minutehand of the clock moves slowly,
The opium eater reclines with rigid head and just-opened lips,
The prostitute draggles her shawl, her bonnet bobs on her tipsy and pimpled neck,
The crowd laugh at her blackguard oaths, the men jeer and wink to each other,
(Miserable! I do not laugh at your oaths nor jeer you,)
The President holds a cabinet council, he is surrounded by the great secretaries,
On the piazza walk five friendly matrons with twined arms;
The crew of the fish-smack pack repeated layers of halibut in the hold,
The Missourian crosses the plains toting his wares and his cattle,
The fare-collector goes through the train—he gives notice by the jingling of loose change,
The floormen are laying the floor—the tinners are tinning the roof—the masons are calling for mortar,
In single file each shouldering his hod pass onward the laborers;
Seasons pursuing each other the indescribable crowd is gathered. . . . it is the Fourth of July. . . . what salutes of cannon at small arms!
Seasons pursuing each other the plougher ploughs and the mower mows and the wintergrain falls in the ground;
Off on the lakes the pikefisher watches and waits by the hole in the frozen surface,
The stumps stand thick round the clearing, the squatter strikes deep with his axe,

The flatboatmen make fast toward dusk near the cottonwood or pekantrees,
The coon-seekers go now through the regions of the Red river, or through those drained by the Tennessee, or through those of the Arkansas,
The torches shine in the dark that hangs on the Chattahoochee or Altamahaw,[4]
Patriarchs sit at supper with sons and grandsons and great grandsons around them,
In walls of adobe, in canvass tents, rest hunters and trappers after their day's sport.
The city sleeps and the country sleeps,
The living sleep for their time. . . . the dead sleep for their time
The old husband sleeps by his wife and the young husband sleeps by his wife;
And these one and all tend inward to me, and I tend outward to them,
And such as it is to be of these more or less I am,
And of these one and all I weave the song of myself.[5]

LEARNING MORE

To read the whole of "Song of Myself" and other poems in *Leaves of Grass,* as well as discover useful links to information about Whitman, see the *Ideas Across Time* website.

QUESTIONING THE TEXT

1. What kinds of people and activities does Whitman choose to include in his song? Try to order his instances into distinct categories.
2. Are all the people and activities Whitman chronicles equal? Explain.
3. What is the relation between the human world and nature in this poem?
4. For the most part, Whitman includes a person in his catalogue of Americans through a phrase or at most a sentence. But sometimes he gives a person or event more space. Have a look at those occasions in the poem, and consider why he wants to draw special attention to these people and occasions.
5. What is American about this list?
6. Restate the last three lines of the poem in your own words.

[4] Chattahoochee or Altamahaw: Georgia rivers.
[5] . . . myself: Whitman added this last line to 1881 edition of *Leaves of Grass.*

ANALYZING THE WRITER'S CRAFT

1. But is there craft here? How does Whitman make this poem more than just a list?
2. Although Whitman does not use rhyme, he does use other devices to establish a rhythmic order in the poem. What stands out for you in the form of the poem that serves in the stead of rhyme?
3. Whitman uses everyday words for his poem—but his vocabulary and his choice of sounds elevate these ordinary words into poetry. What features of Whitman's diction contribute most to his poetic effect?
4. Choose some striking examples of assonance and alliteration to illustrate some of the musical qualities of the poem. Are these words or these rhythms distinctly American? Why or why not?
5. The context of the poem abruptly shifts at line 56, when individuals cease to be the focus of attention and Whitman introduces "Seasons" and later "the city" and "the living" as well as "the dead." What is the effect of this shift of focus? How does this expansion of context affect the poem's meaning?
6. Do you think Whitman uses too many examples? Too few? How does the length of the poem affect your reading experience?

MAKING CONNECTIONS

1. Would students in J. E. B. Stuart High School (pp. 11–19) recognize themselves in this poem?
2. Is "Song of Myself" an eloquent illustration of the melting pot that excites Crevecoeur (pp. 22–27), or does Whitman make it something radically different from anything Crevecoeur could have imagined?
3. The idea of America as a society always in the process of becoming has prompted many different reactions from Americans. How does Whitman's take on the diversity and dynamism of American life compare to how Judith Ortiz Cofer (pp. 45–52) experiences it? Or Richard Rodriguez (Chapter 6, pp. 542–549)?
4. Whereas Americans often embrace or in any event tolerate our cultural diversity, we seem far less pleased by the impact of change in our economic life. Compare and contrast Whitman's attitude toward work and that of Barbara Ehrenreich (Chapter 4, pp. 316–319).
5. "Song of Myself" first appeared in 1855, two years before Thomas Babington Macaulay, in his "Letter on Democracy" (Chapter 5, pp. 385–388), explained why he does not favor democracy. Compare and contrast Whitman's and Macaulay's outlook on popular democracy.

FORMULATING IDEAS FOR WRITING

1. Whitman added the very last line of this poem in preparing the edition of 1881, a quarter century after the poem was first written. Why do you think

Whitman decided, after so many years had passed, that his poem needed this new last line? Do *you* think the poem needs this line? Write an essay that either discusses how the poem is improved and clarified by this last line or that argues that the last line is redundant and Whitman's change was unnecessary.

2. What makes this poem anything more than an inspired list?
3. Write an essay on what this poem has to say about the nature of human experience. In your discussion, consider the poem's attitude toward good and evil, toward death, toward age, toward social class, and toward the place of human beings in nature.
4. How does this poem view American identity?

chapter 2

Belief

The way human beings approach the most central questions—What is the meaning of life? Who are we? Where are we? Where are we going?—has always involved religion. Gregory Rodriguez, in the keynote essay of this chapter, says that more than anything else, religion is the language we use to explore these questions. For this reason, theology, liturgy, and prayer have been at the center of Western culture for centuries, and in analogous forms at the center of all cultures.

But writing in 2006 about his decision to become a practicing Catholic only when in his thirties, Rodriguez also draws attention to the different circumstances in which belief must find its way in present-day America as compared with the past. Despite the visible importance of religion in American life, the power of technology and science has made ours a secular society, one in which religious belief can be looked at as peculiar. At the same time, the separation of church and state in the United States is questioned from within the country while theocratic regimes in other countries have taken aim at the United States as a godless society.

The readings in this chapter explore these urgent issues, beginning with excerpts from the sacred texts of world faiths. These selections from the King James Bible, the Qur'an, the Analects of Confucious, and the Rig Veda and the Upanishad affirm both the all-encompassing power of God and the reliability of religious doctrine. This passage from the Qur'an is representative:

> To God belongs all
> that is in the heavens and the earth;
> and whether you reveal
> what is in your heart or conceal it,
> you will have to account for it to God
> who will pardon whom He please and punish whom He will,
> for God has the power over all things.

The certainty, authority, universality, and confidence of this point of view was—and continues to be—a core belief to large numbers of people. Over the last several centuries, such unequivocal assertions have also been questioned by others and even regarded as superstition. In an excerpt from his *Age of Reason*, the great eighteenth-century rationalist Tom Paine explains that his reason leads him to a belief in "one God," but no further: he rejects all organized religions. Next, the nineteenth-century suffragette Elizabeth Cady Stanton argues that the Bible has long been misunderstood and manipulated by men, and she finds in Genesis a divine sanction for the equality of the sexes. At the end of the nineteenth century, the radical German philosopher Friedrich Nietzsche announces that "God is dead." Humankind—meaning the physicists, the geologists, the evolutionary biologists—has killed Him. For Nietzsche the death of God spells liberation: human beings are free to make their own way in the universe without illusions. Nietzsche predicts that this liberation, with its need for the "revaluation" of all values, will not be a pleasant passage to wisdom but rather a chaotic and possibly violent journey.

In part, the twentieth century confirmed Nietzsche's fears. But it is also the case that in the twentieth century belief not only continued but in certain ways reasserted its centrality as a human attribute. At the very moment that Nietzsche announces the death of God, the influential pragmatist philosopher William James, brother of the great American novelist Henry James, makes his (often wry and gently amusing) claim to the rationality and soundness of "the will to believe."

Belief persists—but incontestably in a transformed context, surrounded by science and our ubiquitous, insistently secular technology. In the middle of the twentieth century, the important theologian Paul Tillich, in a reflective and sober essay, notes that while religious observance, especially in the United States, is statistically high, we have nonetheless lost the "dimension of depth" in religion, which he defines as "being grasped by an infinite concern." The resurgence of participation in organized religion, he says, "is nothing but a desperate and mostly futile attempt to regain what has been lost." The vivacity of secular life, what once was pejoratively known as worldliness, was surely never more seductive or powerful than in our time.

But the new century also reveals an intriguing diversity of spiritual thought. The worldwide popularity of the teaching of the Dalai Llama demonstrates how, as instant communication and the ease of travel make the world a smaller place, many people across the globe are receptive to religious counsel without preconceptions or cultural prejudice. And finally, Karen Armstrong, writing about Islam, explains why a belief in a just God can mean not that people look *beyond* the corrupt history of human societies for justice but rather that they may seek the presence of God *within* history. For the Muslim people, she writes, history is not secular or a realm separated from divinity but rather is the very terrain of the sacred.

KEYNOTE

Catholic Confessions (2006)

Gregory Rodriguez

Gregory Rodriguez is Irvine Senior Fellow at the New America Foundation and a contributing editor to the *Los Angeles Times,* where he writes a Sunday op-ed column. He is the author of *The Emerging Latino Middle Class* (1996) and *From Newcomers to New Americans: The Successful Integration of Immigrants into American Society* (1999). His essay "Mongrel America," which first appeared in *The Atlantic Monthly,* was included in *The Best American Political Writing of 2003.* Rodriguez is at work on a study of the impact of Mexican immigration on U.S. attitudes toward race. The selection below appeared in the *Los Angeles Times* on Easter Sunday, April 16, 2006.

Five years ago this month, I became a Catholic. It wasn't an easy or sudden decision. I had been grappling with the idea since I was in my late teens. Back then, I dreamed of becoming a theologian. I studied religion in college, philosophy mostly, as well as German and Latin, two important languages for Christian theological studies. After college and three years of work in New York, I was even accepted at a high-falutin' East Coast divinity school.

This is not to say that I was a believer. Though I had been baptized, I was raised in an agnostic household by two independent-thinking parents, neither of whom felt a pressing need to give their children a traditional upbringing. My mother and father met at UCLA in the mid-1950s, two among a handful of Mexican American students on campus. Whatever ties they had to traditional religious folkways were lost on their way up the social ladder.

Other than having my grandmother cross and bless me each time I visited her, I had no sustained contact with religion as a child. When I was 7, the same grandmother taught me the Lord's Prayer as a way to help me stop worrying about my parents while they were on vacation across the ocean. I don't recall it working.

But in my sophomore year of college, I read St. Augustine's "Confessions,"[1] and it changed my life. His journey of self-discovery made me realize that without a religion, I had no language with which to tackle the big questions of life and death. That was the semester I changed my major to religious studies.

5 I was not at all sold on the idea of becoming a member of an organized religion. For starters, there were so many to choose from.

A Mexican American priest once told me that, like it or not, I was a cultural Catholic. After all, the religion is inextricably entwined with Mexicanness. Perhaps just as important, my taste for the baroque,[2] another cultural inheritance,

[1] "Confessions": Augustine (354–430) wrote his *Confessions* (397) as the account of his struggle as a young man to overcome his immoral habits and achieve grace. The book is the classic story of sinner-turned-priest.

[2] baroque: an elaborately ornate seventeenth-century architectural and broadly artistic style.

made me predisposed to respond to all the bells, whistles and hocus pocus of the church.

For years, I told people that I was thinking of becoming a Catholic. Invariably, those friends who were raised in the church, and had suffered the stupidity and, sometimes, cruelty of this priest or that nun, accused me of romanticizing the institution.

I plead not guilty. By the time I joined, the molestation scandal was in full swing; I have no illusions about the sanctity of the Catholic Church. Yet I am also not convinced of my ability to lead a fulfilling spiritual life without a religious language, tradition and infrastructure.

As debased as it can be, the church to me is still an extraordinary institution whose liturgy has the ability to focus one's attention on the fundamental questions of life. Like the art-nouveau lamp in the chapel on the final page of *Brideshead Revisited,* Evelyn Waugh's[3] fictional masterpiece, the church is the keeper of a "small red flame—a beaten-copper lamp of deplorable design, relit before the beaten-copper doors of a tabernacle."

10 Most of my contemporaries couldn't believe that I chose to "convert," to go through catechism, to make my first communion in my 30s. "You actually believe that stuff?" one blurted out. Some believe that all religions are merely attempts to simplify life's complexities. They found my decision unworthy of someone who practices rationality, who thinks and writes for a living. I explain that my faith doesn't so much provide me with simple certainties as it gives me a space and a means to grapple with uncertainties. I ask them if they think Christ's parables, the stories that form the core of his teaching, are simple to understand, simple to put to use.

Biblical scholar John Dominic Crossan[4] makes a useful distinction between religious myths and parables. Myths, he writes, give believers the "final word" on reality, while parables "deliberately subvert final words" and challenge us to engage in the questions.

Today, hundreds of millions of Christians will celebrate the joyful and unexpected conclusion to the story of Christ's betrayal, suffering and death. It is a story that, like a parable, is fundamentally unsettling. It points to what lies beyond the limits of reason and gives us hope that, one day, we too will rise above what burdens us.

LEADING QUESTIONS

Rodriguez speaks of religion as a "language." For centuries the language of religion—theology, liturgy, prayer—has helped people grapple with (in Rodriguez' words) "the big questions of life and death." But in our time—

---

[3] Evelyn Waugh: Waugh (1903–1966), a self-consciously Catholic writer, one of the twentieth-century masters of English prose, subtitled his novel *Brideshead Revisited* as *The Sacred and Profane Memories of Capt. Charles Ryder.*

[4] Crossan: John Dominic Crossan (b. 1934) is an Irish-American biblical scholar. He cofounded the Jesus Seminar, a group of academics who seek to "demythologize" Jesus.

secular, often religious in form only—this language has fallen into disuse, or is looked at askance, as Rodriguez's friends have looked at his turning to the Church as an adult. And yet, is there another language with which to address these questions?

Do we expect unequivocal answers from religion? Rodriguez says religion offers him "a space and a means to grapple with uncertainties." He points to Jesus's parables as mysteries rather than certainties. Yet the holy books, especially of the Western tradition, seem often to suggest—especially in their tone—that they are conveying certainties. Aren't the holy books the word of God?

Rodriguez shows that today a grown man who suddenly gets serious about religion is likely to be mocked. We are a secular, "rational" society. Can reason and faith support one another, or must they inevitably clash?

Is religion only about the self and the infinite, the soul and God? Or is religion about being in the world, and thus a force that must show its face in history (see Karen Armstrong on "History and Religion," pp. 137–139)?

LEARNING MORE

Rodriguez makes three pertinent allusions in his essay, each of which reveals something about his outlook. Augustine's *Confessions* are accessible online. You can also find useful links to learn more about Evelyn Waugh and about the Jesus Seminar that John Dominic Crossan helped found on the *Ideas Across Time* website.

QUESTIONING THE TEXT

1. When Rodriguez turned to religion, why did he turn to Catholicism? Does his choice of Catholicism seem a choice of this one Christian denomination above all others, or is it a choice of organized religion over no formal religious practice? Explain.
2. What are the pros and cons of the Church that Rodriguez identified? Why isn't Rodriguez as bothered by the problems within the Church as are his friends?
3. What is Rodriguez looking for in organized religion?
4. Explain in your own words the distinction Rodriguez attributes to John Dominic Crossan, between religious myths and parables. Why does this distinction matter to him?

ANALYZING THE WRITER'S CRAFT

1. How does Rodriguez's essay reveal that it was written for the mass audience of a daily newspaper (it was published in the *Los Angeles Times*)?
2. Does this essay have a thesis? If so, what is it, and where is it stated? If not, what holds the essay together?

3. Rodriguez is forced to reduce a complex experience that occurred over many years into a few hundred words. He therefore has to move the reader efficiently from one idea to the next. Cite two or three of his especially effective transitions, and explain how they create a comfortable bridge between one point and the next. (Look in particular at the beginning of each of his paragraphs.)
4. Rodriguez employs a combination of narrative and argument for his essay. What arguments against active participation in the Church does Rodriguez choose to refute? Does he state these objections fairly? Does he refute them to your satisfaction? Explain.
5. Rodriguez uses three significant allusions to support and amplify his points—one to Augustine's *Confessions* (par. 4), one to Evelyn Waugh's *Brideshead Revisited,* one to John Dominic Crossan. How do these allusions help Rodriguez get his ideas across? Does it matter whether the reader has read Augustine, Waugh, and Crossan? Explain. Do you think Rodriguez expects most of his readers to have read these writers? Explain. What do these allusions add to the essay that could not be contributed by Rodriguez's own words? Do these allusions enrich the essay? Explain.
6. Discuss how Rodriguez's essay explores the contrasts between religion as certainty and religion as mystery.
7. What is the effect of closing the essay with an affirmation of parable? Does this ending clinch Rodriguez's argument? Why or why not?

MAKING CONNECTIONS

1. Judging from this essay, what parts of the holy books (pp. 68–96) do you think Rodriguez would find most meaningful? Would a reading of these texts from Rodriguez' point of view distort the texts by stressing some sections over others?
2. Might reading the Dalai Lama (pp. 132–135) convert Rodriguez to Buddhism?
3. Does what Richard Feynman says about the value of science (Chapter 3, pp. 201–207) offer an alternative approach to the great questions from religion? What do you think Rodriguez might say?
4. Socrates' famous effort to assuage his disciples on his deathbed (Chapter 8, pp. 640–644) is supremely rational. He faces death with equanimity and logic. For Socrates, therefore, it seems nothing "lies beyond the limits of reason" (Rodriguez's words). What is your view?

FORMULATING IDEAS FOR WRITING

1. Many people seem to find comfort in religion precisely because it offers certainty about the big questions to which we have no clear answers, such as whether there is existence after death. But Rodriguez is drawn to religion as a way and a form—a way of questioning, a form of answering—in the terms he chooses, not for the certainty of myth but the mystery of parable.

Write an essay that explores the two aspects of religion that Rodriguez isolates in his essay: certainty and mystery.

2. There has been a great deal of attention devoted in the recent past to sexual abuse of children by priests. These apparently widespread abuses have not only shocked many people but have caused some Catholics to leave the Church. Rodriguez acknowledges the problem but says it is not great enough to overcome the value of the Church. What is your view? Do you find Rodriguez to be complacent or wise?
3. The term *religious myth* is usually applied by believers to other religions, or to the beliefs of the past, such as Greek mythology. But Rodriguez and John Dominic Crossan seem to include Catholic and broadly Christian beliefs in the category of religious myth. Should we see Christ's rising from the dead as a myth? How does viewing Christ's ascension as a myth change the nature of Christian belief? Does this change enlarge and deepen Christian thought, or does it diminish Christian teaching? Why do Rodriguez and Crossan—both believers and practicing Catholics—prefer the mystery of the parables to the certainty of myth? Discuss—and, if you care to, explain your own view.
4. Write an essay modeled on Rodriguez's that explains why you are or are not a practicing member of a religious denomination.

The Rig Veda and the Upanishad

The Rig Veda and the Upanishad are key texts of the Hindu scriptures—the *Shruti*. The Rig Veda (Sanskrit for "praise" plus "knowledge") is the oldest text in the Indo-Iranian language, the earliest of all the holy documents of the Hindu tradition, originating around 1500 BCE. The earliest translation into English was performed by Ralph T. H. Griffith in 1896. The Rig Veda forms the first of the four Vedas—Rig Veda, Yajur Veda, Sama Veda, and Atharva Veda. It is a collection of over one thousand hymns, contained in ten books, mostly devoted to praise for the Vedic gods.

The Upanishad are, in contrast, commentaries on each of the four Vedas. Scholars agree that the Upanishad—literally, "sitting down near," that is, receiving instruction from a Guru—were written before the time of Buddha, though not fully recorded until the seventeenth century. They are mystical and philosophical, detailing the practices of mystic and yoga teachers.

As the selection from the Rig Veda shows, although these scriptures do not begin with creation, they do offer accounts of creation at some point in the text. The Vedas rather are concerned with "being" and "nonbeing"; the beginning, in these texts, is reached not by tracing a line backward but rather by moving from the circumference to the center of things. In the Upanishad, in a related vein, death can lead back to life or can open onto a domain of spiritual freedom. This domain recalls the Christian Heaven but is lacking the element of final judgment and is expressed in an evocative but elusive mystical language.

Creation Accounts in the Vedas*

From the Rig Veda X, 129

1. At first was neither Being nor Nonbeing.
   There was not air nor yet sky beyond.
   What was its wrapping? Where? In whose protection?
   Was Water there, unfathomable and deep?

2. There was no death then, nor yet deathlessness;
   of night or day there was not any sign.
   The One breathed without breath, by its own impulse.
   Other than that was nothing else at all.

3. Darkness was there, all wrapped around by darkness,
   and all was Water indiscriminate. Then
   that which was hidden by the Void, that One, emerging,
   stirring, through power of Ardor, came to be.

4. In the beginning Love arose,
   which was the primal germ cell of the mind.
   The Seers, searching in their hearts with wisdom,
   discovered the connection of Being in Nonbeing.

5. A crosswise line cut Being from Nonbeing.
   What was described above it, what below?
   Bearers of seed there were and mighty forces,

6. Who really knows? Who can presume to tell it?
   Whence was it born? Whence issued this creation?
   Even the Gods came after its emergence.
   Then who can tell from whence it came to be?

7. That out of which creation has arisen,
   whether it held it firm or it did not,
   He who surveys it in the highest heaven,
   He surely knows or maybe He does not!

**The Vedic Experience: Mantra-manjari*, trans., Raimundo Panikkar (New Delhi: Motilal Banarsidas, 1994), p. 58.

What Remains at Death?*

From the Katha Upanishad, Part 5

"By ruling over the city of eleven gates,
the unborn who is not devious-minded does not grieve,
but when set free is truly free.
This truly is that.

"The swan in the sky, the god in the atmosphere,
the priest at the altar, the guest in the house,
in people, in gods, in justice, in the sky,
born in water, born in cattle, born in justice,
born in rock, is justice, the great one.
Upwards it leads the out-breath,
downwards it casts the in-breath.
The dwarf who sits in the center all the gods reverence.
When this incorporate one that is in the body
slips off and is released from the body,
what is there that remains?
This truly is that.

"Not by the out-breath and the in-breath
does any mortal live.
Buy by another do they live
on which these both depend.

"Look, I shall explain to you
the mystery of God, the eternal,
and how the soul fares after reaching death, Gautama.
Some enter a womb for embodiment;
others enter stationary objects
according to their actions and according to their thoughts.

"Whoever is awake in those that sleep,
the Spirit who shapes desire after desire,
that they call the bright one.
That is God; that indeed is called the immortal.
On it all the worlds rest, and no one ever goes beyond it.
This truly is that.

"As one fire has entered the world
and becomes varied in shape

---

*Sanderson Beck, ed. and trans., *Wisdom Bible* (Goleta, Calif.: World Peace Communications, 2002), pp. 79–80.

according to the form of every object,
so the one inner soul in all beings
becomes varied according to whatever form
and also exists outside.

"As one air has entered the world
and becomes varied in shape
according to the form of every object,
so the one inner soul in all beings
becomes varied according to whatever form
and also exists outside.

"As the sun, the eye of the world,
is not defiled by the external faults of the eyes,
so the inner soul in all beings
is not defiled by the evil in the world, being outside it.

"The inner soul in all beings, the one controller,
who makes this one form manifold,
the wise who perceive this standing in oneself,
they and no others have eternal happiness.

"The one eternal among the transient,
the conscious among the conscious,
the one among the many, who grants desires,
the wise who perceive this standing in oneself
they and no others have eternal happiness.

"This is it.
Thus they recognize the ineffable supreme happiness.
How then may I understand this?
Does it shine or does it reflect?
The sun does not shine there, nor the moon and the stars;
lightning does not shine there, much less this fire.
After that shines does everything else shine.
The whole world is illuminated by its light."

LEARNING MORE

Many people devote years—or a lifetime—of study to sacred texts. For the purposes of understanding these more thoroughly, you may want to read more of the texts or to find out more about them. Useful links can be found on the *Ideas Across Time* website.

QUESTIONING THE TEXT

The Rig Veda

1. What existed before the creation?
2. How did the world come to be?
3. What concept of the divine do you find in these passages from the Rig Veda?
4. How do the authors of the Rig Veda claim knowledge of the creation?

The Upanishad

1. What is death?
2. What is the idea of God in the Upanishad?
3. What is the idea of soul in the Upanishad?
4. How do you interpret the repeated phrase "This truly is that"?
5. What concept of afterlife is found in the Upanishad?

ANALYZING THE WRITER'S CRAFT

1. Who is the audience, and how can you tell?
2. What is the purpose of each text? Explain.
3. What is the tone of the writing?
4. How is the deeper truth of these passages revealed to the reader?
5. Why are these texts in an essentially poetic rather than a prosaic form?

MAKING CONNECTIONS

1. Compare and contrast the image of God in the other sacred texts of this chapter.
2. What do the sacred texts of this chapter have in common? In what ways do these texts differ—in terms of form and in terms of content?
3. Do these sacred texts reveal an underlying unity of human religious perspectives, or an underlying diversity?
4. Do these sacred texts confirm Paul Tillich's view of the religious dimension in life (pp. 123–130)? Explain.
5. How do these sacred texts help an individual decide the rights and wrongs of problems like those raised in the keynote essay of this chapter?

FORMULATING IDEAS FOR WRITING

1. The idea of the divine is a perennial theme of human culture. On the basis of the sacred texts in this chapter, write an essay on the concept of the divine. In preparing your essay, consider what these texts say about the outstanding characteristics of God, about the nature of God, about God's

expectations of human beings, and about human expectations of God. What do these texts say about the relation of eternity to time, and of immortality to mortality?

2. Consider the quality of "goodness" as it appears in these texts (or in most of them). Is being good a quality of "inwardness," of the essential inner self, which God recognizes and will reward on the day of resurrection; or is being good a matter of meeting the "external" demands of and fulfilling the obligations prescribed by God? Is there a condition of being that transcends "good"? Is evil implied by good, and vice versa?
3. Which of these texts brings you closest to God? Write an essay that explains your religious response to these sacred texts.
4. Write an essay on the rights and wrongs of cloning using one or more of these sacred texts to support your argument.

The King James Bible

The selections that follow are taken from Genesis and Exodus, the first two of the five books of Moses in the Hebrew Bible or, in Christian terms, the Old Testament; and from the Sermon on the Mount in the Gospel of Matthew, in the New Testament. The books of Moses are assumed to originate around the year 1400 BCE (the earliest record of a Hebrew alphabet is c. 1800 BCE), but it is accepted that these books were compiled in their existing form between 538 BCE, when the Persian king Cyrus allowed the Jews to return to Jerusalem from their Babylonian exile, and around 300 BCE. The gospels were in circulation in book form within sixty years of the death of Jesus. Although it seems impossible to be certain where, when, and even by whom they were written, the four gospels in the New Testament (Matthew, Mark, Luke, John) each tell the story of Jesus, concentrating on his life as a preacher and on his death. The theological import of these gospels is suggested in Paul's use of the singular "gospel" (or "good news," which is what gospel means in early English usage). For Paul, the message of the Christian "gospel" is that the promises of God to the Jews have been fulfilled through Jesus.

The first translations from the Bible to appear in English were composed by John Wyclif (1330–1384) from the Latin Bible that Jerome established between 383 and 405 CE. (Wyclif did not translate the entire Bible.) The King James version of the Bible (sometimes known as the authorized version), published in 1611, is the work of fifty-four scholars named by King James I of England to produce a translation into English for use in church services throughout the realm. King James's committee of churchmen depended heavily on the English translation of the Bible by William Tyndale (1494–1536), who wished to make the Bible accessible to the common man. The King James version, contemporary with the work of Shakespeare, is a monumental example of the glories of the English language at an extraordinarily rich moment in its development. Moreover, more than any other single work, the King James Bible has shaped the modern English language.

Genesis

Chapter 1

In the beginning God created the heaven and the earth.

2 And the earth was without form, and void; and darkness *was* upon the face of the deep. And the Spirit of God moved upon the face of the waters.

3 And God said, Let there be light: and there was light.

4 And God saw the light, that *it was* good: and God divided the light from the darkness.

5 And God called the light Day, and the darkness he called Night. And the evening and the morning were the first day.

6 And God said, Let there be a firmament in the midst of the waters, and let it divide the waters from the waters.

7 And God made the firmament, and divided the waters which *were* under the firmament from the waters which *were* above the firmament: and it was so.

8 And God called the firmament Heaven. And the evening and the morning were the second day.

9 And God said, Let the waters under the heaven be gathered together unto one place, and let the dry *land* appear: and it was so.

10 And God called the dry *land* Earth; and the gathering together of the waters called he Seas: and God saw that *it was* good.

11 And God said, Let the earth bring forth grass, the herb yielding seed, *and* the fruit tree yielding fruit after his kind, whose seed *is* in itself, upon the earth: and it was so.

12 And the earth brought forth grass, *and* herb yielding seed after his kind, and the tree yielding fruit, whose seed *was* in itself, after his kind: and God saw that *it was* good.

13 And the evening and the morning were the third day.

14 And God said, Let there be lights in the firmament of the heaven to divide the day from the night; and let them be for signs, and for seasons, and for days, and years:

15 And let them be for lights in the firmament of the heaven to give light upon the earth: and it was so.

16 And God made two great lights; the greater light to rule the day, and the lesser light to rule the night: *he made* the stars also.

17 And God set them in the firmament of the heaven to give light upon the earth,

18 And to rule over the day and over the night, and to divide the light from the darkness: and God saw that *it was* good.

19 And the evening and the morning were the fourth day.

20 And God said, Let the waters bring forth abundantly the moving creature that hath life, and fowl *that* may fly above the earth in the open firmament of heaven.

21 And God created great whales, and every living creature that moveth, which the waters brought forth abundantly, after their kind, and every winged fowl after his kind: and God saw that *it was* good.

22 And God blessed them, saying, Be fruitful, and multiply, and fill the waters in the seas, and let fowl multiply in the earth.

23 And the evening and the morning were the fifth day.

24 And God said, Let the earth bring forth the living creature after his kind, cattle, and creeping thing, and beast of the earth after his kind: and it was so.

25 And God made the beast of the earth after his kind, and cattle after their kind, and every thing that creepeth upon the earth, after his kind: and God saw that *it was* good.

26 And God said, Let us make man in our image, after our likeness: and let them have dominion over the fish of the sea, and over the fowl of the air, and over the cattle, and over all the earth, and over every creeping thing that creepeth upon the earth.

27 So God created man in his *own* image, in the image of God created he him; male and female created he them.

28 And God blessed them, and God said unto them, Be fruitful, and multiply, and replenish the earth, and subdue it: and have dominion over the fish of the sea, and over the fowl of the air, and over every living thing that moveth upon the earth.

29 And God said, Behold, I have given you every herb bearing seed, which *is* upon the face of all the earth, and every tree, in the which *is* the fruit of a tree yielding seed; to you it shall be for meat.

30 And to every beast of the earth, and to every fowl of the air, and to every thing that creepeth upon the earth, wherein *there is* life, *I have given* every green herb for meat: and it was so.

31 And God saw every thing that he had made, and, behold, *it was* very good. And the evening and the morning were the sixth day.

Chapter 2

Thus the heavens and the earth were finished, and all the host of them.

2 And on the seventh day God ended his work which he had made; and he rested on the seventh day from all his work which he had made.

3 And God blessed the seventh day, and sanctified it: because that in it he had rested from all his work which God created and made.

4 These *are* the generations of the heavens and of the earth when they were created, in the day that the LORD God made the earth and the heavens,

5 And every plant of the field before it was in the earth, and every herb of the field before it grew: for the LORD God had not caused it to rain upon the earth, and *there was* not a man to till the ground.

6 But there went up a mist from the earth, and watered the whole face of the ground.

7 And the LORD God formed man *of* the dust of the ground, and breathed into his nostrils the breath of life; and man became a living soul.

8 And the LORD God planted a garden eastward in Eden; and there he put the man whom he had formed.

9 And out of the ground made the LORD God to grow every tree that is pleasant to the sight, and good for food; the tree of life also in the midst of the garden, and the tree of knowledge of good and evil.

10 And a river went out of Eden to water the garden; and from thence it was parted, and became into four heads.

11 The name of the first *is* Pi'son: that *is* it which compasseth the whole land of Hav'i-lah, where *there is* gold;

12 And the gold of that land *is* good: there *is* bdellium and the onyx stone.

13 And the name of the second river *is* Gi'hon: the same *is* it that compasseth the whole land of E-thi-ópi-a.

14 And the name of the third river *is* Hid'de-kel: that *is* it which goeth toward the east of As-syr'i-a. And the fourth river *is* Eu-phra'tes.

15 And the LORD God took the man, and put him into the garden of Eden to dress it and to keep it.

16 And the LORD God commanded the man, saying, Of every tree of the garden thou mayest freely eat:

17 But of the tree of the knowledge of good and evil, thou shalt not eat of it: for in the day that thou eatest thereof thou shalt surely die.

18 And the LORD God said. *It is* not good that the man should be alone; I will make him an help meet for him.

19 And out of the ground the LORD God formed every beast of the field, and every fowl of the air; and brought *them* unto Adam to see what he would call them: and whatsoever Adam called every living creature, that *was* the name thereof.

20 And Adam gave names to all cattle, and to the fowl of the air, and to every beast of the field; but for Adam there was not found an help meet for him.

21 And the LORD God caused a deep sleep to fall upon Adam, and he slept: and he took one of his ribs, and closed up the flesh instead thereof;

22 And the rib, which the LORD God had taken from man, made he a woman, and brought her unto the man.

23 And Adam said, This *is* now bone of my bones, and flesh of my flesh: she shall be called Woman, because she was taken out of Man.

24 Therefore shall a man leave his father and his mother, and shall cleave unto his wife: and they shall be one flesh.

25 And they were both naked, the man and his wife, and were not ashamed.

Chapter 3

Now the serpent was more subtil than any beast of the field which the LORD God had made. And he said unto the woman, Yea, hath God said, Ye shall not eat of every tree of the garden?

2 And the woman said unto the serpent, We may eat of the fruit of the trees of the garden:

3 But of the fruit of the tree which *is* in the midst of the garden, God hath said, Ye shall not eat of it, neither shall ye touch it, lest ye die.

4 And the serpent said unto the woman, Ye shall not surely die:

5 For God doth know that in the day ye eat thereof, then your eyes shall be opened, and ye shall be as gods, knowing good and evil.

6 And when the woman saw that the tree *was* good for food, and that it *was* pleasant to the eyes, and a tree to be desired to make *one* wise, she took of the fruit thereof, and did eat, and gave also unto her husband with her; and he did eat.

7 And the eyes of them both were opened, and they knew that they *were* naked; and they sewed fig leaves together, and made themselves aprons.

8 And they heard the voice of the LORD God walking in the garden in the cool of the day: and Adam and his wife hid themselves from the presence of the LORD God amongst the trees of the garden.

9 And the LORD God called unto Adam, and said unto him, Where *art* thou?

10 And he said, I heard thy voice in the garden, and I was afraid, because I *was* naked; and I hid myself.

11 And he said, Who told thee that thou *wast* naked? Hast thou eaten of the tree, whereof I commanded thee that thou shouldest not eat?

12 And the man said, The woman whom thou gavest *to be* with me, she gave me of the tree, and I did eat.

13 And the LORD God said unto the woman, What *is* this *that* thou hast done? And the woman said, The serpent beguiled me, and I did eat.

14 And the LORD God said unto the serpent, Because thou hast done this, thou *art* cursed above all cattle, and above every beast of the field; upon thy belly shalt thou go, and dust shalt thou eat all the days of thy life:

15 And I will put enmity between thee and the woman, and between thy seed and her seed; it shall bruise thy head, and thou shalt bruise his heel.

16 Unto the woman he said, I will greatly multiply thy sorrow and thy conception; in sorrow thou shalt bring forth children; and thy desire *shall be* to thy husband, and he shall rule over thee.

17 And unto Adam he said, Because thou hast hearkened unto the voice of thy wife, and hast eaten of the tree, of which I commanded thee, saying, Thou shalt not eat of it: cursed *is* the ground for thy sake; in sorrow shalt thou eat *of* it all the days of thy life;

18 Thorns also and thistles shall it bring forth to thee; and thou shalt eat the herb of the field;

19 In the sweat of thy face shalt thou eat bread, till thou return unto the ground; for out of it wast thou taken: for dust thou *art,* and unto dust shalt thou return.

20 And Adam called his wife's name Eve; because she was the mother of all living.

21 Unto Adam also and to his wife did the LORD God make coats of skins, and clothed them.

22 And the LORD God said, Behold, the man is become as one of us, to know good and evil: and now, lest he put forth his hand, and take also of the tree of life, and eat, and live for ever:

23 Therefore the LORD God sent him forth from the garden of Eden, to till the ground from whence he was taken.

24 So he drove out the man; and he placed at the east of the garden of Eden Cher'u-bims, and a flaming sword which turned every way, to keep the way of the tree of life.

Exodus

Chapter 20

And God spake all these words, saying,

2 I *am* the LORD thy God, which have brought thee out of the land of Egypt, out of the house of bondage.

3 Thou shalt have no other gods before me.

4 Thou shalt not make unto thee any graven image, or any likeness *of any thing* that *is* in heaven above, or that *is* in the earth beneath, or that *is* in the water under the earth:

5 Thou shalt not bow down thyself to them, nor serve them: for I the LORD thy God *am* a jealous God, visiting the iniquity of the fathers upon the children unto the third and fourth *generation* of them that hate me;

6 And shewing mercy unto thousands of them that love me, and keep my commandments.

7 Thou shalt not take the name of the LORD thy God in vain; for the LORD will not hold him guiltless that taketh his name in vain.

8 Remember the sabbath day, to keep it holy.

9 Six days shalt thou labour, and do all thy work:

10 But the seventh day *is* the sabbath of the LORD thy God: *in it* thou shalt not do any work, thou, nor thy son, nor thy daughter, thy manservant, nor thy maidservant, nor thy cattle, nor thy stranger that *is* within thy gates:

11 For *in* six days the LORD made heaven and earth, the sea, and all that in them *is,* and rested the seventh day: wherefore the LORD blessed the sabbath day, and hallowed it.

12 Honour thy father and thy mother: that thy days may be long upon the land which the LORD thy God giveth thee.

13 Thou shalt not kill.

14 Thou shalt not commit adultery.

15 Thou shalt not steal.

16 Thou shalt not bear false witness against thy neighbour.

17 Thou shalt not covet thy neighbour's house, thou shalt not covet thy neighbour's wife, nor his manservant, nor his maidservant, nor his ox, nor his ass, nor any thing that *is* thy neighbour's.

18 And all the people saw the thunderings, and the lightnings, and the noise of the trumpet, and the mountain smoking: and when the people saw *it,* they removed, and stood afar off.

19 And they said unto Moses, Speak thou with us, and we will hear: but let not God speak with us, lest we die.

20 And Moses said unto the people, Fear not: for God is come to prove you, and that his fear may be before your faces, that ye sin not.

21 And the people stood afar off, and Moses drew near unto the thick darkness where God *was.*

22 And the LORD said unto Moses, Thus thou shalt say unto the children of Israel, Ye have seen that I have talked with you from heaven.

23 Ye shall not make with me gods of silver, neither shall ye make unto you gods of gold.

24 An altar of earth thou shalt make unto me, and shalt sacrifice thereon thy burnt offerings, and thy peace offerings, thy sheep, and thine oxen: in all places where I record my name I will come unto thee, and I will bless thee.

25 And if thou wilt make me an altar of stone, thou shalt not build it of hewn stone: for if thou lift up thy tool upon it, thou hast polluted it.

26 Neither shalt thou go up by steps unto mine altar, that thy nakedness be not discovered thereon.

Chapter 21

Now these *are* the judgments which thou shalt set before them.

2 If thou buy an Hebrew servant, six years he shall serve: and in the seventh he shall go out free for nothing.

3 If he came in by himself, he shall go out by himself: if he were married, then his wife shall go out with him.

4 If his master have given him a wife, and she have born him sons or daughters; the wife and her children shall be her master's, and he shall go out by himself.

5 And if the servant shall plainly say, I love my master, my wife, and my children; I will not go out free:

6 Then his master shall bring him unto the judges; he shall also bring him to the door, or unto the door post; and his master shall bore his ear through with an aul; and he shall serve him for ever.

7 And if a man sell his daughter to be a maidservant, she shall not go out as the menservants do.

8 If she please not her master, who hath betrothed her to himself, then shall he let her be redeemed: to sell her unto a strange nation he shall have no power, seeing he hath dealt deceitfully with her.

9 And if he have betrothed her unto his son, he shall deal with her after the manner of daughters.

10 If he take him another *wife;* her food, her raiment, and her duty of marriage, shall he not diminish.

11 And if he do not these three unto her, then shall she go out free without money.

12 He that smiteth a man, so that he die, shall be surely put to death.

13 And if a man lie not in wait, but God deliver *him* into his hand; then I will appoint thee a place whither he shall flee.

14 But if a man come presumptuously upon his neighbour, to slay him with guile; thou shalt take him from mine altar, that he may die.

15 And he that smiteth his father, or his mother, shall be surely put to death.

16 And he that stealeth a man, and selleth him, or if he be found in his hand, he shall surely be put to death.

17 And he that curseth his father, or his mother, shall surely be put to death.

18 And if men strive together, and one smite another with a stone, or with *his* fist, and he die not, but keepeth *his* bed:

19 If he rise again, and walk abroad upon his staff, then shall he that smote *him* be quit: only he shall pay *for* the loss of his time, and shall cause *him* to be thoroughly healed.

20 And if a man smite his servant, or his maid, with a rod, and he die under his hand; he shall be surely punished.

21 Notwithstanding, if he continue a day or two, he shall not be punished; for he *is* his money.

22 If men strive, and hurt a woman with child, so that her fruit depart *from her,* and yet no mischief follow: he shall be surely punished, according as the woman's husband will lay upon him; and he shall pay as the judges *determine.*

23 And if *any* mischief follow, then thou shalt give life for life,

24 Eye for eye, tooth for tooth, hand for hand, foot for foot,

25 Burning for burning, wound for wound, stripe for stripe.

26 And if a man smite the eye of his servant, or the eye of his maid, that it perish; he shall let him go free for his eye's sake.

27 And if he smite out his manservant's tooth, or his maidservant's tooth; he shall let him go free for his tooth's sake.

28 If an ox gore a man or a woman, that they die: then the ox shall be surely stoned, and his flesh shall not be eaten; but the owner of the ox *shall be* quit.

29 But if the ox were wont to push with his horn in time past, and it hath been testified to his owner, and he hath not kept him in, but that he hath killed a man or a woman; the ox shall be stoned, and his owner also shall be put to death.

30 If there be laid on him a sum of money, then he shall give for the ransom of his life whatsoever is laid upon him.

31 Whether he have gored a son or have gored a daughter, according to this judgment shall it be done unto him.

32 If the ox shall push a manservant or a maidservant; he shall give unto their master thirty shekels of silver, and the ox shall be stoned.

33 And if a man shall open a pit, or if a man shall dig a pit, and not cover it, and an ox or an ass fall therein;

34 The owner of the pit shall make *it* good, *and* give money unto the owner of them; and the dead *beast* shall be his.

35 And if one man's ox hurt another's, that he die; then they shall sell the live ox, and divide the money of it; and the dead *ox* also they shall divide.

36 Or if it be known that the ox hath used to push in time past, and his owner hath not kept him in; he shall surely pay ox for ox; and the dead shall be his own.

Matthew

Chapter 7

Judge not, that ye be not judged.

2 For with what judgment ye judge, ye shall be judged: and with what measure ye mete, it shall be measured to you again.

3 And why beholdest thou the mote that is in thy brother's eye, but considerest not the beam that is in thine own eye?

4 Or how wilt thou say to thy brother, Let me pull out the mote out of thine eye; and, behold, a beam *is* in thine own eye?

5 Thou hypocrite, first cast out the beam out of thine own eye; and then shalt thou see clearly to cast out the mote out of thy brother's eye.

6 Give not that which is holy unto the dogs, neither cast ye your pearls before swine, lest they trample them under their feet, and turn again and rend you.

7 Ask, and it shall be given you; seek, and ye shall find; knock, and it shall be opened unto you:

8 For every one that asketh receiveth; and he that seeketh findeth; and to him that knocketh it shall be opened.

9 Or what man is there of you, whom if his son ask bread, will he give him a stone?

10 Or if he ask a fish, will he give him a serpent?

11 If ye then, being evil, know how to give good gifts unto your children, how much more shall your Father which is in heaven give good things to them that ask him?

12 Therefore all things whatsoever ye would that men should do to you, do ye even so to them: for this is the law and the prophets.

13 Enter ye in at the strait gate: for wide *is* the gate, and broad *is* the way, that leadeth to destruction, and many there be which go in thereat:

14 Because strait *is* the gate, and narrow *is* the way, which leadeth unto life, and few there be that find it.

15 Beware of false prophets, which come to you in sheep's clothing, but inwardly they are ravening wolves.

16 Ye shall know them by their fruits. Do men gather grapes of thorns, or figs of thistles?

17 Even so every good tree bringeth forth good fruit; but a corrupt tree bringeth forth evil fruit.

18 A good tree cannot bring forth evil fruit, neither *can* a corrupt tree bring forth good fruit.

19 Every tree that bringeth not forth good fruit is hewn down, and cast into the fire.

20 Wherefore by their fruits ye shall know them.

21 Not every one that saith unto me, Lord, Lord, shall enter into the kingdom of heaven; but he that doeth the will of my Father which is in heaven.

22 Many will say to me in that day, Lord, Lord, have we not prophesied in thy name? and in thy name have cast out devils? and in thy name done many wonderful works?

23 And then will I profess unto them, I never knew you: depart from me, ye that work iniquity.
24 Therefore whosoever heareth these sayings of mine, and doeth them, I will liken him unto a wiseman, which built his house upon a rock:
25 And the rain descended, and the floods came, and the winds blew, and beat upon that house; and it fell not: for it was founded upon a rock.
26 And every one that heareth these sayings of mine, and doeth them not, shall be likened unto a foolish man, which built his house upon the sand:
27 And the rain descended, and the floods came, and the winds blew, and beat upon that house; and it fell: and great was the fall of it.
28 And it came to pass, when Jesus had ended these sayings, the people were astonished at his doctrine:
29 For he taught them as *one* having authority, and not as the scribes.

LEARNING MORE

Many people devote years—or a lifetime—of study to sacred texts. For the purposes of understanding these more thoroughly, you may want to read more of the texts or to find out more about them. Useful links can be found on the *Ideas Across Time* website.

QUESTIONING THE TEXT

1. What picture of God is presented in Genesis? Exodus? Matthew?
2. How does God create the world?
3. How does God create human beings?
4. What roles and responsibilities does God assign to human beings in Genesis?
5. What is the temptation to which Adam and Eve succumb?
6. What are the consequences of Adam and Eve's transgression?
7. What picture of society is implied by Chapters 20 and 21 of Exodus?
8. What notion of justice is expressed by Chapters 20 and 21 of Exodus?
9. What notion of justice is expressed in Matthew?
10. How do you become a good person according to these passages?

ANALYZING THE WRITER'S CRAFT

1. Who is the audience and how can you tell?
2. What is the purpose of each text? Explain.
3. What is the tone of the writing?
4. How is the deeper truth of these passages revealed to the reader?
5. Why are these texts in an essentially poetic rather than a prosaic form?

MAKING CONNECTIONS

1. Compare and contrast the image of God in other sacred texts in this chapter.
2. What do these sacred texts have in common? In what ways do these texts differ—in terms of form and in terms of content?
3. Do these sacred texts reveal an underlying unity of human religious perspectives, or an underlying diversity?
4. Do these sacred texts confirm Paul Tillich's view of the religious dimension in life (pp. 123–130)? Explain.
5. How do these sacred texts help an individual decide the rights and wrongs of of problems like those raised in the keynote essay of this chapter?

FORMULATING IDEAS FOR WRITING

1. The idea of the divine is a perennial theme of human culture. On the basis of the sacred texts in this chapter, write an essay on the concept of the divine. In preparing your essay, consider what these texts say about the outstanding characteristics of God, about the nature of God, about God's expectations of human beings, and about human expectations of God. What do these texts say about the relation of eternity to time, and of immortality to mortality?
2. Consider the quality of "goodness" as it appears in these texts (or in most of them). Is being good a quality of "inwardness," of the essential inner self, which God recognizes and will reward on the day of resurrection; or is being good a matter of meeting the "external" demands of and fulfilling the obligations prescribed by God? Is there a condition of being that transcends "good"? Is evil implied by good, and vice versa?
3. Which of these texts brings you closest to God? Write an essay that explains your religious response to these sacred texts.
4. Write an essay on the rights and wrongs of cloning using one or more of these sacred texts to support your argument.

The Analects of Confucius

The Analects (Sayings) of the Chinese teacher Confucius [K'ung-fu-tzu] (551–479 BCE), not unlike the Christian Gospels, represent the record of the recollections of his disciples. These teachings are assumed to have been put into writing several centuries after Confucius's death. Although some of the sayings are clearly connected by subject or theme, for the most part the Analects are random. Moreover, since this is a record of Confucius's teaching, it does not take the form of an organized exposition of his ideas, or of a treatise, but rather of his responses to students or occasions.

Confucius seems to have been a private tutor to young gentlemen, training them in the virtues appropriate to the governing class. This was the context in which Confucius proselytized for the Way of Goodness. By the twelfth century, when the Analects were adopted as the basic text of all Chinese education, Confucius was universally regarded as a Divine Sage, infallible and omniscient. The aim of Chinese education was to uncover and make available to all the Truth embedded in Confucius's sayings.

Confucianism is a form of devotion that however does not invoke God or a transcendent order. It asserts as wise and proper a posture toward human affairs memorably expressed by the eighteenth-century British poet and satirist Alexander Pope in his famous line "The proper study of mankind is man" ("Essay on Man, Epistle II"). Confucius lived at a time of social and political disorder, and in his teaching harked back to an earlier period of learning, wisdom, and discipline (or ritual) that he believed represented an ideal union of societal ways and *the* Way, a concept that seems to suggest to Confucius the Way of Nature or, as Pope might have said, Nature's God. But Confucius, at least in the Analects, doesn't expound at length on the Way, offering instead glancing observations, partial responses, and pithy comments—all implying a complete underlying system of thought that the reader, or disciple, needs to uncover by attentive, reflective study.

The excerpts from the Analects that follow are in the translation by the authoritative Chinese scholar Arthur Waley.

Book I

1. The Master said, To learn and at due times to repeat what one has learnt, is that not after all a pleasure? That friends should come to one from afar, is this not after all delightful? To remain unsoured even though one's merits are unrecognized by others, is that not after all what is expected of a gentleman?

16. The Master said, (the good man) does not grieve that other people do not recognize his merits. His only anxiety is lest he should fail to recognize theirs.

Book II

14. The Master said, A gentleman can see a question from all sides without bias. The small man is biased and can see a question only from one side.
15. The Master said, He who learns but does not think, is lost. He who thinks but does not learn is in great danger.
16. The Master said, He who sets to work upon a different strand destroys the whole fabric.
17. The Master said, Yu, shall I teach you what knowledge is? When you know a thing, to recognize that you know it, and when you do not know a thing, to recognize that you do not know it. That is knowledge.

Book IV

16. The Master said, A gentleman takes as much trouble to discover what is right as lesser men take to discover what will pay.
17. The Master said, In the presence of a good man, think all the time how you may learn to equal him. In the presence of a bad man, turn your gaze within!

Book VIII

21. The Master said, In Yü I can find no semblance of a flaw. Abstemious in his own food and drink, he displayed the utmost devotion in his offerings to spirits and divinities. Content with the plainest clothes for common wear, he saw to it that his sacrificial apron and ceremonial head-dress were of the utmost magnificence. His place of habitation was of the humblest, and all his energy went into draining and ditching. In him I can find no semblance of a flaw.

Book IX

16. Once when the Master was standing by a stream, he said, Could one but go on and on like this, never ceasing day or night!

Book XII

2. Jan Jung asked about Goodness. The Master said, Behave when away from home as though you were in the presence of an important guest. Deal with the common people as though you were officiating at an important sacrifice. Do not do to others what you would not like yourself. Then there will be no feelings of opposition to you, whether it is the affairs of a State that you are handling or the affairs of a Family.

Book XIV

7. The Master said, It is possible to be a true gentleman and yet lack Goodness. But there has never yet existed a Good man who was not a gentleman.

Book XV

9. Tzu-kung asked how to become Good. The Master said, A craftsman, if he means to do good work, must first sharpen his tools. In whatever State you dwell

   Take service with such of its officers as are worthy,
   Make friends with such of its knights as are Good.

30. The Master said, I once spent a whole day without food and a whole night without sleep, in order to meditate. It was no use. It is better to learn.

Book XVI

4. Master K'ung said, There are three sorts of friend that are profitable, and three sorts that are harmful. Friendship with the upright, with the true-to-death and with those who have heard much is profitable. Friendship with the obsequious, friendship with those who are good at accommodating their principles, friendship with those who are clever at talk is harmful.
5. Master K'ung said, There are three sorts of pleasure that are profitable, and three sorts of pleasure that are harmful. The pleasure got from the due ordering of ritual and music, the pleasure got from discussing the good points in the conduct of others, the pleasure of having many wise friends is profitable. But pleasure got from profligate enjoyments, pleasure got from idle gadding about, pleasure got from comfort and ease is harmful.
6. Master K'ung said, There are three mistakes that are liable to be made when waiting upon a gentleman. To speak before being called upon to do so; this is called forwardness. Not to speak when called upon to do so; this is called secretiveness. To speak without without first noting the expression of his face; this is called "blindness."
7. Master K'ung said, There are three things against which a gentleman is on his guard. In his youth, before his blood and vital humours have settled down, he is on his guard against lust. Having reached his prime, when the blood and vital humours have finally hardened, he is on his guard against strife. Having reached old age, when the blood and vital humours are already decaying, he is on his guard against avarice.
8. Master K'ung said, There are three things that a gentleman fears: he fears the will of Heaven, he fears great men, he fears the words of the Divine Sages. The small man does not know the will of Heaven and so does not fear it. He treats great men with contempt, and scoffs at the words of the Divine Sages.

Book XX

3. The Master said, He who does not understand the will of Heaven cannot be regarded as a gentleman. He who does not know the rites cannot take his stand. He who does not understand words, cannot understand people.

LEARNING MORE

Many people devote years—or a lifetime—of study to sacred texts. For the purposes of understanding these more thoroughly, you may want to read more of the texts or to find out more about them. Useful links can be found on the *Ideas Across Time* website.

QUESTIONING THE TEXT

1. What are the attributes of the good person? How do you become a good person?
2. What is the place of learning and knowledge in moral life?

3. What picture of society is implied by the Analects?
4. What is the relation between "conduct" (see Book XVI, 5) and "goodness"?
5. What is knowledge and how do you attain it?
6. What picture of God is expressed in the Analects?

ANALYZING THE WRITER'S CRAFT

1. Who is the audience and how can you tell?
2. What is the purpose of each text? Explain.
3. What is the tone of the writing?
4. How is the deeper truth of these passages revealed to the reader?
5. Most holy texts are essentially poetic rather than prosaic. Do you find Confucius poetic, too? Explain. Is his language powerful in ways that distinguish his Analects from, say, the Bible or the Qur'an? Explain.

MAKING CONNECTIONS

1. Compare and contrast the image of God in other sacred texts in this chapter.
2. What do these sacred texts have in common? In what ways do these texts differ—in terms of form and in terms of content?
3. Do these sacred texts reveal an underlying unity of human religious perspectives, or an underlying diversity?
4. Do these sacred texts confirm Paul Tillich's view of the religious dimension in life (pp. 123–130)? Explain.
5. How do these sacred texts help an individual decide the rights and wrongs of of problems like those raised in the keynote essay of this chapter?

FORMULATING IDEAS FOR WRITING

1. The idea of the divine is a perennial theme of human culture. One the basis of the sacred texts in this chapter, write an essay on the concept of the divine. In preparing your essay, consider what these texts say about the outstanding characteristics of God, about the nature of God, about God's expectations of human beings, and about human expectations of God. What do these texts say about the relation of eternity to time, and of immortality to mortality?
2. Consider the quality of "goodness" as it appears in these texts (or in most of them). Is being good a quality of "inwardness," of the essential inner self, which God recognizes and will reward on the day of resurrection; or is being good a matter of meeting the "external" demands of and fulfilling the obligations prescribed by God? Is there a condition of being that transcends "good"? Is evil implied by good, and vice versa?
3. Which of these texts brings you closest to God? Write an essay that explains your religious response to these sacred texts.
4. Write an essay on the rights and wrongs of cloning using one or more of these sacred texts to support your argument.

The Qur'an

The Qur'an, the holy book of Islam, is believed to be a text, or collection of messages, transmitted by Allah (God) to humanity through God's prophet Muhammad. Muhammad received these messages, in Arabic, over a period of around twenty-three years (610–622 CE). Followers of Muhammad believe him to be the final messenger of God to humanity, and the Qur'an therefore incorporates the Hebrew and Christian Bibles and supercedes them. Muhammad not only recited the Qur'an but also identified the location of each verse and *surah* (chapter or section), and selected scribes to record his recitation. The first authenticated copy of the whole Qur'an was compiled under the Caliphate of the Prophet's disciple Abu Bakr (632–634 CE).

Two features of the Qur'an are especially characteristic: first, it is an emphatically monotheistic book, stressing over and over that there is one God, and that Muhammad is His prophet. Second, it is totalistic—that is, it contains a complete and exhaustive guide to every aspect of life, from marital relations to economics. Since the Qur'an is understood by believers as Muhammad's direct report of God's word, the Qur'an's prescriptions are read as universal and independent of time and place: they apply to all people everywhere, as much today as when the Prophet first expressed them. The text below is from the Oxford Qur'an of 1900, translated by E.A. Palmer.

2. The Chapter of the Heifer

[157] Your God is one God; there is no God but He, the merciful, the compassionate.

Verily, in the creation of the heavens and the earth, and the alternation of night and day, and in the ship that runneth in the sea with that which profits man, and in what water God sends down from heaven and quickens therewith the earth after its death, and spreads abroad therein all kinds of cattle, and in the shifting of the winds, and in the clouds that are pressed into service betwixt heaven and earth, are signs to people who can understand.

[284] God's is what is in heaven and in the earth, and if ye show what is in your souls, or hide it, God will call you to account; and He forgives whom He will, and punishes whom He will, for God is mighty over all.

[285] The Apostle believes in what is sent down to him from his Lord, and the believers all believe on God, and His angels, and His Books, and His apostles,—we make no difference between any of His apostles,—they say, 'We hear and obey, Thy pardon, O Lord! for to Thee our journey tends. God will not require of the soul save its capacity. It shall have what it has earned, and it shall

owe what has been earned from it. Lord, catch us not up, if we forget or make mistake; Lord, load us not with a burden, as Thou hast loaded those who were before us. Lord, make us not to carry what we have not strength for, but forgive us, and pardon us, and have mercy on us. Thou art our Sovereign, then help us against the people who do not believe!'

3. The Chapter of Imran's Family

O people of the Book, why do ye dispute about Abraham, when the law and the gospel were not revealed until after him? What! do ye not understand? Here ye are, disputing about what ye have some knowledge of; why then do ye dispute about what ye have no knowledge of? God knows and ye know not.

[60] Abraham was not a Jew, nor yet a Christian, but he was a 'Hanîf[1] resigned, and not of the idolaters. Verily, the people most worthy of Abraham are those who follow him and his prophets, and those who believe;—God is the patron of the believers.

A sect of the people of the Book would fain they could lead you astray, but they only lead themselves astray, and they do not perceive.

O people of the Book! why do ye disbelieve in the signs of God, the while ye witness them? O people of the Book! why do ye clothe the truth with falsehood and hide the truth the while ye know?

4. The Chapter of Women

It is not for a believer to kill a believer save by mistake; and whosoever kills a believer by mistake then let him free a believing neck[2]; and the blood-money must be paid to his people save what they shall remit as alms. But if he be from a tribe hostile to you and yet a believer, then let him free a believing neck. And if it be a tribe betwixt whom and you there is an alliance, then let the blood-money be paid to his friends, and let him free a believing neck; but he who cannot find the means, then let him fast for two consecutive months—a penance this from God, for God is knowing, wise.

[95] And whoso kills a believer purposely, his reward is hell, to dwell therein for aye; and God will be wrath with him, and curse him, and prepare for him a mighty woe.

O ye who believe! when ye are knocking about in the way of God be discerning, and do not say to him who offers you a salutation, 'Thou art no believer,' craving after the chances of this world's life,[3] for with God are many spoils! So were ye aforetime, but God was gracious to you, be ye then discerning; verily, God of what ye do is well aware.

---

[1] A righteous person.

[2] Captive.

[3] Because a believer might not be attacked and plundered as an infidel might be.

Not alike are those of the believers who sit at home without harm, and those who are strenuous in God's way with their wealth and their persons. God hath preferred those who are strenuous with their wealth and their persons to those who sit still, by many degrees, and to each hath God promised good, but God hath preferred the strenuous for a mighty hire over those who sit still,—degrees from him, and pardon and mercy, for God is forgiving and merciful.

Verily, the angels when they took the souls of those who had wronged themselves, said, 'What state were ye in?' they say, 'We were but weak in the earth;' they said, 'Was not God's earth wide enough for you to flee away therein?' These are those whose resort is hell, and a bad journey shall it be!

[100] Save for the weak men, and women, and children, who could not compass any stratagem, and were not guided to a way; these it may be God will pardon, for God both pardons and forgives.

Whosoever flees in the way of God shall find in the earth many a spacious refuge; and he who goes forth from his house, fleeing unto God and His prophet, and then death catches him up,—his hire devolves on God, and God is forgiving and merciful.

5. The Chapter of the Table

In the name of the merciful and compassionate God.

[1] O ye who believe! fulfil your compacts.—Lawful for you are brute beasts, save what is here recited to you, not allowing you the chase while ye are on pilgrimage; verily, God ordaineth what He will.

O ye who believe! do not deem the monuments of God to be lawful, nor the sacred month, nor the offering, nor its neck garlands, nor those who sojourn at the sacred house, craving grace from their Lord and His pleasure.

But when ye are in lawful state again, then chase; and let not ill-will against the people who turned you from the Sacred Mosque make you transgress; but help one another in righteousness and piety, and do not help one another to sin and enmity; but fear God,—verily, God is keen to punish.

Forbidden to you is that which dies of itself, and blood, and the flesh of swine, and that which is devoted to other than God, and the strangled and the knocked down, and that which falls down, and the gored, and what wild beasts have eaten—except what ye slaughter in time—and what is sacrificed to idols, and dividing carcases by arrows.

Verily, we have revealed the law in which is guidance and light; the prophets who were resigned did judge thereby those who were Jews, as did the masters and doctors by what they remembered of the Book of God and by what they were witnesses of. Fear not men, but fear me, and sell not my signs for a little price; for whoso will not judge by what God has revealed, these be the misbelievers.

We have prescribed for thee therein 'a life for a life, and an eye for an eye, and a nose for a nose, and an ear for an ear, and a tooth for a tooth, and for wounds retaliation;' but whoso remits it, it is an expiation for him, but he whoso will not judge by what God has revealed, these be the unjust.

[50] And we followed up the footsteps of these (prophets) with Jesus the son of Mary, confirming that which was before him and the law, and we brought him the gospel, wherein is guidance and light, verifying what was before it of the law, and a guidance and an admonition unto those who fear.

Then let the people of the gospel judge by that which is revealed therein, for whoso will not judge by what God has revealed, these be the evildoers.

We have revealed to thee the Book in truth verifying what was before it, and preserving it; judge then between them by what God has revealed, and follow not their lusts, turning away from what is given to thee of the truth.

For each one of you have we made a law and a pathway; and had God pleased He would have made you one nation, but He will surely try you concerning that which He has brought you. Be ye therefore emulous in good deeds; to God is your return altogether, and He will let you know concerning that wherein ye do dispute.

Wherefore judge thou between them by what God has revealed, and follow not their lusts; but beware lest they mislead thee from part of what God has revealed to thee; yet if they turn back, then know that God wishes to fall on them for some sins of theirs,—verily, many men are evildoers.

23. The Chapter of Believers

In the name of the merciful and compassionate God.

Prosperous are the believers who in their prayers are humble, and who from vain talk turn aside, and who in almsgiving are active. [5] And who guard their private parts—except for their wives or what their right hands possess for then, verily, they are not to be blamed;—but whoso craves aught beyond that, they are the transgressors—and who observe their trusts and covenants, and who guard well their prayers: [10] these are the heirs who shall inherit Paradise; they shall dwell therein for aye!

We have created man from an extract of clay; then we made him a clot in a sure depository; then we created the clot congealed blood, and we created the congealed blood a morsel; then we created the morsel bone, and we clothed the bone with flesh; then we produced it another creation; and blessed be God, the best of creators!

[15] Then shall ye after that surely die; then shall ye on the day of resurrection be raised.

And we have created above you seven roads; nor are we heedless of the creation.

And we send down from the heaven water by measure, and we make it rest in the earth; but, verily, we are able to take it away; and we produce for you thereby gardens of palms and grapes wherein ye have many fruits, and whence ye eat.

[20] And a tree growing out of Mount Sinai which produces oil, and a condiment for those who eat.

And, verily, ye have a lesson in the cattle; we give you to drink of what is in their bellies; and ye have therein many advantages, and of them ye eat, and on them and on ships ye are borne!

24. The Chapter of Light

O ye who believe! enter not into houses which are not your own houses, until ye have asked leave and saluted the people thereof, that is better for you; haply ye may be mindful. And if ye find no one therein, then do not enter them until permission is given you, and if it be said to you, 'Go back!' then go back, it is purer for you; for God of what ye do doth know. It is no crime against you that ye enter uninhabited houses,—a convenience for you;—and God knows what ye show and what ye hide.

[30] Say to the believers that they cast down their looks and guard their private parts; that is purer for them; verily, God is well aware of what they do.

And say to the believing women that they cast down their looks and guard their private parts, and display not their ornaments, except those which are outside; and let them pull their kerchiefs over their bosoms and not display their ornaments save to their husbands and fathers, or the fathers of their husbands, or their sons, or the sons of their husbands, or their brothers, or their brothers' sons, or their sisters' sons, or their women, or what their right hands possess, or their male attendants who are incapable, or to children who do not note women's nakedness; and that they beat not with their feet that their hidden ornaments may be known;—but turn ye all repentant to God, O ye believers! haply ye may prosper.

And marry the single amongst you, and the righteous among your servants and your handmaidens. If they be poor, God will enrich them of His grace, for God both comprehends and knows. And let those who cannot find a match, until God enriches them of His grace, keep chaste.

And such of those whom your right hands possess as crave a writing, write it for them, if ye know any good in them, and give them of the wealth of God which He has given you. And do not compel your slave girls to prostitution, if they desire to keep continent, in order to crave the goods of the life of this world; but he who does compel them, then, verily, God after they are compelled is forgiving, compassionate.

Now have we sent down to you manifest signs, and the like of those who have passed away before you, and as an admonition to those who fear.

[35] God is the light of the heavens and the earth; His light is as a niche in which is a lamp, and the lamp is in a glass, the glass is as though it were a glittering star; it is lit from a blessed tree, an olive neither of the east nor of the west, the oil of which would well-nigh give light though no fire touched it,—light upon light!—God guides to His light whom He pleases; and God strikes out parables for men, and God all things doth know.

75. The Chapter of the Resurrection

In the name of the merciful and compassionate God.

I need not swear by the resurrection day!

Nor need I swear by the self-accusing soul!

Does man think that we shall not collect his bones? Able are we to arrange his finger tips!

[5] Nay, but man wishes to be wicked hence-forward! he asks, When is the resurrection day?

But when the sight shall be dazed, and the moon be eclipsed, and the sun and the moon be together, [10] and man shall say upon that day, 'Where is a place to flee to?'—nay, no refuge! and to thy Lord that day is the sure settlement: He will inform man on that day of what He has sent forward or delayed!

Nay, man is an evidence against himself, [15] and even if he thrusts forward his excuses—.

Do not move thy tongue thereby to hasten it. It is for us to collect it and to read it; and when we read it then follow its reading. And again it is for us to explain it.

[20] Nay, indeed, but ye love the transient life, and ye neglect the hereafter!

Faces on that day shall be bright, gazing on their Lord!

And faces on that day shall be dismal!

[25] Thou wilt think that a back-breaking calamity has happened to them!

Nay, but when the [soul] comes up into the throat, and it is said, 'Who will charm it back?' and he will think that it is his parting [hour]. And leg shall be pressed on leg; [30] unto thy Lord on that day shall the driving be.

For he did not believe and did not pray; but he said it was a lie, and turned his back! Then he went to his people haughtily—woe to thee, and woe to thee! again woe to thee, and woe to thee!

Does man think that he shall be left to himself?

Wasn't he a clot of emitted seed? Then he was congealed blood, and (God) created him, and fashioned him, and made of him pairs, male and female.

[35] Is not He able to quicken the dead?

76. The Chapter of Man

In the name of the merciful and compassionate God.

Does there not come on man a portion of time when he is nothing worth mentioning?

Verily, we created man from a mingled clot, to try him; and we gave him hearing and sight. Verily, we guided him in the way, whether he be grateful or ungrateful.

Verily, we have prepared for those who misbelieve chains and fetters and a blaze!

[5] Verily, the righteous shall drink of a cup tempered with Kâfûr, a spring from which God's servants shall drink and make it gush out as they please!

They who fulfil their vows, and fear a day, the evil which shall fly abroad, and who give food for His love to the poor and the orphan and the captive. 'We only feed you for God's sake; we desire not from you either reward or thanks; [10] we fear from our Lord a frowning, calamitous day!'

And God will guard them from the evil of that day and will cast on them brightness and joy; and their reward for their patience shall be Paradise and silk! reclining therein upon couches they shall neither see therein sun nor piercing cold; and close down upon them shall be its shadows; and lowered over them its fruits to cull; [15] and they shall be served round with vessels of silver and goblets that are as flagons—flagons of silver which they shall mete out! and they shall drink therein a cup tempered with Zingabil, a spring therein named Silsabil! and there shall go round about them eternal boys; when thou seest them thou wilt think them scattered pearls; [20] and when thou seest them thou shalt see pleasure and a great estate! On them shall be garments of green embroidered satin and brocade; and they shall be adorned with bracelets of silver; and their Lord shall give them to drink pure drink! Verily, this is a reward for you, and your efforts are thanked.

Verily, we have sent down upon thee the Qur'ân. Wherefore wait patiently for the judgment of thy Lord, and obey not any sinner or misbeliever amongst them. [25] But remember the name of thy Lord morning, and evening, and through the night, and adore Him, and celebrate His praises the whole night long.

Verily, these love the transitory life, and leave behind them a heavy day!

We created them and strengthened their joints; and if we please we can exchange for the likes of them in their stead. Verily, this is a memorial, and whoso will, let him take unto his Lord a way.

[30] But ye will not please except God please! Verily, God is knowing, wise.

He makes whomsoever He pleases to enter into His mercy; but the unjust He has prepared for them a grievous woe!

78. The Chapter of the Information

In the name of the merciful and compassionate God.

Of what do they ask each other?—Of the mighty information whereon they do dispute[4]? nay, they shall know too well! [5] Again, nay, they shall know too well!

Have we not set the earth as a couch, and the mountains as stakes, and created you in pairs, and made your sleep for rest, [10] and made the night a garment, and made the day for livelihood, and built above you seven solid (heavens) and set a burning lamp, and, sent down from the rain-expressing clouds water pouring forth, [15] to bring out thereby the grain and herb and gardens thickly planted?

Verily, the day of decision is an appointed time; and the day when the trumpet shall be blown, and ye shall come in troops, and the heavens shall be opened, and shall be all doors, [20] and the mountains shall be moved, and shall be like a mirage!

Verily, hell is an ambuscade; a reward for the outrageous, to tarry therein for ages. They shall not taste therein cool nor drink, [25] but only boiling water and pus;—a fit reward!

Verily, they did not hope for the account; but they ever said our signs were lies.

Everything have we remembered in a book.

[30] 'Then taste, for we will only increase your torment!'

Verily, for the pious is a blissful place,—gardens and vineyards, and girls with swelling breasts of the same age as themselves, and a brimming cup; [35] they shall hear therein no folly and no lie;—a reward from thy Lord, a sufficient gift! The Lord of the heavens and the earth, and what is between them both,—the Merciful,—they cannot obtain audience of Him!

---

[4] I.e. the news of the resurrection.

The day when the Spirit and the angels shall stand in ranks, they shall not speak save to whom the Merciful permits, and who speaks aright.

That is the true day; and whoso pleases let him take to a resort unto his Lord!

[40] Verily, we have warned you of a torment that is nigh: on a day when man shall see what his two hands have sent forward; and the misbeliever shall say, 'Would that I were dust!'

79. The Chapter of Those Who Tear Out

In the name of the merciful and compassionate God.

By those who tear out violently!

And by those who gaily release[5]!

And by those who float through the air!

And the preceders who precede!

[5] And those who manage the affair!

On the day when the quaking quakes which the following one shall succeed! Hearts on that day shall tremble; eyes thereon be humbled!

[10] They say, 'Shall we be sent back to our old course?—What! when we are rotten bones?' they say, 'That then were a losing return!'

But it will only be one scare, and lo! they will be on the surface!

[15] Has the story of Moses come to you? when his Lord addressed him in the holy valley of Tuvâ, 'Go unto Pharaoh, verily, he is outrageous; and say, "Hast thou a wish to purify thyself, and that I may guide thee to thy Lord, and thou mayest fear?"'

[20] So he showed him the greatest signs; but he called him a liar and rebelled. Then he retreated hastily, and gathered, and proclaimed, and said, 'I am your Lord most High!' [25] but God seized him with the punishment of the future life and of the former.

Verily, in that is a lesson to him who fears!

Are ye harder to create or the heaven that He has built? He raised its height and fashioned it; and made its night to cover it, and brought forth its noonday light; [30] and the earth after that He did stretch out. He brings forth from it its water and its pasture.

And the mountains He did firmly set, a provision for you and for your cattle.

And when the great predominant calamity shall come, [35] on the day when man shall remember what he strove after, and hell shall be brought out for him who sees!

And as for him who was outrageous and preferred the life of this world, verily, hell is the resort!

[40] But as for him who feared the station of his Lord, and prohibited his soul from lust, verily, Paradise is the resort!

They shall ask thee about the Hour, for when it is set. Whereby canst thou mention it? Unto thy Lord its period belongs.

---

[5] Referring to the angel of death and his assistants, who tear away the souls of the wicked violently, and gently release the souls of the good.

[45] Thou art only a warner to him who fears it.

On the day they see it, it will be as though they had only tarried an evening or the noon thereof.

81. The Chapter of the Folding up

In the name of the merciful and compassionate God.

When the sun is folded up,
And when the stars do fall,
And when the mountains are moved,
And when the she-camels ten months' gone with young shall be neglected,
[5] And when the beasts shall be crowded together,
And when the seas shall surge up,
And when souls shall be paired with bodies,
And when the child who was buried alive shall be asked for what sin she was slain,
[10] And when the pages shall be spread out,
And when the heaven shall be flayed,
And when hell shall be set ablaze,
And when Paradise shall be brought nigh,
The soul shall know what it has produced!

[15] I need not swear by the stars that slink back, moving swiftly, slinking into their dens!

Nor by the night when darkness draws on!

Nor by the morn when it first breathes up!

Verily, it is the speech of a noble apostle, [20] mighty, standing sure with the Lord of the throne, obeyed and trusty too!

Your comrade is not mad; he saw him on the plain horizon, nor does he grudge to communicate the unseen.

[25] Nor is it the speech of a pelted devil.

Then whither do ye go?

It is but a reminder to the worlds, to whomsoever of you pleases to go straight:—but ye will not please, except God, the Lord of the world, should please.

112. The Chapter of Unity

In the name of the merciful and compassionate God.

Say, 'He is God alone!
God the Eternal!
He begets not and is not begotten!
Nor is there like unto Him any one!'

LEARNING MORE

Many people devote years—or a lifetime—of study to sacred texts. For the purposes of understanding these more thoroughly, you may want to read more of the texts or to find out more about them. Useful links can be found on the *Ideas Across Time* website.

QUESTIONING THE TEXT

1. What picture of God is presented in these passages?
2. What notion of justice is expressed in these passages?
3. How does God create human beings?
4. How do you become a good person?
5. How does the afterlife affect human choices in this life?

ANALYZING THE WRITER'S CRAFT

1. Who is the audience and how can you tell?
2. What is the purpose of each text? Explain.
3. What is the tone of the writing?
4. How is the deeper truth of these passages revealed to the reader?
5. Why are these texts in an essentially poetic rather than a prosaic form?

MAKING CONNECTIONS

1. Compare and contrast the image of God in other sacred texts in this chapter.
2. What do these sacred texts have in common? In what ways do these texts differ—in terms of form and in terms of content?
3. Do these sacred texts reveal an underlying unity of human religious perspectives, or an underlying diversity?
4. Do these sacred texts confirm Paul Tillich's view of the religious dimension in life (pp. 123–130)? Explain.
5. How do these sacred texts help an individual decide the rights and wrongs of problems like those raised in the keynote essay of this chapter?

FORMULATING IDEAS FOR WRITING

1. The idea of the divine is a perennial theme of human culture. One the basis of the sacred texts in this chapter, write an essay on the concept of the divine. In preparing your essay, consider what these texts say about the outstanding characteristics of God, about the nature of God, about God's expectations of human beings, and about human expectations of God. What do these texts say about the relation of eternity to time, and of immortality to mortality?
2. Consider the quality of "goodness" as it appears in these texts (or in most of them). Is being good a quality of "inwardness," of the essential inner self, which God recognizes and will reward on the day of resurrection; or is being good a matter of meeting the "external" demands of and fulfilling the

obligations prescribed by God? Is there a condition of being that transcends "good"? Is evil implied by good, and vice versa?
3. Which of these texts brings you closest to God? Write an essay that explains your religious response to these sacred texts.
4. Write an essay on the rights and wrongs of cloning using one or more of these sacred texts to support your argument.

What I Believe (1794)

Tom Paine

Even in an era of remarkable public and literary figures, Tom Paine stood out as an especially remarkable man. He was the most lucid and most widely read advocate for the ultimate cause of the eighteenth-century Enlightenment: freedom of thought. His plainspoken eloquence captured the revolutionary aspirations of the age, making him a hero not only of the American but also of the French revolutions, and of radical republicanism in England.

The son of a Quaker corset maker, Paine was born in Thetford, England, on January 29, 1737. Although he attended the local grammar school, he was largely self-taught. Paine's true education occurred in the vibrant radical artisan culture of England, the culture for which his most influential book, *The Rights of Man* (1791), later became an antimonarchist bible. More copies of *The Rights of Man* were in circulation in England in the 1790s than of any other book. After apprenticeship to his father as a corset maker, a stint at sea, work as a grocer and a teacher, and a fiery tenure as a government tax collector—he tried to unionize his fellow workers—Paine finally immigrated to the American colonies at the urging of Benjamin Franklin. He was thirty-seven years old.

Almost immediately, Paine was launched on his history-making career as a radical polemicist. As editor of the *Philadelphia Magazine,* Paine wrote groundbreaking articles favoring rights for women and abolition of slavery. In 1776, he published *Common Sense,* the first pamphlet advocating an immediate break with Britain. It sold an amazing half-million copies and was followed by sixteen broadsides titled *Crisis.* Published during the darkest hours of the revolutionary war, *Crisis* is credited with lifting the morale of George Washington's demoralized troops.

In the postrevolutionary United States, however, Paine never found a suitable role, and in 1787, he returned to England. But the publication of *The Rights of Man* resulted in his being charged with treason, and after only a few years back in his native land, Paine fled to France. These were the early years of the

French Revolution, and Paine was received as a hero, made a citizen, and elected to the revolutionary National Convention. However, when Paine, a fervent opponent of monarchy, nonetheless withheld his support for the execution of Louis XVI, he was arrested, threatened with death, and held in prison for over a year until the intercession of the American ambassador, James Monroe, secured his release. As a patriot of the American Revolution, Paine was granted U.S. citizenship and a safe passage to New York.

While in prison in France, Paine had written *The Age of Reason* (1794), his last work. In it Paine declares his belief in God, but in little else that could be called Christian; he casts a skeptical eye equally on the Old and New Testaments, finding cruelty in the God of the former and contradictions in the preaching of the latter. Consistent in his free-thinking opposition to established systems, Paine prefers a rational humanism to any of the forms of organized belief prevalent in the young nation. But while Paine's "theosophism" later appealed to the generation of Emerson and Thoreau, it found an ill welcome in his "beloved America" at the turn of the nineteenth century. Having left the nation a hero, he returned an "infidel." His remaining years were dark, impoverished, and lonely. He died in 1809 and was buried on his farm in New Rochelle, having had his request for a Quaker grave site denied. A few years later Paine's bones were taken back to his native England by the radical English journalist William Cobbett.

The selections below are taken from first three chapters of *The Age of Reason*.

To My Fellow-Citizens of the UNITED STATES OF AMERICA

I put the following work under your protection. It contains my opinion upon religion. You will do me the justice to remember that I have always strenuously supported the right of every man to his own opinion, however different that opinion might be to mine. He who denies to another this right makes a slave of himself to his present opinion, because he precludes himself the right of changing it.

The most formidable weapon against errors of every kind is reason. I have never used any other, and I trust I never shall.

It has been my intention for several years past to publish my thoughts upon Religion. I am well aware of the difficulties that attend the subject; and from that consideration had reserved it to a more advanced period of life. I intended it to be the last offering I should make to my fellow-citizens of all nations, and that at a time when the purity of the motive that induced me to it could not admit of a question, even by those who might disapprove the work.

5 The circumstance that has now taken place in France,[1] of the total abolition of the whole national order of priesthood and of everything appertaining to compulsive systems of religion and compulsive articles of faith, has not only precipitated my intention, but rendered a work of this kind exceedingly necessary; lest, in the general wreck of superstition, of false systems of government, and false theology, we lose sight of morality, of humanity, and of the theology that is true.

[1] The French Revolution closed the churches.

As several of my colleagues, and others of my fellow-citizens of France, have given me the example of making their voluntary and individual profession of faith, I also will make mine; and I do this with all that sincerity and frankness with which the mind of man communicates with itself.

I believe in one God, and no more; and I hope for happiness beyond this life.

I believe in the equality of man, and I believe that religious duties consist in doing justice, loving mercy, and endeavoring to make our fellow-creatures happy.

But lest it should be supposed that I believe many other things in addition to these, I shall, in the progress of this work, declare the things I do not believe and my reasons for not believing them.

10 I do not believe in the creed professed by the Jewish church, by the Roman church, by the Greek church, by the Turkish church, by the Protestant church, nor by any church that I know of. My own mind is my own church.

All national institutions of churches—whether Jewish, Christian, or Turkish—appear to me no other than human inventions set up to terrify and enslave mankind and monopolize power and profit.

I do not mean by this declaration to condemn those who believe otherwise. They have the same right to their belief as I have to mine. But it is necessary to the happiness of man that he be mentally faithful to himself. Infidelity does not consist in believing or in disbelieving; it consists in professing to believe what he does not believe.

It is impossible to calculate the moral mischief, if I may so express it, that mental lying has produced in society. When a man has so far corrupted and prostituted the chastity of his mind as to subscribe his professional belief to things he does not believe, he has prepared himself for the commission of every other crime. He takes up the trade of a priest for the sake of gain, and, in order to *qualify* himself for that trade, he begins with a perjury. Can we conceive anything more destructive to morality than this?

Soon after I had published the pamphlet, COMMON SENSE, in America, I saw the exceeding probability that a revolution in the system of government would be followed by a revolution in the system of religion. The adulterous connection of church and state, wherever it had taken place, whether Jewish, Christian, or Turkish, had so effectually prohibited, by pains and penalties, every discussion upon established creeds and upon first principles of religion, that until the system of government should be changed those subjects could not be brought fairly and openly before the world; but that whenever this should be done, a revolution in the system of religion would follow. Human inventions and priestcraft would be detected, and man would return to the pure, unmixed, and unadulterated belief of one God, and no more.

15 Every national church or religion has established itself by pretending some special mission from God, communicated to certain individuals. The Jews have their Moses; the Christians their Jesus Christ, their apostles and saints; and the Turks their Mahomet—as if the way to God was not open to every man alike.

Each of those churches show certain books which they call *revelation*, or the word of God. The Jews say that their word of God was given by God to Moses face to face; the Christians say that their word of God came by divine inspiration; and the Turks say that their word of God (the Koran) was brought by an angel from heaven. Each of those churches accuse the other of unbelief; and, for my own part, I disbelieve them all.

As it is necessary to affix right ideas to words, I will, before I proceed further into the subject, offer some observations on the word *revelation*. Revelation, when applied to religion, means something communicated *immediately* from God to man.

No one will deny or dispute the power of the Almighty to make such a communication, if he pleases. But admitting, for the sake of a case, that something has been revealed to a certain person, and not revealed to any other person, it is revelation to that person only. When he tells it to a second person, a second to a third, a third to a fourth, and so on, it ceases to be a revelation to all those persons. It is a revelation to the first person only, and *hearsay* to every other; and, consequently, they are not obliged to believe it. . . .

When Moses told the children of Israel that he received the two tables of commandments from the hand of God, they were not obliged to believe him, because they had no other authority for it than his telling them so; and I have no other authority for it than some historian telling me so. The commandments carry no internal evidence of divinity with them. They contain some good moral precepts, such as any man qualified to be a lawgiver, or a legislator, could produce himself, without having recourse to supernatural intervention.

When I am told that the Koran was written in heaven, and brought to Mahomet by an angel, the account comes too near the same kind of hearsay evidence and secondhand authority as the former. I did not see the angel myself, and therefore I have a right not to believe it.

When also I am told that a woman, called the Virgin Mary, said, or gave out, that that she was with child without any cohabitation with a man, and that her betrothed husband, Joseph, said that an angel told him so, I have a right to believe them or not; such a circumstance required a much stronger evidence than their bare word for it; but we have not even this; for neither Joseph nor Mary wrote any such matter themselves. It is only reported by others that *they said so*. It is hearsay upon hearsay, and I do not choose to rest my belief upon such evidence.

It is, however, not difficult to account for the credit that was given to the story of Jesus Christ being the Son of God. He was born at a time when the heathen mythology had still some fashion and repute in the world, and that mythology had prepared the people for the belief of such a story. Almost all the extraordinary men that lived under the heathen mythology were reputed to be the sons of some of their gods. It was not a new thing, at that time, to believe a man to have been celestially begotten; the intercourse of gods with women was then a matter of familiar opinion. Their Jupiter, according to their accounts, had cohabited with hundreds; the story therefore had nothing in it either new, wonderful, or obscene; it was conformable to the opinions that then prevailed among the people called Gentiles, or mythologists, and it was those people only that believed it. The Jews, who had kept strictly to the belief of one God and no more, and who had always rejected the heathen mythology, never credited the story.

It is curious to observe how the theory of what is called the Christian church sprung out of the tail of the heathen mythology. A direct incorporation took place, in the first instance, by making the reputed founder to be celestially begotten. The trinity of gods that then followed was no other than a reduction of the former plurality, which was about twenty or thirty thousand. The statue of Mary succeeded the statue of Diana of Ephesus. The deification of heroes changed into the canonization of saints. The mythologists had gods for everthing; the Christian mythologists had saints for everything. The church became as crowded with the one as the pantheon had been with the other; and Rome was the place of both. The Christian theory is little else than the idolatry of the ancient mythologists, accommodated to the purposes of power and revenue; and it yet remains to reason and philosophy to abolish the amphibious fraud.

Nothing that is here said can apply, even with the most distant disrespect, to the real character of Jesus Christ. He was a virtuous and an amiable man. The morality that he preached and practiced was of the most benevolent kind; and though similar systems of morality had been preached by Confucius, and by some of the Greek philosophers, many years before, by the Quakers since, and by many good men in all ages, it has not been exceeded by any.

Jesus Christ wrote no account of himself, of his birth, parentage, or anything else. Not a line of what is called the New Testament is of his writing. The history of him is altogether the work of other people; and as to the account given of his resurrection and ascension, it was the necessary counterpart to the story of his birth. His historians, having brought him into the world in supernatural manner, were obliged to take him out again in the same manner, or the first part of the story must have fallen to the ground. . . .

But some perhaps will say: Are we to have no word of God—no revelation? I answer: Yes, there is a word of God; there is a revelation.

THE WORD OF GOD IS THE CREATION WE BEHOLD; and it is in *this* word, which no human invention can counterfeit or alter, that God speaketh universally to man. . . .

It is only in the CREATION that all our ideas and conceptions of a *word of God* can unite. The creation speaketh a universal language, independently of human speech or human languages, multiplied and various as they be. It is an ever existing original which every man can read. It cannot be forged; it cannot be counterfeited; it cannot be lost; it cannot be altered; it cannot be suppressed. It does not depend upon the will of man whether it shall be published or not; it publishes itself from one end of the earth to the other. It preaches to all nations and to all worlds; and this *word of God* reveals to man all that is necessary for man to know of God.

Do we want to contemplate his power? We see it in the immensity of the creation. Do we want to contemplate his wisdom? We see it in the unchangeable order by which the incomprehensible whole is governed. Do we want to contemplate his munificence? We see it in the abundance with which he fills the earth. Do we want to contemplate his mercy? We see it in his not withholding that abundance even from the unthankful. In fine, do we want to know what God is? Search not the book called the Scripture, which any human hand might make, but the scripture called the Creation.

30 The only idea man can affix to the name of God is that of a *first cause,* the cause of all things. And incomprehensibly difficult as it is for man to conceive what a first cause is, he arrives at the belief of it from the tenfold greater difficulty of disbelieving it. It is difficult beyond description to conceive that space can have no end; but it is more difficult to conceive an end. It is difficult beyond the power of man to conceive an eternal duration of what we call time; but, it is more impossible to conceive a time when there shall be no time. In like manner of reasoning, everything we behold carries in itself the internal evidence that it did not make itself. Every man is an evidence to himself that he did not make himself; neither could his father make himself, nor his grandfather, nor any of his race; neither could any tree, plant, or animal make itself; and it is the conviction arising from this evidence that carries us on, as it were, by necessity, to the belief of a first cause eternally existing, of a nature totally different to any material existence we know of, and by the power of which all things exist; and this first cause, man calls God.

It is only by the exercise of reason that man can discover God. Take away that reason and he would be incapable of understanding anything; and, in this case, it would be just as consistent to read even the book called the Bible to a horse as to a man. How then is it that those people pretend to reject reason?

LEARNING MORE

Paine here espouses an intensely rational *deism.* Although this approach to God was common in the eighteenth century, it was much more widely espoused in Europe than in the United States. To learn more about deism, see the *Ideas Across Time* website.

QUESTIONING THE TEXT

1. What appeal to U.S. citizens does Paine make as he begins his essay? Why do you think he begins in this way?
2. On what grounds does Paine reject all churches he knows of?
3. What, for Paine, is the connection between political and religious liberty?
4. On what grounds does Paine reject revelation?
5. How does Paine explain the "credit that was given to the story of Jesus Christ being the Son of God" (par. 22)? What is your view of this explanation?
6. What is Paine's view of Jesus's resurrection?
7. What does Paine believe we should trust in the place of revelation?

8. Although Paine says belief in God is "incomprehensibly difficult" (par. 30), he nonetheless affirms his belief. On what basis does he do so?
9. What human faculty does Paine wish to substitute for faith as a way of discovering God?

ANALYZING THE WRITER'S CRAFT

1. How would Paine's essay have been different had he begun with par. 3 rather than par. 1?
2. Does this selection have a thesis? If so, where is it stated? If not, what maintains the essay's coherence?
3. What is the tone of this essay?
4. Paine took pride in the plainness of his style. Give two or three examples of sentences or passages that represent Paine's style especially well, and analyze Paine's diction and sentence structure. What do you think his diction implies about his intended audience?
5. Although Paine writes plainly, he is nonetheless a masterful rhetoretician. Give two or three examples that illustrate Paine's deft use of stylistic devices.
6. Paine devotes considerable space to arguing against the validity of revelation. Is his reasoning sound? If it is sound, why were many Americans offended by it? If it is not sound, point out its logical flaws.
7. Why does Paine think that "the creation we behold" provides sounder evidence of the "word of God" than revelation?
8. Is Paine's conclusion effective?

MAKING CONNECTIONS

1. What would Paine think of Paul Tillich's notion of religion (pp. 123–130)?
2. Paine's total faith in reason suggests a complete affinity with the scientific worldview. Compare and contrast Paine's use of and attitude toward reason with Francis Bacon's (Chapter 3, pp. 152–155), Albert Einstein's (Chapter 3, pp. 193–200), and Richard Feynman's (Chapter 3, pp. 201–207).
3. Does Paine's writing, addressed to the citizens of the United States, have the ring and tone of American English? Compare his prose to that of Thomas Jefferson (Chapter 5, pp. 354–360).

FORMULATING IDEAS FOR WRITING

1. Write a letter to Tom Paine explaining why you appreciate his unalloyed candor and agree with his deistic point of view; or write a letter that explains why he has not persuaded you to abandon your allegiance to your church (or synagogue or mosque or . . .).
2. Paine argues (par. 14) that the old way of government, in which church and state were one and you had to conform to the established religion, naturally

restricted people's religious thought. He anticipates a new liberation from what he sees as the tyranny of religious institutions under the new democratic forms of government, those that separate church and state. But in the United States today, a significant number of people are saying that the separation of church and state has gone too far and that government should cooperate with and in various ways underwrite organized churches. Write an essay that either supports Paine's view, and supports the separation of church and state, or takes issue with Paine, and argues for a more intimate relation between church and state.

3. Write a refutation of Paine's ideas about revelation.
4. Write a refutation of Paine's argument for the existence and nature of God (pars. 27–32).

The Book of Genesis from *The Woman's Bible* (1895–1898)

Elizabeth Cady Stanton

Elizabeth Cady Stanton was the foremost American feminist of the nineteenth century. She was the driving force behind the Women's Rights Convention held in Seneca Falls, New York, in 1848—the launching event of the women's rights movement in the United States. Stanton went on to a lifelong collaboration with Susan B. Anthony, often drafting the core documents and speeches that established the basis for women's equality, including women's suffrage, property rights for married women, and fair divorce laws. Although recognized as one of the main leaders of the women's movement in the United States until the end of her life, her radicalism also increasingly isolated her from the more religiously conservative mainstream. Her biblical commentaries, collected in *The Woman's Bible* (1895–1898), from which this selection is taken, spelled out her view that masculine theology, translated into religious orthodoxy, effectively blocked women's aspirations to personal, social, and spiritual independence. These views were rejected by the organized woman's movement.

Stanton was born in 1815 into a prominent New York State family. Her father, Daniel Cady, from whom she learned a great deal about the law, became a New York State Supreme Court justice. When Stanton married the abolitionist Henry Brewster Stanton in 1840, she dropped the word "obey" from her marriage vows. The couple had seven children. Stanton met Susan B. Anthony in 1851, and Stanton's role in their remarkable collaboration was mainly that of writer and thinker; Anthony proved far more effective as an organizer. In 1866, with Lucretia Mott and Lucy Stone, they founded the American Equal Rights

Association, and then in 1870, the National Woman Suffrage Association (NWSA). Through the NWSA, Stanton campaigned for women's suffrage, against discrimination in employment and pay, and for the right to divorce. When the NWSA merged with its more conservative rival the American Woman Suffrage Association in 1890, Stanton became the first president of the new organization, the national American Woman Suffrage Association. She was succeeded two years later by Anthony. With Matilda Gage, Stanton wrote a four-volume *History of Woman Suffrage* (1881–1902); her autobiography, *Eighty Years and More,* appeared in 1898. Stanton died in New York City in 1902. It would be another twenty years before American women nationwide would win the right to vote.

The Book of Genesis

Chapter I

Genesis i: 26, 27, 28.

26¶ And God said, Let us make man in our image, after our likeness: and let them have dominion over the fish of the sea, and over the fowl of the air, and over the cattle, and over all the earth, and over every creeping thing that creepeth upon the earth.

27 So God created man in his *own* image, in the image of God created he him; male and female created he them.

28 And God blessed them, and God said unto them, Be fruitful, and multiply, and replenish the earth, and subdue it; and have dominion over the fish of the sea, and over the fowl of the air, and over every living thing that moveth upon the earth.

Here is the sacred historian's first account of the advent of woman; a simultaneous creation of both sexes, in the image of God. It is evident from the language that there was consultation in the Godhead, and that the masculine and feminine elements were equally represented. Scott in his commentaries says, "this consultation of the Gods is the origin of the doctrine of the trinity." But instead of three male personages, as generally represented, a Heavenly Father, Mother, and Son would seem more rational.

The first step in the elevation of woman to her true position, as an equal factor in human progress, is the cultivation of the religious sentiment in regard to her dignity and equality, the recognition by the rising generation of an ideal Heavenly Mother, to whom their prayers should be addressed, as well as to a Father.

If language has any meaning, we have in these texts a plain declaration of the existence of the feminine element in the Godhead, equal in power and glory with the masculine. The Heavenly Mother and Father! "God created man in his *own image, male and female.*" Thus Scripture, as well as science and philosophy, declares the eternity and equality of sex—the philosophical fact, without which there could have been no perpetuation of creation, no growth or development in the animal, vegetable, or mineral kingdoms, no awakening nor progressing in the world of thought. The masculine and feminine elements, exactly equal and balancing each other, are as essential to the maintenance of the equilibrium of the universe as positive and negative electricity, the centripetal and centrifugal forces, the laws of attraction which bind together all we know of this planet whereon we dwell and of the system in which we revolve.

In the great work of creation the crowning glory was realized, when man and woman were evolved on the sixth day, the masculine and feminine forces in the image of God, that must have existed eternally, in all forms of matter and mind. All the persons in the Godhead are represented in the Elohim[1] the divine plurality taking counsel in regard to this last and highest form of life. Who were the members of this high council, and whether a duality or a trinity? Verse 27 declares the image of God male and female. How then is it possible to make woman an afterthought? We find in verses 5–16 the pronoun "he" used. Should it not in harmony with verse 26 be "they," a dual pronoun? We may attribute this to the same cause as the use of "his" in verse 11 instead of "it." The fruit tree yielding fruit after "his" kind instead of after "its" kind. The paucity of a language may give rise to many misunderstandings.

5 The above texts plainly show the simultaneous creation of man and woman, and their equal importance in the development of the race. All those theories based on the assumption that man was prior in the creation, have no foundation in Scripture.

As to woman's subjection, on which both the canon and the civil law delight to dwell, it is important to note that equal dominion is given to woman over every living thing, but not one word is said giving man dominion over woman.

Here is the first title deed to this green earth given alike to the sons and daughters of God. No lesson of woman's subjection can be fairly drawn from the first chapter of the Old Testament.

E. C. S.

LEARNING MORE

As a central figure in the movement for women's rights, Elizabeth Cady Stanton helped pen a number of the foundation documents of modern American feminism. See the *Ideas Across Time* website to read some of these and to learn more about Stanton.

To read the rest of the first books of Genesis, see the *Ideas Across Time* website.

QUESTIONING THE TEXT

1. To whom does Stanton refer as "the sacred historian" (par. 1)? Why does she use this locution?

[1] Elohim, one of the Hebrew names for God in Genesis, is in the plural form.

2. On what basis does Stanton deduce a Trinitarian God in Genesis? On what basis does she claim that this Trinity includes a female divine personage? Do you read these passages in the same way she does? Explain.
3. What does Stanton believe to be the essential first step on the road to full equality for women?
4. How do the passages Stanton quotes from Genesis support her view of the equality of the sexes?
5. How has the "paucity of language" (par. 4) led to a misunderstanding about the relative standing, in God's eyes, of men and women?
6. What is Stanton's main conclusion from her reading of Genesis? Do you agree with her? Why or why not?

ANALYZING THE WRITER'S CRAFT

1. What is the thesis statement of this essay, and where is it found?
2. To whom is this essay addressed? Explain.
3. What is the tone of this essay? Cite some examples to support your reading.
4. Is Stanton's method rigorous; that is, are her conclusions reasonably drawn from the text? Explain.
5. Is Stanton persuasive? What is her strongest argument, or interpretation? Her weakest? Explain.
6. Is her conclusion effective? Why or why not?

MAKING CONNECTIONS

1. The implications for women's well-being of the social roles imposed on them are explored from various perspectives by Harriet Jacobs (Chapter 6, pp. 464–470), Betty Friedan (Chapter 6, pp. 496–509), Jamaica Kincaid (Chapter 6, pp. 552–553), and Stanton. How do the views of these important women compare? How do they differ? Which of these women do you find most appealing? Why?
2. Do you think Louisa May Alcott (Chapter 4, pp. 275–286) would join Stanton in her project to reinterpret the Bible from a woman's point of view? How about Barbara Ehrenreich (Chapter 4, pp. 316–319)? Explain.

FORMULATING IDEAS FOR WRITING

1. Support or critique Stanton's reading of Genesis.
2. Stanton argues that "the first step" in gaining equality for women is gaining equality in religious terms—specifically, gaining recognition for women's equality in the Christian story of creation. Do you agree? Can equality be achieved in social and political terms without first addressing the question of religious equality?
3. Today the role of women remains at least significantly different from the role of men in certain societies and in certain roles—for example, in many

non-Western countries or in those religions that do not permit women to be ordained as priests. How do you think Stanton's reading of the Bible might affect the disputes about whether women should be ordained? In the absence of scriptural authority, what is the ground on which women are denied a role as priests (whatever the religion)? Do you find the arguments against the ordination of women to be persuasive?

4. Stanton reprints the passages from Genesis she is going to discuss. We can all read those passages, and she wants us to have them right there in front of us. Clearly, however, she offers an unorthodox reading of Genesis. How can we explain the different interpretations by people of good will of the very same passages? What principles, if any, can we use to arrive at an appropriate, or even "correct," reading of important texts? How would you persuade someone who altogether disagreed with Stanton that Stanton had indeed read the text properly, or, at least, had read the text in a responsible and plausible way? Conversely, what might you say to Stanton to demonstrate to her that her reading is implausible?

God Is Dead (1887)

Friedrich Nietzsche

The problematic maxim of the twentieth century—"God is dead"—was proclaimed by the German philosopher Friedrich Nietzsche (1844–1900), the son and grandson of Lutheran ministers. More than any writer of his time, Nietzsche took the implications of science, and in particular of Darwinism, to what he considered to be their philosophical conclusions—that human beings must be looked at and understood as what they are: animals; that human institutions and human values must be reexamined in light of our animal nature; and that there is no more purpose or direction to life than there is to the evolution of species (see Chapter 3, pp. 167–180, and pp. 182–185). There is no external standard to judge human actions, he argued, which in any case are no more "willed" than is a thunderstorm or the habits of the chimpanzee. But free of illusion at last, human beings, Nietzsche thought, could now grasp their fates in their own hands, recognizing the inappropriateness of such concepts as good and evil. He rejected Christianity as demeaning. "There was only *one* Christian," he said, "and he died on the cross." The possibilities for human liberation after the death of God, Nietzsche argued, depended on a "revaluation of all values."

Nietzsche studied philology—at that time, the study and interpretation of the classics and the Bible—at the universities of Bonn and Leipzig, soon thereafter

(1869) becoming a professor at the University of Basel, in Switzerland. Here he met the composer Richard Wagner, one of the great figures in nineteenth-century music. Almost exactly the age Nietzsche's father would have been had he lived (the father died of a brain disease when Nietzsche was 4 years old), Wagner deeply influenced Nietzsche during the decade of their intimacy, a close friendship that ended when Nietzsche became revolted by Wagner's fervid nationalism and anti-Semitism. In 1882, Nietzsche proposed to the 21-year-old Lou Andreas-Salome, later an associate of Sigmund Freud. His proposal rejected, Nietzsche, spent the next decade as a kind of wandering scholar after resigning from his university post. During this time, he wrote his most famous books—among them, *Thus Spake Zarathustra* (1883–1885), *Beyond Good and Evil* (1886), and *The Genealogy of Morals* (1887). In 1889, he suffered a mental breakdown, and he remained an invalid until his death in 1900.

The selections below are taken from several of Nietzsche's books in the translation by R. J. Hollingdale (Penguin, 1977).

1. On a Sunday morning we hear the bells ringing we ask ourselves: it is possible! this is going on because of a Jew crucified 2,000 years ago who said he was the son of God. The proof of such an assertion is lacking. In the context of our age the Christian religion is certainly a piece of antiquity intruding out of distant ages past, and that the above-mentioned assertion is believed [. . .] is perhaps the most ancient piece of this inheritance. A god who begets children on a mortal woman; a sage who calls upon us no longer to work, no longer to sit in judgement, but to heed the signs of the imminent end of the world; a justice which accepts an innocent man as a substitute sacrifice; someone who bids his disciples drink his blood; prayers for miraculous interventions; sins perpetrated against a god atoned for by a god; fear of a Beyond to which death is the gateway: the figure of the Cross as a symbol in an age which no longer knows the meaning and shame of the Cross—how gruesomely all this is wafted to us, as if out of the grave of a primeval past! Can one believe that things of this sort are still believed in?

2. The greatest recent event—that "God is dead," that belief in the Christian God has become unbelievable—is already beginning to cast its first shadows over Europe. For the few, at least, whose eyes, the *suspicion* in whose eyes is strong and subtle enough for this spectacle, it seems as though some sun had just gone down, some ancient profound trust had been turned round into doubt: to them our old world must appear daily more crepuscular,[1] untrustworthy, stranger, "older." On the whole, however, one has to say that the event itself is much too great, too distant, too remote from the comprehension of many for news of it even to have *arrived* yet; not to speak of many knowing already *what* has really taken place—and what, now that this belief has been undermined, must now fall in because it was built on this belief, leaned on it, had

[1] crepuscular: having the look and qualities of twilight.

grown into it: for example, our entire European morality. This protracted abundance and succession of demolition, destruction, decline, overturning which now stands before us: who today could divine enough of this to feel obliged to be the teacher and herald of this tremendous logic of terror, the prophet of a darkening and eclipse of the sun such as there has probably never yet been on earth? . . . Even we born readers of riddles, who wait, as it were, on the mountains, set between today and tomorrow and yoked to the contradiction between today and tomorrow, we first-born and premature-born of the coming century, to whom the shadows which must soon envelop Europe *ought* already to have come into sight: why is it that even we lack any real participation in this darkening, above all behold its advent without any care or fear for *ourselves?* Do we perhaps still stand too much within the *immediate consequences* of this event—and these immediate consequences, its consequences for *us,* are, conversely from what one could expect, in no way sad and darkening but, rather, like a new, hard to describe kind of light, happiness, alleviation, encouragement, dawn. . . . We philosophers and "free spirits" in fact feel at the news that the "old God is dead" as if illumined by a new dawn; our heart overflows with gratitude, astonishment, presentiment, expectation—at last the horizon seems to us again free, even if it is not bright, at last our ships can put out again, no matter what the danger, every daring venture of knowledge is again permitted, the sea, *our* sea again lies there open before us, perhaps there has never yet been such an "open sea."

LEARNING MORE

Nietzsche placed his thought in the context of other great German figures, such as Immanuel Kant and Johann Wolfgang von Goethe, as well as, of course, Richard Wagner. To learn more about these men, see the *Ideas Across Time* website.

QUESTIONING THE TEXT

1. Why is Nietzsche incredulous that people still go to church on Sundays?
2. What does Nietzsche foresee as the consequences of the "fact" that God is dead?
3. Why is the death of God a new dawn for philosophers?

ANALYZING THE WRITER'S CRAFT

1. Nietzsche worked to develop a style that would be true to what he saw as his radical break with cultural and philosophical tradition. How would you characterize that style? Offer a few representative examples.
2. Discuss Nietzsche's use of "I" in his writing. Is he being egotistical? Does he mean his "I" to refer literally to himself?
3. Is Nietzsche logical? Explain.

4. What kind of evidence, or supporting material, does Nietzsche use to make his points?
5. Discuss Nietzsche's use of reversal (taking a proposition and turning it on its head). Offer two or three examples. How is the principle of reversal related to Nietzsche's advocacy of "the revaluation of all values"?
6. Do you find Nietzsche's incredulity about the persistence of Christian belief persuasive? Why or why not?

MAKING CONNECTIONS

1. Compare and contrast Tom Paine's (pp. 98–103) and Nietzsche's ways of analyzing belief, as well as their conclusions. Do you think they are essentially kindred spirits or at best casually related thinkers?
2. Does Nietzsche draw proper conclusions about the implications of science for belief? Consider the insights of Charles Darwin (Chapter 3, pp. 167–180), Albert Einstein (Chapter 3, pp. 193–200), and Richard Feynman (Chapter 3, pp. 201–207) as they do or do not support Nietzsche's views.
3. Would Paul Tillich (pp. 123–130) think of Nietzsche as evincing religious concern?
4. Would Nietzsche find confirmation for his views in Alexis de Tocqueville's analysis of the United States (Chapter 6, pp. 458–462)? In Daniel J. Boorstin's analysis of democracy (Chapter 5, pp. 390–402)?

FORMULATING IDEAS FOR WRITING

1. Nietzsche became a favorite philosopher of Adolf Hitler and the Nazi regime. He was perceived as a prophet of Aryan racial superiority and of the violent cult of the "superman" (the leader) as *the* agent of human progress. Nietzsche's supporters have argued that Hitler's delight in Nietzsche depends on a misreading and misunderstanding of Nietzsche's ideas. Write an essay that sides with or against Nietzsche in this dispute about the meaning of his work.
2. Right and wrong seem to depend upon free will: if I cannot control my actions, how can I be held accountable for my actions? Yet Nietzsche argues that people are not in the least accountable for their actions. Is Nietzsche's argument persuasive? If it is, is he arguing for the overthrow of all moral rules and standards? If it is not, show why not.
3. Explain to Nietzsche why so many millions of people are today Christians (or Muslims or Hindus or . . .), despite his arguments about the death of God.
4. Nietzsche believed that his philosophy established the ground for the liberation of humankind from lies and illusions. Some readers have agreed with him and found in his ideas a bracing, liberating way of looking at the world. Others have found him to be nihilistic, depressing, and even dangerous, an enemy of decency and morality. What is your view?

The Will to Believe (1897)

William James

William James was the most influential and widely read of the many American intellectuals who, in the latter half of the nineteenth century, were preoccupied with the relation of religion to science. Perhaps one reason for this was James's unique position in American thought, having initiated the study and teaching of psychology in the United States ("The first lecture in psychology I ever heard," James joked, "was the first I ever gave."), as well as formulating that most American of all philosophies: pragmatism.

James was born in New York City on January 11, 1842. His father, Henry, inherited a considerable fortune, thus ensuring for his children an eccentric but intensely cosmopolitan and religious education, including tutors, wide exposure to the arts, and extended stays abroad. The regimen worked well: William's brother Henry became the foremost American novelist of the late nineteenth and early twentieth centuries, and his sister Alice, though not well known in her time, is now also recognized as a major literary talent. James entered Harvard Medical School in 1864, receiving his doctor's degree in 1869 and commencing work as an instructor in anatomy and physiology at Harvard in 1873. In 1875, he began teaching psychology at Harvard. His two-volume *The Principles of Psychology* (1890), ten years in the making, was a founding text on the subject, and he was the first American to notice the work of Freud. But by 1879, James had already begun to teach philosophy, publishing *The Will to Believe and Other Essays in Popular Philosophy* in 1897. Many of these essays were taken from James's popular public lectures, and "The Will to Believe" was widely quoted and generally lionized in its time. Here James argued that science had failed to disprove the essentials of religion and that the scientific ethos of the age had, without any rational grounds for doing so and without justification, made religious belief seem quaint, old-fashioned, and something no thinking person could seriously pursue. But James obviously was a thinking person, and he devoted his writings on religion to countering what he saw as a wrong-headed and prejudiced dismissal of people's rational desire to believe. James's main contribution to philosophy, *Pragmatism* (1907), was a tough-minded argument for a certain method of assessing the value of ideas, essentially maintaining that the value of a truth inheres in its potential to infuse meaning in someone's actual life. But James's complex methodological argument was quickly transformed by early-twentieth-century American exuberance into an affirmation of a strictly practical outlook: how can we judge the value or truth of something? Answer: if it "works." In 1907, James retired from teaching, and in 1910, he died at his country house in New Hampshire.

In the recently published *Life* by Leslie Stephen of his brother, Fitz-James,[1] there is an account of a school to which the latter went when he was a boy. The teacher, a certain Mr. Guest, used to converse with his pupils in this wise: "Gurney, what is the difference between justification and sanctification?—Stephen, prove the omnipotence of God!" etc. In the midst of our Harvard free-thinking and indifference we are prone to imagine that here at your good old orthodox College conversation continues to be somewhat upon this order; and to show you that we at Harvard have not lost all interest in these vital subjects, I have brought with me to-night something like a sermon on justification by faith to read to you,—I mean an essay in justification *of* faith, a defence of our right to adopt a believing attitude in religious matters, in spite of the fact that our merely logical intellect may not have been coerced. 'The Will to Believe,' accordingly, is the title of my paper.

I have long defended to my own students the lawfulness of voluntarily adopted faith; but as soon as they have got well imbued with the logical spirit, they have as a rule refused to admit my contention to be lawful philosophically, even though in point of fact they were personally all the time chock-full of some faith or other themselves. I am all the while, however, so profoundly convinced that my own position is correct, that your invitation has seemed to me a good occasion to make my statements more clear. Perhaps your minds will be more open than those with which I have hitherto had to deal. . . .

In Pascal's *Thoughts*[2] there is a celebrated passage known in literature as Pascal's wager. In it he tries to force us into Christianity by reasoning as if our concern with truth resembled our concern with the stakes in a game of chance. Translated freely his words are these: You must either believe or not believe what God is—which will you do? Your human reason cannot say. A game is going on between you and the nature of things which at the day of judgment will bring out either heads or tails. Weigh what your gains and your losses would be if you should stake all you have on heads, or God's existence: if you win in such case, you gain eternal beatitude; if you lose, you lose nothing at all. If there were an infinity of chances, and only one for God in this wager, still you ought to stake your all on God; for though you surely risk a finite loss by this procedure, and finite loss is reasonable, even a certain one is reasonable, if there is but the possibility of infinite gain. Go, then, and take holy water, and have masses said; belief will come and stupefy your scruples,—*Cela vous fera croire et vous abêtira*.[3] Why should you not? At bottom, what have you to lose?

You probably feel that when religious faith expresses itself thus, in the language of the gaming-table, it is put to its last trumps. Surely Pascal's own personal belief in masses and holy water had far other springs; and this

[1] Leslie and Fitz-James Stephen: Leslie Stephen (1832–1904), prominent English author and critic, father of Virginia Woolf, editor of the *Dictionary of National Biography*. Leslie Stephen's brother Fitz-James Stephen (1829–1894) was a leading English jurist.

[2] Pascal's Thoughts: Blaise Pascal (1623–1662) was a major French mathematician and theologian, best known for his *Pensées* (*Thoughts*), published in 1670.

[3] *cela . . . abêtira:* French for "This will make you believe and help you on your way."

celebrated page of his is but an argument for others, a last desperate snatch at a weapon against the hardness of the unbelieving heart. We feel that a faith in masses and holy water adopted willfully after such a mechanical calculation would lack the inner soul of faith's reality; and if we were ourselves in the place of the Deity, we would probably take particular pleasure in cutting off believers of this pattern from their infinite reward. It is evident that unless there be some preexisting tendency to believe in masses and holy water, the option offered to the will by Pascal is not a living option. Certainly no Turk ever took to masses and holy water on its account; and even to us Protestants these means of salvation seem such foregone impossibilities that Pascal's logic, invoked for them specifically, leaves us unmoved. . . .

5 The talk of believing by our volition seems, then, from one point of view, simply silly. From another point of view it is worse than silly, it is vile. When one turns to the magnificent edifice of the physical sciences, and sees how it was reared; what thousands of disinterested moral lives of men lie buried in its mere foundations; what patience and postponement, what choking down of preference, what submission to the icy laws of outer fact are wrought into its very stones and mortar; how absolutely impersonal it stands in its vast augustness,—then how besotted and contemptible seems every little sentimentalist who comes blowing his voluntary smoke-wreaths, and pretending to decide things from out of his private dream! Can we wonder if those bred in the rugged and manly school of science should feel like spewing such subjectivism out of their mouths? The whole system of loyalties which grow up in the schools of science go dead against its toleration; so that it is only natural that those who have caught the scientific fever should pass over to the opposite extreme, and write sometimes as if the incorruptibly truthful intellect ought positively to prefer bitterness and unacceptableness to the heart in its cup.

Yet if any one should thereupon assume that intellectual insight is what remains after wish and will and sentimental preference have taken wing, or that pure reason is what then settles our opinions, he would fly quite as directly in the teeth of the facts. . . . As a matter of fact we find ourselves believing, we hardly know how or why. Mr. Balfour[4] gives the name of "authority" to all those influences, born of the intellectual climate, that make hypotheses possible or impossible for us, alive or dead. Here in this room, we all of us believe in molecules and the conservation of energy, in democracy and necessary progress, in Protestant Christianity and the duty of fighting for 'the doctrine of the immortal Monroe,[5] all for no reasons worthy of the name. We see into these matters with no more inner clearness, and probably with much less, than any disbeliever in them might possess. His unconventionality would probably have some grounds to show for its conclusions; but for us, not insight, but the *prestige*

[4] Balfour: Arthur Balfour (1848–1930), British prime minister, in 1917 made the Balfour Declaration, recognizing the right of Jews to have a homeland in Palestine.

[5] Monroe: The Monroe Doctrine (1823) established U.S. dominance in the New World, declaring that any interference by the European powers in the Western Hemisphere would be considered by the United States as an act of war.

of the opinions, is what makes the spark shoot from them and light up our sleeping magazines of faith. Our reason is quite satisfied, in nine hundred and ninety-nine cases out of every thousand of us, if it can find a few arguments that will do to recite in case our credulity is criticized by some one else. Our faith is faith in some one else's faith, and in the greatest matters this is most the case. Our belief in truth itself, for instance, that there is a truth, and that our minds and it are made for each other,—what is it but a passionate affirmation of desire, in which our social system backs us up? We want to have a truth; we want to believe that our experiments and studies and discussions must put us in a continually better and better position towards it; and on this line we agree to fight out our thinking lives. But if a pyrrhonistic[6] sceptic asks us *how we know* all this, can our logic find a reply? Not certainly it cannot. It is just one volition against another,—we willing to go in for life upon a trust or assumption which he, for his part, does not care to make.

Evidently, then, our non-intellectual nature does influence our convictions. There are passional tendencies and volitions which run before and others which come after belief, and it is only the latter that are too late for the fair; and they are not too late when the previous passional work has been already in their own direction. Pascal's argument, instead of being powerless, then seems a regular clincher, and is the last stroke needed to make our faith in masses and holy water complete. The state of things is evidently far from simple; and pure insight and logic, whatever they might do ideally, are not the only things that really do produce our creeds.

Our next duty, having recognized this mixed-up state of affairs, is to ask whether it be simply reprehensible and pathological[7] or whether, on the contrary, we must treat it as a normal element in making up our minds. The thesis I defend is, briefly stated, this: *Our passional nature not only lawfully may, but must, decide an option between propositions, whenever it is a genuine option that cannot by its nature be decided on intellectual grounds; for to say, under such circumstances, "Do not decide, but leave the question open," is itself a passional decision,—just like deciding yes or no,—and is attended with the same risk of losing the truth.* The thesis thus abstractly expressed will, I trust, soon become quite clear. But I must first indulge in a bit more of preliminary work.

It will be observed that for the purposes of this discussion we are on "dogmatic" ground,—ground, I mean, which leaves systematic philosophical scepticism altogether out of account. The postulate that there is truth, and that it is the destiny of our minds to attain it, we are deliberately resolving to make, though the sceptic will not make it. We part company with him, therefore, absolutely, at this point. But the faith that truth exists, and that our minds can find it, may be held in two ways. We may talk of the *empiricist* way and of the *absolutist* way of believing in truth. The absolutists in this matter say that we not only can attain to knowing truth, but we can *know when* we have attained to

[6] pyrrhonistic: radically skeptical, after the Greek philosopher Pyrrho of Ellis (c. 300 BCE).

[7] pathological: caused by (mental) disease.

knowing it; while the empiricists think that although we may attain it, we cannot infallibly know when. To *know* is one thing, and to know for certain *that* we know is another. One may hold to the first being possible without the second; hence the empiricists and the absolutists, although neither of them is a sceptic in the usual philosophic sense of the term, show very different degrees of dogmatism in their lives.

If we look at the history of opinions, we see that the empiricist tendency has largely prevailed in science, while in philosophy the absolutist tendency has had everything its own way. The characteristic sort of happiness, indeed, which philosophies yield has mainly consisted in the conviction felt by each successive school or system that by it bottom-certitude had been attained. "Other philosophies are collections of opinions, mostly false; *my* philosophy gives standing-ground forever,"—who does not recognize in this the keynote of every system worthy of the name? A system, to be a system at all, must come as a *closed* system, reversible in this or that detail, perchance, but in its essential features never!

10 But now, since we are all such absolutists by instinct, what in our quality of students of philosophy ought we to do about the fact? Shall we espouse and indorse it? Or shall we treat it as a weakness of our nature from which we must free ourselves, if we can?

I sincerely believe that the latter course is the only one we can follow as reflective men. Objective evidence and certitude are doubtless very fine ideals to play with, but where on this moonlit and dream-visited planet are they found? I am, therefore, myself a complete empiricist so far as my theory of human knowledge goes. I live, to be sure, by the practical faith that we must go on experiencing and thinking over our experience, for only thus can our opinions grow more true; but to hold any one of them—I absolutely do not care which—as if it never could be reinterpretable or corrigible, I believe to be a tremendously mistaken attitude, and I think that the whole history of philosophy will bear me out. There is but one indefectibly certain truth, and that is the truth that pyrrhonistic scepticism itself leaves standing,—the truth that the present phenomenon of consciousness exists. That, however, is the bare starting-point of knowledge, the mere admission of a stuff to be philosophized about. The various philosophies are but so many attempts at expressing what this stuff really is. And if we repair to our libraries what disagreement do we discover! Where is a certainly true answer found? Apart from abstract propositions of comparison (such as two and two are the same as four), propositions which tell us nothing by themselves about concrete reality, we find no proposition ever regarded by any one as evidently certain that has not either been called a falsehood, or at least had its truth sincerely questioned by some one else. . . . No concrete test of what is really true has ever been agreed upon. . . .

But please observe, now, that when as empiricists we give up the doctrine of objective certitude, we do not thereby give up the quest or hope of truth itself. We still pin our faith on its existence, and still believe that we gain an ever better position towards it by systematically continuing to roll up experiences and think. Our great difference from the scholastic lies in the way we face. The strength of his system lies in the principles, the origin, the *terminus a quo* of his thought; for us the strength is in the outcome, the upshot, the *terminus ad quem.* Not where it comes from but what it leads to is to decide. It matters not to an empiricist from what quarter an hypothesis may come to him: he may have acquired it by fair means or by foul; passion may have whispered or accident suggested it; but if the total drift of thinking continues to confirm it, that is what he means by its being true. . . .

And now, after all this introduction, let us go straight at our question. I have said, and now repeat it, that not only as a matter of fact do we find our passional nature influencing us in our opinions, but that there are some options between opinions in which this influence must be regarded both as an inevitable and as a lawful determinant of our choice. . . .

Religions differ so much in their accidents that in discussing the religious question we must make it very generic and broad. What then do we now mean by the religious hypothesis? Science says things are; morality says some things are better than other things; and religion says essentially two things.

First, she says that the best things are the more eternal things, the overlapping things, the things in the universe that throw the last stone, so to speak, and say the final word. "Perfection is eternal,"—this phrase of Charles Secrétan[8] seems a good way of putting this first affirmation of religion, an affirmation which obviously cannot yet be verified scientifically at all.

The second affirmation of religion is that we are better off even now if we believe her first affirmation to be true.

Now, let us consider what the logical elements of this situation are *in case the religious hypothesis in both its branches be really true.* (Of course, we must admit that possibility at the outset. If we are to discuss the question at all, it must involve a living option. If for any of you religion be a hypothesis that cannot, by any living possibility be true, then you need go no farther. I speak to the "saving remnant" alone.) So proceeding, we see, first, that religion offers itself as a *momentous* option. We are supposed to gain, even now, by our belief, and to lose by our non-belief, a certain vital good. Secondly, religion is a *forced* option, so far as that good goes. We cannot escape the issue by remaining sceptical and waiting for more light, because, although we do avoid error in that way *if religion be untrue,* we lose the good, *if it be true,* just as certainly as if we positively chose to disbelieve. It is as if a man should hesitate indefinitely to ask a certain woman to marry him because he was not perfectly sure that she would prove an angel after he brought her home. Would he not cut himself off from that particular angel-possibility as decisively as if he went and married some one else? Scepticism, then, is not avoidance of option; it is option of a certain particular kind of risk. *Better risk loss of truth than chance of error,*—that is your faith-vetoer's exact position. He is actively playing his stake as much as the believer is; he is backing the field against the religious hypothesis, just as the believer is backing

---

[8] Charles Secrétan: Swiss philosopher (1815–1895) who aimed to reconcile Christianity and rational philosophy.

the religious hypothesis against the field. To preach scepticism to us as a duty until "sufficient evidence" for religion be found, is tantamount therefore to telling us, when in presence of the religious hypothesis, that to yield to our fear of its being error is wiser and better than to yield to our hope that it may be true. It is not intellect against all passions, then; it is only intellect with one passion laying down its law. And by what, forsooth, is the supreme wisdom of this passion warranted? Dupery for dupery, what proof is there that dupery through hope is so much worse than dupery through fear? I, for one, can see no proof; and I simply refuse obedience to the scientist's command to imitate his kind of option, in a case where my own stake is important enough to give me the right to choose my own form of risk. If religion be true and the evidence for it be still insufficient, I do not wish, by putting your extinguisher upon my nature (which feels to me as if it had after all some business in this matter), to forfeit my sole chance in life of getting upon the winning side,—that chance depending, of course, on my willingness to run the risk of acting as if my passional need of taking the world religiously might be prophetic and right.

All this is on the supposition that it really may be prophetic and right, and that, even to us who are discussing the matter; religion is a live hypothesis which may be true. Now, to most of us religion comes in a still further way that makes a veto on our active faith even more illogical. The more perfect and more eternal aspect of the universe is represented in our religions as having personal form. The universe is no longer a mere *It* to us, but a *Thou,* if we are religious; and any relation that may be possible from person to person might be possible here. For instance, although in one sense we are passive portions of the universe, in another we show a curious autonomy, as if we were small active centres on our own account. We feel, too, as if the appeal of religion to us were made to our own active good-will, as if evidence might be forever withheld from us unless we met the hypothesis half-way. To take a trivial illustration: just as a man who in a company of gentlemen made no advances, asked a warrant for every concession, and believed no one's word without proof, would cut himself off by such churlishness from all the social rewards that a more trusting spirit would earn,—so here, one who should shut himself up in snarling logicality and try to make the gods extort his recognition willy-nilly, or not get it at all, might cut himself off forever from his only opportunity of making the gods' acquaintance. This feeling, forced on us we know not whence, that by obstinately believing that there are gods (although not to do so would be so easy both for our logic and our life) we are doing the universe the deepest service we can, seems part of the living essence of the religious hypothesis. If the hypothesis *were* true in all its parts, including this one, then pure intellectualism, with its veto on our making willing advances, would be an absurdity; and some participation of our sympathetic nature would be logically required. I, therefore, for one, cannot see my way to accepting the agnostic[9] rules for truth-seeking, or wilfully agree to keep my willing nature out of the game. I cannot do so for this plain reason, that *a rule of thinking which would absolutely prevent me from*

[9] agnostic: skeptical about the existence of God.

acknowledging certain kinds of truth if those kinds of truth were really there, would be an irrational rule. That for me is the long and short of the formal logic of the situation, no matter what the kinds of truth might materially be.

I confess I do not see how this logic can be escaped. But sad experience makes me fear that some of you may still shrink from radically saying with me, *in abstracto,* that we have the right to believe at our own risk any hypothesis that is live enough to tempt our will. I suspect, however, that if this is so, it is because you have got away from the abstract logical point of view altogether, and are thinking (perhaps without realizing it) of some particular religious hypothesis which for you is dead. The freedom to "believe what we will" you apply to the case of some patent superstition; and the faith you think of is the faith defined by the schoolboy when he said, "Faith is when you believe something that you know ain't true." I can only repeat that this is misapprehension. *In concreto,* the freedom to believe can only cover living options which the intellect of the individual cannot by itself resolve; and living options never seem absurdities to him who has them to consider. When I look at the religious question as it really puts itself to concrete men, and when I think of all the possibilities which both practically and theoretically it involves, then this command that we shall put a stopper on our heart, instincts, and courage, and *wait*—acting of course meanwhile more or less as if religion were *not* true[10]—till doomsday, or till such time as our intellect and senses working together may have raked in evidence enough,—this command, I say, seems to me the queerest idol ever manufactured in the philosophic cave. Were we scholastic absolutists, there might be more excuse. If we had an infallible intellect with its objective certitudes, we might feel ourselves disloyal to such a perfect organ of knowledge in not trusting to it exclusively, in not waiting for its releasing word. But if we are empiricists, if we believe that no bell in us tolls to let us know for certain when truth is in our grasp, then it seems a piece of idle fantasticality to preach so solemnly our duty of waiting for the bell. Indeed we *may* wait if we will,—I hope you do not think that I am denying that,—but if we do so, we do so at our peril as much as if we believed. In either case we *act,* taking our life in our hands. No one of us ought to issue vetoes to the other, nor should we bandy words of abuse. We ought, on the contrary, delicately and profoundly to respect one another's mental freedom: then only shall we bring about the intellectual republic; then only shall we have that spirit of inner tolerance without which all our outer tolerance is soulless, and which is empiricism's glory; then only shall we live and let live, in speculative as well as in practical things.

[10] Since belief is measured by action, he who forbids us to believe religion to be true, necessarily also forbids us to act as we should if we did believe it to be true. The whole defence of religious faith hinges upon action. If the action required or inspired by the religious hypothesis is in no way different from that dictated by the naturalistic hypothesis, then religious faith is a pure superfluity, better pruned away, and controversy about its legitimacy is a piece of idle trifling, unworthy of serious minds. I myself believe, of course, that the religious hypothesis gives to the world an expression which specifically determines our reactions, and makes them in a large part unlike what they might be on a purely naturalistic scheme of belief. [James's note]

20 I began by a reference to Fitz-James Stephen; let me end by a quotation from him. "What do you think of yourself? What do you think of the world? . . . These are questions with which all must deal as it seems good to them. They are riddles of the Sphinx, and in some way or other we must deal with them. . . . In all important transactions of life we have to take a leap in the dark. . . . If we decide to leave the riddles unanswered, that is a choice; if we waver in our answer, that, too, is a choice: but whatever choice we make, we make it at our peril. If a man chooses to turn his back altogether on God and the future, no one can prevent him; no one can show beyond reasonable doubt that he is mistaken. If a man thinks otherwise and acts as he thinks, I do not see that any one can prove that *he* is mistaken. Each must act as he thinks best; and if he is wrong, so much the worse for him. We stand on a mountain pass in the midst of whirling snow and blinding mist, through which we get glimpses now and then of paths which may be deceptive. If we stand still we shall be frozen to death. If we take the wrong road we shall be dashed to pieces. We do not certainly know whether there is any right one. What must we do? 'Be strong and of a good courage.' Act for the best, hope for the best, and take what comes. . . . If death ends all, we cannot meet death better."

LEARNING MORE

James relies for a number of points of departure on Blaise Pascal's famous "wager" in his *Pensées* (*Thoughts*). Find out more about Pascal on the *Ideas Across Time* website.

QUESTIONING THE TEXT

1. What does James maintain is the basis for most of our opinions? Do you agree?
2. What are the two ways in which you can believe the idea that truth exists? Which of these does James favor, and why?
3. What is "truth" to an empiricist?
4. What, for James, is "the religious hypothesis" (par. 14)?
5. What logical options does the religious hypothesis entail?
6. How does James approach Pascal's wager differently at the start of his essay and toward its conclusion?

ANALYZING THE WRITER'S CRAFT

1. What is James's thesis?
2. What kinds of evidence does James use to support his thesis?
3. What evidence in support of James's thesis do you find most convincing? Least convincing?
4. Do you find James's restatement of Pascal's wager (par. 17) a persuasive refutation of the objections against it that he himself raises in par. 3?

5. What is the tone of this essay?
6. Do you find James's allusion to Fitz-James Stephen a good way to begin his essay? Do you find the quotation from Stephen a useful conclusion to his essay?
7. James's style sounds distinctly old-fashioned. Identify two or three features of the writing that make it seem "dated," that is, quite obviously written well before our time.
8. Do you find James's logic to be sound? Explain.
9. What grounds for belief does James fail to examine? Why do you think he looks at only certain roads to belief?

MAKING CONNECTIONS

1. Tom Paine (pp. 98–103) might well be described as a "pyrrhonistic sceptic." Do you think he would assent to James' logical argument for the place of sentiment as a basis for belief?
2. Compare James' account of religion and Paul Tillich's (pp. 123–130).
3. What do you imagine would be James's response to Richard Feynman's argument for the value of science (Chapter 3, pp. 193–200)?

FORMULATING IDEAS FOR WRITING

1. James's allusion, in his opening, to Fitz-James Stephen's schooldays illustrates the place of religion in schooling around two hundred years ago. Students in the early years of school were expected to know the answers to standard theological distinctions (the difference between justification and sanctification, for example) and to be able to recite standard proofs of the nature of God. James displays a mixed response to this long-gone state of affairs, partly an amused reporting of a clunky pedagogy, partly a serious appreciation for the actual questions at hand, and partly a mild but earnest disappointment that such questions have come to seem, by the end of the nineteenth century, archaic, beyond the interest of serious-thinking people. Write an essay that explores, in a reflective but autobiographical way, the place of religion in your own schooling. Be specific. Consider what "religion" was taken to mean (if anything—your essay could report the general absence of religion in your schooling). How did your schooling affect your religious beliefs?
2. Does science imply that religious belief is incompatible with serious thought?
3. James argues that we *feel* certain ideas as inherently persuasive, such as that there is "truth." Do you agree? If you do not agree, explain why not. If you do agree, explain why you are an absolute or empirical believer in truth (see par. 8).
4. Write an essay in praise of James's conclusion as refreshingly candid and persuasive, or in rejection of his conclusion as wishful but flawed.

The Lost Dimension in Religion (1958)

Paul Tillich

One of the great theologians of the twentieth century, Paul Tillich took on the monumental task of affirming faith in the secular culture of popular modern societies. Tillich, however, was neither scornful nor dismissive of the culture of his time. He fully acknowledged the modern condition of skeptical, secular humanism, with its seductive consumerism. He devoted his work to finding a path to God in the light of modern knowledge and in the language of twentieth-century existentialist philosophy. Born in Germany in 1886, the son of a learned Lutheran minister, Tillich was ordained in the Evangelical Church of the Prussian Union—the Protestant state church—in 1912. Service as chaplain in the German army in World War I led to two nervous breakdowns and a crisis of faith that transformed Tillich's religious outlook. His work thereafter might be characterized as a modern quest for God. For Tillich, theology revolves around the issue of being and nonbeing. The way to God is through the full realization of the dread of nonbeing, the dark shadow of every human existence, since we could as easily "not be" as "be." Contemplation of nonbeing raises the question of what sustains us as finite beings. To this philosophical question, Tillich says theology has the answer: God. For whatever force infuses the finite cannot itself be finite but must transcend the terms and conditions of finite being or existence. This transcendent power Tillich calls "being itself" or "the Ground of Being" or "God."

For Tillich, therefore, the everyday evidence of religious belief, such as attendance at church, can be no more than an evasion of the "dimension of depth" in religion, which he defines as "being grasped by an infinite concern." He says we have "lost an answer to the question: What is the meaning of life?" and have even lost the courage to ask the question. Yet without rediscovery of this dimension of depth, belief cannot be glimpsed, let alone achieved.

Tillich's career followed a successful trajectory, leading to the position of professor of philosophy at the University of Frankfurt, until 1933, when he was dismissed from his post by the Nazi government. Several months later, Tillich arrived in New York; he taught at the Union Theological Seminary from 1933 until 1955. From 1955 to 1962, he was University Professor at Harvard, and then Nuveen Professor of Theology in the University of Chicago Divinity School until his death in 1965. Among Tillich's influential works are *The Courage to Be* (1952), *Theology of Culture* (1959), and *The Eternal Now* (1963). His major treatise is the three-volume *Systematic Theology* (1951–1963). The selection below originally appeared in the *Saturday Evening Post* on June 14, 1958.

Every observer of our Western civilization is aware of the fact that something has happened to religion. It especially strikes the observer of the American scene. Everywhere he finds symptoms of what one has called religious revival or more modestly, the revival of interest in religion. He finds them in the churches with their rapidly increasing membership. He finds them in the mushroomlike growth of sects. He finds them on college campuses and in the theological faculties of universities. Most conspicuously he finds them in the tremendous success of men like Billy Graham and Norman Vincent Peale,[1] who attract masses of people Sunday after Sunday, meeting after meeting. The facts cannot be denied, but how should they be interpreted? It is my intention to show that these facts must be seen as expressions of the predicament of Western man in the second half of the twentieth century. But I would even go a step further. I believe that the predicament of man in our period gives us also an important insight into the predicament of man generally—at all times and in all parts of the earth.

There are many analyses of man and society in our time. Most of them show important traits in the picture, but few of them succeed in giving a general key to our present situation. Although it is not easy to find such a key, I shall attempt it and, in so doing, will make an assertion which may be somewhat mystifying at first hearing. The decisive element in the predicament of Western man in our period is his loss of the dimension of depth. Of course "dimension of depth" is a metaphor. It is taken from the spatial realm and applied to man's spiritual life. What does it mean?

It means that man has lost an answer to the question: What is the meaning of life? Where do we come from, where do we go to? What shall we do, what should we become in the short stretch between birth and death? Such questions are not answered or even asked if the "dimension of depth" is lost. And this is precisely what has happened to man in our period of history. He has lost the courage to ask such questions with an infinite seriousness—as former generations did—and he has lost the courage to receive answers to these questions, wherever they may come from.

I suggest that we call the dimension of depth the religious dimension in man's nature. Being religious means asking passionately the question of the meaning of our existence and being willing to receive answers, even if the answers hurt. Such an idea of religion makes religion universally human, but it certainly differs from what is usually called religion. It does not describe religion as the belief in the existence of gods or one God, and as a set of activities and institutions for the sake of relating oneself to these beings in thought, devotion and obedience. No one can deny that the religions which have appeared in history are religions in this sense. Nevertheless, religion in its innermost nature is more than religion in this narrower sense. It is the state of being concerned about one's own being and being universally.

[1] Norman Vincent Peale: popular Christian preacher (1898–1993), for a half-century at the Marble Collegiate Church in Manhattan. The title of his best-known work encapsulates his philosophy: *The Power of Positive Thinking* (1952).

5 There are many people who are ultimately concerned in this way who feel far removed, however, from religion in the narrower sense, and therefore from every historical religion. It often happens that such people take the question of the meaning of their life infinitely seriously and reject any historical religion just for this reason. They feel that the concrete religions fail to express their profound concern adequately. They are religious while rejecting the religions. It is this experience which forces us to distinguish the meaning of religion as living in the dimension of depth from particular expressions of one's ultimate concern in the symbols and institutions of a concrete religion. If we now turn to the concrete analysis of the religious situation of our time, it is obvious that our key must be the basic meaning of religion and not any particular religion, not even Christianity. What does this key disclose about the predicament of man in our period?

If we define religion as the state of being grasped by an infinite concern, we must say: Man in our time has lost such infinite concern. And the resurgence of religion is nothing but a desperate and mostly futile attempt to regain what has been lost.

How did the dimension of depth become lost? Like any important event, it had many causes, but certainly not the one which one hears often mentioned from ministers' pulpits and evangelists' platforms, namely that a widespread impiety of modern man is responsible. Modern man is neither more pious nor more impious than man in any other period. The loss of the dimension of depth is caused by the relation of man to his world and to himself in our period, the period in which nature is being subjected scientifically and technically to the control of man. In this period, life in the dimension of depth is replaced by life in the horizontal dimension. The driving forces of the industrial society of which we are a part go ahead horizontally and not vertically. In popular terms this is expressed in phrases like "better and better," "bigger and bigger," "more and more." One should not disparage the feeling which lies behind such speech. Man is right in feeling that he is able to know and transform the world he encounters without a foreseeable limit. He can go ahead in all directions without a definite boundary.

A most expressive symbol of this attitude of going ahead in the horizontal dimension is the breaking through of the space which is controlled by the gravitational power of the earth into the world-space. It is interesting that one calls this world-space simply "space" and speaks, for instance, of space travel, as if every trip were not travel into space. Perhaps one feels that the true nature of space has been discovered only through our entering into indefinite world-space. In any case, the predominance of the horizontal dimension over the dimension of depth has been immensely increased by the opening up of the space beyond the space of the earth.

If we now ask what does man do and seek if he goes ahead in the horizontal dimension, the answer is difficult. Sometimes one is inclined to say that the mere movement ahead without an end, the intoxication with speeding forward without limits, is what satisfies him. But this answer is by no means sufficient. For on his way into space and time man changes the world he encounters. And the changes made by him change himself. He transforms everything he encounters into a tool; and in doing so he himself becomes a tool. But if he asks, a tool for what, there is no answer.

One does not need to look far beyond everyone's daily experience in order to find examples to describe this predicament. Indeed our daily life in office and home, in cars and airplanes, at parties and conference, while reading magazines and watching television, while looking at advertisements and hearing radio, are in themselves continuous examples of a life which has lost the dimension of depth. It runs ahead, every moment is filled with something which must be done or seen or said or planned. But no one can experience depth without stopping and becoming aware of himself. Only if he has moments in which he does not care about what comes next can he experience the meaning of the moment here and now and ask himself about the meaning of his life. As long as the preliminary, transitory concerns are not silenced, no matter how interesting and valuable and important they may be, the voice of the ultimate concern cannot be heard. This is the deepest root of the loss of the dimension of depth in our period—the loss of religion in its basic and universal meaning.

If the dimension of depth is lost, the symbols in which life in this dimension has expressed itself must also disappear. I am speaking of the great symbols of the historical religions in our Western world, of Judaism and Christianity. The reason that the religious symbols became lost is not primarily scientific criticism, but it is a complete misunderstanding of their meaning; and only because of this misunderstanding was scientific critique able, and even justified, in attacking them. The first step toward the nonreligion of the Western world was made by religion itself. When it defended its great symbols, not as symbols, but as literal stories, it had already lost the battle. In doing so the theologians (and today many religious laymen) helped to transfer the powerful expressions of the dimension of depth into objects or happenings on the horizontal plane. There the symbols lose their power and meaning and become an easy prey to physical, biological and historical attack.

If the symbol of creation which points to the divine ground of everything is transferred to the horizontal plane, it becomes a story of events in a removed past for which there is no evidence, but which contradicts every piece of scientific evidence. If the symbol of the Fall of Man which points to the tragic estrangement of man and his world from their true being is transferred to the horizontal plane, it becomes a story of a human couple a few thousand years ago in what is now present-day Iraq. One of the most profound psychological descriptions of the general human predicament becomes an absurdity on the horizontal plane. If the symbols of the Savior and the salvation through Him which point to the healing power in history and personal life are transferred to the horizontal plane, they become stories of a half-divine being coming from a heavenly place and returning to it. Obviously, in this form, they have no meaning whatsoever for people whose view of the universe is determined by scientific astronomy.

If the idea of God (and the symbols applied to Him) which expresses man's ultimate concern is transferred to the horizontal plane, God becomes a being among others whose existence or nonexistence is a matter of inquiry. Nothing, perhaps, is more symptomatic of the loss of the dimension of depth than the permanent discussion about the existence or nonexistence of God—a discussion in which both sides are equally wrong, because the discussion itself is wrong and possible only after the loss of the dimension of depth.

When in this way man has deprived himself of the dimension of depth and the symbols expressing it, he then becomes a part of the horizontal plane. He loses his self and becomes a thing among things. He becomes an element in the process of manipulated production and manipulated consumption. This is now a matter of public knowledge. We have become aware of the degree to which everyone in our social structure is managed, even if one knows it and even if one belongs himself to the managing group. The influence of the gang mentality on adolescents, of the corporation's demands on the executives, of the conditioning of everyone by public communication, by propaganda and advertising under the guidance of motivation research, et cetera, have all been described in many books and articles.

Under these pressures, man can hardly escape the fate of becoming a thing among the things he produces, a bundle of conditioned reflexes without a free, deciding and responsible self. The immense mechanism, set up by man to produce objects for his use, transforms man himself into an object used by the same mechanism of production and consumption.

But man has not ceased to be man. He resists this fate anxiously, desperately, courageously. He asks the question, for what? And he realizes that there is no answer. He becomes aware of the emptiness which is covered by the continuous movement ahead and the production of means for ends which become means again without an ultimate end. Without knowing what has happened to him, he feels that he has lost the meaning of life, the dimension of depth.

Out of this awareness the religious question arises and religious answers are received or rejected. Therefore, in order to describe the contemporary attitude toward religion, we must first point to the places where the awareness of the predicament of Western man in our period is most sharply expressed. These places are the great art, literature and partly, at least, the philosophy of our time. It is both the subject matter and the style of these creations which show the passionate and often tragic struggle about the meaning of life in a period in which man has lost the dimension of depth. This art, literature, philosophy is not religious in the narrower sense of the word; but it asks the religious question more radically and more profoundly than most directly religious expressions of our time.

It is the religious question which is asked when the novelist describes a man who tries in vain to reach the only place which could solve the problem of his life, or a man who disintegrates under the memory of a guilt which persecutes him, or a man who never had a real self and is pushed by his fate without resistance to death, or a man who experiences a profound disgust of everything he encounters.

It is the religious question which is asked when the poet opens up the horror and the fascination of the demonic regions of his soul, or if he leads us into the deserts and empty places of our being or if he shows physical and moral mud under the surface of life, or if he sings the song of transitoriness, giving words to the ever-present anxiety of our hearts.

It is the religious question which is asked when the playwright shows the illusion of a life in a ridiculous symbol or if he lets the emptiness of a life's work end in self-destruction, or if he confronts us with the inescapable bondage to mutual hate and guilt, or if he leads us into the dark cellar of lost hopes and slow disintegration.

It is the religious question which is asked when the painter breaks the visible surface into pieces, then reunites them into a great picture which has little similarity with the world at which we normally look, but which expresses our anxiety and our courage to face reality.

It is the religious question which is asked when the architect in creating office buildings or churches removes the trimmings taken over from past styles because they cannot be considered an honest expression of our own period. He prefers the seeming poverty of a purpose-determined style to the deceptive richness of imitated styles of the past. He knows that he gives no final answer but he does give an honest answer.

The philosophy of our time, shows the same hiddenly religious traits. It is divided into two main schools of thought, the analytic and the existentialist. The former tries to analyze logical and linguistic forms which are always used and which underlie all scientific research. One may compare them with the painters who dissolve the natural forms of bodies into cubes, planes and lines; or with those architects who want the structural "bones" of their buildings to be conspicuously visible and not hidden by covering features. This self-restriction produces the almost monastic poverty and seriousness of this philosophy. It is religious—without any contact with religion in its method—by exercising the humility of "learned ignorance."

In contrast to this school the existentialist philosophers[2] have much to say about the problems of human existence. They bring into rational concepts what the writers and poets, the painters and architects are expressing in their particular material. What they express is the human predicament in time and space, in anxiety and guilt and the feeling of meaninglessness. From Pascal in the seventeenth century to Heidegger and Sartre[3] in our time, philosophers have emphasized the contrast between human dignity and human misery. And by

---

[2] Existentialist philosophers: Beginning with the French theologian Blaise Pascal (1623–1662), existentialists focused on the essential features of existence as the terrain of understanding of human beings. Their work examines anxiety, dread, death, and the absurd situation of being in the universe. See also footnote 3.

[3] Pascal . . . Sartre: Pascal in his *Pensées* (1670) postulated his famous wager. We cannot know if God exists, so we should bet that he does and behave accordingly. If we're wrong, we will nonetheless have lived a good life. If we're right. . . . The German philosopher Martin Heidegger (1889–1976) and the French thinker Jean-Paul Sartre (1905–1980) are the two most important existentialist philosophers of the twentieth century. Sartre in particular drew from his view of the human condition, which Heidegger defined as being "thrown" into existence, a method for asserting free choice in the full knowledge of the absurdity of our situation as beings in a godless, meaningless universe.

doing so, they have raised the religious question. Some have tried to answer the question they have asked. But if they did so, they turned back to past traditions and offered to our time that which does not fit our time. Is it possible for our time to receive answers which are born out of our time?

Answers given today are in danger of strengthening the present situation and with it the questions to which they are supposed to be the answers. This refers to some of the previously mentioned major representatives of the so-called resurgence of religion as for instance the evangelist Billy Graham and the counseling and healing minister Norman Vincent Peale. Against the validity of the answers given by the former, one must say that in spite of his personal integrity, his propagandistic methods and his primitive theological fundamentalism fall short of what is needed to give an answer to the religious question of our period. In spite of all his seriousness, he does not take the radical question of our period seriously.

The effect that Norman Peale has on large groups of people is rooted in the fact that he confirms the situation which he is supposed to help overcome. He heals people with the purpose of making them fit again for the demands of the competitive and conformist society in which we are living. He helps them to become adapted to the situation which is characterized by the loss of the dimension of depth. Therefore, his advice is valid on this level; but it is the validity of this level that is the true religious question of our time. And this question he neither raises nor answers.

In many cases the increase of church membership and interest in religious activities does not mean much more than the religious consecration of a state of things in which the religious dimension has been lost. It is the desire to participate in activities which are socially strongly approved and give internal and a certain amount of external security. This is not necessarily bad, but it certainly is not an answer to the religious question of our period.

Is there an answer? There is always an answer, but the answer may not be available to us. We may be too deeply steeped in the predicament out of which the question arises to be able to answer it. To acknowledge this is certainly a better way toward a real answer than to bar the way to it by deceptive answers. And it may be that in this attitude the real answer (within available limits) is given. The real answer to the question of how to regain the dimension of depth is not given by increased church membership or church attendance, nor by conversion or healing experiences. But it is given by the awareness that we have lost the decisive dimension of life, the dimension of depth, and that there is no easy way of getting it back. Such awareness is in itself a state of being grasped by that which is symbolized in the term, dimension of depth. He who realizes that he is separated from the ultimate source of meaning shows by this realization that he is not only separated but also reunited. And this is just our situation. What we need above all—and partly have—is the radical realization of our predicament, without trying to cover it up by secular or religious ideologies. The revival of religious interest would be a creative power in our culture if it would develop into a movement of search for the lost dimension of depth.

This does not mean that the traditional religious symbols should be dismissed. They certainly have lost their meaning in the literalistic form into which they have been distorted, thus producing the critical reaction against them. But they have not lost their genuine meaning, namely, of answering the question which is implied in man's very existence in powerful, revealing and saving symbols. If the resurgence of religion would produce a new understanding of the symbols of the past and their relevance for our situation instead of premature and deceptive answers, it would become a creative factor in our culture and a saving factor for many who live in estrangement, anxiety and despair. The religious answer has always the character of "in spite of." In spite of the loss of dimension of depth, its power is present, and most present in those who are aware of the loss and are striving to regain it with ultimate seriousness.

LEARNING MORE

Tillich is considered one the main existentialist theologians of the twentieth century. What are the main tenets of existentialism? What does it mean to be an existentialist theologian? To learn more, see the *Ideas Across Time* website.

QUESTIONING THE TEXT

1. What does Tillich mean by "the dimension of depth"?
2. How does Tillich's definition of religion differ from what is usually called religion?
3. What does Tillich's analysis of religion in our time reveal about our "predicament" (par. 5)?
4. What has caused the loss of the dimension of depth?
5. How does Tillich define "the horizontal dimension" (pars. 7 and 8)?
6. What happens to the symbols of religion when they are transferred to the horizontal plane? What happens to God when He is transferred to the horizontal plane?
7. What way out of the contemporary predicament does Tillich propose?
8. According to Tillich, who succeeds in expressing the religious question in our time?
9. Why does Tillich reject the answers offered by Billy Graham and Norman Vincent Peale?
10. How can Christianity help to answer "the religious question of our period"?

ANALYZING THE WRITER'S CRAFT

1. What is Tillich's thesis?
2. Tillich says he is going to offer an analysis of "man and society in our time." How does he do this? What are the main steps in his analysis?
3. How does Tillich substantiate his claim that we have lost the dimension of depth? Do you find his evidence persuasive? Why or why not?

4. How does Tillich analyze the consequences of life on the horizontal dimension?
5. Tillich's essay appeared in a popular weekly magazine with a mass readership. What aspects of the writing suggest that the essay was intended for a mass audience? Do you think this essay, published fifty years ago, would need to be changed if it were to appear in a mass audience magazine today? Discuss.
6. Discuss two or three examples of Tillich's use of comparison and contrast.
7. Is Tillich's conclusion effective? Does his conclusion satisfactorily answer the question that he poses?

MAKING CONNECTIONS

1. Tillich says that his analysis offers "an important insight into the predicament of man . . . at all times and in all parts of the earth" (par. 1). Compare his account of our predicament with the account expressed in the holy texts (pp. 68–96).
2. Do you think Tillich would say that Nietzsche (pp. 109–112) expresses the religious predicament of modern men and women?
3. Compare and contrast Tillich's ideas about the dimension of depth and the horizontal dimension with Daniel J. Boorstin's notion of attenuation (Chapter 5, pp. 390–402).
4. Compare and contrast Tillich's understanding of modern art with Meyer Schapiro's (Chapter 7, pp. 590–602).

FORMULATING IDEAS FOR WRITING

1. Tillich's essay was written a half-century ago. Write an essay arguing either that his analysis is as valid today as it was when he wrote it or that his analysis is no longer valid because of the changes in society.
2. Explain why you do or do not agree with Tillich's view of what is religious.
3. When Tillich thinks of the contemporary religious predicament, he thinks of writers, artists, and philosophers. In the works of these men and women, Tillich finds the dimension of depth. Write an essay about a figure whose work you think expresses the dimension of depth for the twenty-first century.
4. Write an essay that attempts to explain how Tillich believes we should understand the orthodox symbols, parables, and rituals of Christianity—the expulsion from Eden, the cross, the Mass, and so forth.
5. "He who realizes that he is separated from the ultimate source of meaning," Tillich writes toward the end of his essay, "shows by this realization that he is not only separated but also reunited" (par. 28). Does this sentence contain a profound truth, or is it evidence of Tillich's own failure to answer the religious question in a contemporary way? Explain.

The Art of Happiness (1998)

His Holiness the Dalai Lama

The Dalai Lama, the political and spiritual leader of Tibet, was born in 1935 to a peasant family in a small village in northern Tibet. Five years later, after having been recognized as the fourteenth incarnation of the Buddha of Compassion, he was formally enthroned in his present role. *Dalai* means "ocean" in the Mongolian language, and *Lama* is Tibetan for "guru" or "teacher." In 1959, when China laid claim to all of Tibet, the Dalai Lama was forced into exile, fleeing to India with about 80,000 followers. He took up residence in Dharamsala in northern India, and there established the headquarters of the Tibetan government in exile. In 1989, the Dalai Lama received the Nobel Peace Prize for advocating "peaceful solutions based upon tolerance and mutual respect in order to preserve the historical and cultural heritage of his people."

Through his down-to-earth teaching of Buddhism, the Dalai Lama has earned a worldwide following. He has been notably ecumenical, asserting the need in all human beings for spiritual fulfillment but affirming many religious paths. As he says in this selection, taken from *The Art of Happiness* (1998), written with Howard C. Cutler, M.D., "different people have different mental dispositions. So, the variety of people calls for a variety of religions." The Dalai Lama lives simply in his role as a monk, rising each day at 4 A.M. to meditate. He is fond of saying, "I am just a simple Buddhist monk—no more, nor less."

I believe that it is essential to appreciate our potential as human beings and recognize the importance of inner transformation. This should be achieved through what could be called a process of mental development. Sometimes, I call this having a spiritual dimension in our life.

There can be two levels of spirituality. One level of spirituality has to do with our religious beliefs. In this world, there are so many different people, so many different dispositions. There are five billion human beings and in a certain way I think we need five billion different religions, because there is such a large variety of dispositions. I believe that each individual should embark upon a spiritual path that is best suited to his or her mental disposition, natural inclination, temperament, belief, family, and cultural background.

Now, for example, as a Buddhist monk, I find Buddhism to be most suitable. So, for myself, I've found that Buddhism is best. But that does not mean Buddhism is best for everyone. That's clear. It's definite. If I believed that Buddhism were best for everyone, that would be foolish, because different people have different mental dispositions. So, the variety of people calls for a variety of religions. The purpose of religion is to benefit people, and I think that if we only had one religion, after a while it would cease to benefit many people. If we had a restaurant, for instance, and it only served one dish—day after day, for every meal—that restaurant wouldn't have many customers left after a while. People need and appreciate diversity in their food because there are so many different tastes. In the same way, religions are meant to nourish the human spirit. And I think we can learn to celebrate that diversity in religions and develop a deep appreciation of the variety of religions. So certain people may find Judaism, the Christian tradition, or the Islamic tradition to be most effective for them. Therefore, we must respect and appreciate the value of all the different major world religious traditions.

All of these religions can make an effective contribution for the benefit of humanity. They are all designed to make the individual a happier person, and the world a better place. However, in order for the religion to have an impact in making the world a better place, I think it's important for the individual practitioner to sincerely practice the teachings of that religion. One must integrate the religious teachings into one's life, wherever one is, so one can use them as a source of inner strength. And one must gain a deeper understanding of the religion's ideas, not just on an intellectual level but with a deep feeling, making them part of one's inner experience.

5 I believe that one can cultivate a deep respect for all the different religious traditions. One reason to respect these other traditions is that all of these traditions can provide an ethical framework which can govern one's behavior and have positive effects. For instance, in the Christian tradition a belief in God can provide one with a coherent and clear-cut ethical framework which can govern one's behavior and way of life—and it can be a very powerful approach because there is a certain intimacy created in one's relationship with God, and the way to demonstrate one's love of God, the God who created you, is by showing love and compassion to one's fellow human beings.

I believe that there are many similar reasons to respect other religious traditions as well. All major religions, of course, have provided tremendous benefit for millions of human beings throughout many centuries in the past. And even at this very moment, millions of people still get a benefit, get some kind of inspiration, from these different religious traditions. It is clear. And in the future also, these different religious traditions will give inspiration to millions of coming generations. That is a fact. So therefore, it is very, very important to realize that reality and respect other traditions.

I think that one way of strengthening that mutual respect is through closer contact between those of different religious faiths—personal contact. I have made efforts over the past few years to meet and have dialogues with, for example, the Christian community and the Jewish community, and I think that some really positive results have come of this. Through this kind of closer contact we can learn about the useful contributions that these religions have made to humanity and find useful aspects of the other traditions that we can learn from. We may even discover methods and techniques that we can adopt in our own practice.

So, it is essential that we develop closer bonds among the various religions; through this we can make a common effort for the benefit of humanity. There are so many things that divide humanity, so many problems in the world. Religion should be a remedy to help reduce the conflict and suffering in the world, not another source of conflict.

We often hear people say that all human beings are equal. By this we mean that everyone has the obvious desire of happiness. Everybody has the right to be a happy person. And everyone has the right to overcome suffering. So if someone is deriving happiness or benefit from a particular religious tradition, it becomes important to respect the rights of others; thus we must learn to respect all these major religious traditions. That is clear. . . .

10 So, in speaking of having a spiritual dimension to our lives, we have identified our religious beliefs as one level of spirituality. Now regarding religion, if we believe in any religion, that's good. But even without a religious belief, we can still manage. In some cases, we can manage even better. But that's our own individual right; if we wish to believe, good. If not, it's all right. But then there's another level of spirituality. That is what I call *basic spirituality*—basic human qualities of goodness, kindness, compassion, caring. Whether we are believers or nonbelievers, this kind of spirituality is essential. I personally consider this second level of spirituality to be more important than the first, because no matter how wonderful a particular religion may be, it will still only be accepted by a limited number of human beings, only a portion of humanity. But as long as we are human beings, as long as we are members of the human family, *all* of us need these basic spiritual values. Without these, human existence remains hard, very dry. As a result, none of us can be a happy person, our whole family will suffer, and then, eventually, society will be more troubled. So, it becomes clear that cultivating these kinds of basic spiritual values becomes crucial.

In seeking to cultivate these basic spiritual values, I think we need to remember that out of the, say, five billion human beings on this planet, I think perhaps one or two billion are very sincere, genuine believers in religion. Of course, when I refer to sincere believers, I'm not including those people who simply say, for example, "I am Christian" mainly because their family background is Christian but in daily life may not consider very much about the Christian faith or actively practice it. So excluding these people, I believe that there are perhaps only around one billion who sincerely practice their religion. That means that four billion, the majority of the people on this earth, are nonbelievers. So we must still find a way to try to improve life for this majority of the people, the four billion people who aren't involved in a specific religion—ways to help them become good human beings, moral people, without any religion. Here I think that education is crucial—instilling in people a sense that compassion, kindness, and so on are the basic good qualities of human beings, not just a matter of religious subjects. I think earlier we spoke at greater length about the prime importance of human warmth, affection, and compassion in people's physical health, happiness, and peace of mind. This is a very practical issue, not religious theory or philosophical speculation. It is a key issue. And I think that this is in fact the essence of all the religious teachings of the different traditions.

But it remains just as crucial for those who choose not to follow any particular religion. For those people, I think we can educate them and impress upon them that it's all right to remain without any religion but be a good human being, a sensible human being, with a sense of responsibility and commitment for a better, happier world.

In general, it is possible to indicate your particular religious or spiritual way of life through external means, such as wearing certain clothes, or having a shrine or altar in your house, or doing recitations and chanting, and so on. There are ways of demonstrating that externally. However, these practices or activities are secondary to your conducting a truly spiritual way of life, based on the basic spiritual values, because it is possible that all of these external religious activities can still go along with a person's harboring a very negative state of mind. But true spirituality should have the result of making a person calmer, happier, more peaceful.

All of the virtuous states of mind—compassion, tolerance, forgiveness, caring, and so on—these mental qualities are genuine Dharma, or genuine spiritual qualities, because all of these internal mental qualities cannot coexist with ill feelings or negative states of mind.

So, engaging in training or a method of bringing about inner discipline within one's mind is the essence of a religious life, an inner discipline that has the purpose of cultivating these positive mental states. Thus, whether one leads a spiritual life depends on whether one has been successful in bringing about that disciplined, tamed state of mind and translating that state of mind into one's daily actions. . . .

LEARNING MORE

More of the Dalai Lama's writings, including his Nobel Address, can be found on the *Ideas Across Time* website.

QUESTIONING THE TEXT

1. In his opening paragraph, the Dalai Lama refers to "inner transformation." After reading his essay, what do you think he means by this phrase?
2. What are the two levels of spirituality? Which does the Dalai Lama think is more important, and why?
3. Is it important to respect all the different world religions? Why or why not?
4. What, according to the Dalai Lama, is the purpose of religion? Do you agree? Explain.
5. What constitutes basic spirituality?
6. Why is inner discipline the essence of the religious life?

ANALYZING THE WRITER'S CRAFT

1. What is the thesis statement of this essay?
2. Who is the audience for this essay? How do you know?

3. What is the tone of this essay? Illustrate your answer.
4. How does the Dalai Lama go about trying to get readers to see things his way?
5. What is the Dalai Lama's strongest argument, in your view? Explain. What is his weakest argument, in your view?

MAKING CONNECTIONS

1. The Dalai Lama stresses the importance of respecting all religions, and he seeks moreover to find unifying features in all religions. Do you think his approach can reconcile the varying emphases in the major holy texts (see pp. 88–96)?
2. Which one of the thinkers about religion in this chapter do you think the Dalai Lama would find most compatible with his own outlook? Explain.
3. The Dalai Lama identifies spiritual development with inner peace. Friedrich Nietzsche says, however, that the human quality that evolution favors in homo sapiens is our fierce competitive drive, our basic kill-or-be-killed instincts. Who is right?
4. Is there a particular affinity between Buddhism and the spiritual outlook of Native Americans (see Luther Standing Bear, Chapter 3, pp. 187–191; N. Scott Momaday, Chapter 7, pp. 612–616; and Leslie Marmon Silko, Chapter 8, pp. 693–694)? Explore and explain.

FORMULATING IDEAS FOR WRITING

1. Write a letter to the Dalai Lama seeking clarification or amplification of his views. Take either the position that you are attracted by what he says, but don't understand X or Y, or that you really don't find him convincing, but maybe that is because you haven't fully understood him—could he clarify X or Y?
2. Do you agree that all human beings have the *right* to happiness, as the Dalai Lama says? Is this a right of the inalienable sort, like the rights Jefferson asserts in the Declaration of Independence (see Chapter 5, pp. 354–360)? How did we come by this right? Is the right to happiness affirmed by the Judeo-Christian-Muslim tradition?
3. Do you agree that the purpose of religion is to benefit humanity, as the Dalai Lama says? Would most religious leaders agree with his point of view? How do notions of salvation and damnation square with the Dalai Lama's view of the purpose of religion? Do you agree with the Dalai Lama that the history of religion shows that religion has always benefited millions of people? Or is religion one of the main causes of strife over the centuries?
4. Do you agree with the Dalai Lama that more important than being religious is being a good person? (Can you be a good person without being religious?)

"History and Religion" (2000)

Karen Armstrong

Karen Armstrong (b. 1947), who calls herself a "freelance monotheist," is one of the major, genuinely ecumenical voices in the exploration of spiritual life in contemporary society. Having joined the British convent the Society of the Holy Child Jesus at age seventeen, she left the order seven years later and wrote of her cloistered experience as a nun in her first book, *Through the Narrow Gate* (1981). She produced a six-part television series on the life of Saint Paul in 1983, a project that launched her intensive reexamination of the Abrahamic religions—Judaism, Christianity, and Islam. She has written about the common ground on which these religions have been built, as well as about the history of violence within and between these faiths. Among her best-known books are *A History of God: The 4000-Year Quest of Judaism, Christianity, and Islam* (1993); *Islam, a Short History* (2000), from which the present selection is taken; and, most recently, the autobiographical *The Spiral Staircase: My Climb Out of Darkness* (2004). Armstrong has been honored by the Islamic Center of Southern California for promoting understanding among faiths and is an instructor at London's Leo Baeck College for the Study of Judaism.

The external history of a religious tradition often seems divorced from the raison d'être[1] of faith. The spiritual quest is an interior journey; it is a psychic rather than a political drama. It is preoccupied with liturgy, doctrine, contemplative disciplines and an exploration of the heart, not with the clash of current events. Religions certainly have a life outside the soul. Their leaders have to contend with the state and affairs of the world, and often relish doing so. They fight with members of other faiths, who seem to challenge their claim to a monopoly of absolute truth; they also persecute their co-religionists for interpreting a tradition differently or for holding heterodox beliefs. Very often priests, rabbis, imams and shamans are just as consumed by worldly ambition as regular politicans. But all this is generally seen as an abuse of a sacred ideal. These power struggles are not what religion is really about, but an unworthy distraction from the life of the spirit, which is conducted far from the madding crowd, unseen, silent and unobtrusive. Indeed, in many faiths, monks and mystics lock themselves away from the world, since the clamour and strife of history is regarded as incompatible with a truly religious life.

In the Hindu tradition, history is dismissed as evanescent,[2] unimportant and insubstantial. The philosophers of ancient Greece were concerned with the

[1] *raison d'être:* reason for being.

[2] evanescent: passing with time; tending to vanish.

eternal laws underlying the flux of external events, which could be of no real interest to a serious thinker. In the gospels, Jesus often went out of his way to explain to his followers that his Kingdom was not of this world, but could only be found within the believer. The Kingdom would not arrive with a great political fanfare, but would develop as quietly and imperceptibly as a germinating mustardseed. In the modern West, we have made a point of separating religion from politics; this secularization was originally seen by the *philosophes* of the Enlightenment[3] as a means of liberating religion from the corruption of state affairs, and allowing it to become more truly itself.

But however spiritual their aspirations, religious people have to seek God or the sacred in this world. They often feel that they have a duty to bring their ideals to bear upon society. Even if they lock themselves away, they are inescapably men and women of their time and are affected by what goes on outside the monastery, although they do not fully realize this. Wars, plagues, famines, economic recession and the internal politics of their nation will intrude upon their cloistered existence and qualify their religious vision. Indeed, the tragedies of history often goad people into the spiritual quest, in order to find some ultimate meaning in what often seems to be a succession of random, arbitrary and dispiriting incidents. There is a symbiotic[4] relationship between history and religion, therefore. It is, as the Buddha remarked, our perception that existence is awry that forces us to find an alternative which will prevent us from falling into despair.

Perhaps the central paradox of the religious life is that it seeks transcendence, a dimension of existence that goes beyond our mundane lives, but that human beings can only experience this transcendent reality in earthly, physical phenomena. People have sensed the divine in rocks, mountains, temple buildings, law codes, written texts, or in other men and women. We never experience transcendence directly: our ecstasy is always "earthed," enshrined in something or someone here below. Religious people are trained to look beneath the unpromising surface to find the sacred within it. They have to use their creative imaginations. Jean-Paul Sartre[5] defined the imagination as the ability to think of what is not present. Human beings are religious creatures because they are imaginative; they are so constituted that they are compelled to search for hidden meaning and to achieve an ecstasy that makes them feel fully alive. Each tradition encourages the faithful to focus their attention on an earthly symbol that is peculiarly its own, and to teach themselves to see the divine in it.

5 In Islam, Muslims have looked for God in history. Their sacred scripture, the Quran, gave them a historical mission. Their chief duty was to create a just community in which all members, even the most weak and vulnerable, were treated with absolute respect. The experience of building such a society and

[3] *philosophes:* eighteenth-century French Enlightenment philosophers that included Diderot and Voltaire.

[4] symbiotic: mutually dependent.

[5] Jean-Paul Sartre: Sartre (1905–1980), one of the most important French intellectuals of the twentieth century; the chief figure of French existential philosophy.

living in it would give them intimations of the divine, because they would be living in accordance with God's will. A Muslim had to redeem history, and that meant that state affairs were not a distraction from spirituality but the stuff of religion itself. The political well-being of the Muslim community was a matter of supreme importance. Like any religious ideal, it was almost impossibly difficult to implement in the flawed and tragic conditions of history, but after each failure Muslims had to get up and begin again.

Muslims developed their own rituals, mysticism, philosophy, doctrines, sacred texts, laws and shrines like everybody else. But all these religious pursuits sprang directly from the Muslims' frequently anguished contemplation of the political current affairs of Islamic society. If state institutions did not measure up to the Quranic ideal, if their political leaders were cruel or exploitative, or if their community was humiliated by apparently irreligious enemies, a Muslim could feel that his or her faith in life's ultimate purpose and value was in jeopardy. Every effort had to be expended to put Islamic history back on track, or the whole religious enterprise would fail, and life would be drained of meaning. Politics was, therefore, what Christians would call a sacrament: it was the arena in which Muslims experienced God and which enabled the divine to function effectively in the world. Consequently, the historical trials and tribulations of the Muslim community—political assassinations, civil wars, invasions, and the rise and fall of the ruling dynasties—were not divorced from the interior religious quest, but were of the essence of the Islamic vision. A Muslim would meditate upon the current events of his time and upon past history as a Christian would contemplate an icon, using the creative imagination to discover the hidden divine kernel. An account of the external history of the Muslim people cannot, therefore, be of mere secondary interest, since one of the chief characteristics of Islam has been its sacralization of history.

LEARNING MORE

You can find out more about the Muslim faith and the history of Islam on the *Images Across Time* website.

QUESTIONING THE TEXT

1. Why does Armstrong think that being active in public life is often seen as an abuse of religion? Do you agree?
2. What examples does she offer to support this view?
3. Armstrong also says that there is "a symbiotic relation between history and religion" (par. 3). What does she mean?
4. How does the very physicality and mortality of humans create the central paradox of religious life?
5. Why does Armstrong see history as often tragic?
6. What is the relation between justice and the Muslim view of history?
7. In what way is politics for a Muslim the same as a sacrament for a Christian?

ANALYZING THE WRITER'S CRAFT

1. What is the thesis of this essay, and where is it stated?
2. Armstrong writes about a many-faceted paradox. In a paradox, two things seem to be in contradiction. But deeper examination shows that they are compatible, or at worst in tension. A paradox has something of an "on the one hand/on the other hand" quality. Show how the paradox that is the subject of Armstrong's essay is reflected in the structure of her essay.
3. What qualities does Armstrong associate with history? What qualities does she associate with religion? List the main qualities of each. Do these lists seem compatible? Explain.
4. How does Armstrong's discussion of the paradoxical relation between history and religion lead logically to her discussion of the relation of Islam to history?

MAKING CONNECTIONS

1. Compare and contrast Armstrong's view of the relation of religion and history with that of Marcus Aurelius, the Roman leader and stoic (see Chapter 8, pp. 646–648).
2. Armstrong stresses the inescapable implications of our physical being: we cannot transcend the physical and can only imagine what is beyond through the physical. The Native American writers in this book—Luther Standing Bear (Chapter 3, pp. 187–191), N. Scott Momaday (Chapter 7, pp. 612–616), and Leslie Marmon Silko (Chapter 8, pp. 693–694)—seem to suggest that the American Indian tribes had long ago evolved a spiritual reading on analogous lines. Would you agree? Consider for example how Momaday interprets the very concrete story of the Arrowmaker.
3. What is the relation between history and religion in Sandra Cisneros' story "Little Miracles, Kept Promises" (Chapter 7, pp. 618–626)?
4. American history seems to offer two views of justice. One view, represented in the separation of church and state, is that God's justice transcends politics. Another view is that an American obligation is the realization of justice for all as a politico-religious goal. What is your view? Consider Martin Luther King Jr.'s point of view in "Letter From Birmingham Jail" (Chapter 6, pp. 511–525) before arriving at your answer.

FORMULATING IDEAS FOR WRITING

1. Having just finished Armstrong's essay, you have decided it is must reading for the president of the United States. Write an essay in the form of a letter to the president, explaining to him why you are sending him Armstrong's essay and why it is imperative that he understand what she wishes to convey.

2. If Armstrong is right about how Muslims view history, is their view exactly the same as the Jewish view of history in the books of Moses (the Old Testament)? Discuss.
3. Americans have long believed that our history is the product of God's plan. One of the powerful ideas in our history, for example, is the idea of manifest destiny. Will our tradition of seeing ourselves as God's favored nation help us understand the Islamic view of history? Are the words of the Pledge of Allegiance—"one nation, under God, indivisible, with liberty and justice for all"—a bridge between our culture and the Muslim people?
4. If history is necessarily tragic because it is created by imperfect people in the midst of random or accidental circumstances, then can history truly be imbued with holiness? Is history definitively human, and therefore something that must be transcended in order to reach the divine?
5. Can justice be realized through politics?
6. Should church and state always be separate for the good of both, or is it essential that states be built on religious foundations?

Images of Divinity

The images of divinity in this chapter are not attributed to any specific maker or artist but rather represent common, widely reproduced, and anonymous depictions of the divine from the Buddhist, Hindu, and Christian traditions.

LEARNING MORE

These images represent entire religious traditions. It will help you appreciate these images to know something of the import of those traditions. For useful links, see the *Images Across Time* website.

QUESTIONING THE TEXT

1. What concept or impression of divinity do these images convey? What do these images have in common? What differentiates them?
2. Can these images communicate without context and reference; that is, without knowing anything about Christianity, for example, what might you be able to glean from the image of Christ's body on the cross?
3. What do you find to be the dominant mood, or emotion, conveyed by these images? Explain.
4. These three representations, each in stone, focus differently on the body of the divine person or god: Buddha is portrayed sitting; only Shiva's face is represented; and we see Christ's whole body. How do these images reflect

Sitting Buddha.

the core religious tenets of the holy books of, respectively, Buddhism, Hinduism, and Christianity?

ANALYZING THE ARTIST'S CRAFT

1. Religious images usually involve symbolism, even an allegorical reading. Are there key visual symbols in these representations of divinity, and, if there are, what do they imply?
2. Think of these images as a physical composition, a sculpture. What do you find most striking in the use of mass and line in each of these figures?
3. How do these representations convey the divinity of their subjects? How do we know these are divine beings?

Shiva the Destroyer.

4. How do these representations draw the attention of the eye to their symbolic meaning, to what these divinities "stand for"?
5. How are these divinities clothed, and why are they clothed as they are?
6. Discuss the effect of contrasts in these sculptures—between smooth surfaces and carved, for example, or between flat surfaces and round, or straight lines and curves, and so on.
7. Why do you think none of these representations shows the divine person looking at us?

MAKING CONNECTIONS

1. In matters of belief, visual symbolism has always been employed in consciously argumentative and evocative ways. The symbol of the cross, or a political symbol—the Stars and Stripes, for example—can move people, or evoke allegiance far more effectively than can speeches or writings. Visual

Christ on the Cross.

symbols also establish immediately recognizable tokens of identity for believers, so that believers can find their beliefs condensed, as it were, in an image that at one and the same time moves them deeply and identifies them as Christians or Americans. Compare and contrast these images with the holy texts (pp. 88–96) that try to explain their importance and the nature of their divinity.

2. Which of these images do you think would best accompany Walt Whitman's "Song of Myself" (Chapter 1, pp. 55–59)? Explain.
3. Modern art tends to make its statement through form rather than representation (see Meyer Shapiro, Chapter 7, pp. 590–602). Since religious images are necessarily symbolic, do you think therefore that these images of divinity could be conveyed just as well through abstract art as in the more or less realistic form of these sculptures?

FORMULATING IDEAS FOR WRITING

1. In all religious traditions, worship occurs in the presence of representations of divinity—a mosque, a shrine—or includes representations of divinity, such as a cross or other physical symbol. Consequently, for believers, these holy locations and images can have enormous emotional meaning and arouse deep emotions of awe, peace, and humility, and also of fear or guilt. Write an essay about a place of worship or an image of divinity that has special meaning for you. Explore your own responses and try to make these real to the reader.

2. Some religions—Judaism, Islam—forbid images of divinity. The biblical story of the Golden Calf aptly demonstrates the difference between faith in the unseen and faith mediated by physical symbols. In Genesis, the building of the Calf is a betrayal of God. But a Buddhist may well sit in front of a statue of the Buddha as an aid to contemplation. The image of Buddha is not understood to represent divinity but to symbolize it, to offer a visual aid to going beyond the senses. Different traditions about visual representation of divinity can come into violent conflict over the question of whether it is proper to create a physical image of God or any divine person. Write an essay that explores these different views through an imaginary dialogue on this subject between, say, a Christian and a Jew, or a Muslim and a Buddhist.
3. Representations of Buddha, Shiva, and Christ vary enormously. If you were to make a sculpture or painting of one of these divine persons, how would you represent him? What are the core qualities you think such a representation must convey? What form do you think such a representation should take? Explain.

chapter 3

Science

What *is* science? This chapter opens with a report from the *Los Angeles Times* about the genome of mice. "An international consortium of scientists," the article says, "announced today in the journal *Nature* that it has completed a sophisticated draft of the mouse genome, and has published the first detailed comparison of the genetic codes of mouse and man." The comparison shows that "mice and humans aren't that different" (see pp. 148–151).

This news article seems to suggest that science is a kind of knowledge—sometimes a fairly astonishing kind of knowledge. Science, on this view, is about things we know, about the facts. While often they are in awe of the nature of things as discovered by science and while in education they may insist on a rigorous familiarity with what we know, when you ask scientists about science, they tend to give a different kind of answer. The Renaissance courtier and theorist Francis Bacon, for example, says in the second selection of this chapter, "The Sphinx," that science is concerned with seeking the answers to two riddles, one about "the nature of things" and one about "the nature of man." Bacon proposed a method for solving these riddles, one that involves collecting data in an organized manner, weighing results judiciously, deriving answers to questions in this provisional manner, and checking answers through additional empirical observation and experiment. In short, a method akin to what we today would call the "scientific" method. (Bacon emphasized induction but left out the educated guesses we call theory.)

At the start, in Bacon's day, the assumptions underlying his methodological suggestions implied a revolution in human understanding. For centuries educated people assumed that knowledge attainable by humans was limited or should be derived from authority, by deduction from the established glosses on ancient sources—especially the work of Aristotle or Scripture. Bacon's approach set no limits to knowledge; it asserted that reality is material (what's real about the rock is the matter of which it's composed rather than the "idea" of the rock) and that material reality can be understood by means of organized observation and trial and error.

Nonetheless, it seems likely that we wouldn't think so highly of the method if it weren't for its results. Its results have been, and continue to be, astonishing.

These results have overturned received opinion, transformed the human capacity to be in the world, transformed nature—and ushered in the modern world. We know today that the earth is round and not flat. We know that the earth revolves around the sun, and not the other way around. We know that the earth and everything on it has existed and evolved over millions and millions of years. This knowledge, in particular Charles Darwin's conclusion "that man is descended from some lowly organized form," has been both liberating and deeply upsetting. (Darwin said *The Origin of Species* was based on Bacon's method.) If what we have to conclude from Darwin's findings is that "evolution has no purpose" (see pp. 167–180), then science seems to have advanced knowledge only to leave us in the end with the alarming thought that life has no meaning. Moreover, twentieth-century science, the science of Albert Einstein's theory of relativity, of the uncertainty principle, and of genetics, doesn't conform well to our comfortable idea that we can learn about our world through trial and error, by relying on our senses to tell us what is and what is not so. Science seems to refute "common sense." It may have been hard, for example, when Isaac Newton first explained his theory of gravitation, to believe that actually we are walking upside down on a curved surface, secured in place by a force we cannot see and do not feel. But it is even more difficult to get your mind around the idea that space and time are somehow interchangeable, and anyway "curved," or that light is composed of packets of energy, or simply that the rock against which you have stubbed your toe is actually made of millions of tiny, dynamic gismos with weird names, for the most part so tiny they can't be seen no matter how clever we get. And the universe started as a phenomenal gas explosion and is mostly composed of "dark matter" that, again, we can't see and no one can prove exists.

No wonder our most common image of scientists is of people who are "mad," as in Mary Shelley's prophetic *Frankenstein,* first published in 1818. Dr. Frankenstein, impelled by noble ideals and an admirable thirst for knowledge, overreaches, heedlessly creates a man, and then is horrified by what he has done. And yet, though science may indeed overreach, it nonetheless has yielded such dramatic results that different views from those of Dr. Frankenstein on the relation of humans to nature, and to knowledge, have had difficulty being heard in the modern world. Notions of human life as only one part of a harmonious nature, such as the philosophy of the Lakota (see Luther Standing Bear, pp. 187–191), however important, have not been easily integrated into the story of modernity, which we have been content to oversimplify as the story of a science of awesome potential for good and ill.

The implications of this open-ended aspect of our scientific knowledge for our self-awareness is explored in an unsettling meditation by Annie Dillard in her account of her visit to one of the landmarks of Darwinian legend, the Galapagos Islands. She looks on the creatures living on the islands with awe and wonder, and at the same time, feeling the presence of Darwin, as representatives of our own circumstance, odd creatures living on the rock called Earth. Also in this chapter, the implications for our way of thinking of the tools of science, in this case computers, is examined by the psychologist Sherry Turkle. Can computers, by affecting the way the mind works, change knowledge itself?

As the physicist Richard Feynman says in his essay on "The Value of Science," science is a key—both to heaven and to hell. We have good reason to fear science, for it has brought forth knowledge that can in fact open the door to hell, such as our knowledge of how to create a hydrogen bomb. But science has also enabled an existence that for most of human history would have seemed nothing less than magical. We are in the infancy of the scientific age. In this respect, Feynman modestly suggests that a virtue of science is that it trains us to appreciate uncertainty. More than its immense practical impact on every aspect of our lives, science has taught us that you can't finally be sure that what once was thought of as absolute and universal, and always everywhere equally applicable, as "truth," may need to be reconsidered.

Finally, the photo of the Qafzeh skull projected on a billboard in New York's Times Square (p. 228) illustrates that whatever the heady pleasures of science and technology, nothing can alter our fundamental mortality. Despite the breathtaking advances of sciences, human life remains a mystery.

KEYNOTE

Of Mice and Men: We're Quite Similar, Genetically (2002)

Rosie Mestel

Rosie Mestel is a medical writer at the *Los Angeles Times,* which she joined in 1998. Born in England, Mestel came to the states to pursue her Ph.D. in genetics, but after earning her degree, she entered the science writing program at the University of California at Santa Cruz. Her writing has appeared in *Discover* magazine, *Health, Science,* and *New Scientist.* She writes news and features for the *Times,* as well as a weekly column in the paper's health section. This article appeared in the paper on December 5, 2002.

It has been squeaking around us for millenniums, reviled as a disease-spreading pest or cherished as a collector's curiosity and a powerful scientific tool.

Now, the common laboratory mouse, *Mus musculus,* has scurried out of its hole to show us what it's made of. An international consortium of scientists announced today in the journal *Nature* that it has completed a sophisticated draft of the mouse genome, and has published the first detailed comparison of the genetic codes of mouse and man.

Scientists heralded the advance as every bit as important, if not more, as the decoding of the human genome because of the mouse's critical role in biomedical research.

As it turns out, mice and humans aren't that different. Both species have about 30,000 genes, although the full mouse genome is about 15% smaller. Very few of the genes—less than 1%—are unique to either species. Humans even possess the same set of mouse genes that direct the formation of a tail.

5 The mouse genome adds an important set of data to the human genome and the genomes of other key research species, such as yeast, fruit flies and roundworms.

Scientists say it will ease the ability to tackle medically important or just plain fascinating questions such as how bodies are built, how they decay and die, how diseases are caused, and how to prevent or cure them.

The advance is also crucial because having a blueprint from another mammal helps scientists extract meaning from the human genome's vast code. By directly comparing these two genomes, scientists can deduce which parts are important and which are seemingly useless filler that can mutate and change at will.

"Having sequenced the human genome is all well and good," said Eric Lander, director of the Whitehead/MIT Center for Genome Research, one of the institutes that sequenced the mouse genome.

But "the mouse provides us for the first time with the ability to turn the spotlight on what matters, and what probably doesn't matter, in the human genome."

10 The sequencing of the mouse genome was conducted by scientists of the Mouse Genome Sequencing Consortium at the Whitehead/MIT Institute, Washington University in St. Louis, and the Wellcome Trust Sanger Institute and the European Bioinformatics Institute in Hinxton, England. Researchers from 21 institutes around the world contributed to the analysis published today. The draft sequence covers 96% of the genome. Full completion is expected in the next few years.

A private company, Celera Genomics, has offered a different mouse genome sequence for a fee since 2001. But the availability now of a free version that can be accessed on the Web is a treasure trove for research, scientists say.

They have learned much already.

The mouse genome has helped scientists identify 1,200 new human genes—and 9,000 new mouse genes. While the genes—the key strings of DNA that direct the formation and functioning of organisms—are largely the same in both species, the mouse has expanded numbers of certain types, particularly those that are involved with smell, reproduction and processing certain toxins.

Scientists have also found that mouse and human genes tend to line up in a similar order, although chromosomes have broken and rejoined in all kinds of new patterns over the course of our separate evolutions.

15 Scientists are particularly enthralled by the finding that far more than just the genes appear to be closely conserved between mouse and human. The actual genes make up only 1.5% of the genome: the rest consists of DNA that may be unimportant, involved in turning the genes on and off or serving some other function.

But fully 5% of the genome has been closely preserved for 75 million years, the time when mouse and human split off from their last common ancestor. This percentage of preserved genetic information suggests that far more than just the genes are important.

Mice have long lived around human beings, and odd types with exotic fur, small size or the tendency to "waltz" in circles were bred and prized in Asia for centuries.

In Europe, "fancy" mouse breeding and collecting spawned a "National Mouse Club" in Victorian England.

In the early 20th century, Harvard University scientist William Castle saw that mice also could be eminently useful in the new-fangled science of genetics.

20 Mouse science blossomed, and thousands of different strains of mice are now studied. Scientists can delete or add genes to mice at will, and thus figure out their function. Stem-cell science, with its medical promise, got its start in mice. Mice have helped our understanding of many human maladies, from obesity and heart defects to hearing loss and cancer.

"Mice have taught us most of what we know about disease," said Jake Lusis, a UCLA professor of human genetics and microbiology who uses mice to study heart disease and diabetes.

With the genome in hand, such findings are expected to come at a much faster pace.

For example, in two papers accompanying today's release, scientists used the mouse genome to probe the genes connected with Down syndrome, in which a baby is born with an extra chromosome 21. They surveyed all the known genes on the mouse equivalent to that chromosome to see how each one acted during mouse development. They found genes that are active in the developing brain or heart at crucial times, and thus might be key in the mental retardation and heart abnormalities common with Down syndrome.

The mouse-human comparison may also help illuminate the very process of evolution. Scientists don't yet understand what kinds of genetic changes occur when creatures diverge from each other and form new species with different bodies, behaviors and habits.

25 They are intrigued by the fact that at least half of the mouse and human genomes are wildly different from each other, stuffed with odd DNA elements that hop from place to place in the genome, leaving copies of themselves behind. For unknown reasons, there is a lot more jumping going on in the mouse.

The structure of the mouse genome is also evolving twice as fast as the human genome. But the rates of change are very different from one site in the genome to the next, a surprising finding that may overturn the previous conception of a uniform pace of mutation.

"The greatest fear we had was we'd look at the mouse and human genomes and we'd say, 'Well, that's kind of what we thought,'" said Dr. Francis Collins, director of the National Human Genome Research Institute, a major funder of the mouse genome effort. "We need not have feared."

LEADING QUESTIONS

Science—the investigation of the natural world through observation, experiment, and reasoning—dates back to the earliest recorded time. But modern science, science since Galileo and Newton, provides us with remarkable information. This information is without doubt amazing. It is amazing that we can know anything at all about genetics, never mind to be able to "map" the genomes of animals. Just how is that done? Can ordinary people map a genome, given enough equipment? Or is mapping a genome hopelessly specialized, way out of the reach of most of us? And if so, then are we really taking science mainly on faith?

Most amazing of all in the *Los Angeles Times* report is that we aren't that different from mice. Is this a comforting or uncomfortable piece of information? In mapping human and animal genomes, are scientists crossing some moral line, acquiring knowledge we ought not to have? But is there such knowledge? In the age of science, can we assert that there are things we ought not to know?

Does knowing too much about something knock all the beauty out of it?

LEARNING MORE

Of Mice and Men is the title of a novel by John Steinbeck (1937), itself borrowed from Robert Burns's (1759–1796) lines in his famous poem "To a Mouse": "The best laid schemes o' Mice an' Men / Gang aft agley [Go oft awry]." Does the book or the poem have anything in common with the article?

The findings this article reports are said to have been published in the journal *Nature.* What is that journal? Why would these findings be published there?

QUESTIONING THE TEXT

1. What is the occasion for the article?
2. What's important about mapping the mouse genome?
3. Aside from the mouse, what are "other key research species" (par. 5)? What do you think makes these species so useful for research?
4. What is gained by comparing the genomes of two species that can't be learned from studying one genome in isolation?
5. When did mice and men diverge genetically?
6. What sort of findings have already been made on the basis of the completed mouse genome?
7. What are the most intriguing differences between the mouse and human genomes?

ANALYZING THE WRITER'S CRAFT

1. In what ways is this article formally the same as an essay. In what ways is this article formally an example of print journalism?
2. If you had to edit this article because of lack of space, making it one-quarter its present length, what would you cut out? Explain.
3. What is the thesis of this article?
4. What is the effect of quoting such people as Eric Lander and Jake Lusis?
5. Outline this article. On the basis of your outline, indicate and explain the main transitions in this article.
6. Discuss the effectiveness of the article's introduction and conclusion.

MAKING CONNECTIONS

1. To what extent do the findings reported in this article depend on Darwin's work (see pp. 167–180)? To what extent do the findings confirm Darwin's view of evolution?
2. Does the information reported in this article support Francis Bacon's view of science (pp. 152–156)? Mary Shelley's (pp. 157–165)?
3. Do these findings have any implications for religion?
4. Is using mice for research—say, by altering their genes—justified?

FORMULATING IDEAS FOR WRITING

1. Mestel reports that research on the mouse genome suggests promising directions to follow in understanding and treating Down syndrome. Using this example, write an essay arguing either that using other species for research is a boon to humans or that it is an immoral exploitation by humans of other living creatures.
2. Mestel reports that the new map of the mouse genome has been posted for free on the Internet, but that it has been available for two years from a private company for a fee. Discuss the pros and cons of private versus public funding of basic scientific research.
3. Follow up on research that has been conducted using the mouse genome since this article appeared, and write an article for the science pages of the *Los Angeles Times* based on what you discover.
4. Write a proposal to the Discovery channel for a TV program based on this article.

The Sphinx (1609)

Francis Bacon

This selection is number 28 of Francis Bacon's *Da Sapienta Veterum* (*The Wisdom of the Ancients*, 1609), a collection of interpretations of ancient fables. "Beneath no small number of the fables of the ancient poets," Bacon said, "there lay from the very beginning a mystery and an allegory." In this case, the Sphinx represents science. Bacon was not a scientist, and he seems to have paid little heed to the great scientific work of his time, such as Galileo's astronomy and William Harvey's discovery of the circulation of the blood. But as much as anyone, he furthered the cause of modern science by writing against the received wisdom of his age, which saw knowledge as static, limited, and largely accomplished, in particular by Aristotle, who it was believed had already discovered most of what there was to discover. Bacon advocated a new approach to knowledge, one that was inductive, empirical, inventive, and intended for "the use and benefit of men." In his *New Organon*, published in 1620, Bacon symbolically proposes an advance on Aristotle's *Organon*—the word means "key" or "instrument" in Greek. This new form of practical knowledge, based on, to quote the title of one of his books, *The Advancement of Learning* (1605), would serve as the foundation of historical progress. In this way, Bacon was the chief prophet of our technological age.

Francis Bacon was born in London in 1561, the child of well-connected parents. His father, Nicholas Bacon, was the Lord Keeper of the Seal and had been tutor to the royal family; his mother, Lady Anne Cooke, was sister-in-law to William Cecil, later Lord Burghley, Queen Elizabeth's chief counselor and for a quarter-century the most powerful man in England. Educated in the law, Bacon became a member of Parliament in 1584, and he remained a member for the next 36 years. But his opposition to a new tax levy in 1593 lost him Elizabeth's favor, and he did not advance until James succeeded her in 1603. By this time, he had already completed the first edition of his essays (1597), which he revised and to which he added for the rest of his life. Unlike his great predecessor, Michel de Montaigne (1533–1592), whose *Essays* inaugurated the form, Bacon wrote not about himself but about the world; and unlike his contemporaries, he wrote a simple, unadorned English rather than the cluttered, elaborate, ornate sentences fashionable in his time. The product is a style of worldly aphorisms that both proved immensely popular and opened the way for the supple, accessible prose of the great English writing of the coming centuries.

In 1604, King James appointed Bacon King's Counsel, and in 1605, Bacon completed *The Advancement of Learning*. Now his public career quickly advanced too, culminating in his assumption of his father's former office as Lord Keeper of the Royal Seal in 1617 and, finally, his rise to the post of Lord Chancellor, the nation's chief justice, in 1618. But then abruptly, in 1621, Bacon's enemies conspired to have him arrested on a charge of bribery. Although the practice of accepting gifts from those coming before a judge for trial was common in his day, Bacon did not evade the issue. He said candidly that, whatever the common practice, he ought nevertheless not to have done it. Bacon pleaded guilty, falling from the height of his achievement into humiliating disgrace. He neither sat in Parliament nor held public office ever again. But he accepted his punishment without excuse and threw himself into literary and philosophical work. Among the works he published at this time was an expanded version of *The Advancement*, in Latin, as well as *The New Organon* and his utopia *New Atlantis*, published posthumously but apparently completed in 1624. Bacon died of pneumonia in early spring of 1626. He had apparently been testing on himself some ideas he held on the preservative properties of snow.

Sphinx, says the story, was a monster combining many shapes in one. She had the face and voice of a virgin, the wings of a bird, the claws of a griffin. She dwelt on the ridge of a mountain near Thebes and infested the roads, lying in ambush for travellers, whom she would suddenly attack and lay hold of; and when she had mastered them, she propounded to them certain dark and perplexing riddles, which she was thought to have obtained from the Muses. And if the wretched captives could not at once solve and interpret the same, as they stood hesitating and confused she cruelly tore them to pieces. Time bringing no abatement of the calamity, the Thebans offered to any man who should expound the Sphinx's riddles (for this was the only way to subdue her) the sovereignty of Thebes as his reward. The greatness of the prize induced Œdipus, a man of wisdom and penetration, but lame from wounds in his feet, to accept the condition and make the trial: who presenting himself full of confidence and alacrity before the Sphinx, and being asked what kind of animal it was which was born four-footed, afterwards became two-footed, then three-footed, and at last four-footed again, answered readily that it was man; who at his birth and during his infancy sprawls on all fours, hardly attempting to creep; in a little while walks upright on two feet; in later years leans on a walking-stick and so goes as it were on three; and at last in extreme age and decrepitude, his sinews all failing, sinks into a quadruped again, and keeps his bed. This was the right answer and gave him the victory; whereupon he slew the Sphinx; whose body was put on the back of an ass and carried about in triumph; while himself was made according to compact King of Thebes.

The fable is an elegant and a wise one, invented apparently in allusion to Science; especially in its application to practical life. Science, being the wonder of the ignorant and unskilful, may be not absurdly called a monster. In figure and aspect it is represented as many-shaped, in allusion to the immense variety of matter with which it deals. It is said to have the face and voice of a woman, in respect of its beauty and facility of utterance. Wings are added because the sciences and the discoveries of science spread and fly abroad in an instant; the communication of knowledge being like that of one candle with another, which lights up at once. Claws, sharp and hooked, are ascribed to it with great elegance, because the axioms and arguments of science penetrate and hold fast the mind, so that it has no means of evasion or escape; a point which the sacred philosopher also noted: *The words of the wise are as goads, and as nails driven deep in.*[1] Again, all knowledge may be regarded as having its station on the heights of mountains; for it is deservedly esteemed a thing sublime and lofty, which looks down upon ignorance as from an eminence, and has moreover a spacious prospect on every side, such as we find on hill-tops. It is described as infesting the roads, because at every turn in the journey or pilgrimage of human life, matter and occasion for study assails and encounters us. Again Sphinx proposes to men a variety of hard questions and riddles which she received from the Muses. In these, while they remain with the Muses, there is probably no cruelty; for so-long as the object of meditation and inquiry is merely to know, the understanding

[1] "The words . . . deep in": Ecclesiastes 12:11.

is not oppressed or straitened by it, but is free to wander and expatiate,[2] and finds in the very uncertainty of conclusion and variety of choice a certain pleasure and delight; but when they pass from the Muses to Sphinx, that is from contemplation to practice, whereby there is necessity for present action, choice, and decision, then they begin to be painful and cruel; and unless they be solved and disposed of they strangely torment and worry the mind, pulling it first this way and then that, and fairly tearing it to pieces. Moreover the riddles of the Sphinx have always a twofold condition attached to them; distraction and laceration of mind, if you fail to solve them; if you succeed, a kingdom. For he who understands his subject is master of his end; and every workman is king over his work.

Now of the Sphinx's riddles there are in all two kinds; one concerning the nature of things, another concerning the nature of man; and in like manner there are two kinds of kingdom offered as the reward of solving them; one over nature, and the other over man. For the command over things natural,—over bodies, medicines, mechanical powers, and infinite other of the kind—is the one proper and ultimate end of true natural philosophy; however the philosophy of the School, content with what it finds, and swelling with talk, may neglect or spurn the search after realities and works. But the riddle proposed to Œdipus, by the solution of which he became King of Thebes, related to the nature of man; for whoever has a thorough insight into the nature of man may shape his fortune almost as he will, and is born for empire; as was well declared concerning the arts of the Romans,—

> Be thine the art,
> O Rome, with government to rule the nations,
> And to know whom to spare and whom to abate,
> And settle the condition of the world.[3]

And therefore it fell out happily that Augustus Cæsar, whether on purpose or by chance, used a Sphinx for his seal. For he certainly excelled in the art of politics if ever man did; and succeeded in the course of his life in solving most happily a great many new riddles concerning the nature of man, which if he had not dexterously and readily answered he would many times have been in imminent danger of destruction. The fable adds very prettily that when the Sphinx was subdued, her body was laid on the back of an ass: for there is nothing so subtle and abstruse, but when it is once thoroughly understood and published to the world, even a dull wit can carry it. Nor is that other point to be passed over, that the Sphinx was subdued by a lame man with club feet; for men generally proceed too fast and in too great a hurry to the solution of the Sphinx's riddles; whence it follows that the Sphinx has the better of them, and instead of obtaining the sovereignty by works and effects, they only distract and worry their minds with disputations.

---

[2] expatiate: speak about at some length.

[3] "Be thine the art . . . of the world": Virgil's *Aeneid*, Book One.

LEARNING MORE

How does Bacon come to be familiar with the riddle of the Sphinx? Homer mentions Oedipus but does not say anything about a Sphinx. The earliest version of the story is in Hesiod's *Theogony*, itself elaborated by Apollodorus. Oedipus is the hero of the great Greek tragedy bearing his name, *Oedipus Rex* [*King*], by Sophocles. For more about the Sphinx and Oedipus, see the *Ideas Across Time* website.

QUESTIONING THE TEXT

1. What are the physical features of the Sphinx?
2. What does the Sphinx do?
3. In what ways is the story of the Sphinx an allusion to science?
4. What are the two different rewards that come from solving the two different kinds of riddles posed by the Sphinx?
5. What pleases Bacon about the conclusion of the story of Oedipus and the Sphinx?

ANALYZING THE WRITER'S CRAFT

1. Bacon's essay falls into two parts. In the first, he recounts the story; in the second, he interprets the story. How does Bacon achieve clarity and brevity in his summary of the story?
2. In what ways is Bacon's writing clearly dated, that is, clearly following conventions different from our own? In what ways is Bacon's writing similar to writing in English today?
3. How does Bacon organize his presentation of the Sphinx as an allegory?
4. What qualities of science does Bacon's account emphasize?
5. Do you think Bacon views riddles concerning the nature of things as more or less appropriate to science than those concerning the nature of man?
6. Are you persuaded that the story of the Sphinx was intended from the start, as Bacon asserts, to be read as an allegory about science? Explain.

MAKING CONNECTIONS

1. Compare the way Bacon presents and interprets the story of the Sphinx with the way N. Scott Momaday presents and interprets the story of the arrowmaker (Chapter 7, pp. 612–616).
2. Compare and contrast Bacon's view of science with those of Einstein (pp. 193–200) and Richard Feynman (pp. 201–207).
3. Bacon says that science, like the Sphinx, can be seen as a monster. Compare this interpretation of science with Mary Shelley's (pp. 157–165).

FORMULATINGS IDEAS FOR WRITING

1. Bacon succinctly recounts the fable of the Sphinx. Offer a different, preferably allegorical, interpretation of its meaning.
2. Oedipus, king of Thebes, is one of the most famous figures in Western culture: we know him as the solver of the riddle of the Sphinx; as Sophocles' tragic hero, the man who killed his father and married his mother; and as Freud's most well-known example of the workings of our unconscious, labeled the "Oedipus complex." Write an essay based on research into the Oedipus legend that explores these questions: What does the story of the riddle say about Oedipus? What qualities in Oedipus as solver of the riddle fascinate us?
3. Bacon is a champion of the advancement of knowledge. For him knowledge is progressive and good. Write an essay that sees in the riddle a warning about man's cleverness and our apparently heedless pursuit of knowledge.
4. Write an essay arguing that we should value solving riddles about the nature of human beings more than we should value solving riddles about the nature of things (see par. 3).

Frankenstein (1818)

Mary Wollstonecraft Shelley

On May 14, 1817, Mary Shelley completed her epochal novel *Frankenstein, or The Modern Prometheus*, perhaps the single best-known piece of writing, in any language, of the nineteenth century. Although she was not yet twenty years old, this was but one remarkable event in an extraordinary life, at once triumphant and tragic. And as *Frankenstein* (first published in 1818) illustrates, Shelley's art was deeply rooted in the intellectual core of her age. In her writing, we find merged her own talents and personal visions, good and ill, and the deepest anxieties and expectations of the new century, fueled by the utopian possibilities of science, the true modern Pometheus.

Born in London in 1797, Mary Shelley was the daughter of two leading radicals of that time: the philosopher William Godwin and the feminist Mary Wollstonecraft, author of *Vindication of the Rights of Woman* (1792). She was born not only into a radical household but also into an age of revolution. And the wild, heady, heedless fervor of the French Revolution in politics and of the Romantic reaction to the classical eighteenth century in culture made much of her life a kind of exhilarating torture. In the summer of 1814, a month short of her seventeenth birthday, she eloped to France with the already-married

Percy Bysshe Shelley and her half-sister Jane (later known as Claire) Clairmont, daughter of her father's second wife. Shelley, born into an extremely wealthy family, was the very model of a Romantic poet—dashing, free-thinking, eloquent, good-hearted, charismatic, following passion and thought wherever they might lead (and to whomever they might inspire or harm). Estranged from his father and without money, Percy led Mary on a hectic itinerant life, moving incessantly from place to place, often in flight from creditors. The Shelleys had four children, only one of whom, Percy Florence, lived to adulthood. Mary's first child, a daughter, was born prematurely in 1815 and died a few weeks later; her second child, William, born 1816, died at three years of age; and her third child, Clara, born 1817, died a year later. Percy Florence was born in 1819.

In the summer of 1816, Percy, Mary, and Claire Clairmont joined the most famous poet of his day, Lord Byron, at Villa Diodati on Lake Geneva in Switzerland. The weather was bad, and they were forced to bide their time indoors, so Byron suggested they each write a ghost story. Mary had trouble getting going, but a discussion of galvanism (electricity) and Erasmus Darwin's experiments (he was Charles Darwin's grandfather) finally gave her the idea that she would turn into *Frankenstein*, a work she completed a year later at Albion House in Marlow, England. The Shelleys had returned to England at the end of the summer of 1816. In October, Mary's older half-sister, Fanny Imlay, her mother's daughter by an American lover, Gilbert Imlay, committed suicide by an overdose of sleeping draughts; and one month later, Percy's wife, Harriet, drowned herself. The ambivalence of *Frankenstein* about creation and birth, seeing both as wondrous and horrifying at the same time; its depiction of the scientist Dr. Frankenstein as an idealist who nonetheless harbors within himself huge destructive urges; its cast of motherless characters—Frankenstein, his creation, Frankenstein's fiancée, and so forth—in search of friendship and care; its contrast between a nurturing domesticity and a ruthless, cold male pursuit of the forbidden secrets of nature—all this seems a powerful mix of Mary's inner turmoil and the deepest hopes and fears of her age.

In 1822, Percy and a friend, Edward Williams, drowned while sailing in the Gulf of Spezia in Italy. Mary returned to England a year later with her son, Percy Florence. She never married again but devoted herself to her son and her father. (Godwin died in 1836; Percy Florence inherited his grandfather's estate and title in 1844.) But she also engaged in an active literary life, publishing six novels in addition to *Frankenstein*, as well as numerous stories and reviews. She continued to live at the center of the intellectual culture of her era, and by the time of her death achieved a reputation independent of her husband's. In fact, Mary took charge of Percy's reputation, bringing out a four-volume edition of his poems, with her preface and notes on his life, in 1839. Mary Wollstonecraft Shelley died of a brain tumor in February 1851.

Frankenstein opens with a series of letters from a Captain Robert Walton to his sister in London. The young adventurer Walton, whose first letter is sent from St. Petersburg in Russia, aims to find a passage through the Arctic seas to the East. One day he comes across a half-frozen man afloat on an ice flow—Frankenstein. Once revived, Frankenstein tells Walton his story. Victor Frankenstein comes from a distinguished family in Geneva. His mother died when he was seventeen; he was raised by her and his loving father in the company of a beautiful half-sister, Elizabeth, whom his mother had adopted and to whom Frankenstein is engaged. In the following passages, Frankenstein is a student at the University of Ingolstadt. He had been earlier infatuated with the alchemists, such as Cornelius Agrippa, but has now been won over to science by his professors, M. (Monsieur) Krempe and M. Waldman. The "you" whom Frankenstein occasionally addresses is the sea captain, Walton. The selection is preceded by a facsimile of the title page of the novel's first edition.

FRANKENSTEIN;

OR,

THE MODERN PROMETHEUS.

IN THREE VOLUMES.

Did I request thee, Maker, from my clay
To mould me man? Did I solicit thee
From darkness to promote me?——
PARADISE LOST.

VOL. I.

London:

PRINTED FOR

LACKINGTON, HUGHES, HARDING, MAVOR, & JONES,
FINSBURY SQUARE.

1818.

Facsimile of title page and dedication from the first edition of *Frankenstein.*

Chapter IV

From this day natural philosophy,[1] and particularly chemistry, in the most comprehensive sense of the term, became nearly my sole occupation. I read with ardour those works, so full of genius and discrimination, which modern enquirers have written on these subjects. I attended the lectures, and cultivated the acquaintance, of the men of science of the university; and I found even in M. Krempe a great deal of sound sense and real information, combined, it is true, with a repulsive physiognomy and manners, but not on that account the less valuable. In M. Waldman I found a true friend. His gentleness was never tinged by dogmatism; and his instructions were given with an air of frankness and good nature, that banished every idea of pedantry. In a thousand ways he smoothed for me the path of knowledge, and made the most abstruse enquiries clear and facile to my apprehension. My application was at first fluctuating and uncertain; it gained strength as I proceeded, and soon became so ardent and eager, that the stars often disappeared in the light of morning whilst I was yet engaged in my laboratory.

As I applied so closely, it may be easily conceived that my progress was rapid. My ardour was indeed the astonishment of the students, and my proficiency that of the masters. Professor Krempe often asked me, with a sly smile, how Cornelius Agrippa went on? whilst M. Waldman expressed the most heartfelt exultation in my progress. Two years passed in this manner, during which I paid no visit to Geneva, but was engaged, heart and soul, in the pursuit of some discoveries, which I hoped to make. None but those who have experienced them can conceive of the enticements of science. In other studies you go as far as others have gone before you, and there is nothing more to know; but in a scientific pursuit there is continual food for discovery and wonder. A mind of moderate capacity, which closely pursues one study, must infallibly arrive at great proficiency in that study; and I, who continually sought the attainment of one object of pursuit, and was solely wrapt up in this, improved so rapidly, that, at the end of two years, I made some discoveries in the improvement of some chemical instruments, which procured me great esteem and admiration at the university. When I had arrived at this point, and had become as well acquainted with the theory and practice of natural philosophy as depended on the lessons of any of the professors at Ingolstadt, my residence there being no longer conducive to my improvements, I thought of returning to my friends and my native town, when an incident happened that protracted my stay.

One of the phenomena which had peculiarly attracted my attention was the structure of the human frame, and, indeed, any animal endued with life. Whence, I often asked myself, did the principle of life proceed? It was a bold question, and one which has ever been considered as a mystery; yet with how many things are we upon the brink of becoming acquainted, if cowardice or carelessness did not restrain our enquiries. I revolved these circumstances in my mind, and determined thenceforth to apply myself more particularly to those

[1] natural philosophy: science.

branches of natural philosophy which relate to physiology. Unless I had been animated by an almost supernatural enthusiasm, my application to this study would have been irksome, and almost intolerable. To examine the causes of life, we must first have recourse to death. I became acquainted with the science of anatomy: but this was not sufficient; I must also observe the natural decay and corruption of the human body. In my education my father had taken the greatest precautions that my mind should be impressed with no supernatural horrors. I do not ever remember to have trembled at a tale of superstition, or to have feared the apparition of a spirit. Darkness had no effect upon my fancy; and a churchyard was to me merely the receptacle of bodies deprived of life, which, from being the seat of beauty and strength, had become food for the worm. Now I was led to examine the cause and progress of this decay, and forced to spend days and nights in vaults and charnel-houses.[2] My attention was fixed upon every object the most insupportable to the delicacy of the human feelings. I saw how the fine form of man was degraded and wasted; I beheld the corruption of death succeed to the blooming cheek of life; I saw how the worm inherited the wonders of the eye and brain. I paused, examining and analysing all the minutiæ of causation, as exemplified in the change from life to death, and death to life, until from the midst of this darkness a sudden light broke in upon me—a light so brilliant and wondrous, yet so simple, that while I became dizzy with the immensity of the prospect which it illustrated, I was surprised, that among so many men of genius who had directed their enquiries towards the same science, that I alone should be reserved to discover so astonishing a secret.

Remember, I am not recording the vision of a madman. The sun does not more certainly shine in the heavens, than that which I now affirm is true. Some miracle might have produced it, yet the stages of the discovery were distinct and probable. After days and nights of incredible labour and fatigue, I succeeded in discovering the cause of generation and life; nay, more, I became myself capable of bestowing animation upon lifeless matter.

5 The astonishment which I had at first experienced on this discovery soon gave place to delight and rapture. After so much time spent in painful labour, to arrive at once at the summit of my desires, was the most gratifying consummation of my toils. But this discovery was so great and overwhelming, that all the steps by which I had been progressively led to it were obliterated and I beheld only the result. What had been the study and desire of the wisest men since the creation of the world was now within my grasp. Not that, like a magic scene, it all opened upon me at once: the information I had obtained was of a nature rather to direct my endeavours so soon as I should point them towards the object of my search, than to exhibit that object already accomplished. I was like the Arabian[3] who had been buried with the dead, and found a passage to life, aided only by one glimmering, and seemingly ineffectual, light.

I see by your eagerness, and the wonder and hope which your eyes express, my friend, that you expect to be informed of the secret with which I am

---

[2] charnel-houses: store houses for corpses.

[3] the Arabian: refers to Sindbad's fourth voyage in *The Thousand and One Nights.*

acquainted; that cannot be: listen patiently until the end of my story, and you will easily perceive why I am reserved upon that subject. I will not lead you on, unguarded and ardent as I then was, to your destruction and infallible misery. Learn from me, if not by my precepts, at least by my example, how dangerous is the acquirement of knowledge, and how much happier that man is who believes his native town to be the world, than he who aspires to become greater than his nature will allow.

When I found so astonishing a power placed within my hands, I hesitated a long time concerning the manner in which I should employ it. Although I possessed the capacity of bestowing animation, yet to prepare a frame for the reception of it, with all its intricacies of fibres, muscles, and veins, still remained a work of inconceivable difficulty and labour. I doubted at first whether I should attempt the creation of a being like myself, or one of simpler organization; but my imagination was too much exalted by my first success to permit me to doubt of my ability to give life to an animal as complex and wonderful as man. The materials at present within my command hardly appeared adequate to so arduous an undertaking; but I doubted not that I should ultimately succeed. I prepared myself for a multitude of reverses; my operations might be incessantly baffled, and at last my work be imperfect: yet, when I considered the improvement which every day takes place in science and mechanics, I was encouraged to hope my present attempts would at least lay the foundations of future success. Nor could I consider the magnitude and complexity of my plan as any argument of its impracticability. It was with these feelings that I began the creation of a human being. As the minuteness of the parts formed a great hindrance to my speed, I resolved, contrary to my first intention, to make the being of a gigantic stature; that is to say, about eight feet in height, and proportionably large. After having formed this determination, and having spent some months in successfully collecting and arranging my materials, I began.

No one can conceive the variety of feelings which bore me onwards, like a hurricane, in the first enthusiasm of success. Life and death appeared to me ideal bounds, which I should first break through, and pour a torrent of light into our dark world. A new species would bless me as its creator and source; many happy and excellent natures would owe their being to me. No father could claim the gratitude of his child so completely as I should deserve theirs. Pursuing these reflections, I thought, that if I could bestow animation upon lifeless matter, I might in process of time (although I now found it impossible) renew life where death had apparently devoted the body to corruption.

These thoughts supported my spirits, while I pursued my undertaking with unremitting ardour. My cheek had grown pale with study, and my person had become emaciated with confinement. Sometimes, on the very brink of certainty, I failed; yet still I clung to the hope which the next day or the next hour might realise. One secret which I alone possessed was the hope to which I had dedicated myself; and the moon gazed on my midnight labours, while, with unrelaxed and breathless eagerness, I pursued nature to her hiding-places. Who shall conceive the horrors of my secret toil, as I dabbled among the unhallowed damps of the grave, or tortured the living animal to animate the lifeless clay?

My limbs now tremble, and my eyes swim with the remembrance; but then a resistless, and almost frantic, impulse, urged me forward; I seemed to have lost all soul or sensation but for this one pursuit. It was indeed but a passing trance, that only made me feel with renewed acuteness so soon as, the unnatural stimulus ceasing to operate, I had returned to my old habits. I collected bones from charnel-houses; and disturbed, with profane fingers, the tremendous secrets of the human frame. In a solitary chamber, or rather cell, at the top of the house, and separated from all the other apartments by a gallery and staircase, I kept my workshop of filthy creation: my eye-balls were starting from their sockets in attending to the details of my employment. The dissecting room and the slaughter-house furnished many of my materials; and often did my human nature turn with loathing from my occupation, whilst, still urged on by an eagerness which perpetually increased, I brought my work near to a conclusion.

10 The summer months passed while I was thus engaged, heart and soul, in one pursuit. It was a most beautiful season; never did the fields bestow a more plentiful harvest, or the vines yield a more luxuriant vintage: but my eyes were insensible to the charms of nature. And the same feelings which made me neglect the scenes around me caused me also to forget those friends who were so many miles absent, and whom I had not seen for so long a time. I knew my silence disquieted them; and I well remembered the words of my father: "I know that while you are pleased with yourself, you will think of us with affection, and we shall hear regularly from you. You must pardon me if I regard any interruption in your correspondence as a proof that your other duties are equally neglected."

I knew well therefore what would be my father's feelings; but I could not tear my thoughts from my employment, loathsome in itself, but which had taken an irresistible hold of my imagination. I wished, as it were, to procrastinate all that related to my feelings of affection until the great object, which swallowed up every habit of my nature, should be completed.

I then thought that my father would be unjust if he ascribed my neglect to vice, or faultiness on my part; but I am now convinced that he was justified in conceiving that I should not be altogether free from blame. A human being in perfection ought always to preserve a calm and peaceful mind, and never to allow passion or a transitory desire to disturb his tranquillity. I do not think that the pursuit of knowledge is an exception to this rule. If the study to which you apply yourself has a tendency to weaken your affections, and to destroy your taste for those simple pleasures in which no alloy can possibly mix, then that study is certainly unlawful, that is to say, not befitting the human mind. If this rule were always observed; if no man allowed any pursuit whatsoever to interfere with the tranquillity of his domestic affections, Greece had not been enslaved; Caesar would have spared his country; America would have been discovered more gradually; and the empires of Mexico and Peru had not been destroyed.

But I forget that I am moralising in the most interesting part of my tale; and your looks remind me to proceed.

My father made no reproach in his letters, and only took notice of my silence by enquiring into my occupations more particularly than before. Winter, spring, and summer passed away during my labours; but I did not watch the blossom or the expanding leaves—sights which before always yielded me supreme delight—so deeply was I engrossed in my occupation. The leaves of that year had withered before my work drew near to a close; and now every day showed me more plainly how well I had succeeded. But my enthusiasm was checked by my anxiety, and I appeared rather like one doomed by slavery to toil in the mines, or any other unwholesome trade, than an artist occupied by his favourite employment. Every night I was oppressed by a slow fever, and I became nervous to a most painful degree; the fall of a leaf startled me, and I shunned my fellow-creatures as if I had been guilty of a crime. Sometimes I grew alarmed at the wreck I perceived that I had become; the energy of my purpose alone sustained me: my labours would soon end, and I believed that exercise and amusement would then drive away incipient disease; and I promised myself both of these when my creation should be complete.

Chapter V

15 It was on a dreary night of November, that I beheld the accomplishment of my toils. With an anxiety that almost amounted to agony, I collected the instruments of life around me, that I might infuse a spark of being into the lifeless thing that lay at my feet. It was already one in the morning; the rain pattered dismally against the panes, and my candle was nearly burnt out, when, by the glimmer of the half-extinguished light, I saw the dull yellow eye of the creature open; it breathed hard, and a convulsive motion agitated its limbs.

How can I describe my emotions at this catastrophe, or how delineate the wretch whom with such infinite pains and care I had endeavoured to form? His limbs were in proportion, and I had selected his features as beautiful. Beautiful!—Great God! His yellow skin scarcely covered the work of muscles and arteries beneath; his hair was of a lustrous black, and flowing; his teeth of a pearly whiteness; but these luxuriances only formed a more horrid contrast with his watery eyes, that seemed almost of the same colour as the dun white sockets in which they were set, his shriveled complexion and straight black lips.

The different accidents of life are not so changeable as the feelings of human nature. I had worked hard for nearly two years, for the sole purpose of infusing life into an inanimate body. For this I had deprived myself of rest and health. I had desired it with an ardour that far exceeded moderation; but now that I had finished, the beauty of the dream vanished, and breathless horror and disgust filled my heart. Unable to endure the aspect of the being I had created, I rushed out of the room, and continued a long time traversing my bedchamber, unable to compose my mind to sleep. At length lassitude[4] succeeded to the tumult I had before endured; and I threw myself on the bed in my clothes, endeavouring to seek a few moments of forgetfulness. But it was in vain; I slept, indeed, but I was disturbed by the wildest dreams. I thought I saw Elizabeth, in the bloom of health, walking in the streets of Ingolstadt. Delighted and surprised, I embraced

---

[4] lassitude: fatigue.

her; but as I imprinted the first kiss on her lips, they became livid with the hue of death; her features appeared to change, and I thought that I held the corpse of my dead mother in my arms; a shroud enveloped her form, and I saw the graveworms crawling in the folds of the flannel. I started from my sleep with horror; a cold dew covered my forehead, my teeth chattered, and every limb became convulsed; when, by the dim and yellow light of the moon, as it forced its way through the window shutters, I beheld the wretch—the miserable monster whom I had created. He held up the curtain of the bed; and his eyes, if eyes they may be called, were fixed on me. His jaws opened, and he muttered some inarticulate sounds, while a grin wrinkled his cheeks. He might have spoken, but I did not hear; one hand was stretched out, seemingly to detain me, but I escaped, and rushed down stairs. I took refuge in the courtyard belonging to the house which I inhabited; where I remained during the rest of the night, walking up and down in the greatest agitation, listening attentively, catching and fearing each sound as if it were to announce the approach of the demoniacal corpse to which I had so miserably given life.

Oh! no mortal could support the horror of that countenance. A mummy again endued with animation could not be so hideous as that wretch. I had gazed on him while unfinished; he was ugly then; but when those muscles and joints were rendered capable of motion, it became a thing such as even Dante could not have conceived.

I passed the night wretchedly. Sometimes my pulse beat so quickly and hardly, that I felt the palpitation of every artery; at others, I nearly sank to the ground through languor and extreme weakness. Mingled with this horror, I felt the bitterness of disappointment; dreams that had been my food and pleasant rest for so long a space were now become a hell to me; and the change was so rapid, the overthrow so complete!

Morning, dismal and wet, at length dawned, and discovered to my sleepless and aching eyes the church of Ingolstadt, its white steeple and clock, which indicated the sixth hour. The porter opened the gates of the court, which had that night been my asylum, and I issued into the streets, pacing them with quick steps, as if I sought to avoid the wretch whom I feared every turning of the street would present to my view. I did not dare return to the apartment which I inhabited, but felt impelled to hurry on, although drenched by the rain which poured from a black and comfortless sky. . . .

LEARNING MORE

Shelley subtitles her book *The Modern Prometheus* and quotes a passage from John Milton's epic *Paradise Lost*. It will be helpful to be familiar with the myth of Prometheus, as well as with Milton's poem. For useful links, see the *Ideas Across Time* website.

A look at Percy Bysshe Shelley's poems, and at some of Lord Byron's, will help set Mary Shelley's book in context. See the *Ideas Across Time* website for useful links.

QUESTIONING THE TEXT

1. What, according to Frankenstein, are the unique enticements of science as a branch of knowledge?
2. How does Frankenstein go about discovering the secret of life?
3. What is Frankenstein's frame of mind as he pursues his studies?
4. What lesson does Frankenstein want to bestow on Captain Walton?
5. What did Frankenstein anticipate would be the consequence of his creating a new species?
6. How does Frankenstein think of home during the years of his labors?
7. What test does Frankenstein suggest can tell you whether your pursuit of knowledge is "lawful" (par. 12)?
8. Why does Frankenstein react to his creation with "horror and disgust" (par. 16)?
9. How is Frankenstein's dream a commentary on what he has done?
10. Why does Frankenstein run from his creation? Is he being irresponsible?
11. What is implied by the fact that the first thing Frankenstein sees at dawn is the church of Ingolstadt?

READING FOR WRITING

1. What kind of a person is Frankenstein? How would you describe his character? What are his good qualities? His bad qualities? What would you say are the things he values? Explain and cite specific examples.
2. These passages offer a wealth of contrasts to delineate and develop the novel's themes. Choose three contrasts and discuss their implications.
3. If this were an essay, what would be its thesis?
4. Do these passages confirm, in the emotions of the writing, that knowledge is a dangerous thing and should be avoided? Explain.
5. How are the two allusions of the novel's title page—to Prometheus and to Adam's complaint in *Paradise Lost*—helpful guides to reading these passages?
6. What connections can be made between Frankenstein's attitude toward his studies and his creature, and his attitude toward his father and Elizabeth?
7. Is there anything in this writing to make you think the author is a woman?
8. How does Shelley use nature (the seasons, the weather) in these passages?
9. How does Shelley seek to portray the physical ugliness of the creature? Does she succeed?
10. Is Frankenstein the narrator fully aware of the implications of the actions he narrates? Does he fully understand himself?

MAKING CONNECTIONS

1. Shelley expresses a view of science that clearly has found resonance in our culture for two centuries. Compare and contrast this view with that of Francis Bacon (pp. 152–156) and Richard Feynman (pp. 201–207).

2. The idea that the search for knowledge can be overreaching and unlawful forms a powerful theme in literature—see, for example, Christopher Marlowe's or Goethe's plays about *Faust*. The fundamentals of theme are, of course, expressed in the Prometheus myth and in *Paradise Lost;* but you might also want to look at Byron's play *Manfred* or Bertolt Brecht's *Galileo*. Is being creative a good thing?
3. Is "creativity" a quality of God alone? See Genesis (Chapter 2, pp. 106–107) and the Qur'an (Chapter 2, pp. 88–96)? Is pursuit of knowledge irreligious?

MAKING IDEAS FOR WRITING

1. Choose one of these two titles for an essay: "Knowledge Cannot Be Dangerous" or "Even a Little Knowledge Can Be a Dangerous Thing."
2. Frankenstein says, "A human being in perfection ought always to preserve a calm and peaceful mind, and never allow passion or a transitory desire to disturb his tranquility" (par. 12). Write an essay that explores this idea. Consider how this idea does or does not apply to Frankenstein—to Shelley, to Percy Shelley. Do you think Shelley intends us to read this sentence as if it were an obvious truth, or as something Frankenstein believes (or wants to believe)? Is this your idea of "a human being in perfection"?
3. If Frankenstein had been a different kind of person, would the story have been different? Would the story have been different had Frankenstein been a woman?
4. Write an essay that explores the implications of some of the key contrasts in these passages.
5. In these passages, we hear only Frankenstein's voice. His creation is inarticulate. If the creature could speak, what would it say to Frankenstein?

The Origin of Species and *The Descent of Man* (1859, 1871)

Charles Darwin

Charles Robert Darwin was born in Shrewsbury in the west of England on February 12, 1809—the same day that Abraham Lincoln was born. Darwin's father was a well-known physician, and the son of a famous scientist, Erasmus Darwin; his mother's father was Josiah Wedgwood, whose pottery dishes revolutionized "china" worldwide. (Darwin's wife Emma was also a Wedgwood.)

Darwin was intended to be yet another physician, but he couldn't stand the prospect of surgery without anesthesia. His family tried to persuade him to become a minister. At Cambridge, however, Darwin became friendly with a professor of botany, John S. Henslow, who obtained for him a post as naturalist on the H.M.S. (Her Majesty's Ship) *Beagle*, about to go on a survey voyage of Tierra del Fuego and the South Seas. Darwin was twenty-three.

The journey lasted five years. Darwin was given a corner of the chart room to work in and three drawers for specimens. He was expected to sleep in a hammock over the charts, but he was too tall, and there wasn't room for his feet without removing one of the drawers.

In 1839, Darwin published the best-seller *The Voyage of the Beagle,* which recounted his adventures and presented the early material that later he would turn into *The Origin of Species.* But Darwin didn't publish the latter for twenty more years (1859). After returning from his journey, Darwin retired to domestic life—his health was always unreliable—at Down House in the village of Downe, Kent. But in his retreat, Darwin continued collecting data, occasionally publishing specialized essays. It was not until it seemed that the young naturalist Alfred Russell Wallace was about to publish a work explaining evolution very much along Darwin's own lines that Darwin was stirred to put his ideas into writing.

These ideas, which have influenced many aspects of scientific thought, were nonetheless immediately challenged by the scientific and religious communities of mid-Victorian Britain. Of course, Darwin's ideas did not appear without a supporting scientific context. In *Principles of Geology* (1830–1833), his friend and colleague, Charles Lyell, maintained that the earth's surface records aeons of change under the impact of natural forces operating uniformly over very long stretches of time and that change is constant. But while Lyell's geology directly challenged the biblical account of creation in Genesis, it was Darwin's notion that living things had evolved along the lines of "natural selection," suggesting unity between humans and animals, that most deeply upset theological opinion. In the twentieth century, scientists have filled in the gaps in Darwin's theory and overwhelmingly concur with his outlook, but to this day Darwin's ideas are challenged by some. Darwin followed *Origin* with publication of *The Descent of Man* (1871), explicitly linking human evolution to animal species.

Darwin died in 1882, and despite the fact that he had been reviled as an enemy of the faithful, he was buried ceremoniously in Westminster Abbey, a few feet from another great British scientist, Isaac Newton.

The Origin of Species

. . . Under domestication[1] we see much variability, caused, or at least excited, by changed conditions of life; but often in so obscure a manner, that we are tempted to consider the variations as spontaneous. Variability is governed by

---

[1] domestication: breeding plants or animals for domestic purposes, in the sense that domestic animals are the opposite of wild ones and are kept or bred by people for their own ends, such as eating or hunting. Darwin, writing in a time when agriculture employed more than half the population, used this example to suggest that if humans can breed wild animals for their own ends, think of what nature can do over aeons.

many complex laws,—by correlated growth, compensation, the increased use and disuse of parts, and the definite action of the surrounding conditions. There is much difficulty in ascertaining how largely our domestic productions have been modified; but we may safely infer that the amount has been large, and that modifications can be inherited for long periods. As long as the conditions of life remain the same, we have reason to believe that a modification, which has already been inherited for many generations, may continue to be inherited for an almost infinite number of generations. On the other hand, we have evidence that variability when it has once come into play, does not cease under domestication for a very long period; nor do we know that it ever ceases, for new varieties are still occasionally produced by our oldest domesticated productions.

Variability is not actually caused by man; he only unintentionally exposes organic beings to new conditions of life, and then nature acts on the organisation and causes it to vary. But man can and does select the variations given to him by nature, and thus accumulates them in any desired manner. He thus adapts animals and plants for his own benefit or pleasure. He may do this methodically, or he may do it unconsciously by preserving the individuals most useful or pleasing to him without any intention of altering the breed. It is certain that he can largely influence the character of a breed by selecting, in each successive generation, individual differences so slight as to be inappreciable except by an educated eye. This unconscious process of selection has been the great agency in the formation of the most distinct and useful domestic breeds. That many breeds produced by man have to a large extent the character of natural species, is shown by the inextricable doubts whether many of them are varieties or aboriginally distinct species.

There is no reason why the principles which have acted so efficiently under domestication should not have acted under nature. In the survival of favoured individuals and races, during the constantly-recurrent Struggle for Existence, we see a powerful and ever-acting form of Selection. The struggle for existence inevitably follows from the high geometrical ratio of increase which is common to all organic beings. This high rate of increase is proved by calculation,—by the rapid increase of many animals and plants during a succession of peculiar seasons, and when naturalised in new countries. More individuals are born than can possibly survive. A grain in the balance may determine which individuals shall live and which shall die,—which variety or species shall increase in number, and which shall decrease, or finally become extinct. As the individuals of the same species come in all respects into the closest competition with each other, the struggle will generally be most severe between them; it will be almost equally severe between the varieties of the same species, and next in severity between the species of the same genus. On the other hand the struggle will often be severe between beings remote in the scale of nature. The slightest advantage in certain individuals, at any age or during any season, over those with which they come into competition, or better adaptation in however slight a degree to the surrounding physical conditions, will, in the long run, turn the balance.

With animals having separated sexes, there will be in most cases a struggle between the males for the possession of the females. The most vigorous males, or those which have most successfully struggled with their conditions of life, will generally leave most progeny. But success will often depend on the males having special weapons, or means of defense, or charms; and a slight advantage will lead to victory.

As geology plainly proclaims that each land has undergone great physical changes, we might have expected to find that organic beings have varied under nature, in the same way as they have varied under domestication. And if there has been any variability under nature, it would be an unaccountable fact if natural selection had not come into play. It has often been asserted, but the assertion is incapable of proof, that the amount of variation under nature is a strictly limited quantity. Man, though acting on external characters alone and often capriciously,[2] can produce within a short period a great result by adding up mere individual differences in his domestic productions; and every one admits that species present individual differences. But, besides such differences, all naturalists admit that natural varieties exist, which are considered sufficiently distinct to be worthy of record in systematic works. No one has drawn any clear distinction between individual differences and slight varieties; or between more plainly marked varieties and sub-species, and species. On separate continents, and on different parts of the same continent when divided by barriers of any kind, and on outlying islands, what a multitude of forms exist, which some experienced naturalists rank as varieties, others as geographical races or sub-species, and others as distinct, though closely allied species!

If then, animals and plants do vary, let it be ever so slightly or slowly, why should not variations or individual differences, which are in any way beneficial, be preserved and accumulated through natural selection, or the survival of the fittest? If man can by patience select variations useful to him, why, under changing and complex conditions of life, should not variations useful to nature's living products often arise, and be preserved or selected? What limit can be put to this power, acting during long ages and rigidly scrutinising the whole constitution, structure, and habits of each creature,—favouring the good and rejecting the bad? I can see no limit to this power, in slowly and beautifully adapting each form to the most complex relations of life. The theory of natural selection, even if we look no farther than this, seems to be in the highest degree probable. . . .

On the view that species are only strongly marked and permanent varieties, and that each species first existed as a variety, we can see why it is that no line of demarcation can be drawn between species, commonly supposed to have been produced by special acts of creation, and varities which are acknowledged to have been produced by secondary laws. On this same view we can understand how it is that in a region where many species of a genus[3] have been produced, and where they now flourish, these same species should present many varieties; for where the manufactory of species has been active, we might

[2] capriciously: impulsively; unpredictably.

[3] genus: a class that includes a number of subordinate kinds, known as species. The plural of genus that Darwin employs is genera.

expect, as a general rule, to find it still in action; and this is the case if varieties be incipient[4] species. Moreover, the species of the larger genera, which afford the greater number of varieties or incipient species, retain to a certain degree the character of varieties; for they differ from each other by a less amount of difference than do the species of smaller genera. The closely allied species also of the larger genera apparently have restricted ranges, and in their affinities they are clustered in little groups round other species—in both respects resembling varieties. These are strange relations on the view that each species was independently created, but are intelligible if each existed first as a variety.

As each species tends by its geometrical rate of reproduction to increase inordinately in number; and as the modified descendants of each species will be enabled to increase by as much as they become more diversified in habits and structure, so as to be able to seize on many and widely different places in the economy of nature, there will be a constant tendency in natural selection to preserve the most divergent offspring of any one species. Hence, during a long-continued course of modification, the slight differences characteristic of varieties of the same species, tend to be augmented into the greater differences characteristic of the species of the same genus. New and improved varieties will inevitably supplant and exterminate the older, less improved, and intermediate varieties; and thus species are rendered to a large extent defined and distinct objects. Dominant species belonging to the larger groups within each class tend to give birth to new and dominant forms; so that each large group tends to become still larger, and at the same time more divergent in character. But as all groups cannot thus go on increasing in size, for the world would not hold them, the more dominant groups beat the less dominant. This tendency in the large groups to go on increasing in size and diverging in character, together with the inevitable contingency of much extinction, explains the arrangement of all the forms of life in groups subordinate to groups, all within a few great classes, which has prevailed throughout all time. This grand fact of the grouping of all organic beings under what is called the Natural System, is utterly inexplicable on the theory of creation. . . .

The Descent of Man

General Summary and Conclusion

A brief summary will be sufficient to recall to the reader's mind the more salient[5] points in this work. Many of the views which have been advanced are highly speculative, and some no doubt will prove erroneous; but I have in every case given the reasons which have led me to one view rather than to another. It seemed worthwhile to try how far the principle of evolution would throw light on some of the more complex problems in the natural history of man. False facts are highly injurious to the progress of science, for they often endure long; but

---

[4] incipient: in an initial stage.
[5] salient: prominent; significant.

false views, if supported by some evidence, do little harm, for every one takes a salutary[6] pleasure in proving their falseness and when this is done, one path towards error is closed and the road to truth is often at the same time opened.

The main conclusion here arrived at, and now held by many naturalists who are well competent to form a sound judgment, is that man is descended from some less highly organised form. The grounds upon which this conclusion rests will never be shaken, for the close similarity between man and the lower animals in embryonic development, as well as in innumerable points of structure and constitution, both of high and of the most trifling importance,—the rudiments which he retains, and the abnormal reversions to which he is occasionally liable,—are facts which cannot be disputed. They have long been known, but until recently they told us nothing with respect to the origin of man. Now when viewed by the light of our knowledge of the whole organic world, their meaning is unmistakable. The great principle of evolution stands up clear and firm, when these groups or facts are considered in connection with others, such as the mutual affinities of the members of the same group, their geographical distribution in past and present times, and their geological succession. It is incredible that all these facts should speak falsely. He who is not content to look, like a savage, at the phenomena of nature as disconnected, cannot any longer believe that man is the work of a separate act of creation. He will be forced to admit that the close resemblance of the embryo of man to that, for instance, of a dog—the construction of his skull, limbs and whole frame on the same plan with that of other mammals, independently of the uses to which the parts may be put—the occasional re-appearance of various structures, for instance of several muscles, which man does not normally possess, but which are common to the Quadrumana[7]—and a crowd of analogous facts—all point in the plainest manner to the conclusion that man is the co-descendant with other mammals of a common progenitor.

We have seen that man incessantly presents individual differences in all parts of his body and in his mental faculties. These differences or variations seem to be induced by the same general causes, and to obey the same laws as with the lower animals. In both cases similar laws of inheritance prevail. Man tends to increase at a greater rate than his means of subsistence; consequently he is occasionally subjected to a severe struggle for existence, and natural selection will have effected whatever lies within its scope. A succession of strongly-marked variations of a similar nature is by no means requisite; slight fluctuating differences in the individual suffice for the work of natural selection; not that we have any reason to suppose that in the same species, all parts of the organisation tend to vary to the same degree. We may feel assured that the inherited effects of the long-continued use or disuse of parts will have done much in the same direction with natural selection. Modifications formerly of importance, though no longer of any special use, are long-inherited. When one part is

[6] salutary: healthy.

[7] Quadrumana: order of mammals, including monkeys and apes, whose forefeet can be used as hands.

modified, other parts change through the principle of correlation, of which we have instances in many curious cases of correlated monstrosities. Something may be attributed to the direct and definite action of the surrounding conditions of life, such as abundant food, heat or moisture; and lastly, many characters of slight physiological importance, some indeed of considerable importance, have been gained through sexual selection. . . .

Through the means just specified, aided perhaps by others as yet undiscovered, man has been raised to his present state. But since he attained to the rank of manhood, he has diverged into distinct races, or as they may be more fitly called, sub-species. Some of these, such as the Negro and European, are so distinct that, if specimens had been brought to a naturalist without any further information, they would undoubtedly have been considered by him as good and true species. Nevertheless all the races agree in so many unimportant details of structure and in so many mental peculiarities that these can be accounted for only by inheritance from a common progenitor; and a progenitor thus characterised would probably deserve to rank as man.

It must not be supposed that the divergence of each race from the other races, and of all from a common stock, can be traced back to any one pair of progenitors. On the contrary, at every stage in the process of modification, all the individuals which were in any way better fitted for their conditions of life, though in different degrees, would have survived in greater numbers than the less well-fitted. The process would have been like that followed by man, when he does not intentionally select particular individuals, but breeds from all the superior individuals, and neglects the inferior. He thus slowly but surely modifies his stock, and unconciously forms a new strain. So with respect to modifications acquired independently of selection, and due to variations arising from the nature of the organism and the action of the surrounding conditions, or from changed habits of life, no single pair will have been modified much more than the other pairs inhabiting the same country, for all will have been continually blended through free intercrossing.

By considering the embryological structure of man,—the homologies[8] which he presents with the lower animals,—the rudiments which he retains,—and the reversions to which he is liable, we can partly recall in imagination the former condition of our early progenitors; and can approximately place them in their proper place in the zoological series. We thus learn that man is descended from a hairy, tailed quadruped, probably arboreal in its habits, and an inhabitant of the Old World. This creature, if its whole structure had been examined by a naturalist, would have been classed amongst the Quadrumana, as surely as the still more ancient progenitor of the Old and New World monkeys. The Quadrumana and all the higher mammals are probably derived from an ancient marsupial[9] animal, and this through a long series of diversified forms, from some amphibian-like creature, and this again from some fish-like animal. In the dim obscurity of the past we can see that the early progenitor of all the

---

[8] homologies: direct structural correspondences with a previous form or kind.

[9] marsupial: mammals, such as kangaroos, that carry their young in a body pouch.

Vertebrata[10] must have been an aquatic animal provided with branchiæ,[11] with the two sexes united in the same individual, and with the most important organs of the body (such as the brain and heart) imperfectly or not at all developed. This animal seems to have been more like the larvæ of the existing marine Ascidians[12] than any other known form.

The high standard of our intellectual powers and moral disposition is the greatest difficulty which presents itself, after we have been driven to this conclusion on the origin of man. But every one who admits the principle of evolution, must see that the mental powers of the higher animals, which are the same in kind with those of man, though so different in degree, are capable of advancement. Thus the interval between the mental powers of one of the higher apes and of a fish, or between those of an ant and scale-insect, is immense; yet their development does not offer any special difficulty; for with our domesticated animals, the mental faculties are certainly variable, and the variations are inherited. No one doubts that they are of the utmost importance to animals in a state of nature. Therefore the conditions are favourable for their development through natural selection. The same conclusion may be extended to man; the intellect must have been all-important to him, even at a very remote period, as enabling him to invent and use language, to make weapons, tools, traps, &c., whereby with the aid of his social habits, he long ago became the most dominant of all living creatures.

A great stride in the development of the intellect will have followed, as soon as the half-art and half-instinct of language came into use; for the continued use of language will have reacted on the brain and produced an inherited effect; and this again will have reacted on the improvement of language. As Mr. Chauncey Wright[13] has well remarked, the largeness of the brain in man relatively to his body, compared with the lower animals, may be attributed in chief part to the early use of some simple form of language,—that wonderful engine which affixes signs to all sorts of objects and qualities, and excites trains of thought which would never arise from the mere impression of the senses, or if they did arise could not be followed out. The higher intellectual powers of man, such as those of ratiocination,[14] abstraction, self-consciousness, &c., probably follow from the continued improvement and exercise of the other mental faculties.

The development of the moral qualities is a more interesting problem. The foundation lies in the social instincts, including under this term the family ties. These instincts are highly complex, and in the case of the lower animals give special tendencies towards certain definite actions; but the more important elements are love, and the distinct emotion of sympathy. Animals endowed with

---

[10] Vertebrata: animals that have spines.

[11] branchiae: gills.

[12] marine Ascidians: sea creatures without spines whose young nevertheless show features in common with vertebrates.

[13] . . . Wright: "On the Limits of Natural Selection," in the *North American Review*, Oct. 1870, p. 295 [Darwin's note].

[14] ratiocination: reasoning.

the social instincts take pleasure in one another's company, warn one another of danger, defend and aid one another in many ways. These instincts do not extend to all the individuals of the species, but only to those of the same community. As they are highly beneficial to entire species, they have in all probability been acquired through natural selection.

A moral being is one who is capable of reflecting on his past actions and their motives—of approving of some and disapproving of others; and the fact that man is the one being who certainly deserves this designation, is the greatest of all distinctions between him and the lower animals. But . . . I have endeavoured to shew that the moral sense follows, firstly, from the enduring and ever-present nature of the social instincts; secondly, from man's appreciation of the approbation and disapprobation of his fellows; and thirdly, from the high activity of his mental faculties, with past impressions extremely vivid; and in these latter respects he differs from the lower animals. Owing to this condition of mind, man cannot avoid looking both backwards and forwards, and comparing past impressions. Hence after some temporary desire or passion has mastered his social instincts, he reflects and compares the now weakened impression of such past impulses with the ever-present social instincts; and he then feels that sense of dissatisfaction which all unsatisfied instincts leave behind them, he therefore resolves to act differently for the future,—and this is conscience. Any instinct, permanently stronger or more enduring than another, gives rise to a feeling which we express by saying that it ought to be obeyed. A pointer dog, if able to reflect on his past conduct, would say to himself, I ought (as indeed we say of him) to have pointed at that hare and not have yielded to the passing temptation of hunting it.

Social animals are impelled partly by a wish to aid the members of their community in a general manner, but more commonly to perform certain definite actions. Man is impelled by the same general wish to aid his fellows; but has few or no special instincts. He differs also from the lower animals in the power of expressing his desires by words, which thus become a guide to the aid required and bestowed. The motive to give aid is likewise much modified in man: it no longer consists solely of a blind instinctive impulse, but is much influenced by the praise or blame of his fellows. The appreciation and the bestowal of praise and blame both rest on sympathy; and this emotion, as we have seen, is one of the most important elements of the social instincts. Sympathy, though gained as an instinct, is also much strengthened by exercise or habit. As all men desire their own happiness, praise or blame is bestowed on actions and motives, according as they lead to this end; and as happiness is an essential part of the general good, the greatest-happiness principle indirectly serves as a nearly safe standard of right and wrong. As the reasoning powers advance and experience is gained, the remoter effects of certain lines of conduct on the character of the individual, and on the general good, are perceived; and then the self-regarding virtues come within the scope of public opinion, and receive praise, and their opposites blame. But with the less civilised nations reason often errs, and many bad customs and base superstitions come within the same scope, and are then esteemed as high virtues, and their breach as heavy crimes.

The moral faculties are generally and justly esteemed as of higher value than the intellectual powers. But we should bear in mind that the activity of the mind in vividly recalling past impressions is one of the fundamental though secondary bases of conscience. This affords the strongest argument for educating and stimulating in all possible ways the intellectual faculties of every human being. No doubt a man with a torpid mind, if his social affections and sympathies are well developed, will be led to good actions, and may have a fairly sensitive conscience. But whatever renders the imagination more vivid and strengthens the habit of recalling and comparing past impressions, will make the conscience more sensitive, and may even somewhat compensate for weak social affections and sympathies.

The moral nature of man has reached its present standard, partly through the advancement of his reasoning powers and consequently of a just public opinion, but especially from his sympathies having been rendered more tender and widely diffused through the effects of habit, example, instruction, and reflection. It is not improbable that after long practice virtuous tendencies may be inherited. With the more civilised races, the conviction of the existence of an all-seeing Deity has had a potent influence on the advance of morality. Ultimately man does not accept the praise or blame of his fellows as his sole guide, though few escape this influence, but his habitual convictions, controlled by reason, afford him the safest rule. His conscience then becomes the supreme judge and monitor. Nevertheless the first foundation or origin of the moral sense lies in the social instincts, including sympathy; and these instincts no doubt were primarily gained, as in the case of the lower animals, through natural selection.

The belief in God has often been advanced as not only the greatest, but the most complete of all the distinctions between man and the lower animals. It is however impossible, as we have seen, to maintain that this belief is innate or instinctive in man. On the other hand a belief in all-pervading spiritual agencies seems to be universal; and apparently follows from a considerable advance in man's reason, and from a still greater advance in his faculties of imagination, curiosity and wonder. I am aware that the assumed instinctive belief in God has been used by many persons as an argument for His existence. But this is a rash argument, as we should thus be compelled to believe in the existence of many cruel and malignant spirits, only a little more powerful than man; for the belief in them is far more general than in a beneficent Deity. The idea of a universal and beneficent Creator does not seem to arise in the mind of man, until he has been elevated by long-continued culture.

He who believes in the advancement of man from some low organised form, will naturally ask how does this bear on the belief in the immortality of the soul. The barbarous races of man, as Sir J. Lubbock has shewn, possess no clear belief of this kind; but arguments derived from the primeval beliefs of savages are, as we have just seen, of little or no avail. Few persons feel any anxiety from the impossibility of determining at what precise period in the development of the individual, from the first trace of a minute germinal vesicle, man becomes an immortal being; and there is no greater cause for anxiety because the period cannot possibly be determined in the gradually ascending organic scale.[15]

I am aware that the conclusions arrived at in this work will be denounced by some as highly irreligious; but he who denounces them is bound to shew why it is more irreligious to explain the origin of man as a distinct species by descent from some lower form, through the laws of variation and natural selection, than to explain the birth of the individual through the laws of ordinary reproduction. The birth both of the species and of the individual are equally parts of that grand sequence of events, which our minds refuse to accept as the result of blind chance. The understanding revolts at such a conclusion, whether or not we are able to believe that every slight variation of structure,—the union of each pair in marriage,—the dissemination of each seed,—and other such events, have all been ordained for some special purpose.

Sexual selection has been treated at great length in this work; for, as I have attempted to shew, it has played an important part in the history of the organic world. I am aware that much remains doubtful, but I have endeavoured to give a fair view of the whole case. In the lower divisions of the animal kingdom, sexual selection seems to have done nothing: such animals are often affixed for life to the same spot, or have the sexes combined in the same individual, or what is still more important, their perceptive and intellectual faculties are not sufficiently advanced to allow of the feelings of love and jealousy, or of the exertion of choice. When, however, we come to the Arthropoda[16] and Vertebrata, even to the lowest classes in these two great Sub-Kingdoms, sexual selection has effected much.

In the several great classes of the animal kingdom,—in mammals, birds, reptiles, fishes, insects, and even crustaceans,—the differences between the sexes follow nearly the same rules. The males are almost always the wooers; and they alone are armed with special weapons for fighting with their rivals. They are generally stronger and larger than the females, and are endowed with the requisite qualities of courage and pugnacity. They are provided, either exclusively or in a much higher degree than the females, with organs for vocal or instrumental music, and with odoriferous glands. They are ornamental with infinitely diversified appendages, and with the most brilliant or conspicuous colours, often arranged in elegant patterns, whilst the females are unadorned. When the sexes differ in more important structures, it is the male which is provided with special sense-organs for discovering the female, with locomotive organs for reaching her, and often with prehensile organs for holding her. These various structures for charming or securing the female are often developed in the male during only part of the year, namely the breeding-season. They have in many cases been more or less transferred to the females; and in the latter case they often appear in her as mere rudiments. They are lost or never gained by the males after emasculation.[17] Generally they are not developed in the male during

[15] . . . scale: The Rev. J. A. Picton gives a discussion to this effect in his *New Theories and the Old Faith*, 1870 [Darwin's note].

[16] Anthropoda: diverse animal group that includes insects, crustaceans, spiders, and centipedes.

[17] emasculation: castration; deprivation of procreative power.

early youth, but appear a short time before the age for reproduction. Hence in most cases the young of both sexes resemble each other; and the female somewhat resembles her young offspring throughout life. In almost every great class a few anomalous cases occur, where there has been an almost complete transposition of the characters proper to the two sexes; the females assuming characters which properly belong to the males. This surprising uniformity in the laws regulating the differences between the sexes in so many and such widely separated classes, is intelligible if we admit the action of one common cause, namely sexual selection.

Sexual selection depends on the success of certain individuals over others of the same sex, in relation to the propagation of the species; whilst natural selection depends on the success of both sexes, at all ages, in relation to the general conditions of life. The sexual struggle is of two kinds; in the one it is between individuals of the same sex, generally the males, in order to drive away or kill their rivals, the females remaining passive; whilst in the other, the struggle is likewise between the individuals of the same sex, in order to excite or charm those of the opposite sex, generally the females, which no longer remain passive, but select the more agreeable partners. This latter kind of selection is closely analogous to that which man unintentionally, yet effectually, brings to bear on his domesticated productions, when he preserves during a long period the most pleasing or useful individuals, without any wish to modify the breed. . . .

He who admits the principle of sexual selection will be led to the remarkable conclusion that the nervous system not only regulates most of the existing functions of the body, but has indirectly influenced the progressive development of various bodily structures and of certain mental qualities. Courage, pugnacity, perseverance, strength and size of body, weapons of all kinds, musical organs, both vocal and instrumental, bright colours and ornamental appendages, have all been indirectly gained by the one sex or the other, through the exertion of choice, the influence of love and jealousy, and the appreciation of the beautiful in sound, colour or form; and these powers of the mind manifestly depend on the development of the brain.

Man scans with scrupulous care the character and pedigree of his horses, cattle, and dogs before he matches them; but when he comes to his own marriage he rarely, or never, takes any such care. He is impelled by nearly the same motives as the lower animals, when they are left to their own free choice, though he is in so far superior to them that he highly values mental charms and virtues. On the other hand he is strongly attracted by mere wealth or rank. Yet he might by selection do something not only for the bodily constitution and frame of his offspring, but for their intellectual and moral qualities. Both sexes ought to refrain from marriage if they are in any marked degree inferior in body or mind; but such hopes are Utopian and will never be even partially realised until the laws of inheritance are thoroughly known. Everyone does good service, who aids toward this end. When the principles of breeding and inheritance are better understood, we shall not hear ignorant members of our legislature rejecting with scorn a plan for ascertaining whether or not consanguineous[18] marriages are injurious to man.

The advancement of the welfare of mankind is a most intricate problem: all ought to refrain from marriage who cannot avoid abject poverty for their children; for poverty is not only a great evil, but tends to its own increase by leading to recklessness in marriage. On the other hand, as Mr. Galton[19] has remarked, if the prudent avoid marriage, whilst the reckless marry, the inferior members tend to supplant the better members of society. Man, like every other animal, has no doubt advanced to his present high condition through a struggle for existence consequent on his rapid multiplication; and if he is to advance still higher, it is to be feared that he must remain subject to a severe struggle. Otherwise he would sink into indolence, and the more gifted men would not be more successful in the battle of life than the less gifted. Hence our natural rate of increase, though leading to many and obvious evils, must not be greatly diminished by any means. There should be open competition for all men; and the most able should not be prevented by laws or customs from succeeding best and rearing the largest number of offspring. Important as the struggle for existence has been and even still is, yet as far as the highest part of man's nature is concerned there are other agencies more important. For the moral qualities are advanced, either directly or indirectly, much more through the effects of habit, the reasoning powers, instruction, religion, &c., than through natural selection; though to this latter agency may be safely attributed the social instincts, which afforded the basis for the development of the moral sense.

The main conclusion arrived at in this work, namely, that man is descended from some lowly organised form, will, I regret to think, be highly distasteful to many. But there can hardly be a doubt that we are descended from barbarians. The astonishment which I felt on first seeing a party of Fuegians[20] on a wild and broken shore will never be forgotten by me, for the reflection at once rushed into my mind—such were our ancestors. These men were absolutely naked and bedaubed with paint, their long hair was tangled, their mouths, frothed with excitement, and their expression was wild, startled, and distrustful. They possessed hardly any arts, and like wild animals lived on what they could catch; they had no government, and were merciless to every one not of their own small tribe. He who has seen a savage in his native land will not feel much shame, if forced to acknowledge that the blood of some more humble creature flows in his veins. For my own part I would as soon be descended from that heroic little monkey, who braved his dreaded enemy in order to save the life of his keeper, or from that old baboon, who descending from the mountains, carried away in triumph his young comrade from a crowd of astonished dogs—as

[18] consanguineous: related by blood.

[19] Mr. Galton: Francis Galton (1822–1911), a half-cousin of Darwin's and a pioneer of eugenics and psychometrics, was the first to use statistics to study intelligence.

[20] Fuegians: natives of Tierra del Fuego, where Darwin first traveled on the *Beagle*.

from a savage who delights to torture his enemies, offers up bloody sacrifices, practises infanticide without remorse, treats his wives like slaves, knows no decency, and is haunted by the grossest superstitions.

Man may be excused for feeling some pride at having risen, though not through his own exertions, to the very summit of the organic scale; and the fact of his having thus risen, instead of having been aboriginally placed there, may give him hope for a still higher destiny in the distant future. But we are not here concerned with hopes or fears, only with the truth as far as our reason permits us to discover it; and I have given the evidence to the best of my ability. We must, however, acknowledge, as it seems to me, that man with all his noble qualities, with sympathy which feels for the most debased, with benevolence which extends not only to other men but to the humblest living creature, with his god-like intellect which has penetrated into the movements and constitution of the solar system—with all these exalted powers—Man still bears in his bodily frame the indelible stamp of his lowly origin.

LEARNING MORE

These selections are excerpted from longer chapters of Darwin's two main books, both of which can be read online. A great deal of information about Darwin and Darwinism, too, is available online, as are the main objections to or deviations from the theory of evolution. See the *Ideas Across Time* website for useful links.

QUESTIONING THE TEXT

1. Why does Darwin want to point out the "variability" to be found among domestic animals and/or plants (dogs, cows, corn)?
2. What importance does Darwin attribute to the fact that "more individuals [of any given species] are born than can possibly survive" (par. 3)?
3. What significance does Darwin attribute to the difficulty of distinguishing between "species" and "varieties"?
4. How does Darwin's view of the origin of species challenge the theory of creation?
5. What is Darwin's main conclusion in *The Descent of Man*?
6. What are some of the main pieces of evidence Darwin relies on to arrive at his view of the origin of humans?
7. What does Darwin mean by "survival of the fittest" (par. 6)?
8. How does evolution explain human intellectual powers and human moral tendencies? Do you find Darwin's explanation persuasive?
9. How does Darwin defend himself against the charge that his conclusions are irreligious?
10. What is the difference between "sexual selection" and "natural selection"?
11. What were Darwin's emotions upon first seeing a party of Fuegians (par. 30)?
12. How has "man" risen "to the very summit of the organic scale" (par. 31)?

ANALYZING THE WRITER'S CRAFT

1. Darwin has three main challenges to overcome in these passages: first, how to present a mass of detail in readable fashion; second, how to explain the theory of evolution and its component parts in a clear and persuasive way; and third, how to address the skepticism of the scientific community and the hostility of the religious community. Explain briefly how Darwin solves these problems. In each case, cite an example or two.
2. What is the tone of these selections?
3. Why does Darwin open his discussion of natural selection with reference to domestic animals and plants?
4. What kinds of evidence does Darwin rely on to illustrate the coherence of all living things? Do you find his evidence persuasive? Why or why not?
5. Why is "the high standard of our intellectual powers and moral disposition" a tough thing to explain in terms of natural selection (pars. 15ff.)? Is Darwin's explanation "scientific"?
6. What do you learn about Victorian society from Darwin's remark that "The moral faculties are generally and justly esteemed as of higher value than the intellectual powers" (par. 19, *Descent*)? Do you think this sentence applies to U.S. society today?
7. What, for Darwin, makes one group of people more civilized than another?
8. What evidence is there in these selections to show whether Darwin does or does not believe in God?

MAKING CONNECTIONS

1. The paleontologist Stephen Jay Gould, in the next selection in this chapter (pp. 182–185), aims to summarize and clarify Darwin's main points. Does Gould add to Darwin's own words or simply distill them?
2. Is Darwin's method scientific? What would Francis Bacon say (pp. 152–156)? Richard Feynman (pp. 201–207)?
3. Does Darwin undermine Genesis (see Chapter 2, pp. 106–107)? What do you think Muhammad or Confucius would have to say about the theory of evolution (See Chapter 2, pp. 88–96 and pp. 83–86)?
4. Does Friedrich Nietzsche draw proper conclusions from Darwin's theory (Chapter 2, pp. 109–111)?

FORMULATING IDEAS FOR WRITING

1. Darwin concludes that "man is descended from some less highly organized form." The grounds on which this conclusions rests, he says, "will never be shaken" (par. 9). This seems an unusually assertive statement. In our day, "creationists" and those who subscribe to the "argument from design" question Darwin's account of the origin of species and of human beings in particular. Weigh the evidence and write an essay explaining your conclusion (see the *Ideas Across Time* website for useful links).

2. Darwin's views about the origin of species and the origin of humans are today the views of the scientific community. Write an essay that explains why Darwin's views have prevailed. (How does Darwin's work meet or exceed the standard required by scientists as "proof" or substantiation of a theory? What makes Darwin persuasive? His logic? His evidence? His reading of the evidence? All of the above? More?)
3. Write an essay about Darwin's theory of natural selection from a skeptical perspective, including in your discussion the point he makes that you find most powerful and the point he makes, or evidence he adduces, that you find least persuasive.
4. Write an essay that reverses Darwin's emphasis and argues that "the intellectual powers" should be more highly esteemed than "the moral faculties" (par. 19).
5. Write a response to Darwin's explanation of morality as arising from our "social instincts" (pars. 17–20). If you find his account persuasive, explain why. If you do not, explain why and suggest what *you* think is the origin of "the moral faculties."
6. Darwin cannot test his theory by experiment. Is this a fatal flaw in his theory? Is Darwinism scientific?

Introduction to Darwin (1977)

Stephen Jay Gould

Stephen Jay Gould was born in New York City in 1941. In 1974, he began to write a monthly column ("This View of Life") for *Natural History,* the magazine of the American Museum of Natural History. These monthly essays, which he wrote without interruption for the next quarter century, established Gould as the outstanding scientific essayist of his time. Communicating to a wide audience, Gould promoted a kind of scrupulously humanistic view of science, its ways of operating, its beauties and its horrors, and in particular its implications for human advancement. He has been especially concerned with certain explosive issues within Darwinism, arguing, on the one hand, for the paramount importance of Darwin's core propositions while, on the other hand, offering new ideas to evolutionary theory, as well as a fierce resistance to various strands of contemporary Darwinism that embrace biological determinism or maintain that evolution provides a total explanation for all facets of human nature. He is associated with the idea of "punctuated equilibria," the theory that the gaps in the fossil record suggest that instead of proceeding in a slow, steady, continuous way, evolution proceeds by fits and starts. There are periods, so the theory of punctuated equilibria maintains, when evolution speeds up considerably and large numbers of new species arise. Gould has also written to counter the view that evolution either cancels religion or can be the basis of a new religion. Religion and science, he says, are different modes, different ways of knowing—they are neither compatible nor incompatible, but are different.

The selection that follows comes from Gould's "Prologue" to his first collection of *Natural History* columns, *Ever Since Darwin: Reflections in Natural History* (1977). Here Gould stresses certain key features of Darwin's thought that, he says, challenge "Western attitudes." These key points are that "evolution has no purpose" and that "evolution has no direction: it does not lead inevitably to higher things."

Stephen Jay Gould graduated with a degree in geology from Antioch College in 1963 and went on to receive a Ph.D. in paleontology from Columbia University in 1967. From that time until his death, Gould served as professor of geology and zoology at Harvard University. From 1996 to 2002, he was also Vincent Astor Research Visiting Professor of Biology at New York University. Among Gould's most celebrated books are *The Panda's Thumb* (1981), which won the American Book Award for Science; *The Mismeasure of Man* (1983), winner of the National Book Critics' Circle Award; and *Wonderful Life* (1991), winner of the Science Book Prize. In 1981, Gould received a MacArthur Foundation "genius" award. He was president of the American Society of Naturalists and of the nation's largest scientific organization, the American Association for the Advancement of Science. Gould died of cancer in May 2002. He was sixty.

"One hundred years without Darwin are enough," grumbled the noted American geneticist H. J. Muller in 1959. The remark struck many listeners as a singularly inauspicious[1] way to greet the centenary of the *Origin of Species,* but no one could deny the truth expressed in its frustration.

Why has Darwin been so hard to grasp? Within a decade, he convinced the thinking world that evolution had occurred, but his own theory of natural selection never achieved much popularity during his lifetime. It did not prevail until the 1940s, and even today [1977], though it forms the core of our evolutionary theory, it is widely misunderstood, misquoted, and misapplied. The difficulty cannot lie in complexity of logical structure, for the basis of natural selection is simplicity itself—two undeniable facts and an inescapable conclusion:

1. Organisms vary, and these variations are inherited (at least in part) by their offspring.
2. Organisms produce more offspring than can possibly survive.
3. On average, offspring that vary most strongly in directions favored by the environment will survive and propagate. Favorable variation will therefore accumulate in populations by natural selection.

[1] inauspicious: of ill omen, unfavorable.

These three statements do ensure that natural selection will operate, but they do not (by themselves) guarantee for it the fundamental role that Darwin assigned. The essence of Darwin's theory lies in his contention that natural selection is the creative force of evolution—not just the executioner of the unfit. Natural selection must construct the fit as well; it must build adaptation in stages by preserving, generation after generation, the favorable part of a random spectrum of variation. If natural selection is creative, then our first statement on variation must be amplified by two additional constraints.

First, variation must be random, or at least not preferentially inclined toward adaptation. For, if variation comes prepackaged in the right direction, then selection plays no creative role, but merely eliminates the unlucky individuals who do not vary in the appropriate way. Lamarckism,[2] with its insistence that animals respond creatively to their needs and pass acquired traits to offspring, is a non-Darwinian theory on this account. Our understanding of genetic mutation suggests that Darwin was right in maintaining that variation is not predirected in favorable ways. Evolution is a mixture of chance and necessity—chance at the level of variation, necessity in the working of selection.

5 Secondly, variation must be small relative to the extent of evolutionary change in the foundation of new species. For if new species arise all at once, then selection only has to remove former occupants to make way for an improvement that it did not manufacture. Again, our understanding of genetics encourages Darwin's view that small mutations are the stuff of evolutionary change.

Thus, Darwin's apparently simple theory is not without its subtle complexities and additional requirements. Nonetheless, I believe that the stumbling block to its acceptance does not lie in any scientific difficulty, but rather in the radical philosophical content of Darwin's message—in its challenge to a set of entrenched Western attitudes that we are not yet ready to abandon. First, Darwin argues that evolution has no purpose. Individuals struggle to increase the representation of their genes in future generations, and that is all. If the world displays any harmony and order, it arises only as an incidental result of individuals seeking their own advantage—the economy of Adam Smith transferred to nature.[3] Second, Darwin maintained that evolution has no direction; it does not lead inevitably to higher things. Organisms become better adapted to their local environments, and that is all. The "degeneracy" of a parasite is as perfect as the gait of a gazelle. Third, Darwin applied a consistent philosophy of materialism to his interpretation of nature. Matter is the ground of all existence; mind, spirit, and God as well, are just words that express the wondrous results of neuronal[4] complexity. Thomas Hardy, speaking for nature, expressed his distress at the claim that purpose, direction, and spirit had been banished:

> When I took forth at dawning, pool,
> Field, flock, and lonely tree,

---

[2] Lamrackism: Jean-Baptiste Lamarck (1774–1829), French naturalist and evolutionist, proposed the now-discredited theory of inheritance of acquired traits.

[3] Adam Smith: See Chapter 4, pp. 244–262.

[4] neuronal: relating to neurons, or nerve cells.

All seem to gaze at me
Like chastened children sitting silent in a school;

Upon them stirs in lippings mere
(As if once clear in call,
But now scarce breathed at all)—
"We wonder, ever wonder, why we find us here!"[5]

Yes, the world has been different ever since Darwin. But no less exciting, instructing, or uplifting; for if we cannot find purpose in nature, we will have to define it for ourselves. Darwin was not a moral dolt; he just didn't care to fob off upon nature all the deep prejudices of Western thought. Indeed, I suggest that the true Darwinian spirit might salvage our depleted world by denying a favorite theme of Western arrogance—that we are meant to have control and dominion over the earth and its life because we are the loftiest product of a preordained process.

In any case, we must come to terms with Darwin. . . .

LEARNING MORE

1. Darwin's most significant predecessor as an evolutionist was Jean-Baptiste Lamarck (Gould makes reference to Lamarckism in par. 7). Since his views are similar to but also significantly different from Darwin's, it is helpful to understand Lamarck's ideas—see useful links on the *Ideas Across Time* website.
2. Gould quotes the poet and novelist Thomas Hardy. As a major Victorian eminence, Hardy represents a sensitive late-Victorian response to the implications of Darwin's ideas—and of the advance of science more generally. For more about Hardy, see the *Ideas Across Time* website.

QUESTIONING THE TEXT

1. What does Gould think is the main "stumbling block" to the acceptance of Darwin's "simple theory" (par. 6)?
2. What are the two "undeniable facts" and the "inescapable conclusion" that form the core of Darwinism?
3. What must be true in order for natural selection to be "the creative force of evolution" (par. 3)?
4. Explain in your own words why, for Darwin's theory to hold up, "variation must be random" (par. 4).
5. What are the philosophical implications, according to Gould, of Darwin's "simple theory"?

[5] "When . . . here": From the poem "Nature's Questioning" by the British poet and novelist Thomas Hardy (1840–1928). The full poem can be found on the *Ideas Across Time* website.

ANALYZING THE WRITER'S CRAFT

1. What is Gould's thesis?
2. Gould relies, in these brief passages, on a number of allusions in order to clarify and support his argument. What is his purpose in alluding to Lamarck (par. 4)? In alluding to Adam Smith (par. 6)? In alluding to Thomas Hardy (par. 6)? In alluding to Genesis (par. 6)? How would his essay have been different without these allusions?
3. What is the tone of this essay? Is there any place where the tone changes?
4. Gould uses the word "our" in different ways in this essay. In par. 6, he writes: "then our first statement on variation must be amplified." Here he uses "our" to mean "mine" adhering to the conventions of semiformal writing. How does he use "our" in pars. 4 and 5—"Our understanding of genetic mutation" and "our understanding of genetics"?
5. In this short essay, Gould frequently (three times) employs numerals or explicit listing ("first," "second," . . .) to organize his material. What is the effect of this kind of notation? Why do you think Gould wants to sort his points out in this emphatic way?
6. Gould relies heavily here on a form of argument called *modus ponens* (the method of affirming the antecedent), which schematically looks like this:

   Major premise: If A, then B
   Minor premise: A
   Conclusion: Therefore, B

   In this kind of argument, each premise must be valid or true; otherwise, the whole thing falls apart. Gould tends to use this structure not so much to affirm the antecedent but to affirm its opposite. In par. 4, for example, Gould says:

Major premise:	If variation comes prepackaged in the right direction, then selection plays no creative role.
Minor premise:	Genetic mutation shows that variation is not predirected.
Conclusion:	Therefore, variation is random.

   Examine other examples of this kind of logical argument in the essay, and explain why Gould's arguments are or are not valid.
7. Is Gould's conclusion effective? Why or why not?

MAKING CONNECTIONS

1. Do you find Gould's gloss on Darwin accurate, or does he draw conclusions and find implications in Darwin that you do not see in Darwin's writing (see pp. 167–180)?
2. Is Gould reading Genesis properly (see his conclusion to par. 6)? Does Genesis (see Chapter 2, pp. 106–107) establish a basis for "Western arrogance"?

3. Compare Gould's reading of Darwin with that of Friedrich Nietzsche (Chapter 2, pp. 109–111).
4. Does Gould link Adam Smith and Darwin appropriately (see Chapter 4, pp. 244–262)?

FORMULATING IDEAS FOR WRITING

1. Support or challenge Gould's reading of Darwin.
2. After further reading of Jean-Baptiste Lamarck, explain how his ideas and Darwin's differ, and why the differences matter.
3. If evolution "has no purpose" and "no direction," then should we be joyful at the prospect that we can or must define life's meaning for ourselves, as Gould suggests? Or are these implications of Darwinism indeed so radical as to challenge our basic assumptions and undermine our sense of life's value?
4. Is the idea that human beings are "meant to have control and dominion over the earth and its life" an example, as Gould says, of "Western arrogance"? Or is it the expression of a necessary custodianship of nature on the part of humans, whose intelligence makes them the only creatures on the planet capable both of caring for it and of safeguarding it?

Nature (1933)

Luther Standing Bear

Son of the Sioux chieftain Standing Bear, Luther Standing Bear (1868–1939) was the Oglala chief from 1905 to 1939 and was a member of the last Lakota Sioux generation to be raised in the traditions of his tribe. "My first years were spent living just as my forefathers had lived," he said. But once his people were restricted to reservation life in 1879, his father enrolled him as one of the first students at the Carlisle Indian Industrial School in Carlisle, Pennsylvania. Carlisle was designed to assimilate American Indians into the U.S. mainstream and to provide them with industrial skills. Standing Bear was trained as a tinsmith. But the assimilation was bitter: born Ota Kte (Plenty Kill), Standing Bear was now given the name Luther and, like all his classmates, forced to cut his hair. In 1884, Standing Bear returned to the Rosebud reservation, working at a variety of jobs including teacher, store clerk, and minister's aide. In 1902, he joined Buffalo Bill's Wild West Show and later became a movie actor, eventually leading the Indian Actors' Association. He died on February 19, 1939, during the filming of *Union Pacific*.

When, upon his father's death in 1905, Standing Bear was called to become chief in his stead, he found that he was subject to the authority of the white reservation agent and could not work for his people while remaining on the reservation. He then began a campaign for Indian rights that would last the rest of his life. He traveled to Washington, D.C., to claim his U.S. citizenship so he could travel freely to and from his reservation. On the lecture circuit and in several important books, Standing Bear sought to communicate the depth, wisdom, and dignity of American Indian culture, and to combat the prejudices that tarred his people as "savages." His central works, written with the help of his niece Waste Win (Good Woman), are *My People, the Sioux* (1928), *My Indian Boyhood* (1931), *Land of the Spotted Eagle* (1933)—from which the following selection is taken—and *Stories of the Sioux* (1934).

In this selection, Standing Bear conveys the Lakota apprehension of nature and contrasts it with that of the white man. For the Indian, Standing Bear says, all of creation emanates from the Great Mystery; the aim of Indian study of nature is to achieve harmony between the human and his or her surroundings. For white people, Standing Bear says, nature is alien and dangerous, a "wilderness" that, like sinful human nature, needs to be conquered.

Nature

The Lakota was a true naturist—a lover of Nature. He loved the earth and all things of the earth, the attachment growing with age. The old people came literally to love the soil and they sat or reclined on the ground with a feeling of being close to a mothering power. It was good for the skin to touch the earth and the old people liked to remove their moccasins and walk with bare feet on the sacred earth. Their tipis were built upon the earth and their altars were made of earth. The birds that flew in the air came to rest upon the earth and it was the final abiding place of all things that lived and grew. The soil was soothing, strengthening, cleansing, and healing.

This is why the old Indian still sits upon the earth instead of propping himself up and away from its life-giving forces. For him, to sit or lie upon the ground is to be able to think more deeply and to feel more keenly; he can see more clearly into the mysteries of life and come closer in kinship to other lives about him.

The earth was full of sounds which the old-time Indian could hear, sometimes putting his ear to it so as to hear more clearly. The forefathers of the Lakotas had done this for long ages until there had come to them real understanding of earth ways. It was almost as if the man were still a part of the earth as he was in the beginning, according to the legend of the tribe. This beautiful story of the genesis of the Lakota people furnished the foundation for the love they bore for earth and all things of the earth. Wherever the Lakota went, he was with Mother Earth. No matter where he roamed by day or slept by night, he was safe with her. This thought comforted and sustained the Lakota and he was eternally filled with gratitude.

From Wakan Tanka there came a great unifying life force that flowed in and through all things—the flowers of the plains, blowing winds, rocks, trees, birds, animals—and was the same force that had been breathed into the first man. Thus all things were kindred and brought together by the same Great Mystery.

Kinship with all creatures of the earth, sky, and water was a real and active principle. For the animal and bird world there existed a brotherly feeling that kept the Lakota safe among them. And so close did some of the Lakotas come to their feathered and furred friends that in true brotherhood they spoke a common tongue.

The animal had rights—the right of man's protection, the right to live, the right to multiply, the right to freedom, and the right to man's indebtedness—and in recognition of these rights the Lakota never enslaved the animal, and spared all life that was not needed for food and clothing.

This concept of life and its relations was humanizing and gave to the Lakota an abiding love. It filled his being with the joy and mystery of living; it gave him reverence for all life; it made a place for all things in the scheme of existence with equal importance to all. The Lakota could despise no creature, for all were of one blood, made by the same hand, and filled with the essence of the Great Mystery. In spirit the Lakota was humble and meek. "Blessed are the meek: for they shall inherit the earth," was true for the Lakota, and from the earth he inherited secrets long since forgotten. His religion was sane, normal, and human.

Reflection upon life and its meaning, consideration of its wonders and observation of the world of creatures, began with childhood. The earth, which was called *Maka,* and the sun, called *Anpetuwi,* represented two functions somewhat analogous to those of male and female. The earth brought forth life, but the warming, enticing rays of the sun coaxed it into being. The earth yielded, the sun engendered.

In talking to children, the old Lakota would place a hand on the ground and explain: "We sit in the lap of our Mother. From her we, and all other living things, come. We shall soon pass, but the place where we now rest will last forever." So we, too, learned to sit or lie on the ground and become conscious of life about us in its multitude of forms. Sometimes we boys would sit motionless and watch the swallow, the tiny ants, or perhaps some small animal at its work and ponder on its industry and ingenuity; or we lay on our backs and looked long at the sky and when the stars came out made shapes from the various groups. The morning and evening star always attracted attention, and the Milky Way was a path which was traveled by the ghosts. The old people told us to heed *wa maka skan,* which were the "moving things of earth." This meant, of course, the animals that lived and moved about, and the stories they told of *wa maka skan* increased our interest and delight. The wolf, duck, eagle, hawk, spider, bear, and other creatures had marvelous powers, and each one was useful and helpful to us. Then there were the warriors who lived in the sky and dashed about on their spirited horses during a thunder storm, their lances clashing with the thunder and glittering with the lightning. There was *wiwila,* the living spirit of the spring, and the stones that flew like a bird and talked like a man. Everything was possessed of personality, only differing with us in form. Knowledge was inherent in all things. The world was a library and its books were the stones, leaves, grass, brooks, and the birds and animals that shared, alike with us, the storms and blessings of earth. We learned to do what only the student of nature ever learns, and that was to feel beauty. We never railed at the storms, the furious winds, and the biting frosts and snows. To do so intensified human futility, so whatever came we adjusted ourselves, by more effort and energy if necessary, but without complaint. Even the lightning did us no harm, for whenever it came too close, mothers and grandmothers in every tipi put cedar leaves on the coals and their magic kept danger away. Bright days and dark days were both expressions of the Great Mystery, and the Indian reveled in being close to the Big Holy. His worship was unalloyed, free from the fears of civilization.

I have come to know that the white mind does not feel toward nature as does the Indian mind, and it is because, I believe, of the difference in childhood instruction. I have often noticed white boys gathered in a city by-street or alley jostling and pushing one another in a foolish manner. They spend much time in this aimless fashion, their natural faculties neither seeing, hearing, nor feeling the varied life that surrounds them. There is about them no awareness, no acuteness, and it is this dullness that gives ugly mannerisms full play; it takes from them natural poise and stimulation. In contrast, Indian boys, who are naturally reared, are alert to their surroundings; their senses are not narrowed to observing only one another, and they cannot spend hours seeing nothing, hearing nothing, and thinking nothing in particular. Observation was certain in its rewards; interest, wonder, admiration grew, and the fact was appreciated that life was more than mere human manifestation; that it was expressed in a multitude of forms. This appreciation enriched Lakota existence. Life was vivid and pulsing; nothing was casual and commonplace. The Indian lived—lived in every sense of the word—from his first to his last breath.

The character of the Indian's emotion left little room in his heart for antagonism toward his fellow creatures, this attitude giving him what is sometimes referred to as "the Indian point of view." Every true student, every lover of nature has "the Indian point of view," but there are few such students, for few white men approach nature in the Indian manner. The Indian and the white man sense things differently because the white man has put distance between himself and nature; and assuming a lofty place in the scheme of order of things has lost for him both reverence and understanding. Consequently the white man finds Indian philosophy obscure—wrapped, as he says, in a maze of ideas and symbols which he does not understand. A writer friend, a white man whose knowledge of "Injuns" is far more profound and sympathetic than the average, once said that he had been privileged, on two occasions, to see the contents of an Indian medicine-man's bag in which were bits of earth, feathers, stones, and various other articles of symbolic nature; that a "collector" showed him one and laughed, but a great and world-famous archeologist showed him the other with admiration and wonder. Many times the Indian is embarrassed and baffled by the white man's allusions to nature in such terms as crude, primitive, wild, rude, untamed, and savage. For the Lakota, mountains, lakes, rivers, springs, valleys, and woods were all finished beauty; winds, rain, snow, sunshine, day, night, and change of seasons brought interest; birds, insects, and animals filled the world with knowledge that defied the discernment of man.

But nothing the Great Mystery placed in the land of the Indian pleased the white man, and nothing escaped his transforming hand. Wherever forests have not been mowed down; wherever the animal is recessed in their quiet protection; wherever the earth is not bereft of four-footed life—that to him is an "unbroken wilderness." But since for the Lakota there was no wilderness; since nature was not dangerous but hospitable; not forbidding but friendly, Lakota philosophy was healthy—free from fear and dogmatism. And here I find the great distinction between the faith of the Indian and the white man. Indian faith sought the harmony of man with his surroundings; the other sought the dominance of surroundings. In sharing, in loving all and everything, one people naturally found a measure of the thing they sought; while, in fearing, the other found need of conquest. For one man the world was full of beauty; for the other it was a place of sin and ugliness to be endured until he went to another world, there to become a creature of wings, half-man and half-bird. Forever one man directed his Mystery to change the world He had made; forever this man pleaded with Him to chastise His wicked ones; and forever he implored his Wakan Tanka to send His light to earth. Small wonder this man could not understand the other.

But the old Lakota was wise. He knew that man's heart, away from nature, becomes hard; he knew that lack of respect for growing, living things soon led to lack of respect for humans too. So he kept his youth close to its softening influence.

LEARNING MORE

Useful links to explore more of Luther Standing Bear's writing can be found on *Ideas Across Time* website.

QUESTIONING THE TEXT

1. What is the difference between a "naturist" (par. 1) and a "naturalist"?
2. Why does the "old-time" Indian put his ear to the ground (par. 3)?
3. How does the Christian sentiment "Blessed are the meek: for they shall inherit the earth" (par. 7) apply to the Lakota?
4. How does the Lakota attitude toward nature affect the education of Lakota children?
5. Why does "civilization" fear nature?
6. Explain the responses of the collector and the archeologist to the medicine-man's bag (par. 11).
7. How does observation lead to reverence in Lakota life?
8. How do the Indian and the white man view wilderness differently?
9. Is the Lakota relation to nature scientific?

ANALYZING THE WRITER'S CRAFT

1. How does Standing Bear's use the metaphor of the earth as a mother to explain the Lakota view of nature?
2. What is the thesis statement of this essay, and where is it found?
3. What is the impact in the essay of the introduction of one the most common of Christian sayings—"Blessed are the meek: for they shall inherit the earth"?
4. What audience do you think Standing Bear has in mind for his essay? Explain.
5. The role of study and the acquisition of knowledge are central to Standing Bear's purpose in this essay. How does he define study and knowledge? How are these definitions used to distinguish the Indian and white person's views of life?
6. How does Standing Bear near illustrate the importance, and benefits, of observation for the Lakota, especially the Lakota young?
7. Why does Standing Bear introduce "the Indian point of view" in quotation marks (par. 11)?
8. How does Standing Bear contrast both the Indian and the white attitudes toward nature and the implications of these attitudes?
9. Is Standing Bear's conclusion effective? Why or why not?

MAKING CONNECTIONS

1. Compare and contrast the attitude toward nature of the Lakota with that of the Pueblo people (Chapter 8, pp. 693–694).
2. Do you think the Lakota understanding of creation is mainly like or mainly unlike that expressed in Genesis (Chapter 2, pp. 106–107)?
3. How does the Lakota view of nature compare with that expressed by perhaps the most famous Western naturalist, Charles Darwin (pp. 167–180)?
4. What would Standing Bear have thought of Richard Feynman's view of the value of science (pp. 201–207)? What would Feynman have thought of the Lakota view of nature?

FORMULATING IDEAS FOR WRITING

1. Luther Standing Bear contrasts the being-at-home-in-nature attitude of the Lakota with "the fears of civilization" (par. 9). Is he exaggerating? Is his account of the Lakota philosophy a persuasive critique of Western civilization? Or does he misunderstand Western civilization? Is his account of the Lakota worldview rosier than it likely was in everyday practice?
2. In the Western tradition, from the outset in the Garden of Eden, knowledge is a double-edged sword. On the one hand, knowing things is pleasurable, and human skill—the ability to make chairs, or shoes, or airplanes—has always been a source of pride. On the other hand, we have always been uncomfortable with certain kinds knowledge. God forbids Adam and Eve to

eat of the tree of knowledge; Frankenstein violates our sense of what we should know. But science is primarily a way of knowing, and it now dominates the contemporary world of knowledge. Write an essay reflecting on this puzzling subject, using Standing Bear's essay on nature as a point of departure and including reference to one or two (or more, if you wish) of the following: Bacon's "Sphinx" (pp. 152–156); Einstein's "Scientific Truth" (pp. 193–200); Feynman's "The Value of Science," (pp. 201–207); Genesis (Chapter 2, pp. 106–107).

3. What do you think about the Lakota form of education of the young?
4. Is there an inherent conflict between civilization and nature? For example, should we revere the cockroach invading our kitchen and swarming over our food? Or should we call the exterminator and get rid of the pesky things? Should we let the grass and the weeds bloom, or should we pull the weeds and mow the grass? Is it a violation of the sky to send airplanes across it? Is modern medicine incompatible with reverence for the forces of nature?

On Scientific Truth (1934) and Letters to and from Children (1936–1953)

Albert Einstein

In the seventeenth century, Isaac Newton created modern physics, describing in mathematical terms that could be confirmed by experiment exactly how the universe works. In the first decades of the twentieth century, Albert Einstein created contemporary physics, revising or overturning Newton's laws. Einstein's first set of major breakthroughs occurred in 1905, when he was twenty-six and working full-time in the Swiss Patent Office at Bern. For Newton, the laws of physics were universal and applied everywhere in the same way. Einstein proved this was not true. His special theory of relativity (1905) holds that if, for all sets of circumstances, the speed of light is constant and the same natural laws apply, then both time and motion are relative to the observer. Disconcertingly, Einstein showed that concepts common sense says are absolute, such as time and space, are actually "relative." The length of a yardstick is not the same everywhere but depends on the motion of the observer. His most famous equation—$E = mc^2$—is an extension of the special theory and establishes the equivalence of matter and energy. In the formula $E = mc^2$, "E" represents "energy," which equals the mass of a body (m) multiplied by the speed of light (c) squared. In other words, if you could release the energy within even a small mass, you would get a phenomenal wallop—precisely what occurs in the nuclear explosions that, to Einstein's horror, became the definitive proof of his equation. In the general theory of relativity (1915–1917), Einstein proposed that gravity as well as motion can affect time and space. Gravity, he said, pulling in one direction, is equivalent to acceleration in the opposite direction. (Think of an elevator rushing up to the top of the Empire State Building: the elevator car acceleration is exactly equivalent to the gravity you can feel pulling you downward.) Any mass, therefore, such as the sun, warps the space and time around it. In November 1919, a Royal Society of London expedition to the Gulf of Guinea to measure the solar eclipse of that year (May 29, 1919) announced that it had completed its calculations and that they confirmed not Newton's but Einstein's predictions. Einstein became famous overnight, receiving the Nobel Prize for Physics in 1921 and creating the conceptual frame for contemporary cosmology. The big bang theory, the notion of an expanding universe, and the postulation of black holes all derive from Einstein's general theory.

Albert Einstein was born in 1879 into a German-Jewish family in Ulm, Germany. He was educated at the prestigious Federal Polytechnic Academy in Zurich, Switzerland, from which he graduated in 1900, becoming a Swiss citizen. Soon thereafter, he began working in the patent office in Bern, and in 1903, he married his university sweetheart, Mileva Maric. On the basis of his revolutionary papers of 1905, Einstein was awarded a Ph.D. by the University of Zurich, and he quickly rose in prominence in scientific circles, assuming the post of professor of theoretical physics in Berlin in 1914. When World War I erupted later that year, Einstein's wife and two sons were stranded on vacation in Switzerland, a separation that led to a divorce. In the year of his international acclaim after the solar eclipse of 1919, Einstein married his second cousin, Elsa, and became increasingly active as a public figure, campaigning for peace, socialism, and Zionism. The rise of Adolf Hitler forced Einstein to flee Germany in 1933. He settled in Princeton, New Jersey, where he worked at the Princeton Institute for Advanced Study for the rest of his life. Einstein and Elsa lived a reclusive, unassuming life in a simple, two-story house. In 1939, Einstein wrote to President Roosevelt alerting him to the importance of atomic bomb research. His letter marked the beginning of the Manhattan Project. Though he had no part in this work, Einstein was alarmed by its results and agitated until his death against nuclear weapons and for world government. His scientific work at Princeton involved a search for a unifying theory to meld quantum physics and relativity. Although he did not succeed, he insisted that the universe could not be random, asserting that he put his faith in "Spinoza's God who reveals himself in the harmony of what exists." Einstein died of heart failure in his sleep on April 18, 1955.

"On Scientific Truth" appeared in a collection of Einstein's writing, *Essays in Science*, published in 1934. His letters to children have been collected in *Dear Professor Einstein* by Alice Calaprice.

On Scientific Truth

(1) It is difficult even to attach a precise meaning to the term "scientific truth." So different is the meaning of the word "truth" according to whether we are

dealing with a fact of experience, a mathematical proposition or a scientific theory. "Religious truth" conveys nothing clear to me at all.

(2) Scientific research can reduce superstition by encouraging people to think and survey things in terms of cause and effect. Certain it is that a conviction, akin to religious feeling, of the rationality or intelligibility of the world lies behind all scientific work of a higher order.

(3) This firm belief, a belief bound up with deep feeling, in a superior mind that reveals itself in the world of experience, represents my conception of God. In common parlance this may be described as "pantheistic" (Spinoza).

(4) Denominational traditions I can only consider historically and psychologically; they have no other significance for me.

Albert Einstein's Letters to and from Children

1. From Phyllis, New York

The Riverside Church
January 19, 1936

My dear Dr. Einstein,

We have brought up the question: Do scientists pray? in our Sunday school class. It began by asking whether we could believe in both science and religion. We are writing to scientists and other important men, to try and have our own question answered.

We will feel greatly honored if you will answer our question: Do scientists pray, and what do they pray for?

We are in the sixth grade, Miss Ellis's class.

Respectfully yours,
Phyllis

1a. To Phyllis, New York

January 24, 1936

Dear Phyllis,

I will attempt to reply to your question as simply as I can. Here is my answer:

Scientists believe that every occurrence, including the affairs of human beings, is due to the laws of nature. Therefore a scientist cannot be inclined to believe that the course of events can be influenced by prayer, that is, by a supernaturally manifested wish.

However, we must concede that our actual knowledge of these forces is imperfect, so that in the end the belief in the existence of a final, ultimate spirit rests on a kind of faith. Such belief remains widespread even with the current achievements in science.

But also, everyone who is seriously involved in the pursuit of science becomes convinced that some spirit is manifest in the laws of the universe, one that is vastly superior to that of man. In this way the pursuit of science leads to a religious feeling of a special sort, which is surely quite different from the religiosity of someone more naive.

With cordial greetings,
your A. Einstein

2. *From Tyfanny, South Africa*

10th July, 1946

Dear Sir,

I trust you will not consider it impertinence, but as you are the greatest scientist that ever lived, I would like your autograph. Please do not think that I collect famous people's autographs—I do not. But I would like yours; if you are too busy, it does not matter.

I probably would have written ages ago, only I was not aware that you were still alive. I am not interested in history, and I thought that you had lived in the 18th c., or somewhere around that time. I must have been mixing you up with Sir Isaac Newton or someone. Anyway, I discovered during Maths one day that the mistress (who we can always sidetrack) was talking about the most brilliant scientists. She mentioned that you were in America, and when I asked whether you were buried there, and not in England, she said, Well, you were not dead yet. I was so excited when I heard that, that I all but got a Maths detention!

I am awfully interested in Science, so are quite a lot of people in my form at school. My best friends are the Wilson twins. Every night after Lights Out at school, Pat Wilson and I lean out of our cubicle windows, which are next to each other, and discuss Astronomy, which we both prefer to anything as far as work goes. Pat has a telescope and we study those stars that we can see. For the first part of the year we had the Pleiades, and the constellation of Orion, then Castor and Pollux, and what we thought to be Mars and Saturn. Now they have all moved over, and we usually have to creep past the prefect's room to other parts of the building to carry on our observations. We have been caught a few times now, though, so it's rather difficult.

Pat knows much more about the theoretical side than I do. What worries me most is How can Space go on forever? I have read many books on the subject, but they all say they could not possibly explain, as no ordinary reader would understand. If you do not mind me saying so, I do not really see how it could be spiral. But then, of course you obviously know what you are saying, and I could not contradict!

I must apologise once more if I have taken up some of your valueable time. I am sorry that you have become an American citizen, I would much prefer you in England.

I trust you are well, and will continue to make many more great Scientific discoveries.

I remain,

Yours obediently,
Tyfanny

2a. To Tyfanny, South Africa

August 25, 1946

Dear Tyfanny,

Thank you for your letter of July 10th. I have to apologize to you that I am still among the living. There *will* be a remedy for this, however.

Be not worried about "curved space." You will understand at a later time that for it this status is the easiest it could possibly have. Used in the right sense the word "curved" has not exactly the same meaning as in everyday language.

I hope that yours and your friend's future astronomical investigations will not be discovered anymore by the eyes and ears of your school-government. This is the attitude taken by most good citizens toward their government and I think rightly so.

Yours sincerely,
Albert Einstein

3. From a Father, New York

ca. February 9, 1950

Dear Dr. Einstein,

Last summer my eleven-year-old son died of polio. He was an unusual child, a lad of great promise who verily thirsted after knowledge so that he could prepare himself for a useful life in the community. His death has shattered the very structure of my existence, my very life has become an almost meaningless void—for all my dreams and aspirations were somehow associated with his future and his strivings. I have tried during the past months to find comfort for my anguished spirit, a measure of solace to help me bear the agony of losing one dearer than life itself—an innocent, dutiful, and gifted child who was the victim of such a cruel fate. I have sought comfort in the belief that man has a spirit which attains immortality—that somehow, somewhere my son lives on in a higher world.

I have said to myself: "Is not everything in this universe created in accordance with a fixed purpose and does not everything accomplish its purpose? What would be the purpose of the spirit if with the body it should perish; of what benefit would be to us the faculties of thinking and reasoning if they should attain us no more than they do here on earth and the insight to the full truth be barred to us forever? . . ."

I have said to myself: "it is a law of science that matter can never be destroyed; things are changed but the essence does not cease to be. Take a quantity of matter, divide it and sub-divide it in ten thousand ways, still it exists as the same quantity of matter with unchanged qualities as to its essence and will exist even unto the end of time. Shall we say that matter lives and the spirit perishes; shall the lower outlast the higher?"

I have said to myself: "shall we believe that they who have gone out of life in childhood before the natural measure of their days was full have been forever hurled into the darkness of oblivion? Shall we believe that the millions who have died the death of martyrs for truth, enduring the pangs of persecution, have utterly perished? Without immortality the world is a moral chaos." . . .

I write you all this because I have just read your volume *The World As I See It*. On page 5 of that book you stated: "Any individual who should survive his physical death is beyond my comprehension . . . such notions are for the fears or absurd egoism of feeble souls." And I inquire in a spirit of desperation, is there in your view no comfort, no consolation for what has happened? Am I to believe that my beautiful darling child . . . has been forever wedded into dust, that there was nothing within him which has defied the grave and transcended the power of death? Is there nothing to assuage the pain of an unquenchable longing, an intense craving, an unceasing love for my darling son?

May I have a word from you? I need help badly.

Sincerely yours,
R. M.

3a. *To a Father*

February 12, 1950

Dear Mr. M.,

A human being is part of the whole world, called by us "Universe," a part limited in time and space. He experiences himself, his thoughts and feelings as something separate from the rest—a kind of optical delusion of his consciousness. The striving to free oneself from this delusion is the one issue of true religion. Not to nourish the delusion but to try to overcome it is the way to reach the attainable measure of peace of mind.

With my best wishes,
sincerely yours,
Albert Einstein

4. *From Six Little Scientists, Morgan City, Louisiana*

[1951]

Dear Proffesser,

We are six children who took an interest in Science. We are in sixth grade. In our class we are having an argument. The class took sides. We six are on one side and 21 on the other side. Our teacher is also on the other side so that makes 22. The argument is whether there would be living things on earth if the sun burnt out or if human beings would die. We are not going to say anything we don't believe. We are going to keep what we believe in until it is proved different. We believe there would be living things on the earth if the sun burnt out. Will you tell us what you think. We have some other questions we have been wondering about. If it wouldn't bother you too much could you please answer them? They are: Does the sun give off hydrogen? Are the stars bigger than the sun? Do we have a chance to become scientists? We are:

Linda, age 11 Richard, age 11
Brenda, " 11 Rosalie, " 11
Ubain, " 11 Glenn, " 11

We would like you to join our Six Little Scientists, only now it would be Six Little Scientists and One Big Scientist. Please give us each your autograph so we can use them for club badges and also to help us remember how you helped us and showed us something if we are wrong. Probably there are many things misspelled or done wrong on here because we are not showing this to the teacher. Our teacher's name is Mrs. Smythe.

If you would join our club you must not tell any of our secrets and you would be our special friend and not a proffesser.

Love and lollipops,
Six Little Scientists

—P. S. Linda wrote the letter.

4a. To Six Little Scientists

December 12, 1951

Dear Children:

The minority is sometimes right—but not in your case. Without sunlight there is:

no wheat, no bread,
no grass, no cattle, no meat, no milk,
and everything would be frozen.
No LIFE.

A. Einstein

5. From Carol, Zanesville, Ohio

November 12, 1952

Dear Dr. Einstein,

I am a pupil in the sixth grade at Westview School. We have been talking about animals and plants in Science. There are a few children in our room that do not understand why people are classed as animals. I would appreciate it very much if you would please answer this and explain to me why people are classed as animals.

Thanking you,

Sincerely,
Carol

5a. To the Children of Westview School

January 17, 1953

Dear Children:

We should not ask "What is an animal" but "what sort of thing do we call an animal?" Well, we call something an animal which has certain characteristics: it takes nourishment, it descends from parents similar to itself, it grows, it moves by itself, it dies if its time has run out. That's why we call the worms, the chicken, the dog, the monkey an animal. What about us humans? Think about it in the above mentioned way and then decide for yourselves whether it is a natural thing to regard ourselves as animals.

With kind regards,
Albert Einstein

LEARNING MORE

Einstein claims that his conception of God is like Baruch Spinoza's "pantheistic" conception. To learn more about Spinoza, see the *Ideas Across Time* website.

QUESTIONING THE TEXT

Scientific Truth

1. What are the three kinds of possible scientific truths that Einstein mentions?
2. How can science reduce superstition?
3. What religionlike faith lies behind scientific work?
4. In your own words, express Einstein's view of God.

Letters

1. How do Einstein's comments on religion (letters 1a and 3a) amplify his views of God expressed in "Of Scientific Truth"?
2. What is Tyfanny (letter 2) mainly interested in asking? How does her question derive from Einstein's theories?
3. How does Einstein's answer to letter 5 subtly relay the methods or approaches of science to Carol?

ANALYZING THE WRITER'S CRAFT

Scientific Truth

1. What is the effect of Einstein's presenting his ideas in this listlike format?
2. What is the tone of this writing?
3. Is there a logical order to these paragraphs?
4. Why is Einstein's God not a "religious truth"?
5. What distinguishes Einstein's "religious feeling" (par. 2) from "superstition"?
6. Why does Einstein present his views in such a pithy, aphoristic way? Would this selection be more effective, or powerful, if its ideas were developed at greater length?
7. Why do you think Einstein mentions "denominational traditions"?

Letters

1. What do you learn about Einstein as a person from the letters he writes? Give two or three examples to support your answer.
2. Often questions can be very brief, whereas answers tend to be a good deal longer and more complex. But Einstein's letters in answer to people's

questions are usually a lot shorter than the letters asking the questions in the first place. Why do you think this is so?
3. What features of the letters to Einstein reveal the way convention dominates our writing practices?
4. How does the specificity of audience affect the letters written to Einstein, as well as the letters Einstein writes in reply? Offer two or three examples to support your answer.

MAKING CONNECTIONS

1. Einstein is the modern epitome of the scientist. How does he compare with Dr. Frankenstein (pp. 157–165)? How do the children view Einstein as a preeminent scientist, and how does that compare with the self-definition of scientists? In answering, consider the impression of a scientist that Richard Feynman (pp. 201–207) wishes to convey?
2. How do Einstein's comments about man as an animal (Letter 5a) compare, or contrast, with Darwin's views (pp. 167–180)?
3. Is Einstein's brief definition of God in accord with Spinoza's pantheism?

FORMULATING IDEAS FOR WRITING

1. Is the view that the universe is "rational" (par. 2) in accord with the view of creation and of God in Genesis or the Qur'an? Discuss.
2. Can a religious feeling be meaningful in the absence of denominational traditions? Why or why not?
3. How do you account for Einstein's reluctance to define "scientific truth"? After all, isn't "the world of experience" coherent, according to Einstein?
4. Explain Spinoza's pantheism.
5. What are the implications for morality of Einstein's view of God?
6. If you were to write Einstein a letter today, what would *you* ask him? Draft a letter and try writing Einstein's reply.

The Value of Science (1955)

Richard Feynman

One of the most original and flamboyant of modern physicists, rising to the status of a cult hero, Richard Feynman won the Nobel Prize for his work in quantum electrodynamics in 1965. One of the youngest members of the team that worked on the Manhattan Project to build an atom bomb, Feynman was the only one who was so bothered by the potential ease with which he believed the documents on the bomb could be filched that he became an expert safe-cracker. Always playful and heedless of authority, he would secretly open the safes where his superiors stored research documents and leave teasing notes behind. While at Los Alamos, he patented an atomic submarine and an atomic airplane.

Among Feynman's major scientific contributions that recast the whole of quantum mechanics and electrodynamics, was a simple way to study the interaction of subatomic particles, something existing formulas could not do well. Feynman developed a series of particle interaction diagrams ("the Feynman diagrams") that made accurate calculations of these interactions possible; the diagrams remain in use to this day. His daring addition to the General Theory of Relativity, known as "sum over histories," has shaped current inquiry into the nature of the universe.

In the early 1960s, Feynman was persuaded to interrupt his scientific research and teach the introductory physics sequence at the California Institute of Technology (Caltech). These lectures became the three-volume *Feynman Lectures on Physics*, revolutionizing physics education across the country.

Feynman came to the attention of the national television audience when part of the NASA panel investigating the space shuttle *Challenger* disaster in 1986. Impatient with the bureaucratic nature of the investigation, Feynman dropped a piece of the rocket booster's O-ring material into a cup of ice water on the table in front of him and—with the cameras rolling—quickly showed that the material lost its flexibility at low temperatures. (In the investigating commission's report, Feynman accused NASA of "playing Russian roulette" with the lives of astronauts.)

Born in 1918 in Far Rockaway, Queens, Feynman graduated from the Massachusetts Institute of Technology in 1939 and received his Ph.D. from Princeton University in 1942. For most of his career, he was on the faculty of Caltech. In 1985, Feynman's friend Ralph Leighton compiled speeches and other Feynman material, and published *"Surely You're Joking, Mr. Feynman!"* a book that became a best-seller. Feynman died of abdominal cancer in 1988.

The present selection was delivered as an address at the 1955 autumn meeting of the National Academy of Sciences.

From time to time people suggest to me that scientists ought to give more consideration to social problems—especially that they should be more responsible in considering the impact of science on society. It seems to be generally believed that if the scientists would only look at these very difficult social problems and not spend so much time fooling with less vital scientific ones, great success would come of it.

It seems to me that we *do* think about these problems from time to time, but we don't put a full-time effort into them—the reasons being that we know we don't have any magic formula for solving social problems, that social problems are very much harder than scientific ones, and that we usually don't get anywhere when we do think about them.

I believe that a scientist looking at nonscientific problems is just as dumb as the next guy—and when he talks about a nonscientific matter, he sounds as naive as anyone untrained in the matter. Since the question of the value of science is *not* a scientific subject, this talk is dedicated to proving my point—by example.

The first way in which science is of value is familiar to everyone. It is that scientific knowledge enables us to do all kinds of things and to make all kinds of things. Of course if we make *good* things, it is not only to the credit of science; it is also to the credit of the moral choice which led us to good work. Scientific knowledge is an enabling power to do either good or bad—but it does not carry instructions on how to use it. Such power has evident value—even though the power may be negated by what one does with it.

5 I learned a way of expressing this common human problem on a trip to Honolulu. In a Buddhist temple there, the man in charge explained a little bit about the Buddhist religion for tourists, and then ended his talk by telling them he had something to say to them that they would *never* forget—and I have never forgotten it. It was a proverb of the Buddhist religion:

> *To every man is given the key to the gates of heaven; the same key opens the gates of hell.*

What, then, is the value of the key to heaven? It is true that if we lack clear instructions that enable us to determine which is the gate to heaven and which the gate to hell, the key may be a dangerous object to use.

But the key obviously has value: how can we enter heaven without it?

Instructions would be of no value without the key. So it is evident that, in spite of the fact that it could produce enormous horror in the world, science is of value because it *can* produce *something.*

Another value of science is the fun called intellectual enjoyment which some people get from reading and learning and thinking about it, and which others get from working in it. This is an important point, one which is not considered enough by those who tell us it is our social responsibility to reflect on the impact of science on society.

10 Is this mere personal enjoyment of value to society as a whole? No! But it is also a responsibility to consider the aim of society itself. Is it to arrange matters so that people can enjoy things? If so, then the enjoyment of science is as important as anything else.

But I would like *not* to underestimate the value of the World view which is the result of scientific effort. We have been led to imagine all sorts of things infinitely more marvelous than the imaginings of poets and dreamers of the past. It shows that the imagination of nature is far, far greater than the imagination of man. For instance, how much more remarkable it is for us all to be stuck—half of us upside down—by a mysterious attraction to a spinning ball that has been swinging in space for billions of years than to be carried on the back of an elephant supported on a tortoise swimming in a bottomless sea.

I have thought about these things so many times alone that I hope you will excuse me if I remind you of this type of thought that I am sure many of you have had, which no one could ever have had in the past because people then didn't have the information we have about the world today.

There are the rushing waves
mountains of molecules
each stupidly minding its own business
trillions apart
yet forming white surf in unison.

Ages on ages
before any eyes could see
year after year
thunderously pounding the shore as now.
For whom, for what?
On a dead planet
with no life to entertain.

Never at rest
tortured by energy
wasted prodigiously[1] by the sun
poured into space
A mite makes the sea roar.

Deep in the sea
all molecules repeat
the patterns of one another
till complex new ones are formed.
They make others like themselves
and a new dance starts.

Growing in size and complexity
living things
masses of atoms
DNA, protein
dancing a pattern ever more intricate.

Out of the cradle
onto dry land
here it is
standing:
atoms with consciousness;
matter with curiosity.

Stands at the sea,
wonders at wondering: I

[1] prodigiously: extravagantly.

a universe of atoms
an atom in the universe.

The same thrill, the same awe and mystery, comes again and again when we look at any question deeply enough. With more knowledge comes a deeper, more wonderful mystery, luring one on to penetrate deeper still. Never concerned that the answer may prove disappointing, with pleasure and confidence we turn over each new stone to find unimagined strangeness leading on to more wonderful questions and mysteries—certainly a grand adventure!

It is true that few unscientific people have this particular type of religious experience. Our poets do not write about it; our artists do not try to portray this remarkable thing. I don't know why. Is no one inspired by our present picture of the universe? This value of science remains unsung by singers: you are reduced to hearing not a song or poem, but an evening lecture about it. This is not yet a scientific age.

15 Perhaps one of the reasons for this silence is that you have to know how to read the music. For instance, the scientific article may say, "The radioactive phosphorus content of the cerebrum of the rat decreases to one-half in a period of two weeks." Now what does that mean?

It means that phosphorous that is in the brain of a rat—and also in mine, and yours—is not the same phosphorus as it was two weeks ago. It means the atoms that are in the brain are being replaced: the ones that were there before have gone away.

So what is this mind of ours: what are these atoms with consciousness? Last week's potatoes! They now can *remember* what was going on in my mind a year ago—a mind which has long ago been replaced.

To note that the thing I call my individuality is only a pattern or dance, *that* is what it means when one discovers how long it takes for the atoms of the brain to be replaced by other atoms. The atoms come into my brain, dance a dance, and then go out—there are always new atoms, but always doing the same dance, remembering what the dance was yesterday.

When we read about this in the newspaper, it says "Scientists say this discovery may have importance in the search for a cure for cancer." The paper is only interested in the use of the idea, not the idea itself. Hardly anyone can understand the importance of an idea, it is so remarkable. Except that, possibly, some children catch on. And when a child catches on to an idea like that, we have a scientist. It is too late[2] for them to get the spirit when they are in our universities; so we must attempt to explain these ideas to children.

20 I would now like to turn to a third value that science has. It is a little less direct, but not much. The scientist has a lot of experience with ignorance and doubt and uncertainty, and this experience is of very great importance, I think. When a scientist doesn't know the answer to a problem, he is ignorant. When he has a hunch as to what the result is, he is uncertain. And when he is pretty darn

[2] I would now say, "It is late—although not too late—for them to get the spirit . . ." [Feynman's note].

sure of what the result is going to be, he is still in some doubt. We have found it of paramount importance that in order to progress we must recognize our ignorance and leave room for doubt. Scientific knowledge is a body of statements of varying degrees of certainty—some most unsure, some nearly sure, but none *absolutely* certain.

Now, we scientists are used to this, and we take it for granted that it is perfectly consistent to be unsure, that it is possible to live and *not* know. But I don't know whether everyone realizes this is true. Our freedom to doubt was born out of a struggle against authority in the early days of science. It was a very deep and strong struggle: permit us to question—to doubt—to not be sure. I think that it is important that we do not forget this struggle and thus perhaps lose what we have gained. Herein lies a responsibility to society.

We are all sad when we think of the wondrous potentialities human beings seem to have, as contrasted with their small accomplishments. Again and again people have thought that we could do much better. Those of the past saw in the nightmare of their times a dream for the future. We, of *their* future, see that their dreams, in certain ways surpassed, have in many ways remained dreams. The hopes for the future today are, in good share, those of yesterday.

It was once thought that the possibilities people had were not developed because most of the people were ignorant. With universal education, could all men be Voltaires?[3] Bad can be taught at least as efficiently as good. Education is a strong force, but for either good or evil.

Communications between nations must promote understanding—so went another dream. But the machines of communication can be manipulated. What is communicated can be truth or lie. Communication is a strong force, but also for either good or evil.

The applied sciences should free men of material problems at least. Medicine controls diseases. And the record here seems all to the good. Yet there are some patiently working today to create great plagues and poisons for use in warfare tomorrow.

Nearly everyone dislikes war. Our dream today is peace. In peace, man can develop best the enormous possibilities he seems to have. But maybe future men will find that peace, too, can be good and bad. Perhaps peaceful men will drink out of boredom. Then perhaps drink will become the great problem which seems to keep man from getting all he thinks he should out of his abilities.

Clearly, peace is a great force—as are sobriety, material power, communication, education, honesty, and the ideals of many dreamers. We have more of these forces to control than did the ancients. And maybe we are doing a little better than most of them could do. But what we ought to be able to do seems gigantic compared with our confused accomplishments.

Why is this? Why can't we conquer ourselves?

Because we find that even great forces and abilities do not seem to carry with them clear instructions on how to use them. As an example, the great accumulation of understanding as to how the physical world behaves only

[3] Voltaires: The French writer Voltaire (1694–1778) was a leading figure of the Enlightenment.

convinces one that this behavior seems to have a kind of meaninglessness. The sciences do not directly teach good and bad.

30 Through all ages of our past, people have tried to fathom the meaning of life. They have realized that if some direction or meaning could be given to our actions, great human forces would be unleashed. So very many answers have been given to the question of the meaning of it all. But the answers have been of all different sorts, and the proponents of one answer have looked with horror at the actions of the believers in another—horror, because from a disagreeing point of view all the great potentialities of the race are channeled into a false and confining blind alley. In fact, it is from the history of the enormous monstrosities created by false belief that philosophers have realized the apparently infinite and wondrous capacities of human beings. The dream is to find the open channel.

What, then, is the meaning of it all? What can we say to dispel the mystery of existence?

If we take everything into account—not only what the ancients knew, but all of what we know today that they didn't know—then I think we must frankly admit that *we do not know*.

But, in admitting this, we have probably found the open channel.

This is not a new idea; this is the idea of the age of reason. This is the philosophy that guided the men who made the democracy that we live under. The idea that no one really knew how to run a government led to the idea that we should arrange a system by which new ideas could be developed, tried out, and tossed out if necessary, with more new ideas brought in—a trial-and-error system. This method was a result of the fact that science was already showing itself to be a successful venture at the end of the eighteenth century. Even then it was clear to socially minded people that the openness of possibilities was an opportunity, and that doubt and discussion were essential to progress into the unknown. If we want to solve a problem that we have never solved before, we must leave the door to the unknown ajar.

35 We are at the very beginning of time for the human race. It is not unreasonable that we grapple with problems. But there are tens of thousands of years in the future. Our responsibility is to do what we can, learn what we can, improve the solutions, and pass them on. It is our responsibility to leave the people of the future a free hand. In the impetuous youth of humanity, we can make grave errors that can stunt our growth for a long time. This we will do if we say we have the answers now, so young and ignorant as we are. If we suppress all discussion, all criticism, proclaiming "This is the answer, my friends; man is saved!" we will doom humanity for a long time to the chains of authority, confined to the limits of our present imagination. It has been done so many times before.

It is our responsibility as scientists, knowing the great progress which comes from a satisfactory philosophy of ignorance, the great progress which is the fruit of freedom of thought, to proclaim the value of this freedom; to teach how doubt is not to be feared but welcomed and discussed; and to demand this freedom as our duty to all coming generations.

LEARNING MORE

This is an unusually—and characteristically—accessible address. Feynman relies on only one significant allusion, and that is to the Enlightenment (or the Age of Reason). So it will be useful to know the main outlines of the events and ideas he refers to. For useful links, see the *Ideas Across Time* website.

QUESTIONING THE TEXT

1. According to Feynman, are scientists especially suited to discussing the value of science? Explain.
2. What does Feynman say are the three ways that science is valuable?
3. What is the drawback to science's ability to produce things?
4. According to Feynman, what is the scientific worldview?
5. Why does Feynman think that "[t]his is not yet a scientific age" (par. 14)?
6. What, for Feynman, is the significance of the fact that we do not know the meaning of life?
7. What does Feynman believe is our duty to all coming generations?
8. This talk was delivered in 1955. In what ways might it be a response to the American political context at that time, in the years of the Cold War, when certainty was at a premium?

ANALYZING THE WRITER'S CRAFT

1. Does this essay have a thesis statement? If so, where is it found in the essay? If not, what gives the essay coherence?
2. What aspects of this essay reveal that it was originally a speech?
3. Why does Feynman place certain of his ideas in poetry form? What makes this part of his writing poetry?
4. What is the tone of this essay? How would you characterize the diction in this essay?
5. What do you think is the impact on the reader of Feynman's overwhelming reliance on simple declarative sentences?
6. Why does Feynman bring in the Age of Reason to support his argument?
7. How effective is Feynman's conclusion?

MAKING CONNECTIONS

1. Compare and contrast Feynman's notion of science and its value with Francis Bacon's (pp. 152–155).
2. Compare and contrast what William James (Chapter 2, pp. 113–121), Einstein (pp. 193–200), and Feynman have to say about the relation of science and religion.
3. Compare and contrast Feynman's no-nonsense approach to his subject matter with that of Tom Paine (Chapter 2, pp. 98–103).

4. Compare and contrast Feynman's understanding of the Age of Reason as fostering "a satisfactory philosophy of ignorance" (par. 36) with what the eighteenth-century writers themselves say (see John Locke and Jean-Jacques Rousseau's selections, for example, in Chapters 5 and 6, respectively).

FORMULATING IDEAS FOR WRITING

1. According to Feynman, "social problems are very much harder than scientific ones" (par. 2). What does Feynman have in mind? Do you agree? (How many scientific problems can *you* solve?)
2. Is it accurate to call a sense of wonder at what science reveals a "particular type of religious experience" (par. 14)? Or is Paul Tillich more on the right track about what ought to be called religious in his "The Lost Dimension in Religion" (Chapter 2, pp. 123–130)?
3. What does Feynman imply is the relation between science and democracy? Do you agree? Do Daniel J. Boorstin's ideas in "Technology and Democracy" (Chapter 5, pp. 390–402) add a qualifying note to any discussion of this relationship?
4. Write an essay that assesses Feynman's speech in the context of American politics at the time it was delivered (1955).

Life on the Rocks: The Galápagos (1982)

Annie Dillard

Annie Dillard, born Meta Annie Doak, is one of the most original, as well as unsettling, contemporary observers of the natural world. Born in Pittsburgh, Pennsylvania, in 1945, she is the eldest of three daughters of an affluent family, and she speaks of her childhood with affectionate recollection. She attended Hollis College in Virginia, where, in her sophomore year, she married her writing teacher, the poet R. H. W. Dillard. In 1971, after a near-fatal bout of pneumonia, Annie Dillard began writing an extended meditation on nature that eventually appeared under the title *Pilgrim at Tinker Creek* (1974), for which she won the Pulitzer Prize. The book exhibits her characteristic qualities of acute observation combined with a contemplative, even theological apprehension of the natural world. In 1980, Dillard married her second husband, Gary Clevidence, and with him moved to the Northeast and began teaching at Wesleyan University in Middletown, Connecticut, where she remains today as writer-in-residence. Her memoir *An American Childhood* appeared in 1987, a year before her third marriage, to Robert Richardson. Dillard's most recent work is the nonfiction narrative *For the Time Being* (1999). "Life on the Rocks: The Galápagos," her observations on the famous Galápagos Islands off Ecuador, the place where Darwin is said to have conceived his breakthrough idea of natural selection (see pp. 167–180), is taken from *Teaching a Stone to Talk: Expeditions and Encounters* (1982).

I

First there was nothing, and although you know with your reason that nothing is nothing, it is easier to visualize it as a limitless slosh of sea—say, the Pacific. Then energy contracted into matter, and although you know that even an invisible gas is matter, it is easier to visualize it as a massive squeeze of volcanic lava spattered inchoate[1] from the secret pit of the ocean and hardening mute and intractable on nothing's lapping shore—like a series of islands, an archipelago. Like: the Galápagos.[2] Then a softer strain of matter began to twitch. It was a kind of shaped water; it flowed, hardening here and there at its tips. There were blue-green algae; there were tortoises.

The ice rolled up, the ice rolled back, and I knelt on a plain of lava boulders in the islands called Galápagos, stroking a giant tortoise's neck. The tortoise closed its eyes and stretched its neck to its greatest height and vulnerability. I rubbed that neck, and when I pulled away my hand, my palm was green with a slick of single-celled algae. I stared at the algae, and at the tortoise, the way you stare at any life on a lava flow, and thought: Well—here we all are.

Being here is being here on the rocks. These Galapagonian rocks, one of them seventy-five miles long, have dried under the equatorial sun between five and six hundred miles west of the South American continent; they lie at the latitude of the Republic of Ecuador, to which they belong.

There is a way a small island rises from the ocean affronting all reason. It is a chunk of chaos pounded into visibility *ex nihilo:*[3] here rough, here smooth, shaped just so by a matrix of physical necessities too weird to contemplate, here instead of there, here instead of not at all. It is a fantastic utterance, as though I were to open my mouth and emit a French horn, or a vase, or a knob of telluriun.[4] It smacks of folly, of first causes.

5 I think of the island called Daphnecita, little Daphne, on which I never set foot. It's in half of my few photographs, though, because it obsessed me: a dome of gray lava like a pitted loaf, the size of the Plaza Hotel, glazed with guano and crawling with red-orange crabs. Sometimes I attributed to this island's cliff face a surly, infantile consciousness, as though it were sulking in the silent moment after it had just shouted, to the sea and the sky, "I didn't ask to be born." Or sometimes it aged to a raging adolescent, a kid who's just learned that the game

[1] inchoate: undeveloped; unformed.

[2] Galapagos: group of extremely isolated volcanic islands off the coast of Ecuador in South America that were visited by Charles Darwin in 1835 and that inspired his thinking about evolution.

[3] *ex nihilo:* Latin for "out of nothing."

[4] tellurium: white, shiny, brittle substance; one of the rare elements.

is fixed, demanding, "What did you have me for, if you're just going to push me around?" Daphnecita: again, a wise old island, mute, leading the life of pure creaturehood open to any antelope or saint. After you've blown the ocean sky-high, what's there to say? What if we the people had the sense or grace to live as cooled islands in an archipelago live, with dignity, passion, and no comment?

It is worth flying to Guayaquil, Ecuador, and then to Baltra in the Galápagos just to see the rocks. But these rocks are animal gardens. They are home to a Hieronymus Bosch[5] assortment of windblown, stowaway, castaway, flotsam, and shipwrecked creatures. Most exist nowhere else on earth. These reptiles and insects, small mammals and birds, evolved unmolested on the various islands on which they were cast into unique species adapted to the boulder-wrecked shores, the cactus deserts of the low-lands, or the elevated jungles of the large islands' interiors. You come for the animals. You come to see the curious shapes soft proteins can take, to impress yourself with their reality, and to greet them. . . .

The animals are tame. They have not been persecuted, and show no fear of man. You pass among them as though you were wind, spindrift, sunlight, leaves. The songbirds are tame. On Hood Island I sat beside a nesting waved albatross while a mockingbird scratched in my hair, another mockingbird jabbed at my fingernail, and a third mockingbird made an exquisite progression of pokes at my bare feet up the long series of eyelets in my basketball shoes. The marine iguanas are tame. . . . The wild hawk is tame. The Galápagos hawk is related to North America's Swainson's hawk; I have read that if you take pains, you can walk up and pat it. I never tried. We people don't walk up and pat each other; enough is enough. The animals' critical distance and mine tended to coincide, so we could enjoy an easy sociability without threat of violence or unwonted intimacy. The hawk, which is not notably sociable, nevertheless endures even a blundering approach, and is apparently as content to perch on a scrub tree at your shoulder as anyplace else.

In the Galápagos, even the flies are tame. Although most of the land is Ecuadorian national park, and as such rigidly protected, I confess I gave the evolutionary ball an offsides shove by dispatching every fly that bit me, marveling the while at its pristine ignorance, its blithe failure to register a flight trigger at the sweep of my descending hand—an insouciance that was almost, but not quite, disarming. After you kill a fly, you pick it up and feed it to a lava lizard, a bright-throated four-inch lizard that scavenges everywhere in the arid lowlands. And you walk on, passing among the innocent mobs on every rock hillside; or you sit, and they come to you.

We are strangers and sojourners, soft dots on the rocks. You have walked along the strand and seen where birds have landed, walked, and flown; their tracks begin in sand, and go, and suddenly end. Our tracks do that: but we go down. And stay down. While we're here, during the seasons our tents are pitched in the light, we pass among each other crying "greetings" in a thousand tongues,

---

[5] Hieronymus Bosch: Dutch painter (1450–1516) of surreal landscapes with half-human animals and machines, depicting an agonized human condition.

and "welcome," and "good-bye." Inhabitants of uncrowded colonies tend to offer the stranger famously warm hospitality—and such are the Galápagos sea lions. Theirs is the greeting the first creatures must have given Adam—a hero's welcome, a universal and undeserved huzzah. Go, and be greeted by sea lions.

I was sitting with ship's naturalist Soames Summerhays on a sand beach under cliffs on uninhabited Hood Island. The white beach was a havoc of lava boulders black as clinkers, sleek with spray, and lambent[6] as brass in the sinking sun. To our left a dozen sea lions were body-surfing in the long green combers that rose, translucent, half a mile offshore. When the combers broke, the shoreline boulders rolled. I could feel the roar in the rough rock on which I sat; I could hear the grate inside each long backsweeping sea, the rumble of a rolled million rocks muffled in splashes and the seethe before the next wave's heave.

To our right, a sea lion slipped from the ocean. It was a young bull; in another few years he would be dangerous, bellowing at intruders and biting off great dirty chunks of the ones he caught. Now this young bull, which weighed maybe 120 pounds, sprawled silhouetted in the late light, slick as a drop of quicksilver, his glistening whiskers radii of gold like any crown. He hauled his packed bulk toward us up the long beach; he flung himself with an enormous surge of fur-clad muscle onto the boulder where I sat. "Soames," I said—very quietly, "he's here because *we're* here, isn't he?" The naturalist nodded. I felt water drip on my elbow behind me, then the fragile scrape of whiskers, and finally the wet warmth and weight of a muzzle, as the creature settled to sleep on my arm. I was catching on to sea lions.

Walk into the water. Instantly sea lions surround you, even if none has been in sight. To say that they come to play with you is not especially anthropomorphic.[7] Animals play. The bull sea lions are off patrolling their territorial shores; these are the cows and young, which range freely. A five-foot sea lion peers intently into your face, then urges her muzzle gently against your underwater mask and searches your eyes without blinking. Next she rolls upside down and slides along the length of your floating body, rolls again, and casts a long glance back at your eyes. You are, I believe, supposed to follow, and think up something clever in return. You can play games with sea lions in the water using shells or bits of leaf, if you are willing. You can spin on your vertical axis and a sea lion will swim circles around you, keeping her face always six inches from yours, as though she were tethered. You can make a game of touching their back flippers, say, and the sea lions will understand at once; somersaulting conveniently before your clumsy hands, they will give you an excellent field of back flippers.

And when you leave the water, they follow. They don't want you to go. They porpoise to the shore, popping their heads up when they lose you and casting about, then speeding to your side and emitting a choked series of vocal

[6] lambent: flamelike; radiant.

[7] anthropomorphic: having human form and character.

notes. If you won't relent, they disappear, barking; but if you sit on the beach with so much as a foot in the water, two or three will station with you, floating on their backs and saying, Urr. . . .

II

Charles Darwin[8] came to the Galápagos in 1835, on the *Beagle;* he was twenty-six [sic]. He threw the marine iguanas as far as he could into the water; he rode the tortoises and sampled their meat. He noticed that the tortoises' carapaces[9] varied wildly from island to island; so also did the forms of various mockingbirds. He made collections. Nine years later he wrote in a letter, "I am almost convinced (quite contrary to the opinion I started with) that species are not (it is like confessing a murder) immutable." In 1859 he published *On the Origin of Species,* and in 1871 *The Descent of Man.* It is fashionable now to disparage Darwin's originality; not even the surliest of his detractors, however, faults his painstaking methods or denies his impact.

15 Darwinism today is more properly called neo-Darwinism. It is organic evolutionary theory informed by the spate of new data from modern genetics, molecular biology, paleobiology—from the new wave of the biologic revolution which spread after Darwin's announcement like a tsunami. The data are not all in. Crucial first appearances of major invertebrate groups are missing from the fossil record—but these early forms, sometimes modified larvae, tended to be fragile either by virtue of their actual malleability or by virtue of their scarcity and rapid variation into "hardened," successful forms. Lack of proof in this direction doesn't worry scientists. What neo-Darwinism seriously lacks, however, is a description of the actual mechanism of mutation in the chromosomal nucleotides. . . .

So much for scientists. The rest of us didn't hear Darwin as a signal to dive down into the wet nucleus of a cell and surface with handfuls of strange new objects. We were still worried about the book with the unfortunate word in the title: *The Descent of Man.* It was dismaying to imagine great-grandma and great-grandpa effecting a literal, nimble descent from some liana-covered tree to terra firma, scratching themselves, and demanding bananas.

Fundamentalist Christians, of course, still reject Darwinism because it conflicts with the creation account in Genesis. Fundamentalist Christians have a very bad press. Ill feeling surfaces when, from time to time in small towns, they object again to the public schools' teaching evolutionary theory. Tragically, these people feel they have to make a choice between the Bible and modern science. They live and work in the same world as we, and know the derision they face from people whose areas of ignorance are perhaps different, who dismantled their mangers when they moved to town and threw out the baby with the straw. . . .

---

[8] Darwin: see pp. 167–180.

[9] carapaces: body shells.

Darwin gave us time. Before Darwin (and Huxley, Wallace, et al.)[10] there was in the nineteenth century what must have been a fairly nauseating period: people knew about fossils of extinct species, but did not yet know about organic evolution. They thought the fossils were litter from a series of past creations. At any rate, for many, this creation, the world as we know it, had begun in 4004 B.C., a date set by Irish Archbishop James Ussher in the seventeenth century. We were all crouched in a small room against the comforting back wall, awaiting the millennium which had been gathering impetus since Adam and Eve. Up there was a universe, and down here would be a small strip of man come and gone, created, taught, redeemed, and gathered up in a bright twinkling, like a sprinkling of confetti torn from colored papers, tossed from windows, and swept from the streets by morning.

The Darwinian revolution knocked out the back wall, revealing eerie lighted landscapes as far back as we can see. Almost at once, Albert Einstein and astronomers with reflector telescopes and radio telescopes knocked out the other walls and the ceiling, leaving us sunlit, exposed, and drifting—leaving us puckers, albeit evolving puckers, on the inbound curve of space-time.

III

20 It all began in the Galápagos, with these finches. The finches in the Galápagos are called Darwin's finches; they are everywhere in the islands, sparrowlike, and almost identical but for their differing beaks. At first Darwin scarcely noticed their importance. But by 1839, when he revised his *Journal* of the *Beagle* voyage, he added a key sentence about the finches' beaks: "Seeing this gradation and diversity of structure in one small, intimately related group of birds, one might really fancy that from an original paucity of birds in this archipelago, one species had been taken and modified for different ends." And so it was. . . .

Darwin's finches are not brightly colored; they are black, gray, brown, or faintly olive. Their names are even duller: the large ground finch, the medium ground finch, the small ground finch; the large insectivorous tree finch; the vegetarian tree finch; the cactus ground finch, and so forth. But the beaks are interesting, and the beaks' origins even more so.

Some finches wield chunky parrot beaks modified for cracking seeds. Some have slender warbler beaks, short for nabbing insects, long for probing plants. One sports the long chisel beak of a woodpecker; it bores wood for insect grubs and often uses a twig or cactus spine as a pickle fork when the grub won't dislodge. They have all evolved, fanwise, from one bird.

The finches evolved in isolation. So did everything else on earth. With the finches, you can see how it happened. The Galápagos islands are near enough to the mainland that some strays could hazard there; they are far enough away

---

[10] Huxley and Wallace: Thomas Henry Huxley (1825–1895) was the leading popularizer of science in the Victorian era, known as "Darwin's Bulldog" for his fierce defense of Darwin. Alfred Russel Wallace (1823–1913) was a naturalist whose independent work on the theory of natural selection prompted Darwin to publish *Origin of Species* in 1859.

that those strays could evolve in isolation from parent species. And the separate islands are near enough to each other for further dispersal, further isolation, and the eventual reassembling of distinct species. (In other words, finches blew to the Galápagos, blew to various islands, evolved into differing species, and blew back together again.) The tree finches and the ground finches, the woodpecker finch and the warbler finch, veered into being on isolated rocks. The witless green sea shaped those beaks as surely as it shaped the beaches. Now on the finches in the *palo santo* tree you see adaptive radiation's results, a fluorescent splay of horn. It is as though an archipelago were an arpeggio, a rapid series of distinct but related notes. If the Galápagos had been one unified island, there would be one dull note, one super-dull finch.

IV

Now let me carry matters to an imaginary, and impossible, extreme. If the earth were one unified island, a smooth ball, we would all be one species, a tremulous muck. The fact is that when you get down to this business of species formation, you eventually hit some form of reproductive isolation. Cells tend to fuse. Cells tend to engulf each other; primitive creatures tend to move in on each other and on us, to colonize, aggregate, blur. (Within species, individuals have evolved immune reactions, which help preserve individual integrity; you might reject my liver—or someday my brain.) As much of the world's energy seems to be devoted to keeping us apart as was directed to bringing us here in the first place. All sorts of different creatures can mate and produce fertile offspring: two species of snapdragon, for instance, or mallard and pintail ducks. But they don't. They live apart, so they don't mate. When you scratch the varying behaviors and conditions behind reproductive isolation, you find, ultimately, geographical isolation. Once the isolation has occurred, of course, forms harden out, enforcing reproductive isolation, so that snapdragons will never mate with pintail ducks.

25 Geography is the key, the crucial accident of birth. A piece of protein could be a snail, a sea lion, or a systems analyst, but it had to start somewhere. This is not science; it is merely metaphor. And the landscape in which the protein "starts" shapes its end as surely as bowls shape water.

We have all, as it were, blown back together like the finches, and it's hard to imagine the isolation from parent species in which we evolved. The frail beginnings of great phyla are lost in the crushed histories of cells. Now we see the embellishments of random chromosomal mutations selected by natural selection and preserved in geographically isolate gene pools as *faits accomplis,*[11] as the differentiated fringe of brittle knobs that is life as we know it. The process is still going on, but there is no turning back; it happened, in the cells. Geographical determination is not the cow-caught-in-a-crevice business I make it seem. I'm dealing in imagery, working toward a picture.

Geography is life's limiting factor. Speciation—life itself—is ultimately a matter of warm and cool currents, rich and bare soils, deserts and forests, fresh

[11] *faits accomplis:* French for something already completed and, by implication, irreversible.

and salt waters, deltas and jungles and plains. Species arise in isolation. A plaster cast is as intricate as its mold; life is a gloss on geography. And if you dig your fists into the earth and crumble geography, you strike geology. Climate is the wind of the mineral earth's rondure, tilt, and orbit modified by local geological conditions. The Pacific Ocean, the Negev Desert,[12] and the rain forest in Brazil are local geological conditions. So are the slow carp pools and splashing trout riffles of any backyard creek. It is all, God help us, a matter of rocks.

The rocks shape life like hands around swelling dough. In Virginia, the salamanders vary from mountain ridge to mountain ridge; so do the fiddle tunes the old men play. All this is because it is hard to move from mountain to mountain. These are not merely anomalous details. This is what life is all about: salamanders, fiddle tunes, you and me and things, the split and burr of it all, the fizz into particulars. No mountains and one salamander, one fiddle tune, would be a lesser world. No continents, no fiddlers. No possum, no sop, no taters. The earth, without form, is void.

The mountains are time's machines; in effect, they roll out protoplasm[13] like printers' rollers pressing out news. But life is already part of the landscape, a limiting factor in space; life too shapes life. Geology's rocks and climate have already become Brazil's rain forest, yielding shocking bright birds. To say that all life is an interconnected membrane, a weft of linkages like chain mail, is truism. But in this case, too, the Galápagos islands afford a clear picture.

On Santa Cruz island, for instance, the saddleback carapaces of tortoises enable them to stretch high and reach the succulent pads of prickly pear cactus. But the prickly pear cactus on that island, and on other tortoise islands, has evolved a treelike habit; those lower pads get harder to come by. Without limiting factors, the two populations could stretch right into the stratosphere.

Ça va.[14] It goes on everywhere, tit for tat, action and reaction, triggers and inhibitors ascending in a spiral like spatting butterflies. Within life, we are pushing each other around. How many animal forms have evolved just so because there are, for instance, trees? We pass the nitrogen around, and vital gases; we feed and nest, plucking this and that and planting seeds. The protoplasm responds, nudged and nudging, bearing the news.

And the rocks themselves shall be moved. The rocks themselves are not pure necessity, given, like vast, complex molds around which the rest of us swirl. They heave to their own necessities, to stirrings and prickings from within and without.

The mountains are no more fixed than the stars. Granite, for example, contains much oxygen and is relatively light. It "floats." When granite forms under the earth's crust, great chunks of it bob up, I read somewhere, like dumplings. The continents themselves are beautiful pea-green boats. The Galápagos

---

[12] Negev Desert: desert that constitutes 65 percent of Israel's land; the place where Abraham, Isaac, and Jacob tended their sheep.

[13] protoplasm: substance that constitutes the physical basis of life.

[14] *Ça va:* French for "It goes."

archipelago as a whole is surfing toward Ecuador; South America is sliding toward the Galápagos; North America, too, is sailing westward. We're on floating islands, shaky ground.

So the rocks shape life, and then life shapes life, and the rocks are moving. The completed picture needs one more element: life shapes the rocks.

Life is more than a live green scum on a dead pool, a shimmering scurf like slime mold on rock. Look at the planet. Everywhere freedom twines its way around necessity, inventing new strings of occasions, lassoing time and putting it through its varied and spirited paces. Everywhere live things lash at the rocks. Softness is vulnerable, but it has a will; tube worms bore and coral atolls rise. Lichens in delicate lobes are chewing the granite mountains; forests in serried ranks trammel the hills. Man has more freedom than other live things; anti-entropically,[15] he batters a bigger dent in the given, damming the rivers, planting the plains, drawing in his mind's eye dotted lines between the stars. . . .

Like boys on dolphins, the continents ride their crustal plates. New lands shoulder up from the waves, and old lands buckle under. The very landscapes heave; change burgeons into change. Gray granite bobs up, red clay compresses; yellow sandstone tilts, surging in forests, incised by streams. The mountains tremble, the ice rasps back and forth, and the protoplasm furls in shock waves, up the rock valleys and down, ramifying possibilities, riddling the mountains. Life and the rocks, like spirit and matter, are a fringed matrix, lapped and lapping, clasping and held. It is like hand washing hand. It is like hand washing hand and the whole tumult hurled. The planet spins, rapt inside its intricate mists. The galaxy is a flung thing, loose in the night, and our solar system is one of many dotted campfires ringed with tossed rocks. What shall we sing?

What shall we sing, while the fire burns down? We can sing only specifics, time's rambling tune, the places we have seen, the faces we have known. I will sing you the Galápagos islands, the sea lions soft on the rocks. It's all still happening there, in real light, the cool currents upwelling, the finches falling on the wind, the shearwaters looping the waves. I could go back, or I could go on; or I could sit down, like Kubla Khan:

Weave a circle round him thrice,
  And close your eyes with holy dread,
For he on honey-dew hath fed,
  And drunk the milk of Paradise.[16]

LEARNING MORE

1. The Galápagos were made famous by Charles Darwin (pp. 167–180). His *The Voyage of the Beagle* (1839) recounts his encounter with the unique

[15] anti-entropically: Entropy is a condition of thermodynamic systems that tends toward inert uniformity.

[16] . . . Paradise: from the poem "Kubla Khan" by one of the great English Romantics, Samuel Taylor Coleridge (1772–1834).

species on these islands, and his subsequent writings and letters explain the origin of these species. To read Darwin on the Galápagos, see the *Ideas Across Time* website.

2. Dillard ends her essay with some lines from Samuel Taylor Coleridge's poem "Kubla Khan." For the whole poem and useful links, see the *Ideas Across Time* website.

QUESTIONING THE TEXT

1. Why do you think Dillard begins literally at the beginning, echoing Genesis (see Chapter 2, pp. 106–107)?
2. What do you think Dillard means by "Being here is being here on the rocks" (par. 3)?
3. How does an island smack "of first causes" (par. 4)?
4. What is Dillard's attitude toward the animals of the Galápagos? Illustrate and explain.
5. Why is Darwin's *The Descent of Man* a book with an "unfortunate" title (par. 16)? Why does Dillard think it tragic that fundamentalist Christians "feel they have to make a choice between the Bible and modern science" (par. 17)? What alternative does she propose?
6. Dillard gives a dramatic, albeit disarmingly offhand, abbreviation of the impact of modern science on the human perception of life, encapsulated in the idea that science has knocked out the "comforting back wall" of the "small room" in which "we were all crouched" before Darwin. Just what is it Dillard has in mind here?
7. How do Darwin's finches show how evolution works?
8. Dillard concludes her account of evolution by saying, "It is all, God help us, a matter of rocks" (par. 27). Why is it "a matter of rocks"?
9. How does Dillard imagine the nature of being, of living and nonliving things, in the universe? What is your reaction to this picture? What is the place of human beings in Dillard's picture of the universe?
10. How has Dillard "drunk the milk of Paradise" (par. 37)?
11. How is Dillard's account of the Galápagos different from an evolutionary biologist's? What does she add to a strictly biological account of the islands?

ANALYZING THE WRITER'S CRAFT

1. How does Dillard's introduction establish the set of questions explored in the rest of her essay?
2. What is the effect of Dillard's use of dramatic and somewhat ambiguous topic sentences, such as "Being here is being here on the rocks" (par. 3) or "We are strangers and sojourners, soft dots on the rocks" (par. 9)?
3. What is Dillard's tone in this essay? Illustrate and explain.
4. This is an essay composed of four large sections, each further subdivided into a number of sections. How does Dillard effect the transitions

between sections of and within the sections of her essay? Do you find them effective?

5. Dillard aims through her writing to give readers a graphic, or felt, account of the animals on the Galápagos, so readers can feel as if they too are there on the rocks. Choose a paragraph in which you think she is especially successful at making readers feel they are right there on the islands with Dillard, and discuss how she achieves her effects.
6. Does this essay have a thesis statement? If so, what is it, and where in the essay is it located? If not, how does the essay maintain coherence?
7. What do you think Dillard means by saying, "This is not science; it is merely metaphor" (par. 25)? What metaphor is she referring to? How is metaphor different from science?
8. Is Dillard's conclusion an effective way to close her essay? Explain.

MAKING CONNECTIONS

1. How well does Dillard understand Darwin (pp. 167–180)?
2. Compare and contrast Dillard's view of the animals on the Galápagos and Virginia Woolf's "The Death of a Moth" (Chapter 8, pp. 650–653).
3. Dillard ends her meditation with an aesthetic/religious question: "What shall we sing, while the fire burns down?" Does she imply a special role here for art? What else can assuage as the fire burns down?
4. Dillard wrote her M.A. thesis on Henry David Thoreau's *Walden.* If you have read *Walden*, can you see an affinity between Dillard and Thoreau? Can you see an affinity between this essay of Dillard's and Thoreau's "Civil Disobedience" (Chapter 5, pp. 371–383)?

FORMULATING IDEAS FOR WRITING

1. Is this a comforting or dismaying account of the human place within nature and the cosmos?
2. Using Dillard's description of the sea lions as a point of reference, write an essay about an especially evocative incident (or series of incidents) involving you and animals.
3. Dillard discusses Darwin as if the impact of his work can be separated into impact on scientists—mutation of chromosomal nucleotides still needs explanation—and impact on "the rest of us," still worried about that word "descent" in *The Descent of Man.* Is this an appropriate distinction? Does Darwin's impact on society have more to do with metaphor than science?
4. Why do you think Dillard went to the Galápagos? Did she find there what she went there to find? What impact did her visit have on her outlook on life?
5. How does Dillard's diction help convey her interpretation of the implications of the Galápagos?

How Computers Change the Way We Think (2004)

Sherry Turkle

Sherry Turkle (b. 1948) studies the relation between human emotions and technology, especially computers, work for which she has been dubbed the nation's "cybershrink." Computers can create "a kind of crisis about the simulated and the real," she says, because of the complex confusions of identity the Internet encourages. When an MUD (a multiuser domain) asks you for five nicknames to use on the system, she says, how does a person cope with " 'being' Armaniboy in some online discussions, but Motorcycle-man, Too-serious, Aquinas, and Lipstick in others"?

Born in New York City and educated at Radcliffe and the University of Chicago, Turkle earned a joint Ph.D. in sociology and personality psychology from Harvard in 1976. She is a member of the Boston Psychoanalytical Society and a licensed clinical psychologist. Her books include *The Second Self: Computers and the Human Spirit* (1984) and *Life on the Screen; Identity in the Age of the Internet* (1995). Turkle is editing a three-volume collection for the M.I.T. Press on the relationship between things and thinking: *Evocative Objects: Things We Think With, Objects in Mind: Falling for Science, Technology, and Design,* and *The Inner History of Devices.* She is the Abby Rockefeller Mauze Professor of the Social Studies of Science and Technology at the Massachusetts Institute of Technology as well as director of the M.I.T. Initiative on Technology and the Self, a research center for study of the connections between people and artifacts.

"How Computers Change the Way We Think" first appeared in *The Chronicle of Higher Education,* a journal read mainly by professors and college administrators, in 2004.

The tools we use to think change the ways in which we think. The invention of written language brought about a radical shift in how we process, organize, store, and transmit representations of the world. Although writing remains our primary information technology, today when we think about the impact of technology on our habits of mind, we think primarily of the computer.

My first encounters with how computers change the way we think came soon after I joined the faculty at the Massachusetts Institute of Technology in the late 1970s, at the end of the era of the slide rule and the beginning of the era of the personal computer. At a lunch for new faculty members, several senior professors in engineering complained that the transition from slide rules to calculators had affected their students' ability to deal with issues of scale. When students used slide rules, they had to insert decimal points themselves. The professors insisted that that required students to maintain a mental sense of scale, whereas those who relied on calculators made frequent errors in orders of magnitude. Additionally, the students with calculators had lost their ability to do "back of the envelope" calculations, and with that, an intuitive feel for the material.

That same semester, I taught a course in the history of psychology. There, I experienced the impact of computational objects on students' ideas about their emotional lives. My class had read Freud's essay on slips of the tongue, with its famous first example: The chairman of a parliamentary session opens a meeting by declaring it closed. The students discussed how Freud interpreted such errors as revealing a person's mixed emotions. A computer-science major disagreed with Freud's approach. The mind, she argued, is a computer. And in a computational dictionary—like we have in the human mind—"closed" and "open" are designated by the same symbol, separated by a sign for opposition. "Closed" equals "minus open." To substitute "closed" for "open" does not require the notion of ambivalence or conflict.

"When the chairman made that substitution," she declared, "a bit was dropped; a minus sign was lost. There was a power surge. No problem."

5 The young woman turned a Freudian slip into an information-processing error. An explanation in terms of meaning had become an explanation in terms of mechanism.

Such encounters turned me to the study of both the instrumental and the subjective sides of the nascent computer culture. As an ethnographer and psychologist, I began to study not only what the computer was doing *for* us, but what it was doing *to* us, including how it was changing the way we see ourselves, our sense of human identity.

In the 1980s, I surveyed the psychological effects of computational objects in everyday life—largely the unintended side effects of people's tendency to project thoughts and feelings onto their machines. In the 20 years since, computational objects have become more explicitly designed to have emotional and cognitive effects. And those "effects by design" will become even stronger in the decade to come. Machines are being designed to serve explicitly as companions, pets, and tutors. And they are introduced in school settings for the youngest children.

Today, starting in elementary school, students use e-mail, word processing, computer simulations, virtual communities, and PowerPoint software. In the process, they are absorbing more than the content of what appears on their screens. They are learning new ways to think about what it means to know and understand.

What follows is a short and certainly not comprehensive list of areas where I see information technology encouraging changes in thinking. There can be no simple way of cataloging whether any particular change is good or bad. That is contested terrain. At every step we have to ask, as educators and citizens, whether current technology is leading us in directions that serve our human purposes. Such questions are not technical; they are social, moral, and political.

For me, addressing that subjective side of computation is one of the more significant challenges for the next decade of information technology in higher education. Technology does not determine change, but it encourages us to take certain directions. If we make those directions clear, we can more easily exert human choice.

10 **Thinking about privacy.** Today's college students are habituated to a world of online blogging, instant messaging, and Web browsing that leaves electronic traces. Yet they have had little experience with the right to privacy. Unlike past generations of Americans, who grew up with the notion that the privacy of their mail was sacrosanct, our children are accustomed to electronic surveillance as part of their daily lives.

I have colleagues who feel that the increased incursions on privacy have put the topic more in the news, and that this is a positive change. But middle-school and high-school students tend to be willing to provide personal information online with no safeguards, and college students seem uninterested in violations of privacy and in increased governmental and commercial surveillance. Professors find that students do not understand that in a democracy, privacy is a right, not merely a privilege. In ten years, ideas about the relationship of privacy and government will require even more active pedagogy. (One might also hope that increased education about the kinds of silent surveillance that technology makes possible may inspire more active political engagement with the issue.)

Avatars or a self? Chat rooms, role-playing games, and other technological venues offer us many different contexts for presenting ourselves online. Those possibilities are particularly important for adolescents because they offer what Erik Erikson described as a moratorium, a time out or safe space for the personal experimentation that is so crucial for adolescent development. Our dangerous world—with crime, terrorism, drugs, and AIDS—offers little in the way of safe spaces. Online worlds can provide valuable spaces for identity play.

But some people who gain fluency in expressing multiple aspects of self may find it harder to develop authentic selves. Some children who write narratives for their screen avatars may grow up with too little experience of how to share their real feelings with other people. For those who are lonely yet afraid of intimacy, information technology has made it possible to have the illusion of companionship without the demands of friendship.

From powerful ideas to PowerPoint. In the 1970s and early 1980s, some educators wanted to make programming part of the regular curriculum for K–12 education. They argued that because information technology carries ideas, it might as well carry the most powerful ideas that computer science has to offer. It is ironic that in most elementary schools today, the ideas being carried by information technology are not ideas from computer science like procedural thinking, but more likely to be those embedded in productivity tools like PowerPoint presentation software.

15 PowerPoint does more than provide a way of transmitting content. It carries its own way of thinking, its own aesthetic—which not surprisingly shows up in the aesthetic of college freshmen. In that aesthetic, presentation becomes its own powerful idea.

To be sure, the software cannot be blamed for lower intellectual standards. Misuse of the former is as much a symptom as a cause of the latter. Indeed, the culture in which our children are raised is increasingly a culture of presentation, a corporate culture in which appearance is often more important than reality. In contemporary political discourse, the bar has also been lowered. Use of rhetorical devices at the expense of cogent argument regularly goes without notice. But it is precisely because standards of intellectual rigor outside the educational sphere have fallen that educators must attend to how we use, and when we introduce, software that has been designed to simplify the organization and processing of information.

In "The Cognitive Style of PowerPoint" (Graphics Press, 2003), Edward R. Tufte suggests that PowerPoint equates bulleting with clear thinking. It does not teach students to begin a discussion or construct a narrative. It encourages presentation, not conversation. Of course, in the hands of a master teacher, a PowerPoint presentation with few words and powerful images can serve as the jumping-off point for a brilliant lecture. But in the hands of elementary-school students, often introduced to PowerPoint in the third grade, and often infatuated with its swooshing sounds, animated icons, and flashing text, a slide show is more likely to close down debate than open it up.

Developed to serve the needs of the corporate boardroom, the software is designed to convey absolute authority. Teachers used to tell students that clear exposition depended on clear outlining, but presentation software has fetishized the outline at the expense of the content.

Narrative, the exposition of content, takes time. PowerPoint, like so much in the computer culture, speeds up the pace.

20 **Word processing vs. thinking.** The catalog for the Vermont Country Store advertises a manual typewriter, which the advertising copy says "moves at a pace that allows time to compose your thoughts." As many of us know, it is possible to manipulate text on a computer screen and see how it looks faster than we can think about what the words mean.

Word processing has its own complex psychology. From a pedagogical point of view, it can make dedicated students into better writers because it allows them to revise text, rearrange paragraphs, and experiment with the tone and shape of an essay. Few professional writers would part with their computers; some claim that they simply cannot think without their hands on the keyboard. Yet the ability to quickly fill the page, to see it before you can think it, can make bad writers even worse.

A seventh grader once told me that the typewriter she found in her mother's attic is "cool because you have to type each letter by itself. You have to know what you are doing in advance or it comes out a mess." The idea of thinking ahead has become exotic.

Taking things at interface value. We expect software to be easy to use, and we assume that we don't have to know how a computer works. In the early 1980s, most computer users who spoke of transparency meant that, as with any other machine, you could "open the hood" and poke around. But only a few years later, Macintosh users began to use the term when they talked about seeing their documents and programs represented by attractive and easy-to-interpret icons. They were referring to an ability to make things work without needing to go below the screen surface. Paradoxically, it was the screen's opacity that permitted that kind of transparency. Today, when people say that something is transparent, they mean that they can see how to make it work, not that they know how it works. In other words, transparency means epistemic opacity.

The people who built or bought the first generation of personal computers understood them down to the bits and bytes. The next generation of operating systems were more complex, but they still invited that old-time reductive understanding. Contemporary information technology encourages different habits of mind. Today's college students are already used to taking things at (inter)face value; their successors in 2014 will be even less accustomed to probing below the surface.

25 **Simulation and its discontents.** Some thinkers argue that the new opacity is empowering, enabling anyone to use the most sophisticated technological tools and to experiment with simulation in complex and creative ways. But it is also true that our tools carry the message that they are beyond our understanding. It is possible that in daily life, epistemic opacity can lead to passivity.

I first became aware of that possibility in the early 1990s, when the first generation of complex simulation games were introduced and immediately became popular for home as well as school use. SimLife teaches the principles of evolution by getting children involved in the development of complex ecosystems; in that sense it is an extraordinary learning tool. During one session in which I played SimLife with Tim, a 13-year-old, the screen before us flashed a message: "Your orgot is being eaten up." "What's an orgot?" I asked. Tim didn't know. "I just ignore that," he said confidently. "You don't need to know that kind of stuff to play."

For me, that story serves as a cautionary tale. Computer simulations enable their users to think about complex phenomena as dynamic, evolving systems. But they also accustom us to manipulating systems whose core assumptions we may not understand and that may not be true.

We live in a culture of simulation. Our games, our economic and political systems, and the ways architects design buildings, chemists envisage molecules, and surgeons perform operations all use simulation technology. In ten years the degree to which simulations are embedded in every area of life will have increased exponentially. We need to develop a new form of media literacy: readership skills for the culture of simulation.

We come to written text with habits of readership based on centuries of civilization. At the very least, we have learned to begin with the journalist's traditional questions: who, what, when, where, why, and how. Who wrote these words, what is their message, why were they written, and how are they situated in time and place, politically and socially? A central project for higher education during the next ten years should be creating programs in information-technology literacy, with the goal of teaching students to interrogate simulations in much the same spirit, challenging their built-in assumptions.

30 Despite the ever-increasing complexity of software, most computer environments put users in worlds based on constrained choices. In other words, immersion in programmed worlds puts us in reassuring environments where

the rules are clear. For example, when you play a video game, you often go through a series of frightening situations that you escape by mastering the rules—you experience life as a reassuring dichotomy of scary and safe. Children grow up in a culture of video games, action films, fantasy epics, and computer programs that all rely on that familiar scenario of almost losing but then regaining total mastery: There is danger. It is mastered. A still-more-powerful monster appears. It is subdued. Scary. Safe.

Yet in the real world, we have never had a greater need to work our way out of binary assumptions. In the decade ahead, we need to rebuild the culture around information technology. In that new sociotechnical culture, assumptions about the nature of mastery would be less absolute. The new culture would make it easier, not more difficult, to consider life in shades of gray, to see moral dilemmas in terms other than a battle between Good and Evil. For never has our world been more complex, hybridized, and global. Never have we so needed to have many contradictory thoughts and feelings at the same time. Our tools must help us accomplish that, not fight against us.

Information technology is identity technology. Embedding it in a culture that supports democracy, freedom of expression, tolerance, diversity, and complexity of opinion is one of the next decade's greatest challenges. We cannot afford to fail.

When I first began studying the computer culture, a small breed of highly trained technologists thought of themselves as "computer people." That is no longer the case. If we take the computer as a carrier of a way of knowing, a way of seeing the world and our place in it, we are all computer people now.

LEARNING MORE

Turkle probably knows more than anyone about what computers are doing to us "subjectively." To find more of what she has to say, see the *Ideas Across Time* website.

QUESTIONING THE TEXT

1. What experiences brought Turkle to study how computers change the way we think? Explain her concern about the student who "turned a Freudian slip into an information-processing error" (par. 5). Why did this transformation bother Turkle? Does it bother you? Explain.
2. What is the connection between the lack of privacy on the Internet and political democracy?
3. What is the difference between "multiple aspects of self " displayed in role-playing games on the Internet and "authentic selves" (par. 13)?
4. State Turkle's worries about PowerPoint in your own terms.
5. What is the beauty of the typewriter as compared with word processing?
6. What is "epistemic opacity" (par. 25)?
7. Why is Turkle concerned about the coming decade? What kinds of things does she think most need to be addressed by educators? Do you agree?

ANALYZING THE WRITER'S CRAFT

1. To whom is this essay primarily addressed? How do you know?
2. What is Turkle's thesis? Where is it stated?
3. What is Turkle's purpose in the opening six paragraphs of her essay?
4. Turkle organizes the body of her essay as a list. Is there any rhyme or reason to the order in which she lists things? Could she have presented this material in a different order without affecting her argument? Explain.
5. Turkle needs to persuade the reader that her concerns are based on sound evidence. What kind of evidence does she use to support her observations? Do you find her evidence persuasive? Explain. Does she draw plausible conclusions from her evidence? What piece of evidence do you find most persuasive? Least persuasive? Why?
6. What is Turkle's purpose in the concluding three paragraphs of her essay?
7. Is her closing paragraph an apt conclusion for her essay? Explain.

MAKING CONNECTIONS

1. Turkle is especially concerned with how we know things and with how the things we use to learn affect what we know. How does her approach to these questions compare with Charles Darwin's approach to understanding (pp. 167–180)?
2. Turkle says it is important that new technology serve "our human purposes." What are those purposes? Who should set them? Does she see the role of science in the same way that Richard Feynman does (pp. 201–207)?
3. Turkle makes claim to no overt political position, but a series of political assumptions do emerge from her essay nevertheless. Are these the same assumptions about what kind of society is desirable as those of Vaclav Havel (Chapter 5, pp. 404–412)? Both Havel and Turkle worry about how interaction with things can deprive people of their power to control their lives. Does their thinking usefully coincide, or are they in fact going off in different directions? Explain.
4. Susan Sontag says that today's movies are just vapid commercial extravaganzas (Chapter 7, pp. 602–610), glossy presentations empty of content and meaning. This part of Sontag's argument seems to mirror and reinforce Turkle's analysis of PowerPoint. Are there other ways in which the essays illuminate and support each other? Explain.

FORMULATING IDEAS FOR WRITING

1. Turkle cites many examples of educational experiences with computers that children have in school today. Support or take issue with her analysis of some of these based on your own experience. Be careful to write a clear thesis statement and to develop a coherent essay.

2. Some psychologists see the mind as a computer, a kind of information processor. Is Turkle biased in her dismissal of the view that a Freudian slip is better understood as a processing error? If the mind is like a computer, then how should we understand the word "meaning" in Turkle's sentence "An explanation in terms of meaning had become an explanation in terms of mechanism" (par. 5)? Write an essay that explores the implications of these competing views of mind and meaning.
3. Write an essay that supports or takes issue with Turkle's view that current trends in computing threaten "democracy, freedom of expression, tolerance, diversity, and complexity of opinion" (par. 32).
4. How can new technology be invented, adapted, and introduced into the culture so that it serves rather than undermines "our human purposes"? Is Turkle overly alarmed about new technology? After all, haven't people always said that new technology is going to undermine existing society? Or is there something unprecedented about the computer and the Internet?

Qafzeh Skull

The photo on the next page and its accompanying text first appeared in the *National Geographic* magazine, September 2001.

LEARNING MORE

This skull is identified as being about 100,000 years old. To learn more about this anthropological find, and the implications for what we know, or think we know, about human life on earth, see the *Ideas Across Time* website.

QUESTIONING THE TEXT

1. This photo conveys a great deal of information—but about a very familiar location, Times Square, a place millions of people visit and a place millions of people across the world watch on television every New Year's Eve. How does the projection of the skull alter the familiar picture of the Square?
2. Times Square is famous for its garish advertising. Is there any rhyme or reason to what appears on the spaces of the square? What should we make of the variety of things advertised? Are we intended to buy what is advertised? Is Times Square a testament to globalization? Why or why not?

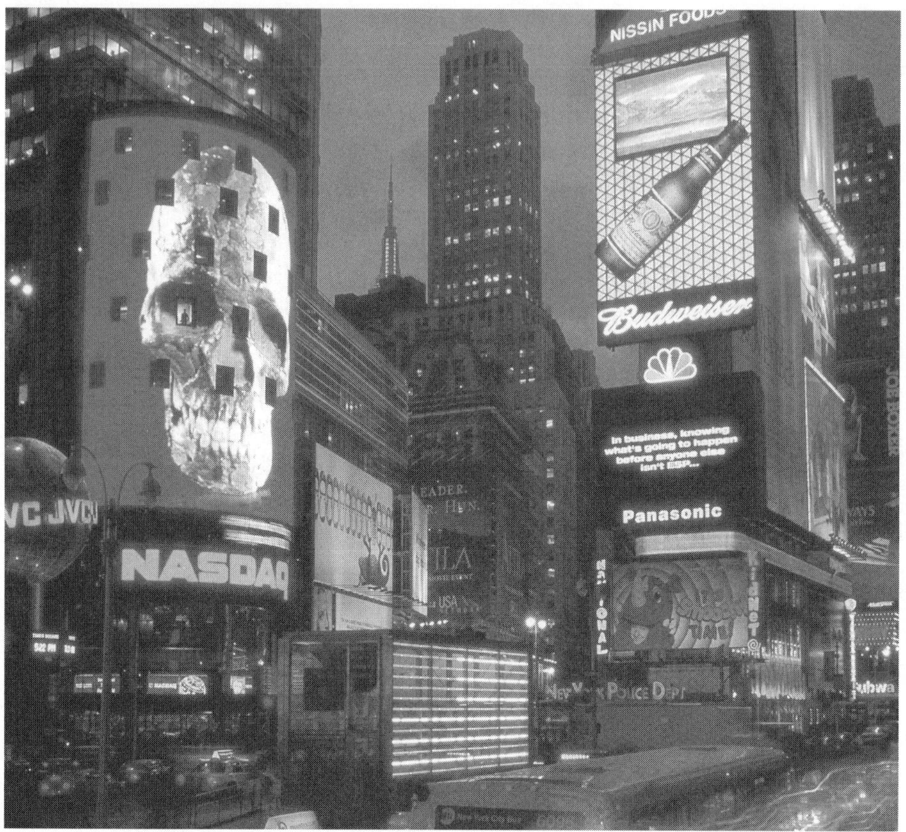

3. In addition to the ads, what else does the photo tell you about the location? Explain.
4. Does this photo make Times Square seem an attractive place?
5. Does the projection of the skull suggest to you that all of our hubbub cannot overcome death? Or that we have come a long way, baby? Or . . .?
6. Why do you think the photographer chose to project this anthropological find onto a building in Times Square?

ANALYZING THE ARTIST'S CRAFT

1. In such a busy visual environment, how does the photo draw the eye to the skull?
2. Discuss the formal contrasts of the photo—contrasts between light and dark, contrasts between shapes, and so on.
3. Discuss the thematic contrasts of the photo, such as the contrast between movement and stasis, present and past, contemporary and older icons

(Empire State Building and the new Times Square buildings, Budweiser and Panasonic), between the frivolous and the deadly serious, and so on.

4. What is the effect of the silhouette of a person in one of the eyes of the skull?
5. How important to the photo is the traffic? Explain.
6. Does the photo effectively convey the age of the skull?
7. For the purposes of the photo, does it matter that the skull is real? Explain.

MAKING CONNECTIONS

1. What view of science do you associate with this photo? Francis Bacon's (pp. 152–156)? Mary Shelley's (pp. 157–165)? Richard Feynman's (pp. 201–207)?
2. What attitude toward death and the dead does this photo suggest? Compare and contrast the attitude toward death and the dead of this photo with the views of Leslie Marmon Silko (Chapter 8, pp. 693–694)?
3. Does this photo reflect Oscar Wilde's view of art (Chapter 7, pp. 587–588)? Explain.
4. Does this photo reflect the flattening of experience discussed by Daniel J. Boorstin (Chapter 5, pp. 390–402)?
5. How does this photo confirm Darwin's view of life on earth (pp. 167–180)?

FORMULATING IDEAS FOR WRITING

1. If you were given the opportunity to project an image onto a building in Times Square in place of the Qafzeh skull, what would you choose? Write an essay explaining your choice and what you would hope to achieve through your choice.
2. Can the Times Square portrayed in this photo be seen as a microcosm of America? Explain. Is the image of the United States conveyed in this photo admirable? Decadent? Representative of democracy? Of American capitalism? Of religious faith?
3. Write an essay that discusses the contrasts depicted in this photo.
4. Write an essay titled "Who Are We?" that uses this photo and the accompanying text as your main points of reference. What does this skull imply about who we are? What does the rest of the photo imply about who we are? How does the effort to date this skull address the question of who we are?

chapter 4

Economic Life

"It is a truth universally acknowledged, that a single man in possession of a good fortune, must be in want of a wife." This witty sentence opens one of the most popular novels of the last two centuries, Jane Austen's *Pride and Prejudice,* first published in 1813. A brilliant comedy of manners, *Pride and Prejudice* recounts the courtships of the five Bennet sisters, daughters of a prominent gentry family residing in the English countryside. The fundamental moral dilemma that the book explores is the relation between love and money, the great theme of the nineteenth-century English novel. In this respect, the book's witty opening announces a new, and perhaps even unprecedented, focus for civilized social life. We know from such tales as *Cinderella* that mothers wanted their daughters to marry rich men well before the modern era. But Austen's sentence nonetheless suggests a new outlook. She proclaims as a universal truth that personal life in its most intimate aspects is animated by what we have come to call economics, making material wealth and well-being the highest value.

The German social philosopher Max Weber published in 1904–1905 an important study under the weighty title *The Protestant Ethic and the Spirit of Capitalism.* (You can read an excerpt from this work on the *Ideas Across Time* website). Weber quotes Benjamin Franklin to make the point that the modern outlook doesn't simply value money as something that can get you what you want, but that because it can get you what you want, it has become desirable in itself. The goal is to get rich not so you can travel the world or enjoy a fruitful leisure but for its own symbolic value as the highest moral state. The richest person is also "the best," an appropriately ambiguous phrase suggesting at once the social elite and the morally superior. Earlier societies, of course, also harbored men and women of great wealth, and money has been around—and has been coveted—for a long time. But whatever the role and desirability of wealth in the past, the greatest human aspirations transcended making money: money was a *means* rather than an *end.*

The closer we come to the present, however, the more comprehensive become the claims of the practical activities having to do with "making a living." And as the opening selection of this chapter, portraying the material conditions of six Chinese men and women of different occupations, ages, and sexes, makes clear, the fixation on material progress is a worldwide signature of modern times. The enormous changes in every aspect of life occurring at a staggering pace and on a vast scale in today's China offer us a unique view of the making of a market economy, an economy that *The New York Times* reports "is popularly called the one-billion-man market."

By "market" the *Times* means not an array of stalls selling baubles but a complex consumer economy. The classic account of "the market" in this sense is found in Adam Smith's enormously influential *The Wealth of Nations* (1776), the next reading in the chapter. Smith, a Scottish professor of moral philosophy at Glasgow University, set out to uncover the true sources of a nation's wealth. In the end, he wrote a book that launched modern economic thought and established not only our understanding of modern capitalism but also many of our key economic practices and attitudes. At the heart of this rich (and long) book lie a few simple but profound ideas. We owe to Smith the modern notion of a "market," which he saw as a self-regulating mechanism for the distribution of goods and the establishment of prices, including the price of labor. We also owe to Smith the notion that competition is inherent in the market and fuels the ingenuity on which the improvement of everyday life depends. Smith also concluded that labor—the human force that, for example, transforms a tree into a table—is the root source of economic value, an idea of great importance in particular for the working-class political movements of the nineteenth century.

The outstanding expression of the outlook of those mass movements is Karl Marx and Friedrich Engels's *Communist Manifesto*. The political sections of that revolutionary document may seem outdated, and are not reprinted here, but its analytical power remains exceptional. More often than not, Marx's analysis reads as an amplification rather than a contradiction of Adam Smith. Moreover, Marx was an imaginative interpreter of the deeper nature of the capitalist economy with its unprecedented inventiveness and destructiveness. The production of the new necessitates the destruction of the old, and this includes old and new values, old and new ideas, and even old and new feelings. And nothing better illustrates these contradictory features of modern economic life than does money, which the writer Gertrude Stein, in an album of comments on money in this chapter, says is "the thing that differentiates man from animals." But, of course, money is so changeable, elusive, and volatile that its importance is significantly different to different people. "There is only one class in the community," says Oscar Wilde, "that thinks more about money than the rich, and that is the poor." Little wonder that in his popular utopian novel *Looking Backward* (1888), Edward Bellamy imagines a society without money. By the end of the nineteenth century, the pillars of individual life in the modern economy—the need to work a number of hours daily and the use of money as the medium of exchange—had come to seem part of an old and archaic order, a transitional moment on the way to a new society.

But that new society has proved elusive. Today almost everyone has to work in order to make money. Indeed, although child labor has receded as a common practice, women's labor has become an ordinary part of contemporary life. Two essays in this chapter illuminate the working experience of women. The first, by Louisa May Alcott, is from the nineteenth century and relates her humiliating but also comic experiences as a servant. The second, by the contemporary social commentator Barbara Ehrenreich, relates her experience as a salesperson for Wal-Mart in Minnesota, and is similarly humiliating and comic. Men's labor is represented in the chapter by a selection from Studs Terkel's book of interviews about life and work, titled *Working*. A contemporary steelworker, Mike Lefevre, speaks for himself. "I'm a dying breed. A laborer," he says. Lefevre strains less against the weariness of his work than against its anonymity: there is no sign of him in the steel he produces. Lefevre's passionate and dignified dissatisfaction is given voice in Bertolt Brecht's poem "A Worker Reads History," which asks, "Who built the seven gates of Thebes?" and answers, "The books are filled with the names of kings."

It is impossible today to think of the economy without almost immediately adding "global"—the global economy. In a later chapter, Benjamin Barber writes about this phenomenon in the essay "Jihad vs. McWorld" (Chapter 5, pp. 414–425). In an essay in this chapter, the ethicist Peter Singer points to an uncomfortable fact of the global economy, namely the extremes of wealth and poverty it encompasses. What is our obligation as citizens of the United States to children starving abroad? Singer says we owe them all the money we have that we don't need for bare necessities.

And yet isn't there poverty at home, too? The chapter closes with competing images of contemporary "American values," one expressed in an ad for an investment corporation, and the other in handwritten placards used by beggars in New York City ("Help Me Please").

KEYNOTE

China Juggles the Conflicting Pressures of a Society in Transition (2002)

Craig S. Smith

This story by reporter Craig S. Smith appeared in *The New York Times* on July 15, 2002.

With China now a member of the World Trade Organization, foreigners have focused on what is popularly called the one-billion-man market. The country is already the world's biggest market for televisions, refrigerators and mobile phones. Its huge population has the potential to become a consumption engine that could someday drive much of the world's economy in the way that the United States' does today.

The numbers are impressive. China's emerging middle class, people with a net income of at least $3,000 a year, numbers nearly 100 million and is growing about 20 percent a year. Because of state-subsidized housing, little of that money is spent on shelter, the biggest household expense in the West, and much of it is saved.

Georges Desvaux, a Beijing-based partner at the consulting firm McKinsey & Company, estimates that five million or six million Chinese have personal assets of $100,000 or more. Perhaps 10,000 have assets exceeding $1 million.

But unemployment is surging, rural incomes are sliding, competition is rising and the government barely has its toe in the waters of political reform. China's leadership acknowledges that the country's internal stresses are building and [that it] is running a race against a potential collapse, patching weak spots while carrying out a major overhaul of society even before having decided what its final shape should be.

5 China's broader population is far less secure than the much-celebrated affluent urbanites in a handful of its cities. The number of people who can afford the wares peddled by the world's multinationals is but a slim slice of the billion-man pie.

Weighted against the country's nascent middle class are 800 million peasants, whose lot in life has worsened in recent years. About 150 million of those people have flocked to the cities or coastal industrial zones to find jobs, usually low-paying ones. As many as 20 million urbanites, meanwhile, are unemployed.

The rising standard of living experienced by many Chinese during the 1980's and early 1990's has stalled. Much of the generation that suffered in childhood through the disastrous Great Leap Forward of the late 1950's and whose education was cut short by the 1966–76 Cultural Revolution is now facing unemployment and a retirement of privation.

Add to the mix an increasing flow of information via radio, satellite television, telephones and, in the cities, the Internet and the future looks more uncertain than ever.

The Communist Party maintains a firm grip on most media and is quick to crush organizations—like the Falun Gong spiritual movement—that pose a potential challenge to its authority.

10 Yet most Chinese want a strong central government and, despite some cynicism about its anachronistic ideology, continue to support the party as a unifying force and a check against the "luan," or chaos, that all Chinese most deeply fear.

The Farmer

A Growing Struggle to Make Ends Meet

China, more than anything else, is a country of peasants, with the centuries of custom and convention that the word implies. About 800 million Chinese are peasants, a total of roughly 215 million households. Despite their role in

LI YONGRONG, 53

HAT bought secondhand for 1 yuan
SHIRT 20 yuan
SWEATER VEST 30 yuan
JACKET AND PANTS
bought secondhand for a total of about 100 yuan
BOOTS Double-Coin brand, made in Shanghai, 20 yuan
CHICKEN raised locally
DOG from a neighbor's litter

$1 = 8.28 yuan

Photographs by Ritz Sino/RS Photos, for The New York Times.

propelling the Communist Party to power more than a half century ago, farming is now often a losing proposition.

Li Yongrong, a farmer in central Anhui Province, says he earns about 5,000 yuan a year from the rice, wheat, canola and pigs he has on four acres he leases from the state. But taxes and fees now eat up about 4,000 yuan of that income. School fees for his two teenage children cost him another 2,000 yuan.

To make ends meet, he transports pigs and produce for fellow farmers in a Flying Tiger pickup truck that he bought four years ago with 10,000 yuan borrowed from relatives and his 3,000 yuan life savings.

The trucking earns him enough to pay his electricity and telephone bills but there is barely enough left over for the red envelopes of cash he is obliged to give as gifts each year during the Lunar New Year holiday and at weddings and funerals. He saves almost nothing and remains deep in debt to relatives.

Besides the truck and the telephone, his grandest possession is a 21-inch color television set that he bought in 1996 and that holds pride of place in his small brick house.

Mr. Li, 53, and his wife, 48, have no pension. Mr. Li wants his children to go to college, but does not know how he will pay for this even if they manage to pass the examinations that allow just 13 percent of China's young people to attend the state-run universities.

The Government Clerk

Perks That Allow Savings for School

Wang Dongfeng, 36, is one of China's roughly 30 million government employees. China's more progressive leaders have vowed to pare down the country's bloated bureaucracy, and the central government has shrunk its payroll sharply in the past few years. But millions of people like Mr. Wang continue to draw substantial salaries from the state. They support the status quo and represent the largest chunk of the country's emerging middle class.

Mr. Wang works for the China Family Planning Association, a state-financed organization that helps coordinate China's one-child policy with more than a million branches or lower-level organizations across the country. He lives with his wife and son in a 690-square-foot, two-bedroom apartment for which he pays 230 yuan a month.

Mr. Wang's government salary is just 1,200 yuan a month, but he receives various benefits from his employer, like free lunches, that effectively increase his monthly income to about 2,000 yuan. His biggest expenses are his son's kindergarten, for which he pays 4,000 yuan a year, and yearly tuition of 10,000 for a two-year course he is taking toward a master's degree in social welfare. Mr. Wang and his wife own a car—a tiny Suzuki made under license by a

WANG DONGFENG, 36

EYEGLASSES Japanese frames, more than 1,000 yuan
SHIRT domestic brand, 170 yuan
TIE a gift
PANTS domestic brand, about 300 yuan
SHOES domestically made Caesar brand, 600 yuan
SON'S SHIRT: 80 yuan
SON'S SWEATER VEST handed down from a cousin
SON'S PANTS handed down from a cousin
SON'S SHOES a gift from his grandmother, 70 yuan

Chinese factory. Besides the car, Mr. Wang's most expensive possessions are a Motorola mobile telephone, a desktop computer assembled from parts by a friend, and an aging color television set. Thanks to Mr. Wang's wife's salary, the couple save about 3,000 yuan a month, and they have put about 60,000 yuan in the bank so far.

The Migrant

Building a New Life in Unwelcoming City

Chen Qun, 28, is one of an estimated 150 million peasants who have left the land to find work in China's swelling cities. Most cities have large populations of these struggling "outsiders," as urban residents call them.

City dwellers regard the migrants with suspicion and regularly blame them for rising crime. The migrants overwhelm railroads and bus lines early each year during an annual migration back to their hometowns for the all-important

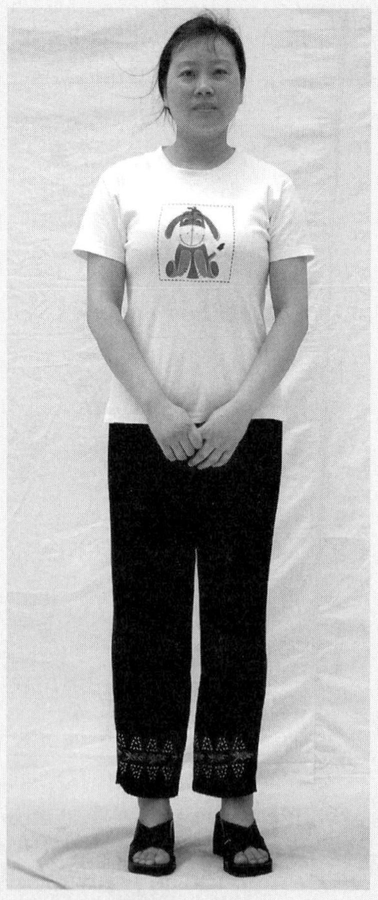

CHEN QUN, 28
T-SHIRT local brand, 20 yuan
PANTS 30 yuan
PIGSKIN SHOES 70 yuan

lunar New Year holiday. But their remittances to their families in the countryside remain the most significant means of distributing the wealth of China's cities and its coastal export belt to the vast, impoverished hinterland.

Two years ago, Ms. Chen left her 4-year-old son with her husband's parents in rural Sichuan province and moved to Shenzhen, just north of Hong Kong, where her husband had found work as a security guard.

She began working as a maid, earning about 500 yuan a month, but she now earns double that as a dispatcher for a small cleaning company. She lives rent-free in the company dormitory and eats free in the company canteen. Her biggest personal expenses are snacks, like bananas and melon seeds, and occasional bits of clothing. She sends about 300 yuan a month back home to pay for her son's school fees and clothes.

She and her husband together earn about 2,800 yuan a month, most of which they save. She said they now have about 60,000 yuan in the bank, "but this is still far from our goal."

She and her husband hope to open a business in Sichuan some day. "And we need to save so that our son can go to college," she said.

The Student

A Tantalizing View of a Bright Future

About six million young Chinese are attending universities and it is to these people that the future holds the most promise and the gravest risks. The current generation of college students is far more concerned with career prospects than with the politics that preoccupied their counterparts in the 1980's. Nationalistic sentiments run high in this group and the Communist Party's leadership goes largely unquestioned. The students' greatest fear, in fact, is political instability that might interfere with their seemingly bright future.

Li Boyu, 20, attends the University of Finance and Economy in Shanghai and hopes to become an actuary in a large insurance company. She grew up in the compound of a state-owned factory in Shaanxi Province, one of the poorer parts of the country.

Ms. Li listens to Western pop music and reads newspapers and magazines, all of which are domestic except the Chinese edition of *Reader's Digest*. She goes to the campus computer lab twice a week to surf the Internet. "The first thing I do is to check my e-mail," she said.

Ms. Li shares a dormitory room with three other young women. She plays Ping-Pong and tennis and for a time was in the campus chorus, where she sang songs like "Without the Communist Party, There Would Be No New China." She spends her vacations at home in Shaanxi watching pirated DVD's of Hollywood films. Her favorite actors are Tom Cruise and Brad Pitt.

She hopes to earn between 5,000 yuan and 8,000 yuan as an actuary. If she finds work in Shanghai, she wants her parents to move to the city so they can "share the light" of her good fortune.

LI BOYU, 20

SILVER NECKLACE mail-order from a Shanghai company, 55 yuan
JACKET bought in Shaanxi, 70 yuan
T-SHIRT domestically made Hong Kong brand, 70 yuan
PANTS 105 yuan
SHOES 50 yuan
BACKPACK Japanese brand, gift from a friend in Beijing
DOLL bought in Shaanxi when she was in high school, 4 yuan

The Businessman

Schmoozing Clients and Making Millions

China's economy remains largely state owned, but its private sector is growing fast. There are now at least 10 million private business owners, not including millions more independent merchants, traders and street hawkers.

Xue Bing, 39, is typical of the new capitalist breed amassing wealth in the transitional economy. While most of these people shun politics, they tend to support the Communist Party as guardian of the stability on which their future depends.

Mr. Xue was a manager in a state-owned construction company until two years ago, when it began to privatize many of its businesses. He invested 80,000 yuan, his life savings, to buy 8 percent of one of the businesses, a company that manufactures paint. He holds a quarter stake in the company's Beijing subsidiary.

XUE BING, 39

SHIRT 300 yuan
PANTS 200 yuan
SHOES Italian-designed local brand, 600 yuan
TIE a gift, about 300 yuan
CROCODILE BELT bought in Thailand, $80
MOBILE TELEPHONE domestically made Motorola, 2,900 yuan
BRIEFCASE domestically made Hong Kong brand, 2,100 yuan

Like most private businessmen in China, Mr. Xue spends much of his time cultivating relationships with officials to win his company business. He spends as much as 20,000 yuan a month on entertaining and gifts, though his company reimburses him for at least half of that.

One of his biggest expenses is his daughter, for whom he spends about 20,000 yuan a year on school fees and an annuity.

Mr. Xue draws a salary of 4,800 yuan a month and his wife earns 1,600 yuan a month as an office worker. But his annual income fluctuates because he can earn as much as 300,000 yuan from a single project. He has also made money on the stock market and today his savings total millions of yuan.

His dream is to take control of the company and then take it public in about five years.

TANG NIANSHAN, 47

BICYCLE Domestically made Forever brand, 400 yuan
WRISTWATCH local brand, 1,000 yuan
VEST 30 yuan
SHIRT 30 yuan
BELT 40 yuan
PANTS 50 yuan
SHOES 70 yuan
CIGARETTE Double Happiness, a domestic brand, 8 yuan a pack.

The Factory Worker

A Workplace Shifts as a Society Changes

China's roughly 60 million factory workers, most of whom are still employed by the state, make up the bulk of the urban work force. As the worst of the state-owned enterprises are shut down, many of these people are being thrown out of work. Accustomed to the security of the state economy and concentrated enough to organize, they represent the most volatile slice of the population.

Tang Nianshan and his wife, Tang Airong, have spent most of their lives working in state-owned factories. Ms. Tang, 43, has been working for the same factory since she was 18. It makes enameled tin washbasins. She earns just under 1,000 yuan a month.

Mr. Tang, 47, quit his factory job when the business began failing in the late 1980's as the government began withdrawing support for state enterprises. Millions of people have lost their jobs in that transition, but Mr. Tang was lucky and found work in a Chinese-Thai joint venture that manufactures auto parts. He earns 2,600 yuan a month on a welding line.

After work, he goes home to a two-bedroom, 490-square-foot apartment that he and his family share with his parents. He and his wife sleep in one bedroom. Their 15-year-old son sleeps in the other with Mr. Tang's parents.

His biggest possessions are his bicycle and a mobile telephone. The family also has three television sets, one in each room, and all three are often going at the same time.

The family saves little money, but Shanghai's rapid development has filled Mr. Tang with hope, particularly for his son, who he wants to go to college someday. "Our generation has seen many, many things," he said. "Today, life is getting better."

LEADING QUESTIONS

When we look at China's remarkable transformation from a vast backward nation into one of the world's greatest industrial powers, we are observing something of a replay in fast speed of the Industrial Revolution of the nineteenth century, itself a very rapid phenomenon. The Chinese experience allows us to reflect on our own, and to think about the future.

Do we admire what we see in China? Enormous entrepreneurial energy, a daunting work ethic, a swiftly rising level of wealth for huge populations, great opportunities for all . . . Is that what attracts our attention? Or do we see instead, alongside Shanghai's ever-rising skyscrapers, the worst air pollution in the world? Spectacular cities and devastated rural areas? Great wealth for a few and poverty for millions?

In these questions is China us in capital letters? What is the *point* of it all? Are we really born to work?

LEARNING MORE

These portraits of contemporary Chinese men and women assume some knowledge of the key events of recent Chinese history. You may want to learn more about the Great Leap Forward, the Cultural Revolution, and the "one child policy." See the *Ideas Across Time* website.

QUESTIONING THE TEXT

Overview

1. The introduction to this article in *The New York Times* portrays China at a crossroad, just on the edge of a qualitative change. One reason cited is the

growth of China's middle class. How big does the writer say it is? What are the implications of the size of this middle class?
2. What are the economically attractive features of the current Chinese situation?
3. What are the economic shortcomings of the current Chinese market?
4. What main problems does the Chinese economy need to overcome?

The Farmer

1. What is the main occupation of people in China? What are the implications of this fact?
2. What does Li Yongrong grow?
3. What percentage of China's young attend university?
4. How would you characterize Li Yongrong's life situation?

The Government Clerk

1. What group represents the largest chunk of China's emerging middle class?
2. What are Wang Dongfeng's biggest expenses?
3. How much do the Wangs save monthly (in dollars)?

The Migrant

1. What is the most significant means of distributing the wealth of China's cities to its countryside?
2. Why isn't Mrs. Chen living with her husband?
3. What is Mrs. Chen's ambition?

The Student

1. What is the greatest fear of China's university students?
2. What are Ms. Li's extracurricular activities?
3. What are Ms. Li's plans once she gets a job?

The Businessman

1. What is the attitude of China's entrepreneurs to the ruling Communist Party?
2. What business is Mr. Xue involved in?
3. How does Mr. Xue occupy most of his work time?
4. What is Mr. Xue's dream?

The Factory Worker

1. Who is the biggest employer of China's factory workers?
2. Why are factory workers "the most volatile slice" of China's population?
3. What jobs do Mr. and Mrs. Tang hold?
4. What is the Tangs' housing situation?

ANALYZING THE WRITER'S CRAFT

1. One of the requirements of a newspaper story like this one is that it condense a great deal of material into a fairly brief space. How is this done in this case? Give one or two examples of especially effective communication of a good deal of information in a highly condensed way in this story (including the portraits).
2. Had space allowed, where would you have provided more information? How could that information have been integrated into the present story (or stories)?
3. How would this story be different without the photos? What information do the photos give you that the words do not/cannot?
4. Discuss the usefulness of the charts accompanying each photo. How would the stories be different without these charts? What do charts convey especially well that can't be done as well in other ways?
5. A newspaper feature such as this one requires especially clear but swift transitions. Provide two or three examples of effective transitions here, and explain why they work well.
6. Discuss the effectiveness of the conclusions of each of the portraits.

MAKING CONNECTIONS

1. Compare/contrast these stories with "Changing America" (Chapter 1, pp. 11–20).
2. Do these stories suggest that China is building a "market" along lines that Adam Smith (pp. 244–262) would recognize? Karl Marx (pp. 264–273)?
3. What overall view of China do you derive from these stories? How are these stories similar to and different from the stories of American life portrayed in Chapter 1?
4. Does the picture of Chinese life portrayed in this story support or question the thesis of "Jihad vs. McWorld" (Chapter 5, pp. 414–425)?
5. What do you think Mike Lefevre (pp. 300–307) would have to say about these stories?

FORMULATING IDEAS FOR WRITING

1. Write a self-portrait along the lines of the ones in this article.
2. Take the point of view of Adam Smith or Karl Marx and reflect on China's present situation and where it is going, or ought to go, in the future.
3. What do these stories suggest about the relation between democracy and economic development? Between economic development and freedom?
4. Supplement these readings with some research, and write a newspaper article about everyday life in today's China.

The Division of Labor and the Origin of Money (1776)

Adam Smith

Adam Smith (1723–1790), the father of modern capitalism, was an endearing and eccentric man, famous for his absent-mindedness. He counted among his many friends some of the greatest figures of his time, such as the philosopher David Hume, the French *savant* Voltaire, and the leading English man of letters, Samuel Johnson. Born in the small town of Kirkcaldy in Scotland, Smith became professor of moral philosophy at the University of Glasgow, one of Europe's centers of learning during the preeminent intellectual movement of the eighteenth century, the Enlightenment. At Glasgow, Smith lectured on law and ethics as well as economics, or what was at the time called "political economy." On the basis of his teaching, he published the book that first propelled him to the front rank of eighteenth-century philosophers, *The Theory of Moral Sentiments,* in 1759. But his most famous work, *An Inquiry into the Nature and the Causes of the Wealth of Nations,* was begun to relieve his boredom as he toured Europe in the role of tutor to the young Duke of Buccleuch. He did not complete this work until twelve years later, in 1776, the same year that the Declaration of Independence was published. Two years afterward, he was awarded the sinecure of commissioner of customs for Edinburgh, where he lived with his mother until his death at the age of sixty-seven.

The Wealth of Nations established modern economics, in terms of both its root ideas and its methods. But even more, the book captured and expressed some of the essential values of the modern world, namely, the idea that well-being means material well-being; that the rational application of understanding to everyday life will create improvement in the conditions of life; and that politics and economics, or as Smith saw it, liberty and the "free" market, are intimately interconnected.

Smith's book is an "inquiry" in the sense that he starts out to discover how things in society work. The society he wants to understand is the commercial society of England and Scotland in his own day. Smith concludes that the cause of Britain's commercial advancement is the division of labor, that is, the breaking up of the process of production into small parts, each performed repetitively by the same person. In the second half of the eighteenth century, British commerce strained against the system of mercantile monopoly, and it was against the idea of monopoly that Smith wished in particular to argue. As well, Smith wrote in a commercial rather than industrial context: the Industrial Revolution was just beginning to gain momentum at the time that *The Wealth of Nations* was published. Nonetheless, Smith's inquiry, directed by his analysis of the implications of the division of labor, applied just as forcefully to the Industrial Revolution as to commercial capitalism, and all in all his main ideas succeeded in shaping how we view economic life to this day.

At the heart of Smith's thinking about economics is "the market." He sees a "propensity in human nature" to barter and trade, and out of this natural human impulse, he maintains, grows the system of exchange, what we are used to calling "the marketplace." Smith uses the word in our contemporary sense; that is, he means by "market" not a local institution of booths and stalls but a large, indeed international, system of exchange. He took pains to stress that a truly commercial nation requires a big enough market to satisfy the processes of commerce. The size of the market results in two other fundamental features of modern economics. The first seems obvious to us: the crucial role of money. Clearly, stability of currency (or currencies) is a precondition for exchange on a large scale. The second is not only Smith's most influential idea but also an idea whose implications have continued to excite and trouble people right up to our own day: this is the idea that the market, left as free as possible of governmental regulation, is guided by an "invisible hand" and is in practice self-regulating. Each individual, or each corporation, seeks its own best interest. But competition among individuals and among corporations ensures that within the apparent chaos of exchange and self-seeking—as, say, on the floor of a busy stock exchange—the laws of the market are at work, regulating prices, wages, and even the distribution of wealth.

Smith is a philosopher, an analyst, and a scientist much more than he is a propagandist. He is not a "capitalist" in the sense of someone who is "for" the owners and "against" the workers. The final passages reproduced here pull no punches, for example, about the unfair advantages that the owner enjoys over the worker when it comes to setting wages. But it is characteristic of Smith's hawk's-eye view that he should conclude that more than anything else it is the increase in national wealth that promotes an increase in wages.

The passages that follow are taken from the first eight chapters of Smith's *The Wealth of Nations.*

Chapter I

Of the Division of Labour

The greatest improvement in the productive powers of labour, and the greater part of the skill, dexterity, and judgment with which it is anywhere directed, or applied, seem to have been the effects of the division of labour.

The effects of the division of labour, in the general business of society, will be more easily understood by considering in what manner it operates in some particular manufactures. It is commonly supposed to be carried furthest in some very trifling ones; not perhaps that it really is carried further in them than in others of more importance: but in those trifling manufactures which are destined to supply the small wants of but a small number of people, the whole number of workmen must necessarily be small; and those employed in every different branch of the work can often be collected into the same workhouse, and placed at once under the view of the spectator. In those great manufactures, on the contrary, which are destined to supply the great wants of the great body of the people, every different branch of the work employs so great a number of workmen that it is impossible to collect them all into the same workhouse. We can seldom see more, at one time, than those employed in one single branch. Though in such manufactures, therefore, the work may really be divided into a much greater number of parts than in those of a more trifling nature, the division is not near so obvious, and has accordingly been much less observed.

To take an example, therefore, from a very trifling manufacture; but one in which the division of labour has been very often taken notice of, the trade of the pin-maker; a workman not educated to this business (which the division of labour has rendered a distinct trade), nor acquainted with the use of the machinery employed in it (to the invention of which the same division of labour has probably given occasion), could scarce, perhaps, with his utmost industry, make one pin in a day, and certainly could not make twenty. But in the way in which this business is now carried on, not only the whole work is a peculiar trade, but it is divided into a number of branches, of which the greater part are likewise peculiar trades. One man draws out the wire, another straights it, a third cuts it, a fourth points it, a fifth grinds it at the top for receiving the head; to make the head requires two or three distinct operations; to put it on is a peculiar business, to whiten the pins is another; it is even a trade by itself to put them into the paper; and the important business of making a pin is, in this manner, divided into about eighteen distinct operations, which, in some manufactories, are all performed by distinct hands, though in others the same man will sometimes perform two or three of them. I have seen a small manufactory of this kind where ten men only were employed, and where some of them consequently performed two or three distinct operations. But though they were very poor, and therefore but indifferently accommodated with the necessary machinery, they could, when they exerted themselves, make among them about twelve pounds of pins in a day. There are in a pound upwards of four thousand pins of a middling size. Those ten persons, therefore, could make among them upwards of forty-eight thousand pins in a day. Each person, therefore, making a tenth part of forty-eight thousand pins, might be considered as making four thousand eight hundred pins in a day. But if they had all wrought separately and independently, and without any of them having been educated to this peculiar business, they certainly could not each of them have made twenty, perhaps not one pin in a day; that is, certainly, not the two hundred and fortieth, perhaps not the four thousand eight hundredth part of what they are at present capable of performing, in consequence of a proper division and combination of their different operations.

In every other art and manufacture, the effects of the division of labour are similar to what they are in this very trifling one; though, in many of them, the labour can neither be so much subdivided, nor reduced to so great a simplicity of operation. The division of labour, however, so far as it can be introduced, occasions, in every art, a proportionable increase of the productive powers of labour. The separation of different trades and employments from one another seems to have taken place in consequence of this advantage. This separation, too, is generally carried furthest in those countries which enjoy the highest degree of industry and improvement; what is the work of one man in a rude state of society being generally that of several in an improved one. In every improved society, the farmer is generally nothing but a farmer; the manufacturer, nothing but a manufacturer. The labour, too, which is necessary to produce any one complete manufacture is almost always divided among a great number of hands. How many different trades are employed in each branch of the linen and woollen manufactures from the growers of the flax and the wool, to the bleachers and smoothers of the linen, or to the dyers and dressers of the cloth! . . .

5 This great increase of the quantity of work which, in consequence of the division of labour, the same number of people are capable of performing, is owing to three different circumstances; first, to the increase of dexterity in every particular workman; secondly, to the saving of the time which is commonly lost in passing from one species of work to another; and lastly, to the invention of a great number of machines which facilitate and abridge labour, and enable one man to do the work of many.

First, the improvement of the dexterity of the workman necessarily increases the quantity of the work he can perform; and the division of labour, by reducing every man's business to some one simple operation, and by making this operation the sole employment of his life, necessarily increases very much the dexterity of the workman. A common smith, who, though accustomed to handle the hammer, has never been used to make nails, if upon some particular occasion he is obliged to attempt it, will scarce, I am assured, be able to make above two or three hundred nails in a day, and those too very bad ones. A smith who has been accustomed to make nails, but whose sole or principal business has not been that of a nailer, can seldom with his utmost diligence make more than eight hundred or a thousand nails in a day. I have seen several boys under twenty years of age who had never exercised any other trade but that of making nails, and who, when they exerted themselves, could make, each of them, upwards of two thousand three hundred nails in a day. The making of a nail, however, is by no means one of the simplest operations. The same person blows the bellows, stirs or mends the fire as there is occasion, heats the iron, and forges every part of the nail: in forging the head too he is obliged to change his tools. The different operations into which the making of a pin, or of a metal button, is subdivided, are all of them much more simple, and the dexterity of the person, of whose life it has been the sole business to perform them, is usually much greater. The rapidity, with which some of the operations of those manufactures are performed, exceeds what the human hand could, by those who had never seen them, be supposed capable of acquiring.

Secondly, the advantage which is gained by saving the time commonly lost in passing from one sort of work to another is much greater than we should at first view be apt to imagine it. It is impossible to pass very quickly from one kind of work to another that is carried on in a different place and with quite different tools. A country weaver, who cultivates a small farm, must lose a good deal of time in passing from his loom to the field, and from the field to his loom. When the two trades can be carried on in the same workhouse, the loss of time is no doubt much less. It is even in this case, however, very considerable. A man commonly saunters a little in turning his hand from one sort of employment to another. When he first begins the new work he is seldom very keen and hearty; his mind, as they say, does not go to it, and for some time he rather trifles than applies to good purpose. The habit of sauntering and of indolent careless application, which is naturally, or rather necessarily acquired by every country workman who is obliged to change his work and his tools every half hour, and to apply his hand in twenty different ways almost every day of his life, renders him almost always slothful and lazy, and incapable of any vigorous application even on the most pressing occasions. Independent, therefore, of his deficiency in point of dexterity, this cause alone must always reduce considerably the quantity of work which he is capable of performing.

Thirdly, and lastly, everybody must be sensible how much labour is facilitated and abridged by the application of proper machinery. It is unnecessary to give any example. I shall only observe, therefore, that the invention of all those machines by which labour is so much facilitated and abridged seems to have been originally owing to the division of labour. Men are much more likely to discover easier and readier methods of attaining any object when the whole attention of their minds is directed towards that single object than when it is dissipated among a great variety of things. But in consequence of the division of labour, the whole of every man's attention comes naturally to be directed towards some one very simple object. It is naturally to be expected, therefore, that some one or other of those who are employed in each particular branch of labour should soon find out easier and readier methods of performing their own particular work, wherever the nature of it admits of such improvement. A great part of the machines made use of in those manufactures in which labour is most subdivided, were originally the inventions of common workmen, who, being each of them employed in some very simple operation, naturally turned their thoughts towards finding out easier and readier methods of performing it. Whoever has been much accustomed to visit such manufactures must frequently have been shown very pretty machines, which were the inventions of such workmen in order to facilitate and quicken their own particular part of the work. In the first fire-engines, a boy was constantly employed to open and shut alternately the communication between the boiler and the cylinder, according as the piston either ascended or descended. One of those boys, who loved to play with his companions, observed that, by tying a string from the handle of the valve which opened this communication to another part of the machine, the valve would open and shut without his assistance, and leave him at liberty to divert himself with his play-fellows. One of the greatest improvements that has been made upon this machine, since it was first invented, was in this manner the discovery of a boy who wanted to save his own labour.

All the improvements in machinery, however, have by no means been the inventions of those who had occasion to use the machines. Many improvements have been made by the ingenuity of the makers of the machines, when to make them became the business of a peculiar trade; and some by that of those who are called philosophers or men of speculation, whose trade it is not to do anything, but to observe everything; and who, upon that account, are often capable of combining together the powers of the most distant and dissimilar objects. In the progress of society, philosophy or speculation becomes, like every other employment, the principal or sole trade and occupation of a particular class of citizens. Like every other employment too, it is subdivided into a great number of different branches, each of which affords occupation to a peculiar tribe or class of philosophers; and this subdivision of employment in philosophy, as well as in every other business, improves dexterity, and saves time. Each individual becomes more expert in his own peculiar branch, more work is done upon the whole, and the quantity of science is considerably increased by it.

10 It is the great multiplication of the productions of all the different arts, in consequence of the division of labour, which occasions, in a well-governed society, that universal opulence,[1] which extends itself to the lowest ranks of the people. Every workman has a great quantity of his own work to dispose of beyond what he himself has occasion for; and every other workman being exactly in the same situation, he is enabled to exchange a great quantity of his own goods for a great quantity, or, what comes to the same thing, for the price of a great quantity of theirs. He supplies them abundantly with what they have occasion for, and they accommodate him as amply with what he has occasion for, and a general plenty diffuses itself through all the different ranks of the society.

Observe the accommodation of the most common artificer or day-labourer in a civilised and thriving country, and you will perceive that the number of people of whose industry a part, though but a small part, has been employed in procuring him this accommodation, exceeds all computation. The woollen coat, for example, which covers the day-labourer, as coarse and rough as it may appear, is the produce of the joint labour of a great multitude of workmen. The shepherd, the sorter of the wool, the wool-comber or carder, the dyer the scribbler, the spinner, the weaver, the fuller, the dresser,[2] with many others, must all join their different arts in order to complete even this homely production. How many merchants and carriers, besides, must have been employed in transporting the materials from some of those workmen to others who often live in a very distant part of the country! how much commerce and navigation in particular, how many ship-builders, sailors, sail-makers, rope-makers, must have been employed in order to bring together the different drugs made use of by the dyer, which often come from the remotest corners of the world! What a variety of labour, too, is necessary in order to produce the tools of the meanest of those workmen! To say nothing of such complicated machines as the ship of the sailor, the mill of the fuller, or even the loom of the weaver, let us consider only what a variety of labour is requisite in order to form that very simple machine, the

---

[1] opulence: wealth

[2] scribbler, fuller, dresser: workers in the production of cloth. The scribbler tends to the scribbling machine, which "teased" the wool of impurities. The fuller beat the cloth to clean and thicken it. The dresser finished the cloth.

shears with which the shepherd clips the wool. The miner, the builder of the furnace for smelting the ore, the seller of the timber, the burner of the charcoal to be made use of in the smelting-house, the brick-maker, the brick-layer, the workmen who attend the furnace, the mill-wright, the forger, the smith, must all of them join their different arts in order to produce them. Were we to examine, in the same manner, all the different parts of his dress and household furniture, the coarse linen shirt which he wears next his skin, the shoes which cover his feet, the bed which he lies on, and all the different parts which compose it, the kitchen-grate at which he prepares his victuals,[3] the coals which he makes use of for that purpose, dug from the bowels of the earth, and brought to him perhaps by a long sea and a long land carriage, all the other utensils of his kitchen, all the furniture of his table, the knives and forks, the earthen or pewter plates upon which he serves up and divides his victuals, the different hands employed in preparing his bread and his beer, the glass window which lets in the heat and the light, and keeps out the wind and the rain, with all the knowledge and art[4] requisite for preparing that beautiful and happy invention, without which these northern parts of the world could scarce have afforded a very comfortable habitation, together with the tools of all the different workmen employed in producing those different conveniences; if we examine, I say, all these things, and consider what a variety of labour is employed about each of them, we shall be sensible that, without the assistance and co-operation of many thousands, the very meanest person in a civilised country could not be provided, even according to what we very falsely imagine the easy and simple manner in which he is commonly accommodated. Compared, indeed, with the more extravagant luxury of the great, his accommodation must no doubt appear extremely simple and easy; and yet it may be true, perhaps, that the accommodation of a European prince does not always so much exceed that of an industrious and frugal peasant as the accommodation of the latter exceeds that of many an African king, the absolute master of the lives and liberties of ten thousand naked savages.

Chapter II

Of the Principle Which Gives Occasion to the Division of Labour

This division of labour, from which so many advantages are derived, is not originally the effect of any human wisdom, which foresees and intends that general opulence to which it gives occasion. It is the necessary, though very slow and gradual consequence of a certain propensity in human nature which has in view no such extensive utility; the propensity to truck, barter, and exchange one thing for another.

Whether this propensity be one of those original principles in human nature of which no further account can be given; or whether, as seems more probable, it be the necessary consequence of the faculties of reason and speech,

---

[3] victuals: food.

[4] art: skill.

it belongs not to our present subject to inquire. It is common to all men, and to be found in no other race of animals, which seem to know neither this nor any other species of contracts. Two greyhounds, in running down the same hare, have sometimes the appearance of acting in some sort of concert. Each turns her towards his companion, or endeavours to intercept her when his companion turns her towards himself. This, however, is not the effect of any contract, but of the accidental concurrence of their passions in the same object at that particular time. Nobody ever saw a dog make a fair and deliberate exchange of one bone for another with another dog. Nobody ever saw one animal by its gestures and natural cries signify to another, this is mine, that yours; I am willing to give this for that. When an animal wants to obtain something either of a man or of another animal, it has no other means of persuasion but to gain the favour of those whose service it requires. A puppy fawns upon its dam, and a spaniel endeavours by a thousand attractions to engage the attention of its master who is at dinner, when it wants to be fed by him. Man sometimes uses the same arts with his brethren, and when he has no other means of engaging them to act according to his inclinations, endeavours by every servile and fawning attention to obtain their good will. He has not time, however, to do this upon every occasion. In civilised society he stands at all times in need of the co-operation and assistance of great multitudes, while his whole life is scarce sufficient to gain the friendship of a few persons. In almost every other race of animals each individual, when it is grown up to maturity, is entirely independent, and in its natural state has occasion for the assistance of no other living creature. But man has almost constant occasion for the help of his brethren, and it is in vain for him to expect it from their benevolence only. He will be more likely to prevail if he can interest their self-love in his favour, and show them that it is for their own advantage to do for him what he requires of them. Whoever offers to another a bargain of any kind, proposes to do this. Give me that which I want, and you shall have this which you want, is the meaning of every such offer; and it is in this manner that we obtain from one another the far greater part of those good offices which we stand in need of. It is not from the benevolence of the butcher, the brewer, or the baker that we expect our dinner, but from their regard to their own interest. We address ourselves, not to their humanity but to their self-love, and never talk to them of our own necessities but of their advantages. . . .

As it is by treaty, by barter, and by purchase that we obtain from one another the greater part of those mutual good offices which we stand in need of, so it is this same trucking disposition which originally gives occasion to the division of labour. In a tribe of hunters or shepherds a particular person makes bows and arrows, for example, with more readiness and dexterity than any other. He frequently exchanges them for cattle or for venison[5] with his companions; and he finds at last that he can in this manner get more cattle and venison than if he himself went to the field to catch them. From a regard to his own interest, therefore, the making of bows and arrows grows to be his chief business, and he becomes a sort of armourer. Another excels in making the frames and covers of

[5] venison: deer.

their little huts or movable houses. He is accustomed to be of use in this way to his neighbours, who reward him in the same manner with cattle and with venison, till at last he finds it his interest to dedicate himself entirely to this employment, and to become a sort of house-carpenter. In the same manner a third becomes a smith or a brazier,[6] a fourth a tanner or dresser of hides or skins, the principal part of the clothing of savages. And thus the certainty of being able to exchange all that surplus part of the produce of his own labour, which is over and above his own consumption, for such parts of the produce of other men's labour as he may have occasion for, encourages every man to apply himself to a particular occupation, and to cultivate and bring to perfection whatever talent or genius he may possess for that particular species of business.

The difference of natural talents in different men is, in reality, much less than we are aware of; and the very different genius which appears to distinguish men of different professions, when grown up to maturity, is not upon many occasions so much the cause as the effect of the division of labour. The difference between the most dissimilar characters, between a philosopher and a common street porter, for example, seems to arise not so much from nature as from habit, custom, and education. When they came into the world, and for the first six or eight years of their existence, they were perhaps very much alike, and neither their parents nor play-fellows could perceive any remarkable difference. About that age, or soon after, they come to be employed in very different occupations. The difference of talents comes then to be taken notice of, and widens by degrees, till at last the vanity of the philosopher is willing to acknowledge scarce any resemblance. But without the disposition to truck, barter, and exchange, every man must have procured to himself every necessary and conveniency of life which he wanted. All must have had the same duties to perform, and the same work to do, and there could have been no such difference of employment as could alone give occasion to any great difference of talents.

As it is this disposition which forms that difference of talents, so remarkable among men of different professions, so it is this same disposition which renders that difference useful. Many tribes of animals acknowledged to be all of the same species derive from nature a much more remarkable distinction of genius, than what, antecedent[7] to custom and education, appears to take place among men. By nature a philosopher is not in genius and disposition half so different from a street porter, as a mastiff is from a greyhound, or a greyhound from a spaniel, or this last from a shepherd's dog. Those different tribes of animals, however, though all of the same species, are of scarce any use to one another. The strength of the mastiff is not, in the least, supported either by the swiftness of the greyhound, or by the sagacity of the spaniel, or by the docility of the shepherd's dog. The effects of those different geniuses and talents, for want of the power or disposition to barter and exchange, cannot be brought into a common stock, and do not in the least contribute to the better accommodation and conveniency of the species. Each animal is still obliged to support and defend itself,

---

[6] brazier: one who works with brass.

[7] antecedent: prior.

separately and independently, and derives no sort of advantage from that variety of talents with which nature has distinguished its fellows. Among men, on the contrary, the most dissimilar geniuses[8] are of use to one another; the different produces of their respective talents; by the general disposition to truck, barter, and exchange, being brought, as it were, into a common stock, where every man may purchase whatever part of the produce of other men's talents he has occasion for.

Chapter III

That the Division of Labour Is Limited by the Extent of the Market

As it is the power of exchanging that gives occasion to the division of labour, so the extent of this division must always be limited by the extent of that power, or, in other words, by the extent of the market. When the market is very small, no person can have any encouragement to dedicate himself entirely to one employment, for want of the power to exchange all that surplus part of the produce of his own labour, which is over and above his own consumption, for such parts of the produce of other men's labour as he has occasion for.

There are some sorts of industry, even of the lowest kind, which can be carried on nowhere but in a great town. A porter, for example, can find employment and subsistence in no other place. A village is by much too narrow a sphere for him; even an ordinary market town is scarce large enough to afford him constant occupation. In the lone houses and very small villages which are scattered about in so desert a country as the Highlands of Scotland, every farmer must be butcher, baker and brewer for his own family. In such situations we can scarce expect to find even a smith, a carpenter, or a mason, within less than twenty miles of another of the same trade. The scattered families that live at eight or ten miles distance from the nearest of them must learn to perform themselves a great number of little pieces of work, for which, in more populous countries, they would call in the assistance of those workmen. Country workmen are almost everywhere obliged to apply themselves to all the different branches of industry that have so much affinity to one another as to be employed about the same sort of materials. A country carpenter deals in every sort of work that is made of Wood: a country smith in every sort of work that is made of iron. The former is not only a carpenter, but a joiner, a cabinet-maker, and even a carver in wood, as well as a wheelwright, a plough-wright, a cart and waggon maker. The employments of the latter are still more various. It is impossible there should be such a trade as even that of a nailer in the remote and inland parts of the Highlands of Scotland. Such a workman at the rate of a thousand nails a day, and three hundred working days in the year, will make three hundred thousand nails in the year. But in such a situation it would be impossible to dispose of one thousand, that is, of one day's work in the year.

---

[8] geniuses: talents.

As by means of water-carriage a more extensive market is opened to every sort of industry than what land-carriage alone can afford it, so it is upon the sea-coast, and along the banks of navigable rivers, that industry of every kind naturally begins to sub-divide and improve itself, and it is frequently not till a long time after that those improvements extend themselves to the inland parts of the country. A broad-wheeled waggon, attended by two men, and drawn by eight horses, in about six weeks' time carries and brings back between London and Edinburgh near four ton weight of goods. In about the same time a ship navigated by six or eight men, and sailing between the ports of London and Leith, frequently carries and brings back two hundred ton weight of goods. Six or eight men, therefore, by the help of water-carriage, can carry and bring back in the same time the same quantity of goods between London and Edinburgh, as fifty broad-wheeled waggons, attended by a hundred men, and drawn by four hundred horses. Upon two hundred tons of goods, therefore, carried by the cheapest land-carriage from London to Edinburgh, there must be charged the maintenance of a hundred men for three weeks, and both the maintenance, and, what is nearly equal to the maintenance, the wear and tear of four hundred horses as well as of fifty great waggons. Whereas, upon the same quantity of goods carried by water, there is to be charged only the maintenance of six or eight men, and the wear and tear of a ship of two hundred tons burden, together with the value of the superior risk, or the difference of the insurance between land and water-carriage. Were there no other communication between those two places, therefore, but by land-carriage, as no goods could be transported from the one to the other, except such whose price was very considerable in proportion to their weight, they could carry on but a small part of that commerce which at present subsists between them, and consequently could give but a small part of that encouragement which they at present mutually afford to each other's industry. There could be little or no commerce of any kind between the distant parts of the world. What goods could bear the expense of land-carriage between London and Calcutta? Or if there were any so precious as to be able to support this expense, with what safety could they be transported through the territories of so many barbarous nations? Those two cities, however, at present carry on a very considerable commerce with each other, and by mutually affording a market, give a good deal of encouragement to each other's industry.

20 Since such, therefore, are the advantages of water-carriage, it is natural that the first improvements of art and industry should be made where this conveniency opens the whole world for a market to the produce of every sort of labour, and that they should always be much later in extending themselves into the inland parts of the country. The inland parts of the country can for a long time have no other market for the greater part of their goods, but the country which lies round about them, and separates them from the sea-coast, and the great navigable rivers. The extent of their market, therefore, must for a long time be in proportion to the riches and populousness of that country, and consequently their improvement must always be posterior to the improvement of that country. In our North American colonies the plantations have constantly followed either the

sea-coast or the banks of the navigable rivers, and have scarce anywhere extended themselves to any considerable distance from both. . . .

Chapter IV

Of the Origin and Use of Money

When the division of labour has been once thoroughly established, it is but a very small part of a man's wants which the produce of his own labour can supply. He supplies the far greater part of them by exchanging that surplus part of the produce of his own labour, which is over and above his own consumption, for such parts of the produce of other men's labour as he has occasion for. Every man thus lives by exchanging, or becomes in some measure a merchant, and the society itself grows to be what is properly a commercial society.

But when the division of labour first began to take place, this power of exchanging must frequently have been very much clogged and embarrassed in its operations. One man, we shall suppose, has more of a certain commodity than he himself has occasion for, while another has less. The former consequently would be glad to dispose of, and the latter to purchase, a part of this superfluity. But if this latter should chance to have nothing that the former stands in need of, no exchange can be made between them. The butcher has more meat in his shop than he himself can consume, and the brewer and the baker would each of them be willing to purchase a part of it. But they have nothing to offer in exchange, except the different productions of their respective trades, and the butcher is already provided with all the bread and beer which he has immediate occasion for. No exchange can, in this case, be made between them. He cannot be their merchant, nor they his customers; and they are all of them thus mutually less serviceable to one another. In order to avoid the inconveniency of such situations, every prudent man in every period of society, after the first establishment of the division of labour, must naturally have endeavoured to manage his affairs in such a manner as to have at all times by him, besides the peculiar produce of his own industry, a certain quantity of some one commodity or other, such as he imagined few people would be likely to refuse in exchange for the produce of their industry.

Many different commodities, it is probable, were successively both thought of and employed for this purpose. In the rude ages of society, cattle are said to have been the common instrument of commerce; and, though they must have been a most inconvenient one, yet in old times we find things were frequently valued according to the number of cattle which had been given in exchange for them. The armour of Diomede, says Homer, cost only nine oxen; but that of Glaucus[9] cost an hundred oxen. Salt is said to be the common instrument of commerce and exchanges in Abyssinia; a species of shells in some parts of the coast of India; dried cod at Newfoundland; tobacco in Virginia; sugar in some of our

---

[9] Diomede . . . Glaucus: In Homer's *Iliad,* Diomedes and Glaucus met on the field of battle, but instead of fighting, they exchanged shields. Glaucus's shield, however, was made of gold.

West India colonies; hides or dressed leather in some other countries; and there is at this day a village in Scotland where it is not uncommon, I am told, for a workman to carry nails instead of money to the baker's shop or the alehouse.[10]

In all countries, however, men seem at last to have been determined by irresistible reasons to give the preference, for this employment, to metals above every other commodity. Metals can not only be kept with as little loss as any other commodity, scarce anything being less perishable than they are, but they can likewise, without any loss, be divided into any number of parts, as by fusion those parts can easily be reunited again; a quality which no other equally durable commodities possess, and which more than any other quality renders them fit to be the instruments of commerce and circulation. The man who wanted to buy salt, for example, and had nothing but cattle to give in exchange for it, must have been obliged to buy salt to the value of a whole ox, or a whole sheep at a time. He could seldom buy less than this, because what he was to give for it could seldom be divided without loss; and if he had a mind to buy more, he must, for the same reasons, have been obliged to buy double or triple the quantity, the value, to wit, of two or three oxen, or of two or three sheep. If, on the contrary, instead of sheep or oxen, he had metals to give in exchange for it, he could easily proportion the quantity of the metal to the precise quantity of the commodity which he had immediate occasion for.

Different metals have been made use of by different nations for this purpose. Iron was the common instrument of commerce among the ancient Spartans; copper among the ancient Romans; and gold and silver among all rich and commercial nations.

Those metals seem originally to have been made use of for this purpose in rude bars, without any stamp or coinage. Thus we are told by Pliny,[11] upon the authority of Timæus, an ancient historian, that, till the time of Servius Tullius, the Romans had no coined money, but made use of unstamped bars of copper, to purchase whatever they had occasion for. These rude bars, therefore, performed at this time the function of money.

The use of metals in this rude state was attended with two very considerable inconveniencies; first, with the trouble of weighing; and, secondly, with that of assaying them. In the precious metals, where a small difference in the quantity makes a great difference in the value, even the business of weighing, with proper exactness, requires at least very accurate weights and scales. The weighing of gold in particular is an operation of some nicety. In the coarser metals, indeed, where a small error would be of little consequence, less accuracy would, no doubt, be necessary. Yet we should find it excessively troublesome, if every time a poor man had occasion either to buy or sell a farthing's[12] worth of goods, he was obliged to weigh the farthing. The operation of assaying[13] is still more difficult, still more tedious, and, unless a part of the metal is fairly melted

[10] alehouse: Smith is referring to his own native village of Kircaldy.
[11] Pliny: famous, and reliable, Roman historian (23–79 CE).
[12] farthing: quarter of a penny.
[13] assaying: process for determining the quality of a metal.

in the crucible, with proper dissolvents, any conclusion that can be drawn from it, is extremely uncertain. Before the institution of coined money, however, unless they went through this tedious and difficult operation, people must always have been liable to the grossest frauds and impositions, and instead of a pound weight of pure silver, or pure copper, might receive in exchange for their goods an adulterated composition of the coarsest and cheapest materials, which had, however, in their outward appearance, been made to resemble those metals. To prevent such abuses, to facilitate exchanges, and thereby to encourage all sorts of industry and commerce, it has been found necessary, in all countries that have made any considerable advances towards improvement, to affix a public stamp upon certain quantities of such particular metals as were in those countries commonly made use of to purchase goods. Hence the origin of coined money, and of those public offices called mints; institutions exactly of the same nature with those of the aulnagers[14] and stampmasters of woollen and linen cloth. All of them are equally meant to ascertain, by means of a public stamp, the quantity and uniform goodness of those different commodities when brought to market.

It is in this manner that money has become in all civilised nations the universal instrument of commerce, by the intervention of which goods of all kinds are bought and sold, or exchanged for one another.

What are the rules which men naturally observe in exchanging them either for money or for one another, I shall now proceed to examine. These rules determine what may be called the relative or exchangeable value of goods.

The word value, it is to be observed, has two different meanings, and sometimes expresses the utility of some particular object, and sometimes the power of purchasing other goods which the possession of that object conveys. The one may be called "value in use;" the other, "value in exchange." The things which have the greatest value in use have frequently little or no value in exchange; and, on the contrary, those which have the greatest value in exchange have frequently little or no value in use. Nothing is more useful than water: but it will purchase scarce anything; scarce anything can be had in exchange for it. A diamond, on the contrary, has scarce any value in use; but a very great quantity of other goods may frequently be had in exchange for it.

In order to investigate the principles which regulate the exchangeable value of commodities, I shall endeavour to show:

First, what is the real measure of this exchangeable value; or, wherein consists the real price of all commodities.

Secondly, what are the different parts of which this real price is composed or made up.

And, lastly, what are the different circumstances which sometimes raise some or all of these different parts of price above, and sometimes sink them below their natural or ordinary rate; or, what are the causes which sometimes hinder the market price, that is, the actual price of commodities, from coinciding exactly with what may be called their natural price.

---

[14] aulnagers: officers appointed to attest to the quality of woolen goods.

I shall endeavour to explain, as fully and distinctly as I can, those three subjects in the three following chapters, for which I must very earnestly entreat both the patience and attention of the reader: his patience in order to examine a detail which may perhaps in some places appear unnecessarily tedious; and his attention in order to understand what may, perhaps, after the fullest explication which I am capable of giving of it, appear still in some degree obscure. I am always willing to run some hazard of being tedious in order to be sure that I am perspicuous,[15] and after taking the utmost pains that I can to be perspicuous, some obscurity may still appear to remain upon a subject in its own nature extremely abstracted.

Chapter V

Of the Real and Nominal Price of Commodities, or Their Price in Labour, and Their Price in Money

Every man is rich or poor according to the degree in which he can afford to enjoy the necessaries, conveniences, and amusements of human life. But after the division of labour has once thoroughly taken place, it is but a very small part of these with which a man's own labour can supply him. The far greater part of them he must derive from the labour of other people, and he must be rich or poor according to the quantity of that labour which he can command, or which he can afford to purchase. The value of any commodity, therefore, to the person who possesses it, and who means not to use or consume it himself, but to exchange it for other commodities, is equal to the quantity of labour which it enables him to purchase or command. Labour, therefore, is the real measure of the exchangeable value of all commodities.

The real price of everything, what everything really costs to the man who wants to acquire it, is the toil and trouble of acquiring it. What everything is really worth to the man who has acquired it, and who wants to dispose of it or exchange it for something else, is the toil and trouble which it can save to himself, and which it can impose upon other people. What is bought with money or with goods is purchased by labour as much as what we acquire by the toil of our own body. That money or those goods indeed save us this toil. They contain the value of a certain quantity of labour which we exchange for what is supposed at the time to contain the value of an equal quantity. Labour was the first price, the original purchase-money that was paid for all things. It was not by gold or by silver, but by labour, that all the wealth of the world was originally purchased; and its value, to those who possess it, and who want to exchange it for some new productions, is precisely equal to the quantity of labour which it can enable them to purchase or command. . . .

. . . When barter ceases, and money has become the common instrument of commerce, every particular commodity is more frequently exchanged for money than for any other commodity. The butcher seldom carries his beef or his mutton

[15] perspicuous: easily understood.

to the baker, or the brewer, in order to exchange them for bread or for beer; but he carries them to the market, where he exchanges them for money, and afterwards exchanges that money for bread and for beer. The quantity of money which he gets for them regulates, too, the quantity of bread and beer which he can afterwards purchase. It is more natural and obvious to him, therefore, to estimate their value by the quantity of money, the commodity for which he immediately exchanges them, than by that of bread and beer, the commodities for which he can exchange them only by the intervention of another commodity; and rather to say that his butcher's meat is worth threepence or fourpence a pound, than that it is worth three or four pounds of bread, or three or four quarts of small beer. Hence it comes to pass that the exchangeable value of every commodity is more frequently estimated by the quantity of money, than by the quantity either of labour or of any other commodity which can be had in exchange for it. . . .

Chapter VIII

Of the Wages of Labour

The produce of labour constitutes the natural recompense or wages of labour.

40 In that original state of things, which precedes both the appropriation of land and the accumulation of stock, the whole produce of labour belongs to the labourer. He has neither landlord nor master to share with him.

Had this state continued, the wages of labour would have augmented with all those improvements in its productive powers to which the division of labour gives occasion. All things would gradually have become cheaper. They would have been produced by a smaller quantity of labour; and as the commodities produced by equal quantities of labour would naturally in this state of things be exchanged for one another, they would have been purchased likewise with the produce of a smaller quantity. . . .

But this original state of things, in which the labourer enjoyed the whole produce of his own labour, could not last beyond the first introduction of the appropriation of land and the accumulation of stock. It was at an end, therefore, long before the most considerable improvements were made in the productive powers of labour, and it would be to no purpose to trace further what might have been its effects upon the recompense or wages of labour.

As soon as land becomes private property, the landlord demands a share of almost all the produce which the labourer can either raise, or collect from it. His rent makes the first deduction from the produce of the labour which is employed upon land.

It seldom happens that the person who tills the ground has wherewithal to maintain himself till he reaps the harvest. His maintenance is generally advanced to him from the stock of a master, the farmer who employs him, and who would have no interest to employ him, unless he was to share in the produce of his labour, or unless his stock was to be replaced to him with a profit. This profit makes a second deduction from the produce of the labour which is employed upon land.

45 The produce of almost all other labour is liable to the like deduction of profit. In all arts and manufactures the greater part of the workmen stand in need of a master to advance them the materials of their work, and their wages and maintenance till it be completed. He shares in the produce of their labour, or in the value which it adds to the materials upon which it is bestowed; and in this share consists his profit.

It sometimes happens, indeed, that a single independent workman has stock sufficient both to purchase the materials of his work, and to maintain himself till it be completed. He is both master and workman, and enjoys the whole produce of his own labour, or the whole value which it adds to the materials upon which it is bestowed. It includes what are usually two distinct revenues, belonging to two distinct persons, the profits of stock, and the wages of labour.

Such cases, however, are not very frequent, and in every part of Europe, twenty workmen serve under a master for one that is independent; and the wages of labour are everywhere understood to be, what they usually are, when the labourer is one person, and the owner of the stock which employs him another.

What are the common wages of labour, depends everywhere upon the contract usually made between those two parties, whose interests are by no means the same. The workmen desire to get as much, the masters to give as little as possible. The former are disposed to combine in order to raise, the latter in order to lower the wages of labour.

It is not, however, difficult to foresee which of the two parties must, upon all ordinary occasions, have the advantage in the dispute, and force the other into a compliance with their terms. The masters, being fewer in number, can combine much more easily; and the law, besides, authorises, or at least does not prohibit their combinations, while it prohibits those of the workmen. We have no acts of parliament against combining to lower the price of work; but many against combining to raise it. In all such disputes the masters can hold out much longer. A landlord, a farmer, a master manufacturer, a merchant, though they did not employ a single workman, could generally live a year or two upon the stocks which they have already acquired. Many workmen could not subsist a week, few could subsist a month, and scarce any a year without employment. In the long-run the workman may be as necessary to his master as his master is to him; but the necessity is not so immediate.

50 We rarely hear, it has been said, of the combinations of masters, though frequently of those of workmen. But whoever imagines, upon this account, that masters rarely combine, is as ignorant of the world as of the subject. Masters are always and everywhere in a sort of tacit, but constant and uniform combination, not to raise the wages of labour above their actual rate. To violate this combination is everywhere a most unpopular action, and a sort of reproach to a master among his neighbours and equals. We seldom, indeed, hear of this combination, because it is the usual, and one may say, the natural state of things, which nobody ever hears of. Masters, too, sometimes enter into particular combinations to sink the wages of labour even below this rate. These are always conducted with the utmost silence and secrecy, till the moment of execution, and when the workmen yield, as they sometimes do, without resistance, though severely felt

by them, they are never heard of by other people. Such combinations, however, are frequently resisted by a contrary defensive combination of the workmen; who sometimes too, without any provocation of this kind, combine of their own accord to raise the price of their labour. Their usual pretences are, sometimes the high price of provisions; sometimes the great profit which their masters make by their work. But whether their combinations be offensive or defensive, they are always abundantly heard of. In order to bring the point to a speedy decision, they have always recourse to the loudest clamour, and sometimes to the most shocking violence and outrage. They are desperate, and act with the folly and extravagance of desperate men, who must either starve, or frighten their masters into an immediate compliance with their demands. The masters upon these occasions are just as clamorous upon the other side, and never cease to call aloud for the assistance of the civil magistrate, and the rigorous execution of those laws which have been enacted with so much severity against the combinations of servants, labourers, and journeymen. The workmen, accordingly, very seldom derive any advantage from the violence of those tumultuous combinations, which, partly from the interposition of the civil magistrate, partly from the superior steadiness of the masters, partly from the necessity which the greater part of the workmen are under of submitting for the sake of present subsistence, generally end in nothing, but the punishment or ruin of the ringleaders. . . .

There are certain circumstances, however, which sometimes give the labourers an advantage, and enable them to raise their wages considerably above this rate; evidently the lowest which is consistent with common humanity.

When in any country the demand for those who live by wages, labourers, journeymen, servants of every kind, is continually increasing; when every year furnishes employment for a greater number than had been employed the year before, the workmen have no occasion to combine in order to raise their wages. The scarcity of hands occasions a competition among masters, who bid against one another, in order to get workmen, and thus voluntarily break through the natural combination of masters not to raise wages.

The demand for those who live by wages, it is evident, cannot increase but in proportion to the increase of the funds which are destined for the payment of wages. These funds are of two kinds; first, the revenue which is over and above what is necessary for the maintenance; and, secondly, the stock which is over and above what is necessary for the employment of their masters.

When the landlord, annuitant,[16] or monied man, has a greater revenue than what he judges sufficient to maintain his own family, he employs either the whole or a part of the surplus in maintaining one or more menial servants. Increase this surplus, and he will naturally increase the number of those servants.

55 When an independent workman, such as a weaver or shoemaker, has got more stock than what is sufficient to purchase the materials of his own work, and to maintain himself till he can dispose of it, he naturally employs one or more journeymen with the surplus, in order to make a profit by their work. Increase this surplus, and he will naturally increase the number of his journeymen.

[16] annuitant: receiver of income from annuities, that is, yearly income from investments or land.

The demand for those who live by wages, therefore, necessarily increases with the increase of the revenue and stock of every country, and cannot possibly increase without it. The increase of revenue and stock is the increase of national wealth. The demand for those who live by wages, therefore, naturally increases with the increase of national wealth, and cannot possibly increase without it.

It is not the actual greatness of national wealth, but its continual increase, which occasions a rise in the wages of labour. It is not, accordingly, in the richest countries, but in the most thriving, or in those which are growing rich the fastest, that the wages of labour are highest. . . .

LEARNING MORE

Smith's writing is easier to understand if you are familiar with the economic and social context in which he wrote. Look up the "mercantile" system, for example, and write a few sentences that explain it. (Online resources that can help answer this question can be found on the *Ideas Across Time* website.)

QUESTIONING THE TEXT

1. Smith says that the division of labor results in improvements in productivity for three main reasons. What are they?
2. How does the division of labor extend "opulence" even to the "lowest ranks of the people" (par. 10)?
3. Paraphrase Smith's thinking about how the division of labor fuels exchange and how exchange in turn fuels commercial society.
4. Explain what Smith means when he says that "it is this same trucking disposition which originally gives occasion to the division of labour" (par. 14).
5. How are the unique talents of individuals essential to the economic well-being of a whole society (par. 16)?
6. Explain the relation between the extent of the division of labor and the extent of the market.
7. What is the measure of "exchangeable value" (see pars. 27–37)?
8. Why do the owners have the advantage over the workers in the setting of wages? Is your view of Smith in any way affected by his account of the relations between workers and owners?
9. What, according to Smith, causes a rise in wages?
10. Are there any circumstances under which the workers have the advantage in the matter of wages and employment?

ANALYZING THE WRITER'S CRAFT

1. Smith offers an *analysis* of a market economy. Cite two or three passages in his essay that illustrate this purpose in his work. (See the discussion of analysis in the Introduction, pp. 1–8.)

2. What kinds of evidence does Smith use to support his general observations? Cite two of his major contentions, and list the evidence he uses in support.
3. Cite three examples of especially effective transitions in Smith's writing.
4. What is the tone of this essay? To whom do you think the essay is addressed? Explain. Include a discussion of Smith's diction in your answer.
5. Write an outline of Smith's essay that highlights the progression of his argument.
6. Is Smith's essay an example of argument or persuasion? Explain.

MAKING CONNECTIONS

1. How might Smith's account of the market have influenced Charles Darwin's view of evolution (Chapter 3, pp. 167–180)? Is there any evidence, one way or the other?
2. Compare/contrast Smith's view of the role of labor with that of Karl Marx (see *The Communist Manifesto*, pp. 264–273).
3. Thomas Hobbes's *Leviathan* is one of the formative books of seventeenth-century British political philosophy. Smith quotes Hobbes with apparent approval. What ideas might Hobbes have contributed to Smith? (See excerpts from *Leviathan* on the *Ideas Across Time* website.)

FORMULATING IDEAS FOR WRITING

1. Are barter, trade, and exchange indeed a "propensity in human nature," or does Smith, looking at men engaged in business, incorrectly generalize from their behavior to the rest of us? Discuss.
2. Is improvement in the way things are made a constant, never-ending process leading to better and better living conditions for people in general, or is it an illusory search for utopian perfection in human life? Discuss.
3. Smith seems to assume that the independent worker is a threatened species, already overcome by the wage laborer employed by someone else. Do a little research to find out if the number of people who are "self-employed" in the United States is on the rise or on the decline (choose—but explain—your own point of comparison to establish "rise" or "decline"). Write an essay that assesses the meaning and/or importance of the trend you uncover.
4. What, in your view, does Smith think is the "purpose" or "goal" of an economy? What do *you* think is the purpose of an economy? What do you think ought to be the purpose of an economy? Formulate an essay that answers these questions.
5. Write an analysis of Smith's "method," that is, of how he goes about studying things and making his points. Include in your essay a discussion of whether you find his way of thinking and writing to be persuasive (see the discussion of analysis, argument, and persuasion in the Introduction, pp. 1–8).

The Communist Manifesto (1848)

Karl Marx and Friedrich Engels

"On the 14th of March [1883], at a quarter to three in the afternoon, the greatest living thinker ceased to think." With these words, Karl Marx's lifelong collaborator, Friedrich Engels (1820–1895), began the eulogy of the man whose economic and political ideas exerted unparalleled influence on millions of people across the globe in the twentieth century. Ironically, Marx was virtually unknown during his lifetime, a lifetime passed in poverty and intense political quarrels within a tiny revolutionary movement. He spent his life in the study and writing of the original works that made his name dangerous across the world and that served to shape all the international socialist and communist movements that, at one time, governed half the globe.

Born on May 5, 1818, from a long line of rabbis on both his father's and mother's side, Karl Marx was raised in an affluent home in Trier, on the Mosel River, in Germany. His father, who had converted to Protestantism to pursue a professional career, was a lawyer. Educated at universities in Bonn, Berlin, and Jena (where he received a Ph.D. in 1841), Marx married Jenny, the daughter of Baron von Westphalen, and began his career as the editor of an influential liberal newspaper in Cologne. But the Prussian authorities shut the paper down to silence Marx's ideas about economics, and he and Jenny were forced abroad. They settled briefly in Paris in 1843. From this point forward, Marx's true home was with the miniscule band of revolutionary German exiles among whom, first in Paris and Brussels and finally in London, he spent the remainder of his life.

He met Engels in Paris in 1844 and with him later wrote *The Communist Manifesto* (1848), as well as other works that shifted the ground on which all previous claims to radical social reform had been based. Where Tom Paine, to take a representative example, had staked his call to arms on "the Rights of Man," Marx, in contrast, based his revolutionary agitation on an economic analysis of history as a relentless evolution toward a state of genuine equality. For Marx, history—periodically taking the form of revolution—is driven by the struggle between classes, between an ever-changing array of oppressors and oppressed—patricians and slaves, feudal lords and vassals. This long history culminated for Marx in the explosive division in Victorian Britain between the owners of factories and material (the bourgeoisie) and the propertyless mass of the population, Marx's famous "working class" (or proletariat). When this working class revolted, Marx confidently predicted, it would inaugurate a new era in the history of humanity: communism. Because this new era would have come about through the revolt of the masses, it would also inaugurate the first truly equal, truly free society, the terminal point of the long evolution of human progress.

How this utopian vision inspired the murder of millions and the totalitarian tyranny over vast populations is a story for a different place. The following passages present instead Marx as analyst of the new capitalist order. His analysis was not only brilliant but even more influential than his politics, outlasting the collapse of communist regimes. No one has articulated in more dramatic or persuasive ways the necessary tumult of a capitalist economy, driven by the quest for profit to achievements beyond the wildest dreams of earlier generations and at the same time forced by the logic of profit-seeking to undermine all traditional ideals, practices, and relationships.

Engels, like Marx, came from a well-off German family. The eldest son of a thriving German industrialist, he had spent two years managing his father's cotton factory in the world's leading center of manufacturing, Manchester in northern England, before meeting Marx. Engels was so shocked by the disparities between wealth and poverty in the city that he wrote (in his early twenties) what remains one of the seminal accounts of the early industrial era, *The Condition of the Working Class in England in 1844.* Engels, who never married, took a subordinate position to Marx throughout their long partnership, judging Marx to be a prophetic thinker and the greatest man of his age. And although Engels supported Marx financially for most of his life, Marx nevertheless raised his family and conducted his research, writing, and political organizing under conditions of extreme poverty.

The Communist Manifesto was written as the party program of the Communist League, a revolutionary organization of German émigrés. Marx and Engels were asked to write the document as the organization's public statement of beliefs, a document to be used for a conference the league was holding in London in early 1848. Its overt propagandistic purpose makes the *Manifesto* one of Marx's most lucid works. Although its timing prophetically coincided with the 1848 wave of revolutions that swept across Europe, the *Manifesto,* published originally in German, was hardly noticed at the time, and the Communist League soon disintegrated. The first English version did not appear for almost forty years.

A specter is haunting Europe—the specter of Communism. All the powers of old Europe have entered into a holy alliance to exorcise this specter: Pope and Czar, Metternich and Guizot, French Radicals[1] and German police spies. Where is the party in opposition that has not been decried as Communistic by its opponents in power? Where the Opposition that has not hurled back the branding reproach of Communism, against the more advanced opposition parties, as well as against its reactionary adversaries?

---

[1] Metternich . . . Radicals: Prince Klemens Metternich (1772–1859), the most important European diplomat of the nineteenth century, led the forces of reaction to republicanism after the fall of Napoleon. François Guizot (1787–1874) was a leading French foe of democracy and proponent of limited monarchy. French Radicals such as Marie-François Marrast (1802–1852) and Alexander Marie (1795–1870) resisted the demands of the workers' parties in mid-nineteenth-century France.

Two things result from this fact:

1. Communism is already acknowledged by all European powers to be itself a power.
2. It is high time that Communists should openly, in the face of the whole world, publish their views, their aims, their tendencies, and meet this nursery tale of the Specter of Communism with a Manifesto of the party itself.

To this end, Communists of various nationalities have assembled in London, and sketched the following Manifesto, to be published in the English, French, German, Italian, Flemish, and Danish languages.

I. Bourgeois and Proletarians[2]

The history of all hitherto existing society[3] is the history of class struggles.

Freeman and slave, patrician and plebeian, lord and serf, guildmaster[4] and journeyman, in a word, oppressor and oppressed, stood in constant opposition to one another, carried on an uninterrupted, now hidden, now open fight, a fight that each time ended, either in a revolutionary reconstitution of society at large, or in the common ruin of the contending classes.

In the earlier epochs of history, we find almost everywhere a complicated arrangement of society into various orders, a manifold gradation of social rank. In ancient Rome we have patricians, knights, plebeians, slaves; in the Middle Ages, feudal lords, vassals, guild-masters, journeymen, apprentices, serfs; in almost all of these classes, again, subordinate gradations. The modern bourgeois society that has sprouted from the ruins of feudal society has not done away with class antagonisms. It has but established new classes, new conditions of oppression, new forms of struggle in place of the old ones.

Our epoch, the epoch of the bourgeoisie, possesses, however, this distinctive feature: It has simplified the class antagonisms. Society as a whole is more and more splitting up into two great hostile camps, into two great classes directly facing each other—Bourgeoisie and Proletariat.

---

[2] Bourgeois and Proletarians: Engels supervised the 1888 English edition of the *Manifesto* and added several clarifying footnotes. This is the first: "By bourgeosie is meant the class of modern capitalists, owners of the means of production and employers of wage-labor; by proletariat, the class of modern wage-laborers who, having no means of production of their own, are reduced to selling their labor power in order to live."

[3] "That is, all written history. In 1837, the pre-history of society, the social organization existing previous to recorded history, was all but unknown. Since then [August von] Haxthuasen [1792–1866] discovered common ownership of land in Russia, [George von] Maurer [1790–1872] proved it to be the social foundation from which all Teutonic races started in history, and, by and by, village communities were found to be, or to have been, the primitive form of society everywhere from India to Ireland. The inner organization of this primitive Communistic society was laid bare, in its typical form by [Lewis H.] Morgan's [1818–1881] crowning discovery of the true nature of the *gens* and its relation to the *tribe*. With the dissolution of these primeval communities, society begins to be differentiated into separate and finally antagonistic classes. I have attempted to retrace this process in *The Origins of the Family, Private Property, and the State*" [Engels's note].

[4] "Guildmaster, that is, a full member of a guild, a master within, not a head of a guild" [Engels's note].

From the serfs of the Middle Ages sprang the chartered burghers[5] of the earliest towns. From these burgesses the first elements of the bourgeoisie were developed.

The discovery of America, the rounding of the Cape, opened up fresh ground for the rising bourgeoisie. The East Indian and Chinese markets, the colonization of America, trade with the colonies, the increase in the means of exchange and in commodities generally, gave to commerce, to navigation, to industry, an impulse never before known, and thereby, to the revolutionary element in the tottering feudal society, a rapid development.

The feudal system of industry, in which industrial production was monopolized by closed guilds,[6] now no longer sufficed for the growing wants of the new markets. The manufacturing system took its place. The guild-masters were pushed aside by the manufacturing middle class; division of labor between the different corporate guilds vanished in the face of division of labor in each single workshop.

Meantime the markets kept ever growing, the demand ever rising. Even manufacture no longer sufficed. Thereupon, steam and machinery revolutionized industrial production. The place of manufacture was taken by the giant, Modern Industry, the place of the industrial middle class, by industrial millionaires—the leaders of whole industrial armies, the modern bourgeois.

Modern industry has established the world market, for which the discovery of America paved the way. This market has given an immense development to commerce, to navigation, to communication by land. This development has, in its turn, reacted on the extension of industry; and in proportion as industry, commerce, navigation, railways extended, in the same proportion the bourgeoisie developed, increased its capital, and pushed into the background every class handed down from the Middle Ages.

We see, therefore, how the modern bourgeoisie is itself the product of a long course of development, of a series of revolutions in the modes of production and of exchange.

Each step in the development of the bourgeoisie was accompanied by a corresponding political advance of that class. An oppressed class under the sway of the feudal nobility, it became an armed and self-governing association in the medieval commune;[7] here independent urban republic (as in Italy and Germany), there taxable "third estate" of the monarchy (as in France); afterwards, in the

[5] chartered burghers: Municipalities that were "chartered" received certain powers from the Crown akin to today's "incorporated" towns or villages. A chartered burgher was a freeman admitted to full political participation in a chartered borough.

[6] closed guilds: In the Middle Ages, craft guilds, that is, organized trades closed to outsiders, enjoyed monopoly rights to produce certain goods in certain markets and imposed detailed regulations on members to govern not only wages and prices but the kinds of tools to be used and similar matters.

[7] "'Commune' was the name taken in France by the nascent towns even before they had conquered from their feudal lords and masters local self-government and political rights as the 'Third Estate.' Generally speaking, for the economic development of the bourgeoisie, England is here taken as the typical country, for its political development, France" [Engels's note].

period of manufacture proper, serving either the semifeudal or the absolute monarchy as a counterpoise against the nobility, and, in fact, cornerstone of the great monarchies in general—the bourgeoisie has at last, since the establishment of Modern Industry and of the world market, conquered for itself, in the modern representative State, exclusive political sway. The executive of the modern State is but a committee for managing the common affairs of the whole bourgeoisie.

15 The bourgeoisie has played a most revolutionary role in history.

The bourgeoisie, wherever it has got the upper hand, has put an end to all feudal, patriarchal, idyllic relations. It has pitilessly torn asunder the motley feudal ties that bound man to his "natural superiors," and has left remaining no other bond between man and man than naked self-interest, than callous "cash payment." It has drowned the most heavenly ecstasies of religious fervor, of chivalrous enthusiasm, of philistine sentimentalism, in the icy water of egotistical calculation. It has resolved personal worth into exchange value, and in place of the numberless indefeasible chartered freedoms has set up that single, unconscionable freedom—Free Trade. In one word, for exploitation, veiled by religious and political illusions, it has substituted naked, shameless, direct, brutal exploitation.

The bourgeoisie has stripped of its halo every occupation hitherto honored and looked up to with reverent awe. It has converted the physician, the lawyer, the priest, the poet, the man of science, into its paid wage laborers.

The bourgeoisie has torn away from the family its sentimental veil, and has reduced the family relation to a mere money relation.

The bourgeoisie has disclosed how it came to pass that the brutal display of vigor in the Middle Ages, which Reactionaries so much admire, found its fitting complement in the most slothful indolence. It has been the first to show what man's activity can bring about. It has accomplished wonders far surpassing Egyptian pyramids, Roman aqueducts, and Gothic cathedrals; it has conducted expeditions that put in the shade all former migrations of nations and crusades.

20 The bourgeoisie cannot exist without constantly revolutionizing the instruments of production, and thereby the relations of production, and with them the whole relations of society. Conservation of the old modes of production in unaltered form, was, on the contrary, the first condition of existence for all earlier industrial classes. Constant revolutionizing of production, uninterrupted disturbance of all social conditions, everlasting uncertainty and agitation distinguish the bourgeois epoch from all earlier ones. All fixed, fast-frozen relations, with their train of ancient and venerable prejudices and opinions, are swept away, all new-formed ones become antiquated before they can ossify. All that is solid melts into air, all that is holy is profaned, and man is at last compelled to face with sober senses his real conditions of life and his relations with his kind.

The need of a constantly expanding market for its products chases the bourgeoisie over the whole surface of the globe. It must nestle everywhere, settle everywhere, establish connections everywhere.

The bourgeoisie has through its exploitation of the world market given a cosmopolitan character to production and consumption in every country. To the great chagrin of reactionaries, it has drawn from under the feet of industry the national ground on which it stood. All old-established national industries have been destroyed or are daily being destroyed. They are dislodged by new industries, whose introduction becomes a life and death question for all civilized nations, by industries that no longer work up indigenous raw material, but raw material drawn from the remotest zones; industries whose products are consumed, not only at home, but in every quarter of the globe. In place of the old wants, satisfied by the production of the country, we find new wants, requiring for their satisfaction the products of distant lands and climes. In place of the old local and national seclusion and self-sufficiency, we have intercourse in every direction, universal interdependence of nations. And as in material, so also in intellectual production. The intellectual creations of individual nations become common property. National one-sidedness and narrow-mindedness become more and more impossible, and from the numerous national and local literatures there arises a world literature.

The bourgeoisie, by the rapid improvement of all instruments of production, by the immensely facilitated means of communication, draws all nations, even the most barbarian, into civilization. The cheap prices of its commodities are the heavy artillery with which it batters down all Chinese walls, with which it forces the barbarians' intensely obstinate hatred of foreigners to capitulate. It compels all nations, on pain of extinction, to adopt the bourgeois mode of production; it compels them to introduce what it calls civilization into their midst, i.e., to become bourgeois themselves. In a word, it creates a world after its own image.

The bourgeoisie has subjected the country to the rule of the towns. It has created enormous cities, has greatly increased the urban population as compared with the rural, and has thus rescued a considerable part of the population from the idiocy of rural life. Just as it has made the country dependent on the towns, so it has made barbarian and semi-barbarian countries dependent on the civilized ones, nations of peasants on nations of bourgeois, the East on the West.

More and more the bourgeoisie keeps doing away with the scattered state of the population, of the means of production, and of property. It has agglomerated[8] population, centralized means of production, and has concentrated property in a few hands. The necessary consequence of this was political centralization. Independent, or but loosely connected provinces, with separate interests, laws, governments, and systems of taxation, became lumped together into one nation, with one government, one code of laws, one national class interest, one frontier, and one customs tariff.

The bourgeoisie, during its rule of scarce one hundred years, has created more massive and more colossal productive forces than have all preceding generations together. Subjection of Nature's forces to man, machinery, application of chemistry to industry and agriculture, steam-navigation, railways, electric telegraphs, clearing of whole continents for cultivation, canalization of rivers, whole populations conjured out of the ground—what earlier century had even a presentiment that such productive forces slumbered in the lap of social labor?

---

[8] agglomerated: clustered.

We see then that the means of production and of exchange, which served as the foundation for the growth of the bourgeoisie, were generated in feudal society. At a certain stage in the development of these means of production and of exchange, the conditions under which feudal society produced and exchanged, the feudal organization of agriculture and manufacturing industry, in a word, the feudal relations of property became no longer compatible with the already developed productive forces; they became so many fetters. They had to be burst asunder; they were burst asunder.

Into their place stepped free competition, accompanied by a social and political constitution adapted to it, and by the economic and political sway of the bourgeois class.

A similar movement is going on before our own eyes. Modern bourgeois society with its relations of production, of exchange and of property, a society that has conjured up such gigantic means of production and of exchange, is like the sorcerer who is no longer able to control the powers of the netherworld whom he has called up by his spells. For many a decade past the history of industry and commerce is but the history of the revolt of modern productive forces against modern conditions of production, against the property relations that are the conditions for the existence of the bourgeoisie and of its rule. It is enough to mention the commercial crises that by their periodical return put the existence of the entire bourgeois society on trial, each time more threateningly. In these crises a great part not only of the existing products, but also of the previously created productive forces, are periodically destroyed. In these crises there breaks out an epidemic that, in all earlier epochs, would have seemed an absurdity—the epidemic of overproduction. Society suddenly finds itself put back into a state of momentary barbarism; it appears as if a famine, a universal war of devastation had cut off the supply of every means of subsistence; industry and commerce seem to be destroyed. And why? Because there is too much civilization, too much means of subsistence, too much industry, too much commerce. The productive forces at the disposal of society no longer tend to further the development of the conditions of bourgeois property; on the contrary, they have become too powerful for these conditions, by which they are fettered, and no sooner do they overcome these fetters than they bring disorder into the whole of bourgeois society, endanger the existence of bourgeois property. The conditions of bourgeois society are too narrow to comprise the wealth created by them. And how does the bourgeoisie get over these crises? On the one hand, by enforced destruction of a mass of productive forces; on the other, by the conquest of new markets, and by the more thorough exploitation of the old ones. That is to say, by paving the way for more extensive and more destructive crises, and by diminishing the means whereby crises are prevented.

The weapons with which the bourgeoisie felled feudalism to the ground are now turned against the bourgeoisie itself.

But not only has the bourgeoisie forged the weapons that bring death to itself; it has also called into existence the men who are to wield those weapons—the modern working class—the proletarians.

In proportion as the bourgeoisie, i.e., capital, is developed, in the same proportion is the proletariat, the modern working class, developed—a class of laborers, who live only so long as they find work, and who find work only so long as their labor increases capital. These laborers, who must sell themselves piecemeal, are a commodity, like every other article of commerce, and are consequently exposed to all the vicissitudes of competition, to all the fluctuations of the market.

Owing to the extensive use of machinery and to division of labor, the work of the proletarians has lost all individual character, and, consequently, all charm for the workman. He becomes an appendage of the machine, and it is only the most simple, most monotonous, and most easily acquired knack, that is required of him. Hence, the cost of production of a workman is restricted, almost entirely, to the means of subsistence that he requires for his maintenance, and for the propagation of his race. But the price of a commodity, and therefore also of labor, is equal to its cost of production. In proportion, therefore, as the repulsiveness of the work increases, the wage decreases. Nay more, in proportion as the use of machinery and division of labor increases, in the same proportion the burden of toil also increases, whether by prolongation of the working hours, by increase of the work exacted in a given time, or by increased speed of the machinery, etc.

Modern industry has converted the little workshop of the patriarchal master into the great factory of the industrial capitalist. Masses of laborers, crowded into the factory, are organized like soldiers. As privates of the industrial army they are placed under the command of a perfect hierarchy of officers and sergeants. Not only are they slaves of the bourgeois class, and of the bourgeois State; they are daily and hourly enslaved by the machine, by the overlooker, and, above all, by the individual bourgeois manufacturer himself. The more openly this despotism proclaims gain to be its end and aim, the more petty, the more hateful and the more embittering it is.

The less the skill and exertion of strength implied in manual labor, in other words, the more modern industry develops, the more is the labor of men superseded by that of women. Differences of age and sex have no longer any distinctive social validity for the working class. All are instruments of labor, more or less expensive to use, according to their age and sex.

No sooner has the laborer received his wages in cash, for the moment escaping exploitation by the manufacturer, than he is set upon by the other portions of the bourgeoisie, the landlord, the shopkeeper, the pawnbroker, etc.

The lower strata of the middle class—the small tradespeople, shopkeepers, and retired tradesmen generally, the handicraftsmen and peasants—all these sink gradually into the proletariat, partly because their diminutive capital does not suffice for the scale on which Modern Industry is carried on, and is swamped in the competition with the large capitalists, partly because their specialized skill is rendered worthless by new methods of production. The proletariat is recruited from all classes of the population.

The proletariat goes through various stages of development. With its birth begins its struggle with the bourgeoisie. At first the contest is carried on by individual laborers, then by the work people of a factory, then by the operatives of one trade, in one locality, against the individual bourgeois who directly exploits them. They direct their attacks not against the bourgeois conditions of production, but against the instruments of production themselves; they destroy imported wares that compete with their labor, they smash machinery to pieces, they set factories ablaze, they seek to restore by force the vanished status of the workman of the Middle Ages.

At this stage the laborers still form an incoherent mass scattered over the whole country, and broken up by their mutual competition. If anywhere they unite to form more compact bodies, this is not yet the consequence of their own active union, but of the union of the bourgeoisie, which class, in order to attain its own political ends, is compelled to set the whole proletariat in motion, and is moreover still able to do so for a time. At this stage, therefore, the proletarians do not fight their enemies, but the enemies of their enemies, the remnants of absolute monarchy, the landowners, the nonindustrial bourgeois, the petty bourgeoisie. Thus the whole historical movement is concentrated in the hands of the bourgeoisie; every victory so obtained is a victory for the bourgeoisie.

But with the development of industry the proletariat not only increases in number; it becomes concentrated in greater masses, its strength grows, and it feels that strength more. The various interests and conditions of life within the ranks of the proletariat are more and more equalized, in proportion as machinery obliterates all distinctions of labor, and nearly everywhere reduces wages to the same low level. The growing competition among the bourgeois, and the resulting commercial crises, make the wages of the workers ever more fluctuating. The unceasing improvement of machinery, ever more rapidly developing, makes their livelihood more and more precarious; the collisions between individual workmen and individual bourgeois take more and more the character of collisions between two classes. . . .

All previous historical movements were movements of minorities, or in the interest of minorities. The proletarian movement is the self-conscious, independent movement of the immense majority, in the interest of the immense majority. The proletariat, the lowest stratum of our present society, cannot stir, cannot raise itself up, without the whole superincumbent strata of official society being sprung into the air.

Though not in substance, yet in form, the struggle of the proletariat with the bourgeoisie is at first a national struggle. The proletariat of each country must, of course, first of all settle matters with its own bourgeoisie.

In depicting the most general phases of the development of the proletariat, we traced the more or less veiled civil war, raging within existing society, up to the point where that war breaks out into open revolution, and where the violent overthrow of the bourgeoisie lays the foundation for the sway of the proletariat.

Hitherto, every form of society has been based, as we have already seen, on the antagonism of oppressing and oppressed classes. But in order to oppress a class, certain conditions must be assured to it under which it can, at least, continue its slavish existence. The serf, in the period of serfdom, raised himself to membership in the commune, just as the petty bourgeois, under the yoke of feudal absolutism, managed to develop into a bourgeois. The modern laborer, on the contrary, instead of rising with the progress of industry, sinks deeper and deeper below the conditions of existence of his own class. He becomes a pauper, and pauperism develops more rapidly than population and wealth. And here it becomes evident, that the bourgeoisie is unfit any longer to be the ruling class in society, and to impose its conditions of existence upon society as an overriding law. It is unfit to rule because it is incompetent to assure an existence to its slave within his slavery, because it cannot help letting him sink into such a state, that it has to feed him, instead of being fed by him. Society can no longer live under this bourgeoisie, in other words, its existence is no longer compatible with society.

45 The essential condition for the existence and sway of the bourgeois class, is the formation and augmentation of capital; the condition for capital is wage-labor. Wage-labor rests exclusively on competition between the laborers. The advance of industry, whose involuntary promoter is the bourgeoisie, replaces the isolation of the laborers, due to competition, by their revolutionary combination, due to association. The development of Modern Industry, therefore, cuts from under its feet the very foundation on which the bourgeoisie produces and appropriates products. What the bourgeoisie therefore, produces, above all, are its own grave-diggers. Its fall and the victory of the proletariat are equally inevitable.

LEARNING MORE

1. To read the whole *Manifesto* see the *Ideas Across Time* website.
2. The revolutions of 1848 were thought, at the time, to be a harbinger of a republican triumph across Europe. To learn more about these revolutions, see useful links on the *Ideas Across Time* website.

QUESTIONING THE TEXT

1. How are "class antagonisms" different in the "epoch of the bourgeoisie" (par. 7) from all other eras?
2. How does Marx say the modern industrial state developed?
3. Explain what Marx means when he says that "The bourgeoisie has played a most revolutionary role in history" (par. 15).
4. Does Marx admire or detest the bourgeoisie?
5. How has the bourgeoisie been "the first to show what man's activity can bring about" (par. 19)?
6. Why can the bourgeoisie not exist "without constantly revolutionizing the instruments of production" (par. 20)?
7. Why does revolutionizing the instruments (or means) of production necessitate revolutionizing "the relations of production" (par. 20)?
8. How does modern industry draw all corners of the world into "civilization"?
9. What is the crisis that Marx says faces the bourgeoisie?

10. What characterizes labor in the age of industrial capitalism?
11. Describe the evolution of the working population from isolated laborers to a self-conscious "class."
12. What distinguishes the present historical movement from all previous historical movements (par. 41)?
13. Why does Marx believe that the fall of the bourgeoisie and the victory of the proletariat "are equally inevitable" (par. 45)?

ANALYZING THE WRITER'S CRAFT

1. At the time it was written, the *Manifesto* was the declaration of beliefs of a tiny, entirely inconsequential, and powerless political group. In what ways does the document reflect the utterly marginal position of the Communist League? In what ways does it read as a major historical document?
2. As a party platform, the *Manifesto* necessarily compresses a complex argument, advancing its views in a limited space (Adam Smith's *Wealth of Nations* and Marx's *Das Kapital* span, by comparison, many hundreds of pages). What is sacrificed to gain this extreme compression? What is gained? Do you find the compression in the document to be effective or confusing? Discuss by specific reference to passages in the text.
3. What is the tone of the document? Does the tone change? Choose two or three examples of Marx and Engels's assertions about the bourgeoisie, and, by analyzing the *tone* of the passages, explain whether you think the writers want us to applaud or abhor the bourgeoisie.
4. What sort of evidence do Marx and Engels rely on to make their argument? Offer two or three examples and discuss their effectiveness.
5. Some paragraphs in the text are long and complex; others are no longer than a sentence. What is the effect of this variation in paragraph length?
6. Where is this piece of writing especially polemical (that is, disputatious or aggressively confrontational rather than objectively analytical)? Illustrate and explain. How do you react to the polemical aspects of the piece?
7. Marx and Engels's analysis of social development stresses *inevitability*. To what extent do you find that the structure of their argument, and its rhetorical flare, reflects a similar force moving the reader inevitably toward Marx and Engels' revolutionary conclusion? Illustrate and explain.
8. Would you say this essay is an illustration of argument or persuasion? Explain.

MAKING CONNECTIONS

1. To what extent does Marx seem to build his views on those of Adam Smith (pp. 244–262)? Where do they differ?
2. To what extent do you think Marx concurs with Jean-Jacques Rousseau (Chapter 6, pp. 451–456) and Alexis de Tocqueville (Chapter 6, 458–460) on individuality and inequality?

3. Do you think that the analyses of Daniel J. Boorstin (Chapter 5, pp. 390–402) and Vaclav Havel (Chapter 5, pp. 404–412) would have induced Marx to revise his stolidly economic conception of change?

FORMULATING IDEAS FOR WRITING

1. Amplify one of Marx's main ideas (for example, "The bourgeoisie has played a most revolutionary role in history," or "[The bourgeoisie] has been the first to show what man's activity can bring about," or "The need of a constantly expanding market for its products chases the bourgeoisie over the whole surface of the globe") by evidence from today's economic or political circumstances. In writing this essay, take some time to explain the main idea, and then line up significant supporting evidence from current events and developments.
2. Do you think Marx's analysis and his prediction of the "inevitable" collapse of capitalism could still prove to be true, just a little delayed? Explain. If not, why not.
3. Is there class warfare in today's society, or are the outlook, values, and needs of all people in society more or less the same?
4. The United States was born of a revolution. Could a second revolution occur in the United States to change the form of our government? What conditions would be essential for such an eventuality (if any conditions *could* lead to such an eventuality)?
5. Write a letter to Marx warning him that his commitment to equality is likely to endanger freedom.

How I Went Out to Service (1874)

Louisa May Alcott

Although best-known for her hugely popular novel *Little Women* (1868), Louisa May Alcott (1832–1888) was a complex, independent figure, writing potboilers for adults under the penname A. M. Barnard and supporting radical causes, including women's and workers' rights, throughout her life.

Alcott grew up in Concord, Massachusetts, in the company of her father's formidable intellectual friends, such as Ralph Waldo Emerson and Henry David Thoreau. Her father, Bronson Alcott, was a well-known Transcendentalist in his own right and a leading educational reformer. But his ventures at launching schools all failed, and the family lived in genteel poverty. Louisa, the second daughter of the family, went to work early as a laundress, tutor, and servant.

The account of her "service" in this selection originally appeared in *The Independent* on June 4, 1874. In 1862, she worked as a nurse for the Civil War wounded. She almost died of typhus and suffered all her life from mercury poisoning caused by the medicine then used for the treatment of that disease. Her nursing experience was translated into *Hospital Sketches* (1863).

The turning point in her life and career was the publication of *Little Women: or, Meg, Jo, Beth and Amy* (1868), an immediate success and one of the classics of American literature. It was followed by the sequel *Good Wives* in 1869, *Little Men* in 1871, and finally *Jo's Boys and How They Turned Out: A Sequel to "Little Men"* in 1886.

Alcott never married, but when her sister May died, leaving behind a daughter, Lulu—named after Louisa—Alcott adopted her. Alcott's beloved mother died in 1877, and her father on March 4, 1888. Two days later, at the age of fifty-six, Alcott finally succumbed to the mercury poisoning she had first contracted nursing wounded soldiers of the Union Army a quarter century earlier.

When I was eighteen I wanted something to do. I had tried teaching for two years, and hated it; I had tried sewing, and could not earn my bread in that way, at the cost of health; I tried story-writing and got five dollars for stories which now bring a hundred; I had thought seriously of going upon the stage, but certain highly respectable relatives were so shocked at the mere idea that I relinquished my dramatic aspirations.

"What *shall* I do?" was still the question that perplexed me. I was ready to work, eager to be independent, and too proud to endure patronage. But the right task seemed hard to find, and my bottled energies were fermenting in a way that threatened an explosion before long.

My honored mother was a city missionary that winter, and not only served the clamorous poor, but often found it in her power to help decayed gentlefolk by quietly placing them where they could earn their bread without the entire sacrifice of taste and talent which makes poverty so hard for such to bear. Knowing her tact and skill, people often came to her for companions, housekeepers, and that class of the needy who do not make their wants known through an intelligence office.

One day, as I sat dreaming splendid dreams, while I made a series of little petticoats out of the odds and ends sent in for the poor, a tall, ministerial gentleman appeared, in search of a companion for his sister. He possessed an impressive nose, a fine flow of language, and a pair of large hands, encased in black kid gloves. With much waving of these somber members, Mr. R. set forth the delights awaiting the happy soul who should secure this home. He described it as a sort of heaven on earth. "There are books, pictures, flowers, a piano, and the best of society," he said. "This person will be one of the family in all respects, and only required to help about the lighter work, which my sister has done herself hitherto, but is now a martyr to neuralgia and needs a gentle friend to assist her."

5 My mother, who never lost her faith in human nature, in spite of many impostures, believed every word, and quite beamed with benevolent interest as she listened and tried to recall some needy young woman to whom this charming home would be a blessing. I also innocently thought:

"That sounds inviting. I like housework and can do it well. I should have time to enjoy the books and things I love, and D— is not far away from home. Suppose I try it."

So, when my mother turned to me, asking if I could suggest any one, I became as red as a poppy and said abruptly:

"Only myself."

"Do you really mean it?" cried my astonished parent.

10 "I really do if Mr. R. thinks I should suit," was my steady reply, as I partially obscured my crimson countenance behind a little flannel skirt, still redder.

The Reverend Josephus gazed upon me with the benign regard which a bachelor of five and thirty may accord a bashful damsel of eighteen. A smile dawned upon his countenance, "sicklied o'er with the pale cast of thought," or dyspepsia; and he softly folded the black gloves, as if about to bestow a blessing as he replied, with emphasis:

"I am sure you would, and we should think ourselves most fortunate if we could secure your society, and—ahem—services for my poor sister."

"Then I'll try it," responded the impetuous maid.

"We will talk it over a little first, and let you know to-morrow, sir," put in my prudent parent, adding, as Mr. R. arose: "What wages do you pay?"

15 "My dear madam, in a case like this let me not use such words as those. Anything you may think proper we shall gladly give. The labor is very light, for there are but three of us and our habits are of the simplest sort. I am a frail reed and may break at any moment; so is my sister, and my aged father cannot long remain; therefore, money is little to us, and any one who comes to lend her youth and strength to our feeble household will not be forgotten in the end, I assure you." And, with another pensive smile, a farewell wave of the impressive gloves, the Reverend Josephus bowed like a well-sweep and departed.

"My dear, are you in earnest?" asked my mother.

"Of course, I am. Why not try this experiment? It can but fail, like all the others."

"I have no objection; only I fancied you were rather too proud for this sort of thing."

"I am too proud to be idle and dependent, ma'am. I'll scrub floors and take in washing first. I do housework at home for love; why not do it abroad for money? I like it better than teaching. It is healthier than sewing and surer than writing. So why not try it?"

20 "It is going out to service, you know, though you are called a companion. How does that suit?"

"I don't care. Every sort of work that is paid for is service; and I don't mind being a companion, if I can do it well. I may find it is my mission to take care of neuralgic old ladies and lackadaisical clergymen. It does not sound exciting, but it's better than nothing," I answered, with a sigh; for it *was* rather a sudden downfall to give up being a Siddons and become a Betcinder.[1]

How my sisters laughed when they heard the new plan! But they soon resigned themselves, sure of fun, for Lu's adventures were the standing joke of the family. Of course, the highly respectable relatives held up their hands in holy horror at the idea of one of the clan degrading herself by going out to service. Teaching a private school was the proper thing for an indigent gentlewoman. Sewing even, if done in the seclusion of home and not mentioned in public, could be tolerated. Story-writing was a genteel accomplishment and reflected credit upon the name. But leaving the paternal roof to wash other people's teacups, nurse other people's ails, and obey other people's orders for hire—this, this was degradation; and headstrong Louisa would disgrace her name forever if she did it.

Opposition only fired the revolutionary blood in my veins, and I crowned my iniquity by the rebellious declaration:

"If doing this work hurts my respectability, I wouldn't give much for it. My aristocratic ancestors don't feed or clothe me and my democratic ideas of honesty and honor won't let me be idle or dependent. You need not know me if you are ashamed of me, and I won't ask you for a penny; so, if I never do succeed in anything, I shall have the immense satisfaction of knowing I am under no obligation to any one."

In spite of the laughter and the lamentation, I got ready my small wardrobe, consisting of two calico dresses and one delaine, made by myself, also several large and uncompromising blue aprons and three tidy little sweeping-caps; for I had some English notions about housework and felt that my muslin hair-protectors would be useful in some of the "light labors" I was to undertake. It is needless to say they were very becoming. Then, firmly embracing my family, I set forth, one cold January day, with my little trunk, a stout heart, and a five-dollar bill for my fortune.

"She will be back in a week," was my sister's prophecy, as she wiped her weeping eye.

"No, she won't, for she has promised to stay the month out and she will keep her word," answered my mother, who always defended the black sheep of her flock.

I heard both speeches, and registered a tremendous vow to keep that promise, if I died in the attempt—little dreaming, poor innocent, what lay before me.

Josephus meantime had written me several remarkable letters, describing the different members of the family I was about to enter. His account was peculiar, but I believed every word of it and my romantic fancy was much excited by the details he gave. The principal ones are as follows, condensed from the voluminous epistles which he evidently enjoyed writing:

"You will find a stately mansion, fast falling to decay, for my father will have nothing repaired, preferring that the old house and its master should

[1] Siddons . . . Betcinder: Sarah Siddons was a famous actress (1755–1831); Betcinder is another name for Cinderella.

crumble away together. I have, however, been permitted to rescue a few rooms from ruin; and here I pass my recluse life, surrounded by the things I love. This will naturally be more attractive to you than the gloomy apartments my father inhabits, and I hope you will here allow me to minister to your young and cheerful nature when your daily cares are over. I need such companionship and shall always welcome you to my abode.

"Eliza, my sister, is a child at forty, for she has lived alone with my father and an old servant all her life. She is a good creature, but not lively, and needs stirring up, as you will soon see. Also I hope by your means to rescue her from the evil influence of Puah, who, in my estimation, is a *wretch*. She has gained entire control over Eliza, and warps her mind with great skill, prejudicing her against *me* and thereby desolating my home. Puah hates *me* and always has. Why I know not, except that I will not yield to her control. She ruled here for years while I was away, and my return upset all her nefarious plans. It will always be my firm opinion that she has tried to *poison me,* and may again. But even this dark suspicion will not deter me from my duty. I cannot send her away, for both my deluded father and my sister have entire faith in her, and I cannot shake it. She is faithful and kind to them, so I submit and remain to guard them, even at the risk of my life.

"I tell you these things because I wish you to know all and be warned, for this old hag has a specious tongue, and I should grieve to see you deceived by her lies. Say nothing, but watch her silently, and help me to thwart her evil plots; but do not trust her, or beware."

Now this was altogether romantic and sensational, and I felt as if about to enter one of those delightfully dangerous houses we read of in novels, where perils, mysteries, and sins freely disport themselves, till the newcomer sets all to rights, after unheard of trials and escapes.

I arrived at twilight, just the proper time for the heroine to appear; and, as no one answered my modest solo on the rusty knocker, I walked in and looked about me. Yes, here was the long, shadowy hall, where the ghosts doubtless walked at midnight. Peering in at an open door on the right, I saw a parlor full of ancient furniture, faded, dusty, and dilapidated. Old portraits stared at me from the walls and a damp chill froze the marrow of my bones in the most approved style.

"The romance opens well," I thought, and, peeping in at an opposite door, beheld a luxurious apartment, full of the warm glow of firelight, the balmy breath of hyacinths and roses, the white glimmer of piano keys, and tempting rows of books along the walls.

The contrast between the two rooms was striking, and, after an admiring survey, I continued my explorations, thinking that I should not mind being "ministered to" in that inviting place when my work was done.

A third door showed me a plain, dull sitting room, with an old man napping in his easy-chair. I heard voices in the kitchen beyond, and, entering there, beheld Puah the fiend. Unfortunately, for the dramatic effect of the tableaux, all I saw was a mild-faced old woman, buttering toast, while she conversed with her familiar, a comfortable gray cat.

The old lady greeted me kindly, but I fancied her faded blue eye had a weird expression and her amiable words were all a snare, though I own I was rather disappointed at the commonplace appearance of this humble Borgia.

She showed me to a tiny room, where I felt more like a young giantess than ever, and was obliged to stow away my possessions as snugly as in a ship's cabin. When I presently descended, armed with a blue apron and "a heart for any fate," I found the old man awake and received from him a welcome full of ancient courtesy and kindliness. Miss Eliza crept in like a timid mouse, looking so afraid of her buxom companion that I forgot my own shyness in trying to relieve hers. She was so enveloped in shawls that all I could discover was that my mistress was a very nervous little woman, with a small button of pale hair on the outside of her head and the vaguest notions of work inside. A few spasmodic remarks and many awkward pauses brought me to teatime, when Josephus appeared, as tall, thin, and cadaverous as ever. After his arrival there was no more silence, for he preached all suppertime something in this agreeable style.

"My young friend, our habits, as you see, are of the simplest. We eat in the kitchen, and all together, in the primitive fashion; for it suits my father and saves labor. I could wish more order and elegance; but *my* wishes are not consulted and I submit. I live above these petty crosses, and, though my health suffers from bad cookery, I do not murmur. Only, I must say, in passing, that if you *will* make your battercakes green with saleratus,[2] Puah, I shall feel it my duty to throw them out of the window. *I* am used to poison; but I cannot see the coals of this blooming girl's stomach destroyed, as mine have been. And, speaking of duties, I may as well mention to you, Louisa (I call you so in a truly fraternal spirit), that I like to find my study in order when I come down in the morning; for I often need a few moments of solitude before I face the daily annoyances of my life. I shall permit *you* to perform this light task, for *you* have some idea of order (I see it in the formation of your brow), and feel sure that *you* will respect the sanctuary of thought. Eliza is so blind she does not see dust, and Puah enjoys devastating the one poor refuge I can call my own this side the grave. We are all waiting for you, sir. My father keeps up the old formalities, you observe; and I endure them, though *my* views are more advanced."

The old gentleman hastily finished his tea and returned thanks, when his son stalked gloomily away, evidently oppressed with the burden of his wrongs, also, as I irreverently fancied, with the seven "green" flapjacks he had devoured during the sermon.

I helped wash up the cups, and during that domestic rite Puah chatted in what I should have considered a cheery, social way had I not been darkly warned against her wiles.

"You needn't mind half Josephus says, my dear. He likes to hear himself talk and always goes on so before folks. I sometimes thinks his books and new ideas have sort of muddled his wits, for he is as full of notions as a paper is of pins; and he gets dreadfully put out if we don't give in to 'em. But, gracious me! they are so redicklus sometimes and so selfish I can't allow him to make a fool

[2] saleratus: a form of bicarbonate (of potash) used in backing powders.

of himself or plague Lizy. She don't dare to say her soul is her own; so I have to stand up for her. His pa don't know half his odd doings; for I try to keep the old gentleman comfortable and have to manage 'em all, which is not an easy job I do assure you."

I had a secret conviction that she was right, but did not commit myself in any way, and we joined the social circle in the sitting room. The prospect was not a lively one, for the old gentleman nodded behind his newspaper; Eliza, with her head pinned up in a little blanket, slumbered on the sofa, Puah fell to knitting silently; and the plump cat dozed under the stove. Josephus was visible, artistically posed in the luxurious recesses of his cell, with the light beaming on his thoughtful brow, as he pored over a large volume or mused with upturned eye.

45 Having nothing else to do, I sat and stared at him, till, emerging from a deep reverie, with an effective start, he became conscious of my existence and beckoned me to approach the "sanctuary of thought" with a dramatic waft of his large hand.

I went, took possession of an easy chair, and prepared myself for elegant conversation. I was disappointed, however; for Josephus showed me a list of his favorite dishes, sole fruit of all that absorbing thought, and, with an earnestness that flushed his saffron countenance, gave me hints as to the proper preparation of these delicacies.

I mildly mentioned that I was not a cook; but was effectually silenced by being reminded that I came to be generally useful, to take his sister's place, and see that the flame of life which burned so feebly in this earthly tabernacle was fed with proper fuel. Mince pies, Welsh rarebits, sausages, and strong coffee did not strike me as strictly spiritual fare; but I listened meekly and privately resolved to shift this awful responsibility to Puah's shoulders.

Detecting me in gape, after an hour of this high converse, he presented me with an overblown rose, which fell to pieces before I got out of the room, pressed my hand, and dismissed me with a fervent "God bless you, child. Don't forget the dropped eggs for breakfast."

I was up betimes next morning and had the study in perfect order before the recluse appeared, enjoying a good prowl among the books as I worked and becoming so absorbed that I forgot the eggs, till a gusty sigh startled me, and I beheld Josephus, in dressing gown and slippers, languidly surveying the scene.

50 "Nay, do not fly," he said, as I grasped my duster in guilty haste. "It pleases me to see you here and lends a sweet, domestic charm to my solitary room. I like that graceful cap, that housewifely apron, and I beg you to wear them often; for it refreshes my eye to see something tasteful, young, and womanly about me. Eliza makes a bundle of herself and Puah is simply detestable."

He sank languidly into a chair and closed his eyes, as if the mere thought of his enemy was too much for him. I took advantage of this momentary prostration to slip away, convulsed with laughter at the looks and words of this bald-headed sentimentalist.

After breakfast I fell to work with a will, eager to show my powers and glad to put things to rights, for many hard jobs had evidently been waiting for a stronger arm than Puah's and a more methodical head than Eliza's.

Everything was dusty, moldy, shiftless, and neglected, except the domain of Josephus. Up-stairs the paper was dropping from the walls, the ancient furniture was all more or less dilapidated, and every hold and corner was full of relics tucked away by Puah, who was a regular old magpie. Rats and mice reveled in the empty rooms and spiders wove their tapestry undisturbed, for the old man would have nothing altered or repaired and his part of the house was fast going to ruin.

I longed to have a grand "clearing up"; but was forbidden to do more than to keep things in livable order. On the whole, it was fortunate, for I soon found that my hands would be kept busy with the realms of Josephus, whose ethereal being shrank from dust, shivered at a cold breath, and needed much cosseting with dainty food, hot fires, soft beds, and endless service, else, as he expressed it, the frail reed would break.

I regret to say that a time soon came when I felt supremely indifferent as to the breakage, and very skeptical as to the fragility of a reed that ate, slept, dawdled, and scolded so energetically. The rose that fell to pieces so suddenly was a good symbol of the rapid disappearance of all the romantic delusions I had indulged in for a time. A week's acquaintance with the inmates of this old house quite settled my opinion, and further developments only confirmed it.

Miss Eliza was a nonentity and made no more impression on me than a fly. The old gentleman passed his days in a placid sort of doze and took no notice of what went on about him. Puah had been a faithful drudge for years, and, instead of being a "wretch," was, as I soon satisfied myself, a motherly old soul, with no malice in her. The secret of Josephus's dislike was that the reverend tyrant ruled the house, and all obeyed him but Puah, who had nursed him as a baby, boxed his ears as a boy, and was not afraid of him even when he became a man and a minister. I soon repented of my first suspicions, and grew fond of her, for without my old gossip I should have fared ill when my day of tribulation came.

At first I innocently accepted the fraternal invitations to visit the study, feeling that when my day's work was done I earned a right to rest and read. But I soon found that this was not the idea. I was not to read; but to be read to. I was not to enjoy the flowers, pictures, fire, and books; but to keep them in order for my lord to enjoy. I was also to be a passive bucket, into which he was to pour all manner of philosophic, metaphysical, and sentimental rubbish. I was to serve his needs, soothe his sufferings, and sympathize with all his sorrows—be a galley slave, in fact.

As soon as I clearly understood this, I tried to put an end to it by shunning the study and never lingering there an instant after my work was done. But it availed little, for Josephus demanded much sympathy and was bound to have it. So he came and read poems while I washed dishes, discussed his pet problems all meal-times, and put reproachful notes under my door, in which were comically mingled complaints of neglect and orders for dinner.

I bore it as long as I could, and then freed my mind in a declaration of independence, delivered in the kitchen, where he found me scrubbing the hearth. It was not an impressive attitude for an orator, nor was the occupation one a girl would choose when receiving calls; but I have always felt grateful for the intense discomfort of that moment, since it gave me the courage to rebel outright. Stranded on a small island of mat, in a sea of soapsuds, I brandished a scrubbing brush, as I indignantly informed him that I came to be a companion to his sister, not to him, and I should keep that post or none. This I followed up by reproaching him with the delusive reports he had given me of the place and its duties, and assuring him that I should not stay long unless matters mended.

60 "But I offer you lighter tasks, and you refuse them," he began, still hovering in the doorway, whither he had hastily retired when I opened my batteries.

"But I don't like the tasks, and consider them much worse than hard work," was my ungrateful answer, as I sat upon my island, with the softsoap conveniently near.

"Do you mean to say you prefer to scrub the hearth to sitting in my charming room while I read Hegel to you?" he demanded, glaring down upon me.

"Infinitely," I responded promptly, and emphasized my words by beginning to scrub with a zeal that made the bricks white with foam.

"Is it possible!" and, with a groan at my depravity, Josephus retired, full of ungodly wrath.

65 I remember that I immediately burst into jocund song, so that no doubt might remain in his mind, and continued to warble cheerfully till my task was done. I also remember that I cried heartily when I got to my room, I was so vexed, disappointed, and tired. But my bower was so small I should soon have swamped the furniture if I had indulged copiously in tears; therefore I speedily dried them up, wrote a comic letter home, and waited with interest to see what would happen next.

Far be it from me to accuse one of the nobler sex of spite or the small revenge of underhand annoyances and slights to one who could not escape and would not retaliate; but after that day a curious change came over the spirit of that very unpleasant dream. Gradually all the work of the house had been slipping into my hands; for Eliza was too poorly to help and direct, and Puah too old to do much besides the cooking. About this time I found that even the roughest work was added to my share, for Josephus was unusually feeble and no one was hired to do his chores. Having made up my mind to go when the month was out, I said nothing, but dug paths, brought water from the well, split kindlings, made fires, and sifted ashes, like a true Cinderella.

There never had been any pretense of companionship with Eliza, who spent her days mulling over the fire, and seldom exerted herself except to find odd jobs for me to do—rusty knives to clean, sheets to turn, old stockings to mend, and, when all else failed, some paradise of moths and mice to be cleared up; for the house was full of such "glory holds."

If I remonstrated, Eliza at once dissolved into tears and said she must do as she was told; Puah begged me to hold on till spring, when things would be much better; and pity pleaded for the two poor souls. But I don't think I could have stood it if my promise had not bound me, for when the fiend said "Budge" honor said "Budge not" and I stayed.

But, being a mortal worm, I turned now and then when ireful Josephus trod upon me too hard, especially in the matter of boot-blacking. I really don't know why that is considered such humiliating work for a woman; but so it is, and there I drew the line. I would have cleaned the old man's shoes without a murmur; but he preferred to keep their native rustiness intact. Eliza never went out, and Puah affected carpet-slippers of the Chinese-junk pattern. Josephus, however, plumed himself upon his feet, which, like his nose, were large, and never took his walks abroad without having his boots in a high state of polish. He had brushed them himself at first; but soon after the explosion I discovered a pair of muddy boots in the shed, set suggestively near the blacking-box. I did not take the hint; feeling instinctively that this amiable being was trying how much I would bear for the sake of peace.

The boots remained untouched; and another pair soon came to keep them company, whereat I smiled wickedly as I chopped just kindlings enough for my own use. Day after day the collection grew, and neither party gave in. Boots were succeeded by shoes, then rubbers gave a pleasing variety to the long line, and then I knew the end was near.

"Why are not my boots attended to?" demanded Josephus, one evening, when obliged to go out.

"I'm sure I don't know," was Eliza's helpless answer.

"I told Louizy I guessed you'd want some of 'em before long," observed Puah with an exasperating twinkle in her old eye.

"And what did she say?" asked my lord with an ireful whack of his velvet slippers as he cast them down.

"Oh! she said she was so busy doing your other work you'd have to do that yourself; and I thought she was about right."

"Louizy" heard it all through the slide, and could have embraced the old woman for her words, but kept still till Josephus had resumed his slippers with a growl and retired to the shed, leaving Eliza in tears, Puah chuckling, and the rebellious handmaid exulting in the china-closet.

Alas! for romance and the Christian virtues, several pairs of boots were cleaned that night, and my sinful soul enjoyed the spectacle of the reverend bootblack at his task. I even found my "fancy work," as I called the evening job of pairing a bucketful of hard russets with a dull knife, much cheered by the shoe-brush accompaniment played in the shed.

Thunder-clouds rested upon the martyr's brow at breakfast, and I was as much ignored as the cat. And what a relief that was! The piano was locked up, so were the bookcases, the newspapers mysteriously disappeared, and a solemn silence reigned at table, for no one dared to talk when that gifted tongue was mute. Eliza fled from the gathering storm and had a comfortable fit of neuralgia in her own room, where Puah nursed her, leaving me to skirmish with the enemy.

It was not a fair fight, and that experience lessened my respect for mankind immensely. I did my best, however—grubbed about all day and amused my dreary evenings as well as I could; too proud even to borrow a book, lest it should seem like a surrender. What a long month it was, and how eagerly I counted the hours of that last week, for my time was up Saturday and I hoped to be off at once. But when I announced my intention such dismay fell upon Eliza that my heart was touched, and Puah so urgently begged me to stay till they could get some one that I consented to remain a few days longer, and wrote posthaste to my mother, telling her to send a substitute quickly or I should do something desperate.

80 That blessed woman, little dreaming of all the woes I had endured, advised me to be patient, to do the generous thing, and be sure I should not regret it in the end. I groaned, submitted, and did regret it all the days of my life.

Three mortal weeks I waited; for, though two other victims came, I was implored to set them going, and tried to do it. But both fled after a day or two, condemning the place as a very hard one and calling me a fool to stand it another hour. I entirely agreed with them on both points, and, when I had cleared up after the second incapable lady, I tarried not for the coming of a third, but clutched my property and announced my departure by the next train.

Of course, Eliza wept, Puah moaned, the old man politely regretted, and the younger one washed his hands of the whole affair by shutting himself up in his room and forbidding me to say farewell because "he could not bear it." I laughed, and fancied it done for effect then; but I soon understood it better and did not laugh.

At the last moment, Eliza nervously tucked a sixpenny pocketbook into my hand and shrouded herself in the little blanket with a sob. But Puah kissed me kindly and whispered, with an odd look: "Don't blame us for anything. Some folks is liberal and some ain't." I thanked the poor old soul for her kindness to me and trudged gayly away to the station, whither my property had preceded me on a wheelbarrow, hired at my own expense.

I never shall forget that day. A bleak March afternoon, a sloppy, lonely road, and one hoarse crow stalking about a field, so like Josephus that I could not resist throwing a snowball at him. Behind me stood the dull old house, no longer either mysterious or romantic in my disenchanted eyes; before me rumbled the barrow, bearing my dilapidated wardrobe; and in my pocket reposed what I fondly hoped was, if not a liberal, at least an honest return for seven weeks of the hardest work I ever did.

85 Unable to resist the desire to see what my earnings were, I opened the purse and beheld *four dollars*.

I have had a good many bitter minutes in my life; but one of the bitterest came to me as I stood there in the windy road, with the sixpenny pocket-book open before me, and looked from my poor chapped, grimy, chill-blained hands to the paltry sum that was considered reward enough for all the hard and humble labor they had done.

A girl's heart is a sensitive thing. And mine had been very full lately; for it had suffered many of the trials that wound deeply yet cannot be told; so I think it as but natural that my first impulse was to go straight back to that sacred study and fling this insulting money at the feet of him who sent it. But I was so boiling over with indignation that I could not trust myself in his presence, lest I should be unable to resist the temptation to shake him, in spite of his cloth.

No, I would go home, show my honorable wounds, tell my pathetic tale, and leave my parents to avenge my wrongs. I did so; but over that harrowing scene I drop a veil, for my feeble pen refuses to depict the emotions of my outraged family. I will merely mention that the four dollars went back and the reverend Josephus never heard the last of it in that neighborhood.

My experiment seemed a dire failure and I mourned it as such for years; but more than once in my life I have been grateful for that serio-comico experience, since it has taught me many lessons. One of the most useful of these has been the power of successfully making a companion, not a servant, of those whose aid I need, and helping to gild their honest wages with the sympathy and justice which can sweeten the humblest and lighten the hardest task.

LEARNING MORE

To learn more about Louisa May Alcott's lesser known works, see the *Ideas Across Time* website.

QUESTIONING THE TEXT

1. What expectations do Alcott's introductory paragraphs raise about the nature of the job she's about to take up (pars. 1–32)? What hints do we have of how things might turn out?
2. What do you learn about the role of women from Alcott's predicament as an unemployed, unmarried eighteen-year-old girl?
3. How do you interpret Alcott's mother's warning—"It is going out to service"—and Alcott's response—"Every sort of work that is paid for is service"?
4. What kind of person is Alcott at eighteen?
5. How are Alcott's expectations rewarded when she first arrives at her new place of employment?
6. What sort of man does the Reverend Josephus reveal himself to be? Is he properly described as a "tyrant"?
7. Describe the tasks that Alcott is required daily to perform?
8. What does Alcott say she learned from her experience? Are there other lessons perhaps that she leaves unmentioned?

ANALYZING THE WRITER'S CRAFT

1. This essay depends more than usual on tone of voice. What is the tone of this essay? Explain and use illustrative examples. Why is the tone here so important? Are there places in the essay where the tone changes?
2. Alcott's narrative is about a number of profoundly serious subjects: the role of women, the nature of work and of the relations between workers and masters, hypocrisy, exploitation, and Christian charity. How does Alcott's

persona—the "Louisa" who narrates the essay—affect the way we think about these subjects as they arise in the essay?

3. Is this piece of writing best described as an "essay" or a "story"? Explain.
4. Show how Alcott's introductory paragraphs establish the points of reference for the essay. Discuss her use of contrasts, especially between the opening and the closing of the story.
5. Alcott is often ironic. She calls herself a "heroine" (par. 34), for example, and Josephus an "amiable being" (par. 69). How would you characterize this irony? Is it angry? Harsh? Gently mocking? Is her irony effective or excessive?
6. How does Alcott capture the qualities of personality through dialogue?
7. How would this account be different if it were written not as a narrative but, say, as an argument for better conditions and better pay for servants?

MAKING CONNECTIONS

1. Barbara Ehrenreich (pp. 316–319) can perhaps be looked at as a contemporary "sister" of Louisa May Alcott, certainly insofar as they are both wry commentators on women's employment. Discuss their similarities and differences.
2. If Barbara Ehrenreich might be a contemporary sister of Alcott's, is there a sibling relationship, too, with Mike Lefevre (pp. 300–307)?
3. Compare and contrast Alcott's situation as an upper-middle-class woman in the nineteenth century and the situation of the women whom Betty Friedan portrays in "The Problem Without a Name" (Chapter 6, pp. 496–509).
4. Tone matters a great deal in Alcott's essay. Compare and contrast her narrative tone of voice and Jamaica Kincaid's in "Girl" (Chapter 6, pp. 552–553). Which do you find most effective? Explain.

FORMULATING IDEAS FOR WRITING

1. Write an essay on a work experience of your own that began with high expectations and ended with angry disillusionment.
2. If you have read *Little Women,* you might want to compare the character of Jo in that novel and the "Louisa" in this essay.
3. Research the role of women in mid-nineteenth-century America, and discuss Alcott's essay as social commentary or a precursor to what today we would call investigative journalism.
4. Alcott does not comment explicitly on the fact that her employer is a Christian minister. How important is Josephus's Christian calling to the essay? Is there a religious moral to the essay?
5. Discuss Alcott's essay as a well-crafted narrative (see the Introduction, pp. 1–8). Comment on its structure, diction, and use of characterization.

Album: Money Matters (1493–1991)

Christopher Columbus, Gertrude Stein, W. H. Auden, Henry Mayhew, Oscar Wilde, Edward Bellamy, and Dana Gioia

The selections below are taken from a fascinating volume in the authoritative Oxford Books series, *The Oxford Book of Money* (ed. Kevin Jackson, 1995). Each addresses this unspoken question: what *is* money? Since money is all around us, and since we can as little do without money as we can do without water, you would think the question could be easily answered. But it turns out that ideas about money are no fewer than the uses of money.

In the first selection, Christopher Columbus gives us a glimpse of an almost unimaginable time before money. Writing half a millennium ago to a friend in Europe, he remarks on a discovery almost as startling as the discovery of the Americas itself: the discovery of a people for whom barter, "purchase," and property seem meaningless. "They never refuse to give any thing away which is demanded of them," Columbus says. His men shamelessly exploit these innocents, exchanging bits of china for ounces of gold. Columbus has to intervene and ban this "traffic," probably our first record of the epochal misunderstandings between civilizations that are signatures of modernity.

The writer Gertrude Stein (1874–1946), mentor of Ernest Hemingway and James Joyce, was a key figure in the community of writers and artists living in Paris in the years between World Wars I and II. She was an early champion of some of the great modernist painters, such as Pablo Picasso and Henri Matisse. Although only *The Autobiography of Alice B. Toklas* (1933), Stein's idiosyncratic biography of her lifelong companion, reached a wide public, she was well known among writers as a daring and eccentric experimentalist in prose. In this selection, some of her qualities of mind and style are apparent. Stein is acutely conscious of the mysteries of money. She notes, for example, that the government expends money in even numbers—say, $80,000,000—but collects money, such as in taxes, in odd numbers—say, $79,987,472. What happens to the difference, she shrewdly asks? Not only are the intrinsic qualities of money intriguing, but so too is the vexing relation between money and worth, that is, the intrinsic quality of an individual, which nonetheless we talk about in monetary terms—worth.

The poet W. H. Auden (1907–1973) compares Europe and America by examining their respective attitudes toward money. The leading poetic voice of his generation, Auden, born in York, England, immigrated to the United States in 1939 and became a U.S. citizen. A prolific writer in many forms, he exhibits a supreme verbal facility and wide-ranging intellectual interests. As a young man, he was an ardent publicist for radical left-wing political causes, as well as psychoanalysis; in his maturity, he espoused a stoic Christianity and became learned in Protestant theology. His unusual position as a trans-Atlantic intellectual gave his cultural observations an especial authority. The European, Auden says in the selection here reprinted, has always understood that "wealth could only be acquired at the expense of other human beings" whereas the American has always exploited "poor Mother Earth," and as a consequence has always expected, generation after generation, to get richer. If you are not richer than your father, it must be your "fault."

A chilling passage from *London Labour and the London Poor,* one of the classic documents of investigative journalism, written at the high point of the Industrial Revolution, shows that self-blame is not just a clever abstraction. Here the editor and journalist Henry Mayhew (1812–1887) records the dismal words of a starving boy struggling to be good on the ruthless London streets. In the next selection, the usually effervescent Oscar Wilde (1854–1900), known for his witty plays, also takes up the question of rich and poor. Enormously successful as a writer of elegant and entertaining dramas—such as *Lady Windermere's Fan* (1873) and the masterpiece *The Importance of Being Earnest* (1895)—Wilde, though married, was homosexual and sentenced late in his life to two years' hard labor for gross indecency. Although he enjoyed the company of the wealthy and aristocratic, Wilde was a committed socialist, and he saw lucidly both the life of the privileged and that of the exploited. In this selection, Wilde offers a humane gloss on Jesus's teaching about the poor. Money and riches are external, and easily lost, Wilde understands Jesus to say. But in "the treasury-house of your soul, there are infinitely precious things."

Be that as it may, when the utopian movements of the late nineteenth century plotted happiness for humankind, they seemed to stress fulfillment not only for spirit but often for body too. In the version of utopia represented by Edward Bellamy (1850–1898) in his popular novel *Looking Backward* (1888), for example, we have a kind of reversal of Columbus: society has reverted to a condition without money and trade. But not without the satisfactions that previously only money could buy. It's just that now those things once available only to the wealthy are available to all. Bellamy's utopians think that "buying and selling is essentially anti-social" and produces "a very low grade of civilization." The market is abolished by a goodwill not unlike that of the people whom Columbus encountered, generous to a fault, who "exhibit a great friendship toward everyone."

The final selection, a poem about money by Dana Gioia (b. 1950), concludes the album by wittily employing the innumerable words and phrases we use to describe money for a wry observation on the affinities between these two energies of human creation—money and words. Gioia is currently chair of the National Endowment for the Arts.

Christopher Columbus to Rafael Sanchez, 14 March 1493

They never refuse to give any thing away which is demanded of them, and will even themselves entreat an acceptance of their property. They exhibit a great friendship towards every one, and will give whatever they have for a trifle or nothing at all. I forbade my men to purchase any thing of them with such worthless articles as bits of earthenware, fragments of platters, broken glass, nails, and thongs of leather, although when they got possession of any such thing they valued it as highly as the most precious jewel in the world. In this manner of bartering, a sailor has acquired for a leather strap or piece of rope, gold to the amount of three *sueldos*. Others have obtained as much for a matter of still lower value. For new Spanish coins they would give any thing asked of them, as an ounce and a half or two ounces of gold, or thirty or forty pounds of cotton. Thus they would trade away their cotton and gold like idiots, for broken hoops, platters and glass. I prohibited their traffic on account of its injustice, and made them many presents of useful things which I had carried with me, for the purpose of gaining their affection, in order that they may receive the faith of Jesus Christ, be well disposed towards us, and inclined to submit to the King and Queen our Princes, and all the Spaniards, and furthermore that they may furnish us with the commodities which abound among them and we are in want of.

Gertrude Stein, *Saturday Evening Post*, 22 August 1936

It is very funny about money. The thing that differentiates man from animals is money. All animals have the same emotions and the same ways as men. Anybody who has lots of animals around knows that. But the thing no animal can do is count, and the thing no animal can know is money.

Men can count, and they do, and that is what makes them have money.

And so, as long as the earth turns around there will be men on it, and as long as there are men on it, they will count, and they will count money.

Everybody is always counting money.

5 The queen was in the parlor eating bread and honey the king was in his counting house counting out his money.

That is the way it is and the only trouble comes when they count money without counting it as money.

Counting is funny.

When you see a big store and see so many of each kind of anything that is in it, and on the counters, it is hard to believe that one more or less makes any difference to any one. When you see a cashier in a bank with drawers filled with money, it is hard to realize that one more or less makes any difference. But it does, if you buy it, or if you take it away or if you sell it, or if you make a mistake in giving it out. Of course it does. But a government, well a government does just that, it does not really believe that when there is such a lot that one more or less does make any difference. It is funny, if you buy anything well it may cost four dollars and fifty-five cents or four hundred and eighty-nine dollars or any other sum, but when government votes money it is always even money. One or five or fifteen or thirty-six more or less does not make any difference. The minute it gets to be billions it does not make any difference, fifteen or twenty-five or thirty-six more or less. Well, everybody has to think about that, because when it is made up it has to be made up by all sorts of odd numbers, everybody who pays taxes knows that, and it does make a difference.

All these odd pieces of money have to go to make that even money that is voted, but does it. It is voted even but it is collected odd. Everybody has to think about that.

The Dyer's Hand, 1963

W. H. Auden

Political and technological developments are rapidly obliterating all cultural differences and it is possible that, in a not remote future, it will be impossible to distinguish human beings living on one area of the earth's surface from those living on any other, but our different pasts have not yet been completely erased and cultural differences are still perceptible. The most striking difference between an American and a European is the difference in their attitudes towards money. Every European knows, as a matter of historical fact, that, in Europe, wealth could only be acquired at the expense of other human beings, either by conquering them or by exploiting their labor in factories. Further, even after the Industrial Revolution began, the number of persons who could rise from poverty to wealth was small; the vast majority took it for granted that they would not be much richer nor poorer than their fathers. In consequence, no European associates wealth with personal merit or poverty with personal failure.

To a European, money means power, the freedom to do as he likes, which also means that, consciously or unconsciously, he says: "I want to have as much money as possible myself and others to have as little money as possible."

In the United States, wealth was also acquired by stealing, but the real exploited victim was not a human being but poor Mother Earth and her creatures who were ruthlessly plundered. It is true that the Indians were expropriated or exterminated, but this was not, as it had always been in Europe, a matter of the conqueror seizing the wealth of the conquered, for the Indian had never realized the potential riches of his country. It is also true that, in the Southern states, men lived on the labor of slaves, but slave labor did not make them fortunes; what made slavery in the South all the more inexcusable was that, in addition to being morally wicked, it didn't even pay off handsomely.

Thanks to the natural resources of the country, every American, until quite recently, could reasonably look forward to making more money than his father, so that, if he made less, the fault must be his; he was either lazy or inefficient. What an American values, therefore, is not the possession of money as such, but his power to make it as a proof of his manhood; once he has proved himself by making it, it has served its function and can be lost or given away. In no society in history have rich men given away so large a part of their fortunes. A poor American feels guilty at being poor, but less guilty than an American *rentier*[1] who has inherited wealth but is doing nothing to increase it; what can the latter do but take to drink and psychoanalysis?

[1] *rentier:* a person whose income comes from property or investments.

5 In the Fifth Circle on the Mount of Purgatory,[2] I do not think that many Americans will be found among the Avaricious; but I suspect that the Prodigals may be almost an American colony. The great vice of Americans is not materialism but a lack of respect for matter.

London Labour and the London Poor, 1861

Henry Mayhew

The last statement I took was that of a boy of thirteen. I can hardly say that he was clothed at all. He had no shirt, and no waistcoat; all his neck and a great part of his chest being bare. A ragged cloth jacket hung about him, and was tied, so as to keep it together, with bits of tape. What he had wrapped round for trousers did not cover one of his legs, while one of his thighs was bare. He wore two old shoes; one tied to his foot with an old ribbon, the other a woman's old boot. He had an old cloth cap. His features were distorted somewhat, through being swollen with the cold. "I was begging, sometimes taking me with her; at other times she left me at the lodging-house in Hadley. She went in the country, round about Tunbridge and there, begging. Sometimes she had a day's work. We had plenty to eat then, but I haven't had much lately. My mother died at Hadley a year ago. I didn't know how she was buried. She was ill a long time, and I was out begging; for she sent me out to beg for myself a good while before that, and when I got back to the lodging-house they told me she was dead. I had sixpence in my pocket, but I couldn't help crying to think I'd lost my mother. I cry about it still. I didn't wait to see her buried, but I started on my own account. I met two navvies[3] in Bromley, and they paid my first night's lodging; and there was a man passing, going to London with potatoes, and the navvies gave the man a pot of beer to take me up to London in the van, and they went that way with me. I came to London to beg, thinking I could get more there than anywhere else, hearing that London was such a good place. I begged; but sometimes wouldn't get a farthing[4] in a day; often walking about the streets all night. I have been begging about all the time till now. I am very weak—starving to death. I never stole anything: I always kept my hands to myself. A boy wanted me to go with him to pick a gentleman's pocket. We was mates for two days, and then he asked me to go picking pockets; but I wouldn't. I know it's wrong, though I can neither read nor write. The boy asked me to do it to get into prison, as that would be better than the streets. He picked pockets to get into prison. He was starving about the streets like me. I never slept in a bed since I've been in London: I am sure I haven't: I generally slept under the dry arches in Weststreet, where they're building houses—I mean the arches for the cellars. I begged chiefly from the Jews about Petticoat-lane, for they all give away bread that their children leave—pieces of crust, and such-like. I would do anything to be out of this misery."

---

[2] The Fifth Circle on the Mount of Purgatory: in Canto 19 of Dante's (1265–1321) *Divine Comedy,* avarice is cleansed on the fifth circle of Purgatory.

[3] navvies: building trade laborers.

[4] farthing: quarter of a penny.

The Soul of Man under Socialism, 1891

Oscar Wilde

When Jesus talks about the poor he simply means personalities, just as when he talks about the rich he simply means people who have not developed their personalities. Jesus moved in a community that allowed the accumulation of private property just as ours does, and the gospel that he preached was, not that in such a community it is an advantage for a man to live on scanty, unwholesome food, to wear ragged, unwholesome clothes, to sleep in horrid, unwholesome dwellings, and a disadvantage for a man to live under healthy, pleasant, and decent conditions. Such a view would have been wrong there and then, and would, of course, be still more wrong now and in England; for as man moves northward the material necessities of life become of more vital importance, and our society is infinitely more complex, and displays far greater extremes of luxury and pauperism than any society of the antique world. What Jesus meant was this. He said to man, "You have a wonderful personality. Develop it. Be yourself. Don't imagine that your perfection lies in accumulating or possessing external things. Your affection is inside of you. If only you could realize that, you would not want to be rich. Ordinary riches can be stolen from a man. Real riches cannot. In the treasury-house of your soul, there are infinitely precious things, that may not be taken from you. And so, try to so shape your life that external things will not harm you. And try also to get rid of personal property. It involves sordid preoccupation, endless industry, continual wrong. Personal property hinders Individualism at every step." It is to be noted that Jesus never says that impoverished people are necessarily good, or wealthy people necessarily bad. That would not have been true. Wealthy people are, as a class, better than impoverished people, more moral, more intellectual, more well-behaved. There is only one class in the community that thinks more about money than the rich, and that is the poor. The poor can think of nothing else. That is the misery of being poor.

Looking Backward, 1888

Edward Bellamy

"You were surprised," he said, "at my saying that we got along without money or trade, but a moment's reflection will show that trade existed and money was needed in your day simply because the business of production was left in private hands, and that, consequently, they are superfluous now."

"I do not at once see how that follows," I replied.

"It is very simple," said Dr Leete. "When innumerable, unrelated, and independent persons produced the various things needful to life and comfort, endless exchanges between individuals were requisite in order that they might supply themselves with what they desired. These exchanges constituted trade, and money was essential as their medium. But as soon as the nation became the sole producer of all sorts of commodities, there was no need of exchanges between individuals that they might get what they required. Everything was procurable from one source, and nothing could be procured anywhere else. A system of direct distribution from the national storehouses took the place of trade, and for this money was unnecessary."

"How is this distribution managed?" I asked.

5 "On the simplest possible plan," replied Dr Leete. "A credit corresponding to his share of the annual product of the nation is given to every citizen on the public books at the beginning of each year, and a credit card issued him with which he procures at the public storehouses, found in every community, whatever he desires whenever he desires it. This arrangement, you will see, totally obviates the necessity for business transactions of any sort between individuals and consumers. Perhaps you would like to see what our credit cards are like?

"You observe," he pursued, as I was curiously examining the piece of pasteboard he gave me, "that this card is issued for a certain number of dollars. We have kept the old word but not the substance. The term, as we use it, answers to no real thing, but merely serves as an algebraical symbol for comparing the values of products with one another. For this purpose they are all priced in dollars and cents, just as in your day. The value of what I procure on this card is checked off by the clerk, who pricks out of these tiers of squares the price of what I order."

"If you wanted to buy something of your neighbour could you transfer part of your credit to him as consideration?" I inquired.

"In the first place," replied Dr Leete, "our neighbours have nothing to sell us, but in any event our credit would not be transferable, being strictly personal. Before the nation could even think of honouring any such transfer as you speak of, it would be bound to inquire into all the circumstances of the transaction, so as to be able to guarantee its absolute equity. It would have been reason enough, had there been no other, for abolishing money, that its possession was no indication of rightful title to it. In the hands of the man who had stolen it, or murdered for it, it was as good as in those which had earned it by industry. People nowadays interchange gifts and favours out of friendship, but buying and selling is considered absolutely inconsistent with the mutual benevolence and disinterestedness which should prevail between citizens and the sense of community of interests which supports our social system. According to our ideas, buying and selling is essentially anti-social in all its tendencies. It is an education in self-seeking at the expense of others, and no society whose citizens are trained in such a school can possibly rise above a very low grade of civilization."

"What if you have to spend more than your card in any one year?" I asked.

10 "The provision is so ample that we are more likely not to spend it all," replied Dr Leete. "But if extraordinary expenses should exhaust it, we can obtain a limited advance on the next year's credit, though this practice is not encouraged, and a heavy discount is charged to check it."

"If you don't spend your allowance, I suppose it accumulates?"

"That is also permitted to a certain extent, when a special outlay is anticipated. But unless notice to the contrary is given, it is presumed that the citizen who does not fully expend his credit did not have occasion to do so, and the balance is turned into the general surplus."

"Such a system does not encourage saving habits on the part of citizens," I said.

"It is not intended to," was the reply. "The nation is rich, and does not wish the people to deprive themselves of any good thing. In your day, men were bound to lay up goods and money against coming failure of the means of support and for their children. This necessity made parsimony a virtue. But now it would have no such laudable object, and, having lost its utility, it has ceased to be regarded as a virtue. No man any more has any care for the morrow, either for himself or his children, for the nation guarantees the nurture, education, and comfortable maintenance of every citizen, from the cradle to the grave."

"Money," from *The Lions of Winter,* 1991

Dana Gioia

Money is a kind of poetry.
WALLACE STEVENS

Money, the long green,
cash, stash, rhino, jack
or just plain dough.

Chock it up, fork it over,
shell it out. Watch it
burn holes through pockets.

To be made of it! To have it
to burn! Greenbacks, double eagles,
megabucks and Ginnie Maes.

It greases the palm, feathers a nest,
holds heads above water,
makes both ends meet.

Money breeds money.
Gathering interest, compounding daily.
Always in circulation.

Money. You don't know where it's been,
but you put it where your mouth is.
And it talks.

LEARNING MORE

You have probably studied something about Christopher Columbus. If you are interested in learning more about Gertrude Stein, W. H. Auden, Henry Mayhew, Edward Bellamy, or Dana Gioia, see the *Ideas Across Time* website.

QUESTIONING THE TEXT

Columbus

1. Who are "they"?
2. What is Columbus's attitude toward "them"?
3. Columbus says he banned the "traffic" of his men with the native population "on account of its injustice." What do you think he means by "injustice"? Explain.
4. What does this passage say about what makes things valuable?
5. What does this passage suggest is the relation of commerce and religion?

Stein

1. What's funny about money?
2. Is Stein serious, or is she writing tongue-in-cheek? What makes you think so?
3. According to Stein, what "makes" men have money? What do you think of her explanation?
4. What do you think Stein means to convey in par. 6?
5. Put in your own words what Stein means when she says "counting is funny."
6. Why does it matter that the government allocates money in even sums and collects it in odd sums?

Auden

1. What, according to Auden, characterizes the European attitude toward wealth and poverty? Why does he think this is so?
2. What characterizes the American attitude toward money? Explain.
3. Why do Americans give away so much of their money?
4. What do you think Auden means by his last sentence?
5. Do you think Auden favors the Europeans or the Americans? Why do you think so?

Mayhew

1. Where did the boy live when he was with his mother?
2. How does the boy get to London?
3. Why won't the boy pick pockets?
4. Why does his friend pick pockets?
5. Where does the boy sleep?
6. What do you think Mayhew wants us to take away from reading this passage? Understanding? Compassion? Anger? A determination to act . . . ? Why do you think so?

Wilde

1. In what ways was the economy of Jesus's world similar to that of Wilde's turn-of-the-century London?

2. What are the virtues of wealth, in Jesus's time and in Wilde's?
3. What are the bad things about poverty, in Jesus's time and in Wilde's?
4. Since poverty is not in itself desirable, Wilde reinterprets Jesus's sayings about the poor. How does he do this? What is Wilde's restatement of Jesus's teaching? Do you think Wilde is being fair to Jesus's meaning, or is he imposing his own views on Jesus's words?
5. How, according to Wilde, are the rich better than the poor? Do you agree? Why or why not?

Bellamy

1. According to Bellamy's utopian, Dr. Leete, why was money necessary in the "old days"?
2. How has national production abolished money?
3. How is the distribution of goods different in Dr. Leete's utopian society of the year 2000 and the pre-utopian society of 1888? (The full title of the book is *Looking Backward: 2000 to 1888*.)
4. Why do the utopians disapprove of buying and selling?
5. Why is parsimony no longer a virtue in the year 2000?
6. The year 2000 has come and gone—and no utopia. Can we read Bellamy and appreciate his ideas as readers in 1888, when he published the book, would have? Explain.

Gioia

1. What is the point of this poem?
2. What qualities of money are conveyed in each stanza?
3. How does the epigraph, from the poet Wallace Stevens (who was also a lawyer and worked most of his life as an insurance company executive), apply to the poem? Is poetry a kind of money?

ANALYZING THE WRITER'S CRAFT

Columbus

1. How do you think Columbus's audience affected his writing of this letter?
2. Is Columbus trying to illustrate something—say, his captainship—or is he describing a process?
3. How important are the details to Columbus's purpose? Could he have achieved his purpose in writing just as well without these details? (Consider, for example, his third sentence.)
4. Is this passage written from a position of power? From a merely observational vantage point? What, in short, is the impact of the writer's point of view on the writing?

Stein

1. What are the outstanding qualities of Stein's style?
2. How would you characterize Stein's diction?

3. Who is Stein's audience? What relation to the audience does this writing convey?
4. Why does Stein use a nursery rhyme to get her point across?
5. What is the effect of Stein's repetitions—for example, the repetition of the word "funny"?
6. How does Stein take advantage of the fact that words often have several meanings and connotations? (Again, think of "funny.")

Auden

1. Is Auden's passage anything more than a string of assertions? Is he conducting an argument, that is, proceeding by a train of reasoning? Explain and illustrate.
2. Why does Auden employ so many incisive generalizations—"Every European knows . . ." (par. 1), "every American . . . could reasonably . . ." (par. 4), "In no society in history . . ." (par. 4)? Do his generalizations expose common truths or ideas you have not encountered before? How does Auden's way of putting things add to or detract from his argument?
3. In the last paragraph, Auden refers to Dante's famous poem *The Divine Comedy,* which is about hell, purgatory, and heaven. Dante casts the avaricious into purgatory. Do you think that's a fair judgment?

Mayhew

1. Who is Mayhew's audience?
2. Does Mayhew want to report or to persuade his audience to act?
3. What distinguishes the language of the writer from the language of the boy?
4. Why does the boy—who is, after all, uneducated—not speak in dialect?
5. What is the effect of conveying the boy's words directly, in direct speech and in his own words, rather than indirectly through the writer?

Wilde

1. What does Wilde's diction suggest about his intended audience?
2. This brief passage is full of rhetorical variety and artful use of language. Discuss the effect, for example, of Wilde's deft employment of long and short sentences, or his use of repetition.
3. What methods does Wilde use to highlight the comparisons and contrasts he wishes to make—between the rich and the poor, and between Jesus's time and his own?
4. This passage comes from a book by Wilde called *The Soul of Man under Socialism,* in which Wilde lays out his social ideas. In what ways is this a "socialist" piece of writing?
5. Is this passage persuasive? Why or why not?
6. How does this passage resemble or differ from Oscar Wilde's preface to *Dorian Gray* (Chapter 7, pp. 587–588)?

Bellamy

1. *Looking Backward* is a novel. Which elements of this passage are novelistic? Which are not? What are the advantages to Bellamy of presenting his ideas in novel rather than in essay form?
2. Like Wilde, Bellamy is contrasting one time period and its way of life with another. How does he manage these contrasts?
3. How does Bellamy aim to show that the values of his time (1888) are not all that they might be?
4. Is Bellamy's account of life in the year 2000 attractive? Credible? Explain.

Gioia

1. Could Gioia make the same point in prose? Explain.
2. Is there a progression to Gioia's poem, or is it really just an arbitrary list of qualities?
3. How does the metrical pattern of this poem reinforce its "meaning"?
4. Is the ending effective—formally, rhetorically, intellectually?

MAKING CONNECTIONS

1. Compare/contrast this ensemble of views about money with those of Adam Smith (pp. 244–262). What qualities of money seem to emerge from this comparison and contrast?
2. Compare/contrast Auden's view of American attitudes about money with the illustrations at the end of this chapter (pp. 324–326).
3. Compare/contrast Auden's view of American values with those of James Baldwin (Chapter 1, pp. 29–35).

FORMULATING IDEAS FOR WRITING

1. Is money the root of all evil? Use quotations from the selections to support your view.
2. Are private values ever truly "individual" or "unique" (as in the often-heard observation "We're all different"), or are private values permeated by public values (for example, "American values")? Discuss with reference to money.
3. Write an essay that explains, or amplifies, or takes issue with W. H. Auden's provocative idea that "the great vice of Americans is not materialism but a lack of respect for matter."
4. Are utopian ideas just a waste of time—since they cannot ever be realized—or a helpful way to think about improving society? Discuss with reference to Bellamy.
5. Write two more stanzas for Gioia's poem.

Mike Lefevre, Steelworker (1974)

Studs Terkel

For more than half a century, Louis (Studs) Terkel has devoted himself to recording the lives of ordinary Americans of every class, age, and race. "What's it like," Terkel asks, "to be that goofy little soldier, scared stiff, with his bayonet pointed at Christ? What's it like to have been a woman in a defense-plant job during World War II? What's it like to be a kid at the front lines?" The tapes of his famous radio program on Chicago station WFMT, "The Studs Terkel Program," which ran from 1952 to 1997, and his many books of interviews, form an unparalled record of the personal stories of Americans from all walks of life in the twentieth century.

Born in the Bronx, New York, in 1912, Terkel was the third son of Russian-Jewish immigrants. His father was a tailor and his mother a seamstress, but when Terkel was ten, they moved to Chicago and opened first a boarding house and later a small hotel near Bughouse Square. Terkel says his fascination with all kinds of people can be traced to the diverse crowds that gathered in that square, including religious fanatics, labor organizers, and the spectrum of employed and unemployed people. Terkel received a law degree in 1934 but never practiced law, following a varied career in radio and writing. He proved to have an unusual gift for getting people to talk. His first book of oral history was *Division Street: America* (1967), for which he spoke to seventy people who had lived in Chicago. His next book recorded the experience of the Depression (*Hard Times*, 1967); it was followed by his interviews with people about work (*Working*, 1974), from which the present selection is taken. His interviews about people's experiences during World War II, contained in *The Good War* (1985), won him the Pulitzer Prize. His most recent publications are *Will the Circle Be Unbroken: Reflections on Death, Rebirth, and the Hunger for Faith* (2001) and *And They All Sang: Adventures of an Eclectice Disk Jockey* (2006). Terkel, who is Distinguished Scholar-in-Residence at the Chicago Historical Society, says his next-to-last book is about redemption. "Anybody can be redeemed," he says, pointing to his interview with C. P. Ellis, a former Ku Klux Klan leader who ended up fighting for the rights of black janitors, accompanied by his partner, an African-American woman.

It is a two-flat dwelling, somewhere in Cicero, on the outskirts of Chicago. He is thirty-seven. He works in a steel mill. On occasion, his wife Carol works as a waitress in a neighborhood restaurant; otherwise, she is at home, caring for their two small children, a girl and a boy.

At the time of my first visit, a sculpted statuette of Mother and Child was on the floor, head severed from body. He laughed softly as he indicated his three-year-old daughter: "She Doctor Spock'd it."

I'm a dying breed. A laborer. Strictly muscle work . . . pick it up, put it down, pick it up, put it down. We handle between forty and fifty thousand pounds of steel a day. (Laughs.) I know this is hard to believe—from four hundred pounds to three- and four-pound pieces. It's dying.

You can't take pride any more. You remember when a guy could point to a house he built, how many logs he stacked. He built it and he was proud of it. I don't really think I could be proud if a contractor built a home for me. I would be tempted to get in there and kick the carpenter in the ass (laughs), and take the saw away from him. 'Cause I would have to be part of it, you know.

5 It's hard to take pride in a bridge you're never gonna cross, in a door you're never gonna open. You're mass-producing things and you never see the end result of it. (Muses.) I worked for a trucker one time. And I got this tiny satisfaction when I loaded a truck. At least I could see the truck depart loaded. In a steel mill, forget it. You don't see where nothing goes.

I got chewed out by my foreman once. He said, "Mike, you're a good worker but you have a bad attitude." My attitude is that I don't get excited about my job. I do my work but I don't say whoopee-doo. The day I get excited about my job is the day I go to a head shrinker. How are you gonna get excited about pullin' steel? How are you gonna get excited when you're tired and want to sit down?

It's not just the work. Somebody built the pyramids. Somebody's going to build something. Pyramids, Empire State Building—these things just don't happen. There's hard work behind it. I would like to see a building, say, the Empire State, I would like to see on one side of it a foot-wide strip from top to bottom with the name of every bricklayer, the name of every electrician, with all the names. So when a guy walked by, he could take his son and say, "See, that's me over there on the forty-fifth floor. I put the steel beam in." Picasso can point to a painting. What can I point to? A writer can point to a book. Everybody should have something to point to.

It's the not-recognition by other people. To say a woman is *just* a housewife is degrading, right? Okay. *Just* a housewife. It's also degrading to say *just* a laborer. The difference is that a man goes out and maybe gets smashed.

When I was single, I could quit, just split. I wandered all over the country. You worked just enough to get a poke, money in your pocket. Now I'm married and I got two kids . . . (trails off). I worked on a truck dock one time and I was single. The foreman came over and he grabbed my shoulder, kind of gave me a shove. I punched him and knocked him off the dock. I said, "Leave me alone. I'm doing my work, just stay away from me, just don't give me the with-the-hands business."

10 Hell, if you whip a damn mule he might kick you. Stay out of my way, that's all. Working is bad enough, don't bug me. I would rather work my ass off for eight hours a day with nobody watching me than five minutes with a guy watching me. Who you gonna sock? You can't sock General Motors, you can't sock anybody in Washington, you can't sock a system.

A mule, an old mule, that's the way I feel. Oh yeah. See. (Shows black and blue marks on arms and legs, burns.) You know what I heard from more than one guy at work? "If my kid wants to work in a factory, I am going to kick the hell out of him." I want my kid to be an effete snob. Yeah, mm-hmm. (Laughs.) I want him to be able to quote Walt Whitman, to be proud of it.

If you can't improve yourself, you improve your posterity. Otherwise life isn't worth nothing. You might as well go back to the cave and stay there. I'm sure the first caveman who went over the hill to see what was on the other side—I don't think he went there wholly out of curiosity. He went there because he wanted to get his son out of the cave. Just the same way I want to send my kid to college.

I work so damn hard and want to come home and sit down and lay around. *But I gotta get it out.* I want to be able to turn around to somebody and say, "Hey, fuck you." You know? (Laughs.) The guy sitting next to me on the bus too. 'Cause all day I wanted to tell my foreman to go fuck himself, but I can't.

So I find a guy in a tavern. To tell him that. And he tells me too. I've been in brawls. He's punching me and I'm punching him, because we actually want to punch somebody else. The most that'll happen is the bartender will bar us from the tavern. But at work, you lose your job.

15 This one foreman I've got, he's a kid. He's a college graduate. He thinks he's better than everybody else. He was chewing me out and I was saying, "Yeah, yeah, yeah." He said, "What do you mean, yeah, yeah, yeah. Yes, *sir*." I told him, "Who the hell are you, Hitler? What is this *'Yes, sir'* bullshit? I came here to work, I didn't come here to crawl. There's a fuckin' difference." One word led to another and I lost.

I got broke down to a lower grade and lost twenty-five cents an hour, which is a hell of a lot. It amounts to about ten dollars a week. He came over—after breaking me down. The guy comes over and smiles at me. I blew up. He didn't know it, but he was about two seconds and two feet away from a hospital. I said, "Stay the fuck away from me." He was just about to say something and was pointing his finger. I just reached my hand up and just grabbed his finger and I just put it back in his pocket. He walked away. I grabbed his finger because I'm married. If I'd a been single, I'd a grabbed his head. That's the difference.

You're doing this manual labor and you know that technology can do it. (Laughs.) Let's face it, a machine can do the work of a man; otherwise they wouldn't have space probes. Why can we send a rocket ship that's unmanned and yet send a man in a steel mill to do a mule's work?

Automation? Depends how it's applied. It frightens me if it puts me out on the street. It doesn't frighten me if it shortens my work week. You read that little thing: what are you going to do when this computer replaces you? Blow up computers. (Laughs.) Really. Blow up computers. I'll be goddamned if a computer is gonna eat before I do! I want milk for my kids and beer for me. Machines can either liberate man or enslave 'im, because they're pretty neutral. It's man who has the bias to put the thing one place or another.

If I had a twenty-hour workweek, I'd get to know my kids better, my wife better. Some kid invited me to go on a college campus. On a Saturday. It was summertime. Hell, if I have a choice of taking my wife and kids to a picnic or going to a college campus, it's gonna be the picnic. But if I worked a twenty-hour week, I could go do both. Don't you think with that extra twenty hours people could really expand? Who's to say? There are some people in factories just by force of circumstance. I'm just like the colored people. Potential Einsteins don't have to be white. They could be in cotton fields, they could be in factories.

The twenty-hour week is a possibility today. The intellectuals, they always say there are potential Lord Byrons, Walt Whitmans, Roosevelts, Picassos working in construction or steel mills or factories. But I don't think they believe it. I think what they're afraid of is the potential Hitlers and Stalins that are there too. The people in power fear the leisure man. Not just the United States. Russia's the same way.

What do you think would happen in this country if, for one year, they experimented and gave everybody a twenty-hour week? How do they know that the guy who digs Wallace today doesn't try to resurrect Hitler tomorrow? Or the guy who is mildly disturbed at pollution doesn't decide to go to General Motors and shit on the guy's desk? You can become a fanatic if you had the time. The whole thing is time. That is, I think, one reason rich kids tend to be fanatic about politics: they have time. Time, that's the important thing.

It isn't that the average working guy is dumb. He's tired, that's all. I picked up a book on chess one time. That thing laid in the drawer for two or three weeks, you're too tired. During the weekends you want to take your kids out. You don't want to sit there and the kid comes up: "Daddy, can I go to the park?" You got your nose in a book? Forget it.

I know a guy fifty-seven years old. Know what he tells me? "Mike, I'm old and tired *all* the time." The first thing happens at work: when the arms start moving, the brain stops. I punch in about ten minutes to seven in the morning. I say hello to a couple of guys I like, I kid around with them. One guy says good morning to you and you say good morning. To another guy you say fuck you. The guy you say fuck you to is your friend.

I put on my hard hat, change into my safety shoes, put on my safety glasses, go to the bonderizer. It's the thing I work on. They rake the metal, they wash it, they dip it in a paint solution, and we take it off. Put it on, take it off, put it on, take it off, put it on, take it off . . .

I say hello to everybody but my boss. At seven it starts. My arms get tired about the first half-hour. After that, they don't get tired any more until maybe the last half-hour at the end of the day. I work from seven to three thirty. My arms are tired at seven thirty and they're tired at three o'clock. I hope to God I never get broke in, because I always want my arms to be tired at seven thirty and three o'clock. (Laughs.) 'Cause that's when I know that there's a beginning and there's an end. That I'm not brainwashed. In between, I don't even try to think.

If I were to put you in front of a dock and I pulled up a skid in front of you with fifty hundred-pound sacks of potatoes and there are fifty more skids just like it; and this is what you're gonna do all day, what would you think about—potatoes? Unless a guy's a nut, he never thinks about work or talks about it. Maybe about baseball or about getting drunk the other night or he got laid or he didn't get laid. I'd say one out of a hundred will actually get excited about work.

Why is it that the communists always say they're for the workingman, and as soon as they set up a country, you got guys singing to tractors? They're singing about how they love the factory. That's where I couldn't buy communism. It's the intellectuals' utopia, not mine. I cannot picture myself singing to a tractor, I just can't. (Laughs.) Or singing to steel. (Singsongs.) Oh whoop-dee-doo, I'm at the bonderizer, oh how I love this heavy steel. No thanks. Never hoppen.

Oh yeah, I daydream. I fantasize about a sexy blonde in Miami who's got my union dues. (Laughs.) I think of the head of the union the way I think of the head of my company. Living it up. I think of February in Miami. Warm weather, a place to lay in. When I hear a college kid say, "I'm oppressed," I don't believe him. You know what I'd like to do for one year? Live like a college kid. Just for one year. I'd love to. Wow! (Whispers.) Wow! Sports car! Marijuana! (Laughs.) Wild, sexy broads. I'd love that, hell yes, I would.

Somebody has to do this work. If my kid ever goes to college, I just want him to have a little respect, to realize that his dad is one of those somebodies. This is why even on—(muses) yeah, I guess, sure—on the black thing . . . (Sighs heavily.) I can't really hate the colored fella that's working with me all day. The black intellectual I got no respect for. The white intellectual I got no use for. I got no use for the black militant who's gonna scream three hundred years of slavery to me while I'm busting my ass. You know what I mean? (Laughs.) I have one answer for that guy: go see Rockefeller. See Harriman. Don't bother me. We're in the same cotton field. So just don't bug me. (Laughs.)

After work I usually stop off at a tavern. Cold beer. Cold beer right away. When I was single, I used to go into hillbilly bars, get in a lot of brawls. Just to explode. I got a thing on my arm here (indicates scar). I got slapped with a bicycle chain. Oh, wow! (Softly) Mmm. I'm getting older. (Laughs.) I don't explode as much. You might say I'm broken in. (Quickly) No, I'll never be broken in. (Sighs.) When you get a little older, you exchange the words. When you're younger, you exchange the blows.

When I get home, I argue with my wife a little bit. Turn on TV, get mad at the news. (Laughs.) I don't even watch the news that much. I watch Jackie Gleason. I look for any alternative to the ten o'clock news. I don't want to go to bed angry. Don't hit a man with anything heavy at five o'clock. He just can't be bothered. This is his time to relax. The heaviest thing he wants is what his wife has to tell him.

When I come home, know what I do for the first twenty minutes? Fake it. I put on a smile. I got a kid three years old. Sometimes she says, "Daddy, where've you been?" I say, "Work." I could have told her I'd been in Disneyland. What's work to a three-year-old kid? If I feel bad, I can't take it out on the kids. Kids are born innocent of everything but birth. You can't take it out on your wife either. This is why you go to a tavern. You want to release it there rather than do it at home. What does an actor do when he's got a bad movie? I got a bad movie every day.

I don't even need the alarm clock to get up in the morning. I can go out drinking all night, fall asleep at four, and bam! I'm up at six—no matter what I do. (Laughs.) It's a pseudo-death, more or less. Your whole system is paralyzed and you give all the appearance of death. It's an ingrown clock. It's a thing you just get used to. The hours differ. It depends. Sometimes my wife wants to do something crazy like play five hundred rummy or put a puzzle together. It could be midnight, could be ten o'clock, could be nine thirty.

What do you do weekends?

35 Drink beer, read a book. See that one? *Violence in America.* It's one of them studies from Washington. One of them committees they're always appointing. A thing like that I read on a weekend. But during the weekdays, gee . . . I just thought about it. I don't do that much reading from Monday through Friday. Unless it's a horny book. I'll read it at work and go home and do my homework. (Laughs.) That's what the guys at the plant call it—homework. (Laughs.) Sometimes my wife works on Saturday and I drink beer at the tavern.

I went out drinking with one guy, oh, a long time ago. A college boy. He was working where I work now. Always preaching to me about how you need violence to change the system and all that garbage. We went into a hillbilly joint. Some guy there, I didn't know him from Adam, he said, "You think you're smart." I said, "What's your pleasure?" (Laughs.) He said, "My pleasure's to kick your ass." I told him I really can't be bothered. He said, "What're you, chicken?" I said, "No, I just don't want to be bothered." He came over and said something to me again. I said, "I don't beat women, drunks, or fools. Now leave me alone."

The guy called his brother over. This college boy that was with me, he came nudging my arm, "Mike, let's get out of here." I said, "What are you worried about?" (Laughs.) This isn't unusual. People will bug you. You fend it off as much as you can with your mouth and when you can't, you punch the guy out.

It was close to closing time and we stayed. We could have left, but when you go into a place to have a beer and a guy challenges you—if you expect to go in that place again, you don't leave. If you have to fight the guy, you fight.

I got just outside the door and one of these guys jumped on me and grabbed me around the neck. I grabbed his arm and flung him against the wall. I grabbed him here (indicates throat), and jiggled his head against the wall quite a few times. He kind of slid down a little bit. This guy who said he was his brother took a swing at me with a garrison belt. He just missed and hit the wall. I'm looking around for my junior Stalin (laughs), who loves violence and everything. He's gone. Split. (Laughs.) Next day I see him at work. I couldn't get mad at him, he's a baby.

40 He saw a book in my back pocket one time and he was amazed. He walked up to me and he said, "You read?" I said, "What do you mean, I read?" He said, "All these dummies read the sports pages around here. What are you doing with a book?" I got pissed off at the kid right away. I said, "What do you mean, all these dummies? Don't knock a man who's paying somebody else's way through college." He was a nineteen-year-old effete snob.

Yet you want your kid to be an effete snob?

Yes. I want my kid to look at me and say, "Dad, you're a nice guy, but you're a fuckin' dummy." Hell yes, I want my kid to tell me that he's not gonna be like me . . .

If I were hiring people to work, I'd try naturally to pay them a decent wage. I'd try to find out their first names, their last names, keep the company as small as possible, so I could personalize the whole thing. All I would ask a man is a handshake, see you in the morning. No applications, nothing. I wouldn't be interested in the guy's past. Nobody ever checks the pedigree on a mule, do they? But they do on a man. Can you picture walking up to a mule and saying, "I'd like to know who his granddaddy was?"

I'd like to run a combination bookstore and tavern. (Laughs.) I would like to have a place where college kids came and a steelworker could sit down and talk. Where a workingman could not be ashamed of Walt Whitman and where a college professor could not be ashamed that he painted his house over the weekend.

If a carpenter built a cabin for poets, I think the least the poets owe the carpenter is just three or four one-liners on the wall. A little plaque: Though we labor with our minds, this place we can relax in was built by someone who can work with his hands. And his work is as noble as ours. I think the poet owes something to the guy who builds the cabin for him.

I don't think of Monday. You know what I'm thinking about on Sunday night? Next Sunday. If you work real hard, you think of a perpetual vacation. Not perpetual sleep . . . What do I think of on a Sunday night? Lord, I wish the fuck I could do something else for a living.

I don't know who the guy is who said there is nothing sweeter than an unfinished symphony. Like an unfinished painting and an unfinished poem. If he creates this thing one day—let's say, Michelangelo's Sistine Chapel. It took him a long time to do this, this beautiful work of art. But what if he had to create this Sistine Chapel a thousand times a year? Don't you think that would even dull Michelangelo's mind? Or if da Vinci had to draw his anatomical charts thirty, forty, fifty, sixty, eighty, ninety, a hundred times a day? Don't you think that would even bore da Vinci?

Way back, you spoke of the guys who built the pyramids, not the pharaohs, the unknowns. You put yourself in their category?

Yes. I want my signature on 'em, too. Sometimes, out of pure meanness, when I make something, I put a little dent in it. I like to do something to make it really unique. Hit it with a hammer. I deliberately fuck it up to see if it'll get by, just so I can say I did it. It could be anything. Let me put it this way: I think God invented the dodo bird so when we get up there we could tell Him, "Don't you ever make mistakes?" and He'd say, "Sure, look." (Laughs.) I'd like to make my imprint. My dodo bird. A mistake, *mine.* Let's say the whole building is nothing but red bricks. I'd like to have just the black one or the white one or the purple one. Deliberately fuck up.

This is gonna sound square, but my kid is my imprint. He's my freedom. There's a line in one of Hemingway's books. I think it's from *For Whom the Bell*

Tolls. They're behind the enemy lines, somewhere in Spain, and she's pregnant. She wants to stay with him. He tells her no. He says, "if you die, I die," knowing he's gonna die. But if you go, I go. Know what I mean? The mystics call it the brass bowl. Continuum. You know what I mean? This is why I work. Every time I see a young guy walk by with a shirt and tie and dressed up real sharp, I'm lookin' at my kid, you know? That's it.

LEARNING MORE

A job in the steel factories was once a sought-after position within a key industry. Is this still true today? To learn more about the steel industry in the second half of the twentieth century, see the *Ideas Across Time* website.

QUESTIONING THE TEXT

1. Why does Lefevre think "You can't take pride any more"?
2. What does Lefevre think should be found on the side of every building? Why?
3. How does Lefevre deal with his anger? What is he angry about?
4. What is Lefevre's attitude toward education?
5. What does Lefevre want for his son? How do you think his hopes will turn out?

ANALYZING THE WRITER'S CRAFT

1. How would this piece be different if Terkel or Lefevre had written it? What is gained from an oral transcription? What is lost?
2. What sort of person is Lefevre? Cite passages that reveal him to you.
3. What do you make of Lefevre's allusions, such as his references to writers?
4. Edit this selection, cutting it to half its length, and write a brief explanation for your deletions.

MAKING CONNECTIONS

1. At the outset of the American adventure, St. John de Crevecoeur (Chapter 1, pp. 22–27) describes a nation of modest prosperity and universal equality. Does Lefevre's story suggest that Crevecoeur's vision has evaporated?
2. How does Lefevre's account of the shopfloor worker compare with the view Marx presents (pp. 264–273)?
3. Does Lefevre's personal witness qualify Vaclav Havel's view of how the powerless might become powerful (Chapter 5, pp. 404–412)?
4. How does Lefevre view of work compare and contrast with those of Louisa May Alcott (pp. 275–286) and Barbara Ehrenreich (pp. 316–319)?

FORMULATING IDEAS FOR WRITING

1. Interview someone who fits Lefevre's description of himself—a "laborer"—and write a brief comparison of the two interviews.
2. Is Lefevre accurate in his view of himself—that is, is he right to say that laborers are a dying breed? Do some statistical research and use your own experience to provide an answer. (Consider, too: Do you want to pursue a working career as a laborer? Why or why not? Do you know people who do wish to work as laborers?)
3. How does what Lefevre says confirm or challenge your preconceptions about laborers?
4. What does Lefevre's experience say about equality in America?

The Singer Solution to World Poverty (1999)

Peter Singer

Peter Singer is a controversial ethicist, a philosopher concerned with applying intellectual discipline to the solution of urgent ethical issues such as poverty and abortion. Singer defines himself as a utilitarian, by which he means that he approaches issues "by seeking the solution that has the best consequences for all affected."

Singer first rose to prominence with the publication of his book *Animal Liberation* (1975). Here he argues against "speciesism," or discrimination on the grounds of belonging to a certain species. Against this often unstated but clearly dominant human view, Singer maintains that the interest of all beings capable of suffering are worthy of equal consideration. Using animals for food, therefore, is without justification because it creates unnecessary suffering; for Singer, the best diet is the vegan diet.

In his most comprehensive book, *Practical Ethics* (1979), Singer uses his utilitarian methodology to address such issues as abortion, euthanasia, and the obligations of the wealthy to those in poverty. Since for Singer beings deserve consideration on the basis of their interests, beings that have no interests, or cannot suffer, such as a fetus or severely disabled infants, do not command equal consideration. He has on this basis advocated euthanasia under certain circumstances for severely disabled infants, a conclusion that has shocked and outraged many people.

Born in 1946 in Melbourne, Australia, Singer is the child of Viennese Jews who fled to Australia in 1938, just prior to the Second World War. He studied at

Oxford University in England but has spent most of his career in Australia where he has served as chair of the Department of Philosophy at Monash University in Melbourne. He is the founder of that university's Centre for Human Bioethics. His other books include *One World: The Ethics of Globalization* (2002), *Pushing Time Away: My Grandfather and the Tragedy of Jewish Vienna* (2003), and *The President of Good and Evil: The Ethics of George W. Bush* (2004). In 1996, Singer ran unsuccessfully as a Green candidate for the Australian Senate. He now divides his time between Melbourne and New Jersey, where he is the Ira W. DeCamp Professor of Bioethics at Princeton University.

"The Singer Solution to World Poverty" first appeared in *The New York Times* on September 5, 1999.

In the Brazilian film "Central Station," Dora is a retired schoolteacher who makes ends meet by sitting at the station writing letters for illiterate people. Suddenly she has an opportunity to pocket $1,000. All she has to do is persuade a homeless 9-year-old boy to follow her to an address she has been given. (She is told he will be adopted by wealthy foreigners.) She delivers the boy, gets the money, spends some of it on a television set and settles down to enjoy her new acquisition. Her neighbor spoils the fun, however, by telling her that the boy was too old to be adopted—he will be killed and his organs sold for transplantation. Perhaps Dora knew this all along, but after her neighbor's plain speaking, she spends a troubled night. In the morning Dora resolves to take the boy back.

Suppose Dora had told her neighbor that it is a tough world, other people have nice new TV's too, and if selling the kid is the only way she can get one, well, he was only a street kid. She would then have become, in the eyes of the audience, a monster. She redeems herself only by being prepared to bear considerable risks to save the boy.

At the end of the movie, in cinemas in the affluent nations of the world, people who would have been quick to condemn Dora if she had not rescued the boy go home to places far more comfortable than her apartment. In fact, the average family in the United States spends almost one-third of its income on things that are no more necessary to them than Dora's new TV was to her. Going out to nice restaurants, buying new clothes because the old ones are no longer stylish, vacationing at beach resorts—so much of our income is spent on things not essential to the preservation of our lives and health. Donated to one of a number of charitable agencies, that money could mean the difference between life and death for children in need.

All of which raises a question: In the end, what is the ethical distinction between a Brazilian who sells a homeless child to organ peddlers and an American who already has a TV and upgrades to a better one—knowing that the money could be donated to an organization that would use it to save the lives of kids in need?

5 Of course, there are several differences between the two situations that could support different moral judgments about them. For one thing, to be able to consign a child to death when he is standing right in front of you takes a

chilling kind of heartlessness; it is much easier to ignore an appeal for money to help children you will never meet. Yet for a utilitarian philosopher like myself—that is, one who judges whether acts are right or wrong by their consequences—if the upshot of the American's failure to donate the money is that one more kid dies on the streets of a Brazilian city, then it is, in some sense, just as bad as selling the kid to the organ peddlers. But one doesn't need to embrace my utilitarian ethic to see that, at the very least, there is a troubling incongruity in being so quick to condemn Dora for taking the child to the organ peddlers while, at the same time, not regarding the American consumer's behavior as raising a serious moral issue.

In his 1996 book, "Living High and Letting Die," the New York University philosopher Peter Unger presented an ingenious series of imaginary examples designed to probe our intuitions about whether it is wrong to live well without giving substantial amounts of money to help people who are hungry, malnourished or dying from easily treatable illnesses like diarrhea. Here's my paraphrase of one of these examples:

Bob is close to retirement. He has invested most of his savings in a very rare and valuable old car, a Bugatti, which he has not been able to insure. The Bugatti is his pride and joy. In addition to the pleasure he gets from driving and caring for his car, Bob knows that its rising market value means that he will always be able to sell it and live comfortably after retirement. One day when Bob is out for a drive, he parks the Bugatti near the end of a railway siding and goes for a walk up the track. As he does so, he sees that a runaway train, with no one aboard, is running down the railway track. Looking farther down the track, he sees the small figure of a child very likely to be killed by the runaway train. He can't stop the train and the child is too far away to warn of the danger, but he can throw a switch that will divert the train down the siding where his Bugatti is parked. Then nobody will be killed—but the train will destroy his Bugatti. Thinking of his joy in owning the car and the financial security it represents, Bob decides not to throw the switch. The child is killed. For many years to come, Bob enjoys owning his Bugatti and the financial security it represents.

Bob's conduct, most of us will immediately respond, was gravely wrong. Unger agrees. But then he reminds us that we, too, have opportunities to save the lives of children. We can give to organizations like Unicef or Oxfam America. How much would we have to give one of these organizations to have a high probability of saving the life of a child threatened by easily preventable diseases? (I do not believe that children are more worth saving than adults, but since no one can argue that children have brought their poverty on themselves, focusing on them simplifies the issues.) Unger called up some experts and used the information they provided to offer some plausible estimates that include the cost of raising money, administrative expenses and the cost of delivering aid where it is most needed. By his calculation, $200 in donations would help a sickly 2-year-old transform into a healthy 6-year-old—offering safe passage through childhood's most dangerous years. To show how practical philosophical argument can be, Unger even tells his readers that they can easily donate funds by using their credit card and calling one of these toll-free numbers: (800) 367-5437 for Unicef; (800) 693-2687 for Oxfam America.

Now you, too, have the information you need to save a child's life. How should you judge yourself if you don't do it? Think again about Bob and his Bugatti. Unlike Dora, Bob did not have to look into the eyes of the child he was sacrificing for his own material comfort. The child was a complete stranger to him and too far away to relate to in an intimate, personal way. Unlike Dora, too, he did not mislead the child or initiate the chain of events imperiling him. In all these respects, Bob's situation resembles that of people able but unwilling to donate to overseas aid and differs from Dora's situation.

10 If you still think that it was very wrong of Bob not to throw the switch that would have diverted the train and saved the child's life, then it is hard to see how you could deny that it is also very wrong not to send money to one of the organizations listed above. Unless, that is, there is some morally important difference between the two situations that I have overlooked.

Is it the practical uncertainties about whether aid will really reach the people who need it? Nobody who knows the world of overseas aid can doubt that such uncertainties exist. But Unger's figure of $200 to save a child's life was reached after he had made conservative assumptions about the proportion of the money donated that will actually reach its target.

One genuine difference between Bob and those who can afford to donate to overseas aid organizations but don't is that only Bob can save the child on the tracks, whereas there are hundreds of millions of people who can give $200 to overseas aid organizations. The problem is that most of them aren't doing it. Does this mean that it is all right for you not to do it?

Suppose that there were more owners of priceless vintage cars—Carol, Dave, Emma, Fred and so on, down to Ziggy—all in exactly the same situation as Bob, with their own siding and their own switch, all sacrificing the child in order to preserve their own cherished car. Would that make it all right for Bob to do the same? To answer this question affirmatively is to endorse follow-the-crowd ethics—the kind of ethics that led many Germans to look away when the Nazi atrocities were being committed. We do not excuse them because others were behaving no better.

We seem to lack a sound basis for drawing a clear moral line between Bob's situation and that of any reader of this article with $200 to spare who does not donate it to an overseas aid agency. These readers seem to be acting at least as badly as Bob was acting when he chose to let the runaway train hurtle toward the unsuspecting child. In the light of this conclusion, I trust that many readers will reach for the phone and donate that $200. Perhaps you should do it before reading further.

15 Now that you have distinguished yourself morally from people who put their vintage cars ahead of a child's life, how about treating yourself and your partner to dinner at your favorite restaurant? But wait. The money you will spend at the restaurant could also help save the lives of children overseas! True, you weren't planning to blow $200 tonight, but if you were to give up dining out just for one month, you would easily save that amount. And what is one

month's dining out, compared to a child's life? There's the rub. Since there are a lot of desperately needy children in the world, there will always be another child whose life you could save for another $200. Are you therefore obliged to keep giving until you have nothing left? At what point can you stop?

Hypothetical examples can easily become farcical. Consider Bob. How far past losing the Bugatti should he go? Imagine that Bob had got his foot stuck in the track of the siding, and if he diverted the train, then before it rammed the car it would also amputate his big toe. Should he still throw the switch? What if it would amputate his foot? His entire leg?

As absurd as the Bugatti scenario gets when pushed to extremes, the point it raises is a serious one: only when the sacrifices become very significant indeed would most people be prepared to say that Bob does nothing wrong when he decides not to throw the switch. Of course, most people could be wrong; we can't decide moral issues by taking opinion polls. But consider for yourself the level of sacrifice that you would demand of Bob, and then think about how much money you would have to give away in order to make a sacrifice that is roughly equal to that. It's almost certainly much, much more than $200. For most middle-class Americans, it could easily be more like $200,000.

Isn't it counterproductive to ask people to do so much? Don't we run the risk that many will shrug their shoulders and say that morality, so conceived, is fine for saints but not for them? I accept that we are unlikely to see, in the near or even medium-term future, a world in which it is normal for wealthy Americans to give the bulk of their wealth to strangers. When it comes to praising or blaming people for what they do, we tend to use a standard that is relative to some conception of normal behavior. Comfortably off Americans who give, say, 10 percent of their income to overseas aid organizations are so far ahead of most of their equally comfortable fellow citizens that I wouldn't go out of my way to chastise them for not doing more. Nevertheless, they should be doing much more, and they are in no position to criticize Bob for failing to make the much greater sacrifice of his Bugatti.

At this point various objections may crop up. Someone may say: "If every citizen living in the affluent nations contributed his or her share I wouldn't have to make such a drastic sacrifice, because long before such levels were reached, the resources would have been there to save the lives of all those children dying from lack of food or medical care. So why should I give more than my fair share?" Another, related, objection is that the Government ought to increase its overseas aid allocations, since that would spread the burden more equitably across all taxpayers.

20 Yet the question of how much we ought to give is a matter to be decided in the real world—and that, sadly, is a world in which we know that most people do not, and in the immediate future will not, give substantial amounts to overseas aid agencies. We know, too, that at least in the next year, the United States Government is not going to meet even the very modest United Nations–recommended target of 0.7 percent of gross national product; at the moment it lags far below that, at 0.09 percent, not even half of Japan's 0.22 percent or a

tenth of Denmark's 0.97 percent. Thus, we know that the money we can give beyond that theoretical "fair share" is still going to save lives that would otherwise be lost. While the idea that no one need do more than his or her fair share is a powerful one, should it prevail if we know that others are not doing their fair share and that children will die preventable deaths unless we do more than our fair share? That would be taking fairness too far.

Thus, this ground for limiting how much we ought to give also fails. In the world as it is now, I can see no escape from the conclusion that each one of us with wealth surplus to his or her essential needs should be giving most of it to help people suffering from poverty so dire as to be life-threatening. That's right: I'm saying that you shouldn't buy that new car, take that cruise, redecorate the house or get that pricey new suit. After all, a $1,000 suit could save five children's lives.

So how does my philosophy break down in dollars and cents? An American household with an income of $50,000 spends around $30,000 annually on necessities, according to the Conference Board, a nonprofit economic research organization. Therefore, for a household bringing in $50,000 a year, donations to help the world's poor should be as close as possible to $20,000. The $30,000 required for necessities holds for higher incomes as well. So a household making $100,000 could cut a yearly check for $70,000. Again, the formula is simple: whatever money you're spending on luxuries, not necessities, should be given away.

Now, evolutionary psychologists tell us that human nature just isn't sufficiently altruistic to make it plausible that many people will sacrifice so much for strangers. On the facts of human nature, they might be right, but they would be wrong to draw a moral conclusion from those facts. If it is the case that we ought to do things that, predictably, most of us won't do, then let's face that fact head-on. Then, if we value the life of a child more than going to fancy restaurants, the next time we dine out we will know that we could have done something better with our money. If that makes living a morally decent life extremely arduous, well, then that is the way things are. If we don't do it, then we should at least know that we are failing to live a morally decent life—not because it is good to wallow in guilt but because knowing where we should be going is the first step toward heading in that direction.

When Bob first grasped the dilemma that faced him as he stood by that railway switch, he must have thought how extraordinarily unlucky he was to be placed in a situation in which he must choose between the life of an innocent child and the sacrifice of most of his savings. But he was not unlucky at all. We are all in that situation.

LEARNING MORE

Many of Peter Singer's views have roused admiration and, often just as fervently, condemnation. See the *Ideas Across Time* website to see what people have said.

QUESTIONING THE TEXT

1. State in your own words the dilemma Singer wants to illustrate by his reference to Dora.
2. Singer says Dora's new TV is not necessary to her. What do you think he means by "necessary"? Offer some evidence from the essay for your answer. In Singer's terms, is your TV necessary?
3. In par. 4, Singer restates the problem in more provocative terms. "In the end," he asks, "what is the ethical distinction . . . ?" Since this is a philosopher talking, just what does he mean by "In the end" and by "ethical distinction"?
4. How does Singer arrive at the conclusion that it's just as bad to sell a child to organ peddlers as it is to buy a new TV? Is his argument sound? Explain.
5. Singer offers his readers several opportunities during the course of his essay to stop and donate money to poor children. Did you call Unicef or Oxfam America and donate money? If so, why? If not, why not?
6. Singer, in an aside, says, "I do not believe that children are more worth saving than adults" (par. 8). He does not explain his reasoning, but since you are familiar now with how he thinks, take a crack at explaining how he arrives at this view.
7. What objections to his conclusion—that we ought to be donating a substantial part of our incomes to aid poor children abroad—does Singer identify? Are there other objections that he has not raised? Are you satisfied with his refutation of the objections that he does raise? Explain.
8. Singer says he is a practical philosopher. But it does not seem practical to believe that a family earning $100,000 will donate $70,000 every year to overseas aid organizations. So why does Singer make this proposal?
9. Singer ends his essay by saying that, although at first blush the hypothetical problem of Bob, his Bugatti, the train, and the child seems far-fetched, in fact Bob's situation is the situation of us all. Do you, at the end of the essay, agree? Why or why not?

ANALYZING THE WRITER'S CRAFT

1. What is the tone of this essay? Offer some evidence to support your view.
2. Are there places where Singer is too preachy? If so, what makes these parts of his essay preachy? Even if he is being preachy, does his preachiness serve a purpose? Explain.
3. Why doesn't Singer come right out and say what he means instead of using the complicated examples of Dora and Bob, which are not, after all, real?
4. Singer maintains that the examples of Dora and Bob illustrate for us the real situation we find ourselves in. But artificial problems, like Dora's and Bob's, necessarily leave out most real-life complexity. By doing so, do these examples usefully clarify our everyday situations or merely evade their complexity? Explain.

5. Is Singer's presentation of our situation fair? Why or why not?
6. What rhetorical purpose leads Singer to include the phone numbers of Unicef and Oxfam in his essay? Do you find the inclusion of these phone numbers effective? Explain.
7. The first sentence of par. 14 reads like a challenge. Singer says, "We seem to lack a sound basis for drawing a clear moral line" between Bob's case and ours, and so ought to donate right now. Is he right, or is there a basis to distinguish between Bob's case and ours? Explain.
8. In par. 23, Singer acknowledges that most people, despite his essay, will not donate when they ought to or as much as they ought to. But he believes that there is a moral virtue to having made his case. In effect, he asks the reader to judge whether his essay has been worth it. What's your opinion?

MAKING CONNECTIONS

1. Rigorous application of logic seems on occasion to produce conclusions that do appear logically sound but that many, if not most people are nonetheless unwilling to accept. Socrates, for example, rigorously explains (Chapter 8, pp. 640–644) why we need not fear death—yet for centuries after him, most people seem to have feared death regardless. Tom Paine (Chapter 2, pp. 98–103) explains logically why be believes in God but not in organized religion. Again, he applies reason reasonably, and yet most people participate in organized religion anyway. Do these works have something in common that might explain why their logic fails to persuade the large majority of people?
2. Singer observes that "evolutionary psychologists"—people who explain human behavior on the basis of Charles Darwin's theory of evolution—would caution that it goes against human nature to be as altruistic as Singer thinks we ought to be (par. 23). But Darwin, like Singer, believed that our moral qualities are our highest qualities, those qualities in our makeup that not only make us most human but of which we can be most proud (see Chapter 3, pp. 167–180). Compare and contrast Darwin's and Singer's views of the place and origin of morals in human life.
3. The great denunciation of the extremes of riches and poverty in the modern era was, of course, made by Karl Marx (pp. 264–273). How do Marx's and Singer's views agree? How do they diverge?
4. Singer asks us to donate significant sums to overseas aid organizations. But as Barbara Ehrenreich shows (pp. 316–319), not all Americans are affluent, or anywhere near affluent. What might she say to Singer?

FORMULATING IDEAS FOR WRITING

1. How persuasive is Singer's notion of what's necessary? Is a television, for example, or a computer, or a car a luxury? Write an essay that explores the idea of what is necessary, agreeing with or taking issue with Singer.

2. If you did not pick up the phone and donate money to Unicef or Oxfam America, write an essay in the form of a letter to Singer explaining to him why he failed to persuade you to make that call.
3. What would happen to the American economy if even a small percentage of those earning $100,000 contributed $70,000 annually to Unicef? Why doesn't Singer take the impact of spending on the American economy, and therefore on employment and poverty in the United States, into account? Why doesn't he care about the people working in all those restaurant kitchens? Is this omission a flaw in his analysis? Or do you think Singer is well aware of this omission but wants to make a different point? Discuss.
4. Singer was candidate for the Australian Senate in 1996; he lost. If Singer were running for public office in your state, would you vote for him? Write an essay explaining why you would or would not.

Selling in Minnesota (2001)

Barbara Ehrenreich

A political activist and prolific social commentator, Barbara Ehrenreich was born in Butte, Montana, in 1941. Her father, a copper miner, eventually became an executive with the Gillette company. Ehrenreich attended Reed College in Oregon and went on to earn a Ph.D. in biology from the Rockefeller University in New York City. But the Vietnam War ended her scientific career, and she has been a left-leaning political essayist ever since. She is the author of thirteen books and numerous essays for such publications as *The Atlantic, The New Republic,* and *The New York Times.* From 1991 to 1997, Ehrenreich wrote a regular column for *Time* magazine. Her most recent book is *Bait and Switch* (2005), about white-collar work in America.

This selection is taken from her best-seller *Nickel and Dimed: On (Not) Getting By in America* (2001). The book originated in a lunch conversation with the editor of *Harper's,* Lewis Lapham, during which Ehrenreich wondered how people can survive on $6 or $7 an hour. To find out, Ehrenreich, assuming the role of a divorced homemaker, took a series of low-paying jobs in various parts of the country: as a waitress, a housecleaner, and a clerk in the world's largest retailer, Wal-Mart.

In my second week [of working at Wal-Mart], two things change. My shift changes from 10:00–6:00 to 2:00–11:00, the so-called closing shift, although the store remains open 24/7. No one tells me this; I find it out by studying the schedules that are posted, under glass, on the wall outside the break room. Now

I have nine hours instead of eight, and my two fifteen-minute breaks, which seemed almost superfluous on the 10:00–6:00 shift, now become a matter of urgent calculation. Do I take both before dinner, which is usually about 7:30, leaving an unbroken two-and-a-half-hour stretch when I'm weariest, between 8:30 and 11:00? Or do I try to go two and a half hours without a break in the afternoon, followed by a nearly three-hour marathon before I can get away for dinner? Then there's the question of how to make the best use of a fifteen-minute break when you have three or more urgent, simultaneous needs—to pee, to drink something, to get outside the neon and into the natural light, and most of all, to sit down. I save about a minute by engaging in a little time theft and stopping at the rest room before I punch out for the break. From the time clock it's a seventy-five second walk to the store exit; if I stop at the Radio Grill, I could end up wasting a full four minutes waiting in line, not to mention the fifty-nine cents for a small-sized iced tea. So if I treat myself to an outing in the tiny fenced-off area beside the store, I get about nine minutes off my feet.

The other thing that happens is that the post–Memorial Day weekend lull definitely comes to an end. Now there are always a dozen or more shoppers rooting around in ladies'. New tasks arise, such as bunching up the carts left behind by customers and steering them to their place in the front of the store every half hour or so. Now I am picking up not only dropped clothes but all the odd items customers carry off from foreign departments and decide to leave with us in ladies'—pillows, upholstery hooks, Pokémon cards, earrings, sunglasses, stuffed animals, even a package of cinnamon buns. And always there are the returns, augmented now by the huge volume of items that have been tossed on the floor or carried fecklessly[1] to inappropriate sites. If I pick up misplaced items as quickly as I replace the returns, my cart never empties and things back up dangerously at the fitting room, where Rhoda or her nighttime replacement is likely to hiss: "You've got three carts waiting, Barb. What's the *problem?*"

Still, for the first half of my shift, I am the very picture of good-natured helpfulness. Amazingly, I get praised by Isabelle, the thin little seventyish lady who seems to be Ellie's adjutant: I am doing "wonderfully," she tells me, and—even better—am "great to work with." But then, somewhere around 6:00 or 7:00, when the desire to sit down becomes a serious craving, a Dr. Jekyll/Mr. Hyde transformation sets in. I cannot ignore the fact that it's the customers' sloppiness and idle whims that make me bend and crouch and run. They are the shoppers, I am the antishopper, whose goal is to make it look as if they'd never been in the store. At this point, "aggressive hospitality" gives way to aggressive hostility. Their carts bang into mine, their children run amok.

It's the clothes I relate to, not the customers. And now a funny thing happens to me here on my new shift: I start thinking they're mine, not mine to take home and wear, because I have no such designs on them, just mine to organize and rule over. Same with ladies' wear as a whole. I patrol the perimeter with my cart, darting in to pick up misplaced and fallen items, making everything look spiffy from the outside. I don't fondle the clothes, the way customers do; I slap

[1] fecklessly: in a feeble way.

them into place, commanding them to hang straight, at attention, or lie subdued on the shelves in perfect order. In this frame of mind, the last thing I want to see is a customer riffling around, disturbing the place. In fact, I hate the idea of things being sold—uprooted from their natural homes, whisked off to some closet that's in God-knows-what state of disorder. I want ladies' wear sealed off in a plastic bubble and trucked away to some place of safety, some museum of retail history.

5 One night I come back bone-tired from my last break and am distressed to find a new person folding T-shirts in the [turtlenecks] area, *my* [turtlenecks] area. It's already been a vexing evening. Earlier, when I'd returned from dinner, the evening fitting room lady upbraided me for being late—which I actually wasn't—and said that if Howard knew, he probably wouldn't yell at me this time because I'm still pretty new, but if it happened again. . . . And I'd snapped back that I could care less if Howard yelled at me. So I'm a little wary with this intruder in [turtlenecks], and, sure enough, after our minimal introductions, she turns on me.

"Did you put anything away here today?" she demands.

"Well, yes, sure." In fact I've put something away everywhere today, as I do on every other day.

"Because this is not in the right place. See the fabric—it's different," and she thrusts the errant[2] item up toward my chest.

True, I can see that this olive-green shirt is slightly ribbed while the others are smooth. "You've *got* to put them in their right places," she continues. "Are you checking the UPC numbers?"

10 Of course I am not checking the ten or more digit UPC numbers, which lie just under the bar codes—nobody does. What does she think this is, the National Academy of Sciences? I'm not sure what kind of deference, if any, is due here: Is she my supervisor now? But I don't care, she's messing with my stuff. So I say, only without the numerals or the forbidden curse word, that (1) plenty of other people work here during the day, not to mention all the customers coming through, so why is she blaming me? (2) it's after 10:00 and I've got another cart full of returns to go, and wouldn't it make more sense if we both worked on the carts, instead of zoning the goddamn T-shirts?

To which she responds huffily, "I don't *do* returns. My job is to *fold*."

I leave that night shaken by my response to the intruder. If she's a supervisor, I could be written up for what I said, but even worse is what I thought. Am I turning mean here, and is that a normal response to the end of a nine-hour shift? There was another outbreak of mental wickedness that night. I'd gone back to the counter by the fitting room to pick up the next cart full of returns and found the guy who answers the phone at the counter at night, a pensive young fellow in a wheelchair, staring into space, looking even sadder than usual. And my uncensored thought was, At least you get to sit down.

This is not me, at least not any version of me I'd like to spend much time with. What I have to face is that "Barb," the name on my ID tag, is not exactly the same person as Barbara. "Barb" is what I was called as a child, and still am by my siblings, and I sense that at some level I'm regressing.[3] Take away the career and

[2] errant: straying.

[3] regressing: returning to a former state.

the higher education, and maybe what you're left with is this original Barb, the one who might have ended up working at Wal-Mart for real if her father hadn't managed to climb out of the mines. So it's interesting, and more than a little disturbing, to see how Barb turned out—that she's meaner and slyer than I am, more cherishing of grudges, and not quite as smart as I'd hoped.

LEARNING MORE

Barbara Erhenreich reports in this essay on her experience selling at Wal-Mart. Is her reporting reliable? Is what she finds representative of all Wal-Marts? Useful links to more information about Wal-Mart can be found on *Ideas Across Time* website.

QUESTIONING THE TEXT

1. What sort of work does Ehrenreich do at Wal-Mart? What skills do you think this work requires? Did the essay change your view of this kind of work?
2. How do the changes that occur in week two affect Ehrenreich's working conditions?
3. How is Ehrenreich's behavior different in the first and the second halves of her shift?
4. How does her attitude toward her work change from the first to the second half of her shift? How does she explain that change?
5. Why is Ehrenreich "shaken" (par. 12) by the worker she calls "the intruder"?
6. Is Ehrenreich right in saying she is "regressing" (par. 13) on the job?
7. Do you think everyone would respond to working at Wal-Mart as Ehrenreich does? Or is her response due to the fact that she's an educated professional and doesn't have to work at Wal-Mart for a living?

ANALYZING THE WRITER'S CRAFT

1. Is there a thesis statement in this essay? If so, what is it? If not, how does Ehrenreich keep the essay coherent?
2. What is the tone of this essay? Give two or three examples? Does the tone change anywhere in the essay? Explain.
3. Who is the audience for this essay? How does the tone establish a bond with the audience? How does the tone convey the "message" of the essay?
4. Ehrenreich reports on events that happened to her. How does she persuade the reader of her observations and judgments about what happened?
5. Is Ehrenreich mainly an observer in this essay, or is she an important character in her own narrative? Illustrate and explain.
6. How does Ehrenreich's language reflect the changes in her feelings as the essay progresses?
7. How do Ehrenreich's examples contribute to the essay?
8. Did you find Ehrenreich's conclusion effective? Explain.

MAKING CONNECTIONS

1. Ehrenreich focuses mainly on other women working at Wal-Mart. How is the plight of these women illuminated by Betty Friedan's "The Problem Without a Name" (Chapter 6, pp. 496–509)?
2. Is what we do the real definition of our lives? How does Ehrenreich's experience compare and contrast with Louisa May Alcott's (pp. 275–286).
3. Would it be fair to speculate that the forces making for conformity at Wal-Mart are the same as, or very similar to, those Vaclav Havel describes in "The Power of the Powerless" (Chapter 5, pp. 404–412)?

FORMULATING IDEAS FOR WRITING

1. Using Ehrenreich's essay as a model, write a narrative account of a job experience.
2. Defend Wal-Mart against Ehrenreich's implied criticisms.
3. Ehrenreich takes her job at Wal-Mart under false pretenses: she doesn't really need the job, and she intends to write about her experiences. Is this ethical? Once on the job, she can't help getting involved, including suggesting that the workers organize a union. Is this irresponsible? Discuss.
4. Write an essay that demonstrates why, on the basis of the essay alone, you trust Ehrenreich, believe her account of her experiences, and concur in most of her judgments; or, you distrust Ehrenreich, don't believe her account of her experiences, and don't concur in her judgments.

A Worker Reads History (1947)

Bertolt Brecht

One of the greatest German poets and playwrights of the twentieth century, Bertolt Brecht was an iconoclastic, revolutionary figure in his life and in his art. He was representative of his generation, Germans who came of age during the First World War, and was bitterly disillusioned with the "civilization"—he would have put the word in ironic quotation marks—that exploded in that war. His work sought to unmask hypocrisy and attack the complacency of bourgeois life. To this end, his dramas aimed to prod the audience into thought and action by use of what he styled the "A Effect"—the alienation effect. He trained his actors to do everything rather than allow the audience the illusion that what is happening on stage is real. Rather than encourage the traditional "suspension of disbelief" in the audience, Brecht developed an epic theater that insisted on drawing attention to the artifice of the theater, and he often bellowed lessons at the audience. These were, for Brecht, political lessons. He wrote in a plain, highly colloquial, often ribald German and espoused the cause of the common man.

Brecht was born in Augsburg in 1898. His father was a director of a paper company. Brecht studied medicine, but after the First World War, he began to write. His first international success was *The Threepenny Opera* (1928), loosely based on John Gay's *The Beggar's Opera.* With music by Kurt Weill, the drama broke the mold of the well-made play and launched a new form. These lines, spoken by one of the play's professional beggars, illustrate its tone and message: "First feed the face, / And then talk right and wrong."

When Hitler came to power, Brecht's poems and plays were banned, and Brecht, a member of the Communist Party, went into exile, eventually settling in the United States. However, the anti-communism crusade in this country following the Second World War forced Brecht to flee the states, and he eventually settled once more in Berlin. After Berlin was divided into separate sectors, he remained in Communist East Berlin, where he launched a famous theatrical company to perform his work, the Berliner Ensemble. Despite his difficulties with the Communist authorities—the actuality of Communism diverged from the theory—Brecht lived in East Berlin until his death from a heart attack in 1956.

Many of Brecht's plays have become classics of twentieth-century theater, including *Mother Courage and Her Children* (1939), considered by many the greatest antiwar play ever written; *Galileo* (1938–1939); *The Good Woman of Setzuan* (1939); and *The Caucasian Chalk Circle* (1944–1945). The following poem is a translation from the original German. It's from Brecht's collection of poems and essays, *Calendar Stories.*

Who built the seven gates of Thebes?
The books are filled with names of kings.
Was it the kings who hauled the craggy blocks of stone?
And Babylon, so many times destroyed.
Who built the city up each time? In which of Lima's houses,
That city glittering with gold, lived those who built it?
In the evening when the Chinese wall was finished
Where did the masons go? Imperial Rome
Is full of arcs of triumph. Who reared them up? Over whom
Did the Caesars triumph? Byzantium lives in song.
Were all her dwellings palaces? And even in Atlantis of the legend
The night the seas rushed in,
The drowning men still bellowed for their slaves.

Young Alexander conquered India.
He alone?
Caesar beat the Gauls.
Was there not even a cook in his army?
Phillip of Spain wept as his fleet
was sunk and destroyed. Were there no other tears?
Frederick the Great triumphed in the Seven Years War.
Who triumphed with him?

Each page a victory
At whose expense the victory ball?

Every ten years a great man,
Who paid the piper?

So many particulars.
So many questions.

LEARNING MORE

Brecht is as well known for his plays as for his poems. If you want to learn more, useful links to his plays and poems can be found on the *Ideas Across Time* website.

QUESTIONING THE TEXT

1. What is the traditional answer to the poem's opening question? What is the answer Brecht seeks?
2. What kind of human achievements and what sorts of historical figures does Brecht include in his list of questions? Why does he choose these kinds of events, achievements, and persons?
3. Why does the poem fail to provide answers to its many questions?
4. What is suggested by the contrast in the concluding stanza between "particulars" and "questions"?

ANALYZING THE WRITER'S CRAFT

1. State Brecht's argument in your own words.
2. Why does Brecht mainly ask questions in this poem? How do we know what he expects us to answer?
3. Could an essay have been constructed in the way Brecht constructed his poem? Explain.
4. How would you characterize Brecht's diction in this poem?
5. What is the tone of this poem?
6. Why doesn't Brecht use any events or persons from contemporary history in his poem?
7. What is the effect of the declarative sentence that concludes the opening stanza?
8. How are the questions and answers of the second stanza different from those of the first?
9. Why does Brecht move from particulars to generalizations in the next-to-last stanza?
10. Is his concluding couplet effective?
11. Does this poem make a persuasive political point? Explain.

MAKING CONNECTIONS

1. Studs Terkel bases the title for his introductory interview for his book *Working* ("Mike Lefevre, Steelworker" pp. 300–307) on this poem. How

does the poem illuminate Terkel's interview? How do you think Mike Lefevre would respond to Brecht's poem?
2. Brecht is usually thought of as an artist within the Communist tradition. Does this poem reflect Karl Marx's views (see pp. 264–273)? Explain.
3. Do you think St. John de Crevecoeur (Chapter 1, pp. 22–27) would consider "the American" as breaking the historical pattern that Brecht suggests in his poem? What about Alexis de Tocqueville (pp. 458–460)?
4. Does Gish Jen's story "In the American Society" (Chapter 5, pp. 427–438) suggest that the historical circumstances Brecht points to persist today? Explain.

FORMULATING IDEAS FOR WRITING

1. Write an essay showing how "A Worker Reads History" is or is not a Marxist poem.
2. Like all apparently simple works of art, this one is highly crafted. Discuss this poem with reference to its diction, its allusions, its images and details, and its organization. How does form reflect or express content in this poem?
3. Rewrite this poem substituting contemporary references for Brecht's historical ones. Justify your choice of substitutions.
4. Is Brecht's point overly simple? That is, could Alexander's soldiers, for example, have conquered India without him? History is full of generals, but there are few Alexanders in human history. So doesn't Alexander deserve credit for his achievements?

American Values

American Values appeared as an advertisement in the December 9, 2002, edition of *The New Yorker* magazine.

QUESTIONING THE TEXT

1. How is this ad about American values?
2. If you removed the title, what values would you conclude that this ad promotes?
3. How does the photo support the "argument" of the ad?
4. This ad, including the photo, appeared in black and white. Why do you think it was not done in color?
5. According to the ad, what two things have remained constant at American Century?

Every day, our founder has the same lunch. It isn't lobster tail.

It's a true story. At noon, he sits down in the cafeteria and eats a peanut butter sandwich. When he's done, he folds up his paper sack so it can be used again tomorrow.

It's a tradition around here. One of the many we've created in our 44 years of managing investments. Over time we've grown, but two things have remained constant. His lunch. And our values. Your success is still our first priority. The proof is in the peanut butter.

AMERICAN CENTURY.
Investment Managers

Please call 1-877-44-AMCEN or visit www.americancentury.com to obtain a prospectus with more complete information, including charges, expenses and minimums. Be sure to read it carefully before you invest or send money.
American Century Investment Services, Inc. © 2002 American Century Services Corporation

ANALYZING THE WRITER'S CRAFT

1. What is the relation in the photo between the foreground and the background?
2. How does the photo suggest admirable values, such as integrity?
3. Analyze the way the photo is put together, aesthetically, to support the "argument" of the words in the ad.
4. Is the written text grammatical? Explain how it is or is not.
5. Is the written text logical? Explain how it is or is not.

6. Is what is portrayed actually a tradition? What are the connotations of the word "tradition"? What other words might have been used instead, and what would have been the impact of different word choices on the reader?
7. Discuss your response to the final sentence.
8. Is what this ad says true? How could you find out?
9. Explain why you do or do not find this ad persuasive.

MAKING CONNECTIONS

1. What would St. John de Crevecoeur (Chapter 1, pp. 22–27), James Baldwin (Chapter 1, pp. 29–35), and Richard Rodriguez (Chapter 6, pp. 542–549) think of this ad's use of "American"? What about "tradition"?
2. What would Adam Smith (pp. 244–262) and Karl Marx (pp. 264–273) think of the founder of American Century?
3. Does this ad support or question Paul Tillich's view of American values (Chapter 2, pp. 123–130)?
4. Does this ad support or question Daniel J. Boorstin's ideas about equality in America (Chapter 5, pp. 390–402)?

FORMULATING IDEAS FOR WRITING

1. Using this same photo, and inventing a fictional firm of some sort, write two versions of possible written copy for an ad—one serious, one funny or satirical.
2. Write an analysis of the visual and written features of this ad that maintains either that the ad is or that the ad is not effective.
3. You are a young executive in the public relations office at American Century and are assigned the task of discovering whether your new ad campaign—"American Values"—is working. The vice president to whom you report wants both an analysis and a recommendation about whether the campaign should be continued, altered, or scrapped. After conducting some actual and fictitious research, write a memo to your boss summarizing your conclusions. (In this memo, begin by stating the question you are investigating, then describe your methodology, and then write your analysis, conclusions, and recommendations.)

Signs of the Times

Signs of the Times appeared on the Op-Ed page of the *New York Times* on January 6, 2003.

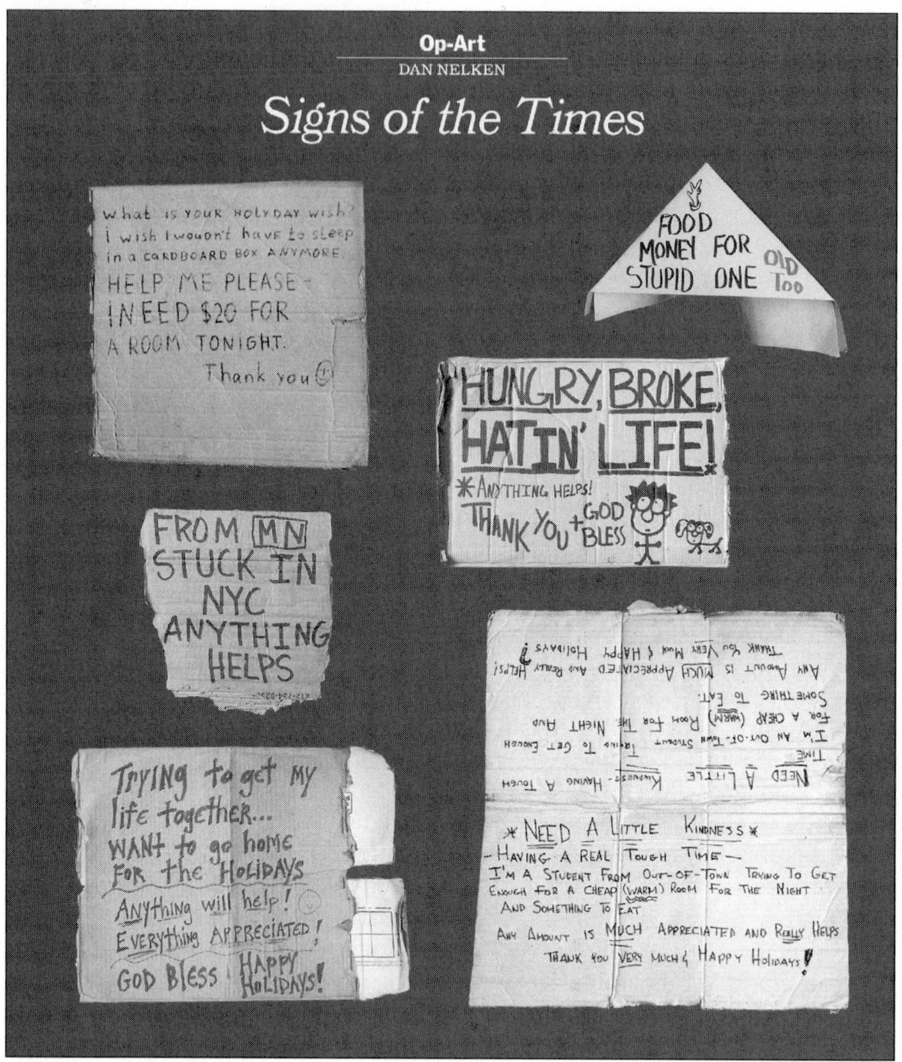

These photographs of placards were taken in New York City in 2002.

LEARNING MORE

What is the source for this title? How does it matter? See the *Ideas Across Time* website for links to other works of the same title.

QUESTIONING THE TEXT

1. Who wrote these placards?
2. What are the common themes of these placards?

3. At what time of year were most of the photos of these placards taken?
4. What do the writers of these placards think of themselves?
5. Why did *The New York Times* (on January 6, 2003) choose to print the photos of these placards?
6. Do these placards tell the truth? Does it matter?

ANALYZING THE WRITER'S CRAFT

1. Would you give money to the writers of these placards? If so, why; if not, why not?
2. Which of these placards do you find most effective? Least effective?
3. How literate are the writers of these placards? Explain.
4. These writers have an urgent mission: they want you to give them money. What strategies do they employ to succeed? Which of these strategies do you find most persuasive? Explain.
5. A placard doesn't allow for a lot of verbiage. What strategies do these writers use to compress their message?
6. One of these placards includes drawings of two stick figures, a man and a dog. What impression do these drawings make on you? Does the presence of these drawings make a significant difference in the communicative power of the placard? Explain.
7. What visual devices do these writers use to reinforce their points? Which of these placards do you think is the best designed? The worst? Explain.

MAKING CONNECTIONS

1. Do you think that Karl Marx (pp. 244–262) would read these placards as evidence of individual failure or of systemic flaws in capitalism? Explain.
2. Are there distinctly American qualities to these pleas for help, or could these messages be found anywhere on the globe? Discuss by reference to any of the readings in Chapter 1.
3. Compare and contrast these photos with the ad "American Values" (p. 324).
4. Do these placards suggest an evident religiosity among the writers? Discuss in relation to any of the readings in Chapter 2.

FORMULATING IDEAS FOR WRITING

1. Write a fictitious interview with the writer of one of these placards. (Or interview a homeless person and write your interview up as a story for *The New York Times*.)
2. Log onto the website of the Bureau of Labor Statistics (www.bls.gov), and use their data to write an essay arguing that homelessness and poverty in the United States are or are not an especially important social issue.
3. Spend a day at a nearby Salvation Army center or at a church soup kitchen, and write an account of your day.

chapter 5

Democratic Society

The evolution of American society can be understood as a complex, sometimes highly acrimonious dialogue among three hugely evocative ideas: liberty (or freedom), equality, and democracy. We explore the relation among these ideas in this chapter and the next, titled "Equality: Race and Gender." In contemporary usage, these three words are often employed as if they were synonymous or, at the very least, mutually supportive. But in the keynote essay of this chapter, the distinguished American journalist Fareed Zakaria suggests that today democracy has become a threat to liberty. In light of the abiding American mission in the world from the time of Woodrow Wilson to the present—that is, to "make the world safe for democracy"—Zakaria's claim is astonishing. How can such a claim have any validity? Zakariah, however, argues forcefully that our unquenchable desire to give everyone a say, without difference or distinction, can produce the unintended result of making things less free *and un*democratic. He explains, for example, how the permeability of legislatures, open as they now are to every interest group, has created legislative gridlock, blocking necessary legislation for the social good. Zakariah also maintains that American democracy has succeeded precisely because so much has been invested in *un*democratic institutions such as the Supreme Court. (Could the Supreme Court ever have come into being if it had had to depend on the assent of a political society like today's United States?)

Liberty is a word that still comes to us accompanied by the drumrolls and fanfares of the eighteenth-century revolutions in America and France. Liberty may include freedoms beyond political freedoms, but its essential meaning, derived from John Locke and Jean-Jacques Rousseau, is political and specifically antimonarchist. For Locke and Rousseau, the signal event in the evolution of human institutions is the voluntary renunciation of the anarchic state of nature, a renunciation enacted through a de facto social contract. Each individual exchanges his or her untrammeled and unchecked liberty for the guarantee of order in the rule-bound precincts of society. This original exchange is daily affirmed—tacitly or explicitly—by each member of society. If we did not agree to live together, we could not live together. For Locke, the emergence of society from the consent of each person abolishes the privileges of monarchy, setting the authority of any ruler squarely on the consent of the governed. In this broad Enlightenment view, liberty derives from the equality of persons and is realized in the political exercise of the common good.

From this distance of time, the arguments of the late-eighteenth century democrats seem not only remarkably confident and disdainful of the opposition but also fiercely rational. Reason leads these writers to assert rights and duties for humanity that still seem radical today. Jefferson's Declaration of Independence, as he tells us in his *Autobiography,* would have been yet more radical had the original version he penned been adopted without change (see pp. 354–360). Mary Wollstonecraft, in her revolutionary *A Vindication of the Rights of Woman* (1792), goes even further than Jefferson, extending the democratic logic of the Enlightenment to make the case for the emancipation of women.

But as the practice of democracy translated into the exercise of power, the difficulty of enacting the vaulting ideals of the founders in the real world of conflicting political interests could be seen as a check on the validity of these ideals. Already in the Renaissance, Niccolo Machiavelli, in what many consider the first work of political science, *The Prince,* had posed a fundamental challenge to democracy. There are many ways to come to power, in Machiavelli's view, but the objects of power are always the same—security, order, and the maintenance of power. This applies to a democratic ruler as much as to any other ruler. For Machiavelli, rule and morality have nothing in common. Three centuries later, Thomas Babington Macaulay, the main spokesman for liberal capitalism in nineteenth-century England, voices another objection to egalitarian democracy. For Macaulay, it is one thing to extend political rights beyond the aristocracy to an educated elite, men who understand the exercise of power; it is quite another thing to cast the fortunes of the state into the untutored hands of any Tom, Dick, or Harry. Henry David Thoreau, a New Englander who had little in common with aristocrats, takes a different view. The purpose of government, for Thoreau, is not government but rather justice. When the government is unjust, a just person must resist that government. But Thoreau does not preach revolution. Rather, he advocates civil disobedience, in effect an appeal to the democratic conscience of his fellow citizens. Thoreau's civil disobedience is a vote of confidence not in those in power but in the common man.

In the twentieth century, there were plenty of obvious challenges to democracy, such as Fascism and Communism. There were also more subtle and insidious challenges, coming from within our own way of life. For example, Daniel J. Boorstin, the long-time Librarian of Congress, maintains that the marriage of technology and democracy has flattened and homogenized experience, draining everyday life of authenticity, genuineness, and memorable particularity. Similarly, the Czech playwright Vaclav Havel, writing as an imprisoned dissident under Communism, asks whether modern consumer society, with its overvaluation of material comforts and devaluation of "spiritual and moral integrity," may not invite some form of dictatorial ideology. And the noted political scientist Benjamin Barber, in a now famous (and prophetic) essay titled

"Jihad vs. McWorld" (1992), also sees a world future inhospitable to either political liberty or democracy. He observes two antithetical movements in global society. One, McWorld, is familiar to us today under "globalization"; the earth is one market, requiring stability of currencies and societies, as well as freedom of trade and communications, and some human rights, but it is indifferent to democracy and political liberty. In contrast, Jihad is reactionary, with the claim to locality and exclusive culture and religion, the rejection of global interdependence, and indifference to democracy and political liberty. Often, in practice, Jihad has taken the form of fundamentalist theocracy.

It seems appropriate to end the chapter with Gish Jen's story "In the American Society" and David Hume Kennerly's photographs of the United States in the year 2000. In a telling study of the generations, Jen subtly explores the social maze of opportunities, hidden codes, and obscured prejudices that faces the new Americans, the upwardly mobile immigrants who continue to define the nation (see Joel L. Swerdlow's "Changing America," Chapter 1, pp. 11–19). The photographs by David Hume Kennerly are taken from his book *Photo du Jour,* which Kennerly says records "a picture-a-day journey through the first year of the New Millenium." Kennerly's journey gives visual form to the themes of this chapter, with its dramatic contrasts between vaulting ideas and practical achievements, and persistent inequalities and equally persistent disenchantments.

KEYNOTE

The Democratic Age (2003)

Fareed Zakaria

Fareed Zakaria, named by *Esquire* magazine as "one of the 21 most important people of the 21st century," is editor of *Newsweek International* and a political analyst for ABC News. After receiving a B.A. from Yale and a Ph.D. from Harvard, Zakaria became the youngest person to hold the post of managing editor of *Foreign Affairs,* the authoritative English-language journal on international politics. Zakaria is author of *From Wealth to Power: The Unusual Origins of America's World Role* (1998) and *The Future of Freedom: Illiberal Democracy at Home and Abroad* (2003), from which the selection below is taken. He is also regularly featured on *This Week with George Stephanopoulos.* Calling ours a "democratic age," Zakaria argues that not only are liberty and democracy not synonymous but the seemingly insatiable desire to democratize everything can in practice threaten liberty.

We live in a democratic age. Over the last century the world has been shaped by one trend above all others—the rise of democracy. In 1900 not a single country had what we would today consider a democracy: a government created by elections in which every adult citizen could vote. Today 119 do, comprising 62 percent of all countries in the world. What was once a peculiar practice of a handful of states around the North Atlantic has become the standard form of government for humankind. Monarchies are antique, fascism and communism utterly discredited. Even Islamic theocracy appeals only to a fanatical few. For the vast majority of the world, democracy is the sole surviving source of political legitimacy. Dictators such as Egypt's Hosni Mubarak and Zimbabwe's Robert Mugabe go to great effort and expense to organize national elections—which, of course, they win handily. When the enemies of democracy mouth its rhetoric and ape its rituals, you know it has won the war.

We live in a democratic age in an even broader sense. From its Greek root, "democracy" means "the rule of the people." And everywhere we are witnessing the shift of power downward. I call this "democratization," even though it goes far beyond politics, because the process is similar: hierarchies are breaking down, closed systems are opening up, and pressures from the masses are now the primary engine of social change. Democracy has gone from being a form of government to a way of life.

Consider the economic realm. What is truly distinctive and new about today's capitalism is not that it is global or information-rich or technologically driven—all that has been true at earlier points in history—but rather that it is *democratic.* Over the last half-century economic growth has enriched hundreds of millions in the industrial world, turning consumption, saving, and investing into a mass phenomenon. This has forced the social structures of societies to adapt. Economic power, which was for centuries held by small groups of businessmen, bankers, and bureaucrats, has, as a result, been shifting downward. Today most companies—indeed most countries—woo not the handful that are rich but the many that are middle class. And rightly so, for the assets of the most exclusive investment group are dwarfed by those of a fund of workers' pensions.

Culture has also been democratized. What was once called "high culture" continues to flourish, of course, but as a niche product for the elderly set, no longer at the center of society's cultural life, which is now defined and dominated by popular music, blockbuster movies, and prime-time television. Those three make up the canon of the modern age, the set of cultural references with which everyone in society is familiar. The democratic revolution coursing through society has changed our very definition of culture. The key to the reputation of, say, a singer in an old order would have been *who* liked her. The key to fame today is *how many* like her. And by that yardstick Madonna will always trump Jessye Norman.[1] Quantity has become quality.

5 What has produced this dramatic shift? As with any large-scale social phenomenon, many forces have helped produce the democratic wave—a technological revolution, growing middle-class wealth, and the collapse of alternative systems and ideologies that organized society. To these grand systemic causes add another: America. The rise and dominance of America—a country whose

[1] Jessye Norman: one of the world's leading opera stars.

politics and culture are deeply democratic—has made democratization seem inevitable. Whatever its causes, the democratic wave is having predictable effects in every area. It is breaking down hierarchies, empowering individuals, and transforming societies well beyond their politics. Indeed much of what is distinctive about the world we live in is a consequence of the democratic idea.

We often read during the roaring 1990s that technology and information had been democratized. This is a relatively new phenomenon. In the past, technology helped reinforce centralization and hierarchy. For example, the last great information revolution—in the 1920s involving radio, television, movies, megaphones—had a centralizing effect. It gave the person or group with access to that technology the power to reach the rest of society. That's why the first step in a twentieth-century coup or revolution was always to take control of the country's television or radio station. But today's information revolution has produced thousands of outlets for news that make central control impossible and dissent easy. The Internet has taken this process another huge step forward, being a system where, in the columnist Thomas Friedman's words, "everyone is connected but no one is in control."[2]

The democratization of technology and information means that most anyone can get his hands on anything. Like weapons of mass destruction. We now know that Osama bin Laden was working on a serious biological-weapons program during the 1990s. But what is most astonishing is that the scientific information and manuals found in Al Qaeda's Kabul safe houses were not secrets stolen from government laboratories. They were documents downloaded from the Internet. Today if you want to find sources for anthrax, recipes for poison, or methods to weaponize chemicals, all you need is a good search engine. These same open sources will, unfortunately, soon help someone build a dirty bomb. The components are easier to get than ever before. Mostly what you need is knowledge, and that has been widely disseminated over the last decade. Even nuclear technology is now commonly available. It is, after all, fifty-year-old know-how, part of the world of AM radios and black-and-white television. Call it the democratization of violence.

It's more than a catchy phrase. The democratization of violence is one of the fundamental—and terrifying—features of the world today. For centuries the state has had a monopoly over the legitimate use of force in human societies. This inequality of power between the state and the citizen created order and was part of the glue that held modern civilization together. But over the last few decades the state's advantage has been weakened; now small groups of people can do dreadful things. And while terrorism is the most serious blow to state authority, central governments have been under siege in other ways as well. Capital markets, private businesses, local governments, nongovernmental organizations have all been gaining strength, sapping the authority of the state. The illegal flow of people, drugs, money, and weapons rising around the world attests to its weakness. This diffusion of power will continue because it is fueled by broad technological, social, and economic changes. In the post–September 11

[2] Thomas Friedman: columnist for *The New York Times*.

world the state has returned, with renewed power and legitimacy. This too will endure. The age of terror will thus be marked by a tension, between the forces that drive the democratization of authority on the one hand and the state on the other.

To discuss these problems is not to say that democracy is a bad thing. Overwhelmingly it has had wonderful consequences. Who among us would want to go back to an age with fewer choices and less individual power and autonomy? But like any broad transformation, democracy has its dark sides. Yet we rarely speak about them. To do so would be to provoke instant criticism that you are "out of sync" with the times. But this means that we never really stop to understand these times. Silenced by fears of being branded "antidemocratic" we have no way to understand what might be troubling about the ever-increasing democratization of our lives. We assume that no problem could ever be caused by democracy, so when we see social, political, and economic maladies we shift blame here and there, deflecting problems, avoiding answers, but never talking about the great transformation that is at the center of our political, economic, and social lives.

Democracy and Liberty

10 "Suppose elections are free and fair and those elected are racists, fascists, separatists," said the American diplomat Richard Holbrooke about Yugoslavia in the 1990s. "That is the dilemma." Indeed it is, and not merely in Yugoslavia's past but in the world's present. Consider, for example, the challenge we face across the Islamic world. We recognize the need for democracy in those often-repressive countries. But what if democracy produces an Islamic theocracy or something like it? It is not an idle concern. Across the globe, democratically elected regimes, often ones that have been re-elected or reaffirmed through referenda, are routinely ignoring constitutional limits on their power and depriving their citizens of basic rights. This disturbing phenomenon—visible from Peru to the Palestinian territories, from Ghana to Venezuela—could be called "illiberal democracy."

For people in the West, democracy means "liberal democracy": a political system marked not only by free and fair elections but also by the rule of law, a separation of powers, and the protection of basic liberties of speech, assembly, religion, and property. But this bundle of freedoms—what might be termed "constitutional liberalism"—has nothing intrinsically to do with democracy and the two have not always gone together, even in the West. After all, Adolf Hitler became chancellor of Germany via free elections. Over the last half-century in the West, democracy and liberty have merged. But today the two strands of liberal democracy, interwoven in the Western political fabric, are coming apart across the globe. Democracy is flourishing; liberty is not. . . .

. . . Let's be clear what we mean by political democracy. From the time of Herodotus[3] it has been defined, first and foremost, as the rule of the people.

[3] Herodotus: ancient Greek historian (484–425 BCE).

This definition of democracy as a process of selecting governments is now widely used by scholars. In *The Third Wave,* the eminent political scientist Samuel P. Huntington explains why:

> Elections, open, free and fair, are the essence of democracy, the inescapable *sine qua non.* Governments produced by elections may be inefficient, corrupt, shortsighted, irresponsible, dominated by special interests, and incapable of adopting policies demanded by the public good. These qualities make such governments undesirable but they do not make them undemocratic. Democracy is one public virtue, not the only one, and the relation of democracy to other public virtues and vices can only be understood if democracy is clearly distinguished from the other characteristics of political systems.

This definition also accords with the commonsense view of the term. If a country holds competitive, multiparty elections, we call it "democratic." When public participation in a country's politics is increased—for example, through the enfranchisement of women—that country is seen as having become more democratic. Of course elections must be open and fair, and this requires some protections for the freedom of speech and assembly. But to go beyond this minimal requirement and label a country democratic only if it guarantees a particular catalog of social, political, economic, and religious rights—which will vary with every observer—makes the word "democracy" meaningless. After all, Sweden has an economic system that many argue curtails individual property rights, France until recently had a state monopoly on television, and Britain has a state religion. But they are all clearly and identifiably democracies. To have "democracy" mean, subjectively, "a good government" makes it analytically useless.

Constitutional liberalism, on the other hand, is not about the procedures for selecting government but, rather, government's goals. It refers to the tradition, deep in Western history, that seeks to protect an individual's autonomy and dignity against coercion, whatever the source—state, church, or society. The term marries two closely connected ideas. It is liberal[4] because it draws on the philosophical strain, beginning with the Greeks and Romans, that emphasizes individual liberty. It is constitutional because it places the rule of law at the center of politics. Constitutional liberalism developed in Western Europe and the United States as a defense of an individual's right to life and property and the freedoms of religion and speech. To secure these rights, it emphasized checks on the power of government, equality under the law, impartial courts and tribunals, and the separation of church and state. In almost all of its variants, constitutional liberalism argues that human beings have certain natural (or "inalienable") rights and that governments must accept a basic law, limiting its own powers, to secure them. Thus in 1215 at Runnymede, England's barons forced

---

[4] I use the term "liberal" in the nineteenth-century sense, meaning concerned with individual economic, political, and religious liberty, which is sometimes called "classical liberalism," not in the modern, American sense, which associates it with the welfare state, affirmative action, and other policies [Zakaria's note].

the king to limit his own authority. In the American colonies these customs were made explicit, and in 1638 the town of Hartford adopted the first written constitution in modern history. In 1789 the American Constitution created a formal framework for the new nation. In 1975 Western nations set standards of behavior even for nondemocratic regimes. Magna Carta, the Fundamental Orders of Connecticut, the American Constitution, and the Helsinki Final Act are all expressions of constitutional liberalism.

Since 1945 Western governments have, for the most part, embodied both democracy and constitutional liberalism. Thus it is difficult to imagine the two apart, in the form of either illiberal democracy or liberal autocracy.

Americans in particular have trouble seeing any tension between democracy and liberty because it is not a dominant theme in our own history—with one huge exception. Slavery and segregation were entrenched in the American South through the democratic system. From the founding of the republic, those who abhorred slavery faced the problem that the majority of southern voters defended it passionately. In the end, slavery died not because it was lost in a vote but because the forces of the North crushed the South. Eventually the Jim Crow system that succeeded slavery in the South was destroyed during the 1950s and 1960s not by democracy but despite it. Although the final act of emancipation, the Civil Rights Act of 1964, was passed by Congress, all previous progress took place through the executive branch's fiat—as with the desegregation of the armed forces—or the Supreme Court's writ—as with school desegregation. In America's greatest tragedy, liberty and democracy were often at odds.

It is odd that the United States is so often the advocate of unrestrained democracy abroad. What is distinctive about the American system is not how democratic it is but rather how undemocratic it is, placing as it does multiple constraints on electoral majorities. The Bill of Rights, after all, is a list of things that the government may not do, regardless of the wishes of the majority. Of America's three branches of government, the Supreme Court—arguably the paramount branch—is headed by nine unelected men and women with life tenure. The U.S. Senate is the most unrepresentative upper house in the world, with the lone exception of the House of Lords, which is powerless and in any event on the verge of transformation. Each American state sends two senators to Washington, D.C., regardless of its population. Thus California's 30 million people have as many votes in the Senate as Arizona's 3.7 million—hardly one man, one vote.[5] In state and local legislatures all over the United States, what is striking is not the power of the majority party but the protections accorded to the minority party, often to an individual legislator. Private businesses and other nongovernmental groups—what Alexis de Tocqueville called "intermediate associations"—make up yet another crucial stratum within society. This rich fabric of civil society has been instrumental in shaping the character of American democracy.

[5] This particular aspect of American democracy has had mostly terrible effects, giving small states with tiny populations huge political influence and massive subsidies. Still, American democracy benefits greatly from most of its "undemocratic" features [Zakaria's note].

But it is wearing thin, producing America's own version of illiberal democracy. America's problems are different from—and much smaller than—those that face Third World countries. But they are related. In America, laws and rights are firmly established. The less-formal constraints, however, that are the inner stuffing of liberal democracy are disappearing. Many of these social and political institutions—political parties, professions, clubs, and associations—are undemocratic in their structure. They are all threatened by a democratic ideology that judges the value of every idea and institution by one simple test: Is power as widely dispersed as it can be? Are they, in other words, as democratic as they can be? Thus the U.S. Congress, although by definition democratic, used to function in a hierarchical and closed manner, at some distance from public pressures. Now it is a transparent body, utterly open to its constituents' views and pressures. Congress has become a more responsive, more democratic, and more dysfunctional body. . . .

Freedom and Restraint

The people, on the other hand, sense a problem. Americans have a lower regard for their political system than ever before. In this they are not alone. Most Western countries show the same historically low regard for their politics. In fact the recent rise of anti-establishment populism in every European country suggests that these feelings may already have become quite strong. This rising trend of dissatisfaction and anger with existing political systems comes at a bad time. Western democracies are under stress as they confront fundamental new challenges such as terrorism, demographic shifts, immigration, and cultural clashes. Governments have to protect societies from new dangers, revamp the welfare state, and encourage immigration without producing cultural war—a tall order at any time. But the political system has never been as dysfunctional. Perpetual campaigning and pandering, money-raising, special interests, and lobbying—most acute in America—have all discredited the system in people's eyes and voter turnouts are shockingly low. Western democracy remains the model for the rest of the world, but is it possible that like a supernova, at the moment of its blinding glory in distant universes, Western democracy is hollowing out at the core?

20 Many believe the contrary—that the increasing democratization of all spheres of society is an unqualified good. Out of the breakdown of the old systems, the opening up of access, and the empowerment of everyman will come ever-increasing individual freedom and happiness. During the last years of the heady 1990s the consulting firm Accenture published advertisements to tout its farseeing analysis. One of these was a mock newspaper headline that read, "THE INTERNET WILL BRING DEMOCRACY TO CHINA," followed by their tagline, "*Now* It Gets Interesting." While the fervor of the dot-com era has faded, technology enthusiasts point out that the Internet is in its infancy and eventually it will bring democracy to China, prosperity to India, and make us all our own bankers, lawyers, editors, and even legislators. The last trend is already visible in states like California, where government-by-referendum is well underway. Others are following the lead. How can you argue against more democracy?

But what if liberty comes not from chaos but from some measure of order as well—not from unfettered, direct democracy but from regulated, representative democracy? What if, as in much of life, we need guides and constraints? And what if liberty is truly secure only when these guardrails are strong? This alternate theory is, at any rate, what produced modern, liberal democracy. The democracy we have lived with in the West has always been what Aristotle called a "mixed regime." It had an elected government, to be sure, but also constitutional laws and rights, an independent judiciary, strong political parties, churches, businesses, private associations, and professional elites. Political democracy was an essential, indeed crucial, element of the whole—the people had ultimate power—but the system was a complex one with many parts, not all of them subject to elections. Indeed the purpose of many of these undemocratic institutions and groups was to temper public passions, educate citizens, guide democracy, and thereby secure liberty. When the Harvard Law School hands its graduates their diplomas, it reminds them to think of law as "the wise restraints that make men free." The national hymn, "America the Beautiful," declares, "America, America/God mend thine every flaw./Confirm thy soul in self-control/Thy liberty in law."

. . . There can be such a thing as too much democracy—too much of an emphatically good thing. The essence of liberal democratic politics is the construction of a rich, complex social order, not one dominated by a single idea. America's founding fathers, for example, sought to create such a pluralistic society when many believed that a single religious ideology should dominate societies. Democracy is also a single ideology, and, like all such templates, it has its limits. What works in a legislature might not work in a corporation.

To undertake a restoration is not to seek the return of an old order. We like the democratic changes that we have lived through and cherish their achievements. The goal is liberal democracy not as it was practiced in the nineteenth century but as it should be practiced in the twenty-first century. Democratic societies need new buffers and guides, designed for modern problems and times. And yet any such undertaking must begin with a return to history, to the struggle for liberty and democracy that began in the West and spread elsewhere. If we want to renew the perennial quest for life, liberty, and the pursuit of happiness, we must recall the forces that produced them in the first place. Only by understanding freedom's past can we help secure its future.

LEADING QUESTIONS

The Founding Fathers had at the forefront of their minds two powerful realities: the oppressive practices of absolute monarchy and the groundbreaking theories of the Englightenment thinkers. One experience taught them what to avoid, the other what to aspire to.

Today, however, we are a long way from oppression by a king and wild hopes based on new political theories. And yet today, too, the United States not only represents democracy in the world but seeks actively to promote it. Critics contend that we are hypocritical about democracy both at home and abroad. At home huge disparities in wealth and rule by entrenched officials don't seem exactly what Thomas Jefferson had in mind. And abroad we seem to want the appearance of democracy without appreciating how liberty might be understood by local populations.

So have we lost our way politically? The essays in this chapter reveal both what the original thinkers who created our democracy believed, and why they believed it, and what insightful commentators observe about the present challenges of democracy.

LEARNING MORE

To read more of Fareed Zakaria's work, as well as access links to relevant discussions of democracy, see the *Ideas Across Time* website.

QUESTIONING THE TEXT

1. What does Zakaria have in mind when he says that "we live in a democratic age" (par. 1)?
2. In what ways has democracy become a way of life? What examples does Zakaria offer to illustrate what he means?
3. How is the influence of technology and information different today from what it was in the past?
4. What is the "dark side" of democracy, according to Zakaria (par. 9)?
5. What distinguishes "constitutional liberalism" from "illiberal democracy"?
6. What is the outstanding example of illiberal democracy in the history of the United States?
7. Why does Zakaria believe that what's distinctive about American democracy is how *un*democratic it is?
8. How can democracy be a threat to liberty?
9. What does Zakaria believe we can do to make our democracy more compatible with liberty?

ANALYZING THE WRITER'S CRAFT

1. What is the essay's thesis statement?
2. Cite two or three especially effective transitions in this essay and explain why they are effective.
3. What kinds of evidence does Zakaria mainly rely on? Give two or three examples.
4. Zakaria relies on a number of major contrasts to get his argument across. Cite two and explain why they are effective.
5. Do you find Zakaria's argument persuasive? Why or why not?

MAKING CONNECTIONS

1. Zakaria's probing of American democracy illustrates a persistent paradox in American life—that is, that the impulse toward ever greater equality in America, the democratizing impulse, works against liberty and can even, unintentionally, undermine liberty. Democratizing implies fewer and fewer restraints or limits, and yet liberty seems to require restraints and limits. How would St. John de Crevecoeur (Chapter 1, pp. 22–27) view the dilemma that Zakaria is highlighting?
2. Do you think W. E. B. Du Bois (Chapter 6, pp. 472–479) would agree with Zakaria that there can be such a thing as too much democracy?
3. Zakaria maintains that today's decentralizing technology is not liberating but potentially dangerous. What do you think Daniel J. Boorstin would say (pp. 390–402)?
4. Are Zakaria and Alexis de Tocqueville both interested in liberty rather than democracy? Compare and contrast Zakaria's argument with that of Tocqueville (Chapter 6, pp. 458–462).

FORMULATING IDEAS FOR WRITING

1. Write an essay based on your own experience that illustrates how too much democracy can be a bad thing.
2. Write an essay based on your own experience that illustrates how democratization can lead to greater inclusiveness and diversity.
3. Do you agree with Zakaria that "democracy is flourishing; liberty is not" (par. 11)?
4. On the basis of Zakaria's essay, do you think America can/ought to export our democracy to the world?
5. Is freedom a qualitative good that cannot be achieved by quantitative (democratic) means?

On the Exercise of Power (1513)

Niccolo Machiavelli

The Italy of Machiavelli's lifetime was really a cultural grouping of independent city-states—Florence (his home), Venice, and Milan. These city-states competed for power among themselves and with the papacy through ceaseless, brutal wars. This turmoil forms the background of Machiavelli's great work. Having served for fifteen years at the high levels of Florentine government,

Machiavelli was arrested, tortured, and then exiled upon the resumption of Medici rule in Florence in 1512. He hoped to regain favor through his book *The Prince,* which was a kind of handbook on how to exercise power.

Unlike other earlier writers on politics, Machiavelli says his aim is to speak of things as they are and not as they might or ought to be. He is interested in the exercise of power. His considerable experience as civil servant, soldier, and diplomat gives him plenty of examples to support his premise—that the purpose of power is to serve neither moral nor immoral ends but rather the ends of rule, which are stability, order, and security. In politics, he says, there is only one standard: whether an action is successful or unsuccessful. In this respect, his work represents a challenge to ideas of democratic society based on morality. Even an elected ruler in what he calls a "constitutional principality" has to rule, and the tools and principles by means of which he must do so, in Machiavelli's estimation, are exactly the same as those of a monarch.

Niccolo Machiavelli was born into a poor family of aristocratic lineage. Little is known about his early life. In 1498, he was elected Secretary to the Second Chancery (or government) of Florence and became an active figure in political life. He accompanied Cesare Borgia in his famous campaign to unite Romagna, the central Italian provinces, under papal rule. (Borgia was a cardinal and son of the sitting pope, Alexander VI.) With the return of the Medici, Machiavelli was forced to return to his farm near San Casciano, where he lived with his wife and six children and passed his time writing. In addition to *The Prince,* Machiavelli wrote *Mandragola* (1518), *The Art of War* (1521), and *The History of Florence* (1525). After almost fifteen years in exile, Machiavelli achieved a reconciliation with the Medici and returned briefly to public office. He died in Florence in 1527.

The selections below on how to exercise power are from *The Prince.*

IX. The Constitutional Principality

But now we come to the other case, where a private citizen becomes the ruler of his country neither by crime nor by any other outrageous act of violence[1] but by the favour of his fellow citizens (and this we can call a constitutional principality, to become the ruler of which one needs neither prowess alone nor fortune, but rather a lucky astuteness). I say that one becomes a prince in this case with the favour of the people or of the nobles. These two different dispositions are found in every city; and the people are everywhere anxious not to be dominated or oppressed by the nobles, and the nobles are out to dominate and oppress the people. These opposed ambitions bring about one of three results: a principality, a free city, or anarchy.

A principality is created either by the people or by the nobles, according to whether the one or the other of these two classes is given the opportunity. What happens is that when the nobles see they cannot withstand the people, they start to increase the standing of one of their own numbers, and they make him prince

[1] violence: Machiavelli discussed becoming a ruler through these methods in the preceding sections of *The Prince.*

in order to be able to achieve their own ends under his cloak. The people in the same way, when they see they cannot withstand the nobles, increase the standing of one of themselves and make him prince in order to be protected by his authority. A man who becomes prince with the help of the nobles finds it more difficult to maintain his position than one who does so with the help of the people. As prince, he finds himself surrounded by many who believe they are his equals, and because of that he cannot command or manage them the way he wants. A man who becomes prince by favour of the people finds himself standing alone, and he has near him either no one or very few not prepared to take orders. In addition, it is impossible to satisfy the nobles honourably, without doing violence to the interests of others; but this can be done as far as the people are concerned. The people are more honest in their intentions than the nobles are, because the latter want to oppress the people, whereas they want only not to be oppressed. Moreover, a prince can never make himself safe against a hostile people: there are too many of them. He can make himself safe against the nobles, who are few. The worst that can happen to a prince when the people are hostile is for him to be deserted; but from the nobles, if hostile, he has to fear not only desertion but even active opposition. The nobles have more foresight and are more astute, they always act in time to safeguard their interests, and they take sides with the one whom they expect to win. Again, a prince must always live with the same people, but he can well do without the nobles, since he can make and unmake them every day, increasing and lowering their standing at will.

To clarify the discussion further, I say that there are two main considerations to be remembered in regard to the nobles: either they conduct themselves in such a way that they come to depend entirely on your fortunes, or they do not. Those who become dependent, and are not rapacious, must be honoured and loved; those who remain independent of you do so for two different reasons. They may do so because they are pusillanimous[2] and naturally lacking in spirit; if so you should make use of them, especially those who are capable of giving sensible advice, since they will respect you when you are doing well, and you will have nothing to fear from them in times of adversity. But when they deliberately and for reasons of ambition remain independent of you, it is a sign that they are more concerned about themselves than about you. Against nobles such as these, a prince must safeguard himself, fearing them as if they were his declared enemies, because in times of adversity they will always help to ruin him.

A man who is made a prince by the favour of the people must work to retain their friendship; and this is easy for him because the people ask only not to be oppressed. But a man who has become prince against the will of the people and by the favour of the nobles should, before anything else, try to win the people over; this too is easy if he takes them under his protection. When men receive favours from someone they expected to do them ill, they are under a greater obligation to their benefactor; just so the people can in an instant become more amicably disposed towards the prince than if he had seized power by their favour. And there are many ways in which a prince can win them over. These vary according to circumstances, so no definite rule can be given and I shall not deal

[2] pusillanimous: cowardly.

with them here. I shall only conclude that it is necessary for a prince to have the friendship of the people; otherwise he has no remedy in times of adversity.

Nabis,[3] prince of the Spartans, withstood the whole of Greece and a triumphant Roman army, and successfully defended his country and his own authority against them. All he had to do, when danger threatened, was to take steps against a few of his subjects; but this would not have been enough had the people been hostile to him. Let no one contradict this opinion of mine with that trite proverb, that he who builds on the people builds on mud. That may be so when a private citizen bases his power on the people and takes it for granted that the people will rescue him if he is in danger from enemies or from the magistrates. (In this case, he could often find he had made a mistake, as happened with the Gracchi in Rome and messer Giorgio Scali in Florence.[4]) But if it is a prince who builds his power on the people, one who can command and is a man of courage, who does not despair in adversity, who does not fail to take precautions, and who wins general allegiance by his personal qualities and the institutions he establishes, he will never be let down by the people; and he will be found to have established his power securely.

Principalities usually come to grief when the transition is being made from limited power to absolutism. Princes taking this step rule either directly or through magistrates. In the latter case, their position is weaker and more dangerous, because they rely entirely on the will of those citizens who have been put in office; and these, especially in times of adversity, can very easily depose them either by positive action against them or by not obeying them. And when danger comes, the prince has no time to seize absolute authority, because the citizens and subjects, accustomed to taking orders from the magistrates, will not take them from him in a crisis. In disturbed times, also, men whom the prince can trust will be hard to find. So such a prince cannot rely on what he has experienced in times of tranquillity, when the citizens have need of his government. When things are quiet, everyone dances attendance, everyone makes promises, and everybody would die for him so long as death is far off. But in times of adversity, when the state has need of its citizens, there are few to be found. And this test of loyalty is all the more dangerous since it can be made only once. Therefore a wise prince must devise ways by which his citizens are always and in all circumstances dependent on him and on his authority; and then they will always be faithful to him.

XV. The Things for Which Men, and Especially Princes, Are Praised or Blamed

It now remains for us to see how a prince must govern his conduct towards his subjects or his friends. I know that this has often been written about before, and

---

[3] Nabis: the last ruler (207–192 BCE) of independent Sparta.

[4] the Gracchi . . . Giorgio Scali: The Gracchi brothers, Tiberius (166–133 BCE) and Gaius (154–121 BCE), both tribunes, were killed by members of the Roman Senate for fostering policies favorable to the lower classes of Rome. Giorgio Scali, as leader of the wool workers' revolt in Florence in 1378, was elected one of the rulers of the city but was soon beheaded. Machiavelli, who did not think well of Scali, wrote of these events in his *History of Florence*.

so I hope it will not be thought presumptuous for me to do so, as, especially in discussing this subject, I draw up an original set of rules. But since my intention is to say something that will prove of practical use to the inquirer, I have thought it proper to represent things as they are in real truth, rather than as they are imagined. Many have dreamed up republics and principalities which have never in truth been known to exist; the gulf between how one should live and how one does live is so wide that a man who neglects what is actually done for what should be done learns the way to self-destruction rather than self-preservation. The fact is that a man who wants to act virtuously in every way necessarily comes to grief among so many who are not virtuous. Therefore if a prince wants to maintain his rule he must learn how not to be virtuous, and to make use of this or not according to need.

So leaving aside imaginary things, and referring only to those which truly exist, I say that whenever men are discussed (and especially princes, who are more exposed to view), they are noted for various qualities which earn them either praise or condemnation. Some, for example, are held to be generous, and others miserly (I use the Tuscan word rather than the word avaricious: we call a man who is mean with what he possesses, miserly, and a man who wants to plunder others, avaricious).[5] Some are held to be benefactors, others are called grasping; some cruel, some compassionate; one man faithless, another faithful; one man effeminate and cowardly, another fierce and courageous; one man courteous, another proud; one man lascivious, another pure; one guileless, another crafty; one stubborn, another flexible; one grave, another frivolous; one religious, another sceptical; and so forth. I know everyone will agree that it would be most laudable if a prince possessed all the qualities deemed to be good among those I have enumerated. But, because of conditions in the world, princes cannot have those qualities, or observe them completely. So a prince has of necessity to be so prudent that he knows how to escape the evil reputation attached to those vices which could lose him his state, and how to avoid those vices which are not so dangerous, if he possibly can; but, if he cannot, he need not worry so much about the latter. And then, he must not flinch from being blamed for vices which are necessary for safeguarding the state. This is because, taking everything into account, he will find that some of the things that appear to be virtues will, if he practises them, ruin him, and some of the things that appear to be vices will bring him security and prosperity.

XVIII. How Princes Should Honour Their Word

Everyone realizes how praiseworthy it is for a prince to honour his word and to be straightforward rather than crafty in his dealings; nonetheless contemporary experience shows that princes who have achieved great things have been those who have given their word lightly, who have known how to trick men with their cunning, and who, in the end, have overcome those abiding by honest principles.

---

[5] avaricious: Machiavelli uses the words *misero* and *avaro*.

10 You must understand, therefore, that there are two ways of fighting: by law or by force. The first way is natural to men, and the second to beasts. But as the first way often proves inadequate one must needs have recourse to the second. So a prince must understand how to make a nice use of the beast and the man. The ancient writers taught princes about this by an allegory, when they described how Achilles and many other princes of the ancient world were sent to be brought up by Chiron, the centaur, so that he might train them his way. All the allegory means, in making the teacher half beast and half man, is that a prince must know how to act according to the nature of both, and that he cannot survive otherwise.

So, as a prince is forced to know how to act like a beast, he must learn from the fox and the lion; because the lion is defenceless against traps and a fox is defenceless against wolves. Therefore one must be a fox in order to recognize traps, and a lion to frighten off wolves. Those who simply act like lions are stupid. So it follows that a prudent ruler cannot, and must not, honour his word when it places him at a disadvantage and when the reasons for which he made his promise no longer exist. If all men were good, this precept would not be good; but because men are wretched creatures who would not keep their word to you, you need not keep your word to them. And no prince ever lacked good excuses to colour his bad faith. One could give innumerable modern instances of this, showing how many pacts and promises have been made null and void by the bad faith of princes: those who have known best how to imitate the fox have come off best. But one must know how to colour one's actions and to be a great liar and deceiver. Men are so simple, and so much creatures of circumstance, that the deceiver will always find someone ready to be deceived.

There is one fresh example I do not want to omit. Alexander VI[6] never did anything, or thought of anything, other than deceiving men; and he always found victims for his deceptions. There never was a man capable of such convincing asseverations,[7] or so ready to swear to the truth of something, who would honour his word less. Nonetheless his deceptions always had the result he intended, because he was a past master in the art.

A prince, therefore, need not necessarily have all the good qualities I mentioned above, but he should certainly appear to have them. I would even go so far as to say that if he has these qualities and always behaves accordingly he will find them harmful; if he only appears to have them they will render him service. He should appear to be compassionate, faithful to his word, kind, guileless, and devout. And indeed he should be so. But his disposition should be such that, if he needs to be the opposite, he knows how. You must realize this: that a prince, and especially a new prince, cannot observe all those things which give men a reputation for virtue, because in order to maintain his state he is often forced to act in defiance of good faith, of charity, of kindness, of

---

[6] Alexander VI: Rodrigo Borgia, father of Cesare and Lucrezia Borgia, was elected Pope Alexander VI in 1492.

[7] asseverations: emphatic statements.

religion. And so he should have a flexible disposition, varying as fortune and circumstances dictate. As I said above, he should not deviate from what is good, if that is possible, but he should know how to do evil, if that is necessary.

A prince, then, must be very careful not to say a word which does not seem inspired by the five qualities I mentioned earlier. To those seeing and hearing him, he should appear a man of compassion, a man of good faith, a man of integrity, a kind and a religious man. And there is nothing so important as to seem to have this last quality. Men in general judge by their eyes rather than by their hands; because everyone is in a position to watch, few are in a position to come in close touch with you. Everyone sees what you appear to be, few experience what you really are. And those few dare not gainsay the many who are backed by the majesty of the state. In the actions of all men, and especially of princes, where there is no court of appeal, one judges by the result. So let a prince set about the task of conquering and maintaining his state; his methods will always be judged honourable and will be universally praised. The common people are always impressed by appearances and results. In this context, there are only common people, and there is no room for the few when the many are supported by the state. A certain contemporary ruler, whom it is better not to name,[8] never preaches anything except peace and good faith; and he is an enemy of both one and the other, and if he had ever honoured either of them he would have lost either his standing or his state many times over.

LEARNING MORE

The complete texts of Machiavelli's main works, including *The Prince* and *The History of Florence*, are accessible online. See the *Ideas Across Time* website.

QUESTIONING THE TEXT

1. How is a constitutional principality distinguishable from all other principalities?
2. Why does a man who becomes a prince through the help of the nobility have a harder time than if aided by the people?
3. Why is the good opinion of the people easy to keep but the favor of the nobles hard to sustain?
4. How can the magistrates (the civil bureaucracy) become a danger to a prince?
5. How can virtues ruin a prince?

---

[8] name: Ferdinand II of Aragon (1452–1516). Scholars have said that Machiavelli disguises his admiration of Ferdinand by usually praising Cesare Borgia in his stead. This is the Ferdinand of Ferdinand and Isabella, who commissioned Christopher Columbus's journey. Ferdinand unified Spain into the most powerful country in Europe. After conquering the last remaining Islamic kingdom in Spain, he also expelled the Jews in 1492.

6. A prince must be half-beast and half-man, Machiavelli says. What does Machiavelli associate with beastliness? With manhood?
7. How is it useful for a prince to appear—but only appear—to be a good man?
8. Machiavelli says that in the action of princes the only standard is results. Do you agree?
9. Should every newly elected American president learn his "trade" by reading Machiavelli before assuming office? Explain.

ANALYZING THE WRITER'S CRAFT

1. Machiavelli advances his argument by setting up many contraries, such as nobles and people, what is actually done and what should be done, and honesty and deceit. Choose two of these oppositions, and discuss how they help Machiavelli get his point across.
2. We know that the intended audience of this writing is the prince or the prospective prince; and we know such men would have been familiar with Machiavelli's experience as a soldier and statesman. Nonetheless, Machiavelli chooses to ballast his generalizations with supporting examples. Analyze Machiavelli's use of examples to consider why he resorts to examples in certain cases and not in others, and what else he gains from his examples other than factual support for his analysis.
3. Machiavelli is fond of aphorisms (pithy statements of commonly held truths), such as "the people are everywhere anxious not to be dominated or oppressed by the nobles, and the nobles are out to dominate and oppress the people." What does he gain through his use of aphorisms? Are there any drawbacks to their use?
4. Did you find Machiavelli's allusion to Chiron, the centaur, effective? Explain. How about the examples of the fox and the lion—do these references work just as well?
5. What is the tone of Machiavelli's writing? Offer two or three examples to support your answer.
6. Machiavelli wants to be read as a practical teacher. Does his version of the unvarnished truth give his teaching authority, or does he seem less a reliable teacher than a cynic?

MAKING CONNECTIONS

1. Karl Marx (Chapter 4, pp. 264–273) sees history as the record of class struggle between the oppressor and the oppressed. Are Machiavelli's oppositions of interests an early example of Marx's way of thinking? Explain.
2. Machiavelli seems largely to ignore economics. Both Adam Smith (Chapter 4, pp. 244–262) and Karl Marx (Chapter 4, pp. 264–273), however, see

economics as the basis of power and the test of political success. Why doesn't Machiavelli devote more time to economics? How much control can a prince have over prosperity?

3. Vaclav Havel (pp. 404–412) is also concerned with power. What do Havel and Machiavelli have in common? What separates them?
4. Another pioneer of political science is Alexis de Tocqueville, whose method of analysis is also a precursor of modern political study. How do Machiavelli and Tocqueville (Chapter 6, pp. 458–462) point to contemporary social analysis? In what ways do the two men approach their analysis differently?
5. The greatest statesman and soldier whose writing is collected in this textbook is the Roman emperor Marcus Aurelius (Chapter 8, pp. 646–648). To what extent do Aurelius and Machiavelli see eye to eye?
6. Henry David Thoreau (pp. 371–383) makes the classic case for appeal to a higher authority than government in determining action. If the government is immoral, following its laws is also immoral and should be resisted by moral people. Machiavelli says that such a view is impossible for a prince, for whom results are all that counts. Whose side do you take, Thoreau's or Machiavelli's?

FORMULATING IDEAS FOR WRITING

1. "In the actions of all men, and especially of princes, where there is no court of appeal, one judges by the result," writes Machiavelli. In the view of some—see, for example, Henry Thoreau (pp. 371–383) or Martin Luther King Jr. (Chapter 6, pp. 511–525)—there is always a court of appeal, a higher standard of morality against which all actions should be judged. Machiavelli says the idea of a moral standard is imaginary and indeed dangerous. "To maintain his rule he [a prince] must learn how not to be virtuous" (par. 7). What is your view?
2. Machiavelli advises the prince to *appear* to be compassionate, a man of integrity, a religious man (par. 13). This suggests that most people value these qualities and expect their leader to embody them. But for Machiavelli these are no more than tools of government, useful if they serve an end and useless if they don't. Since there is always a prince or governor or president in office, why don't people notice the discrepancy between the leader's appearance and the reality of his actions? Are people easily fooled, as Machiavelli says? Or is there some other explanation you might offer?
3. Did the turmoil and butchery of his times lead Machiavelli to overestimate the importance of security and order? Or are all eras ones of turmoil and butchery? Even in the context of turmoil and butchery, are there more important goals for a prince?
4. Is Machiavelli's analysis a fatal critique of a democratic politics? Write an essay that tries to arrive at a persuasive answer. Choose carefully among historical examples to support your argument.

The Social Contract (1690)

John Locke

John Locke (1623–1704) was one of an extraordinary cadre of thinkers in an extraordinary age, the English seventeenth century. On the intellectual side, this was the century of Locke's friend Isaac Newton and of Locke's Oxford tutor the chemist Robert Boyle. On the political side, it was the century that established the modern British state as an Anglican constitutional monarchy, though this outcome was hardly certain at the time. The century was marked by conflict between the king and Parliament and among Puritans, Anglicans, and Catholics, contentions that erupted into civil war in the 1640s. The Parliamentary party, led by Oliver Cromwell, overthrew and killed the king, Charles I, and abolished the monarchy, the House of Lords, and the Anglican Church. Cromwell's Protectorate of the 1650s was an early experiment in republican government. Upon Cromwell's death, however, the monarchy and all its institutions were restored.

This was the world into which Locke was born. His parents were Puritans of modest means. His father fought in a cavalry company on the Puritan side in the civil war. Through the intervention of the local Member of Parliament, Locke gained admission to the most important school of the age, Westminster School, and from there went on to the most important college, Christ Church, Oxford. He studied to be a physician. An accident of fate brought him into the ambit of Anthony Ashley Cooper, later First Lord Shaftesbury, one of the wealthiest and most powerful men in the nation. He first worked as Shaftesbury's personal physician but soon became an indispensable assistant and close friend. Locke seems to have saved Shaftesbury's life through a timely operation, arranged the marriage of Shaftesbury's heir, and directed the education of Shaftesbury's grandson. Attending on Shaftesbury, Locke found himself at the epicenter of English politics.

Shaftesbury took a leading role in the faction that sought to exclude the Catholic James, then Duke of York, from succeeding to the throne. As a consequence, Shaftesbury was imprisoned in the Tower of London in 1681 but later acquitted. When an assassination attempt on the king and his brother failed, however, Shaftesbury fled to Holland and died there in January 1683. Fearing for his life because of his association with Shaftesbury, Locke also fled the country, not to return until William and Mary finally took the throne in 1688.

It was while in exile that Locke penned his two major works, both subsequently published in 1690—*An Essay Concerning Human Understanding* and *Two Treatises on Government*. Still wary, Locke published these political treatises anonymously. The *Two Treatises* had a profound influence on political theory, and it paved the way for the American and French revolutions. The First Treatise was an extended, even pedantic assault on Robert Filmer's now happily forgotten apology for absolute monarchy and the divine right of kings, titled *Patriarcha* (1680). But it was in the Second Treatise, from which the excerpts below are taken, that Locke set out his version of the social contract. According to Locke, men—Locke does not consider the role of women—leave the dangers to their persons and their property in the state of nature by a voluntary association into community, which requires that they cede to a central authority—government—some of their natural rights in exchange for the stability and order of civil society. But all people retain their natural rights, and it is by the guarantee of their voluntary association that these rights remain inalienable. Since government in this way derives from the consent of the governed, any government or ruler that fails to sustain people's natural rights can justly be deposed by the people. Locke did not anticipate that this doctrine would be turned to revolutionary purposes against kings in general. Although he wrote the *Treatises* before the Glorious Revolution of 1688, he published them later and expressly made the argument as a defense of the assumption of the throne by "our great restorer, the present King William."

Locke indeed served King William in various civil service posts until his death on October 28, 1704.

Chapter II: Of the State of Nature

4. To understand political power aright, and derive it from its original, we must consider what state all men are naturally in, and that is, a state of perfect freedom to order their actions and dispose of their possessions and persons as they think fit, within the bounds of the law of nature, without asking leave, or depending upon the will of any other man.

A state also of equality, wherein all the power and jurisdiction is reciprocal, no one having more than another; there being nothing more evident than that creatures of the same species and rank, promiscuously born to all the same advantages of nature, and the use of the same faculties, should also be equal one amongst another without subordination or subjection, unless the Lord and Master of them all should, by any manifest declaration of His will, set one above another, and confer on him by an evident and clear appointment an undoubted right to dominion and sovereignty. . . .

Chapter IV: Of Slavery

22. The natural liberty of man is to be free from any superior power on earth, and not to be under the will or legislative authority of man, but to have only the law of nature for his rule. The liberty of man in society is to be under no other legislative power but that established by consent in the commonwealth; nor under the dominion of any will or restraint of any law, but what that legislative shall enact according to the trust put in it. Freedom then is not . . . "a liberty for every one to do what he lists, to live as he pleases, and not to be tied by any

laws." But freedom of men under government is to have a standing rule to live by, common to every one of that society, and made by the legislative power erected in it; a liberty to follow my own will in all things, where that rule prescribes not; and not to be subject to the inconstant, uncertain, unknown, arbitrary will of another man: as freedom of nature is to be under no other restraint but the law of nature. . . .

Chapter VII: Of Political or Civil Society

87. Man being born, as has been proved, with a title to perfect freedom, and an uncontrolled enjoyment of all the rights and privileges of the law of Nature equally with any other man or number of men in the world, hath by nature a power not only to preserve his property—that is, his life, liberty, and estate—against the injuries and attempts of other men, but to judge of and punish the breaches of that law in others as he is persuaded the offense deserves, even with death itself, in crimes where the heinousness of the fact in his opinion requires it. But because no political society can be nor subsist without having in itself the power to preserve the property, and, in order thereunto, punish the offenses of all those of that society, there, and there only, is political society, where every one of the members hath quitted this natural power, resigned it up into the hands of the community in all cases that exclude him not from appealing for protection to the law established by it. And thus all private judgment of every particular member being excluded, the community comes to be umpire; and by understanding indifferent rules and men authorized by the community for their execution, decides all the differences that may happen between any members of that society concerning any matter of right, and punishes those offenses which any member hath committed against the society with such penalties as the law has established; whereby it is easy to discern who are and who are not in political society together. Those who are united into one body, and have a common established law and judicature to appeal to, with authority to decide controversies between them and punish offenders, are in civil society one with another; but those who have no such common appeal—I mean on earth—are still in the state of Nature, each being, where there is no other, judge for himself and executioner, which is, as I have before shown it, the perfect state of Nature.

88. And thus the commonwealth comes by a power to set down what punishment shall belong to the several transgressions which they think worthy of it committed amongst the members of that society, which is the power of making laws, as well as it has the power to punish any injury done unto any of its members by anyone that is not of it, which is the power of war and peace; and all this for the preservation of the property of all the members of that society as far as is possible. But though every man entered into civil society has quitted his power to punish offenses against the law of Nature in prosecution of his own private judgment, yet with the judgment of offenses, which he has given up to the legislative in all cases where he can appeal to the magistrate, he has given a right to the commonwealth to employ his force for the execution of the judgments of the commonwealth whenever he shall be called to it; which, indeed, are his own judgments, they being made by himself or his representative. And herein we

have the original of the legislative and executive power of civil society, which is to judge by standing laws how far offenses are to be punished when committed within the commonwealth, and also by occasional judgments founded on the present circumstances of the fact, how far injuries from without are to be vindicated; and in both these to employ all the force of all the members when there shall be need.

89. Wherever, therefore, any number of men so unite into one society, as to quit everyone his executive power of the law of Nature, and to resign it to the public, there, and there only, is a political or civil society. And this is done wherever any number of men, in the state of Nature, enter into society to make one people, one body politic, under one supreme government, or else when anyone joins himself to, and incorporates with, any government already made. For hereby he authorizes the society, or, which is all one, the legislative thereof, to make laws for him, as the public good of the society shall require, to the execution whereof his own assistance (as to his own decrees) is due. And this puts men out of a state of Nature into that of a commonwealth, by setting up a judge on earth with authority to determine all the controversies and redress the injuries that may happen to any member of the commonwealth; which judge is the legislative, or magistrates appointed by it. And wherever there are any number of men, however associated, that have no such decisive power to appeal to, there they are still in the state of Nature.

90. Hence it is evident that absolute monarchy, which by some men is counted the only government in the world, is indeed inconsistent with civil society, and so can be no form of civil government at all. . . .

Chapter VIII: Of the Beginning of Political Societies

. . . 96. For when any number of men have, by the consent of every individual, made a community, they have thereby made that community one body, with a power to act as one body, which is only by the will and determination of the majority. For that which acts any community being only the consent of the individuals of it, and it being one body must move one way, it is necessary the body should move that way whither the greater force carries it, which is the consent of the majority; or else it is impossible it should act or continue one body, one community which the consent of every individual that united into it agreed that it should; and so everyone is bound by that consent to be concluded by the majority. And therefore we see that in assemblies empowered to act by positive laws, where no number is set by that positive law which empowers them, the act of the majority passes for the act of the whole, and of course determines, as having by the law of nature and reason the power of the whole.

97. And thus every man, by consenting with others to make one body politic under one government, puts himself under an obligation to every one of that society, to submit to the determination of the majority, and to be concluded by it; or else this original compact, whereby he with others incorporates into one society, would signify nothing, and be no compact, if he be left free and under no other ties than he was in before in the state of nature. For what appearance would there be of any compact? . . .

Chapter IX: Of the Ends of Political Society and Government

123. If man in the state of Nature be so free, as has been said, if he be absolute lord of his own person and possessions, equal to the greatest, and subject to nobody, why will he part with his freedom, this empire, and subject himself to the dominion and control of any other power? To which, it is obvious to answer, that though in the state of Nature he hath such a right, yet the enjoyment of it is very uncertain, and constantly exposed to the invasions of others. For all being kings as much as he, every man his equal, and the greater part no strict observers of equity and justice, the enjoyment of the property he has in this state is very unsafe, very unsecure. This makes him willing to quit this condition, which, however free, is full of fears and continual dangers; and it is not without reason that he seeks out and is willing to join in society with others, who are already united, or have a mind to unite, for the mutual preservation of their lives, liberties, and estates, which I call by the general name, property.

124. The great and chief end, therefore, of men's uniting into commonwealths, and putting themselves under government, is the preservation of their property; to which in the state of nature there are many things wanting.

First, There wants an established, settled, known law, received and allowed by common consent to be the standard of right and wrong, and the common measure to decide all controversies between them. For though the law of nature be plain and intelligible to all rational creatures; yet men, being biased by their interest, as well as ignorant for want of study of it, are not apt to allow of it as a law binding to them in the application of it to their particular cases.

125. Secondly, In the state of Nature there wants a known and indifferent judge, with authority to determine all differences according to the established law. For everyone in that state, being both judge and executioner of the law of nature, men being partial to themselves, passion and revenge is very apt to carry them too far, and with too much heat in their own cases, as well as negligence and unconcernedness, to make them too remiss in other men's. . . .

LEARNING MORE

To read more of Locke's *Treatise* and to access useful information about his life and thought, see the *Ideas Across Time* website.

QUESTIONING THE TEXT

1. What are the main characteristics of the human condition in the state of nature?
2. What does Locke mean by "property"?
3. How does Locke distinguish between the state of nature and "political society" (par. 4)?

4. Why does Locke see legislative power and society as synonymous?
5. What gives the community the power to act?
6. If men are completely free in the state of nature, why do they consent to join together in political society?
7. Why does Locke say that monarchy is inconsistent with civil society?

ANALYZING THE WRITER'S CRAFT

1. Locke presents his argument step by step, building one point on the previous one. Write an outline of those steps.
2. Is Locke's foundational premise—that in the state of nature men are completely free and also completely equal—valid? Explain.
3. Whom does Locke imagine as his audience? How do you know?
4. What is the effect of Locke's using "property" to include "life, liberty, and estate" (par. 4)?
5. Would Locke's evidence for his views be adequate today as a basis of persuading others of the soundness of his views? Why or why not?
6. Quote the definitions that are the building blocks of Locke's argument.

MAKING CONNECTIONS

1. Does St. John de Crevecoeur's portrait of early America (Chapter 1, pp. 22–27) confirm Locke's view of man in a state of nature? Or in civil society?
2. Distinguish between Locke's notion of equality and Alexis de Tocqueville's (Chapter 6, pp. 458–462).
3. Does Charles Darwin's account of the state of nature (Chapter 4, pp. 167–180) undermine or support Locke's?
4. In addition to Locke's view of civil society, that of Adam Smith (Chapter 4, pp. 244–262) is probably the model that has most influenced contemporary U.S. society. Compare and contrast these two influential concepts of civil society. Can we truly follow both?

FORMULATING IDEAS FOR WRITING

1. Write an account of civil society based on a Darwinian picture of the state of nature.
2. Locke ascribes onerous obligations to people in civil society. Do we in the United States today feel as committed to the fulfillment of our civil obligations as Locke suggests we must be once we leave the state of nature and enter into "commonwealth"?
3. Locke attributes significant value, maybe the greatest social value, to what he calls "property." Is his belief in the goodness of property naïve, or is he an early prophet of the core values of the future?

4. For Locke, "society" and "legislature" are one. Similarly, he views judges and legislators as making "our" judgments and speaking "our" opinions because they are "our" representatives. Is Locke's view just the unrealistic idealism of a philosopher, or has the evolution of society from Locke's time to our own demonstrated the soundness of his views?

The Original Declaration of Independence (1776)

Thomas Jefferson

Thomas Jefferson's eloquent, learned, principled, and often fierce opposition to tyranny in any form reverberates through American history as our standard of unalloyed commitment to human freedom and faith in the abiding wisdom of the citizens. But he was a complex individual, a man of many contradictions: a slaveholder, he was nonetheless a passionate public opponent of slavery; an agrarian aristocrat, he championed the primary role of ordinary people in politics; a skeptic about federal power, he used the authority of the president in an unprecedented way to make the Louisiana Purchase; one of the most persuasive writers in American history, he was a poor public speaker and famously said nothing during the entire session of the Second Continental Congress, when he penned the Declaration of Independence. The original document is on display in the Rotunda for the Charters of Freedom in the National Archives Building in Washington, D.C.

Jefferson was born in Shadwell, Virginia, in 1743. His mother came from one of the leading families in Virginia, and when his father died in 1757, he left Jefferson 2,750 acres of land. By Jefferson's death, the estate had doubled in size. Jefferson studied at the College of William and Mary and was admitted to the bar in Williamsburg, then the capital of Virginia; he was elected to the Virginia House of Burgesses in 1769. His open letter to King George, *A Summary View of the Rights of British America* (1774), contributed to his election as delegate to the Second Continental Congress. On June 11, 1776, he was appointed to the committee established to draft a declaration of independence, along with Benjamin Franklin, John Adams, Roger Sherman (of Connecticut), and Robert Livingston (of New York). It was Jefferson, however, who composed the document. Jefferson's draft was amended by Congress, often in ways that displeased him. Congress, for example, refused to include a strong statement against slavery. The text of the Declaration of Independence in this selection comes from Jefferson's *Autobiography* (1821), where he prints his original text and indicates what was changed by Congress.

In 1779, Jefferson was elected governor of Virginia, and in 1790, George Washington appointed him the first secretary of state of the new republic. In 1796, he was defeated for the office of president by John Adams and became vice-president. However, in 1800, he was at last elected to the office and became the first president to be inaugurated in the new capital, Washington, that he helped plan. Indeed, Jefferson was a man of many talents. He was a great patron of the arts; his library formed the core of the new Library of Congress; he designed not only his own home at Monticello but the stunning and original buildings for the University of Virginia, which he founded. To the end, he was an indefatigable correspondent and writer: the most recent edition of his works runs to sixty volumes. In the most uncanny coincidence in American history, Jefferson died on the 4th of July, 1826, followed in death a few hours later by his long-time rival and friend, John Adams.

Congress proceeded the same day to consider the Declaration of Independence, which had been reported and lain on the table the Friday preceding, and on Monday referred to a committee of the whole. The pusillanimous[1] idea that we had friends in England worth keeping terms with, still haunted the minds of many. For this reason, those passages which conveyed censures on the people of England were struck out, lest they should give them offense. The clause too, reprobating the enslaving the inhabitants of Africa, was struck out in complaisance to South Carolina and Georgia, who had never attempted to restrain the importation of slaves, and who, on the contrary, still wished to continue it. Our northern brethren also, I believe, felt a little tender under those censures; for though their people had very few slaves themselves, yet they had been pretty considerable carriers of them to others. The debates, having taken up the greater parts of the 2d, 3d, and 4th days of July, were, on the evening of the last, closed; the Declaration was reported by the committee, agreed to by the House, and signed by every member present, except Mr. Dickinson.[2] As the sentiments of men are known not only by what they receive, but what they reject also, I will state the form of the Declaration as originally reported. The parts struck out by Congress shall be distinguished by a black line drawn under them, and those inserted by them shall be placed in the margin, or in a concurrent column.

A Declaration by the Representatives of the United States of America, in General Congress Assembled

When, in the course of human events, it becomes necessary for one people to dissolve the political bands which have connected them with another, and to assume among the powers of the earth the separate and equal station to which the laws of nature and of nature's God entitle

[1] pusillanimous: cowardly.
[2] Dickinson: John Dickinson of Pennsylvania, who opposed it.

them, a decent respect to the opinions of mankind requires that they should declare the causes which impel them to the separation.

We hold these truths to be self evident: that all men are created equal; that they are endowed by their Creator with inherent and in- **certain**
alienable rights; that among these are life, liberty, and the pursuit of happiness; that to secure these rights, governments are instituted among men, deriving their just powers from the consent of the governed; that whenever any form of government becomes destructive of these ends, it is the right of the people to alter or to abolish it, and to institute new government, laying its foundation on such principles, and organizing its powers in such form, as to them shall seem most likely to effect their safety and happiness. Prudence, indeed, will dictate that governments long established should not be changed for light and transient causes; and accordingly all experience hath shown that mankind are more disposed to suffer while evils are sufferable, than to right themselves by abolishing the forms to which they are accustomed. But when a long train of abuses and usurpations, begun at a distinguished[3] period and pursuing invariably the same object, evinces a design to reduce them under absolute despotism, it is their right, it is their duty to throw off such government, and to provide new guards for their future security. Such has been the patient sufferance of these colonies; and such is now the necessity which constrains
them to expunge their former systems of government. The history of **alter**
the present king of Great Britain is a history of unremitting injuries **repeated**
and usurpations, among which appears no solitary fact to contradict **all having**
the uniform tenor of the rest, but all have in direct object the establishment of an absolute tyranny over these states. To prove this, let facts be submitted to a candid[4] world for the truth of which we pledge a faith yet unsullied by falsehood.

5 He has refused his assent to laws the most wholesome and necessary for the public good.

He has forbidden his governors to pass laws of immediate and pressing importance, unless suspended in their operation till his assent should be obtained; and, when so suspended, he has utterly neglected to attend to them.

He has refused to pass other laws for the accommodation of large districts of people, unless those people would relinquish the right of representation in the legislature, a right inestimable to them, and formidable to tyrants only.

He has called together legislative bodies at places unusual, uncomfortable, and distant from the depository of their public records, for the sole purpose of fatiguing them into compliance with his measures.

---

[3] distinguished: discernible.

[4] candid: impartial.

He has dissolved representative houses repeatedly and continually for opposing with manly firmness his invasions on the rights of the people.

10 He has refused for a long time after such dissolutions to cause others to be elected, whereby the legislative powers, incapable of annihilation, have returned to the people at large for their exercise, the state remaining, in the meantime, exposed to all the dangers of invasion from without and convulsions within.

He has endeavored to prevent the population of these states; for that purpose obstructing the laws for naturalization of foreigners, refusing to pass others to encourage their migrations hither, and raising the conditions of new appropriations of lands.

He has suffered the administration of justice totally to cease in some of these states refusing his assent to laws for establishing judiciary powers.

obstructed by

He has made our judges dependent on his will alone for the tenure of their offices, and the amount and payment of their salaries.

He has erected a multitude of new offices, by a self-assumed power and sent hither swarms of new officers to harass our people and eat out their substance.

15 He has kept among us in times of peace standing armies and ships of war without the consent of our legislatures.

He has affected to render the military independent of, and superior to, the civil power.

He has combined with others to subject us to a jurisdiction foreign to our constitutions and unacknowledged by our laws, giving his assent to their acts of pretended legislation for quartering large bodies of armed troops among us; for protecting them by a mock trial from punishment for any murders which they should commit on the inhabitants of these states; for cutting off our trade with all parts of the world; for imposing taxes on us without our consent; for depriving us [ ] of the benefits of trial by jury; for transporting us beyond seas to be tried for pretended offenses; for abolishing the free system of English laws in a neighboring province, establishing therein an arbitrary government, and enlarging its boundaries, so as to render it at once an example and fit instrument for introducing the same absolute rule into these states; for taking away our charters, abolishing our most valuable laws, and altering fundamentally the forms of our governments; for suspending our own legislatures, and declaring themselves invested with power to legislate for us in all cases whatsoever.

in many cases

colonies;

He has abdicated government here withdrawing his governors, and declaring us out of his allegiance and protection.

by declaring us out of his protection, and waging war against us.

He has plundered our seas, ravaged our coasts, burnt our towns, and destroyed the lives of our people.

20 He is at this time transporting large armies of foreign mercenaries to complete the works of death, desolation and tyranny already begun

with circumstances of cruelty and perfidy [ ] unworthy the head of a civilized nation.

scarcely paralleled in the most barbarous ages, and totally

He has constrained our fellow citizens taken captive on the high seas, to bear arms against their country, to become the executioners of their friends and brethren, or to fall themselves by their hands.

He has [ ] endeavored to bring on the inhabitants of our frontiers, the merciless Indian savages, whose known rule of warfare is an undistinguished destruction of all ages, sexes and conditions of existence.

excited domestic insurrection among us, and has

He has incited treasonable insurrections of our fellow citizens, with the allurements of forfeiture and confiscation of our property.

He has waged cruel war against human nature itself, violating its most sacred rights of life and liberty in the persons of a distant people who never offended him, captivating and carrying them into slavery in another hemisphere, or to incur miserable death in their transportation thither. This piratical warfare, the opprobrium of INFIDEL powers, is the warfare of the CHRISTIAN king of Great Britain. Determined to keep open a market where MEN should be bought and sold, he has prostituted his negative for suppressing every legislative attempt to prohibit or to restrain this execrable commerce. And that this assemblage of horrors might want no fact of distinguished die, he is now exciting those very people to rise in arms among us, and to purchase that liberty of which he has deprived them, by murdering the people on whom he also obtruded them: thus paying off former crimes committed against the LIBERTIES of one people, with crimes which he urges them to commit against the LIVES of another.

25 In every stage of these oppressions we have petitioned for redress in the most humble terms: our repeated petitions have been answered only by repeated injuries.

A prince whose character is thus marked by every act which may define a tyrant is unfit to be the ruler of a [ ] people who mean to be free. Future ages will scarcely believe that the hardiness of one man adventured, within the short compass of twelve years only, to lay a foundation so broad and so undisguised for tyranny over a people fostered and fixed in principles of freedom.

free

Nor have we been wanting in attentions to our British brethren. We have warned them from time to time of attempts by their legislature to extend a jurisdiction over these our states. We have reminded them of the circumstances of our emigration and settlement here, no one of which could warrant so strange a pretension: that these were effected at the expense of our own blood and treasure, unassisted by the wealth or the strength of Great Britain: that in constituting indeed our several forms of government, we had adopted one common king, thereby laying a foundation for perpetual league and amity with them: but that submission to their parliament was no part of our constitution, nor ever in

an unwarrantable/us

idea, if history may be credited: and, we [ ] appealed to their native justice and magnanimity as well as to the ties of our common kindred to disavow these usurpations which were likely to interrupt our connection and correspondence. They too have been deaf to the voice of justice and of consanguinity,[5] and when occasions have been given them, by the regular course of their laws, of removing from their councils the disturbers of our harmony, they have, by their free election, reestablished them in power. At this very time too, they are permitting their chief magistrate to send over not only soldiers of our common blood, but Scotch and foreign mercenaries to invade and destroy us. These facts have given the last stab to agonizing affection, and manly spirit bids us to renounce forever these unfeeling brethren, we must endeavor to forget our former love for them, and hold them as we hold the rest of mankind, enemies in war, in peace friends. We might have been a free and a great people together; but a communication of grandeur and of freedom, it seems, is below their dignity. Be it so, since they will have it. The road to happiness and to glory is open to us, too. We will tread it apart from them, and acquiesce in the necessity which denounces[6] our eternal separation [ ]!

have and we have conjured them by would inevitably

We must therefore and hold them as we hold the rest of mankind; enemies in war, in peace friends.

We therefore the representatives of the United States of America in General Congress assembled, do in the name, and by the authority of the good people of these states reject and renounce all allegiance and subjection to the kings of Great Britain and all others who may hereafter claim by, through or under them; we utterly dissolve all political connection which may heretofore have subsisted between us and the people or parliament of Great Britain: and finally we do assert and declare these colonies to be free and independent states, and that as free and independent states, they have full power to levy war, conclude peace, contract alliances, establish commerce, and to do all other acts and things which independent states may of right do.

And for the support of this declaration, we mutually pledge to each other our lives, our fortunes, and our sacred honor.

We, therefore, the representatives of the United States of America in General Congress assembled, appealing to the supreme judge of the world for the rectitude of our intentions, do in the name, and by the authority of the good people of these colonies, solemnly publish and declare, that these united colonies are, and of right ought to be free and independent states; that they are absolved from all allegiance to the British crown, and that all political connection between them and the state of Great Britain is, and ought to be, totally dissolved; and that as free and independent states, they have full power to levy war, conclude peace, contract alliances, establish commerce, and to do all other acts and things which independent states may of right do.

---

[5] consanguinity: close relation, usually by blood.

[6] denounces: proclaims.

And for the support of this declaration, with a firm reliance on the protection of divine providence, we mutually pledge to each other our lives, our fortunes, and our sacred honor.

The Declaration thus signed on the 4th, on paper, was engrossed[7] on parchment, and signed again on the 2d of August.

LEARNING MORE

As an iconic figure in U.S. history, Jefferson has naturally attracted a great deal of attention, some adulatory and some not. His voluminous papers are available from the Library of Congress online. For a short guide to learning more about Jefferson, see the *Ideas Across Time* website.

QUESTIONING THE TEXT

1. What passages that Jefferson wrote into his original draft does he say Congress rejected? Why did Congress reject these passages?
2. What is the necessary thing Jefferson declares in the first few words of the Declaration? What impact do you think this necessity would have had on the documents' readers?
3. What is a "self-evident" truth?
4. What is the function of government, according to the Declaration?
5. How does this view of government justify the American Revolution?
6. What is the main evidence, as you see it, that Jefferson adduces to show that the British king has traduced the rights of the colonists?
7. Do the grievances Jefferson names justify revolution?

ANALYZING THE WRITER'S CRAFT

1. What is a declaration? How would this document have been different if it had been conceived as a proclamation or a defense?
2. How does Jefferson distinguish between the American and the British people? Why is he at such pains to make this distinction?
3. Rewrite par. 3 as a sequence of logical propositions or as a syllogism (see Introduction, pp. 1–8).
4. Can the evidence Jefferson uses to justify revolution against Britain be categorized into major groupings? If so, show how. If not, are these charges coherent? Explain.
5. What is the tone of this Declaration?
6. What is the diction of this Declaration?
7. What is the audience for this Declaration?
8. Do you find the concluding sentence of the Declaration effective? Explain.

---

[7] engrossed: written in legal form.

9. Are there changes that Congress made that you think improve on the original? Explain.
10. If you had sat in Congress, would you have taken the side of the majority and voted for the main changes that were made in the original draft, or would you have sided with Jefferson?

MAKING CONNECTIONS

1. St. John de Crevecoeur was a Loyalist and opposed to the American Revolution. Yet his definition of an American (Chapter 1, pp. 22–27), while obviously not as much a foundation of American thought and identity as the Declaration, is nonetheless a seminal and enormously influential portrait of "the American." What do these two works have in common? How do they differ? Does it seem to you that there really ought not to have been any political differences between Jefferson and Crevecoeur, or is it obvious that they would be unlikely to see eye to eye?
2. Alexis de Tocqueville, a French aristocrat, viewed democracy with fascinated skepticism (Chapter 6, pp. 458–462). What in the Declaration do you think might have troubled him?
3. How much of John Locke (pp. 348–352) and Jean-Jacques Rousseau (Chapter 6, pp. 451–456) can you find in the Declaration?
4. How might American history have been different if Jefferson's attack on slavery had been left in the Declaration (see James Baldwin, Chapter 1, pp. 29–35)?
5. What do you imagine Jefferson's response might have been to Henry David Thoreau's ideas about civil disobedience (pp. 371–383)?

FORMULATING IDEAS FOR WRITING

1. Did Congress improve or weaken Jefferson's original draft? Explain.
2. It is tempting to imagine the effect on American history of Jefferson's original draft. Do you think that slavery would have been abolished sooner, for example? Or that questions about the separation between church and state would have been less likely to arise (many references to God or divinity were added by Congress)?
3. The Declaration has stood the test of time as a piece of writing, and is generally acknowledged to be one of the greatest examples of inspiring political rhetoric in American history. What rhetorical and stylistic features make the Declaration so effective?
4. The Declaration makes a strong case for a right to revolution. Do you agree with Jefferson's argument? Why or why not? If not, do you believe the American Revolution was unjustified? In a different vein, do you think most Americans today continue to believe that we as a people have the right to take up arms against our government?

The Rights and Involved Duties of Mankind Considered (1792)

Mary Wollstonecraft

Mary Wollstonecraft was a central figure in the late-eighteenth-century radical London circle of the printer and publisher Joseph Johnson, a circle that included the poet William Blake, the political philosopher Tom Paine, the important dissenting minister Richard Price, and Wollstonecraft's future husband, the philosopher William Godwin. Even in this company, Wollstonecraft's views were considered shocking. A formidable stylist and rationalist, Wollstonecraft lucidly argued against the conditions in which women were raised and educated, maintaining that ignorance and helpless docility not only bound women into an unjust dependency but demeaned men as much as women. Making beautiful slaves of women corrupted both master and slave, she said. She called marriage "legal prostitution." It is important to note that before Wollstonecraft presented these ideas, in her book *A Vindication of the Rights of Woman* (1792), she first wrote *A Vindication of the Rights of Men* (1790), a significant response to Edmund Burke's *Reflections on the Revolution in France*. The democratic ideas of *A Vindication of the Rights of Men* formed the basis of *Rights of Woman*. In Wollstonecraft's view, the former led naturally to the latter, as is well illustrated in this selection taken from the first chapter of *Rights of Woman*. But while democracy took firm hold in the United States and then in Europe, notions of equality for women did not achieve similar success until well into the twentieth century.

Wollstonecraft was born in 1759, the second of seven children and the oldest girl. Although her grandfather was a wealthy silk merchant, her father squandered the family's money, turning to drink and often becoming violent toward his wife. Mary assumed the role of protector of the children. Prior to the time her family moved to London, when Mary was fifteen, she had received the usual education for girls. But from the outset, she read to educate herself, an activity that became more intense once she moved to London. Moreover, in London, Wollstonecraft came under the mentorship of Fanny Blood who encouraged her to think of employment and independence. After the death of Wollstonecraft's mother in 1782, she went to live with Blood and joined her in establishing a school. But in 1785, Fanny Blood, recently married, died in childbirth with Wollstonecraft in attendance.

Wollstonecraft then turned to writing. Her first book, *Thoughts on the Education of Daughters,* was published by Joseph Johnson in 1787 and was followed by a decade of works that have achieved increasing eminence over time. These include *Mary: A Fiction* (1788), *An Historical and Moral View of the French Revolution* (1794), and the posthumous *Letters on the Management of Infants* (1798).

By all accounts a vivacious and magnetic person, Wollstonecraft had a personal life filled with tumult. After a disastrous relationship with Gilbert Imlay, with whom she had one child, Fanny, she finally married William Godwin, but tragically she died shortly after giving birth to their daughter Mary. That daughter later became Mary Shelley, author of *Frankenstein* (1818), excerpted elsewhere in this book (see Chapter 3, pp. 157–165).

Wollstonecraft's introduction to *A Vindication of the Rights of Women*, reprinted here, is largely a sharp analysis of and a departure from the ideas of Jean-Jacques Rousseau (see pp. 451–456). In particular it questions his view that human beings are noblest in a state of nature and become corrupted by civilization. Wollstonecraft attacks Rousseau from two sides. On the one side, she advances the claims of first principles (see pars. 1–6), arguing that reason, virtue, and passion are the basis of human happiness and civilization. On the other, she says Rousseau must somehow have forgotten the barbarity of the state of nature, as well as the initial steps from that state as civilization progressed. She notes, for example, that monarchy is an advance on brute living even as it falls far short of rational government. Instead of advocating a "ferocious flight back to the night of sensual ignorance," Rousseau would do better, she concludes, "to contemplate the perfection of man in the establishment of true civilization." These are the arguments that Wollstonecraft considers to be the necessary preconditions for the advocacy of equality for women.

In the present state of society it appears necessary to go back to first principles in search of the most simple truths, and to dispute with some prevailing prejudice every inch of ground. To clear my way, I must be allowed to ask some plain questions, and the answers will probably appear as unequivocal as the axioms on which reasoning is built; though, when entangled with various motives of action, they are formally contradicted, either by the words or conduct of men.

In what does man's pre-eminence over the brute creation consist? The answer is as clear as that a half is less than the whole; in Reason.

What acquirement exalts one being above another? Virtue; we spontaneously reply.

For what purpose were the passions implanted? That man by struggling with them might attain a degree of knowledge denied to the brutes; whispers Experience.

5 Consequently the perfection of our nature and capability of happiness, must be estimated by the degree of reason, virtue, and knowledge, that distinguish the individual, and direct the laws which bind society: and that from the exercise of reason, knowledge and virtue naturally flow, is equally undeniable, if mankind be viewed collectively.

The rights and duties of man thus simplified, it seems almost impertinent to attempt to illustrate truths that appear so incontrovertible; yet such deeply rooted prejudices have clouded reason, and such spurious qualities have assumed the name of virtues, that it is necessary to pursue the course of reason as it has been perplexed and involved in error, by various adventitious[1] circumstances, comparing the simple axiom with casual deviations. Men, in general, seem to employ their reason to justify prejudices, which they have imbibed, they can scarcely trace how, rather than to root them out. The mind must be strong that resolutely forms its own principles; for a kind of intellectual cowardice prevails which makes many men shrink from the task, or only do it by halves. Yet the imperfect conclusions thus drawn, are frequently very plausible, because they are built on partial experience, on just, though narrow, views. . . .

That the society is formed in the wisest manner, whose constitution is founded on the nature of man, strikes, in the abstract, every thinking being so forcibly, that it looks like presumption to endeavour to bring forward proofs; though proof must be brought, or the strong hold of prescription will never be forced by reason; yet to urge prescription as an argument to justify the depriving men (or women) of their natural rights, is one of the absurd sophisms which daily insult common sense.

The civilization of the bulk of the people of Europe is very partial; nay, it may be made a question, whether they have acquired any virtues in exchange for innocence, equivalent to the misery produced by the vices that have been plastered over unsightly ignorance, and the freedom which has been bartered for splendid slavery. The desire of dazzling by riches, the most certain preeminence that man can obtain, the pleasure of commanding flattering sycophants, and many other complicated low calculations of doting self-love, have all contributed to overwhelm the mass of mankind, and make liberty a convenient handle for mock patriotism. For whilst rank and titles are held of the utmost importance, before which Genius "must hide its diminished head,"[2] it is, with a few exceptions, very unfortunate for a nation when a man of abilities, without rank or property, pushes himself forward to notice.—Alas! what unheard of misery have thousands suffered to purchase a cardinal's hat for an intriguing obscure adventurer, who longed to be ranked with princes, or lord it over them by seizing the triple crown![3]

Such, indeed, has been the wretchedness that has flowed from hereditary honours, riches, and monarchy, that men of lively sensibility have almost uttered blasphemy in order to justify the dispensations of providence. Man has been held out as independent of his power who made him, or as a lawless planet darting from its orbit to steal the celestial fire of reason; and the vengeance of heaven, lurking in the subtile flame, like Pandora's pent up mischiefs, sufficiently punished his temerity, by introducing evil into the world.[4]

---

[1] adventitious: accidental.

[2] "must . . . head": Wollstonecraft is quoting Milton's *Paradise Lost*, IV, 34–35.

[3] triple crown: papal crown.

[4] Pandora . . . world: To punish Prometheus for his theft of fire from the gods, Zeus sent Pandora, the first woman, into the world bearing a jar containing all evils.

10 Impressed by this view of the misery and disorder which pervaded society, and fatigued with jostling against artificial fools, Rousseau became enamoured of solitude, and, being at the same time an optimist, he labours with uncommon eloquence to prove that man was naturally a solitary animal.[5] Misled by his respect for the goodness of God, who certainly—for what man of sense and feeling can doubt it!—gave life only to communicate happiness, he considers evil as positive, and the work of man; not aware that he was exalting one attribute at the expence of another, equally necessary to divine perfection.

Reared on a false hypothesis his arguments in favour of a state of nature are plausible, but unsound. I say unsound; for to assert that a state of nature is preferable to civilization, in all its possible perfection, is, in other words, to arraign supreme wisdom; and the paradoxical exclamation, that God has made all things right, and that error has been introduced by the creature, whom he formed, knowing what he formed, is as unphilosophical as impious.[6]

When that wise Being who created us and placed us here, saw the fair idea, he willed, by allowing it to be so, that the passions should unfold our reason, because he could see that present evil would produce future good. Could the helpless creature whom he called from nothing break loose from his providence, and boldly learn to know good by practising evil, without his permission? No.—How could that energetic advocate for immortality argue so inconsistently? Had mankind remained for ever in the brutal state of nature, which even his magic pen cannot paint as a state in which a single virtue took root, it would have been clear, though not to the sensitive unreflecting wanderer, that man was born to run the circle of life and death, and adorn God's garden for some purpose which could not easily be reconciled with his attributes.

But if, to crown the whole, there were to be rational creatures produced, allowed to rise in excellence by the exercise of powers implanted for that purpose; if benignity itself thought fit to call into existence a creature above the brutes,[7] who could think and improve himself, why should that inestimable gift, for a gift it was, if man was so created as to have a capacity to rise above the state in which sensation produced brutal ease, be called, in direct terms, a curse? A curse it might be reckoned, if the whole of our existence were bounded by our continuance in this world; for why should the gracious fountain of life give us passions, and the power of reflecting, only to imbitter our days and inspire us with mistaken notions of dignity? Why should he lead us from love of ourselves to the sublime emotions which the discovery of his wisdom and goodness excites, if

---

[5] animal: Rousseau in his *Confessions* tells of his love of solitude. On Rousseau, see also pp. 451–456.

[6] impious: "All things are good as their Creator made them," Rousseau wrote, "but everything degenerates in the hands of man."

[7] Contrary to the opinion of anatomists, who argue by analogy from the formation of the teeth, stomach, and intestines, Rousseau will not allow a man to be a carnivorous animal. And, carried away from nature by a love of system, he disputes whether man be a gregarious animal, though the long and helpless state of infancy seems to point him out as particularly impelled to pair the first step towards herding [Wollstonecraft's note].

these feelings were not set in motion to improve our nature, of which they make a part,[8] and render us capable of enjoying a more godlike portion of happiness? Firmly persuaded that no evil exists in the world that God did not design to take place, I build my belief on the perfection of God.

Rousseau exerts himself to prove that all *was* right originally: a crowd of authors that all *is* now right: and I, that all will *be* right.

But, true to his first position, next to a state of nature, Rousseau celebrates barbarism, and apostrophizing the shade of Fabricius, he forgets that, in conquering the world, the Romans never dreamed of establishing their own liberty on a firm basis, or of extending the reign of virtue. Eager to support his system, he stigmatizes, as vicious, every effort of genius; and, uttering the apotheosis of savage virtues, he exalts those to demi-gods, who were scarcely human—the brutal Spartans, who, in defiance of justice and gratitude, sacrificed, in cold blood, the slaves who had shewn themselves heroes to rescue their oppressors.[9]

Disgusted with artificial manners and virtues, the citizen of Geneva,[10] instead of properly sifting the subject, threw away the wheat with the chaff, without waiting to inquire whether the evils which his ardent soul turned from indignantly, were the consequence of civilization or the vestiges of barbarism. He saw vice trampling on virtue, and the semblance of goodness taking place of the reality; he saw talents bent by power to sinister purposes, and never thought of tracing the gigantic mischief up to arbitrary power, up to the hereditary distinctions that clash with the mental superiority that naturally raises a man above his fellows. He did not perceive that regal power, in a few generations, introduces idiotism into the noble stem, and holds out baits to render thousands idle and vicious.

Nothing can set the regal character in a more contemptible point of view, than the various crimes that have elevated men to the supreme dignity.—Vile intrigues, unnatural crimes, and every vice that degrades our nature, have been the steps to this distinguished eminence; yet millions of men have supinely allowed the nerveless limbs of the posterity of such rapacious prowlers to rest quietly on their ensanguined thrones.[11]

What but a pestilential vapour can hover over society when its chief director is only instructed in the invention of crimes, or the stupid routine of childish

[8] What would you say to a mechanic whom you had desired to make a watch to point out the hour of the day, if, to shew his ingenuity, he added wheels to make it a repeater, etc. that perplexed the simple mechanism; should he urge, to excuse himself—had you not touched a certain spring, you would have known nothing of the matter, and that he should have amused himself by making *an experiment* without doing you any harm: would you not retort fairly upon him, by insisting that if he had not added those needless wheels and springs, the accident could not have happened [Wollstonecraft's note]?

[9] oppressors: Rousseau praises the Roman general Fabricius, who urged the Romans to conquer the world. The Spartans betrayed their enslaved soldiers, the helots, by saying that those who claimed to have fought most bravely would be made free men but then, when men stepped forward, slaughtered them as the ones most likely to head a rebellion.

[10] Geneva: Rousseau, a native of Geneva, was often called "the citizen of Geneva."

[11] Could there be a greater insult offered to the rights of man than the beds of justice in France, when an infant was made the organ of the detestable Dubois [Wollstonecraft's note]?

ceremonies? Will men never be wise?—will they never cease to expect corn from tares, and figs from thistles?[12]

It is impossible for any man, when the most favourable circumstances concur, to acquire sufficient knowledge and strength of mind to discharge the duties of a king, entrusted with uncontrouled power; how then must they be violated when his very elevation is an insuperable bar to the attainment of either wisdom or virtue; when all the feelings of a man are stifled by flattery, and reflection shut out by pleasure! Surely it is madness to make the fate of thousands depend on the caprice of a weak fellow creature, whose very station sinks him *necessarily* below the meanest of his subjects! But one power should not be thrown down to exalt another—for all power inebriates weak man; and its abuse proves that the more equality there is established among men, the more virtue and happiness will reign in society. But this and any similar maxim deduced from simple reason, raises an outcry—the church or the state is in danger, if faith in the wisdom of antiquity is not implicit; and they who, roused by the sight of human calamity, dare to attack human authority, are reviled as despisers of God, and enemies of man. These are bitter calumnies, yet they reached one of the best of men,[13] whose ashes still preach peace, and whose memory demands a respectful pause, when subjects are discussed that lay so near his heart.

After attacking the sacred majesty of Kings, I shall scarcely excite surprise by adding my firm persuasion that every profession, in which great subordination of rank constitutes its power, is highly injurious to morality.

A standing army, for instance, is incompatible with freedom; because subordination and rigour are the very sinews of military discipline; and despotism is necessary to give vigour to enterprizes that one will directs. A spirit inspired by romantic notions of honour, a kind of morality founded on the fashion of the age, can only be felt by a few officers, whilst the main body must be moved by command, like the waves of the sea; for the strong wind of authority pushes the crowd of subalterns forward, they scarcely know or care why, with headlong fury.

Besides, nothing can be so prejudicial to the morals of the inhabitants of country towns as the occasional residence of a set of idle superficial young men, whose only occupation is gallantry, and whose polished manners render vice more dangerous, by concealing its deformity under gay ornamental drapery. An air of fashion, which is but a badge of slavery, and proves that the soul has not a strong individual character, awes simple country people into an imitation of the vices, when they cannot catch the slippery graces, of politeness. Every corps is a chain of despots, who, submitting and tyrannizing without exercising their reason, become dead weights of vice and folly on the community. A man of rank or fortune, sure of rising by interest, has nothing to do but to pursue

[12] thistles: Matthew 7:16: "Ye shall know them by their fruits. Do men gather grapes of thorns, or figs of thistles?"

[13] men: Dr. Richard Price (1723–1791), whose speech praising the French Revolution, *A Discourse on the Love of Our Country* (1789), prompted Edmund Burke's more famous response, *Reflections on the Revolution in France* (1790), to which in turn Wollstonecraft responded with *A Vindication of the Rights of Men* (1790) and Tom Paine with *Rights of Man* (1794).

some extravagant freak; whilst the needy *gentleman,* who is to rise, as the phrase turns, by his merit, becomes a servile parasite or vile pander.

Sailors, the naval gentlemen, come under the same description, only their vices assume a different and grosser cast. They are more positively indolent, when not discharging the ceremonials of their station; whilst the insignificant fluttering of soldiers may be termed active idleness. More confined to the society of men, the former acquire a fondness for humour and mischievous tricks; whilst the latter, mixing frequently with well-bred women, catch a sentimental cant.—But mind is equally out of the question, whether they indulge the horse-laugh, or polite simper.

May I be allowed to extend the comparison to a profession where more mind is certainly to be found; for the clergy have superior opportunities of improvement, though subordination almost equally cramps their faculties? The blind submission imposed at college to forms of belief serves as a novitiate to the curate, who must obsequiously respect the opinion of his rector or patron, if he mean to rise in his profession. Perhaps there cannot be a more forcible contrast than between the servile dependent gait of a poor curate and the courtly mien of a bishop. And the respect and contempt they inspire render the discharge of their separate functions equally useless.

It is of great importance to observe that the character of every man is, in some degree, formed by his profession. A man of sense may only have a cast of countenance that wears off as you trace his individuality, whilst the weak, common man has scarcely ever any character, but what belongs to the body; at least, all his opinions have been so steeped in the vat consecrated by authority, that the faint spirit which the grape of his own vine yields cannot be distinguished.

Society, therefore, as it becomes more enlightened, should be very careful not to establish bodies of men who must necessarily be made foolish or vicious by the very constitution of their profession.

In the infancy of society, when men were just emerging out of barbarism, chiefs and priests, touching the most powerful springs of savage conduct, hope and fear, must have had unbounded sway. An aristocracy, of course, is naturally the first form of government. But, clashing interests soon losing their equipoise,[14] a monarchy and hierarchy break out of the confusion of ambitious struggles, and the foundation of both is secured by feudal tenures. This appears to be the origin of monarchical and priestly power, and the dawn of civilization. But such combustible materials cannot long be pent up; and, getting vent in foreign wars and intestine insurrections, the people acquire some power in the tumult, which obliges their rulers to gloss over their oppression with a shew of right. Thus, as wars, agriculture, commerce, and literature, expand the mind, despots are compelled, to make covert corruption hold fast the power which was formerly snatched by open force.[15] And this baneful lurking gangrene is

[14] equipoise: equilibrium.

[15] Men of abilities scatter seeds that grow up and have a great influence on the forming opinion; and when once the public opinion preponderates, through the exertion of reason, the overthrow of arbitrary power is not very distant [Wollstonecraft's note].

most quickly spread by luxury and superstition, the sure dregs of ambition. The indolent puppet of a court first becomes a luxurious monster, or fastidious sensualist, and then makes the contagion which his unnatural state spread, the instrument of tyranny.

It is the pestiferous purple which renders the progress of civilization a curse, and warps the understanding, till men of sensibility doubt whether the-expansion of intellect produces a greater portion of happiness or misery. But the nature of the poison points out the antidote; and had Rousseau mounted one step higher in his investigation, or could his eye have pierced through the foggy atmosphere, which he almost disdained to breathe, his active mind would have darted forward to contemplate the perfection of man in the establishment of true civilization, instead of taking his ferocious flight back to the night of sensual ignorance.

LEARNING MORE

The full text of *A Vindication of the Rights of Woman,* as well as other writings of Wollstonecraft and information about her, are readily available online. See the *Ideas Across Time* website for useful links.

QUESTIONING THE TEXT

1. Why does Wollstonecraft feel the need to begin a book about the rights of women by going "back to first principles" (par. 1)?
2. What conclusions does Wollstonecraft draw from her first principles? Do these conclusions seem valid to you?
3. Why is so much of Wollstonecraft's introduction to her treatise devoted to Rousseau?
4. How has the state of civilization in Europe led Rousseau astray?
5. What is Wollstonecraft's critique of Rousseau's assertion that human beings are happiest and best in a state of nature? Do you agree with Rousseau or with Wollstonecraft? Explain.
6. Considering Wollstonecraft's bitter denunciation of monarchy and of every social form "in which great subordination constitutes its power" (par. 20), it would seem that rather than quarrel with Rousseau she should agree with him. Why doesn't she?
7. Does Wollstonecraft believe in progress? Explain, and cite your evidence.

ANALYZING THE WRITER'S CRAFT

1. Wollstonecraft opens her essay with a series of "axioms" (par. 1), that is, propositions that answer essential questions about the "the rights and duties of man" (par. 6). Are these the best questions she could have asked to arrive at first principles? Do you agree with her answers? Does she draw

logical conclusions from her answers (see "Deductive Reasoning" in the Introduction, pp. 1–8)?
2. What does Wollstonecraft's opening suggest about her intended audience?
3. What does Wollstonecraft's opening suggest about the capabilities of women?
4. Is Wollstonecraft's explanation of evil (pars. 12–13) in accord with Christian doctrine? Is her critique of Rousseau dependent on her view of God? Explain.
5. How does Wollstonecraft's diction in the passages that analyze kingship reflect her point of view? Is her diction consistent with rational analysis, or does her diction appeal to emotion? Explain and illustrate.
6. "Rousseau," Wollstonecraft writes, "exerts himself to prove that all *was* right originally: a crowd of authors that all *is* now right: and I, that all will *be* right" (par. 14). Do you think she proves that all will be right? Explain.
7. Is the essay's conclusion effective? Does the conclusion adequately lay the ground for an analysis of the condition of women?

MAKING CONNECTIONS

1. Tom Paine (Chapter 2, pp. 98–103) and Wollstonecraft were close political allies. Are their views of God compatible, too?
2. Would Wollstonecraft have been delighted with Elizabeth Cady Stanton's account of Genesis (Chapter 2, pp. 106–107)? Explain.
3. Look further in *A Vindication of the Rights of Woman* (see the *Ideas Across Time* website), and decide to what extent Wollstonecraft anticipates the arguments of Betty Friedan in *The Feminine Mystique* (Chapter 6, pp. 496–509).
4. Like Thomas Jefferson (pp. 354–360), Wollstonecraft opens her argument with "self-evident" truths. How do these sets of "truths," or "first principles" compare? Would Jefferson and Wollstonecraft have accepted each other's first principles? Explain. How do you account for the differences between their first principles?
5. Compare and contrast Wollstonecraft's and Karl Marx's (Chapter 4, pp. 264–273) reasons for belief in progress.
6. Do you think Wollstonecraft could in any way respond sympathetically to Fareed Zakaria's argument that today freedom is threatened by too much democracy (pp. 330–337)? Explain.

FORMULATING IDEAS FOR WRITING

1. Although Wollstonecraft wrote well before Karl Marx (Chapter 4, pp. 264–273), she nonetheless expresses a strong faith in the perfectibility of human beings—once liberated from oppression. Write an essay that explores the way their views of progress concur and diverge.
2. Using Wollstonecraft as a model, write the opening paragraphs of an essay on the condition of women today. Use these opening paragraphs to

establish the first principles that you believe necessary to form the basis of such an analysis.

3. The core values and the methods of argument and analysis of eighteenth-century writers (Rousseau, Jefferson, Wollstonecraft) seem at once significantly different from our own—curious, strange, quaint—and surprisingly contemporary. Sometimes their ideas seem clearly to have formed our own; and yet their ideas also can seem distant from or foreign to or even irrelevant to our own. Discuss.
4. Wollstonecraft says that society should be based on "the nature of man" (par. 7). Discuss how her essay demonstrates this statement. Consider how a proponent of monarchy, or of some other authoritarian or hierarchical system, might make a case for those systems as being based on human nature. Does Wollstonecraft's essay show how she might respond to the position of these proponents of authoritarian systems?
5. Wollstonecraft's essay is the introductory chapter of a book that calls for equality for women. Yet this essay vehemently attacks monarchy, standing armies, the clergy, and so forth. Do these attacks seem to you useful as a way of illuminating the plight of women? Or are the issues Wollstonecraft raises distractions from her main focus, the plight of women? Must every analysis of the condition of women begin by considering "the rights and duties of mankind"?

Civil Disobedience (Resistance to Civil Government) (1849)

Henry David Thoreau

He never married; he never had an occupation; he quarreled with most people who came too near him, even his closest friend Ralph Waldo Emerson (see Chapter 7, pp. 581–585); he lived almost his entire life in the village of Concord, Massachusetts, where he irritated his neighbors by his (sometimes vocal) dissent from more or less all aspects of nineteenth-century American life; and he published only two books in his lifetime. But one of those books was *Walden* (1854), a book that exemplifies the original genius, the independence of mind and character, and the prickly New England individualism of Henry David Thoreau, now embraced as an essential American prophet.

Thoreau was born in Concord in 1817. He attended Harvard College and then accepted a job as schoolteacher in Concord, but he quickly left rather than inflict corporal punishment. From that point on, he took up odd jobs, serving as a handyman for Emerson, writing occasional reviews and articles, and working in the family pencil factory. As he might have said, he lived rather than worked. His devotion to simplifying his life and needs is amply illustrated by his retreat for two years to a corner of Emerson's property by Walden Pond. Here he occupied a cabin that he built himself and observed himself and nature. The book that eventually emerged from this experience aimed to answer directly the question of how one should live. The upshot, Thoreau's *Walden,* a blend of sharp insight, memoir, and life philosophy, offered in a style of exceptional economy and evocativeness, has been the source of inspired liberation for generations of readers worldwide.

On one of Thoreau's walks from Walden into town, he appears to have run into the tax collector and, upon his refusal to pay up, landed for a night in jail. This experience prompted "Resistance to Civil Government," first delivered as a lecture at the Concord Lyceum in January 1848 and printed the following year in the journal *Aesthetic Papers,* edited by Nathaniel Hawthorne's sister-in-law Elizabeth Peabody. (Although best known as "Civil Disobedience," the essay seems never to have been given that title by Thoreau.) A fierce opponent of slavery, Thoreau raises several fundamental political questions in this essay, questions that go to the heart of American political philosophy: What is the individual's responsibility to society, or government? If the government acts in a manner profoundly contrary to the individual's moral convictions, say, by endorsing slavery, to whom does the individual owe allegiance—conscience or community? If individuals cannot in good conscience follow their government, what course of action can they pursue? In arguing for "civil disobedience," Thoreau profoundly influenced twentieth-century political movements, in particular Mahatma Ghandi's resistance to British colonialism and Martin Luther King Jr.'s resistance to American racial discrimination. Even after abolitionist John Brown's attack on Harper's Ferry, Thoreau spoke vividly in defense of Brown.

Thoreau's posthumous works, compiled from his extensive journals and from his uncollected periodical publications, reveal him to be a formidable naturalist and a pioneer of the modern environmental movement. He was an acute observer, especially attuned to the interactions between living things, their physical world, and the climate. Tragically, Thoreau died in Concord from tuberculosis at the age of 45.

Resistance to Civil Government[1]

I heartily accept the motto,—"That government is best which governs least,"[2] and I should like to see it acted up to more rapidly and systematically. Carried out, it finally amounts to this, which also I believe,—"That government is best which governs not at all"; and when men are prepared for it, that will be the

[1] Resistance . . . Government: Although this essay is widely known as "Civil Disobedience," Thoreau in fact titled it "Resistance to Civil Government."

[2] "That . . . least": This motto appeared on the masthead of *The Democratic Review.*

kind of government which they will have. Government is at best but an expedient; but most governments are usually, and all governments are sometimes, inexpedient. The objections which have been brought against a standing army, and they are many and weighty, and deserve to prevail, may also at last be brought against a standing government. The standing army is only an arm of the standing government. The government itself, which is only the mode which the people have chosen to execute their will, is equally liable to be abused and perverted before the people can act through it. Witness the present Mexican war, the work of comparatively a few individuals using the standing government as their tool; for, in the outset, the people would not have consented to this measure.[3]

This American government,—what is it but a tradition, though a recent one, endeavoring to transmit itself unimpaired to posterity, but each instant losing some of its integrity? It has not the vitality and force of a single living man; for a single man can bend it to his will. It is a sort of wooden gun to the people themselves; and, if ever they should use it in earnest as a real one against each other, it will surely split. But it is not the less necessary for this; for the people must have some complicated machinery or other, and hear its din, to satisfy that idea of government which they have. Governments show thus how successfully men can be imposed on, even impose on themselves, for their own advantage. It is excellent, we must all allow; yet this government never of itself furthered any enterprise, but by the alacrity with which it got out of its way. *It* does not keep the country free. *It* does not settle the West. *It* does not educate. The character inherent in the American people has done all that has been accomplished; and it would have done somewhat more, if the government had not sometimes got in its way. For government is an expedient by which men would fain succeed in letting one another alone; and, as has been said, when it is most expedient, the governed are most let alone by it. Trade and commerce, if they were not made of India rubber, would never manage, to bounce over the obstacles which legislators are continually putting in their way; and, if one were to judge these men wholly by the effects of their actions, and not partly by their intentions, they would deserve to be classed and punished with those mischievous persons who put obstructions on the railroads.

But, to speak practically and as a citizen, unlike those who call themselves no-government men, I ask for, not at once no government, but *at once* a better government. Let every man make known what kind of government would command his respect, and that will be one step toward obtaining it.

After all, the practical reason why, when the power is once in the hands of the people, a majority are permitted, and for a long period continue, to rule, is not because they are most likely to be in the right, not because this seems fairest to the minority, but because they are physically the strongest. But a government in which the majority rule in all cases cannot be based on justice, even as far as men understand it. Can there not be a government in which majorities do not

[3] measure: the Mexican War (1845–1848), which evoked the same kind of protests as did the Vietnam War.

virtually decide right and wrong, but conscience?—in which majorities decide only those questions to which the rule of expediency is applicable? Must the citizen ever for a moment, or in the least degree, resign his conscience to the legislator? Why has every man a conscience, then? I think that we should be men first, and subjects afterward. It is not desirable to cultivate a respect for the law, so much as for the right. The only obligation which I have a right to assume, is to do at any time what I think right. It is truly enough said, that a corporation has no conscience; but a corporation of conscientious men is a corporation *with* a conscience. Law never made men a whit more just; and, by means of their respect for it, even the well-disposed are daily made the agents of injustice. A common and natural result of an undue respect for law is, that you may see a file of soldiers, colonel, captain, corporal, privates, powder-monkeys and all, marching in admirable order over hill and dale to the wars, against their wills, aye, against their common sense and consciences, which makes it very steep marching indeed, and produces a palpitation of the heart. They have no doubt that it is a damnable business in which they are concerned; they are all peaceably inclined. Now, what are they? Men at all? or small moveable forts and magazines,[4] at the service of some unscrupulous man in power? Visit the Navy Yard and behold a marine, such a man as an American government can make, or such as it can make a man with its black arts, a mere shadow and reminiscence of humanity a man laid out alive and standing, and already, as one may say, buried under arms with funeral accompaniments, though it may be

"Not a drum was heard, not a funeral note,
  As his corse to the rampart we hurried;
Not a soldier discharged his farewell shot
  O'er the grave where our hero we buried."[5]

5 The mass of men serve the State thus, not as men mainly, but as machines, with their bodies. They are the standing army, and the militia, jailers, constables, *posse comitatus*,[6] &c. In most cases there is no free exercise whatever of the judgment or of the moral sense; but they put themselves on a level with wood and earth and stones, and wooden men can perhaps be manufactured that will serve the purpose as well. Such command no more respect than men of straw, or a lump of dirt. They have the same sort of worth only as horses and dogs. Yet such as these even are commonly esteemed good citizens. Others, as most legislators, politicians, lawyers, ministers, and office-holders, serve the State chiefly with their heads; and, as they rarely make any moral distinctions, they are as likely to serve the devil, without intending it, as God. A very few, as heroes, patriots, martyrs, reformers in the great sense, and *men*, serve the State with their consciences also, and so necessarily resist it for the most part; and they are commonly treated by it as enemies. . . .

---

[4] magazines: storehouses for ammunition.

[5] "Not . . . buried": from "The Burial of Sir John Moore After Corunna" by Charles Wolfe (1791–1823). The complete poem is on the *Ideas Across Time* website.

[6] *posse comitatus:* literally "the force of the county"; a body of men enlisted to suppress civil discord.

How does it become a man to behave toward this American government today? I answer that he cannot without disgrace be associated with it. I cannot for an instant recognize that political organization as *my* government which is the *slave's* government also.

All men recognize the right of revolution; that is, the right to refuse allegiance to and the resist the government, when its tyranny or its inefficiency are great and unendurable. But almost all say that such is not the case now. But such was the case, they think, in the Revolution of '75. If one were to tell me that this was a bad government because it taxed certain foreign commodities brought to its ports, it is most probable that I should not make an ado about it, for I can do without them: all machines have their friction; and possibly this does enough good to counterbalance the evil. At any rate, it is a great evil to make a stir about it. But when the friction comes to have its machine, and oppression and robbery are organized, I say, let us not have such a machine any longer. In other words, when a sixth of the population of a nation which has undertaken to be the refuge of liberty are slaves, and a whole country is unjustly overrun and conquered by a foreign army, and subjected to military law, I think that it is not too soon for honest men to rebel and revolutionize. What makes this duty the more urgent is the fact, that the country so overrun is not our own, but ours is the invading army.

Paley,[7] a common authority with many on moral questions, in his chapter on the "Duty of Submission to Civil Government," resolves all civil obligation into expediency; and he proceeds to say, "that so long as the interest of the whole society requires it, that is, so long as the established government cannot be resisted or changed without public inconveniency, it is the will of God that the established government be obeyed, and no longer." . . . "This principle being admitted, the justice of every particular case of resistance is reduced to a computation of the quantity of the danger and grievance on the one side, and of the probability and expense of redressing it on the other." Of this, he says, every man shall judge for himself. But Paley appears never to have contemplated those cases to which the rule of expediency does not apply, in which a people, as well as an individual, must do justice, cost what it may. If I have unjustly wrested a plank from a drowning man, I must restore it to him though I drown myself. This, according to Paley, would be inconvenient. But he that would save his life, in such a case, shall lose it. This people must cease to hold slaves, and to make war on Mexico, though it cost them their existence as a people.

In their practice, nations agree with Paley; but does any one think that Massachusetts does exactly what is right at the present crisis?

"A drab of state, a cloth-o'-silver slut,
To have her train borne up, and her soul trail in the dirt."[8]

Practically speaking, the opponents to a reform in Massachusetts are not a hundred thousand politicians at the South, but a hundred thousand merchants and

[7] Paley: William Paley (1743–1805), an English churchman who taught at Cambridge, maintained that resistance to government was an affront to God.

[8] "A drab . . . dirt": from *The Revenger's Tragedy,* IV, iv by Cyril Tourneur (1575?–1626).

farmers here, who are more interested in commerce and agriculture than they are in humanity, and are not prepared to do justice to the slave and to Mexico, *cost what it may.* I quarrel not with far-off foes, but with those who, near at home, co-operate with, and do the bidding of those far away, and without whom the latter would be harmless. We are accustomed to say, that the mass of men are unprepared; but improvement is slow, because the few are not materially wiser or better than the many. It is not so important that many should be as good as you, as that there be some absolute goodness somewhere; for that will leaven the whole lump. There are thousands who are *in opinion* opposed to slavery and to the war, who yet in effect do nothing to put an end to them; who, esteeming themselves children of Washington and Franklin, sit down with their hands in their pockets, and say that they know not what to do, and do nothing; who even postpone the question of freedom to the question of free-trade, and quietly read the prices-current along with the latest advices from Mexico, after dinner, and, it may be, fall asleep over them both. What is the price-current of an honest man and patriot to-day? They hesitate, and they regret, and sometimes they petition; but they do nothing in earnest and with effect. They will wait, well-disposed, for others to remedy the evil, that they may no longer have it to regret. At most, they give only a cheap vote, and a feeble countenance and God-speed, to the right, as it goes by them. There are nine hundred and ninety-nine patrons of virtue to one virtuous man; but it is easier to deal with the real possessor of a thing than with the temporary guardian of it.

10 All voting is a sort of gaming, like chequers or backgammon, with a slight moral tinge to it, a playing with right and wrong, with moral questions; and betting naturally accompanies it. The character of the voters is not staked. I cast my vote, perchance, as I think right; but I am not vitally concerned that that right should prevail. I am willing to leave it to the majority. Its obligation, therefore, never exceeds that of expediency. Even voting *for the right* is *doing* nothing for it. It is only expressing to men feebly your desire that it should prevail. A wise man will not leave the right to the mercy of chance, nor wish it to prevail through the power of the majority. There is but little virtue in the action of masses of men. When the majority shall at length vote for the abolition of slavery, it will be because they are indifferent to slavery, or because there is but little slavery left to be abolished by their vote. *They* will then be the only slaves. Only *his* vote can hasten the abolition of slavery who asserts his own freedom by his vote. . . .

I do not hesitate to say, that those who call themselves abolitionists should at once effectually withdraw their support, both in person and property, from the government of Massachusetts, and not wait till they constitute a majority of one, before they suffer the right to prevail through them. I think that it is enough if they have God on their side, without waiting for that other one. Moreover, any man more right than his neighbors, constitutes a majority of one already.

I meet this American government, or its representative the State government, directly, and face to face, once a year, no more, in the person of its tax-gatherer; this is the only mode in which a man situated as I am necessarily meets it; and it then says distinctly, Recognize me; and the simplest, the most effectual, and, in the present posture of affairs, the indispensablest mode of treating with it on this head, of expressing your little satisfaction with and love for it, is to deny it then. My civil neighbor, the tax-gatherer, is the very man I have to deal with,—for it is, after all, with men and not with parchment that I quarrel,—and he has voluntarily chosen to be an agent of the government. How shall he ever know well what he is and does as an officer of the government, or as a man, until he is obliged to consider whether he shall treat me, his neighbor, for whom he has respect, as a neighbor and well-disposed man, or as a maniac and disturber of the peace, and see if he can get over this obstruction to his neighborliness without a ruder and more impetuous thought or speech corresponding with his action? I know this well, that if one thousand, if one hundred, if ten men whom I could name,—if ten *honest* men only,—aye, if *one* HONEST man, in this State of Massachusetts, *ceasing to hold slaves,* were actually to withdraw from this copartnership, and be locked up in the county jail therefor, it would be the abolition of slavery in America. For it matters not how small the beginning may seem to be: what is once well done is done for ever. . . .

Under a government which imprisons any unjustly, the true place for a just man is also a prison. The proper place to-day, the only place which Massachusetts has provided for her freer and less desponding spirits, is in her prisons, to be put out and locked out of the State by her own act, as they have already put themselves out by their principles. It is there that the fugitive slave, and the Mexican prisoner on parole, and the Indian come to plead the wrongs of his race, should find them; on that separate, but more free and honorable ground, where the State places those who are not *with* her but *against* her,—the only house in a slave-state in which a free man can abide with honor. If any think that their influence would be lost there, and their voices no longer afflict the ear of the State, that they would not be as an enemy within its walls, they do not know by how much truth is stronger than error, nor how much more eloquently and effectively he can combat injustice who has experienced a little in his own person. Cast your whole vote, not a strip of paper merely, but your whole influence. A minority is powerless while it conforms to the majority; it is not even a minority then; but it is irresistible when it clogs by its whole weight. If the alternative is to keep all just men in prison, or give up war and slavery, the State will not hesitate which to choose. If a thousand men were not to pay their tax-bills this year, that would not be a violent and bloody measure, as it would be to pay them, and enable the State to commit violence and shed innocent blood. This is, in fact, the definition of a peaceable revolution, if any such is possible. If the tax-gatherer, or any other public officer, asks me, as one has done, "But what shall I do?" my answer is, "If you really wish to do any thing, resign your office." When the subject has refused allegiance, and the officer has resigned his office, then the revolution is accomplished. But even suppose blood should flow. Is there not a sort of blood shed when the conscience is wounded? Through this wound a man's real manhood and immortality flow out, and he bleeds to an everlasting death. I see this blood flowing now.

I have contemplated the imprisonment of the offender, rather than the seizure of his goods,—though both will serve the same purpose,—because they who assert the purest right, and consequently are most dangerous to a corrupt State, commonly have not spent much time in accumulating property. To such the State renders comparatively small service, and a slight tax is wont to appear exorbitant, particularly if they are obliged to earn it by special labor with their hands. If there were one who lived wholly without the use of money, the State itself would hesitate to demand it of him. But the rich man—not to make any invidious comparison—is always sold to the institution which makes him rich. Absolutely speaking, the more money, the less virtue; for money comes between a man and his objects; and obtains them for him; and it was certainly no great virtue to obtain it. It puts to rest many questions which he would otherwise be taxed to answer; while the only new question which it puts is the hard but superfluous one, how to spend it. Thus his moral ground is taken from under his feet. The opportunities of living are diminished in proportion as what are called the "means" are increased. The best thing a man can do for his culture when he is rich is to endeavour to carry out those schemes which he entertained when he was poor. Christ answered the Herodians according to their condition. "Show me the tribute-money," said he;—and one took a penny out of his pocket;—If you use money which has the image of Caesar on it, and which he has made current and valuable, that is, *if you are men of the State,* and gladly enjoy the advantages of Caesar's government, then pay him back some of his own when he demands it; "Render therefore to Caesar that which is Caesar's, and to God those things which are God's,"—leaving them no wiser than before as to which was which; for they, did not wish to know.

When I converse with the freest of my neighbors, I perceive that, whatever they may say about the magnitude and seriousness of the question, and their regard for the public tranquillity, the long and the short of the matter is, that they cannot spare the protection of the existing government, and they dread the consequences of disobedience to it to their property and families. For my own part, I should not like to think that I ever rely on the protection of the State. But, if I deny, the authority of the State when it presents its tax-bill, it will soon take and waste all my property, and so harass me and my children without end. This is hard. This makes it impossible for a man to live honestly and at the same time comfortably in outward respects. It will not be worth the while to accumulate property; that would, be sure to go again. You must hire or squat somewhere, and raise but a small crop, and eat that soon. You must live within yourself, and depend upon yourself, always tucked up and ready for a start, and not have many affairs.[9] A man may grow rich in Turkey even, if he will be in all respects a good subject of the Turkish government. Confucius said,—"If a State is governed by the principles of reason, poverty and misery are subjects of shame; if a State is not governed by the principles of reason, riches and honors are the subjects of shame." No: until I want the protection of Massachusetts to be extended to me in some distant southern port, where my liberty is endangered, or until I am bent solely on building up an estate at home by peaceful enterprise, I can afford to refuse allegiance, to Massachusetts, and

[9] many affairs: much business.

her right to my property and life. It costs me less in every sense to incur the penalty of disobedience to the State, than it would to obey. I should feel as if I were worth less in that case. . . .

I have paid no poll-tax for six years. I was put into a jail once on this account, for one night; and, as I stood considering the walls of solid stone, two or three feet thick, the door of wood and iron, a foot thick, and die iron grating which strained the light, I could not help being struck with the foolishness of that institution which treated me as if I were mere flesh and blood and bones, to be locked up. I wondered that it should have concluded at length that this was the best use it could put me to, and had never thought to avail itself of my services in some way. I saw that, if there was a wall of stone between me and my townsmen, there was a still more difficult one to climb or break through, before they could get to be as free as I was. I did not for a moment feel confined, and the walls seemed a great waste of stone and mortar. I felt as if I alone of all my townsmen had paid my tax. They plainly did not know how to treat me, but behaved like persons who are underbred. In every threat and in every compliment there was a blunder; for they thought that my chief desire was to stand the other side of that stone wall. I could not but smile to see how industriously they locked the door on my meditations, which followed them out again without let or hinderance, and *they* were really all that was dangerous. As they could not reach me, they had resolved to punish my body; just as boys, if they cannot come at some person against whom they have a spite, will abuse his dog. I saw that the State was half-witted, that it was timid as a lone woman with her silver spoons, and that it did not know its friends from its foes, and I lost all my remaining respect for it; and pitied it.

Thus the State never intentionally confronts a man's sense, intellectual or moral, but only his body, his senses. It is not armed with superior wit or honesty, but with superior physical strength. I was not born to be forced. I will breathe after my own fashion. Let us see who is the strongest. What force has a multitude? They only can force me who obey a higher law than I. They force me to become like themselves. I do not hear of *men* being *forced* to live this way or that by masses of men. What sort of life were that to live? When I meet a government which says to me, "Your money or your life;" why should I be in haste to give it my money? It may be in a great strait, and not know what to do: I cannot help that. It must help itself; do as I do. It is not worth the while to snivel about it. I am not responsible for the successful working of the machinery of society. I am not the son of the engineer. I perceive that, when an acorn and a chestnut fall side by side, the one does not remain inert to make way for the other, but both obey their own laws, and spring and grow and flourish as best they can, till one, perchance, overshadows and destroys the other. If a plant cannot live according to its nature, it dies; and so a man.

The night in prison was novel and interesting enough. The prisoners in their shirt-sleeves were enjoying a chat and the evening air in the door-way, when I entered. But the jailer said, "Come, boys, it is time to lock up"; and so they dispersed, and I heard the sound of their steps returning into the hollow apartments. My roommate was introduced to me by the jailer, as "a first-rate fellow and a clever man." When the door was locked, he showed me where to hang my hat, and how he managed matters there. The rooms were whitewashed once a month; and this one, at least, was the whitest, most simply furnished, and probably the neatest apartment in the town. He naturally wanted to know where I came from, and what brought me there; and, when I had told him, I asked him in turn how he came there, presuming him to be an honest man, of course; and as the world goes, I believe, he was. "Why," said be, "they accused me of burning a barn; but I never did it." As near as I could discover, he had probably gone to bed in a barn when drunk, and smoked his pipe there; and so a barn was burnt. He had the reputation of being a clever man, had been there some three months waiting for his trial to come on, and would have to wait as much longer; but he was quite domesticated and contented, since he got his board for nothing, and thought that he was well treated.

He occupied one window, and I the other, and I saw, that, if one stayed there long, his principal business would be to look out the window. I had soon read all the tracts that were left there, and examined where former prisoners had broken out, and where a grate had been sawed off, and heard the history of the various occupants of that room; for I found that even here there was a history and a gossip which never circulated beyond the walls of the jail. Probably this is the only house in the town where verses are composed, which are afterward printed in a circular form, but not published. I was shown quite a long list of verses which were composed by some young men who had been detected in an attempt to escape, who avenged themselves by singing them.

I pumped my fellow-prisoner as dry as I could, for fear I should never see him again; but at length he showed me which was my bed, and left me to blow out the lamp.

It was like traveling into a far country, such as I had never expected to behold, to lie there for one night. It seemed to me that I never had heard the town-clock strike before, nor the evening sounds of the village, for we slept with the windows open, which were inside the grating. It was to see my native village in the light of the middle ages, and our Concord was turned into a Rhine stream, and visions of knights and castles passed before me. They were the voices of old burghers that I heard in the streets. I was an involuntary spectator and auditor of whatever was done and said in the kitchen of the adjacent village-inn,—a wholly new and rare experience to me. It was a closer view of my native town. I was fairly inside of it. I never had seen its institutions before. This is one of its peculiar institutions; for it is a shire town. I began to comprehend what its inhabitants were about.

In the morning, our breakfasts were put through the hole in the door, in small oblong square tin pans, made to fit, and holding a pint of chocolate, with brown bread and an iron spoon. When they called for the vessels again, I was green enough to return what bread I had left; but my comrade seized it, and said that I should lay that up for lunch or dinner. Soon after, he was let out to work at haying in a neighboring field, whither he went every day, and would not be back till noon; so he bade me good-day, saying that he doubted if he should see me again.

When I came out of prison,—for some one interfered, and paid the tax,—I did not perceive that great changes had taken place on the common, such as he observed who went in a youth, and emerged a tottering and grayheaded man; and yet a change had to my eyes come over the scene,—the town, and State and country,—greater than any that mere time could effect. I saw yet more distinctly the State in which I lived. I saw to what extent the people among whom I lived could be trusted as good neighbors and friends; that their friendship was for summer weather only; that they did not greatly purpose to do right; that they were a distinct race from me by their prejudices and superstitions, as the Chinamen and Malays are; that in their sacrifices to humanity, they ran to risks, not even to their property, that, after all, they were not so noble but they treated the thief as he had treated them, and hoped, by a certain outward observance and a few prayers, and by walking in a particular straight though useless path from time to time, to save their souls. This may be to judge my neighbors harshly; for I believe that most of them are not aware that they have such an institution as the jail in their village.

It was formerly the custom in our village, when a poor debtor came out of jail, for his acquaintances to salute him, looking through their fingers, which were crossed to represent the grating of a jail window, "How do ye do?" My neighbors did not thus salute me, but first looked at me, and then at one another, as if I had returned from a long journey. I was put into jail as I was going to the shoemaker's to get a shoe which was mended. When I was let out the next morning, I proceeded to finish my errand, and, having put on my mended shoe, joined a huckleberry party, who were impatient to put themselves under my conduct; and in half an hour,—for the horse, was soon tackled[10]*—was in the midst of a huckleberry field, on one of our highest hills, two miles off; and then the State was nowhere to be seen.*

This is the whole history of "My Prisons."

I have never declined paying the highway tax, because I am as desirous of being a good neighbor as I am of being a bad subject; and, as for supporting schools, I am doing my part to educate my fellow-countrymen now. It is for no particular item in the tax-bill that I refuse to pay it. I simply wish to refuse allegiance to the State, to withdraw and stand aloof from it effectually. I do not care to trace the course of my dollar, if I could till it buys a man, or a musket to shoot one with,—the dollar is innocent,—but I am concerned to trace the effects of my allegiance. In fact, I quietly declare war with the State, after my fashion, though I will still make what use and get what advantage of her I can, as is usual in such cases. . . .

I do not wish to quarrel with any man or nation. I do not wish to split hairs, to make fine distinctions, or set myself up as better than my neighbors. I seek rather, I may say, even an excuse for conforming to the laws of the land. I am but too ready to conform to them. Indeed I have reason to suspect myself on this head; and each year, as the tax-gatherer comes round, I find myself disposed to review the acts and position of the general and state governments, and the spirit of the people, to discover a pretext for conformity. I believe that the State will soon be able to take all my work of this sort out of my hands, and then I shall be no better a patriot than my fellow countrymen. Seen from a lower point of view, the Constitution, with all its faults, is very good; the law and the courts are very respectable; even this State and this American government are, in many respects, very admirable and rare things, to be thankful for, such as a great many have described them; but seen from a point of view a little higher, they are what

[10] tackled: harnessed.

I have described them; seen from a higher still, and the highest, who shall say what they are, or that they are worth looking at or thinking of at all?

However, the government does not concern me much, and I shall bestow the fewest possible thoughts on it. It is not many moments that I live under a government, even in this world. If a man is thought-free, fancy-free, imagination-free, that which *is not* never for a long time appearing *to be* to him, unwise rulers or reformers cannot fatally interrupt him.

I know that most men think differently from myself; but those whose lives are by profession devoted to the study of these or kindred subjects, content me as little as any. Statesmen and legislators, standing so completely within the institution, never distinctly and nakedly behold it. They speak of moving society, but have no resting-place without it. They may be men of a certain experience and discrimination, and have no doubt invented ingenious and even useful systems, for which we sincerely thank them; but all their wit and usefulness lie within certain not very wide limits. They are wont to forget that the world is not governed by policy and expediency. Webster[11] never goes behind government, and so cannot speak with authority about it. His words are wisdom to those legislators who contemplate no essential reform in the existing government; but for thinkers, and those who legislate for all time, he never once glances at the subject. I know of those whose serene and wise speculations on this theme would soon reveal the limits of his mind's range and hospitality. Yet, compared with the cheap professions of most reformers; and the still cheaper wisdom and eloquence of politicians in general, his are almost the only sensible and valuable words, and we thank Heaven for him. Comparatively, he is always strong, original, and, above all, practical. Still his quality is not wisdom, but prudence. The lawyer's truth is not Truth, but consistency, or a consistent expediency. Truth is always in harmony with herself, and is not concerned chiefly to reveal the justice that may consist with wrong-doing. He well deserves to be called, as he has been called, the Defender of the Constitution. There are really no blows to be given by him but defensive ones. He is not a leader, but a follower. His leaders are the men of '87. "I have never made an effort," he says, "and never propose to make an effort; I have never countenanced an effort, and never mean to countenance an effort, to disturb the arrangement as originally made, by which the various States came into the Union." Still thinking of the sanction which the Constitution gives to slavery, he says, "Because it was a part of the original compact,—let it stand." Notwithstanding his special acuteness and ability, he is unable to take a fact out of its merely political relations, and behold it as lies absolutely to be disposed of by the intellect,—what, for instance, it behoves a man to-do here in America to-day with regard to slavery,—but ventures, or is driven, to make some such desperate answer as the following, while professing to speak absolutely, and as a private man,—from which what new and singular code of social duties might be inferred?—"The manner," says he "in which the governments of those States where slavery exists are to regulate it, is for their

[11] Webster: Daniel Webster (1782–1852), one of the leading politicians of the time, supported strict enforcement of the Fugitive Slave Act as a means of sustaining the union and the Constitution.

own consideration, under their responsibility to their constituents, to the general laws of propriety, humanity, and justice, and to God. Associations formed elsewhere, springing from a feeling of humanity, or any other cause, have nothing whatever to do with it. They have never received any encouragement from me, and they never will."[12]

30 They who know of no purer sources of truth, who have traced up its stream no higher, stand, and wisely stand, by the Bible and the Constitution, and drink at it there with reverence and humility; but they who behold where it comes trickling into this lake or that pool, gird up their loins once more, and continue their pilgrimage toward its fountain-head. . . .

The authority of government, even such as I am willing to submit to,—for I will cheerfully obey those who know and can do better than I, and in many things even those who neither know nor can do so well,—is still an impure one: to be strictly just, it must have the sanction and consent of the governed. It can have no pure right over my person and property but what I concede to it. The progress from an absolute to a limited monarchy, from a limited monarchy to a democracy, is a progress toward a true respect for the individual. Is a democracy, such as we know it, the last improvement possible in government? Is it not possible to take a step further towards recognizing and organizing the rights of man? There will never be a really free and enlightened State, until the State comes to recognize the individual as a higher and independent power, from which all its own power and authority are derived, and treats him accordingly. I please myself with imagining a State at last which can afford to be just to all men, and to treat the individual with respect as a neighbor; which even would not think it inconsistent with its own repose, if a few were to live aloof from it, not meddling with it, nor embraced by it, who fulfilled all the duties of neighbors and fellow men. A State which bore this kind of fruit, and suffered it to drop off as fast as it ripened, would prepare the way for a still more perfect and glorious State, which also I have imagined, but not yet anywhere seen.

LEARNING MORE

There is a wealth of information about Thoreau online, including online versions of his major works. To learn more about Thoreau, see the *Ideas Across Time* website.

QUESTIONING THE TEXT

1. Thoreau says government is "but an expedient" (par. 1). What do you think he means? Is he making light of government or trying to define it accurately?

---

[12] "These extracts have been inserted since the Lecture was read" [Thoreau's note].

2. Why does Thoreau think so little of government in general and of the American government in particular?
3. What is Thoreau's opinion of majority rule? Do you agree?
4. Since the American government recognizes slavery, how does Thoreau view that government?
5. What is Thoreau's quarrel with William Paley's views on the obligations of a citizen to his government (par. 8)?
6. How should citizens act toward their government if they do not think the government is acting in the right?
7. Thoreau says, "It costs me less in every sense to incur the penalty of disobedience to the State, than it would to obey" (par. 15). What does he mean?
8. How does Thoreau characterize his night in prison? Why does he say he was more free in prison than his neighbors outside of it? Is he right?
9. How does Thoreau differ from Daniel Webster on how one should view the Constitution?
10. What sort of government would Thoreau be happy to follow?

ANALYZING THE WRITER'S CRAFT

1. How important to Thoreau's essay as a whole are his opening quotations in par. 1? Explain.
2. What is the thesis statement of this essay? Where is it found?
3. What is the tone of this essay?
4. Thoreau is arguing for a position that he acknowledges few will share. How does he appeal to the majority in his audience?
5. This essay is full of famous aphorisms (terse statements of memorable truths). Choose two or three, and show how they express the essay's main argument and why they are effective.
6. Write an outline of Thoreau's essay. Is it coherent? Is it well developed?
7. Thoreau quotes two prominent authorities in order to dissent from their views—Paley and Webster. Is Thoreau fair in his allusion to these thinkers? How do his quotations help him lay the ground for his own argument?
8. Is Thoreau's extended discussion of his night in jail (pars. 18–25) essential to his essay? How would the essay have been different had he omitted this material? Would you have included or excluded this material if this had been your essay?
9. Where does Thoreau's conclusion begin? Is his conclusion effective?

MAKING CONNECTIONS

1. Compare and contrast Thoreau's view of the obligations a citizen owes his government and John Locke's view (pp. 348–352).
2. Thoreau seems to advance an anarchist's position on government—the best government is no government; government should privilege the individual and not the masses. How do you imagine Thoreau might have reacted to

Fareed Zakaria's argument that today our liberty is threatened by too *much* democracy (pp. 330–337)?

3. Vaclav Havel (pp. 404–412) seems closest to Thoreau in his profoundly moral approach to politics (and in willing to spend time in jail for his ideals). To what extent do these writers see eye to eye? Explain.
4. Thoreau bases his position on moral grounds, on doing right. To what extent is his position also dependent on religion? Do you think Thoreau is closer to his fellow rebel Tom Paine (Chapter 2, pp. 98–103) or to the theologian Paul Tillich (Chapter 2, pp. 123–130)?

FORMULATING IDEAS FOR WRITING

1. Is Thoreau right in saying that the motto "That government is best which governs least," if taken to its logical conclusion, leads to "That government is best which governs not at all"? Explain.
2. Thoreau assaults two powerful positions, those of William Paley and Daniel Webster. Refute Thoreau's position by presenting arguments in favor of either Paley's or Webster's views.
3. How could a government be organized that took the individual as its main point of reference instead of the majority? Thoreau says, "There will never be a really free and enlightened State, until the State comes to recognize the individual as a higher and independent power" (par. 31). Explain what he means. Do you agree?
4. Thoreau states, "Under a government which imprisons any unjustly, the true place for a just man is also a prison" (par. 13). Do you agree? Why or why not?

Letter on Democracy (1857)

Thomas Babington Macaulay

Thomas Babington Macaulay was one of the great figures of the liberal establishment of Victorian England—politician, administrator, orator, conversationalist, and especially historian. His *History of England from the Accession of James the Second* (1848–1861) was hugely popular, a monument of Victorian culture and an emblem of the Whig view of history. In these books, Macaulay narrated the triumph of progress in England under the Protestant Whig settlement. Macaulay wrote in ringing, declamatory rhetoric that England rose to the pinnacle of world power because of the policies and rule of liberal Whig politicians and men of business. Although Macaulay's version of history dominated nineteenth-century England, it was even then seen—affectionately—as partisan. Lord Melbourne is said to have remarked, "I wish I were as cocksure of any one thing as Macaulay is of everything."

Macaulay was born in 1800. His father, Zachary, had been governor of Sierra Leone and was a leading opponent of the slave trade. After graduating from Cambridge, Macaulay began to write for the reformist *Edinburgh Review,* in whose pages he made his name first as a writer. He entered Parliament in 1830 under the patronage of Lord Landsdowne and spoke in favor of the Reform Bill of 1832, which extended the franchise and launched the transition from a Parliament based on the landed and commercial interests to a Parliament based on the principle of one-man (and eventually one-person), one-vote. He followed his father, too, as an opponent of slavery. But as this selection makes clear, Macaulay was by no means a democrat in our sense of the word. He was, rather, an establishment reformer, supporting rule by educated men at a time when "educated" included no more than a minority of the population. From 1834 to 1838, Macaulay served on the Supreme Council of the East India Company, in effect the ruling cabinet of the colony, and composed a widely admired legal code for India. He also headed the reform of the Indian educational system, imposing English as the language of instruction. In 1839, he returned to England and to Parliament, serving as secretary of war in Lord Melbourne's ministry. But increasingly he withdrew from active politics and devoted himself to writing, in particular of his great *History.* Lord Palmerston, as prime minister, made him a peer in 1857; as Baron Macaulay of Rothley, however, he sat but never spoke in the House of Lords. Macaulay never married, devoting himself instead to the family of his sister Hannah and her children. He died in 1859.

The "Letter on Democracy," addressed to Commodore H. S. Randall of the New York Yacht Club in 1857, was originally published in the *Review of Reviews and World's Work* in July 1934.

Holly Lodge, Kensington, London,
MAY 23,1857

Dear Sir:

You are surprised to learn that I have not a high opinion of Mr. Jefferson[1] and I am surprised at your surprise. I am certain that I never wrote a line, and that I never in Parliament—a place where it is the fashion to court the populace—uttered a word, indicating an opinion that the Supreme authority in a State ought to be trusted to the majority of citizens told by the head;[2] in other words to the poorest and most ignorant part of society. I have long been convinced that institutions purely democratic must, sooner or later destroy liberty or civilization, or both. In Europe, where the population is dense, the effect of such institutions would be instantaneous.

[1] Jefferson: Thomas Jefferson.
[2] head: counted by individuals; that is, universal manhood suffrage.

What happened lately in France is an example. In 1848 a pure democracy was established there.[3] During a short time there was reason to expect a general spoliation, a national bankruptcy, a new partition of the soil, a maximum of prices, a ruinous load of taxation laid on the rich for the purpose of supporting the poor in idleness. Such a system would, in twenty years, have made France as poor and barbarous as the France of the Carlovingians.[4] Happily, the danger was averted; and now there is a despotism, a silent tribune, an enslaved press. Liberty is gone but civilization has been saved.

I have not the smallest doubt that, if we had a purely democratic Government here, the effect would be the same. Either the poor would plunder the rich and civilization would perish, or order and prosperity would be saved by a strong military government, and liberty would perish.

You may think that your country enjoys an exemption from these evils; I will frankly own to you that I am of a very different opinion. Your fate I believe to be certain, though it is deferred by a physical cause. As long as you have a boundless extent of fertile and unoccupied land, your laboring population will be far more at ease than the laboring population of the old world; and while that is the case the Jefferson politics may continue to exist without causing any fatal calamity. But the time will come when New England will be as thickly settled as Old England. Wages will be as low, and will fluctuate as much with you as with us. You will have your Manchesters and Birminghams.[5] And in those Manchesters and Birminghams hundreds and thousands of artisans will sometimes be out of work. Then your institutions will be fairly brought to the test. Distress everywhere makes the labourer mutinous and discontented, and inclines him to listen with eagerness to agitators, who tell him that it is a monstrous iniquity that one man should have a million while another cannot get a full meal.

5 In bad years there is plenty of grumbling here, and sometimes a little rioting; but it matters little, for here the sufferers are not the rulers. The supreme power is in the hands of a class numerous indeed, but select—of an educated class—of a class which is and knows itself to be, deeply interested in the security of property and the maintenance of order. Accordingly, the malcontents are gently but firmly restrained. The bad time is got over without robbing the wealthy to relieve the indigent.[6] The springs of national prosperity soon begin to flow again; work is plentiful, wages rise and all is tranquillity and cheerfulness. I have seen England pass, three or four times, through such critical seasons as I have described.

Through such seasons the United States will have to pass in the course of the next century, if not of this. How will you pass through them? I heartily wish you good deliverance. But my reason is quite plain that your Government will never be able to restrain a distressed and discontented majority. For, with you the majority is the government, and has the rich, who are always the minority,

---

[3] In 1848 . . . there: on February 24, 1848, the Second French Republic was established. It instituted universal suffrage and imposed socialist reforms but soon collapsed, to be followed by the emperorship of Louis-Napoleon.

[4] Carlovingians: the second dynasty of Frankish kings (762–987), named after the greatest of them, Charlemagne (742–814).

[5] Manchester and Birmingham: the main industrial cities of nineteenth-century England.

[6] indigent: poor.

absolutely at its mercy. The day will come when in the State of New York, a multitude of people, none of whom has had more than half a breakfast, or expects to have more than half a dinner, will choose a Legislature. Is it possible to doubt what sort of Legislature will be chosen? On one side is a statesman preaching patience, respect for vested rights, strict observance of public faith; on the other is a demagogue, ranting about the tyranny of the capitalists and usurers, and asking why anybody should be permitted to drink champagne and to ride in a carriage while thousands of honest folks are in want of necessaries. Which of the two candidates is likely to be preferred by a workman who hears his children cry for bread?

I seriously apprehend you will, in some season of adversity as I have described, do things that will prevent prosperity from returning; that you will act like people who should, in a season of scarcity, partake of absolute famine. There will be, I fear, spoliation. The spoliation will increase the distress. The distress will produce fresh spoliation. There is nothing to stop you. Your Constitution is all sail and no anchor.

As I said before, when a society has entered on its downward progress either civilization or liberty must perish. Either some Caesar or Napoleon will seize the rein of Government with a strong hand or your republic will be as fearfully plundered and laid waste by barbarians in the Twentieth Century as the Roman Empire was in the Fifth—with this difference that the Huns and Vandals who ravaged the Roman Empire came from without, and that your Huns and Vandals have been engendered within your country by your own institutions.

Thinking this, of course, I cannot reckon Jefferson among the benefactors of mankind.

Yours respectfully,
Thomas Babington Macaulay.

LEARNING MORE

To access Macaualy's *History,* see the *Ideas Across Time* website.

QUESTIONING THE TEXT

1. Macaulay is a democrat, but an opponent of "institutions purely democratic" (par. 1). What sort of democracy does he favor? Why is he opposed to "pure" democracy?
2. How does the example of the revolution of 1848 in France support Macaulay's argument?
3. What exempts the United States from the evils of pure democracy?
4. Why has revolution not come to England?
5. What is Macaulay's prediction for the consequences of democracy in the United States? Do you think he had good grounds for his prediction? Why or why not?

ANALYZING THE WRITER'S CRAFT

1. What is the thesis statement of Macaulay's essay? Where is it found?
2. What is the tone of Macaulay's essay? To what extent do you think his tone is dictated by the purpose of and audience for his essay? Explain.
3. Is Macaulay presenting a fair and impartial view of events and their likely outcomes, or does he "load the dice"? Does his diction betray his prejudices? Illustrate.
4. Does this essay reflect Macaulay's training as a parliamentary orator? Explain.
5. What sorts of evidence does Macaulay use to support his case?
6. Is Macaulay persuasive? Explain.
7. Is Macaulay's conclusion effective? Why or why not?

MAKING CONNECTIONS

1. How might Karl Marx (Chapter 4, pp. 264–273) have responded to Macaulay's fear of democracy?
2. How might Thomas Jefferson (pp. 354–360) have responded to Macaulay's fear of democracy?
3. Is Macaulay's view of democracy a forerunner of Fareed Zakaria's contemporary argument (pp. 330–337) that liberty is today threatened by *too much* democracy? Discuss.

FORMULATING IDEAS FOR WRITING

1. The idea of one-person, one-vote is so deeply ingrained in our way of life that perhaps we are unable to assess it objectively. Does Macaulay raise points that you might not have previously given any attention? Or is Macaulay both dated and prejudiced against ordinary people? Shouldn't democracy require educated participation by informed individuals? What safeguards against rule by an impassioned but ignorant mob does the U.S. Constitution provide?
2. Why didn't things in the United States turn out the way Macaulay was sure that they would?
3. Macaulay is quite straightforward about the boom-and-bust cycle of Victorian capitalism. How do Karl Marx (Chapter 4, pp. 264–273) and Adam Smith (Chapter 4, pp. 244–262) explain this economic fact of Victorian life? Which explanation do you find most persuasive, and why? Does Macaulay's cool, and perhaps even cruel, account undermine any, or all, of these explanations by the economic and political theorists?
4. Is Macaulay's "pure" democracy a nineteenth-century version of Fareed Zakaria's complaint (pp. 330–337) that we now have too much democracy? How are the views of these two experienced men the same? How do they

differ? What would Zakaria have thought of Macaulay had he lived in the nineteenth century? What would Macaulay think of Zakaria if he were to come back to life and enjoy another turn on earth as a contemporary American?

Technology and Democracy (1974)

Daniel J. Boorstin

One of the most celebrated chroniclers of the American experience, Daniel J. Boorstin is something in the nature of an old-fashioned patriot, someone whose very passion for democracy drives him to sound the alarm about its vulnerability to threats from the nature of democratic practice itself and from the inevitable complacency that success breeds. In the selection that follows, from his book *Democracy and Its Discontents: Reflections on Everyday America* (1974), Boorstin argues the paradoxical thesis that the nation's "problems arise not so much from our failures as from our successes." In particular, he analyzes the unsettling implications for democratic life of bourgeoning technology. He shows through a series of unexpected examples—such as the invention of the refrigerator and the car—that as we succeed in abolishing every form of distinction, such as the distinction between the seasons, we at the same time dilute experience, poisoning our success by making things monotonous and bland. Our very exuberance in applying our root values to all corners of everyday living, Boorstin shows, threatens to transform what we dearly desired into something pointless and worthless.

For over a decade Librarian of Congress (1975–1987), Boorstin, born in 1914, also served as director of the National Museum of American History and for twenty-five years as professor of history at the University of Chicago. His widely read and praised work includes the trilogy *The Americans*, the final volume of which—*The Americans: The Democratic Experience* (1975)—was awarded the Pulitzer Prize. *The Discoverers* (1983), a history of the great scientific discoveries, and *The Creators* (1994), an account of achievement in the arts, were both Book-of-the-Month Club best-sellers. In 1989, Boorstin, a graduate of Harvard, Yale, and Oxford, received the National Book Award for Distinguished Contributions to American Letters. His latest publication is *The Daniel J. Boorstin Reader* (1995).

One of the most interesting and characteristic features of democracy is, of course, the difficulty of defining it. And this difficulty has been compounded in the United States, where we have been giving new meanings to almost everything. It is, therefore, especially easy for anyone to say that democracy in America has failed.

"Democracy," according to political scientists, usually describes a form of government by the people, either directly or through their elected representatives. But I prefer to describe a democratic society as one which is governed by a spirit of equality and dominated by the desire to equalize, to give everything to everybody. In the United States the characteristic wealth and skills and know-how and optimism of our country have dominated this quest.

My first and overshadowing proposition is that our problems arise not so much from our failures as from our successes. Of course no success is complete; only death is final. But we have probably come closer to attaining our professed objectives than any other society of comparable size and extent, and it is from this that our peculiarly American problems arise.

The use of technology to democratize our daily life has given a quite new shape to our hopes. In this final chapter I will explore some of the consequences of democracy, not for government but for experience. What are the consequences for everybody every day of this effort to democratize life in America? And especially the consequences of our fantastic success in industry and technology and in invention?

5 There have been at least four of these consequences. I begin with what I call *attenuation,* which means the thinning out or the flattening of experience. We might call this the democratizing of experience. It might otherwise be described as the decline of poignancy. One of the consequences of our success in technology, of our wealth, of our energy and our imagination, has been the removal of distinctions, not just between people but between everything and everything else, between every place and every other place, between every time and every other time. For example, television removes the distinction between being here and being there. And the same kind of process, of thinning out, of removing distinctions, has appeared in one area after another of our lives.

For instance, in the seasons. One of the great unheralded achievements of American civilization was the rise of transportation and refrigeration, the development of techniques of canning and preserving meat, vegetables, and fruits in such a way that it became possible to enjoy strawberries in winter, to enjoy fresh meat at seasons when the meat was not slaughtered, to thin out the difference between the diet of winter and the diet of summer. There are many unsung heroic stories in this effort.

One of them, for example, was the saga of Gustavus Swift in Chicago. In order to make fresh meat available at a relatively low price to people all over the country, it was necessary to be able to transport it from the West, where the cattle were raised, to the Eastern markets and the cities where population was concentrated. Gustavus Swift found the railroad companies unwilling to manufacture refrigerator cars. They were afraid that, if refrigeration was developed, the cattle would be butchered in the West and then transported in a more concentrated form than when the cattle had to be carried live. The obvious consequence, they believed, would be to reduce the amount of freight. So they refused to develop the refrigerator car. Gustavus Swift went ahead and developed it, only to find that he had more cars than he had use for. The price of fresh meat went down in the Eastern cities, and Gustavus Swift had refrigerator cars on his hands. He then sent agents to the South and to other parts of the country, and tried to encourage people to raise produce which had to be carried in refrigerator cars. One of the consequences of this was the development of certain strains of fruit and vegetables, especially of fruit, which would travel well. And Georgia became famous for the peaches which were grown partly as a result of Swift's efforts to encourage people to raise something that he could carry in his refrigerator cars.

There were other elements in this story which we may easily forget—for example, how central heating and air conditioning have affected our attitude toward the seasons, toward one time of year or another. Nowadays visitors from abroad note that wherever they are in our country, it is not unusual to find that in winter it is often too warm indoors, and in summer, often too cool.

But the development of central heating during the latter part of the nineteenth century had other, less obvious consequences. For example, as people built high-rise apartments in the cities they found it impossible to have a fireplace in every room. You could not construct a high building with hundreds of apartments and have enough room for all the chimneys. So central heating was developed and this became a characteristic of city life. As central heating was developed it was necessary to have a place to put the machinery, and the machinery went in the cellar. But formerly people, even in the cities, had used their cellars to store fruit and vegetables over the winter. When the basement was heated by a furnace, of course it was no longer possible to store potatoes or other vegetables or fruit there. This increased the market for fresh fruits and vegetables that were brought in from truck farms just outside the cities or by refrigerator cars from greater distances. And this was another way of accelerating the tendency toward equalizing the seasons and equalizing the diet of people all over the country.

10 Also important in attenuating experience was the development of what I would call homogenized space, especially the development of vertical space as a place to live in. There is a great deal less difference between living on the thirty-fifth floor and living on the fortieth floor of an apartment building than there is between living in a house in the middle of a block and living on the corner. The view is pretty much the same as you go up in the air. Vertical space is much more homogenized, and as we live in vertical space more and more, we live in places where "where we are" makes much less difference than it used to.

An important element in this which has been a product of American technology is, of course, glass. We forget that the innovations in the production of glass resulting in large sheets which you could look through was an achievement largely of American technology in the nineteenth century. Of course, one by-product was the development of the technology of bottling, which is related to some of the levelings-out of the seasons which I mentioned before in relation to food. But we forget that when we admire those old leaded-glass windows which we see in medieval or early modern buildings, what we are admiring is the inability of people to produce plate glass.

When a large plate of glass became technologically possible, this affected daily life in the United States. It affected merchandising, for example, because the "show window" became possible in which you could, with a relatively unobstructed view, display garments and other large objects in a way to make them appealing to people who passed by. But glass was also important in producing one of the main characteristics of modern American architecture—an architecture in which there is relatively less difference between the indoors and the outdoors than elsewhere. And that is one of the great functions of glass in modern architecture.

Along with the attenuation of places and time comes the attenuation of occasions and events. One of the more neglected aspects of modern technology is what I have called the rise of "repeatable experience." It used to be thought that one of the characteristics of life, one of the things that distinguished being alive from being dead, was the uniqueness of the individual moment. Something happened which could never happen again. If you missed it then, you were out of luck. But the growth of popular photography, which we can trace from about 1888 when Kodak #1 went on the market, began to allow everybody to make his own experience repeatable. If you had not seen this baby when he was so cute, you could still see him that way right now if you were so unlucky as to be in the living room with the parents who wanted to show you. Kodak #1 was a great achievement and was the beginning of our taking for granted that there was such a thing as a repeatable experience.

The phonograph, of course, beginning about 1877, created new opportunities to repeat audible experience. If you want to hear the voice of Franklin Delano Roosevelt now, you can hear him on a record. At the opening of the Woodrow Wilson Center for International Scholars at the Smithsonian Institution in 1971, part of the dedicating ceremony was the playing of a record with the voice of Woodrow Wilson. It was not a very warm voice, but it was identifiable and distinctive. The growth of the phonograph, then, has accustomed us to the fact that experience is not a one-time thing.

15 When we watch the Winter Olympics in our living room and see the ski jumper in the seventy-meter jump who makes a mistake or who performs very well, we can see the same performance just a minute later with all the failures and successes pointed out. Is instant replay the last stage in the technology of repeatable experience?

In the attenuating of events there is another element which I call the "pseudo-event." As more and more of the events which have public notice are planned in advance, as the accounts of them are made available before they happen, then it becomes the responsibility of the event to live up to its reputation. In this way the spontaneity of experience, the unpredictableness of experience, dissolves and disappears. The difference between the present and the future becomes less and less.

Another aspect of this is what I have called the "neutralization of risks," a result of the rise of insurance. For insurance, too, is a way of reducing the difference between the future and the present. You reduce risks by assuring yourself that if your house burns down, at least you will have the money so you can rebuild it. In this sense, insurance, and especially casualty insurance, provides a way of thinning out the difference between present and future, removing the suspense and the risk of experience.

What have been the everyday consequences of the democratizing of property for our experience of property? In his classic defense of property in his essay *On Civil Government* (1690), John Locke argued that because property is the product of the mixing of a person's labor with an object, no government has the right to take it without his consent. This simplistic conception of property has dominated a great deal of political and economic thinking. It was prominent in the thinking of the authors of the Declaration of Independence and of the Founding Fathers of the Constitution. It was based on a simpler society where there was something poignant and characteristic about the experience of ownership. Owning meant the right to exclude people. You had the pleasure of possession.

But what has happened to property in our society? Of course, the most important new form of property in modern American life is corporate property: shares of stock in a corporation. And the diffusion of the ownership of shares is one of the most prominent features of American life. There are companies like AT&T, for example, which have as many as a million stockholders. What does it mean to be a stockholder? You are a lucky person. You own property and you have some shares. So what? One doesn't need to be rich or even middle-class in this country to own shares of stock. But very few of my friends who own shares of stock know precisely what it means or what their legal powers are as stockholders. They are solicited to send in their proxies—by somebody who has a special interest in getting them to vote for something or other. They feel very little pleasure of control; they don't have the sense of wreaking themselves on any object. Yet this—a share of stock—is the characteristic and most important form of property in modern times. This property, too, is attenuated.

20 Other developments in American life concerning property have had a similar effect. For example, installment and credit buying. This phenomenon first grew in connection with the wide marketing of the sewing machine and then in relation to the cash register, but its efflorescence has come with the automobile. When it became necessary to sell millions of automobiles—and necessary in order to keep the machinery of our society going to sell them to people who could not afford to lay out the full cost of an automobile—it was necessary to find ways of financing their purchases. Installment and credit buying was developed. One of the results was that people became increasingly puzzled over whether they did or did not (and if so in what sense) own their automobile. Of course, it is not uncommon for people to divest themselves of their physical control of an object like an automobile or a color television set before they have really acquired full ownership—and then to enter on another ambiguous venture of part ownership.

Another aspect of this is the rise of franchising: the development of what I would call the "semi-independent businessman." In the United States today, between 35 percent and 50 percent of all retail merchandising is done through franchised outlets. Well, of course, we all know what a franchised outlet is; a typical example would be a McDonald's hamburger stand or any other outlet in which the person who is in control of the shop has been authorized to use a nationally advertised name like Midas Mufflers or Colonel Sanders' Kentucky Fried Chicken. He is then instructed in the conduct of his business. He must meet certain standards in order to be allowed to continue to advertise as a Holiday Inn or Howard Johnson or whatever. And he is in business "for himself." Now, what does that mean? If you go into a franchised outlet and you find the hamburger unsatisfactory, what can you do? Whom would you complain to? The man who runs the shop has received his instructions and his materials from the people who have franchised him. It is not his fault. And, of course, it's not the fault of the people at the center who franchised him, because the shop is probably badly run by the franchisee.

This phenomenon grew out of the needs of the automobile because in order to sell Fords or any other makes, it was necessary to have an outlet which would take continuous responsibility for stocking parts. Then the purchaser could replace that part at the outlet where he had purchased the car. After automobile franchising came the franchising of filling stations. People wanted some assurance about the quality of the fuel they put in their cars; they were given this by the identification of what they purchased with some nationally advertised brand in which they had confidence.

Now, perhaps the most important example of attenuation, of the decline of poignancy in our experience in relation to property, is so obvious and so universal that it has hardly been discussed. That is packaging. Until relatively recently if you went into a store to buy coffee, you would have to bring a container to the grocery store, and the grocer would ladle out the coffee to you.

Packaging began to develop in this country after the Civil War. In a sense it was a by-product of the Civil War because the necessities of the war (especially the need to package flour) produced certain innovations which were important. And later there were decisive, although what seem to us rather trivial, innovations. For example, the invention of the folding box was important. Until there was a way to make boxes which could be transported and stored compactly, it was impossible or impractical to use them for industrial purposes. The folding box and certain improvements in the paper bag, such as the paper bag that had a square bottom so that it could stand up, and on the side of which you could print an advertisement—these were American inventions.

25 If we will risk seeming pompous or pedantic, we can say that the most important consequences of packaging have been epistemological. They have had to do with the nature of knowledge and they have especially had the effect of confusing us about what knowledge is, and what's real, about what's form and what's substance. When you think about a Winston cigarette, you don't think about the tobacco inside the cigarette. You think about the package. And in one area after another of American life, the form and the content become confused, and the form becomes that which dominates our consciousness. One area perhaps in which this has ceased to be true, happily or otherwise, is the area which I have always thought of as an aspect of packaging—namely, clothing. In the

United States we have developed ready-made clothing, too, in such a way as to obscure the differences of social class and even of sex.

All around us we see attenuation—as our technology has succeeded, as we have tried to make everything available to everybody. The very techniques we use in preparing our food, in transporting our food, in controlling the climate and temperature of the rooms we live in, the shapes of the buildings in which we do business and reside, the ways we look at past experiences—in all these ways our experience becomes attenuated. As we democratize experience, the poignancy of the moment, of the season, of the control of the object, of the spontaneous event, declines.

Now to a second consequence of the success of our technology for our daily experience. This is what I would call the *decline of congregation.* Or it might be called a new segregation. This is the consequence of increasingly organized and centralized sources of anything and everything. Example: Rebecca at the well.[1] When I wrote an article for the issue of *Life* magazine which was intended to celebrate the twenty-fifth anniversary of the introduction of television in this country, I entitled the article at first "Rebecca at the TV Set." But my friends at *Life* said, "Rebecca who?" Deferring to their greater, wider knowledge of American life and of the literariness of the American people, instead we called it simply "The New Segregation."

When Rebecca lived in her village and needed to get water for the household, she went to the well. At the well she met the other women of the village; she heard the gossip; she met her fiancé there, as a matter of fact. And then what happened? With the progress of democracy and technology, running water was introduced; and Rebecca stayed in the kitchenette of her eighth-floor apartment. She turned the faucet on and got the water out of the faucet; she didn't have to go to the well any more. She had only the telephone to help her collect gossip and she would have to find other ways to meet her fiancé. This is a parable of the problem of centralizing sources of everything.

The growth of centralized plumbing was itself, of course, a necessary by-product of the development of the skyscraper and the concentration of population in high buildings. You had to have effective sanitary facilities. But we forget other features of this development. Even those of us who have never made much use of the old "privy" know that the privy characteristically had more than one hole in it. Why was this? The plural facility was not peculiar simply to the privy; it was also found in the sanitary arrangements of many older buildings, including some of the grandest remaining medieval structures. The development of centralized plumbing led to privatizing; "privy" was the wrong word for the old facility. The privatizing of the bodily functions made them less sociable. People engaged in them in private.

30 The most dramatic example today of the privatizing of experience by centralizing a facility is, of course, television. We could start with the newspaper, for that matter. The town crier communicated the news to people in their presence. If you wanted to hear it you had to be there, or talk to somebody

[1] Rebecca . . . well: see Genesis 24.

else who was there when he brought the news. But as the newspaper developed, with inexpensive printing, the messages were brought to you and you could look at them privately as you sat by yourself at breakfast. Television is perhaps one of the most extreme examples of the decline of congregation. Until the development of television, if you wanted to see a play you had to go out to a theater; if you wanted to hear a concert you had to go to a concert hall. These performances were relatively rare. They were special events. But with the coming of television, everybody acquired his private theater. Rebecca had her theater in her kitchen. She no longer needed to go out for entertainment.

The centralized source, the centralizing of the source, then, led to the isolating of the consumer. Of course, much was gained by this. But one of the prices paid was the decline of congregation—congregation being the drawing together of people where they could enjoy and react to and respond to the reactions and feelings of their fellows.

There is a third consequence of our technological success in democratic America, which I would call the new determinism, or *the rising sense of momentum.* Technology has had a deep and pervasive effect on our attitude toward history, and especially on the citizen's attitude toward his control over the future. In the seventeenth century the Puritans spoke about Providence; that was their characteristic way of describing the kind of control that God exercised over futurity. In the nineteenth century, when people became more scientifically minded, they still retained some notion of divine foresight in the form of the concept of destiny or mission or purpose. But in our time in this country we have developed a different kind of approach toward futurity; and this is what I would call the sense of momentum.

Momentum in physics is the product of a body's mass and its linear velocity. Increasing scale and speed of operation increase the momentum. One of the characteristics of our technology and especially of our most spectacular successes has been to increase this sense of momentum. I will mention three obvious examples. It happens that each of these developments came, too, as a result of overwhelming international pressure. When such pressures added to the forces at work inside the nation, in each case they produced a phenomenon of great mass and velocity which became very difficult to stop.

The first example is, of course, atomic research. The large-scale concerted efforts in this country to build an atomic bomb began and were accelerated at the time of World War II because of rumors that the Nazis were about to succeed in nuclear fission. When this information became available, national resources were massed and organized in an unprecedented fashion; futurity was scheduled and groups were set to work in all parts of the continent exploring different possible ways of finding the right form of uranium or of some other element. And the search for the first atomic chain reaction, which was accomplished at my University of Chicago, went on.

One of the more touching human aspects of this story is the account, now well chronicled by several historians, of the frantic efforts of the atomic scientists, the people who had been most instrumental in getting this process started

(Albert Einstein, Leo Szilard, and James Franck,[2] among others), when they saw that the atomic bomb was about to become possible, to persuade the President of the United States either not to use the bomb or to use it only in a demonstration in the uninhabited mid-Pacific. Such a use, they urged, would so impress the enemy with the horrors of the bomb that he would surrender, eliminating the need for us to use the bomb against a live target. They pursued this purpose—trying to put the brakes on military use of the bomb—with a desperation that even exceeded the energy they had shown in developing the bomb. But, of course, they had no success.

They could develop the bomb, but they couldn't stop it. Why? There were many reasons, including President Truman's reasonable belief that use of the bomb could in the long run save the hundreds of thousands of Japanese and American lives that would have been lost in an invasion, and also would shorten the war. But surely one reason was that there had already been too much investment in the bomb. Billions of dollars had gone into the making of it. People were organized all over the country in various ways. It was impossible to stop.

Another example of this kind of momentum is the phenomenon of space exploration. I happen to be an enthusiast for space exploration, so by describing this momentum I do not mean to suggest that I think the space enterprise itself has not been a good thing. Nevertheless, as a historian I am increasingly impressed by the pervasive phenomenon of momentum in our time. Billions of dollars have been spent in developing the machinery for going off to the moon or going then to Mars or elsewhere. The mass of the operation has been enormous. The velocity of it is enormous, and it becomes virtually impossible to stop. The recent problem with the SST is a good example. For when any enterprise in our society has reached a certain scale, the consequences in unemployment and in dislocation of the economy are such that it becomes every year more difficult to cease doing what we are already doing.

A third example, more in the area of institutions, is foreign aid: the international pressures to give foreign aid to one country or another. We have an enormous mass of wealth being invested, a great velocity with lots of people going off all over the world and performing this operation of giving aid, and it becomes almost impossible to stop it. The other countries resent the decline of aid and consider it a hostile act, even though they might not have felt that way if we hadn't started the aid in the first place. Foreign aid is, I think, the most characteristic innovation in foreign policy in this century.

Each of these three enterprises illustrates the attitude of the American citizen in the later twentieth century toward his control over experience. Increasingly, the citizen comes to feel that events are moving, and moving so fast with such velocity and in such mass that he has very little control. The sense of momentum itself becomes possible only because of our success in achieving these

[2] Leo Szilard, James Franck: The Hungarian-American physicist Leo Szilard (1898–1964) developed the idea of the nuclear chain reaction; the German-American quantum physicist James Franck (1882–1964) was awarded the Nobel Prize in 1925.

large purposes which no other democratic society, no other society before us, had even imagined.

40 Now, what does this bring us to? Before I come to my fourth and concluding point on the ways in which the successes of democracy have affected our experience, I would like briefly to recall some of the remedies that have been suggested for the ills of democracy and the problems of democracy in the past. Al Smith[3] once said, "All the ills of democracy can be cured by more democracy." I must confess, though I admire Al Smith for some of his enterprises, the Empire State Building for example, I think he was on the wrong track here. In fact, I would take an almost contrary position. Even at the risk of seeming flip, I might sum up the democratic paradoxes that I have been describing: "Getting there is *all* the fun."

Is there a law of democratic impoverishment? Is it possible that while *democratizing* enriches experience, *democracy* dilutes experience?

Example: photography. Before the invention of photography, it was a remarkable experience to see an exact likeness of the Sphinx or of Notre Dame or of some exotic animal or to see a portrait of an ancestor. Then, as photography was publicized in the 1880's and thoroughly popularized in this century, it opened up a fantastic new range of experience for everybody. Suddenly people were able to see things they had never been able to see before. And then what happened? Everyone had a camera, or two or three cameras; and everywhere he went he took pictures and when he came home he had to find a victim, somebody to show the pictures to. And this became more and more difficult.

While photography was being introduced, it was life-enriching and vista-opening; but once it was achieved, once everybody had a camera, the people were looking in their cameras instead of looking at the sight they had gone to see. It had an attenuating effect. A picture came to mean less and less, simply because people saw pictures everywhere. And the experience of being there also somehow meant less because the main thing people saw everywhere was the inside of their viewfinders, and their concern over their lens cap and finding the proper exposure made it hard for them to notice what was going on around them at the moment.

Another example is, of course, the phonograph. Has the phonograph—in its universal late-twentieth-century uses—necessarily made people more appreciative of music? In the 1920's when I was raised in Tulsa, Oklahoma, I had never heard an opera, nor had I really heard any classical music properly performed by an orchestra. But in our living room we had a windup Victrola, and I heard Galli-Curci singing arias from *Rigoletto,* and I heard Caruso, and I heard some symphonies, and it was fantastic. And then hi-fi came and everybody had a phonograph, a hi-fi machine or a little transistor radio which you could carry with you and hear music any time.

---

[3] Al Smith: The dominant political figure in New York State Democratic politics, Al Smith (1873–1944) ran for president on the Democratic ticket in 1928; he was defeated by Herbert Hoover.

45 Today when I walk into the elevator in an office building, it is not impossible that I will hear Beethoven or Verdi. Sitting in the airplane I hear Mozart coming out of the public-address system. Wherever we go we hear music whether we want to hear it or not, whether we are in the mood for it or not. It becomes an everywhere, all-the-time thing. The experience is attenuated.

And one of the most serious consequences of all this, finally, is the attenuation of community itself. What holds people together? What has held people together in the past? For the most part it has been their sense of humanity, their pleasure in the presence of one another, their feeling for another person's expression, the sound of a voice, the look on his or her face. But the kind of community I describe increasingly becomes attenuated. People are trying to enjoy the community all by themselves.

We are led to certain desperate quests in American life. These, the byproducts of our success, are clues to the vitality and energy of our country, to the quest for novelty to keep life interesting and vistas open, to the quest for community and the quest for autonomy. Can we inoculate ourselves against these perils of our technological success? Samuel Butler[4] once said, "If I die prematurely, at any rate I shall be saved from being bored by my own success." Our problem, too, is partly that.

And now a fourth characteristic of the relation of technology to democracy in our time: *the belief in solutions.* One of the most dangerous popular fallacies—nourished by American history and by some of our most eloquent and voluble patriots—is the notion that democracy is attainable. There is a subtle difference between American democratic society and many earlier societies in the extent to which their ideals could be attained. The objectives of other societies have for the most part been definable and attainable. Aristocracy and monarchy do present attainable ideals. Even totalitarianism presents objectives which can be attained in the sense in which the objectives of democracy never can be.

This nation has been a place of renewal, of new beginnings for nations and for man. Vagueness has been a national resource: the vagueness of the continent, the mystery of our resources, the vagueness of our social classes, the misty miasma of our hopes.

50 Our society has been most distinctively a way of reaching for rather than of finding. American democracy, properly speaking, has been a process and not a product, a quest and not a discovery. But a great danger which has been nourished by our success in technology has been the belief in solutions. For technological problems there *are* solutions. It is possible to set yourself the task of developing an economic and workable internal-combustion engine, a prefabricated house, or a way of reaching the moon. Technological problems are capable of solutions.

We are inclined, then, using the technological problem as our prototype, to believe that somehow democracy itself is a solution, a dissolving of the human condition. But we should have learned, and even the history of technology—especially the history of technology in our democratic society—should have taught us otherwise.

---

[4] Samuel Butler: English writer (1835–1902) and satirist.

In human history in the long run there are no solutions, only problems. This is what I have suggested in my description of "self-liquidating" ideals. And the examples are all around us—in our effort to create a pluralistic society by assimilating and Americanizing people, in our effort to give everybody an uncrowded wilderness vacation, in our effort to find an exciting new model each year.

Every seeming solution is a new problem. When you democratize the speedy automobile and give everybody an automobile, the result is a traffic jam; and this is the sense in which the "solution" of technological problems presents us with obstacles to the fulfillment of what is human in our society. When we think about American democratic society, then, we must learn not to think about a condition, but about a process; not about democracy, but about the quest for democracy, which we might call "democratizing."

The most distinctive feature of our system is not a system, but a quest, not a neat arrangement of men and institutions, but a flux. What other society has ever committed itself to so tantalizing, so fulfilling, so frustrating a community enterprise?

To prepare ourselves for this view of American democracy there are two sides to our personal need. One is on the side of prudence and wisdom; the other on the side of poetry and imagination.

On the side of prudence, there is a need for a sense of history. Only by realizing the boundaries that we have been given can we discover how to reach beyond them. Only so can we have the wisdom not to mistake passing fads for great movements, not to mistake the fanaticisms of a few for the deep beliefs of the many, not to mistake fashion for revolution. This wisdom is necessary if we are to secure sensibly the benefits of a free society for those who have for whatever reason been deprived of its benefits. We were not born yesterday, nor was the nation. And between the day before yesterday and yesterday, crucial events have happened. We can discover these and come to terms with them only through history. As Pascal[5] said, "It is only by knowing our condition that we can transcend it." Our technology brings us the omnipresent present. It dulls our sense of history, and if we are not careful it can destroy it.

We in the U.S.A. are always living in an age of transition. Yet we have tended to believe that our present is always the climax of history, even though American history shows that the climax is always in the future. By keeping suspense alive, we can prepare ourselves for the shocks of change.

And finally, on the side of poetry and imagination, how do we keep alive the spirit of adventure, what I would call the exploring spirit? This should be the easiest because it is the most traditional of our achievements and efforts. We must remember that we live in a new world. We must keep alive the exploring spirit. We must not sacrifice the infinite promise of the unknown, of man's unfulfilled possibilities in the universe's untouched mysteries, for the cozy satisfactions of predictable, statistical benefits. Space exploration is a symbol.

---

[5] Pascal: Blaise Pascal (1623–1662), French mathematician, churchman, and philosopher, a forerunner of existentialist thought.

Recently I had the pleasure of talking with Thor Heyerdahl, the *Kon Tiki* man, whose latest venture was the Ra expedition, in which he explored the possibilities of men having come from Egypt or elsewhere in the Mediterranean to this continent long ago in boats made of reeds. He and his crew, to test their hypothesis, actually crossed the Atlantic in a reed boat. And as I talked to Thor Heyerdahl about the Ra expedition, I said that it must have been a terrible feeling of risk when you suddenly left the sight of land and got out into the open sea. It seemed to me that the fear and perils of the open sea would be the greatest. Thor Heyerdahl said not at all: the great dangers, the dangers of shoals and rocks, existed along the shore. The wonderful sense of relief, he observed, came when he went out on the ocean where there was openness all around, although also high waves and strong currents. The promise of American democracy, I suggest, depends on our ability to stay at sea, to work together in community while we all reach to the open horizon.

LEARNING MORE

1. A large chunk of this essay is devoted to examples of what the writer calls *attenuation*, something he defines in par. 5. Since so much hangs on this concept, it will be useful to look the word up and consider its usual meanings, as well as the one especially employed by Boorstin.
2. Boorstin depends heavily on examples to substantiate his analysis. Find out more about Gustavus Swift and the Kodak camera on the *Ideas Across Time* website.

QUESTIONING THE TEXT

1. In his opening paragraph, Boorstin says it's easy to say democracy in America has failed because democracy is so hard to define. Having read Boorstin's essay, explain what you think Boorstin believes—that is, does he believe democracy in America has failed, or does he think it has succeeded? Be sure to marshal sufficient evidence to support your view.
2. Our problems, Boorstin says, derive from our successes. Choose two or three successes that Boorstin isolates, and indicate how these have led to problems.
3. What do you think Boorstin means by "experience" in par. 4?
4. How does the high-rise apartment building exemplify the problems that follow from the marriage of democracy and technology?
5. What does packaging have to do with epistemology (see pars. 24–25)?
6. How does reference to Rebecca (pars. 27–28) serve Boorstin's argument?
7. Can you think of additional examples of the problematic consequences of the success of democracy and technology? Can you think of examples of the success of democracy and technology that are not subject to the problematic consequences Boorstin illustrates?
8. Do you find Boorstin's examples persuasive? Explain.

ANALYZING THE WRITER'S CRAFT

1. What is Boorstin's thesis, and where is it stated?
2. Boorstin advances his thesis by definition and illustration. Why do you think he finds it necessary to define his main propositions? Why do you think he uses so many illustrations? How he could have made his point differently?
3. What do you think is Boorstin's strongest example? Why? What do you think is Boorstin's weakest example? Why?
4. Why do you think that, before getting to his fourth consequence, Boorstin takes a detour starting in par. 40 to discuss some remedies often proposed for the ills of democracy?
5. Explain why you do or do not find Boorstin's conclusion to be effective.

MAKING CONNECTIONS

1. Do you think Boorstin embraces the points of view of both St. John de Crevecoeur (Chapter 1, pp. 22–27) and Alexis de Tocqueville (Chapter 6, pp. 458–462), or does he lean more toward one or the other?
2. Does Boorstin anticipate the impact of technology on our way of thinking that Sherry Turkle studies (Chapter 3, pp. 220–225)?
3. Does Susan Sontag's history of the movies (Chapter 7, pp. 604–610) display the influence of Boorstin's analysis?

FORMULATING IDEAS FOR WRITING

1. On the basis of this essay, would you say that Boorstin is a champion of democracy or one of those who think democracy in America has failed? Discuss.
2. Support or take issue with Boorstin's contention that the successes of democracy and technology have only led to more problems.
3. What do you think about Boorstin's enthusiasm for American democracy as a never-fulfilled quest, an endless *process?* Is this a persuasive analysis of your experience of life in the United States? Do you find the idea of always seeking and never finding attractive? Discuss.
4. Boorstin and Alexis de Tocqueville (Chapter 6, pp. 458–462) both deplore the excessive individualism, or isolation, of life in America. They seem to long for, or to value more, some image of community and community life. Is community one of those things everyone favors in the abstract but no one wants actually to experience? Or is it something essential for social and political health? Is community a conservative, aristocratic ideal or a liberal, democratic ideal? Discuss.

The Power of the Powerless (1978)

Vaclav Havel

Perhaps the greatest moral drama of the latter half of the twentieth century occurred in the nations of central and eastern Europe during the final decades of Communism. Few suspected that the years between roughly 1960 and the fall of the Berlin Wall in 1989 were *in fact* the final decades of Communism. On the contrary, the possibilities for change even within the Communist system seemed, to most informed observers of the time, to be slim. Precisely because genuine reform seemed so unlikely, the concerted opposition to totalitarianism by a small but remarkable minority riveted the attention both of Communist authorities and of Western observers. This minority—"dissidents," as they were known—exhibited in their actions and their writing qualities that remain rare in public life: honesty, moral (and often physical) courage, and seriousness of thought. From their vantage point, the dissidents were able to speak persuasively about the inestimable value of the mundane features of civil society—and also about how these qualities were threatened not only under Communism but equally in capitalist societies. As we enter the twenty-first century, we can see more clearly that although Communism for the most part differed fundamentally from liberal democracy, in other respects both societies have been equally subject to the relentless forces of modernity, such as secularism, consumerism, mass communication, and the impoverishment of civil life. No writer has explored this terrain with greater insight and clarity than Vaclav Havel. In this selection, written while the author was imprisoned for fostering subversive ideas, the first president of the post-Communist Czech Republic observes in our contemporary condition a moral crisis brought on by "the trivializing temptations of modern civilization." For Havel, the essential integrity of the individual is at risk, and he believes that integrity is the necessary foundation for civil society.

Havel's thoughts about contemporary society carry a unique authority earned not only through his years in jail but also through his modest bravery and self-doubting honesty as the first post-Communist president of the Czech Republic. In power he speaks in the hesitating tones of the common citizen, just as when a common citizen, he spoke with the authority of the nation.

Vaclav (pronounced *vahts-lavf*) Havel was born on October 5, 1936, to a well-to-do family in Prague. After the Communist coup in Czechoslovakia in 1948, the family's property was confiscated, and Havel found himself classified as a "class enemy." His education was blocked by the authorities, and Havel completed high school by working as a lab technician by day and attending school at night. He could not enroll in any liberal arts college and was forced to matriculate in the University of Technology, where he studied economics. Afterward, from 1957–1959, he served two compulsory years in the army. He became interested in the theater and in 1960 became resident writer for the Prague "Theater on the Balustrade," for which he wrote plays in the absurdist tradition, such as his satires of bureaucracy *The Garden Party* (1963) and *The Memorandum* (1965).

When the Soviet invasion of 1968 ended the period of Czech liberalization (known as the "Prague Spring"), Havel's plays were banned; he could find employment only as a laborer at a brewery, loading beer barrels. In 1977, Havel became one of three spokespersons for a protest manifesto, "Charter 77," calling for the fulfillment in Czechoslovakia of the human rights provisions of the Helsinki Accord, to which the nation ostensibly subscribed. For these activities, Havel spent nearly five years in prison between 1977 and 1989. It was at this time that he wrote "The Power of the Powerless" (1978). By the 1980s, he was the undisputed leader of the Czechoslovak human rights movement, and in 1989, he formed a new civic group, the Civic Forum, that spearheaded the "Velvet Revolution," which ended Communism in Czechoslovakia. Havel became the first president of Czechoslovakia in the elections following the fall of Communism. When the Slovak and Czech republics split into two separate nations in 1993, Havel was elected the first president of the new Czech Republic, a position he held until 2003.

The manager of a fruit and vegetable shop places in his window, among the onions and carrots, the slogan: "Workers of the world, unite."[1] Why does he do it? What is he trying to communicate to the world? Is he genuinely enthusiastic about the idea of unity among the workers of the world? Is his enthusiasm so great that he feels an irrepressible impulse to acquaint the public with his ideals? Has he really given more than a moment's thought to how such a unification might occur and what it would mean?

I think it can safely be assumed that the overwhelming majority of shopkeepers never think about the slogans they put in their windows, nor do they use them to express their real opinions. That poster was delivered to our greengrocer from the enterprise headquarters along with the onions and carrots. He put them all into the window simply because it has been done that way for years, because everyone does it, and because that is the way it has to be. If he were to refuse, there could be trouble. He could be reproached for not having the proper "decoration" in his window; someone might even accuse him of disloyalty. He does it because these things must be done if one is to get along in life. It is one of the thousands of details that guarantee him a relatively tranquil life "in harmony with society," as they say.

Obviously the greengrocer is indifferent to the semantic[2] content of the slogan on exhibit; he does not put the slogan in his window from any personal

[1] "Workers . . . unite": Karl Marx closed *The Communist Manifesto* (1848) with this slogan; see Chapter 4, pp. 264–273.

[2] semantic: relating to meaning; that is, what the sign actually says.

desire to acquaint the public with the ideal it expresses. This, of course, does not mean that his action has no motive or significance at all, or that the slogan communicates nothing to anyone. The slogan is really a *sign,* and as such it contains a subliminal but very definite message. Verbally, it might be expressed this way: "I, the greengrocer XY, live here and I know what I must do. I behave in the manner expected of me. I can be depended upon and am beyond reproach. I am obedient and therefore I have the right to be left in peace." This message, of course, has an addressee: it is directed above, to the greengrocer's superior, and at the same time it is a shield that protects the greengrocer from potential informers. The slogan's real meaning, therefore, is rooted firmly in the greengrocer's existence. It reflects his vital interests. But what are those vital interests?

Let us take note: if the greengrocer had been instructed to display the slogan, "I am afraid and therefore unquestioningly obedient," he would not be nearly as indifferent to its semantics, even though the statement would reflect the truth. The greengrocer would be embarrassed and ashamed to put such an unequivocal statement of his own degradation in the shop window, and quite naturally so, for he is a human being and thus has a sense of his own dignity. To overcome this complication, his expression of loyalty must take the form of a sign which, at least on its textual surface, indicates a level of disinterested conviction. It must allow the greengrocer to say, "What's wrong with the workers of the world uniting?" Thus the sign helps the greengrocer to conceal from himself the low foundations of his obedience, at the same time concealing the low foundations of power. It hides them behind the façade of something high. And that something is *ideology.*

5 Ideology is a specious[3] way of relating to the world. It offers human beings the illusion of an identity, of dignity, and of morality while making it easier for them to *part* with them. As the repository of something "supra-personal" and objective, it enables people to deceive their conscience and conceal their true position and their inglorious *modus vivendi,*[4] both from the world and from themselves. It is a very pragmatic, but at the same time an apparently dignified, way of legitimizing what is above, below, and on either side. It is directed towards people and towards God. It is a veil behind which human beings can hide their own "fallen existence," their trivialization, and their adaptation to the status quo. It is an excuse that everyone can use, from the greengrocer, who conceals his fear of losing his job behind an alleged interest in the unification of the workers of the world, to the highest functionary, whose interest in staying in power can be cloaked in phrases about service to the working class. The primary excusatory function of ideology, therefore, is to provide people, both as victims and pillars of the post-totalitarian system, with the illusion that the system is in harmony with the human order and the order of the universe.

The smaller a dictatorship and the less stratified by modernization the society under it, the more directly the will of the dictator can be exercised. In other

[3] specious: false.

[4] *modus vivendi:* a working arrangement.

words, the dictator can employ more or less naked discipline, avoiding the complex processes of relating to the world and of self-justification which ideology involves. But the more complex the mechanisms of power become, the larger and more stratified the society they embrace, and the longer they have operated historically, the more individuals must be connected to them from outside, and the greater the importance attached to the ideological excuse. It acts as a kind of bridge between the regime and the people, across which the regime approaches the people and the people approach the regime. This explains why ideology plays such an important role in the post-totalitarian system: that complex machinery of units, hierarchies, transmission belts, and indirect instruments of manipulation which ensure in countless ways the integrity of the regime, leaving nothing to chance, would be quite simply unthinkable without ideology acting as its all-embracing excuse and as the excuse for each of its parts.

We have seen that the real meaning of the greengrocer's slogan has nothing to do with what the text of the slogan actually says. Even so, this real meaning is quite clear and generally comprehensible because the code is so familiar: the greengrocer declares his loyalty (and he can do no other if his declaration is to be accepted) in the only way the regime is capable of hearing; that is, by accepting the prescribed *ritual,* by accepting appearances as reality, by accepting the given rules of the game. In doing so, however, he has himself become a player in the game, thus making it possible for the game to go on, for it to exist in the first place.

If ideology was originally a bridge between the system and the individual as an individual, then the moment he or she steps on to this bridge it becomes at the same time a bridge between the system and the individual as a component of the system. That is, if ideology originally facilitated (by acting outwardly) the constitution of power by serving as a psychological excuse, then from the moment that excuse is accepted, it constitutes power inwardly, becoming an active component of that power. It begins to function as the principal instrument of ritual communication *within* the system of power.

The whole power structure (and we have already discussed its physical articulation) could not exist at all if there were not a certain "metaphysical" order binding all its components together, interconnecting them and subordinating them to a uniform method of accountability, supplying the combined operation of all these components with rules of the game, that is, with certain regulations, limitations, and legalities. This metaphysical order is fundamental to, and standard throughout, the entire power structure; it integrates its communication system and makes possible the internal exchange and transfer of information and instructions. It is rather like a collection of traffic signals and directional signs, giving the process shape and structure. This metaphysical order guarantees the inner coherence of the totalitarian power structure. It is the glue holding it together, its binding principle, the instrument of its discipline. Without this glue the structure as a totalitarian structure would vanish; it would disintegrate into individual atoms chaotically colliding with one another in their unregulated particular interests and inclinations. The entire pyramid of totalitarian power, deprived of the element that binds it together, would collapse in upon itself, as it were, in a kind of material implosion.

As the interpretation of reality by the power structure, ideology is always subordinated ultimately to the interests of the structure. Therefore, it has a natural tendency to disengage itself from reality, to create a world of appearances, to become ritual. In societies where there is public competition for power and therefore public control of that power, there also exists quite naturally public control of the way that power legitimates itself ideologically. Consequently, in such conditions there are always certain correctives that effectively prevent ideology from abandoning reality altogether. Under totalitarianism, however, these correctives disappear, and thus there is nothing to prevent ideology from becoming more and more removed from reality, gradually turning into what it has already become in the post-totalitarian system: a world of appearances, a mere ritual, a formalized language deprived of semantic contact with reality and transformed into a system of ritual signs that replace reality with pseudo-reality.

10 Yet, as we have seen, ideology becomes at the same time an increasingly important component of power, a pillar providing it with both excusatory legitimacy and an inner coherence. As this aspect grows in importance, and as it gradually loses touch with reality, it acquires a peculiar but very real strength. It becomes reality itself, albeit a reality altogether self-contained, one that on certain levels (chiefly inside the power structure) may have even greater weight than reality as such. Increasingly, the virtuosity of the ritual becomes more important than the reality hidden behind it. The significance of phenomena no longer derives from the phenomena themselves, but from their *locus*[5] as concepts in the ideological context. Reality does not shape theory, but rather the reverse. Thus power gradually draws closer to ideology than it does to reality; it draws its strength from theory and becomes entirely dependent on it. This inevitably leads, of course, to a paradoxical result: rather than theory, or rather ideology, serving power, power begins to serve ideology. It is as though ideology had appropriated power from power, as though it had become dictator itself. It then appears that theory itself, ritual itself, ideology itself, makes decisions that affect people, and not the other way around.

If ideology is the principal guarantee of the inner consistency of power, it becomes at the same time an increasingly important guarantee of its *continuity.* Whereas succession to power in classical dictatorships is always a rather complicated affair (the pretenders having nothing to give their claims reasonable legitimacy, thereby forcing them always to resort to confrontations of naked power), in the post-totalitarian system power is passed on from person to person, from clique to clique, and from generation to generation in an essentially more regular fashion. In the selection of pretenders, a new "king-maker" takes part: it is ritual legitimation, the ability to rely on ritual, to fulfil it and use it, to allow oneself, as it were, to be borne aloft by it. Naturally, power struggles exist in the post-totalitarian system as well, and most of them are far more brutal than in an open society, for the struggle is not open, regulated by democratic

[5] *locus*: place, location.

rules, and subject to public control, but hidden behind the scenes. (It is difficult to recall a single instance in which the First Secretary of a ruling Communist Party has been replaced without the various military and security forces being placed at least on alert.) This struggle, however, can never (as it can in classical dictatorships) threaten the very essence of the system and its continuity. At most it will shake up the power structure, which will recover quickly precisely because the binding substance—ideology—remains undisturbed. No matter who is replaced by whom, succession is only possible against the backdrop and within the framework of a common ritual. It can never take place by denying that ritual.

Because of this dictatorship of the ritual, however, power becomes clearly *anonymous.* Individuals are almost dissolved in the ritual. They allow themselves to be swept along by it and frequently it seems as though ritual alone carries people from obscurity into the light of power. Is it not characteristic of the post-totalitarian system that, on all levels of the power hierarchy, individuals are increasingly being pushed aside by faceless people, puppets, those uniformed flunkeys of the rituals and routines of power?

The automatic operation of a power structure thus dehumanized and made anonymous is a feature of the fundamental automatism of this system. It would seem that it is precisely the *diktats*[6] of this automatism which select people lacking individual will for the power structure, that it is precisely the *diktat* of the empty phrase which summons to power people who use empty phrases as the best guarantee that the automatism of the post-totalitarian system will continue.

VI

Why in fact did our greengrocer have to put his loyalty on display in the shop window? Had he not already displayed it sufficiently in various internal or semi-public ways? At trade union meetings, after all, he had always voted as he should. He had always taken part in various competitions. He voted in elections like a good citizen. He had even signed the "anti-Charter." Why, on top of all that, should he have to declare his loyalty publicly? After all, the people who walk past his window will certainly not stop to read that, in the greengrocer's opinion, the workers of the world ought to unite. The fact of the matter is, they don't read the slogan at all, and it can be fairly assumed they don't even see it. If you were to ask a woman who had stopped in front of his shop what she saw in the window, she could certainly tell whether or not they had tomatoes today, but it is highly unlikely that she noticed the slogan at all, let alone what it said.

It seems senseless to require the greengrocer to declare his loyalty publicly. But it makes sense nevertheless. People ignore his slogan, but they do so because such slogans are also found in other shop windows, on lamp posts, bulletin boards, in apartment windows, and on buildings; they are everywhere, in fact. They form part of the panorama of everyday life. Of course, while they

[6] *diktats:* decrees.

ignore the details, people are very aware of that panorama as a whole. And what else is the greengrocer's slogan but a small component in that huge backdrop to daily life?

The greengrocer had to put the slogan in his window, therefore, not in the hope that someone might read it or be persuaded by it, but to contribute, along with thousands of other slogans, to the panorama that everyone is very much aware of. This panorama, of course, has a subliminal meaning as well: it reminds people where they are living and what is expected of them. It tells them what everyone else is doing, and indicates to them what they must do as well, if they don't want to be excluded, to fall into isolation, alienate themselves from society, break the rules of the game, and risk the loss of their peace and tranquility and security.

The woman who ignored the greengrocer's slogan may well have hung a similar slogan just an hour before in the corridor of the office where she works. She did it more or less without thinking, just as our greengrocer did, and she could do so precisely because she was doing it against the background of the general panorama and with some awareness of it, that is, against the background of the panorama of which the greengrocer's shop window forms a part. When the greengrocer visits her office, he will not notice her slogan either, just as she failed to notice his. Nevertheless their slogans are mutually dependent: both were displayed with some awareness of the general panorama and, we might say, under its *diktat*. Both, however, assist in the creation of that panorama, and therefore they assist in the creation of that *diktat* as well. The greengrocer and the office worker have both adapted to the conditions in which they live, but in doing so, they help to create those conditions. They do what is done, what is to be done, what must be done, but at the same time—by that very token—they confirm that it must be done in fact. They conform to a particular requirement and in so doing they themselves perpetuate that requirement. Metaphysically speaking, without the greengrocer's slogan the office worker's slogan could not exist, and vice versa. Each proposes to the other that something be repeated and each accepts the other's proposal. Their mutual indifference to each other's slogans is only an illusion: in reality, by exhibiting their slogans, each compels the other to accept the rules of the game and to confirm thereby the power that requires the slogans in the first place. Quite simply, each helps the other to be obedient. Both are objects in a system of control, but at the same time they are its subjects as well. They are both victims of the system and its instruments.

If an entire district town is plastered with slogans that no one reads, it is on the one hand a message from the district secretary to the regional secretary, but it is also something more: a small example of the principle of social *auto-totality* at work. Part of the essence of the post-totalitarian system is that it draws everyone into its sphere of power, not so they may realize themselves as human beings, but so they may surrender their human identity in favour of the identity of the system, that is, so they may become agents of the system's general automatism and servants of its self-determined goals, so they may participate in the common responsibility for it, so they may be pulled into and ensnared by it, like

Faust with Mephistopheles.[7] More than this: so they may create through their involvement a general norm and, thus, bring pressure to bear on their fellow citizens. And further: so they may learn to be comfortable with their involvement, to identify with it as though it were something natural and inevitable and, ultimately, so they may—with no external urging—come to treat any non-involvement as an abnormality, as arrogance, as an attack on themselves, as a form of dropping out of society. By pulling everyone into its power structure, the post-totalitarian system makes everyone instruments of a mutual totality, the auto-totality of society.

Everyone, however, is in fact involved and enslaved, not only the greengrocers but also the prime ministers. Differing positions in the hierarchy merely establish differing degrees of involvement: the greengrocer is involved only to a minor extent, but he also has very little power. The prime minister, naturally, has greater power, but in return he is far more deeply involved. Both, however, are unfree, each merely in a somewhat different way. The real accomplice in this involvement, therefore, is not another person, but the system itself. Position in the power hierarchy determines the degree of responsibility and guilt, but it gives no one unlimited responsibility and guilt, nor does it completely absolve anyone. Thus the conflict between the aims of life and the aims of the system is not a conflict between two socially defined and separate communities; and only a very generalized view (and even that only approximative) permits us to divide society into the rulers and the ruled. Here, by the way, is one of the most important differences between the post-totalitarian system and classical dictatorships, in which this line of conflict can still be drawn according to social class. In the post-totalitarian system, this line runs *de facto*[8] through each person, for everyone in his or her own way is both a victim and a supporter of the system. What we understand by the system is not, therefore, a social order imposed by one group upon another, but rather something which permeates the entire society and is a factor in shaping it, something which may seem impossible to grasp or define (for it is in the nature of a mere principle), but which is expressed by the entire society as an important feature of its life.

20 The fact that human beings have created, and daily create, this self-directed system through which they divest themselves of their innermost identity, is not therefore the result of some incomprehensible misunderstanding of history, nor is it history somehow gone off its rails. Neither is it the product of some diabolical higher will which has decided, for reasons unknown, to torment a portion of humanity in this way. It can happen and did happen only because there is obviously in modern humanity a certain tendency towards the creation, or at least the toleration, of such a system there is obviously something in human beings which responds to this system, something they reflect and accommodate, something within them which paralyses every effort of their better selves to revolt. Human beings are compelled to live within a lie, but they can be compelled to do so only because they are in fact capable of living in this way. Therefore not

[7] Faust with Mephistopheles: Faust gave his soul to the Devil in exchange for absolute knowledge.
[8] *de facto:* in reality.

only does the system alienate humanity, but at the same time alienated humanity supports this system as its own involuntary masterplan, as a degenerate image of its own degeneration, as a record of people's own failure as individuals.

The essential aims of life are present naturally in every person. In everyone there is some longing for humanity's rightful dignity, for moral integrity, for free expression of being and a sense of transcendence over the world of existence. Yet, at the same time, each person is capable, to a greater or lesser degree, of coming to terms with living within the lie. Each person somehow succumbs to a profane trivialization of his or her inherent humanity, and to utilitarianism. In everyone there is some willingness to merge with the anonymous crowd and to flow comfortably along with it down the river of pseudo-life. This is much more than a simple conflict between two identities. It is something far worse: it is a challenge to the very notion of identity itself.

In highly simplified terms, it could be said that the post-totalitarian system has been built on foundations laid by the historical encounter between dictatorship and the consumer society. Is it not true that the far-reaching adaptability to living a lie and the effortless spread of social *auto-totality* have some connection with the general unwillingness of consumption-oriented people to sacrifice some material certainties for the sake of their own spiritual and moral integrity? With their willingness to surrender higher values when faced with the trivializing temptations of modern civilization? With their vulnerability to the attractions of mass indifference? And in the end, is not the greyness and the emptiness of life in the post-totalitarian system only an inflated caricature of modern life in general? And do we not in fact stand (although in the external measures of civilization, we are far behind) as a kind of warning to the West, revealing to it its own latent tendencies?

LEARNING MORE

Vaclav Havel wrote this essay during the time when Czechoslovakia was under Communist rule. How was society organized under Communism? Find out what you can about the "Prague Spring" and "Charter 77." See the *Ideas Across Time* website for useful online links.

QUESTIONING THE TEXT

1. How, according to Havel, is the slogan's "real meaning . . . rooted firmly in the greengrocer's existence" (par. 3)?
2. What is the "primary excusatory function" of ideology (par. 5)?
3. How does ideology act as a bridge between "the regime and the people" and between "the system and the individual" (pars. 6–8)?
4. How does ideology guarantee the continuity of power (par. 11)?
5. Restate par. 14 in your own words.
6. What is "the principle of social auto-totality" (par. 19)?

7. How does the greengrocer, by placing the poster in his window, contribute to his own enslavement?
8. Why do you think Havel refers to the social system he is analyzing as "post-totalitarian"?
9. Do you agree that what Havel has been describing reveals "latent tendencies" in American society (par. 22)?
10. What is the power of the powerless?

ANALYZING THE WRITER'S CRAFT

1. Havel opens his essay with a series of questions. How do these questions help him to organize his essay?
2. What is the difference between the slogan the greengrocer puts in the window and the slogan "I am afraid and therefore unquestionaingly obedient" (par. 4)?
3. Write an outline of Havel's essay based on his main transitional phrases or sentences (such as, for example, the first sentence of par. 8).
4. At a number of points in this essay, Havel relies on rhetorical questions to advance his argument. Cite two or three that you think are especially effective, and explain why you find them to be effective.
5. Is the essay's conclusion appropriate and effective? Why or why not?

MAKING CONNECTIONS

1. Alexis de Tocqueville (Chapter 6, pp. 458–462) concludes from observing American democracy that few people love liberty but that all value equality. Do you think Havel's essay supports or questions this conclusion?
2. What ideas from Daniel Boorstin (pp. 390–402) do you think Havel might have incorporated into his own essay?
3. Compare and contrast Havel's analysis of society with Karl Marx's (Chapter 4, pp. 264–273).
4. What do you think Havel might have said to Rudy Guiliani about his intention to shut down the controversial exhibition at the Brooklyn Museum (Chapter 7, pp. 560–563)?

FORMULATING IDEAS FOR WRITING

1. Havel says that "post-totalitarian" society exists "because there is in modern humanity a certain tendency towards the creation, or at least the toleration, of such a system" (par. 20). Write an essay that confirms or takes issue with this statement.
2. "Consumption-oriented people," says Havel, are unwilling "to sacrifice some material certainties for the sake of their own spiritual and moral

integrity" (par. 22). Write an essay explaining your assessment of this fairly severe indictment of, well, most of us.

3. Write an essay explaining why Havel would—or would not—make a good president of the United States.
4. The situation of the individual in post-totalitarian societies, according to Havel, is a warning to us in liberal democracies. Have we heeded that warning? Are we also "powerless"?

Jihad vs. McWorld (1992)

Benjamin Barber

Benjamin Barber's prescient and influential essay "Jihad vs. McWorld" appeared in *The Atlantic* in March, 1992. He later expanded it into an international best-seller under the same name in 1995, and there is now a post-9/11 edition as well. Barber lucidly analyzes two powerful, anatagonistic forces in the contemporary world: one tends toward a homogenized globalism driven by market imperatives, and another holds fast to the life of the village and is committed to traditional, often xenophobic values. Neither force, Barber contends, has any need or love for democracy.

An active consultant to leading political figures, Barber received his Ph.D. from Harvard University and is currently professor of civil society and distinguished university professor at the University of Maryland. His seventeen books include *Strong Democracy* (1984), which established Barber as a major political theorist; *A Passion for Democracy* (1999); and *Fear's Empire: War, Terrorism, and Democracy* (2003). He is completing a new study, to be titled *The Decline of Capitalism and the Infantalist Ethos.*

Just beyond the horizon of current events lie two possible political futures—both bleak, neither democratic. The first is a retribalization of large swaths of humankind by war and bloodshed; a threatened Lebanonization of national states in which culture is pitted against culture, people against people, tribe against tribe—a Jihad in the name of a hundred narrowly conceived faiths against every kind of interdependence, every kind of artificial social cooperation and civic mutuality. The second is being borne in on us by the onrush of economic and ecological forces that demand integration and uniformity and that mesmerize the world with fast music, fast computers, and fast food—with MTV, Macintosh, and McDonald's, pressing nations into one commercially homogenous global network: one McWorld tied together by technology, ecology, communications, and commerce. The planet is falling precipitantly apart *and* coming reluctantly together at the very same moment.

These two tendencies are sometimes visible in the same countries at the same instant: thus Yugoslavia, clamoring just recently to join the New Europe, is exploding into fragments; India is trying to live up to its reputation as the world's largest integral democracy while powerful new fundamentalist parties like the Hindu nationalist Bharatiya Janata Party, along with nationalist assassins, are imperiling its hard-won unity. States are breaking up or joining up: the Soviet Union has disappeared almost overnight, its parts forming new unions with one another or with like-minded nationalities in neighboring states. The old interwar national state based on territory and political sovereignty looks to be a mere transitional development.

The tendencies of what I am here calling the forces of Jihad and the forces of McWorld operate with equal strength in opposite directions, the one driven by parochial[1] hatreds, the other by universalizing markets, the one re-creating ancient subnational and ethnic borders from within, the other making national borders porous from without. They have one thing in common: neither offers much hope to citizens looking for practical ways to govern themselves democratically. If the global future is to pit Jihad's centrifugal whirlwind against McWorld's centripetal black hole, the outcome is unlikely to be democratic—or so I will argue.

McWorld, or the Globalization of Politics

Four imperatives make up the dynamic of McWorld: a market imperative, a resource imperative, an information-technology imperative, and an ecological imperative. By shrinking the world and diminishing the salience[2] of national borders, these imperatives have in combination achieved a considerable victory over factiousness[3] and particularism, and not least of all over their most virulent traditional form—nationalism. It is the realists who are now Europeans, the utopians who dream nostalgically of a resurgent England or Germany, perhaps even a resurgent Wales or Saxony. Yesterday's wishful cry for one world has yielded to the reality of McWorld.

5 *The market imperative.* Marxist and Leninist theories of imperialism assumed that the quest for ever-expanding markets would in time compel nation-based capitalist economies to push against national boundaries in search of an international economic imperium. Whatever else has happened to the scientistic predictions of Marxism, in this domain they have proved farsighted. All national economies are now vulnerable to the inroads of larger, transnational markets within which trade is free, currencies are convertible, access to banking is open, and contracts are enforceable under law. In Europe, Asia, Africa, the South Pacific, and the Americas such markets are eroding national sovereignty

[1] parochial: in the sense of narrowly provincial.
[2] salience: prominence.
[3] factiousness: caused by factions or excessive partisanship.

and giving rise to entities—international banks, trade associations, transnational lobbies like OPEC and Greenpeace,[4] world news services like CNN and the BBC, and multinational corporations that increasingly lack a meaningful national identity—that neither reflect nor respect nationhood as an organizing or regulative principle.

The market imperative has also reinforced the quest for international peace and stability, requisites of an efficient international economy. Markets are enemies of parochialism, isolation, fractiousness, war. Market psychology attenuates the psychology of ideological and religious cleavages and assumes a concord among producers and consumers—categories that ill fit narrowly conceived national or religious cultures. Shopping has little tolerance for blue laws, whether dictated by pub-closing British paternalism, Sabbath-observing Jewish Orthodox fundamentalism, or no-Sunday-liquor-sales Massachusetts puritanism. In the context of common markets, international law ceases to be a vision of justice and becomes a workaday framework for getting things done—enforcing contracts, ensuring that governments abide by deals, regulating trade and currency relations, and so forth.

Common markets demand a common language, as well as a common currency, and they produce common behaviors of the kind bred by cosmopolitan city life everywhere. Commercial pilots, computer programmers, international bankers, media specialists, oil riggers, entertainment celebrities, ecology experts, demographers, accountants, professors, athletes—these compose a new breed of men and women for whom religion, culture, and nationality can seem only marginal elements in a working identity. Although sociologists of everyday life will no doubt continue to distinguish a Japanese from an American mode, shopping has a common signature throughout the world. Cynics might even say that some of the recent revolutions in Eastern Europe have had as their true goal not liberty and the right to vote but well-paying jobs and the right to shop (although the vote is proving easier to acquire than consumer goods). The market imperative is, then, plenty powerful; but, notwithstanding some of the claims made for "democratic capitalism," it is not identical with the democratic imperative.

The resource imperative. Democrats once dreamed of societies whose political autonomy rested firmly on economic independence. The Athenians idealized what they called autarky, and tried for a while to create a way of life simple and austere enough to make the polis genuinely self-sufficient. To be free meant to be independent of any other community or polis. Not even the Athenians were able to achieve autarky, however: human nature, it turns out, is dependency. By the time of Pericles,[5] Athenian politics was inextricably bound up with a flowering empire held together by naval power and commerce—an empire that,

---

[4] OPEC and Greenpeace: the Organization of Petroleum Exporting Countries (OPEC) is the central organization of the world's oil-producing nations (excluding the United States, Russia, and China). Greenpeace is an international nonprofit organization devoted to environmental causes and known for its aggressive protest tactics.

[5] Pericles: Pericles (495–429 BCE) ruled Athens during the golden age of classical Greece.

even as it appeared to enhance Athenian might, ate away at Athenian independence and autarky. Master and slave, it turned out, were bound together by mutual insufficiency.

The dream of autarky briefly engrossed nineteenth-century America as well, for the underpopulated, endlessly bountiful land, the cornucopia of natural resources, and the natural barriers of a continent walled in by two great seas led many to believe that America could be a world unto itself. Given this past, it has been harder for Americans than for most to accept the inevitability of interdependence. But the rapid depletion of resources even in a country like ours, where they once seemed inexhaustible, and the maldistribution of arable soil and mineral resources on the planet, leave even the wealthiest societies ever more resource-dependent and many other nations in permanently desperate straits.

10 Every nation, it turns out, needs something another nation has; some nations have almost nothing they need.

The information-technology imperative. Enlightenment science and the technologies derived from it are inherently universalizing. They entail a quest for descriptive principles of general application, a search for universal solutions to particular problems, and an unswerving embrace of objectivity and impartiality.

Scientific progress embodies and depends on open communication, a common discourse rooted in rationality, collaboration, and an easy and regular flow and exchange of information. Such ideals can be hypocritical covers for power-mongering by elites, and they may be shown to be wanting in many other ways, but they are entailed by the very idea of science and they make science and globalization practical allies.

Business, banking, and commerce all depend on information flow and are facilitated by new communication technologies. The hardware of these technologies tends to be systemic and integrated—computer, television, cable, satellite, laser, fiber-optic, and microchip technologies combining to create a vast interactive communications and information network that can potentially give every person on earth access to every other person, and make every datum, every byte, available to every set of eyes. If the automobile was, as George Ball[6] once said (when he gave his blessing to a Fiat factory in the Soviet Union during the Cold War), "an ideology on four wheels," then electronic telecommunication and information systems are an ideology at 186,000 miles per second—which makes for a very small planet in a very big hurry. Individual cultures speak particular languages; commerce and science increasingly speak English; the whole world speaks logarithms and binary mathematics.

Moreover, the pursuit of science and technology asks for, even compels, open societies. Satellite footprints do not respect national borders; telephone wires penetrate the most closed societies. With photocopying and then fax machines having infiltrated Soviet universities and *samizdat*[7] literary circles in the eighties, and computer modems having multiplied like rabbits in communism's

[6] George Ball: American statesman (1909–1994); served as under secretary of state 1961–1966.

[7] *samizdat:* underground publications.

bureaucratic warrens thereafter, *glasnost*[8] could not be far behind. In their social requisites, secrecy and science are enemies.

15 The new technology's software is perhaps even more globalizing than its hardware. The information arm of international commerce's sprawling body reaches out and touches distinct nations and parochial cultures, and gives them a common face chiseled in Hollywood, on Madison Avenue, and in Silicon Valley. Throughout the 1980s one of the most-watched television programs in South Africa was *The Cosby Show.* The demise of apartheid was already in production. Exhibitors at the 1991 Cannes film festival expressed growing anxiety over the "homogenization" and "Americanization" of the global film industry when, for the third year running, American films dominated the awards ceremonies. America has dominated the world's popular culture for much longer, and much more decisively. In November of 1991 Switzerland's once insular culture boasted best-seller lists featuring *Terminator 2* as the No. 1 movie, *Scarlett* as the No. 1 book, and Prince's *Diamonds and Pearls* as the No. 1 record album. No wonder the Japanese are buying Hollywood film studios even faster than Americans are buying Japanese television sets. This kind of software supremacy may in the long term be far more important than hardware superiority, because culture has become more potent than armaments. What is the power of the Pentagon compared with Disneyland? Can the Sixth Fleet keep up with CNN? McDonald's in Moscow and Coke in China will do more to create a global culture than military colonization ever could. It is less the goods than the brand names that do the work, for they convey life-style images that alter perception and challenge behavior. They make up the seductive software of McWorld's common (at times much too common) soul.

Yet in all this high-tech commercial world there is nothing that looks particularly democratic. It lends itself to surveillance as well as liberty, to new forms of manipulation and covert control as well as new kinds of participation, to skewed, unjust market outcomes as well as greater productivity. The consumer society and the open society are not quite synonymous. Capitalism and democracy have a relationship, but it is something less than a marriage. An efficient free market after all requires that consumers be free to vote their dollars on competing goods, not that citizens be free to vote their values and beliefs on competing political candidates and programs. The free market flourished in junta-run Chile, in military-governed Taiwan and Korea, and, earlier, in a variety of autocratic European empires as well as their colonial possessions.

The ecological imperative. The impact of globalization on ecology is a cliché even to world leaders who ignore it. We know well enough that the German forests can be destroyed by Swiss and Italians driving gas-guzzlers fueled by leaded gas. We also know that the planet can be asphyxiated by greenhouse gases because Brazilian farmers want to be part of the twentieth century and are burning down tropical rain forests to clear a little land to plough, and because

[8] *glasnost:* political openness or transparency.

Indonesians make a living out of converting their lush jungle into toothpicks for fastidious Japanese diners, upsetting the delicate oxygen balance and in effect puncturing our global lungs. Yet this ecological consciousness has meant not only greater awareness but also greater inequality, as modernized nations try to slam the door behind them, saying to developing nations, "The world cannot afford *your* modernization; ours has wrung it dry!"

Each of the four imperatives just cited is transnational, transideological, and transcultural. Each applies impartially to Catholics, Jews, Muslims, Hindus, and Buddhists; to democrats and totalitarians; to capitalists and socialists. The Enlightenment dream of a universal rational society has to a remarkable degree been realized—but in a form that is commercialized, homogenized, depoliticized, bureaucratized, and, of course, radically incomplete, for the movement toward McWorld is in competition with forces of global breakdown, national dissolution, and centrifugal corruption. These forces, working in the opposite direction, are the essence of what I call Jihad.

Jihad, or the Lebanonization of the World

OPEC, the World Bank, the United Nations, the International Red Cross, the multinational corporation . . . there are scores of institutions that reflect globalization. But they often appear as ineffective reactors to the world's real actors: national states and, to an ever greater degree, subnational factions in permanent rebellion against uniformity and integration—even the kind represented by universal law and justice. The headlines feature these players regularly: they are cultures, not countries; parts, not wholes; sects, not religions; rebellious factions and dissenting minorities at war not just with globalism but with the traditional nation-state. Kurds, Basques, Puerto Ricans, Ossetians, East Timoreans, Quebecois, the Catholics of Northern Ireland, Abkhasians, Kurile Islander Japanese, the Zulus of Inkatha, Catalonians, Tamils, and, of course, Palestinians—people without countries, inhabiting nations not their own, seeking smaller worlds within borders that will seal them off from modernity.

20 A powerful irony is at work here. Nationalism was once a force of integration and unification, a movement aimed at bringing together disparate clans, tribes, and cultural fragments under new, assimilationist flags. But as Ortega y Gasset[9] noted more than sixty years ago, having won its victories, nationalism changed its strategy. In the 1920s, and again today, it is more often a reactionary and divisive force, pulverizing the very nations it once helped cement together. The force that creates nations is "inclusive," Ortega wrote in *The Revolt of the Masses*. "In periods of consolidation, nationalism has a positive value, and is a lofty standard. But in Europe everything is more than consolidated, and nationalism is nothing but a mania. . . ."

---

[9] Ortega y Gasset: Spanish philosopher and essayist (1883–1956). His book, *Revolt of the Masses* (1929), characterized the modern era as dominated by the mediocrity of mass culture.

This mania has left the post–Cold War world smoldering with hot wars; the international scene is little more unified than it was at the end of the Great War, in Ortega's own time. There were more than thirty wars in progress last year, most of them ethnic, racial, tribal, or religious in character, and the list of unsafe regions doesn't seem to be getting any shorter. Some new world order!

The aim of many of these small-scale wars is to redraw boundaries, to implode states and resecure parochial identities: to escape McWorld's dully insistent imperatives. The mood is that of Jihad: war not as an instrument of policy but as an emblem of identity, an expression of community, an end in itself. Even where there is no shooting war, there is fractiousness, secession, and the quest for ever smaller communities. Add to the list of dangerous countries those at risk: In Switzerland and Spain, Jurassian and Basque separatists still argue the virtues of ancient identities, sometimes in the language of bombs. Hyperdisintegration in the former Soviet Union may well continue unabated—not just a Ukraine independent from the Soviet Union but a Bessarabian Ukraine independent from the Ukrainian republic; not just Russia severed from the defunct union but Tatarstan severed from Russia. Yugoslavia makes even the disunited, ex-Soviet, nonsocialist republics that were once the Soviet Union look integrated, its sectarian fatherlands springing up within factional motherlands like weeds within weeds within weeds. Kurdish independence would threaten the territorial integrity of four Middle Eastern nations. Well before the current cataclysm Soviet Georgia made a claim for autonomy from the Soviet Union, only to be faced with its Ossetians (164,000 in a republic of 5.5 million) demanding their own self-determination within Georgia. The Abkhasian minority in Georgia has followed suit. Even the good will established by Canada's once promising Meech Lake protocols is in danger, with Francophone Quebec again threatening the dissolution of the federation. In South Africa the emergence from apartheid was hardly achieved when friction between Inkatha's Zulus and the African National Congress's tribally identified members threatened to replace Europeans' racism with an indigenous tribal war. After thirty years of attempted integration using the colonial language (English) as a unifier, Nigeria is now playing with the idea of linguistic multiculturalism—which could mean the cultural breakup of the nation into hundreds of tribal fragments. Even Saddam Hussein has benefited from the threat of internal Jihad, having used renewed tribal and religious warfare to turn last season's mortal enemies into reluctant allies of an Iraqi nationhood that he nearly destroyed.

The passing of communism has torn away the thin veneer of internationalism (workers of the world unite!) to reveal ethnic prejudices that are not only ugly and deep-seated but increasingly murderous. Europe's old scourge, anti-Semitism, is back with a vengeance, but it is only one of many antagonisms. It appears all too easy to throw the historical gears into reverse and pass from a Communist dictatorship back into a tribal state.

Among the tribes, religion is also a battlefield. ("Jihad" is a rich word whose generic meaning is "struggle"—usually the struggle of the soul to avert evil. Strictly applied to religious war, it is used only in reference to battles where the faith is under assault, or battles against a government that denies the practice of Islam. My use here is rhetorical, but does follow both journalistic practice and history.) Remember the Thirty Years War?[10] Whatever forms of Enlightenment universalism might once have come to grace such historically related forms of monotheism as Judaism, Christianity, and Islam, in many of their modern incarnations they are parochial rather than cosmopolitan, angry rather than loving, proselytizing[11] rather than ecumenical, zealous rather than rationalist, sectarian rather than deistic,[12] ethnocentric rather than universalizing. As a result, like the new forms of hypernationalism, the new expressions of religious fundamentalism are fractious and pulverizing, never integrating. This is religion as the Crusaders knew it: a battle to the death for souls that if not saved will be forever lost.

25 The atmospherics of Jihad have resulted in a breakdown of civility in the name of identity, of comity in the name of community. International relations have sometimes taken on the aspect of gang war—cultural turf battles featuring tribal factions that were supposed to be sublimated as integral parts of large national, economic, postcolonial, and constitutional entities.

The Darkening Future of Democracy

These rather melodramatic tableaux vivants do not tell the whole story, however. For all their defects, Jihad and McWorld have their attractions. Yet, to repeat and insist, the attractions are unrelated to democracy. Neither McWorld nor Jihad is remotely democratic in impulse. Neither needs democracy; neither promotes democracy.

McWorld does manage to look pretty seductive in a world obsessed with Jihad. It delivers peace, prosperity, and relative unity—if at the cost of independence, community, and identity (which is generally based on difference). The primary political values required by the global market are order and tranquillity, and freedom—as in the phrases "free trade," "free press," and "free love." Human rights are needed to a degree, but not citizenship or participation—and no more social justice and equality than are necessary to promote efficient economic production and consumption. Multinational corporations sometimes seem to prefer doing business with local oligarchs, inasmuch as they can take confidence from dealing with the boss on all crucial matters. Despots who slaughter their own populations are no problem, so long as they leave markets in place and refrain from making war on their neighbors (Saddam Hussein's fatal mistake). In trading partners, predictability is of more value than justice.

The Eastern European revolutions that seemed to arise out of concern for global democratic values quickly deteriorated into a stampede in the general direction of free markets and their ubiquitous, television-promoted shopping

[10] Thirty Years War: was fought mainly in what is now Germany, between 1618–1648, caused by conflict between Protestants and Catholics in the German principalities.

[11] proselytizing: actively committed to conversion of others to one's faith.

[12] deistic: nonsectarian belief in a deity.

malls. East Germany's Neues Forum, that courageous gathering of intellectuals, students, and workers which overturned the Stalinist regime in Berlin in 1989, lasted only six months in Germany's mini-version of McWorld. Then it gave way to money and markets and monopolies from the West. By the time of the first all-German elections, it could scarcely manage to secure three percent of the vote. Elsewhere there is growing evidence that *glasnost* will go and *perestroika*—defined as privatization and an opening of markets to Western bidders—will stay. So understandably anxious are the new rulers of Eastern Europe and whatever entities are forged from the residues of the Soviet Union to gain access to credit and markets and technology—McWorld's flourishing new currencies—that they have shown themselves willing to trade away democratic prospects in pursuit of them: not just old totalitarian ideologies and command-economy production models but some possible indigenous experiments with a third way between capitalism and socialism, such as economic cooperatives and employee stock-ownership plans, both of which have their ardent supporters in the East.

Jihad delivers a different set of virtues: a vibrant local identity, a sense of community, solidarity among kinsmen, neighbors, and countrymen, narrowly conceived. But it also guarantees parochialism and is grounded in exclusion. Solidarity is secured through war against outsiders. And solidarity often means obedience to a hierarchy in governance, fanaticism in beliefs, and the obliteration of individual selves in the name of the group. Deference to leaders and intolerance toward outsiders (and toward "enemies within") are hallmarks of tribalism—hardly the attitudes required for the cultivation of new democratic women and men capable of governing themselves. Where new democratic experiments have been conducted in retribalizing societies, in both Europe and the Third World, the result has often been anarchy, repression, persecution, and the coming of new, noncommunist forms of very old kinds of despotism. During the past year, Havel's velvet revolution in Czechoslovakia was imperiled by partisans of "Czechland" and of Slovakia as independent entities. India seemed little less rent by Sikh, Hindu, Muslim, and Tamil infighting than it was immediately after the British pulled out, more than forty years ago.

30 To the extent that either McWorld or Jihad has a *natural* politics, it has turned out to be more of an antipolitics. For McWorld, it is the antipolitics of globalism: bureaucratic, technocratic, and meritocratic, focused (as Marx predicted it would be) on the administration of things—with people, however, among the chief things to be administered. In its politico-economic imperatives McWorld has been guided by laissez-faire market principles that privilege efficiency, productivity, and beneficence at the expense of civic liberty and self-government.

For Jihad, the antipolitics of tribalization has been explicitly antidemocratic: one-party dictatorship, government by military junta, theocratic fundamentalism—often associated with a version of the *Führerprinzip* that empowers an individual to rule on behalf of a people. Even the government of India, struggling for decades to model democracy for a people who will soon number a billion, longs for great leaders; and for every Mahatma Gandhi, Indira Gandhi, or Rajiv Gandhi taken from them by zealous assassins, the Indians appear to seek a replacement who will deliver them from the lengthy travail of their freedom.

The Confederal Option

How can democracy be secured and spread in a world whose primary tendencies are at best indifferent to it (McWorld) and at worst deeply antithetical to it (Jihad)? My guess is that globalization will eventually vanquish retribalization. The ethos of material "civilization" has not yet encountered an obstacle it has been unable to thrust aside. Ortega may have grasped in the 1920s a clue to our own future in the coming millennium.

> Everyone sees the need of a new principle of life. But as always happens in similar crises—some people attempt to save the situation by an artificial intensification of the very principle which has led to decay. This is the meaning of the "nationalist" outburst of recent years . . . things have always gone that way. The last flare, the longest; the last sigh, the deepest. On the very eve of their disappearance there is an intensification of frontiers—military and economic.

Jihad may be a last deep sigh before the eternal yawn of McWorld. On the other hand, Ortega was not exactly prescient; his prophecy of peace and internationalism came just before blitzkrieg, world war, and the Holocaust tore the old order to bits. Yet democracy is how we remonstrate with reality, the rebuke our aspirations offer to history. And if retribalization is inhospitable to democracy, there is nonetheless a form of democratic government that can accommodate parochialism and communitarianism, one that can even save them from their defects and make them more tolerant and participatory: decentralized participatory democracy. And if McWorld is indifferent to democracy, there is nonetheless a form of democratic government that suits global markets passably well—representative government in its federal or, better still, confederal variation.

With its concern for accountability, the protection of minorities, and the universal rule of law, a confederalized representative system would serve the political needs of McWorld as well as oligarchic bureaucratism or meritocratic elitism is currently doing. As we are already beginning to see, many nations may survive in the long term only as confederations that afford local regions smaller than "nations" extensive jurisdiction. Recommended reading for democrats of the twenty-first century is not the U.S. Constitution or the French Declaration of Rights of Man and Citizen but the Articles of Confederation, that suddenly pertinent document that stitched together the thirteen American colonies into what then seemed a too loose confederation of independent states but now appears a new form of political realism, as veterans of Yeltsin's[13] new Russia and the new Europe created at Maastricht will attest.

By the same token, the participatory and direct form of democracy that engages citizens in civic activity and civic judgment and goes well beyond just

---

[13] Yeltsin: born in 1931, Boris Yeltsin was the first democratically elected president of Russia (1991–1999) after the collapse of Communism.

voting and accountability—the system I have called "strong democracy"—suits the political needs of decentralized communities as well as theocratic and nationalist party dictatorships have done. Local neighborhoods need not be democratic, but they can be. Real democracy has flourished in diminutive settings: the spirit of liberty, Tocqueville[14] said, is local. Participatory democracy, if not naturally apposite to tribalism, has an undeniable attractiveness under conditions of parochialism.

Democracy in any of these variations will, however, continue to be obstructed by the undemocratic and antidemocratic trends toward uniformitarian globalism and intolerant retribalization which I have portrayed here. For democracy to persist in our brave new McWorld, we will have to commit acts of conscious political will—a possibility, but hardly a probability, under these conditions. Political will requires much more than the quick fix of the transfer of institutions. Like technology transfer, institution transfer rests on foolish assumptions about a uniform world of the kind that once fired the imagination of colonial administrators. Spread English justice to the colonies by exporting wigs. Let an East Indian trading company act as the vanguard to Britain's free parliamentary institutions. Today's well-intentioned quick-fixers in the National Endowment for Democracy and the Kennedy School of Government, in the unions and foundations and universities zealously nurturing contacts in Eastern Europe and the Third World, are hoping to democratize by long distance. Post Bulgaria a parliament by first-class mail. FedEx the Bill of Rights to Sri Lanka. Cable Cambodia some common law.

Yet Eastern Europe has already demonstrated that importing free political parties, parliaments, and presses cannot establish a democratic civil society; imposing a free market may even have the opposite effect. Democracy grows from the bottom up and cannot be imposed from the top down. Civil society has to be built from the inside out. The institutional superstructure comes last. Poland may become democratic, but then again it may heed the Pope, and prefer to found its politics on its Catholicism, with uncertain consequences for democracy. Bulgaria may become democratic, but it may prefer tribal war. The former Soviet Union may become a democratic confederation, or it may just grow into an anarchic and weak conglomeration of markets for other nations' goods and services.

Democrats need to seek out indigenous democratic impulses. There is always a desire for self-government, always some expression of participation, accountability, consent, and representation, even in traditional hierarchical societies. These need to be identified, tapped, modified, and incorporated into new democratic practices with an indigenous flavor. The tortoises among the democratizers may ultimately outlive or outpace the hares, for they will have the time and patience to explore conditions along the way, and to adapt their gait to changing circumstances. Tragically, democracy in a hurry often looks something like France in 1794 or China in 1989.[15]

[14] Tocqueville: see pp. 458–462.

[15] France in 1794, China in 1989: refers to the French Terror following the French Revolution and to the violent suppression of student protest in Beijing's Tiananmen Square in 1989.

It certainly seems possible that the most attractive democratic ideal in the face of the brutal realities of Jihad and the dull realities of McWorld will be a confederal union of semi-autonomous communities smaller than nation-states, tied together into regional economic associations and markets larger than nation-states—participatory and self-determining in local matters at the bottom, representative and accountable at the top. The nation-state would play a diminished role, and sovereignty would lose some of its political potency. The Green movement adage "Think globally, act locally" would actually come to describe the conduct of politics.

40 This vision reflects only an idea, however—one that is not terribly likely to be realized. Freedom, Jean-Jacques Rousseau[16] once wrote, is a food easy to eat but hard to digest. Still, democracy has always played itself out against the odds. And democracy remains both a form of coherence as binding as McWorld and a secular faith potentially as inspiriting as Jihad.

LEARNING MORE

At the close of his essay, Barber suggests that the Articles of Confederation may be a more useful model for political organization worldwide in the future than the Constitution. See for yourself. Check out the Articles of Confederation on the *Ideas Across Time* website.

QUESTIONING THE TEXT

1. Briefly, what characterizes the "two possible political futures" (par. 1) that Barber foresees?
2. What are the main features of the "four imperatives" (par. 4) of McWorld?
3. Why is the strong emergence of "Jihad" in the contemporary period ironic?
4. What is the role of war in Jihad?
5. Why do science and technology support social stability and communication but not democracy?
6. What are the virtues of Jihad?
7. If Jihad favors strong communities, why, according to Barber, does it not favor democracy?
8. Explain the alternative Barber proposes to Jihad and McWorld. Do you find it persuasive? Why or why not?

ANALYZING THE WRITER'S CRAFT

1. If McWorld promotes peace and Jihad promotes community, why should we be concerned that neither favors democracy?
2. Barber wrote this essay in 1992. What aspects of his analysis gain greater weight because of the events of 9/11?

[16] Jean-Jacques Rousseau: see pp. 451–456.

3. Barber argues for a world moving rapidly in two opposed directions. What evidence does he cite to support this main point? What pieces of his evidence do you find most persuasive? What pieces of his evidence do you find least persuasive? Explain.
4. Barber uses three rhetorical methods in particular: comparison and contrast, definition, and analysis. Cite two or three examples of each. Explain why you find these examples to be particularly effective—or discuss ways in which they might have been made more effective.
5. What is the audience for this essay? How do you know?
6. What kinds of logic does Barber employ to advance his argument? Offer some examples.
7. Are Barber's introduction and conclusion effective? Where does Barber locate his thesis statement?
8. Do you find Barber's analysis persuasive? Explain.

MAKING CONNECTIONS

1. What does Craig S. Smith say (Chapter 4, pp. 232–241) about whether China will go the way of Jihad or McWorld?
2. Barber says Marx was right when he argued that capitalism compels nation-based industries to go global. What is Marx's full argument (see Chapter 4, pp. 264–273)? Are there other parts of Marx's analysis that Barber's essay also shows to have been prophetic?
3. How does Barber's analysis of the unintended (or unanticipated) consequences of technological development compare and contrast with that of Daniel J. Boorstin (pp. 390–402)?

FORMULATING IDEAS FOR WRITING

1. Is Barber right? Can McWorld really thrive without democracy? Aren't the essential motives of Jihad—local control of everyday life—ultimately democratic? Discuss.
2. Assess Barber's confederal option by reference to the Articles of Confederation. How are the conditions active in the world today like those that led to the Articles of Confederation? Why did the Articles last no more than a decade? Does the longevity of the Constitution that supplanted the Articles suggest that a world constitution might be a better way to go than Barber's confederal option?
3. Why is democracy a greater value than peace and community? That is, since Barber maintains that McWorld favors peace, open communication, and human rights, and that Jihad favors vibrant community, just what is it about democracy that is *more* desirable than what either McWorld or Jihad have to offer?
4. Barber's essay has assumed the standing of a kind of prophetic icon because of the events of 9/11. Is Barber's essay a useful explanation of the

events of 9/11, or is there only an apparent connection, encouraged, for example, by his terminology (Jihad)?

In the American Society (1991)

Gish Jen

A first-generation American, born in New York in 1955, Gish Jen is the daughter of parents from Shanghai who emigrated (separately) to the United States during the Second World War. Jen attended Harvard, where she majored in English and was also premed. She went on to study at the Stanford Business School and the Iowa Writers Workshop, where she earned an M.F.A.

"I think of Americanness," Jen has said, "as a preoccupation with identity." Her books and stories explore life in the United States from the displaced perspective of those who encounter American life after having been raised elsewhere or who are themselves raised by parents who were born outside the country. Her first novel, *Typical American* (1991), for example, follows the career of Ralph Chang, the father in this selection. In her second novel, *Mona in the Promised Land* (1996), Chang's daughter Mona—the Mona of "In the American Society"—converts to Judaism, startling her father. Her latest novel, *The Love Wife* (2004), is a complex, often comic study of what happens to the marriage of a Chinese-American and his WASP wife (named "Blondie") when the husband's Chinese relative, a survivor of the Chinese Cultural Revolution, comes to serve as their nanny. Jen lives in Cambridge, Massachusetts.

I. His Own Society

When my father took over the pancake house, it was to send my little sister Mona and me to college. We were only in junior high at the time, but my father believed in getting a jump on things. "Those Americans always saying it," he told us. "Smart guys thinking in advance." My mother elaborated, explaining that businesses took bringing up, like children. They could take years to get going, she said, years.

In this case, though, we got rich right away. At two months we were breaking even, and at four, those same hotcakes that could barely withstand the weight of butter and syrup were supporting our family with ease. My mother bought a station wagon with air conditioning, my father an oversized, red vinyl recliner for the back room; and as time went on and the business continued to thrive, my father started to talk about his grandfather and the village he had reigned over in China—things my father had never talked about when he worked for other people. He told us about the bags of rice his family would give out to the poor at New Year's, and about the people who came to beg, on their hands and knees, for his grandfather to intercede for the more wayward of their relatives. "Like that Godfather in the movie," he would tell us as, his feet up, he distributed paychecks. Sometimes an employee would get two green envelopes instead of one, which meant that Jimmy needed a tooth pulled, say, or that Tiffany's husband was in the clinker again.

"It's nothing, nothing," he would insist, sinking back into his chair. "Who else is going to take care of you people?"

My mother would mostly just sigh about it. "Your father thinks this is China," she would say, and then she would go back to her mending. Once in a while, though, when my father had given away a particularly large sum, she would exclaim, outraged, "But this here is the U—S—of—A!"—this apparently having been what she used to tell immigrant stock boys when they came in late.

5 She didn't work at the supermarket anymore; but she had made it to the rank of manager before she left, and this had given her not only new words and phrases, but new ideas about herself, and about America, and about what was what in general. She had opinions, now, on how downtown should be zoned; she could pump her own gas and check her own oil; and for all she used to chide Mona and me for being "copycats," she herself was now interested in espadrilles, and wallpaper, and most recently, the town country club.

"So join already," said Mona, flicking a fly off her knee.

My mother enumerated the problems as she sliced up a quarter round of watermelon: There was the cost. There was the waiting list. There was the fact that no one in our family played either tennis or golf.

"So what?" said Mona.

"It would be waste," said my mother.

10 "Me and Callie can swim in the pool."

"Plus you need that recommendation letter from a member."

"Come *on*," said Mona. "Annie's mom'd write you a letter in *sec*."

My mother's knife glinted in the early summer sun. I spread some more newspaper on the picnic table.

"*Plus* you have to eat there twice a month. You know what that means." My mother cut another, enormous slice of fruit.

15 "No, I *don't* know what that means," said Mona.

"It means Dad would have to wear a jacket, dummy," I said.

"Oh! Oh! Oh!" said Mona, clasping her hand to her breast. "Oh! Oh! Oh! Oh! Oh!"

We all laughed: my father had no use for nice clothes, and would wear only ten-year-old shirts, with grease-spotted pants, to show how little he cared what anyone thought.

"Your father doesn't believe in joining the American society," said my mother. "He wants to have his own society."

20 "So go to dinner without him." Mona shot her seeds out in long arcs over the lawn. "Who cares what he thinks?"

But of course we all did care, and knew my mother could not simply up and do as she pleased. For in my father's mind, a family owed its head a degree of loyalty that left no room for dissent. To embrace what he embraced was to love; and to embrace something else was to betray him.

He demanded a similar sort of loyalty of his workers, whom he treated more like servants than employees. Not in the beginning, of course. In the beginning all he wanted was for them to keep on doing what they used to do, and to that end he concentrated mostly on leaving them alone. As the months passed, though, he expected more and more of them, with the result that for all his largesse, he began to have trouble keeping help. The cooks and busboys complained that he asked them to fix radiators and trim hedges, not only at the restaurant, but at our house; the waitresses that he sent them on errands and made them chauffeur him around. Our head waitress, Gertrude, claimed that he once even asked her to scratch his back.

"It's not just the blacks don't believe in slavery," she said when she quit.

My father never quite registered her complaint, though, nor those of the others who left. Even after Eleanor quit, then Tiffany, then Gerald, and Jimmy, and even his best cook, Eureka Andy, for whom he had bought new glasses, he remained mostly convinced that the fault lay with them.

"All they understand is that assembly line," he lamented. "Robots, they are. They want to be robots."

There *were* occasions when the clear running truth seemed to eddy, when he would pinch the vinyl of his chair up into little peaks and wonder if he was doing things right. But with time he would always smooth the peaks back down; and when business started to slide in the spring, he kept on like a horse in his ways.

By the summer our dishboy was overwhelmed with scraping. It was no longer just the hashbrowns that people were leaving for trash, and the service was as bad as the food. The waitresses served up French pancakes instead of German, apple juice instead of orange, spilt things on laps, on coats. On the Fourth of July some green-horn sent an entire side of fries slaloming down a lady's *massif centrale.* Meanwhile in the back room, my father labored through articles on the economy.

"What is housing starts?" he puzzled. "What is GNP?"

Mona and I did what we could, filling in as busgirls and bookkeepers and, one afternoon, stuffing the comments box that hung by the cashier's desk. That was Mona's idea. We rustled up a variety of pens and pencils, checked boxes for an hour, smeared the cards up with coffee and grease, and waited. It took a few days for my father to notice that the box was full, and he didn't say anything about it for a few days more. Finally, though, he started to complain of fatigue; and then he began to complain that the staff was not what it could be. We encouraged him in this—pointing out, for instance, how many dishes got chipped—but in the end all that happened was that, for the first time since we took over the restaurant, my father got it into his head to fire someone. Skip, a skinny busboy who was saving up for a sports-car, said nothing as my father mumbled on about the price of dishes. My father's hands shook as he wrote out the severance check; and he spent the rest of the day napping in his chair once it was over.

30 As it was going on midsummer, Skip wasn't easy to replace. We hung a sign in the window and advertised in the paper, but no one called the first week, and the person who called the second didn't show up for his interview. The third week, my father phoned Skip to see if he would come back, but a friend of his had already sold him a Corvette for cheap.

Finally a Chinese guy named Booker turned up. He couldn't have been more than thirty, and was wearing a lighthearted seersucker suit, but he looked as though life had him pinned: his eyes were bloodshot and his chest sunken, and the muscles of his neck seemed to strain with the effort of holding his head up. In a single dry breath he told us that he had never bussed tables but was willing to learn, and that he was on the lam from the deportation authorities.

"I do not want to lie to you," he kept saying. He had come to the United States on a student visa, had run out of money, and was now in a bind. He was loath to go back to Taiwan, as it happened—he looked up at this point, to be sure my father wasn't pro-KMT—but all he had was a phony social security card and a willingness to absorb all blame, should anything untoward come to pass.

"I do not think, anyway, that it is against law to hire me, only to be me," he said, smiling faintly.

Anyone else would have examined him on this, but my father conceived of laws as speed bumps rather than curbs. He wiped the counter with his sleeve, and told Booker to report the next morning.

35 "I will be good worker," said Booker.

"Good," said my father.

"Anything you want me to do, I will do."

My father nodded.

Booker seemed to sink into himself for a moment. "Thank you," he said finally. "I am appreciate your help. I am very, very appreciate for everything." He reached out to shake my father's hand.

40 My father looked at him. "Did you eat today?" he asked in Mandarin.

Booker pulled at the hem of his jacket.

"Sit down," said my father. "Please, have a seat."

My father didn't tell my mother about Booker, and my mother didn't tell my father about the country club. She would never have applied, except that Mona, while over at Annie's, had let it drop that our mother wanted to join. Mrs. Lardner came by the very next day.

"Why, I'd be honored and delighted to write you people a letter," she said. Her skirt billowed around her.

45 "Thank you so much," said my mother. "But it's too much trouble for you, and also my husband is . . ."

"Oh, it's no trouble at all, no trouble at all. I tell you." She leaned forward so that her chest freckles showed. "I know just how it is. It's a secret of course, but you know, my natural father was Jewish. Can you see it? Just look at my skin."

"My husband," said my mother.

"I'd be honored and delighted," said Mrs. Lardner with a little wave of her hands. "Just honored and delighted."

Mona was triumphant. "See, Mom," she said, waltzing around the kitchen when Mrs. Lardner left. "What did I tell you? 'I'm just honored and delighted, just honored and delighted.'" She waved her hands in the air.

50 "You know, the Chinese have a saying," said my mother. "To do nothing is better than to overdo. You mean well, but you tell me now what will happen."

"I'll talk Dad into it," said Mona, still waltzing. "Or I bet Callie can. He'll do anything Callie says."

"I can try, anyway," I said.

"Did you hear what I said?" said my mother. Mona bumped into the broom closet door. "You're not going to talk anything; you've already made enough trouble." She started on the dishes with a clatter.

Mona poked diffidently at a mop.

55 I sponged off the counter. "Anyway," I ventured. "I bet our name'll never even come up."

"That's if we're lucky," said my mother.

"There's all these people waiting," I said.

"Good," she said. She started on a pot.

I looked over at Mona, who was still cowering in the broom closet. "In fact, there's some black family's been waiting so long, they're going to sue," I said.

60 My mother turned off the water. "Where'd you hear that?"

"Patty told me."

She turned the water back on, started to wash a dish, then put it back down and shut the faucet.

"I'm sorry," said Mona.

"Forget it," said my mother. "Just forget it."

65 Booker turned out to be a model worker, whose boundless gratitude translated into a willingness to do anything. As he also learned quickly, he soon knew not only how to bus, but how to cook, and how to wait table, and how to keep the books. He fixed the walk-in door so that it stayed shut, reupholstered the torn seats in the dining room, and devised a system for tracking inventory. The only stone in the rice was that he tended to be sickly; but, reliable even in illness, he would always send a friend to take his place. In this way we got to know Ronald, Lynn, Dirk, and Cedric, all of whom, like Booker, had problems with their legal status and were anxious to please. They weren't all as capable as Booker, though, with the exception of Cedric, whom my father often hired even when Booker was well. A round wag of a man who called Mona and me *shou hou*—skinny monkeys—he was a professed non-smoker who was nevertheless always begging drags off of other peoples cigarettes. This last habit drove our head cook, Fernando, crazy, especially since, when refused a hit, Cedric would occasionally snitch one. Winking impishly at Mona and me, he would steal up to an ashtray, take a quick puff, and then break out laughing so that the smoke came rolling out of his mouth in a great incriminatory cloud. Fernando accused him of stealing fresh cigarettes too, even whole packs.

"Why else do you think he's weaseling around in the back of the store all the time," he said. His face was blotchy with anger. "The man is a frigging thief."

Other members of the staff supported him in this contention and joined in on an "Operation Identification," which involved numbering and initialing their cigarettes—even though what they seemed to fear for wasn't so much their cigarettes as their jobs. Then one of the cooks quit; and rather than promote someone, my father hired Cedric for the position. Rumors flew that he was taking only half the normal salary, that Alex had been pressured to resign, and that my father was looking for a position with which to placate Booker, who had been bypassed because of his health.

The result was that Fernando categorically refused to work with Cedric.

"The only way I'll cook with that piece of slime," he said, shaking his huge tattooed fist, "is if it's his ass frying on the grill."

70 My father cajoled and cajoled, to no avail, and in the end was simply forced to put them on different schedules.

The next week Fernando got caught stealing a carton of minute steaks. My father would not tell even Mona and me how he knew to be standing by the back door when Fernando was on his way out, but everyone suspected Booker. Everyone but Fernando, that is, who was sure Cedric had been the tip-off. My father held a staff meeting in which he tried to reassure everyone that Alex had left on his own, and that he had no intention of firing anyone. But though he was careful not to mention Fernando, everyone was so amazed that he was being allowed to stay that Fernando was incensed nonetheless.

"Don't you all be putting your bug eyes on me," he said. "*He's* the frigging crook." He grabbed Cedric by the collar.

Cedric raised an eyebrow. "Cook, you mean," he said.

At this Fernando punched Cedric in the mouth; and the words he had just uttered notwithstanding, my father fired him on the spot.

75 With everything that was happening, Mona and I were ready to be getting out of the restaurant. It was almost time: the days were still stuffy with summer, but our window shade had started flapping in the evening as if gearing up to go out. That year the breezes were full of salt, as they sometimes were when they came in from the East, and they blew anchors and docks through my mind like so many tumbleweeds, filling my dreams with wherries and lobsters and grainy-faced men who squinted, day in and day out, at the sky.

It was time for a change, you could feel it; and yet the pancake house was the same as ever. The day before school started my father came home with bad news.

"Fernando called police," he said, wiping his hand on his pant leg.

My mother naturally wanted to know what police; and so with much coughing and hawing, the long story began, the latest installment of which had the police calling immigration, and immigration sending an investigator. My mother sat stiff as whalebone as my father described how the man summarily refused lunch on the house and how my father had admitted, under pressure, that he knew there were "things" about his workers.

"So now what happens?"

80 My father didn't know. "Booker and Cedric went with him to the Jail," he said. "But me, here I am." He laughed uncomfortably.

The next day my father posted bail for "his boys" and waited apprehensively for something to happen. The day after that he waited again, and the day after that he called our neighbor's law student son, who suggested my father call the immigration department under an alias. My father took his advice; and it was thus that he discovered that Booker was right: it was illegal for aliens to work, but it wasn't to hire them.

In the happy interval that ensued, my father apologized to my mother, who in turn confessed about the country club, for which my father had no choice but to forgive her. Then he turned his attention back to "his boys."

My mother didn't see that there was anything to do.

"I like to talking to the judge," said my father.

85 "This is not China," said my mother.

"I'm only talking to him. I'm not give him money unless he wants it."

"You're going to land up in jail."

"So what else I should do?" My father threw up his hands. "Those are my boys."

"Your boys!" exploded my mother. "What about your family? What about your wife?"

90 My father took a long sip of tea. "You know," he said finally. "In the war my father sent our cook to the soldiers to use. He always said it—the province comes before the town, the town comes before the family."

"A restaurant is not a town," said my mother.

My father sipped at his tea again. "You know, when I first come to the United States, I also had to hide-and-seek with those deportation guys. If people did not helping me, I'm not here today."

My mother scrutinized her hem.

After a minute I volunteered that before seeing a judge, he might try a lawyer.

95 He turned. "Since when did you become so afraid like your mother?"

I started to say that it wasn't a matter of fear, but he cut me off.

"What I need today," he said, "is a son."

My father and I spent the better part of the next day standing in lines at the immigration office. He did not get to speak to a judge, but with much persistence he managed to speak to a judge's clerk, who tried to persuade him that it was not her place to extend him advice. My father, though, shamelessly plied her with compliments and offers of free pancakes until she finally conceded that she personally doubted anything would happen to either Cedric or Booker.

"Especially if they're 'needed workers,'" she said, rubbing at the red marks her glasses left on her nose. She yawned. "Have you thought about sponsoring them to become permanent residents?"

100 Could he do that? My father was overjoyed. And what if he saw to it right away? Would she perhaps put in a good word with the judge?

She yawned again, her nostrils flaring. "Don't worry," she said. "They'll get a fair hearing."

My father returned jubilant. Booker and Cedric hailed him as their savior, their Buddha incarnate. He was like a father to them, they said; and laughing and clapping, they made him tell the story over and over, sorting over the details like jewels. And how old was the assistant judge? And what did she say?

That evening my father tipped the paperboy a dollar and bought a pot of mums for my mother, who suffered them to be placed on the dining room table. The next night he took us all out to dinner. Then on Saturday, Mona found a letter on my father's chair at the restaurant.

> Dear Mr. Chang,
>
> You are the grat boss. But, we do not like to trial, so will runing away now. Plese to excus us. People saying the law in America is fears, like dragon. Here is only $140. We hope some day we can pay back the rest bale. You will getting intrest, as you diserving, so grat a boss you are. Thank you for every thing. In next life you will be burn in rich family, with no more pancaks.
>
> Yours truley,
> Booker + Cedric

105 In the weeks that followed my father went to the pancake house for crises, but otherwise hung around our house, fiddling idly with the sump pump and boiler in an effort, he said, to get ready for winter. It was as though he had gone into retirement, except that instead of moving south, he had moved to the basement. He even took to showering my mother with little attentions, and to calling her "old girl," and when we finally heard that the club had entertained all the applications it could for the year, he was so sympathetic that he seemed more disappointed than my mother.

II. In the American Society

Mrs. Lardner tempered the bad news with an invitation to a bon voyage "bash" she was throwing for a friend of hers who was going to Greece for six months.

"Do come," she urged. "You'll meet everyone, and then, you know, if things open up in the spring . . ." She waved her hands.

My mother wondered if it would be appropriate to show up at a party for someone they didn't know, but "the honest truth" was that this was an annual affair. "If it's not Greece, it's Antibes," sighed Mrs. Lardner. "We really just do it because his wife left him and his daughter doesn't speak to him, and poor Jeremy just feels so *unloved*."

She also invited Mona and me to the goings on, as "*demi*-guests" to keep Annie out of the champagne. I wasn't too keen on the idea, but before I could say anything, she had already thanked us for so generously agreeing to honor her with our presence.

110 "A pair of little princesses, you are!" she told us. "A pair of princesses!"

The party was that Sunday. On Saturday, my mother took my father out shopping for a suit. As it was the end of September, she insisted that he buy a worsted rather than a seersucker, even though it was only ten, rather than fifty percent off. My father protested that it was as hot out as ever, which was true—a thick Indian summer had cozied murderously up to us—but to no avail. Summer clothes, said my mother, were not properly worn after Labor Day.

The suit was unfortunately as extravagant in length as it was in price, which posed an additional quandary, since the tailor wouldn't be in until Monday. The salesgirl, though, found a way of tacking it up temporarily.

"Maybe this suit not fit me," fretted my father.

"Just don't take your jacket off," said the salesgirl.

115 He gave her a tip before they left, but when he got home refused to remove price tag.

"I like to asking the tailor about the size," he insisted.

"You mean you're going to *wear* it and then *return* it?" Mona rolled her eyes.

"I didn't say I'm return it," said my father stiffly. "I like to asking the tailor, that's all."

The party started off swimmingly, except that most people were wearing bermudas or wrap skirts. Still, my parents carried on, sharing with great feeling the complaints about the heat. Of course my father tried to eat a cracker full of shallots and burnt himself in an attempt to help Mr. Lardner turn the coals of the barbeque; but on the whole he seemed to be doing all right. Not nearly so well as my mother, though, who had accepted an entire cupful of Mrs. Lardner's magic punch, and seemed indeed to be under some spell. As Mona and Annie skirmished over whether some boy in their class inhaled when he smoked, I watched my mother take off her shoes, laughing and laughing as a man with a beard regaled her with navy stories by the pool. Apparently he had been stationed in the Orient and remembered a few words of Chinese, which made my mother laugh still more. My father excused himself to go to the men's room then drifted back and weighed anchor at the hors d'oeuvres table, while my mother sailed on to a group of women, who tinkled at length over the clarity of her complexion. I dug out a book I had brought.

120 Just when I'd cracked the spine, though, Mrs. Lardner came by to bewail her shortage of servers. Her caterers were criminals, I agreed; and the next thing I knew I was handing out bits of marine life, making the rounds as amiably as I could.

"Here you go, Dad," I said when I got to the hors d'oeuvres table.

"Everything is fine," he said.

I hesitated to leave him alone; but then the man with the beard zeroed in on him, and though he talked of nothing but my mother, I thought it would be okay to get back to work. Just that moment, though, Jeremy Brothers lurched our way, an empty, albeit corked, wine bottle in hand. He was a slim, well-proportioned man, with a Roman nose and small eyes and a nice manly jaw that he allowed to hang agape.

"Hello," he said drunkenly. "Pleased to meet you."

125 "Pleased to meeting you," said my father.

"Right," said Jeremy. "Right. Listen. I have this bottle here, this most recalcitrant bottle. You see that it refuses to do my bidding. I bid it open sesame, please, and it does nothing." He pulled the cork out with his teeth, then turned the bottle upside down.

My father nodded.

"Would you have a word with it please?" said Jeremy. The man with the beard excused himself. "Would you please have a goddamned word with it?"

My father laughed uncomfortably.

130 "Ah!" Jeremy bowed a little. "Excuse me, excuse me, excuse me. You are not my man, not my man at all." He bowed again and started to leave, but then circled back. "Viticulture is not your forte, yes I can see that, see that plainly. But may I trouble you on another matter? Forget the damned bottle." He threw it into the pool, and winked at the people he splashed. "I have another matter. Do you speak Chinese?"

My father said he did not, but Jeremy pulled out a handkerchief with some characters on it anyway, saying that his daughter had sent it from Hong Kong and that he thought the characters might be some secret message.

"Long life," said my father.

"But you haven't looked at it yet."

"I know what it says without looking." My father winked at me.

135 "You do?"

"Yes, I do."

"You're making fun of me, aren't you?"

"No, no, no," said my father, winking again.

"Who are you anyway?" said Jeremy.

140 His smile fading, my father shrugged.

"Who are you?"

My father shrugged again.

Jeremy began to roar. "This is my party, *my party,* and I've never seen you before in my life." My father backed up as Jeremy came toward him. *"Who are you? WHO ARE YOU?"*

Just as my father was going to step back into the pool, Mrs. Lardner came running up. Jeremy informed her that there was a man crashing his party.

145 "Nonsense," said Mrs. Lardner. "This is Ralph Chang, who I invited extra especially so he could meet you." She straightened the collar of Jeremy's peach-colored polo shirt for him.

"Yes, well, we've had a chance to chat," said Jeremy.

She whispered in his ear; he mumbled something; she whispered something more.

"I do apologize," he said finally.

My father didn't say anything.

150 "I do." Jeremy seemed genuinely contrite. "Doubtless you've seen drunks before, haven't you? You must have them in China."

"Okay," said my father.

As Mrs. Lardner glided off, Jeremy clapped his arm over my father's shoulder. "You know, I really am quite sorry, quite sorry."

My father nodded.

"What can I do, how can I make it up to you?"

155 "No thank you."

"No, tell me, tell me," wheedled Jeremy. "Tickets to casino night?" My father shook his head. "You don't gamble. Dinner at Bartholomew's?" My father shook his head again. "You don't eat." Jeremy scratched his chin. "You know, my wife was like you. Old Annabelle could never let me make things up—never, never, never, never, never."

My father wriggled out from under his arm.

"How about sport clothes? You are rather overdressed, you know, excuse me for saying so. But here." He took off his polo shirt and folded it up. "You can have this with my most profound apologies." He ruffled his chest hairs with his free hand.

"No thank you," said my father.

"No, take it, take it. Accept my apologies." He thrust the shirt into my father's arms. "I'm so very sorry, so very sorry. Please, try it on."

Helplessly holding the shirt, my father searched the crowd for my mother.

"Here, I'll help you off with your coat."

My father froze.

Jeremy reached over and took his jacket off. "Milton's, one hundred twenty-five dollars reduced to one hundred twelve-fifty," he read. "What a bargain, what a bargain!"

"Please give it back," pleaded my father. "Please."

"Now for your shirt," ordered Jeremy.

Heads began to turn.

"Take off your shirt."

"I do not take orders like a servant," announced my father.

"Take off your shirt, or I'm going to throw this jacket right into the pool, just right into this little pool here." Jeremy held it over the water.

"Go ahead."

"One hundred twelve-fifty," taunted Jeremy. "One hundred twelve . . ."

My father flung the polo shirt into the water with such force that part of it bounced back up into the air like a fluorescent fountain. Then it settled into a soft heap on top of the water. My mother hurried up.

"You're a sport!" said Jeremy, suddenly breaking into a smile and slapping my father on the back. "You're a sport! I like that. A man with spirit, that's what you are. A man with panache. Allow me to return to you your jacket." He handed it back to my father. "Good value you got on that, good value."

My father hurled the coat into the pool too. "We're leaving," he said grimly. "Leaving!"

"Now, Ralphie," said Mrs. Lardner, bustling up; but my father was already stomping off.

"Get your sister," he told me. To my mother: "Get your shoes."

"That was *great,* Dad," said Mona as we walked down to the car. "You were *stupendous.*"

"Way to show 'em," I said.

"What? " said my father offhandedly.

Although it was only just dusk, we were in a gulch, which made it hard to see.

"It was all my fault," began my mother.

"Forget it," said my father grandly. Then he said, "The only trouble is I left keys in my jacket pocket."

"Oh *no*," said Mona.

185 "Oh no is right," said my mother.

"So we'll walk home," I said.

"But how're we going to get into the *house*," said Mona.

The noise of the party churned through the silence.

"Someone has to going back," said my father.

190 "Let's go to the pancake house first," suggested my mother "We can wait there until the party is finished, and then call Mrs. Lardner."

Having all agreed that that was a good plan, we started walking again.

"God, just think," said Mona. "We're going to have to *dive* for them."

My father stopped a moment. We waited.

"You girls are good swimmers," he said finally "Not like me."

195 Then his shirt started moving again, and we trooped up the hill after it, into the dark.

LEARNING MORE

Links to more works by and commentary about Gish Jen can be found on the *Ideas Across Time* website.

QUESTIONING THE TEXT

1. The narrator's mother says, "'Your father thinks this is China'" (par. 4). How is his thinking and behavior more appropriate to China than the United States? Is the narrator's mother completely right in her judgment? What was the father's status and experience in China? Is his experience in China inapplicable to life in the United States? How? Why? Does our view of Mr. Chang's attitudes and values change as the story goes on?
2. How do you respond to the idea of this family as owners of a pancake house?
3. Why is it the mother rather than the father who applies for membership in the country club?
4. Why do the girls want to join the country club?
5. Why doesn't the mother tell the father about her application?
6. Mr. Chang demands—or expects—great loyalty from his workers. How does this land him in trouble?
7. Explain Booker's role in the story. (Why doesn't the father tell the mother about Booker?)
8. Is it admirable or foolish of Mr. Chang to go to so much trouble to help Booker and Cedric with their immigration woes?
9. Is Mrs. Lardner a hypocrite?
10. How do Mr. Chang's attributes "in his own society" translate into his behavior "in the American society"?

11. How should we interpret the "gleam" of Mr. Chang's shirt at the end of the story?
12. Has the attitude of the girls toward their father changed from the beginning of the story to the end? Explain.

ANALYZING THE WRITER'S CRAFT

1. This story is divided into two parts. How are these two parts related? What qualities of one feed into the other? Does reading the second part change your understanding of the first part? Explain.
2. Many things in this story are ironic. Some are gently ironic, such as the fact that this Chinese-American family runs something as quintessentially American as a pancake house; some are more sharply ironic, such as Mrs. Lardner calling Mr. Chang "Ralphie" at the end of the story. Discuss the uses of irony in this story by reference to two specific examples.
3. What is the tone of this story? How much of the tone reflects the narrator? What do you learn about the narrator through the story? How would the story be different if someone else in the family were narrating? How would the story be different if it were told in the third person?
4. What do we learn from the differences in the language used by the daughters and by the parents? Would the story be significantly changed if the parents spoke the same American as the daughters?
5. Why do Booker and Cedric not have Chinese names?
6. How does Mrs. Chang's Chinese saying ("To do nothing is better than to overdo," par. 50) foreshadow the ending of the story? Does Mrs. Chang's use of this saying reveal a difference in understanding of life between the daughters and the mother (and perhaps the father)?
7. "The party started off swimmingly," Jen writes as she moves her story to a conclusion (par. 119). This is but one instance of a seemingly unremarkable word, phrase, or image than turns out to carry more meaning than we first notice. Choose one or two other examples as illustrations of how Jen builds meaning in the story.
8. How does the ending bring the thematic strands of the story together at the close?
9. Jen's story explores values and relationships through the forms of fiction. What does her story achieve that an essay might not be able to? What would be gained and lost, for example, if Jen had to fashion a thesis statement for this story?

MAKING CONNECTIONS

1. What does this story say about what it means to be an American? Compare and contrast the story with James Baldwin's "The Discovery of What It Means to Be an American" (Chapter 1, pp. 22–27).

2. W. E. B. Du Bois recounts his shock when, as a boy, he was dismissed as an "other" by a schoolmate (Chapter 6, pp. 472–479). To what extent is the Changs' family experience at the hands of Mrs. Lardner similar to Du Bois'? What are the differences?
3. Why is Ralph Chang's attitude toward his workers portrayed as un-American, or Chinese, and yet the attitude and behavior of Louis May Alcott's employer is automatically accepted as American (Chapter 4, pp. 275–286)? Would Alcott have been a happy worker for Mr. Chang?

FORMULATING IDEAS FOR WRITING

1. The translation of values from one society to another always seems imperfect, liable to confusions and misunderstandings. What does this story say about the dangers and the benefits of applying the values of one culture to another?
2. Is this story a critique or an exploration of American society?
3. Rewrite some part of this story from Mr. Chang's point of view.
4. Discuss the structure of this story, that is, its explicit division into two titled parts—"His Own Society" and "In the American Society." How do these two parts reflect each other? Draw out the thematic and structural connections and differences between part 1 and part 2. When, in the first part, Mrs. Chang says her husband thinks he is still in China and does not understand that he is in the United States, do you tend to agree with her? Explain. How do you view Mrs. Chang's judgment by the end of the story? Does the attitude of the daughters toward their father change between part 1 and part 2?

Photographs Across America (2002)

David Hume Kennerly

One of the nation's preeminent photo-journalists, David Hume Kennerly chose to record the new millennium by departing from his usual hectic pace on assignment by keeping "a visual diary of what I saw as we entered the 21st century." For a year, Kennerly crisscrossed the United States and the globe, traveling 250,000 miles, visiting 38 states and over 300 cities, towns, and villages. The photos that follow are from the resulting book, *Photo du Jour: A Picture-a-Day Journey Through the First Year of the New Millenium* (2002).

Born in 1947, Kennerly began his career in Roseburg, Oregon, taking photos for his school paper, *The Orange R*. From that time on, Kennerly has been present

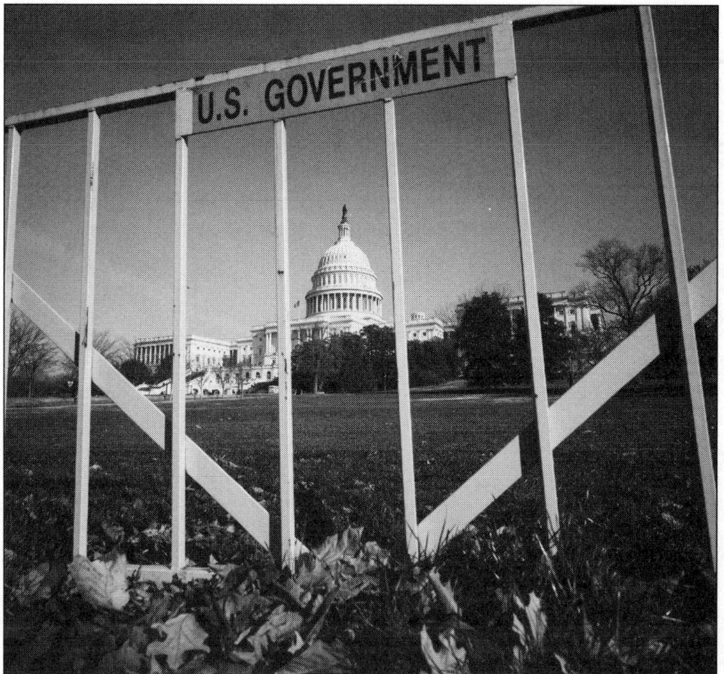

The U.S. Capitol behind bars.

to photograph virtually every major event of U.S. history in the closing years of the millennium. He captured Robert Kennedy as he raised his arms in celebration of winning the California presidential primary on June 5, 1968, just moments before he was shot and killed. He photographed Richard Nixon's last wave to the press corps as he left the White House in disgrace. He was there when Egyptian president Anwar Sadat flew to Israel to conclude a peace treaty, when President Reagan sat down with Mikhail Gorbachev, and when Bill Clinton was impeached. From 1971 to 1973, he shot the war in Vietnam, receiving the Pultizer Prize for this work in 1972. In addition to the Pulitzer, Kennerly has won numerous prizes and honors, including a prize for the best coverage of the 2000 presidential campaign. In March 2001, the *Washingtonian* magazine named him one of the top fifty journalists in the nation's capital. Kennerly served as President Gerald Ford's personal photographer and has been contributing editor for *Newsweek* magazine. His autobiography, *Shooter,* appeared in 1979, and a selection of his photographs spanning thirty years, *Photo Op,* was published in 1995. Kennerly lives in Santa Monica, California.

QUESTIONING THE TEXT

1. How do you think these photos portray the U.S. government?
2. Do you think these photos make ironic observations about what they see?

Inside the Capitol Rotunda.

3. What do you make of the size of the painting in back of the crowd in the Capitol Rotunda? What effect on the viewer do you think the size of the painting would have?
4. How does the Rotunda painting compare and contrast with the visitors to the Capitol, and vice versa?
5. Speculate about the tourists in the Rotunda photo. Who are they? Are they having a good time? Are they bored? Explain.
6. What does the gate in the "behind bars" photo suggest about government?
7. What do these photos convey that words could not?

ANALYZING THE ARTIST'S CRAFT

1. Do you think that framing the Capitol in a gate as Kennerly does is a cheap trick or an effective visual comment?
2. Compare and contrast the frame of the painting in the Rotunda with Kennerley's framing of his photos.
3. How does Kennerly focus our attention in the "behind bars" photo? In the Rotunda photo? What do you think is the center of interest in the Rotunda photo? Explain.

4. What is the effect of the guide's upraised arm on the composition of the Rotunda photo?
5. Why has Kennerly chosen that particular painting in the Rotunda as the backdrop for his photo?

MAKING CONNECTIONS

1. Do you think either of these photos might be used to illustrate any of the essays in this chapter? Explain your choices.
2. How do the two photos contribute to the discussion of the impact of technology on democracy (see Boorstin, pp. 390–402)?
3. What do you think the people pictured in Craig Smith's story about China (Chapter 4, pp. 232–241) would say about these photos?

FORMULATING IDEAS FOR WRITING

1. Write an extended caption for each photo so that, together, these paragraphs establish a coherent commentary on U.S. society today.
2. Write an appreciation of one or both of the photos as visual compositions.

chapter 6

Equality: Race and Gender

Many essays in this book attest to the unique American commitment to equality. Jefferson's words in the Declaration of Independence (Chapter 5, pp. 354–360) are simple and unequivocal: "All men are created equal." But over two hundred years after those words were written, everyday reality forces us to acknowledge not only the persistence of inequalities in America among men, between men and women, and among the races but also, as the Keynote selection of this chapter illustrates, the persistence of deeply ingrained prejudices and misunderstandings.

This tension between an ideal and social reality is already present in the thinking of the formative philosophers whose ideas inspired the democratic revolutions of the late-eighteenth and nineteenth centuries, John Locke (Chapter 5, pp. 348–352) and Jean-Jacques Rousseau (pp. 451–456). Locke and Rousseau begin their speculations about human society in the same place: the imagined moment when human beings abandon the complete freedom of the state of nature and willingly join together to form stable societies. For Locke, this social contract creates not just security but also liberty. Rousseau, however, also sees the social contract as making inequalities permanent. According to Rousseau, the reward for each individual for entering into the social contract is a system of law. But on the morning after, as it were, what most people discover is that wealth is now protected by law. Society is thus necessarily the guarantor of inequality.

The societies established by the American and French revolutions chafed against the implications of Rousseau's analysis. As Alexis de Tocqueville wisely observed of early-eighteenth-century America, democracy is taken to mean equality, and equality is thought to be realized in individuality. All people are equally free to do as they like. However, Tocqueville observes that not only is equality not the same thing as liberty but individualism leads ultimately to isolation rather than community. Like the social contract for Rousseau, individualism can have the unintended result of guaranteeing inequality.

Inequality, however, is not just an abstract concept of political theory. By the mid-nineteenth century, previously silenced persons, such as slaves and women, began to speak and write for themselves. The result was not only a dramatic and emotional widening of the written human record but a passionate new phase of the struggle for equality. Harriet Jacobs's story of her sexual persecution by her slave master and, after harrowing struggle, her ultimate escape to freedom is a notable contribution both to the historical narrative and to the political debate. The experience of African-Americans often turned this political debate on its head because bitter experience taught the ex-slave that freedom does not necessarily translate into equality. As W. E. B. Du Bois argues eloquently, the ex-slave became not an equal citizen but a "problem." This "problem" figure, Du Bois says, had a simple yearning: "He simply wished to make it possible for a man to be both a negro and an American." In the twentieth century, the achievement of equality continued to lie beyond the horizon for African-Americans. More than half a century after Du Bois wrote his eloquent analysis of the condition of black Americans, *The Souls of Black Folk* (1903), Martin Luther King Jr. again called on the nation to fulfill the promise of its founders to establish a republic of free and equal citizens.

The struggle of women in the twentieth century parallels in some respects the struggle of African-Americans, as Simone de Beauvoir notes in her pioneering analysis of the role of women, *The Second Sex* (1949). But Beauvoir also says that the role of woman as "Other" differs from the role of African-Americans insofar as woman's subservience to man dates from the beginning of time. The unique difficulties for women in their search for an identity equal to but independent of men is that social and intellectual norms are defined by and occur within the world of men. Betty Friedan, who is credited with launching the modern feminist movement in the United States, echoes both Du Bois and Beauvoir. The despair of women in the 1950s, when Friedan began writing, is "the problem without a name," a problem denied and all but obliterated by male society. Like Beauvoir, Friedan argues that an authentic identity for women cannot derive from the definitions of men. Jamaica Kincaid's story "Girl" shows how comprehensive the imposition of identity on women can be.

The traditions of African-American and feminist thought come together in the work of bell hooks, who prefers to write her name in lowercase. In her writing, hooks seeks to show how the oppression of women is the consequence of interconnected dominant systems, including the economic system and the cultural system of white male supremacy. In a different way, these traditions of thought also enter the work of Richard Rodriguez. Like Walt Whitman (see Chapter 1, pp. 55–59), Rodriguez celebrates the "impurity" of America, stressing less the inequalities of the society and more its often anarchic mixture, including its mixture of races and genders. This mixing of ideas and peoples, Rodriguez argues, produces on the palette of culture a color that is uniquely expressive of American experience—the color brown.

KEYNOTE

Black and White (2006)

Gloria Goodale

Gloria Goodale is arts and entertainment correspondent for *The Christian Science Monitor* in Los Angeles. Born in Detroit in 1954, Goodale is a graduate of Stanford University. She began her career as a reporter for the *Monitor* at its home office in Boston. In 1986, she opened the West Coast bureau of the newspaper's public radio program *MonitoRadio* and then worked on the Monitor's news program *World Monitor* on the Discovery Channel. She returned to the newspaper as an arts reporter in 1996.

This article appeared in *The Christian Science Monitor* on March 3, 2006.

LOS ANGELES—Next week, a new reality TV show will push the hottest button in the national psyche: race. Through Hollywood makeup wizardry two families—one black, one white—swap skin colors to experience life on the other side of the racial divide for six weeks.

The series on FX, titled "Black.White," observes the dads as they find work and buy shoes. It follows the kids as they go to parties and school. And it homes in on the dinner-time conversations of the two families, who share the same house in a Los Angeles suburb during the experiment. The show, whose premise is reminiscent of John Howard Griffin's 1959 book "Black Like Me," examines the often contentious and emotionally charged issues that come up as the families try to see life through new eyes. They discover that racism may be more subtle, but it is still very much what many have dubbed "the third rail of American public life"—the issue nobody wants to touch.

The *Monitor,* as it has done with other landmark shows, convened a TV panel—in this case, a mixed audience—to watch the first episode and discuss the issues it raises. Perhaps not surprisingly, the ensuing, sometimes heated, conversation often mirrored many of the comments made by the show's participants as they confront their own and each others' views on living in a society where racism seems to be just below the skin.

The participants include Bonnie Davis and Angel Gomez, a married white couple; Lionel Douglass, an African-American actor and author; Gwen Allen, an African-American grandmother; and Julian McLean, her grandson.

5 As the group settles into a lunch of hummus, tabouleh, and grape leaves, Bonnie and Lionel make it clear that the show has touched raw spots in the hearts and minds of our panel members.

Lionel says: "Wherever you go, people think about color."

Bonnie replies: "It is about color, but it's also more complex than that."

The group has just watched the first hour of the series in which, among other things, the black dad in white face buys shoes and has them slipped on his feet "for the first time in my life," and later has a conversation with the white dad in black face about whether he imagines or actually experiences racism. The moments that seem to have stuck in everyone's mind revolve around differences in perception about racism. Throughout the show, Bruno Marcotulli, the white man in black face, seems committed to the notion that racism is something you create. At one point, he even tells Brian Sparks, the African-American in the show: "You're looking for it."

Panel member Lionel responds with an emphatic rebuttal, just as his TV counterpart does. "Race is definitely still a factor in America," says Lionel, anxious to get his thoughts on record even before the group has fully settled in at the table. "Bruno may not see it or feel it, but it's there."

10 Both Bonnie and Angel wonder if Bruno is deliberately taking an extreme position, either for the dramatic purposes of the show or to prove that he is not racist. But even if it isn't a consciously extreme position, Bonnie suggests that mental attitude is extremely important in determining experience. "It's a way of approaching things," says Bonnie. "If you have nothing and you feel you'll achieve something if you work hard, then you'll achieve more than if you think you won't."

The discussion about this idea—whether or not blacks bring racism into their experience by looking for it—grows intense, with all sides weighing in, including 12-year-old Julian. "Stereotypes are everywhere," he says. "You can't help but have an opinion about someone based on their hair or their dress or their skin color. It's just the way things are."

At one point, the effort to come to a single position on the subject dissolves and Bonnie and Lionel break off into their own discussion about assumptions. "I would never assume that I understand the black experience," she says, to which Lionel is willing to agree. "You can't really know anything well," he says, "until you experience it."

This observation brings the group back to the question at the core of the show, namely, what will the families learn from six weeks of color shifting?

Brian Sparks, the black father from "Black.White," opines: "Whites will get more from this show than blacks."

15 This comment underlines what Lionel calls the nuclear button of American life. "Nobody wants to talk about race because it makes them uncomfortable," he says. He concludes that the difference for blacks and whites is that blacks think about it all the time because they are constantly making adjustments to a culture that is dominated by the white experience.

But one of the interesting twists in the show is that both sides realize how much they don't know about the other. In an interview, the show's African-American dad says, "I knew racism was there, but I was shocked." He has just finished a stint bartending as a white person in an all-white neighborhood. Patrons, who assume he is one of them, discuss at length the virtues of keeping their white neighborhood "pure."

"Black.White" offers other eye-opening lessons about cultural differences.

Gwen, the grandmother on the panel, says she has experienced many of the issues that came up on the show. Take the issue of minding one's own business, she says. When the two wives trade tips for fitting in, the black mom advises her white counterpart to "ask fewer questions."

Black people, she says, do not ask questions about other people's lives and don't like such inquiries, either.

20 "I almost didn't want to come today," says Gwen, "because I was worried that I might get asked all sorts of questions about things that are none of anyone's business." It is interesting to realize that this is not personal so much as cultural, she says. Whites do not shy away from personal questions as blacks do.

Toward the end of the lunch, the conversation moves into a sort of Rorscharch test of its own. Gwen brings up a poem written by the white teen, Rose, for an all-black teen poetry class which she joins in her black guise. Rose anguishes over how to fit into the class and comes up with a poem that ends with several graphic references to sex.

"She did that because she thinks that's what blacks relate to," says Gwen, shaking her head in disapproval over the hoary stereotype.

Lionel agrees with Gwen. "I think she did this to fit in," he says, adding, "did you see the way she walked when she came in? It was a deliberately sexy walk."

But Bonnie suggests that this is not a racist move on the 17-year-old's part, rather a reflection of her age. "She's a teenager, and that's what's on her mind."

25 Bonnie's husband Angel, who has been more reserved than the rest of the panel, sums up what he believes the message of the show will be. "Whites tend to underestimate racism," he says, "while blacks tend to overestimate it."

LEADING QUESTIONS

At the outset of the twenty-first century, have we come very close to achieving the American dream of equality for all, or is the realization of this ideal still a good way off? When the *Christian Science Monitor* convenes a panel in Los Angeles to view the FX show "Black.White," it includes in this "mixed audience" an illuminating group, at least judging by their names. The married white couple is called Bonnie Davis and Angel Gomez; the grandson of Gwen Allen, an African-American woman, is called Julian McLean. In the TV show, the white father is called Bruno Marcotulli, and the African-American father is called Brian Sparks. The luncheon includes hummus, tabouleh, and grape leaves. These names and this food suggest that America remains a melting pot. Moreover, the very ability of this group to sit, eat, and talk as equals suggests a sea change in American life. The different last names of the married couple equally attest to new cultural realities, in this case affirming the independent identity of the woman in marriage (see Betty Friedan, pp. 496–509).

At the same time, the initial idealism of earlier generations (see W. E. B. Du Bois, pp. 472–479, and Martin Luther King Jr., pp. 511–525) seems distinctly qualified both by the participants in the TV show and by the *Monitor* audience. Racism and racist attitudes persist. Both white and African-American participants in the show and on the panel see the society as white-dominated. The excerpted article ends: "Whites tend to underestimate racism, while blacks tend to overestimate it." Is this judgment a sign of enormous progress or evidence that inequalities just cannot be overcome? How do the essays in this chapter illuminate these questions?

LEARNING MORE

In 1959, John Howard Griffin, a white Texan from a privileged background, darkened his skin in a New Orleans hotel room and traveled Mississippi as a black man, turning his experiences into the book *Black Like Me,* published in 1961 (not 1959, as the article states). The book remains in print, and you may want to compare it with the FX show "Black.White."

QUESTIONING THE TEXT

1. What part of the TV show did everyone who watched it find most memorable? Can we draw any conclusions about race from this common reaction to the show?
2. Julian is quoted as intervening to say, "Stereotypes are everywhere," and people can't help having opinions based on stereotypes (par. 11). Do you agree? Explain.
3. What is the "nuclear button of American life," according to Lionel Douglass (par. 15)? What is his evidence for this statement? Do the other panel members agree with Lionel? Do you? Why or why not?
4. Which of the issues that came up in the show did the grandmother, Gwen, choose to emphasize? What does this issue suggest about racial attitudes?
5. Lionel and Bonnie have different interpretations of Rose's poem and "sexy walk." With whom do you agree, and why?
6. What does the article conclude that the two families in the show will learn from their experience? Does this conclusion seem fair to you, based on the evidence presented in the article? Is this conclusion an accurate reflection of American attitudes today? Discuss.

ANALYZING THE WRITER'S CRAFT

1. Would this article have been written differently in a newspaper directed at African-Americans? Explain.
2. Discuss how Goodale organizes her material for this article. What determines the order in which she presents information in pars. 1–7? What does she select for special emphasis, and how is that emphasis achieved?
3. Much of this article relies on direct quotation from the panel participants. Do you find the writer's use of quotations effective? Discuss two or three examples.
4. Does the writer reveal her own opinions in this article, or is the article an objective account of the views of others? Explain.

5. The writer draws her article to a conclusion by reference to the "Rorscharch test" of Rose's participation in the all-black poetry class (par. 21). How is Rose's writing and behavior a Rorscharch test? If you were writing this article, would you have placed these facts elsewhere in the story, or maybe not used them at all? Explain.
6. Does the story's conclusion fairly encapsulate the whole discussion, or does it impose an artificial ending on a complex conversation? Explain.

MAKING CONNECTIONS

1. Compare and contrast the attitudes expressed by the people in this article with the attitudes of the students in J. E. B. Stuart High School (Chapter 1, pp. 11–19).
2. Mary Gordon (Chapter 1, pp. 37–42) argues that the determining experience for her and Americans like her is immigration. Does the information in this article suggest that race is a larger issue than immigration, or is race one part of the story of the American melting pot today?
3. Do you think James Baldwin (Chapter 1, pp. 29–35) and Martin Luther King Jr. (pp. 511–525) would take comfort from this article, or would they find in it depressing evidence of the persistence of racism? Explain.
4. Richard Rodriguez (pp. 542–549) sees the melting pot as the best metaphor for America, but also as a dreadful metaphor. How does this article confirm or qualify these two sides of the melting pot?

FORMULATING IDEAS FOR WRITING

1. Is race "the hottest button in the national psyche" (par. 1)? Or is it necessary to say so in order for the media to be able to produce an audience for TV shows and newspaper articles? In answering, be sure to pay special attention to your evidence. On what evidence are you going to base your answer? What gives you confidence that your evidence is sound and reliable?
2. How great a role does perception play in issues that may divide society, such as racism and sexism? Is perception more of an issue for whites than for people of color, or more for men than for women? If a person feels that he or she has experienced racism, can this be analyzed as mainly a matter of perception? How can racism or sexism be assessed in ways that are not subjective?
3. Julian says that "stereotypes are everywhere." Is the existence of stereotypes an obstacle to respectful human relations? Or are stereotypes essential for human communication? Could it be a matter of degree?
4. Read *Black Like Me* and discuss the question of whether racism has significantly changed in the United States in the last forty years.
5. Write an essay about race and minding your own business (see pars. 18–20). Interview some friends, neighbors, fellow students, and others to provide some additional material for your discussion.

On the Origin of Inequality (1755)

Jean-Jacques Rousseau

In *Discourse on the Origin of Inequality* (1755), from which this selection is taken, and in his later *The Social Contract* (1762), Jean-Jacques Rousseau aims to explain the origin of society and the consequences flowing from the way society came into being. Does society liberate or enslave? In answering this question, Rousseau amends but also canonizes John Locke's idea of the social contract (see Chapter 5, pp. 348–352). For Locke, the state of nature is a condition of freedom and equality, but it is also a dangerous condition, unstable and insecure. The social contract involves the ceding of some rights in exchange for the order and security of society. But for Rousseau, the social contract also fixes forever the inequalities of persons and conditions under the protection of law. Consequently, he opens *The Social Contract* with the famous sentence "Man is born free; and everywhere he is in chains."

Rousseau was born in Geneva in 1712. His mother died a few days after he was born, and his father abandoned him when he was ten years old. Under the care of his uncle, Rousseau was apprenticed to an engraver, but after several unhappy years, he ran away to make his fortune. He eventually entered Paris in 1742 to pursue a career in music. Only one of his operas, *Le Devin du village* (*The Village Soothsayer*), survives. (It was performed before Louis XVI in 1746.) The self-taught Rousseau wrote about an extraordinary range of subjects—botany, religion, language, and education. His ideas on education, expressed in *Emile* (1762), profoundly influenced modern practice. The child, Rousseau says, is something of a "noble savage," liable to corruption by the falseness of social mores. A child's education should be an education of the emotions, drawing out the child's natural morality and compassion. It should focus less on book-learning and more on experience.

Rousseau's *Confessions*, published from 1781 to 1788 (after Rousseau's death), reveal another ground for his fame. Although the Enlightenment is often also called the Age of Reason, Rousseau turned his attention inward to feelings. He looked for meaning in an extended, unalloyed, and unstinting look at himself, delving into his behavior and motives. Who am I? What am I? The inner person—fallible, misguided, egotistical, and certainly flawed—would provide the answer to these questions, unveiling the poignancy of being human.

Rousseau was famously difficult, tending to paranoia. Brilliant and iconoclastic, his ideas repelled authority, and he was forced to flee Paris in 1762. Banned from Paris and Geneva, he wandered from place to place, living for a time in Scotland at the invitation of David Hume. He was finally permitted to return to Paris on sufferance in 1770, but the warrant for his arrest was never rescinded. In Paris, he felt the eyes of his enemies upon him and accepted an invitation to leave the capital for Ermenonville, where he died in 1778.

The cultivation of the earth necessarily brought about its distribution; and property, once recognized, gave rise to the first rules of justice, for, to secure each man his own, it had to be possible for each to have something. Besides, as men began to look forward to the future, and all had something to lose, every one had reason to apprehend that reprisals would follow any injury he might do to another. This origin is so much the more natural, as it is impossible to conceive how property can come from anything but manual labor: for what else can a man add to things which he does not originally create, so as to make them his own property? It is the husbandman's[1] labor alone that, giving him a title to the produce of the ground he has tilled, gives him a claim also to the land itself, at least till harvest; and so, from year to year, a constant possession which is easily transformed into property. When the ancients, says Grotius, gave to Ceres[2] the title of Legislatrix, and to a festival celebrated in her honor the name of Thesmophoria,[3] they meant by that that the distribution of lands had produced a new kind of right: that is to say, the right of property, which is different from the right deducible from the law of nature.

In this state of affairs, equality might have been sustained, had the talents of individuals been equal, and had, for example, the use of iron and the consumption of commodities always exactly balanced each other; but, as there was nothing to preserve this balance, it was soon disturbed; the strongest did most work; the most skillful turned his labor to best account; the most ingenious devised methods of diminishing his labor: the husbandman wanted more iron, or the smith more corn,[4] and, while both labored equally, the one gained a great deal by his work, while the other could hardly support himself. Thus natural inequality unfolds itself insensibly with that of combination, and the difference between men, developed by their different circumstances, becomes more sensible and permanent in its effects, and begins to have an influence, in the same proportion, over the lot of individuals.

Matters once at this pitch, it is easy to imagine the rest. I shall not detain the reader, with a description of the successive invention of other arts, the development of language, the trial and utilization of talents, the inequality of fortunes, the use and abuse of riches, and all the details connected with them which the reader can easily supply for himself. I shall confine myself to a glance at mankind in this new situation.

---

[1] husbandman: farmer.

[2] Grotius . . . Ceres: Hugo Grotius (1583–1645), Dutch jurist, is the originator of the modern philosophy of international law. Ceres is the Roman goddess of plants, especially grains (hence "cereal"), and of motherly love.

[3] Thesmophoria: Festival in ancient Greece in honor of Demeter Thesmophorus (in Roman mythology called Ceres) and her daughter Persephone. It commemorated the third of the year when Demeter/Ceres abstained from her role of goddess of the harvest. The festival was held in about October and was attended only by women.

[4] corn: wheat.

Behold then all human faculties developed, memory and imagination in full play, egoism interested, reason active, and the mind almost at the highest point of its perfection. Behold all the natural qualities in action, the rank and condition of every man assigned him; not merely his share of property and his power to serve or injure others, but also his wit, beauty, strength or skill, merit or talents: and these being the only qualities capable of commanding respect, it soon became necessary to possess or to affect them.

5 It now became the interest of men to appear what they really were not. To be and to seem became two totally different things; and from this distinction sprang insolent pomp and cheating trickery, with all the numerous vices that go in their train. On the other hand, free and independent as men were before, they were now, in consequence of a multiplicity of new wants, brought into subjection, as it were, to all nature, and particularly to one another; and each became in some degree a slave even in becoming the master of other men: if rich, they stood in need of the services of others; if poor, of their assistance; and even a middle condition did not enable them to do without one another. Man must now, therefore, have been perpetually employed in getting others to interest themselves in his lot, and in making them, apparently at least, if not really, find their advantage in promoting his own. Thus he must have been sly and artful in his behavior to some, and imperious and cruel to others; being under a kind of necessity to ill-use all the persons of whom he stood in need, when he could not frighten them into compliance, and did not judge it his interest to be useful to them. Insatiable ambition, the thirst of raising their respective fortunes, not so much from real want as from the desire to surpass others, inspired all men with a vile propensity to injure one another, and with a secret jealousy, which is the more dangerous, as it puts on the mask of benevolence, to carry its point with greater security. In a word, there arose rivalry and competition on the one hand, and conflicting interests on the other, together with a secret desire on both of profiting at the expense of others. All these evils were the first effects of property, and the inseparable attendants of growing inequality.

Before the invention of signs to represent riches, wealth could hardly consist in anything but lands and cattle, the only real possessions men can have. But, when inheritances so increased in number and extent as to occupy the whole of the land, and to border on one another, one man could aggrandise himself only at the expense of another; at the same time the supernumeraries,[5] who had been too weak or too indolent to make such acquisitions, and had grown poor without sustaining any loss, because, while they saw everything change around them, they remained still the same, were obliged to receive their subsistence, or steal it, from the rich; and this soon bred, according to their different characters, dominion and slavery, or violence and rapine. The wealthy, on their part, had no sooner begun to taste the pleasure of command, than they disdained all others, and, using their old slaves to acquire new, thought of nothing but subduing and enslaving their neighbors; like ravenous wolves, which,

[5] supernumeraries: excess or superfluous people; in this case, more than have profited from the distribution of land.

having once tasted human flesh, despise every other food and thenceforth seek only men to devour.

Thus, as the most powerful or the most miserable considered their might or misery as a kind of right to the possessions of others, equivalent, in their opinion, to that of property, the destruction of equality was attended by the most terrible disorders. Usurpations by the rich, robbery by the poor, and the unbridled passions of both, suppressed the cries of natural compassion and the still feeble voice of justice, and filled men with avarice, ambition and vice. Between the title of the strongest and that of the first occupier, there arose perpetual conflicts, which never ended but in battles and bloodshed. The new-born state of society thus gave rise to a horrible state of war; men thus harassed and depraved were no longer capable of retracing their steps or renouncing the fatal acquisitions they had made, but, laboring by the abuse of the faculties which do them honor, merely to their own confusion, brought themselves to the brink of ruin. . . .

It is impossible that men should not at length have reflected on so wretched a situation, and on the calamities that overwhelmed them. The rich, in particular, must have felt how much they suffered by a constant state of war, of which they bore all the expense; and in which, though all risked their lives, they alone risked their property. Besides, however speciously[6] they might disguise their usurpations, they knew that they were founded on precarious[7] and false titles; so that, if others took from them by force what they themselves had gained by force, they would have no reason to complain. Even those who had been enriched by their own industry, could hardly base their proprietorship on better claims. It was in vain to repeat, "I built this well; I gained this spot by my industry." Who gave you your standing, it might be answered, and what right have you to demand payment of us for doing what we never asked you to do? Do you not know that numbers of your fellow-creatures are starving, for want of what you have too much of? You ought to have had the express and universal consent of mankind, before appropriating more of the common subsistence than you needed for your own maintenance. Destitute of valid reasons to justify and sufficient strength to defend himself, able to crush individuals with ease, but easily crushed himself by a troop of bandits, one against all, and incapable, on account of mutual jealousy, of joining with his equals against numerous enemies united by the common hope of plunder, the rich man, thus urged by necessity, conceived at length the profoundest plan that ever entered the mind of man: this was to employ in his favor the forces of those who attacked him, to make allies of his adversaries, to inspire them with different maxims, and to give them other institutions as favorable to himself as the law of nature was unfavorable.

With this view, after having represented to his neighbors the horror of a situation which armed every man against the rest, and made their possessions as burdensome to them as their wants, and in which no safety could be expected either in riches or in poverty, he readily devised plausible arguments to make them close with his design. "Let us join," said he, "to guard the weak from

---

[6] speciously: falsely.

[7] precarious: insecure.

oppression, to restrain the ambitious, and secure to every man the possession of what belongs to him: let us institute rules of justice and peace, to which all without exception may be obliged to conform; rules that may in some measure make amends for the caprices of fortune, by subjecting equally the powerful and the weak to the observance of reciprocal obligations. Let us, in a word, instead ofturning our forces against ourselves, collect them in a supreme power which may govern us by wise laws, protect and defend all the members of the association, repulse their common enemies, and maintain eternal harmony among us."

Far fewer words to this purpose would have been enough to impose on men so barbarous and easily seduced; especially as they had too many disputes among themselves to do without arbitrators, and too much ambition and avarice to go long without masters. All ran headlong to their chains, in hopes of securing their liberty; for they had just wit enough to perceive the advantages of political institutions, without experience enough to enable them to foresee the dangers. The most capable of foreseeing the dangers were the very persons who expected to benefit by them; and even the most prudent judged it not inexpedient to sacrifice one part of their freedom to ensure the rest; as a wounded man has his arm cut off to save the rest of his body.

Such was, or may well have been, the origin of society and law, which bound new fetters on the poor, and gave new powers to the rich; which irretrievably destroyed natural liberty, eternally fixed the law of property and inequality, converted clever usurpation into unalterable right, and, for the advantage of a few ambitious individuals, subjected all mankind to perpetual labor, slavery and wretchedness. It is easy to see how the establishment of one community made that of all the rest necessary, and how, in order to make head against united forces, the rest of mankind had to unite in turn.

I know that some writers have given other explanations of the origin of political societies, such as the conquest of the powerful, or the association of the weak. It is, indeed, indifferent to my argument which of these causes we choose. That which I have just laid down, however, appears to me the most natural for the following reasons. First: because, in the first case, the right of conquest, being no right in itself, could not serve as a foundation on which to build any other; the victor and the vanquished people still remained with respect to each other in the state of war, unless the vanquished, restored to the full possession of their liberty, voluntarily made choice of the victor for their chief. For till then, whatever capitulation may have been made being founded on violence, and therefore *ipso facto*[8] void, there could not have been on this hypothesis either a real society or body politic, or any law other than that of the strongest. Secondly: because the words *strong* and *weak* are, in the second case, ambiguous; for during the interval between the establishment of a right of property, or prior occupancy, and that of political government, the meaning of these words is better expressed by the terms *rich* and *poor:* because, in fact, before the institution of laws, men had no other way of reducing their equals to

[8] *ipso facto:* by that very fact.

submission, than by attacking their goods, or making some of their own over to them. Thirdly: because, as the poor had nothing but their freedom to lose, it would have been in the highest degree absurd for them to resign voluntarily the only good they still enjoyed, without getting anything in exchange: whereas the rich having feelings, if I may so express myself, in every part of their possessions, it was much easier to harm them, and therefore more necessary for them to take precautions against it; and, in short, because it is more reasonable to suppose a thing to have been invented by those to whom it would be of service, than by those whom it must have harmed.

LEARNING MORE

The whole of *Discourse on the Origin of Inequality,* as well as *The Social Contract,* can be accessed online. See the *Ideas Across Time* website.

QUESTIONING THE TEXT

1. Rousseau focuses on what he suggests must have been the condition of human societies just at the point of transition from nomadic life to settled communities organized around agriculture. According to Rousseau, how does the introduction of agriculture also "necessarily" lead to the introduction of property (par. 1)?
2. The equality of preagricultural society might have been maintained even in settled communities, Rousseau says. How? Why did inequality come about instead?
3. How does society, a form of human organization "everyone" willingly subscribed to, also enslave everyone?
4. What do you think Rousseau means, in the last sentence of par. 6, by "the law of nature"?
5. How is the "horror" of the law of nature overcome?
6. Why, according to Rousseau does lawful society enshrine inequality? Do you agree with his analysis? Are there any alternatives?
7. In his long final paragraph, Rousseau refutes two alternative speculations about the origin of society and law. Do you find his refutations persuasive? Why or why not?
8. For what purpose do you think Rousseau explores the origin of society and law?

ANALYZING THE WRITER'S CRAFT

1. Rousseau writes about the origin of society and law, a subject about which there is no hard evidence. In the absence of evidence, on what does Rousseau base his analysis? Does Rousseau ever acknowledge that his explanations have no more evidence to back them up than any other explanations ? Where?

2. Rousseau relies heavily on logical inference for his argument, and much depends on his assumptions. Do you find his assumptions to be sound? Why or why not? Are you happy that he has derived logical conclusions from his assumptions? Discuss. If his assumptions and his logic are both sound, his conclusions must also be sound. In that case, must everyone agree with his conclusions? Explain.
3. The story Rousseau has to tell, the story of the origin of society and of law, could be a rather dull subject. How does Rousseau hold our attention?
4. Rousseau proceeds by definite steps in both logic and time. Discuss two of his transitions, showing how they emphasize that one step in his argument is completed and we are now moving on to the next step.
5. Rousseau couches his insights in often striking examples, metaphors, or language. In this way, his logical analysis is given an emotional coloring. Discuss two examples of Rousseau's writing where the way he makes his points adds an emotional edge to the point.
6. Rousseau closes his argument by refuting two alternative views of the same subject. Do you find this to be an effective close? How could he have handled these objections in a different way?

MAKING CONNECTIONS

1. John Locke (Chapter 5, pp. 348–352) does not seem to have the same kinds of reservations about the social contract as does Rousseau. Do their views complement or contradict each other?
2. Is Rousseau a democrat? How does his thinking compare and contrast with that of Mary Wollstonecraft, for example (Chapter 5, pp. 362–369)?
3. Does Rousseau's analysis of inequality support or undermine Karl Marx's view (Chapter 4, pp. 264–273)?
4. Is Rousseau's approach scientific—in the sense of "science" offered by Francis Bacon (Chapter 3, pp. 152–156) and Richard Feynman (Chapter 3, pp. 201–207). Insofar as his work is scientific, does it display the power and beauty of science or the limitations of science when applied to human affairs?
5. Are Rousseau's ideas about "natural inequality" compatible or incompatible with those of Charles Darwin (Chapter 3, pp. 167–180)? Explain.

FORMULATING IDEAS FOR WRITING

1. In this selection, Rousseau writes on something that might be called speculative anthropology, that is, the study of the origin of human society based on speculation about what might have happened thousands of years before recorded history. Write an essay that explores whether anthropologists today support or question Rousseau's account.
2. If human beings necessarily compete against one another for more or less everything on the basis of "natural inequality" (par. 2), as Rousseau says, then what should be the role of society with respect to that competition?

3. The destruction of the equality of existence by agriculture, Rousseau says, resulted in "the most terrible disorders." That early society was more a state of war than of order. Rousseau says that as a consequence men banded together to establish lawful society. But if you look around today, do you see genuine lawful society or a masked state of war?
4. In a memorable phrase, Rousseau says of the impetus toward lawful society, "All ran headlong to their chains, in hopes of securing their liberty" (par. 10). Discuss this sentence as the kernel of Rousseau's analysis of our condition in society. Do you think of yourself as being in chains now that you have read Rousseau? Explain. Is Rousseau painting too static an analysis, neglecting the continuing dynamic of social life, the constants shifts and changes and adjustments that occur?

Equality and Individualism (1840)

Alexis de Tocqueville

Alexis de Tocqueville was a prominent figure among a remarkable generation of mid-nineteenth-century European political thinkers—men and women with roots in the aristocracies of the Old World who nonetheless devoted their careers and their lives to the practice and theory of liberal democracy. Like the English poet Lord Byron, who gave up his life for Greek liberty, or the Russian aristocrat Alexander Herzen, who championed republican ideals from exile in Paris and London, Tocqueville took a stand for democracy. But Tocqueville's embrace of democracy was hardly unreserved. He thought that grand human ideals, lofty achievements, and high ambitions could flourish best in aristocratic society, and he understood that the bedrock of American democracy was a commitment not to political and individual liberty but rather to equality. Despite his profound grasp of the benefits and wide implications of American egalitarianism, Tocqueville thought democracy came at the price of a diminished conception of human possibilities and a complacent or dangerously indifferent regard for liberty.

Alexis-Charles-Henri Clérel de Tocqueville, the son of a Norman nobleman and the granddaughter of one of France's great statesmen, Chrétien de Malesherbes, was born in Paris on June 29, 1805. His father became prefect of Versailles, the most influential post of its kind in France, when Tocqueville was twenty-one. A year later, the elder Tocqueville was made a peer by the Bourbon king, Charles X. But the July Revolution of 1830 drastically altered the careers of both father and son. Charles X was overthrown, and in his place, Louis-Philippe came to the throne as a constitutional monarch. Tocqueville's father was forced to give up his peerage and never assumed important public office again. The younger Tocqueville, aware of his precarious position under the new regime, persuaded the authorities to allow him to travel to the United States, ostensibly to study penal institutions. Traveling with his life-long friend Gustave de Beaumont, Tocqueville observed American life intensively over an eighteen-month period beginning in May 1831. Although Beaumont and Tocqueville's study of the American penal system won a prestigious award from the powerful French Academy, it was Tocqueville's far more ambitious reflection on American life, *Democracy in America,* that made his reputation. The first part of Tocqueville's great work was published in France in 1835; its eighth edition, in 1840, included the book's second and final part. A success in its own day, the book stands today as perhaps the most insightful of all books on the practices, virtues, and limits of American democratic life and institutions.

Tocqueville returned to active French politics in 1839 when he was elected to the Chamber of Deputies. He was seen as an expert on prisons and slavery; his official report recommending immediate emancipation of all slaves in French territories was republished by the Society for the Abolition of Slavery. Although opposed to the Revolution of 1848 that brought Louis-Napoleon to power, Tocqueville nonetheless was elected to the new Constituent Assembly and to the committee designated to draft the constitution for the Second Republic. He served briefly as Louis-Napoleon's foreign minister but then was imprisoned overnight for his opposition to Louis' coup d'état of December 2, 1851, and barred from public office. He retired to his family seat, the village of Tocqueville, where he died of tuberculosis on May 10, 1859.

The following selections have been taken from the second volume of *Democracy in America.*

I. Why Democratic Nations Show a More Ardent and Enduring Love of Equality Than of Liberty

The first and most intense passion that is produced by equality of condition is, I need hardly say, the love of that equality. My readers will therefore not be surprised that I speak of this feeling before all others.

Everybody has remarked that in our time, and especially in France, this passion for equality is every day gaining ground in the human heart. It has been said a hundred times that our contemporaries are far more ardently and tenaciously attached to equality than to freedom; but as I do not find that the causes of the fact have been sufficiently analyzed, I shall endeavor to point them out.

It is possible to imagine an extreme point at which freedom and equality would meet and blend. Let us suppose that all the people take a part in the government, and that each one of them has an equal right to take a part in it. As no one is different from his fellows, none can exercise a tyrannical power; men will be perfectly free because they are all entirely equal; and they will all be perfectly equal because they are entirely free. To this ideal state democratic nations tend. This is the only complete form that equality can assume upon earth; but there are a thousand others which, without being equally perfect, are not less cherished by those nations.

The principle of equality may be established in civil society without prevailing in the political world. There may be equal rights of indulging in the same pleasures, of entering the same professions, of frequenting the same places; in a word, of living in the same manner and seeking wealth by the same means, although all men do not take an equal share in the government. A kind of equality may even be established in the political world though there should be no political freedom there. A man may be the equal of all his countrymen save one, who is the master of all without distinction and who selects equally from among them all the agents of his power. Several other combinations might be easily imagined by which very great equality would be united to institutions more or less free or even to institutions wholly without freedom.

5 Although men cannot become absolutely equal unless they are entirely free, and consequently equality, pushed to its furthest extent, may be confounded with freedom, yet there is good reason for distinguishing the one from the other. The taste which men have for liberty and that which they feel for equality are, in fact, two different things; and I am not afraid to add that among democratic nations they are two unequal things.

Upon close inspection it will be seen that there is in every age some peculiar and preponderant fact with which all others are connected; this fact almost always gives birth to some pregnant idea or some ruling passion, which attracts to itself and bears away in its course all the feelings and opinions of the time; it is like a great stream towards which each of the neighboring rivulets seems to flow.

Freedom has appeared in the world at different times and under various forms; it has not been exclusively bound to any social condition, and it is not confined to democracies. Freedom cannot, therefore, form the distinguishing characteristic of democratic ages. The peculiar and preponderant fact that marks those ages as its own is the equality of condition; the ruling passion of men in those periods is the love of this equality. Do not ask what singular charm the men of democratic ages find in being equal, or what special reasons they may have for clinging so tenaciously to equality rather than to the other advantages that society holds out to them: equality is the distinguishing characteristic of the age they live in; that of itself is enough to explain that they prefer it to all the rest.

But independently of this reason there are several others which will at all times habitually lead men to prefer equality to freedom.

If a people could ever succeed in destroying, or even in diminishing, the equality that prevails in its own body, they could do so only by long and laborious efforts. Their social condition must be modified, their laws abolished, their opinions superseded, their habits changed, their manners corrupted. But political liberty is more easily lost; to neglect to hold it fast is to allow it to escape. Therefore not only do men cling to equality because it is dear to them; they also adhere to it because they think it will last forever.

10 That political freedom in its excesses may compromise the tranquillity, the property, the lives of individuals is obvious even to narrow and unthinking minds. On the contrary, none but attentive and clear-sighted men perceive the perils with

which equality threatens us, and they commonly avoid pointing them out. They know that the calamities they apprehend are remote and flatter themselves that they will only fall upon future generations, for which the present generation takes but little thought. The evils that freedom sometimes brings with it are immediate; they are apparent to all, and all are more or less affected by them. The evils that extreme equality may produce are slowly disclosed; they creep gradually into the social frame; they are seen only at intervals; and at the moment at which they become most violent, habit already causes them to be no longer felt.

The advantages that freedom brings are shown only by the lapse of time, and it is always easy to mistake the cause in which they originate. The advantages of equality are immediate, and they may always be traced from their source.

Political liberty bestows exalted pleasures from time to time upon a certain number of citizens. Equality every day confers a number of small enjoyments on every man. The charms of equality are every instant felt and are within the reach of all; the noblest hearts are not insensible to them, and the most vulgar souls exult in them. The passion that equality creates must therefore be at once strong and general. Men cannot enjoy political liberty unpurchased by some sacrifices, and they never obtain it without great exertions. But the pleasures of equality are self-proffered; each of the petty incidents of life seems to occasion them, and in order to taste them, nothing is required but to live. . . .

II. Of Individualism in Democratic Countries

I have shown how it is that in ages of equality every man seeks for his opinions within himself; I am now to show how it is that in the same ages all his feelings are turned towards himself alone. *Individualism* is a novel expression, to which a novel idea has given birth. Our fathers were only acquainted with *égoïsme* (selfishness). Selfishness is a passionate and exaggerated love of self, which leads a man to connect everything with himself and to prefer himself to everything in the world. Individualism is a mature and calm feeling, which disposes each member of the community to sever himself from the mass of his fellows and to draw apart with his family and his friends, so that after he has thus formed a little circle of his own, he willingly leaves society at large to itself. Selfishness originates in blind instinct; individualism proceeds from erroneous judgment more than from depraved feelings; it originates as much in deficiencies of mind as in perversity of heart.

Selfishness blights the germ of all virtue; individualism, at first, only saps the virtues of public life; but in the long run it attacks and destroys all others and is at length absorbed in downright selfishness. Selfishness is a vice as old as the world, which does not belong to one form of society more than to another; individualism is of democratic origin, and it threatens to spread in the same ratio as the equality of condition.

Among aristocratic nations, as families remain for centuries in the same condition, often on the same spot, all generations become, as it were, contemporaneous. A man almost always knows his forefathers and respects them; he thinks he already sees his remote descendants and he loves them. He willingly imposes duties on himself towards the former and the latter, and he will frequently sacrifice his personal gratifications to those who went before and to those who will come after him. Aristocratic institutions, moreover, have the effect of closely binding every man to several of his fellow citizens. As the classes of an aristocratic people are strongly marked and permanent, each of them is regarded by its own members as a sort of lesser country, more tangible and more cherished than the country at large. As in aristocratic communities all the citizens occupy fixed positions, one above another, the result is that each of them always sees a man above himself whose patronage is necessary to him, and below himself another man whose co-operation he may claim. Men living in aristocratic ages are therefore almost always closely attached to something placed out of their own sphere, and they are often disposed to forget themselves. It is true that in these ages the notion of human fellowship is faint and that men seldom think of sacrificing themselves for mankind; but they often sacrifice themselves for other men. In democratic times, on the contrary, when the duties of each individual to the race are much more clear, devoted service to any one man becomes more rare; the bond of human affection is extended, but it is relaxed.

Among democratic nations new families are constantly springing up, others are constantly falling away, and all that remain change their condition; the woof[1] of time is every instant broken and the track of generations effaced. Those who went before are soon forgotten; of those who will come after, no one has any idea: the interest of man is confined to those in close propinquity[2] to himself. As each class gradually approaches others and mingles with them, its members become undifferentiated and lose their class identity for each other. Aristocracy had made a chain of all the members of the community, from the peasant to the king; democracy breaks that chain and severs every link of it.

As social conditions become more equal, the number of persons increases who, although they are neither rich nor powerful enough to exercise any great influence over their fellows, have nevertheless acquired or retained sufficient education and fortune to satisfy their own wants. They owe nothing to any man, they expect nothing from any man; they acquire the habit of always considering themselves as standing alone, and they are apt to imagine that their whole destiny is in their own hands.

Thus not only does democracy make every man forget his ancestors, but it hides his descendants and separates his contemporaries from him; it throws him back forever upon himself alone and threatens in the end to confine him entirely within the solitude of his own heart.

LEARNING MORE

Tocqueville's *Democracy in America* is widely regarded as one of the best books ever written about America. Tocqueville—an aristocrat—is consequently a hero

[1] woof: cloth; specifically the threads that cross the warp in a woven fabric.
[2] propinquity: nearness, often of kinship.

to individuals from all ends of the political spectrum. To learn more about contemporary views of Tocqueville, see the *Ideas Across Time* website.

QUESTIONING THE TEXT

1. Tocqueville distinguishes between freedom or liberty and equality in a variety of ways. What, for Tocqueville, distinguishes one from the other? Why does he think that in democracies freedom and equality "are two unequal things" (par. 5)?
2. Why does Tocqueville say that people prefer equality to freedom?
3. What are the virtues of aristocracy that Tocqueville identifies?
4. Why does Tocqueville think that freedom is not especially characteristic of democracies?
5. How, according to Tocqueville, is democracy the enemy of community?
6. Why, according to Tocqueville, does democracy threaten to confine each person "entirely within the solitude of his own heart" (par. 19)? Do you agree? Why or why not?

ANALYZING THE WRITER'S CRAFT

1. Much of Tocqueville's writing in these selections involves comparison and contrast. In the passages on individualism (pars. 13–19), for example, he offers an extended review of significant features of life under democracy and aristocracy. Write an outline of these paragraphs or, if you prefer, a chart indicating his main comparisons and contrasts.
2. On what kind of evidence is Tocqueville's analysis built? Do you find his evidence authentic? Persuasive?
3. "Men living in aristocratic ages are *therefore* almost always closely attached to something placed out of their own sphere . . ." (par. 15, emphasis added). How does Tocqueville arrive at this conclusion? Is he being logical?
4. Do you think Tocqueville's conclusion to his discussion of individualism (par. 19) is warranted by the facts as he presents them? Explain.

MAKING CONNECTIONS

1. Compare and contrast Tocqueville's analysis of the American love of equality with that of Daniel Boorstin (Chapter 5, pp. 390–402).
2. Is Richard Rodriguez (pp. 542–549) forcing a contemporary set of values on Tocqueville's attitudes on race, or is he drawing out from Tocqueville what we can only grasp clearly at this distance of time?
3. What does it mean to be an American? Compare and contrast the answers to this question by St. John de Crevecoeur (Chapter 1, pp. 22–27), James Baldwin (Chapter 1, pp. 29–35), and Tocqueville.
4. Compare and contrast Tocqueville's and Adam Smith's (Chapter 4, pp. 244–262) views on consequences for society of the pursuit of self-interest.

FORMULATING IDEAS FOR WRITING

1. Write an essay that discusses how reading Tocqueville modified your understanding of democracy and/or aristocracy.
2. The United States today considers "democracy" to be the essential ingredient of the sociopolitical life of nations. We frown on nations that are perceived to be undemocratic, sometimes imposing sanctions and even employing force to effect change; and we foster the growth of democratic institutions. Write an essay that reflects on this policy stance in light of Tocqueville's analysis of aristocracy and democracy. Is our single-minded support of democracy also simple-minded?
3. Individualism, says Tocqueville, "threatens in the end to confine [every person] entirely within the solitude of his [or her] own heart" (par. 19). Almost two hundred years have passed since these words were written. Write an essay that examines the extent to which Tocqueville's fears about individualism have or have not proved true.
4. Tocqueville displays a high regard for participation in public life, which he equates with political freedom. For this reason, he worries about individualism, something that he believes "saps the virtues of public life" (par. 14). Write an essay that either supports or questions Tocqueville's analysis by reference to life in the United States today. (Bear in mind that if you support Tocqueville, you are going to show how in today's United States individualism has undermined public life; and if you question Tocqueville's views, you are going to show how in today's United States, contrary to his fears, individualism is compatible with a vigorous public life.)

Incidents in the Life of a Slave Girl (1861)

Harriet Ann Jacobs

The life of Harriet Ann Jacobs (1813–1897), born a slave in Edenton, North Carolina, and her book *Incidents in the Life of a Slave Girl* are equally remarkable. Jacobs's life is a wrenching example of the ordeals and tragedies of slave women in the American South before the Civil War, but her story is also remarkable for its instances of magnanimity, bravery, and triumph. Jacobs's book, written under the pen name Linda Brent, narrates her determined resistance to the sexual overtures of an obsessed master, her desperate effort to liberate her children from slavery, and finally her escape and her work for feminism and abolitionism.

Jacobs's mother, Delilan, was the slave of a tavern-keeper, John Horniblow; her father, Daniel Jacobs, was a white slave of Dr. Andrew Knox. Jacobs's travail commenced upon the death of her father in 1825. She was now the slave of

Dr. James Norcom, and as she grew into adolescence, he subjected her to an unrelenting sexual harassment that was not to cease until Jacobs gained her freedom many years later. To prevent Norcom from forcing her to be his slave mistress, at sixteen Jacobs entered a sexual relationship with a white neighbor, Samuel Tredwell Sawyer, with whom she had two children.

Her life was shaped by her determination to free her children from bondage. Learning that Norcom planned to take her children from her free grandmother's care, Jacobs decided to run away to save them. She hid with sympathetic neighbors, and as she had hoped, Norcom sold her children to their father, who allowed them to remain with their grandmother. But Norcom's pursuit of Jacobs was so ceaseless that for almost seven years Jacobs was forced to spend most of her days in a tiny nook in her grandmother's house.

Finally, in 1842, Jacobs escaped North to work in the home of a man of letters, Nathaniel Parker Willis. She eventually joined her brother in Rochester, New York, where she ran the local Anti-Slavery Reading Room. Norcom pursued Jacobs North until Nathaniel Willis bought her freedom in 1852. For several years, Jacobs struggled with the idea of writing her life story. She was concerned that in relaying the truth of her experience she would have to expose herself as a "fallen woman," reveal a side of slavery that would make the prudish public uncomfortable, and open herself to danger and attack. In the end, she decided to write under a pen name and to change the names of all the major personages in her life. After several false starts, she published her ground-breaking tale in 1861.

During the Civil War, Jacobs was active in the organized movement to aid slaves and former slaves, serving in Washington, D.C., and in Georgia. In 1868, Jacobs returned North to spend her remaining years with her daughter in Cambridge, Massachusetts. She is buried in Mount Auburn Cemetery in Cambridge alongside such New England notables as Oliver Wendell Holmes and Henry Wadsworth Longfellow.

VI. The Jealous Mistress

[Linda Brent was willed to her late mistress's little niece Emily Flint and sent to the Flint house to live.]

I would ten thousand times rather that my children should be the half-starved paupers of Ireland than to be the most pampered among the slaves of America. I would rather drudge out my life on a cotton plantation, till the grave opened to give me rest, than to live with an unprincipled master and a jealous mistress. The felon's home in a penitentiary is preferable. He may repent, and turn from the error of his ways, and so find peace; but it is not so with a favorite slave. She is not allowed to have any pride of character. It is deemed a crime in her to wish to be virtuous!

Mrs. Flint possessed the key to her husband's character before I was born. She might have used this knowledge to counsel and to screen the young and the innocent among her slaves; but for them she had no sympathy. They were the objects of her constant suspicion and malevolence. She watched her husband with unceasing vigilance; but he was well practised in means to evade it. What he could not find opportunity to say in words he manifested in signs. He invented more than were ever thought of in a deaf and dumb asylum. I let them pass, as if I did not understand what he meant; and many were the curses and threats bestowed on me for my stupidity. One day he caught me teaching myself to write. He frowned, as if he was not well pleased; but I suppose he came to the conclusion that such an accomplishment might help to advance his favorite scheme. Before long, notes were often slipped into my hand. I would return them, saying, "I can't read them, sir." "Can't you?" he replied; "then I must read them to you." He always finished the reading by asking, "Do you understand?" Sometimes he would complain of the heat of the tea room, and order his supper to be placed on a small table in the piazza. He would seat himself there with a well-satisfied smile, and tell me to stand by and brush away the flies. He would eat very slowly, pausing between the mouthfuls. These intervals were employed in describing the happiness I was so foolishly throwing away, and in threatening me with the penalty that finally awaited by stubborn disobedience. He boasted much of the forbearance he had exercised towards me, and reminded me that there was a limit to his patience. When I succeeded in avoiding opportunities for him to talk to me at home, I was ordered to come to his office, to do some errand. When there, I was obliged to stand and listen to such language as he saw fit to address to me. Sometimes I so openly expressed my contempt for him that he would become violently enraged, and I wondered why he did not strike me. Circumstanced as he was, he probably thought it was better policy to be forbearing. But the state of things grew worse and worse daily. In desperation I told him that I must and would apply to my grandmother for protection.[1] He threatened me with death, and worse than death, if I made any complaint to her. Strange to say, I did not despair. I was naturally of a buoyant disposition, and always I had a hope of somehow getting out of his clutches. Like many a poor, simple slave before me, I trusted that some threads of joy would yet be woven into my dark destiny.

I had entered my sixteenth year, and every day it became more apparent that my presence was intolerable to Mrs. Flint. Angry words frequently passed between her and her husband. He had never punished me himself, and he would not allow any body else to punish me. In that respect, she was never satisfied; but, in her angry moods, no terms were too vile for her to bestow upon me. Yet I, whom she detested so bitterly, had far more pity for her than he had, whose duty it was to make her life happy. I never wronged her, or wished to wrong her; and one word of kindness from her would have brought me to her feet.

5 After repeated quarrels between the doctor and his wife, he announced his intention to take his youngest daughter, then four years old, to sleep in his apartment. It was necessary that a servant should sleep in the same room, to be on hand if the child stirred. I was selected for that office, and informed for what purpose that arrangement had been made. By managing to keep within sight of people, as much as possible, during the day time, I had hitherto succeeded in eluding my master, though a razor was often held to my throat to force me to change this line of policy. At night I slept by the side of my great aunt, where I felt safe. He was too prudent to come into her room. She was an old woman,

[1] grandmother for protection: Jacobs's maternal grandmother was a free black woman.

and had been in the family many years. Moreover, as a married man, and a professional man, he deemed it necessary to save appearances in some degree. But he resolved to remove the obstacle in the way of his scheme; and he thought he had planned it so that he should evade suspicion. He was well aware how much I prized my refuge by the side of my old aunt, and he determined to dispossess me of it. The first night the doctor had the little child in his room alone. The next morning, I was ordered to take my station as nurse the following night. A kind Providence interposed in my favor. During the day Mrs. Flint heard of this new arrangement, and a storm followed. I rejoiced to hear it rage.

After a while my mistress sent for me to come to her room. Her first question was, "Did you know you were to sleep in the doctor's room?"

"Yes, ma'am."

"Who told you?"

"My master."

10 "Will you answer truly all the questions I ask?"

"Yes, ma'am."

"Tell me, then, as you hope to be forgiven, are you innocent of what I have accused you?"

"I am."

She handed me a Bible, and said, "Lay your hand on your heart, kiss this holy book, and swear before God that you tell me the truth."

15 I took the oath she required, and I did it with a clear conscience.

"You have taken God's holy word to testify your innocence," said she. "If you have deceived me, beware! Now take this stool, sit down, look me directly in the face, and tell me all that has passed between your master and you."

I did as she ordered. As I went on with my account her color changed frequently, she wept, and sometimes groaned. She spoke in tones so sad, that I was touched by her grief. The tears came to my eyes; but I was soon convinced that her emotions arose from anger and wounded pride. She felt that her marriage vows were desecrated, her dignity insulted; but she had no compassion for the poor victim of her husband's perfidy. She pitied herself as a martyr; but she was incapable of feeling for the condition of shame and misery in which her unfortunate, helpless slave was placed.

Yet perhaps she had some touch of feeling for me; for when the conference was ended, she spoke kindly, and promised to protect me. I should have been much comforted by this assurance if I could have had confidence in it; but my experiences in slavery had filled me with distrust. She was not a very refined woman, and had not much control over her passions. I was an object of her jealousy, and, consequently, of her hatred; and I knew I could not expect kindness or confidence from her under the circumstances in which I was placed. I could not blame her. Slaveholders' wives feel as other women would under similar circumstances. The fire of her temper kindled from small sparks, and now the flame became so intense that the doctor was obliged to give up his intended arrangement.

I knew I had ignited the torch, and I expected to suffer for it afterwards; but I was too thankful to my mistress for the timely aid she rendered me to care much about that. She now took me to sleep in a room adjoining her own. There I was an object of her especial care, though not of her especial comfort, for she spent many a sleepless night to watch over me. Sometimes I woke up, and found her bending over me. At other times she whispered in my ear, as though it was her husband who was speaking to me, and listened to hear what I would answer. If she startled me, on such occasions, she would glide stealthily away; and the next morning she would tell me I had been talking in my sleep, and ask who I was talking to. At last, I began to be fearful for my life. It had been often threatened; and you can imagine, better than I can describe, what an unpleasant sensation it must produce to wake up in the dead of night and find a jealous woman bending over you. Terrible as this experience was, I had fears that it would give place to one more terrible.

My mistress grew weary of her vigils; they did not prove satisfactory. She changed her tactics. She now tried the trick of accusing my master of crime, in my presence, and gave my name as the author of the accusation. To my utter astonishment, he replied, "I don't believe it: but if she did acknowledge it, you tortured her into exposing me." Tortured into exposing him! Truly, Satan had no difficulty in distinguishing the color of his soul! I understood his object in making this false representation. It was to show me that I gained nothing by seeking the protection of my mistress; that the power was still all in his own hands. I pitied Mrs. Flint. She was a second wife, many years the junior of her husband; and the hoary-headed miscreant was enough to try the patience of a wiser and better woman. She was completely foiled, and knew not how to proceed. She would gladly have had me flogged for my supposed false oath; but, as I have already stated, the doctor never allowed any one to whip me. The old sinner was politic. The application of the lash might have led to remarks that would have exposed him in the eyes of his children and grandchildren. How often did I rejoice that I lived in a town where all the inhabitants knew each other! If I had been on a remote plantation, or lost among the multitude of a crowded city, I should not be a living woman at this day.

The secrets of slavery are concealed like those of the Inquisition. My master was, to my knowledge, the father of eleven slaves. But did the mothers dare to tell who was the father of their children? Did the other slaves dare to allude to it, except in whispers among themselves? No, indeed! They knew too well the terrible consequences.

My grandmother could not avoid seeing things which excited her suspicions. She was uneasy about me, and tried various ways to buy me; but the never-changing answer was always repeated: "Linda does not belong to *me*. She is my daughter's property, and I have no legal right to sell her." The conscientious man! He was too scrupulous to *sell* me; but he had no scruples whatever about committing a much greater wrong against the helpless young girl placed under his guardianship, as his daughter's property. Sometimes my persecutor would ask me whether I would like to be sold. I told him I would rather be sold to any body than to lead such a life as I did. On such occasions he would assume the air of a very injured individual, and reproach me for my ingratitude. "Did I not take you into the house, and make you the companion of my own children?" he would say.

"Have I ever treated you like a negro? I have never allowed you to be punished, not even to please your mistress. And this is the recompense I get, you ungrateful girl!" I answered that he had reasons of his own for screening me from punishment, and that the course he pursued made my mistress hate me and persecute me. If I wept, he would say, "Poor child! Don't cry! don't cry! I will make peace for you with your mistress. Only let me arrange matters in my own way. Poor, foolish girl! you don't know what is for your own good. I would cherish you. I would make a lady of you. Now go, and think of all I have promised you."

I did think of it.

Reader, I draw no imaginary pictures of southern homes. I am telling you the plain truth. Yet when victims make their escape from this wild beast of Slavery, northerners consent to act the part of bloodhounds, and hunt the poor fugitive back into his den, "full of dead men's bones, and all uncleanness."[2] Nay, more, they are not only willing, but proud, to give their daughters in marriage to slaveholders. The poor girls have romantic notions of a sunny clime, and of the flowering vines that all the year round shade a happy home. To what disappointments are they destined! The young wife soon learns that the husband in whose hands she has placed her happiness pays no regard to his marriage vows. Children of every shade of complexion play with her own fair babies, and too well she knows that they are born unto him of his own household. Jealousy and hatred enter the flowery home, and it is ravaged of its loveliness.

Southern women often marry a man knowing that he is the father of many little slaves. They do not trouble themselves about it. They regard such children as property, as marketable as the pigs on the plantation; and it is seldom that they do not make them aware of this by passing them into the slavetrader's hands as soon as possible, and thus getting them out of their sight. I am glad to say there are some honorable exceptions.

I have myself known two southern wives who exhorted their husbands to free those slaves towards whom they stood in a "parental relation"; and their request was granted. These husbands blushed before the superior nobleness of their wives' natures. Though they had only counselled them to do that which it was their duty to do, it commanded their respect, and rendered their conduct more exemplary. Concealment was at an end, and confidence took the place of distrust.

Though this bad institution deadens the moral sense, even in white women, to a fearful extent, it is not altogether extinct. I have heard southern ladies say of Mr. Such a one, "He not only thinks it no disgrace to be the father of those little niggers, but he is not ashamed to call himself their master. I declare, such things ought not to be tolerated in any decent society!"

> [Linda Brent was subjected to unrelenting sexual harrassment by Dr. Flint. When she was in her early teens, she fell in love with a free black man, but Flint, who wanted her for himself, forbade her to marry.]

---

[2] "Woe unto you, scribes and Pharisees, hypocrites! for ye are like unto whited sepulchres, which indeed appear beautiful outward, but are within full of dead men's bones, and of all uncleanness" (Matthew 23:27) [Jacobs's note].

LEARNING MORE

The full text of *Incidents in the Life of a Slave Girl*, as well as useful links, can be accessed through the *Ideas Across Time* website.

QUESTIONING THE TEXT

1. Why does Jacobs see the plight of "a favorite slave" (par. 1) as worse than starvation or jail? What does this say about her character?
2. Why is Dr. Flint kind to Jacobs? What privileges does he allow her? What is Jacobs' response to his forebearance? Do you think Jacobs's assessment of Flint's kindness is fair?
3. Why does Flint want his youngest child, four years old, to sleep in his room? What does this decision suggest about the nature of life in a southern home at that time?
4. What is Mrs. Flint's view of Jacobs? What is Jacobs's view of Mrs. Flint? Whose situation do you find more pitiable?
5. Why is Jacobs not very optimistic about whether her mistress will in fact protect her?
6. Jacobs says of Mrs. Flint, "She was not a very refined woman, and had not much control over her passions" (par. 18). What do you think Jacobs means by "refined"? What are your associations with that word? Does it make sense to think of Jacobs as a typical Victorian?
7. What are the benefits that Jacobs derives from living in a small town?
8. Jacobs says (par. 21) that "The secrets of slavery are concealed like those of the Inquisition." What does her reference to the Inquisition suggest about Jacobs? What secrets does Jacobs reveal? To what extent has Jacobs's revelation of the oppression of women slaves remained obscured to this day?
9. What, according to Jacobs, are the implications of slavery for women as a whole—white and black, mistresses and slaves, northerners and southerners?
10. In her concluding two paragraphs, Jacobs offers examples of behavior by women that are "honorable exceptions" (par. 25) to the norm of feminine acceptance of miscegenation by their husbands. Do you agree with Jacobs that these exceptions are indeed admirable?

ANALYZING THE WRITER'S CRAFT

1. Par. 24 opens, "Reader, I draw no imaginary pictures of southern homes. I am telling you the plain truth." Whom do you think Jacobs has in mind as the "Reader" of her tale? Jacobs says her account is not "imaginary" but it is written under a pen name and in the form of fiction. How does she establish the fact that she is telling "the plain truth"?
2. Later in par. 24, Jacobs quotes from the Bible (from a famous passage in Matthew). What does this quotation tell you about her assumptions regarding the readers of her story? What does it tell you about Jacobs?

3. Why is it important that this story be told in the first person?
4. What is the importance of literacy for this story?
5. Although Jacobs for the most part narrates her story (see Introduction, pp. 1–8), she does depart from the narrative in several places to draw out the moral of her situation, and indeed to stress the implications of her situation for society as a whole (as, for example, in par. 21 and again in par. 25). Should Jacobs simply have allowed her story to speak for itself?
6. Discuss the impact of dialogue in Jacobs's story.
7. Jacobs's story makes an uncomfortable point: that power in southern society and the southern home resides totally in the hands of the master. How does her narrative drive that point home? Do you think the same point could have been made as effectively without using narrative?
8. Despite her unusual directness and her exposure of an aspect of slavery no one wanted to talk about, Jacobs is nonetheless herself evasive at certain points in her story. Mrs. Flint, for example, instead of stating her accusation against Jacobs explicitly, asks, "are you innocent of what I have accused you?" Do you think that in this respect Jacobs reflects the mores of her time?

MAKING CONNECTIONS

1. Jacobs's story seems to qualify or amplify many of the other accounts of American identity in this chapter. How does her story illuminate, for example, the accounts of slavery in St. John de Crevecoeur (Chapter 1, pp. 22–27) and Tocqueville (pp. 458–463)?
2. Jacobs's awareness of herself, and her understanding of her experience, stands in complex relation both to W. E. B. Du Bois's view of the "twoness" of African-American experience (pp. 472–479) and James Baldwin's view of the same (Chapter 1, pp. 29–35). Consider the ways in which these three essential accounts of African-American experience qualify and amplify each other.
3. Compare and contrast the situation of Mrs. Flint with that of the American woman of the 1950s whom Betty Friedan (pp. 496–509) writes about.
4. Compare and contrast Jacobs' experience in the Flint household with Louisa May Alcott's experience as a servant (Chapter 4, pp. 275–286).
5. How do you imagine Jacobs might have responded to Mary Wollstonecraft's "The Rights and Involved Duties of Mankind Considered" (Chapter 5, pp. 362–369).

FORMULATING IDEAS FOR WRITING

1. Write an essay that explores what Jacobs added to the nation's understanding of slavery. (If you wish, you may include in your discussion reference to pertinent accounts of slavery found in this book, such as those of Crevecoeur and Du Bois.)
2. Every aspect of the publishing history of *Incidents in the Life of a Slave Girl* provokes reflection. To begin, Jacobs was torn about whether she ought to

write her story down at all—among other reasons because it would expose her and expose others. Once her story was written, she could not find a publisher, and it was the addition of an introduction by a well-known woman writer and editor that finally secured the book's publication. Doubt was cast on the authenticity of the work, including doubt as to whether a slave woman could have in fact written such a book. Write an essay that explores the relation between the subject matter of Jacobs's story and its publishing history.

3. From beginning to end, Jacobs is concerned with virtue; she concludes by exposing the profound corruption caused by social tolerance of white men's sexual exploitation of slave girls and women. Discuss Jacobs's story as a moral tale.
4. Although there are not many religious allusions in Jacobs's story, they are nonetheless important, such as her reference to the Inquisition (par. 21) and Matthew (par. 25). Write an essay that explores Jacobs's recourse to religion as a way to understand her experience and to shape her story (including the language of her story).

Of Our Spiritual Strivings (1903)

W. E. B. Du Bois

In the opening paragraph of *The Souls of Black Folk,* W. E. B. Du Bois said prophetically that "the problem of the Twentieth Century is the problem of the color-line." His book appeared in 1903, just as the new century was dawning and at a critical turning point both in his career and in the history of African-Americans.

Born William Edward Burghardt Du Bois into the long-established African-American community of Great Barrington, Massachusetts, Du Bois began life in 1868, a moment of hope and promise. The Civil War over, the nation's commitment to the realization of freedom for African-Americans was embodied in the Reconstruction amendments to the U.S. Constitution that explicitly ensured a broad range of civil liberties to all Americans. But before Du Bois reached his thirtieth year, the undermining of these amendments and of the public consensus that created them was symbolized by the Supreme Court's decision in *Plessy v. Fergusson* (1896), the decision that promulgated the "separate but equal" doctrine, thereby giving legal legitimacy to racial segregation. From this point forward, the African-American community was increasingly divided, often bitterly, about how to achieve full citizenship. Broadly speaking, on one side stood the most powerful African-American of his time, Booker T. Washington, who advocated respectful compliance and industry, saving the claims to equality for a later day when whites had come to appreciate the abilities and material successes of blacks. On the other side, Du Bois, in a measured but direct attack on Washington in *The Souls of Black Folk,* argued that Washington's position served in practice to retard the progress of African-Americans, threatening a never-ending perpetuation of inferior status. After helping to found the interracial National Association for the Advancement of Colored People (NAACP) in 1909, Du Bois promoted his views in the organization's magazine, *The Crisis,* which he edited for the next quarter century.

The Souls of Black Folk represented an important departure in Du Bois's career in another respect as well. Educated as an undergraduate at Fisk University and at Harvard, Du Bois spent two years at the University of Berlin, familiarizing himself with the new methodology being developed there for the scientific study of society. Upon his return to Harvard, Du Bois applied these methods in his dissertation and became the first African-American to earn a Ph.D. from Harvard. Furthermore, his dissertation, *The Suppression of the Slave Trade in the United States of America, 1638–1870,* was published as the first volume of the Harvard Historical Studies series. But by 1900, Du Bois had come to see that his rigorous academic writing had little influence on public awareness. In *The Souls of Black Folk,* he crafted instead an evocative, poetic, eloquent style that aimed not just to inform but especially to sway and to move his audience.

In 1934, Du Bois was fired as editor of *Crisis,* and although he returned to the post from 1944 to 1948, his attention increasingly was turned to Pan Africanism—the view that all people of African origin or descent are one people whose fate depends on their common strategy for liberation. In 1951, Du Bois was indicted for his political views under the McCarran Act and was accused of being an unregistered agent of a foreign power. Although cleared, Du Bois abandoned hope in the United States. After joining the U.S. Communist Party in 1961, he emigrated to Ghana, renouncing his American citizenship. When he died in 1963, the Ghanian president, Kwame Nkrumah, awarded him a state funeral as befitting one of the greatest figures of the twentieth century. Sadly, no official representative of the United States was in attendance.

O water, voice of my heart, crying in the sand,
All night long crying with a mournful cry,
As I lie and listen, and cannot understand
The voice of my heart in my side or the voice of the sea,
O water, crying for rest, is it I, is it I?
All night long the water is crying to me.

Unresting water, there shall never be rest
Till the last moon droop and the last tide fail,
And the fire of the end begin to burn in the west;
And the heart shall be weary and wonder and cry like the sea,

All life long crying without avail,
As the water all night long is crying to me.

Arthur Symons[1]

[2]

Between me and the other world there is ever an unasked question: unasked by some through feelings of delicacy; by others through the difficulty of rightly framing it. All nevertheless, flutter round it. They approach me in a half-hesitant sort of way, eye me curiously or compassionately, and then, instead of saying directly, How does it feel to be a problem? they say, I know an excellent colored man in my town; or, I fought at Mechanicsville;[3] or, Do not these Southern outrages make your blood boil? At these I smile, or am interested, or reduce the boiling to a simmer, as the occasion may require. To the real question, How does it feel to be a problem? I answer seldom a word.

And yet, being a problem is a strange experience,—peculiar even for one who has never been anything else, save perhaps in babyhood and in Europe. It is in the early days of rollicking boyhood that the revelation first burst upon one, all in a day, as it were. I remember well when the shadow swept across me. I was a little thing, away up in the hills of New England, where the dark Housatonic winds between Hoosac and Taghkanic[4] to the sea. In a wee wooden schoolhouse, something put in into the boys' and girls' heads to buy gorgeous visiting-cards (ten cents a package) and exchange. The exchange was merry, till one girl, a tall newcomer, refused my card,—refused it peremptorily,[5] with a glance. Then it dawned upon me with a certain suddenness that I was different from the others; or like, mayhap, in heart and life and longing, but shut out from their world by a vast veil. I had thereafter no desire to tear down the veil, to creep through; I held all beyond it in common contempt, and lived above it in a region of blue sky and great wandering shadows. That sky was bluest when I could beat my mates at examination-time, or beat them at a foot-race, or even beat their stringy heads. Alas, with the years all this fine contempt began to fade; for the words I longed for, and all their dazzling opportunities, were theirs, not mine. But they should not keep these prizes, I said; some, all, I would wrest from them. Just how I would do it I could never decide: by reading law, by healing the sick, by telling the wonderful tales that swam in my head,—some way. With other black boys the strife was not so fiercely sunny: their youth

---

[1] Arthur Symons: British poet (1865–1945), one of the "Decadents"; the poem is "The Crying of the Water."

[2] The musical epigraph: Du Bois begins each of his chapters with a musical epigraph from the spirituals; this is "Nobody Knows the Trouble I've Seen."

[3] Mechanicsville: 1862 Civil War battle in Virginia that resulted in large Confederate losses.

[4] Hoosac and Taghkanic: Mountain ranges in Massacusetts and Vermont; the Housatonic river is in western Massachusetts.

[5] peremptorily: brooking no contradiction.

shrunk into tasteless sycophancy,[6] or into silent hatred of the pale world about them and mocking distrust of everything white; or wasted itself in a bitter cry. Why did God make me an outcast and a stranger in mine own house? The shades of the prison-house closed round about us all: walls straight and stubborn to the whitest, but relentlessly narrow, tall, and unscalable to sons of night who must plod darkly on in resignation, or beat unavailing palms against the stone, or steadily, half hopelessly, watch the streak of blue above.

After the Egyptian and Indian, the Greek and Roman, the Teuton and Mongolian, the Negro is a sort of seventh son, born with a veil, and gifted with second-sight in this American world,—a world which yields him no true self-consciousness, but only lets him see himself through the revelation of the other world. It is a peculiar sensation this double-consciousness, this sense of always looking at one's self through the eyes of others, of measuring one's soul by the tape of a world that looks on in amused contempt and pity. One ever feels his twoness,—an American, a Negro; two souls, two thoughts, two unreconciled strivings; two warring ideals in one dark body, whose dogged strength alone keeps it from being torn asunder.

The history of the American Negro is the history of this strife,—this longing to attain self-conscious manhood, to merge his double self into a better and truer self. In this merging he wishes neither of the older selves to be lost. He would not Africanize America, for America has too much to teach the world and Africa. He would not bleach his Negro soul in a flood of white Americanism, for he knows that Negro blood has a message for the world. He simply wished to make it possible for a man to be both a negro and an American, without being cursed and spit upon by his fellows, without having the doors of opportunity closed roughly in his face.

5 This, then, is the end of his striving: to be a co-worker in the kingdom of culture, to escape both death and isolation, to husband and use his best powers and his latent genius. These powers of body and mind have in the past been strangely wasted, dispersed, or forgotten. The shadow of a mighty Negro past flits through the tale of Ethiopia the Shadowy and of Egypt the Sphinx. Through history, the powers of single black men flash here and there like falling stars, and die sometimes before the world has rightly gauged their brightness. Here in America, in the few days since Emancipation, the black man's turning hither and thither in hesitant and doubtful striving has often made his very strength to lose effectiveness, to seem like absence of power, like weakness. And yet it is not weakness,—it is the contradiction of double aims. The double-aimed struggle of the black artisan—on the one hand to escape with contempt for a nation of mere hewers of wood and drawers of water, and on the other hand to plough and nail and dig for a poverty-stricken horde—could only result in making him a poor craftsman, for he had but half a heart in either cause. By the poverty and ignorance of his people, the Negro minister or doctor was tempted toward quackery and demagogy; and by the criticism of the other world, toward ideals that made

[6] sycophancy: servile flattery.

him ashamed of his lowly tasks. The would-be black savant[7] was confronted by the paradox that the knowledge his people needed was a twice-told tale to his white neighbors, while the knowledge which would teach the white harmony and beauty that set the ruder souls of his people a-dancing and a-singing raised but confusion and doubt in the soul of the black artist; for the beauty revealed to him was the soul-beauty of a race which his larger audience despised, and he could not articulate the message of another people. This waste of double aims, this seeking to satisfy two unreconciled ideals, has wrought sad havoc with the courage and faith and deeds of ten thousand people,—has sent them often wooing false gods and invoking false means of salvation and at times has even seemed about to make them ashamed of themselves.

Away back in the days of bondage they thought to see in one divine event the end of all doubt and disappointment; few men ever worshipped Freedom with half such unquestioning faith as did the American Negro for two centuries. To him, so far as he thought and dreamed, slavery was indeed the sum of all villainies, the cause of all sorrow, the root of all prejudice; Emancipation was the key to a promised land of sweeter beauty than ever stretched before the eyes of wearied Israelites. In song and exhortation swelled one refrain—Liberty; in his tears and curses the God he implored had Freedom in his right hand. At last it came,—suddenly, fearfully, like a dream. With one wild carnival of blood and passion came the message in his own plaintive cadences:

"Shout, O Children!
Shout you're free!
For God has brought your liberty!"

Years have passed away since then,—ten, twenty, forty; forty years of national life, forty years of renewal and development, and yet the swarthy spectre sits in its accustomed seat at the Nation's feast. In vain do we cry to this our vastest social problem:

"Take any shape but that, and my firm nerves
Shall never tremble!"[8]

The Nation has not yet found peace from its sins; the freedman has not yet found in freedom his promised land. Whatever of good may have come in these years of change, the shadow of a deep disappointment rests upon the Negro people,—a disappointment all the more bitter because the unattained ideal was unbounded save by the simple ignorance of a lowly people.

The first decade was merely a prolongation of the vain search for freedom, the boon that seemed ever barely to elude their grasp,—like a tantalizing will-o'-the-wisp, maddening and misleading the headless host. The holocaust of war, the terrors of the Ku-Klux Klan, the lies of carpet-baggers,[9] the disorganization

---

[7] savant: man of learning.

[8] "Take . . . tremble": *Macbeth* 3.2.99.

[9] carpetbagger: Name given to people from the North who, carrying their goods in bags made of carpeting, came to the South during Reconstruction to profit from the devastation of the Civil War.

of industry, and the contradictory advice of friends and foes left the bewildered serf with no new watchword beyond the old cry for freedom. As the time flew, however, he began to grasp a new idea. The ideal of liberty demanded for its attainment powerful means, and these the Fifteenth Amendment[10] gave him. The ballot, which before he had looked upon as a visible sign of freedom, he now regarded as the chief means of gaining and perfecting the liberty with which war had partially endowed him. And why not? Had not votes made war and emancipated millions? Had not voters enfranchised the freedmen? Was anything impossible to a power that enfranchised the freedmen? Was anything impossible to a power that had done all this? A million black men started with renewed zeal to vote themselves in the kingdom. So the decade flew away, the revolution of 1876[11] came, and left the half-free serf weary, wondering, but still inspired. Slowly but steadily, in the following years a new vision began gradually to replace the dream of political power,—a powerful movement, the rise of another ideal to guide the unguided, another pillar of fire by night after a clouded day. It was the ideal of "book-learning"; the curiosity born of compulsory ignorance, to know and test the power of the cabalistic[12] letters of the white man, the longing to know. Here at last seemed to have been discovered the mountain path to Canaan;[13] longer than the highway of Emancipation and law, steep and rugged, but straight, leading to heights high enough to overlook life.

Up the new path the advance guard toiled, slowly, heavily, doggedly; only those who have watched and guided the faltering feet, the misty minds, the dull understandings, of the dark pupils of these schools know how faithfully, how piteously, this people strove to learn. It was weary work. The cold statistician wrote down the inches of progress here and there, noted also where here and there a foot had slipped or some one had fallen. To the tired climbers, the horizon was ever dark, the mists were often cold, Canaan was always dim and far away. If, however, the vistas disclosed as yet no goal, no resting-place, little but flattery and criticism, the journey at least gave leisure for reflection and self-examination; it changed the child of Emancipation to the youth with dawning self-consciousness, self-realization, self-respect. In those somber forests of his striving his own soul rose before him, and he saw himself,—darkly as through a veil; and yet he saw in himself some faint revelation of his power, of his mission. He began to have a dim feeling that, to attain his place in the world, he must be himself, and not another. For the first time he sought to analyze the burden he bore upon his back, that dead-weight of social degradation partially masked behind a half-named Negro problem. He felt his poverty; without a cent, without a home, without land, tools, or savings, he had entered into competition with rich, landed, skilled neighbors. To be a poor man is hard, but to be a poor race in a land of dollars is the very bottom of hardships. He felt the

---

[10] Fifteenth Amendment: The 1870 amendment to the Constitution that assured voting rights for African-American men.

[11] 1876: After the election of 1876, opposition grew in Congress to the continuation of Reconstruction.

[12] cabalistic: obscurely mystical.

[13] Canaan: the promised land.

weight of his ignorance,—not simply of letters, but of life, of business, of the humanities; the accumulated sloth and shirking and awkwardness of decades and centuries shackled his hands and feet. Nor was his burden all poverty and ignorance. The red stain of bastardy, which two centuries of systematic legal defilement of Negro women had stamped upon his race, meant not only the loss of ancient African chastity, but also the hereditary weight of a mass of corruption from white adulterers, threatening almost the obliteration of the Negro home.

A people thus handicapped ought not to be asked to race with the world but rather allowed to give all its time and thought to its own social problems. But alas! while sociologists gleefully count his bastards and his prostitutes, the very soul of the toiling, sweating black man is darkened by the shadow of a vast despair. Men call the shadow prejudice and learnedly explain it as the natural defence of culture against barbarism, learning against ignorance, purity against crime, the "higher" against the "lower" races. To which the Negro cries Amen! and swears that to so much of this strange prejudice as is founded on just homage to civilization, culture righteousness, and progress, he humbly bows and meekly does obeisance. But before that nameless prejudice that leaps beyond all this he stands helpless, dismayed, and well-nigh speechless; before that personal disrespect and mockery, the ridicule and systematic humiliation, the distortion of fact and wanton license of fancy, the cynical ignoring of the better and the boisterous welcoming of the worse, the all-pervading desire to inculcate[14] disdain for everything black, from Toussaint[15] to the devil,—before this there rises a sickening despair that would disarm and discourage any nation save that black host to whom "discouragement" is an unwritten word.

10 But the facing of so vast a prejudice could not but bring the inevitable self-questioning, self-disparagement, and lowering of ideals which ever accompany repression and breed in an atmosphere of contempt and hate. Whisperings and portents came borne upon the four winds: Lo! we are diseased and dying, cried the dark hosts; we cannot write, our voting is vain; what need of education since we must always cook and serve? And the Nation echoed and enforced this self-criticism, saying: Be content to be servants, and nothing more; what need of higher culture for halfmen? Away with the black man's ballot, by force or fraud,—and behold the suicide of a race! Nevertheless, out of the evil came something of good,—the more careful adjustment of education to real life, the clearer perception of the Negroes' social responsibilities, and the sobering realization of the meaning of the process.

So dawned the time of Sturm and Drang:[16] storm and stress to-day rock our little boat on the mad waters of the world-sea; there is within and without the sound of conflict, the burning of body and rending of soul; inspiration strives with doubt, and faith with vain questioning. The bright ideals of the

---

[14] inculcate: instill.

[15] Touissant: Touissant L'Overture (1743–1803) was the slave-born leader of the peasant revolt in Haiti against the French in 1791.

[16] Sturm und Drang: German for "storm and stress."

past,—physical freedom, political power, the training of brains and the training of hands,—all these in turn have waxed and waned, until even the last grows dim and overcast. Are they all wrong,—all false? No, not that, but each alone was over-simple and incomplete,—the dreams of a credulous race-childhood, or the fond imaginings of the other world which does not know and does not want to know our power. To be really true, all these ideals must be melted and welded into one. The training of the schools we need to-day more than ever,—the training of deft hands, quick eyes and ears, and above all the broader, deeper, higher culture of gifted minds and pure hearts. The power of the ballot we need in sheer self-defence,—else what shall save us from a second slavery? Freedom, too, the long-sought, we still seek,—the freedom of life and limb, the freedom to work and think, the freedom to love and aspire. Work, culture, liberty,—all these we need, not singly but together, not successively but together, each growing and aiding each, and all striving toward that vaster ideal that swims before the Negro people, the ideal of human brotherhood, gained through the unifying ideal of Race; the ideal of fostering and developing the traits and talents of the Negro, not in opposition to or contempt for other races, but rather in large conformity to the greater ideals of the American Republic, in order that some day on American soil two worked-races may give each to each those characteristics both so sadly lack. We the darker ones come even now not altogether empty-handed: there are to-day no truer exponents of the pure human spirit of the Declaration of Independence than the American Negroes; there is no true American music but the wild sweet melodies of the Negro slave; the American fairy tales and folk-lore are Indian and African; and, all in all, we black men seem the sole oasis of simple faith and reverence in a dusty desert of dollars and smartness. Will America be poorer if she replace her brutal dyspeptic blundering with light-hearted but determined Negro humility? or her coarse and cruel wit with loving jovial good humor? or the vulgar music with the soul of the Sorrow Songs?

Merely a concrete test of the underlying principles of the great republic is the Negro Problem, and the spiritual striving of the freedmen's son is the travail[17] of souls whose burden is almost beyond the measure of their strength, but who bear it in the name of an historic race, in the name of this the land of their fathers' fathers, and in the name of human opportunity.

LEARNING MORE

Du Bois's chapter is supported by numerous allusions, in particular of two kinds, to songs or poems, and to the history of African-Americans in the half-century after the Civil war.

1. Find out more about the musical and poetic allusions in the essay. The musical epigraph is from the spiritual "Nobody Knows the Trouble I've Seen." The second quotation in par. 6 is from Shakespeare's *Macbeth* (3.2.99).

[17] travail: toil and trouble.

"Shades of the prison house closed round about us all" is taken from William Wordsworth's poem "Intimations of Immortality." All these can be found on the *Ideas Across Time* website.

2. In tracing the history of the post–Civil War era, Du Bois makes particular allusion to carpetbaggers, "the revolution of 1876," and the Fifteenth Amendment. Sources for learning more about these topics can be found on the *Ideas Across Time* website.

QUESTIONING THE TEXT

1. In what sense are the "strivings" Du Bois describes "spiritual"?
2. Explain how the two epigraphs—Symons's poem and the musical epigraph—illuminate or encapsulate the essay.
3. What is the "other world" of Du Bois's opening sentence?
4. How does Du Bois illustrate the fact that "being a problem is a strange experience" (par. 2)?
5. What are the main features of the "twoness" of the African-American?
6. In Du Bois's rendering, what are the chief obstacles to the African-American's desire "to be a co-worker in the kingdom of culture" (par. 5)?
7. What has made the disappointment of African-Americans in the period after the Civil War "all the more bitter" (par. 6)?
8. What are the steps toward the African-American's self-realization that Du Bois outlines (pars. 7 and 8)?
9. Restate the argument of par. 9 in your own words.
10. By what steps did the consciousness of the African-American arrive at the "storm and stress" of today (the first years of the twentieth century)?
11. In what ways, according to Du Bois, is "the Negro Problem" "merely a concrete test of the underlying principles" of the United States (par. 12)?

ANALYZING THE WRITER'S CRAFT

1. What is the effect of opening this essay with a poem and a bar of music?
2. Du Bois's rhetorical challenge has at least three formidable components. First, whom is he going to address? An educated reader? But wouldn't that exclude many African-Americans of his generation? Second, how is he to trace a complex history in a brief space? Third, how is he to rouse and trouble his readers, and then lift them to a new awareness of "the problem"? To begin, then, what audience do you think Du Bois is writing for? Give evidence for your answer.
3. Explain how Du Bois compresses a complicated, detailed history into a short space by discussing his methods in par. 7.
4. How does Du Bois rouse the feelings of his audience?
5. What would you say is the tone of this essay?
6. How would you characterize Du Bois's diction (his word choice)?
7. What gives this essay some of the qualities of oratory?

MAKING CONNECTIONS

1. Compare and contrast Du Bois's analysis of the condition of the African-American with those of St. John de Crevecoeur (Chapter 1, pp. 22–27).
2. How much kinship do you find between Du Bois and James Baldwin (Chapter 1, pp. 29–35)?
3. Is Du Bois closer in his thinking to Baldwin or to Richard Rodriguez (pp. 542–549)?
4. Compare and contrast Du Bois's and Vaclav Havel's ideas about the power of the powerless (Chapter 5, pp. 404–312).
5. Would Du Bois recognize an inheritor of his concerns in bell hooks (pp. 528–539)? Explain.

FORMULATING IDEAS FOR WRITING

1. Write an analysis of Du Bois's essay that illustrates how his quotations and allusions articulate his main themes.
2. Discuss Du Bois's use of metaphor and synechdoche (using a part to represent the whole [fifty *sail* for fifty *ships*]).
3. Write an autobiographical essay about "twoness."
4. Du Bois ventures in several directions in this essay, unmasking the hurt of African-Americans and their power, and also unmasking how that hurt has been inflicted and that power minimized. Discuss Du Bois's idea of the "veil" as a source of solace, a retreat from pain, and a way of nurturing power.
5. Is this an idealistic or pessimistic essay? Discuss.

Woman as Other (1949)

Simone de Beauvoir

The French thinker Simone de Beauvoir (1908–1986), one of the major intellectual figures of the twentieth century, represented in her work and in her life the reasoned aspirations of her generation, a generation that came of age in the time of Fascism, Communism, and the trauma of the Second World War. Through *Les Tempes Modernes* (*Modern Times*), the journal she edited with her lifelong companion Jean-Paul Sartre, the leading philosopher of his day; through her novels, notably *The Mandarins* (1954), for which she was awarded the Prix Goncourt, the most coveted French literary prize; and in particular, through *The Second Sex,* the foundation text of contemporary feminism, Beauvoir championed what she called "existential ethics." As she writes in this selection, which opens her study of the condition of woman in *The Second Sex,* every person feels the need "to transcend" him- or herself, by which she seems to mean to chose liberty by continually engaging in "freely chosen projects." This is the essence of an authentic existence, the goal of existential ethics. She writes that she is "interested in the fortunes of the individual as defined not in terms of happiness but in terms of liberty."

Beauvoir was raised in Paris and studied at the Sorbonne, where she became the youngest person ever to complete a degree in philosophy. There she met Sartre, and they established what at the time was a daring, if not scandalous, liaison. They had a publicly open relationship (although he proposed, she refused to marry him), and they vowed complete honesty and freedom to pursue sexual relations with others. They remained intimate companions and soul mates their entire lives, even though they did not have children and often did not live together.

Beauvoir's feminism is rooted in her existentialist outlook. Since, in Sartre's famous phrase, "existence precedes essence," a person is not born a woman, but becomes one by choice. According to Beauvoir, woman in all human societies has been seen as the Other, a social construction of dependence on the male that is the root of women's oppression. As the Other, women usually think of the male as the norm. (Beauvoir thinks that even Mary Wollstonecraft—see Chapter 5, pp. 362–369—considered male ideals to be the ones women too should aim to reach.) The precondition for the liberation of women into an authentic freedom, then, is a freely chosen identity independent of the age-old dichotomies of male and female, One and Other. In 1970, Beauvoir helped start the French women's liberation movement by signing the Abortion Rights Manifesto of the 343. In 1973, she launched a feminist section in *Les Temps Modernes,* which she helped edit until the time of her death. She is buried next to Sartre at the Cimetière du Montparnasse in Paris.

For a long time I have hesitated to write a book on woman. The subject is irritating, especially to women; and it is not new. Enough ink has been spilled in the quarreling over feminism, now practically over, and perhaps we should say no more about it. It is still talked about, however, for the voluminous nonsense uttered during the last century seems to have done little to illuminate the problem. After all, is there a problem? And if so, what is it? Are there women, really? Most assuredly the theory of the eternal feminine still has its adherents who will whisper in your ear: "Even in Russia women still are *women*"; and other erudite persons—sometimes the very same—say with a sigh: "Woman is losing her way, woman is lost." One wonders if women still exist, if they will always exist, whether or not it is desirable that they should, what place they occupy in this world, what their place should be. "What has become of women?" was asked recently in an ephemeral magazine.

But first we must ask: what is a woman? *"Tota mulier in utero,"* says one, "woman is a womb." But in speaking of certain women, connoisseurs declare that they are not women, although they are equipped with a uterus like the rest.

All agree in recognizing the fact that females exist in the human species; today as always they make up about one half of humanity. And yet we are told that femininity is in danger; we are exhorted to be women, remain women, become women. It would appear, then, that every female human being is not necessarily a woman; to be so considered she must share in that mysterious and threatened reality known as femininity. Is this attribute something secreted by the ovaries? Or is it a Platonic essence, a product of the philosophic imagination? Is a rustling petticoat enough to bring it down to earth? Although some women try zealously to incarnate this essence, it is hardly patentable. It is frequently described in vague and dazzling terms that seem to have been borrowed from the vocabulary of the seers, and indeed in the times of St. Thomas[1] it was considered an essence as certainly defined as the somniferous virtue of the poppy. . . .

In truth, to go for a walk with one's eyes open is enough to demonstrate that humanity is divided into two classes of individuals whose clothes, faces, bodies, smiles, gaits, interests, and occupations are manifestly different. Perhaps these differences are superficial, perhaps they are destined to disappear. What is certain is that right now they do most obviously exist.

If her functioning as a female is not enough to define woman, if we decline also to explain her through "the eternal feminine," and if nevertheless we admit, provisionally, that women do exist, then we must face the question: what is a woman?

To state the question is, to me, to suggest, at once, a preliminary answer. The fact that I ask it is in itself significant. A man would never get the notion of writing a book on the peculiar situation of the human male. But if I wish to define myself, I must first of all say: "I am a woman"; on this truth must be based all further discussion. A man never begins by presenting himself as an individual of a certain sex; it goes without saying that he is a man. The terms *masculine* and *feminine* are used symmetrically only as a matter of form, as on legal papers. In actuality the relation of the two sexes is not quite like that of two electrical poles, for man represents both the positive and the neutral, as is indicated by the common use of *man* to designate human beings in general; whereas woman represents only the negative, defined by limiting criteria, without reciprocity. In the midst of an abstract discussion it is vexing to hear a man say: "You think thus and so because you are a woman"; but I know that my only defense is to reply: "I think thus and so because it is true," thereby removing my subjective self from the argument. It would be out of the question to reply: "And you think the contrary because you are a man," for it is understood that the fact of being a man is no peculiarity. A man is in the right in being a man; it is the woman who is in the wrong. It amounts to this: just as for the ancients there was an absolute vertical with reference to which the oblique was defined, so there is an absolute human type, the masculine. Woman has ovaries, a uterus; these peculiarities imprison her in her subjectivity, circumscribe her within the limits of her own nature. It is often said that she thinks with her glands. Man superbly ignores the fact that his anatomy also includes

[1] St. Thomas: Thomas Aquinas (1225–1274), the greatest Catholic theologian of the Middle Ages.

glands, such as the testicles, and that they secrete hormones. He thinks of his body as a direct and normal connection with the world, which he believes he apprehends objectively, whereas he regards the body of woman as a hindrance, a prison, weighed down by everything peculiar to it. "The female is a female by virtue of a certain *lack* of qualities," said Aristotle; "we should regard the female nature as afflicted with a natural defectiveness." And St. Thomas for his part pronounced woman to be an "imperfect man," an "incidental" being. This is symbolized in Genesis where Eve is depicted as made from what Bossuet[2] called "a supernumerary bone" of Adam.

5 Thus humanity is male and man defines woman not in herself but as relative to him; she is not regarded as an autonomous being. Michelet[3] writes: "Woman, the relative being. . . ." And Benda[4] is most positive in his *Rapport d'Uriel:* "The body of man makes sense in itself quite apart from that of woman, whereas the latter seems wanting in significance by itself. . . . Man can think of himself without woman. She cannot think of herself without man." And she is simply what man decrees; thus she is called "the sex," by which is meant that she appears essentially to the male as a sexual being. For him she is sex—absolute sex, no less. She is defined and differentiated with reference to man and not he with reference to her; she is the incidental, the inessential as opposed to the essential. He is the Subject, he is the Absolute—she is the Other.

The category of the *Other* is as primordial as consciousness itself. In the most primitive societies, in the most ancient mythologies, one finds the expression of a duality—that of the Self and the Other. This, duality was not originally attached to the division of the sexes; it was not dependent upon any empirical facts. It is revealed in such works as that of Granet[5] on Chinese thought and those of Dumézil[6] on the East Indies and Rome. The feminine element was at first no more involved in such pairs as Varuna-Mitra,[7] Uranus-Zeus,[8] Sun-Moon, and Day-Night than it was in the contrasts between Good and Evil, lucky and unlucky auspices, right and left, God and Lucifer. Otherness is a fundamental category of human thought.

Thus it is that no group ever sets itself up as the One without at once setting up the Other over against itself. If three travelers chance to occupy the same compartment, that is enough to make vaguely hostile "others" out of all the rest of the passengers on the train. In small-town eyes all persons not belonging to

---

[2] Bossuet: Jacques-Benigne Bossuet (1627–1704), famous orator and theologian, who originated the doctrine of the divine right of kings.

[3] Michelet: Jules Michelet (1798–1874), historian, who wrote the classic nineteenth-century account of the French Revolution.

[4] Benda: Julian Benda (1867–1956), historian and sociologist, who accused intellectuals of abandoning scholarship for right-wing nationalism in his celebrated book *The Betrayal of the Intellectuals* (1927).

[5] Granet: Marcel Granet (1884–1940), sociologist and student of China.

[6] Dumézil: Georges Dumézil (1898–1986), one of the leading French humanists.

[7] Varuna-Mitra: two of the Vedic gods.

[8] Uranus-Zeus: Uranus, the primordial god of the Greeks, leader of the Titans, was overthrown by Zeus.

the village are "strangers" and suspect; to the native of a country all who inhabit other countries are "foreigners"; Jews are "different" for the anti-Semite, Negroes are "inferior" for American racists, aborigines are "natives" for colonists, proletarians are the "lower class" for the privileged.

Lévi-Strauss,[9] at the end of a profound work on the various forms of primitive societies, reaches the following conclusion: "Passage from the state of Nature to the state of Culture is marked by man's ability to view biological relations as a series of contrasts; duality, alternation, opposition, and symmetry, whether under definite or vague forms, constitute not so much phenomena to be explained as fundamental and immediately given data of social reality."[10] These phenomena would be incomprehensible if in fact human society were simply a *Mitsein* or fellowship based on solidarity and friendliness. Things become clear, on the contrary, if, following Hegel,[11] we find in consciousness itself a fundamental hostility toward every other consciousness; the subject can be posed only in being opposed—he sets himself up as the essential, as opposed to the other, the inessential, the object.

But the other consciousness, the other ego, sets up a reciprocal claim. The native traveling abroad is shocked to find himself in turn regarded as a "stranger" by the natives of neighboring countries. As a matter of fact, wars, festivals, trading, treaties, and contests among tribes, nations, and classes tend to deprive the concept *Other* of its absolute sense and to make manifest its relativity; willy-nilly, individuals and groups are forced to realize the reciprocity of their relations. How is it, then, that this reciprocity has not been recognized between the sexes, that one of the contrasting terms is set up as the sole essential, denying any relativity in regard to its correlative and defining the latter as pure otherness? Why is it that women do not dispute male sovereignty? No subject will readily volunteer to become the object, the inessential; it is not the Other who, in defining himself as the Other, establishes the One. The Other is posed as such by the One in defining himself as the One. But if the Other is not to regain the status of being the One, he must be submissive enough to accept this alien point of view. Whence comes this submission in the case of woman?

10 There are, to be sure, other cases in which a certain category has been able to dominate another completely for a time. Very often this privilege depends upon inequality of numbers—the majority imposes its rule upon the minority or persecutes it. But women are not a minority, like the American Negroes or the Jews; there are as many women as men on earth. Again, the two groups concerned have often been originally independent; they may have been formerly unaware of each other's existence, or perhaps they recognized each other's autonomy. But a historical event has resulted in the subjugation of the weaker by the stronger. The scattering of the Jews, the introduction of slavery into

[9] Lévi-Strauss: Claude Lévi-Strauss (b. 1908), the major twentieth-century student of anthropology.

[10] "Passage . . . social reality": From Lévi-Strauss's *Elementary Structure of Kinship* (1949). Beauvoir quoted from the proofs of this book, which Lévi-Strauss had lent her as she worked on her own.

[11] Hegel: Georg Friedrich Hegel (1770–1831), enormously influential German idealist philosopher. Marx is said to have turned Hegel's philosophy of history on its head.

America, the conquests of imperialism are examples in point. In these cases the oppressed retained at least the memory of former days; they possessed in common a past, a tradition, sometimes a religion or a culture.

The parallel drawn by Bebel[12] between women and the proletariat is valid in that neither ever formed a minority or a separate collective unit of mankind. And instead of a single historical event it is in both cases a historical development that explains their status as a class and accounts for the membership of *particular individuals* in that class. But proletarians have not always existed, whereas there have always been women. They are women in virtue of their anatomy and physiology. Throughout history they have always been subordinated to men, and hence their dependency is not the result of a historical event or a social change—it was not something that *occurred.* The reason why otherness in this case seems to be an absolute is in part that it lacks the contingent or incidental nature of historical facts. A condition brought about at a certain time can be abolished at some other time, as the Negroes of Haiti and others have proved; but it might seem that a natural condition is beyond the possibility of change. In truth, however, the nature of things is no more immutably given, once for all, than is historical reality. If woman seems to be the inessential which never becomes the essential, it is because she herself fails to bring about this change. Proletarians say "We"; Negroes also. Regarding themselves as subjects, they transform the bourgeois, the whites, into "others." But women do not say "We," except at some congress of feminists or similar formal demonstrations; men say "women," and women use the same word in referring to themselves. They do not authentically assume a subjective attitude. The proletarians have accomplished the revolution in Russia, the Negroes in Haiti, the Indo-Chinese are battling for it in Indo-China; but the women's effort has never been anything more than a symbolic agitation. They have gained only what men have been willing to grant; they have taken nothing, they have only received.

The reason for this is that women lack concrete means for organizing themselves into a unit which can stand face to face with the correlative unit. They have no past, no history, no religion of their own; and they have no such solidarity of work and interest as that of the proletariat. They are not even promiscuously herded together in the way that creates community feeling among the American Negroes, the ghetto Jews, the workers of Saint-Denis, or the factory hands of Renault. They live dispersed among the males, attached through residence, housework, economic condition, and social standing to certain men—fathers or husbands—more firmly than they are to other women. If they belong to the bourgeoisie, they feel solidarity with men of that class, not with proletarian women; if they are white, their allegiance is to white men, not to Negro women. The proletariat can propose to massacre the ruling class, and a sufficiently fanatical Jew or Negro might dream of getting sole possession of the atomic bomb and making humanity wholly Jewish or black; but woman cannot even dream of exterminating the males. The bond that unites her to her

[12] Bebel: August Bebel (1840–1913), one of the founders of the German Social Democratic Party, and author of *Women and Socialism.*

oppressors is not comparable to any other. The division of the sexes is a biological fact, not an event in human history. Male and female stand opposed within a primordial *Mitsein,* and woman has not broken it. The couple is a fundamental unity with its two halves riveted together, and the cleavage of society along the line of sex is impossible. Here is to be found the basic trait of woman: she is the Other in a totality of which the two components are necessary to one another.

One could suppose that this reciprocity might have facilitated the liberation of woman. When Hercules sat at the feet of Omphale[13] and helped with her spinning, his desire for her held him captive; but why did she fail to gain a lasting power? To revenge herself on Jason, Medea[14] killed their children; and this grim legend would seem to suggest that she might have obtained a formidable influence over him through his love for his offspring. In *Lysistrata* Aristophanes[15] gaily depicts a band of women who joined forces to gain social ends through the sexual needs of their men; but this is only a play. In the legend of the Sabine women,[16] the latter soon abandoned their plan of remaining sterile to punish their ravishers. In truth woman has not been socially emancipated through man's need—sexual desire and the desire for offspring—which makes the male dependent for satisfaction upon the female.

Master and slave, also, are united by a reciprocal need, in this case economic, which does not liberate the slave. In the relation of master to slave the master does not make a point of the need that he has for the other; he has in his grasp the power of satisfying this need through his own action; whereas the slave, in his dependent condition, his hope and fear, is quite conscious of the need he has for his master. Even if the need is at bottom equally urgent for both, it always works in favor of the oppressor and against the oppressed. That is why the liberation of the working class, for example, has been slow.

15 Now, woman has always been man's dependent, if not his slave; the two sexes have never shared the world in equality. And even today woman is heavily handicapped, though her situation is beginning to change. Almost nowhere is her legal status the same as man's, and frequently it is much to her disadvantage. Even when her rights are legally recognized in the abstract, longstanding custom prevents their full expression in the mores. In the economic sphere men and women can almost be said to make up two castes; other things being equal, the former hold the better jobs, get higher wages, and have more opportunity for success than their new competitors. In industry and politics men have a great many more positions and they monopolize the most important posts. In addition to all this, they enjoy a traditional prestige that the education of children tends in every way to support, for the present enshrines the

[13] Omphale: Queen of Lydia in Asia Minor. Hercules was punished by being made her slave.

[14] Medea: With Medea's help, Jason stole the Golden Fleece from Medea's father, King Aeetes. When Jason later forsook Medea, she took her revenge by murdering their two children.

[15] Aristophanes: Classical Greek comic playwright. In *Lysistrata,* the women of warring Athens and Sparta deny their men sex until they stop fighting.

[16] Sabine women: Short of women, the early Romans snatched the Sabine women from their families to populate the young city. The Sabines were from the Apennine region.

past—and in the past all history has been made by men. At the present time, when women are beginning to take part in the affairs of the world, it is still a world that belongs to men—they have no doubt of it at all and women have scarcely any. To decline to be the Other, to refuse to be a party to the deal—this would be for women to renounce all the advantages conferred upon them by their alliance with the superior caste. Man-the-sovereign will provide woman-the-liege with material protection and will undertake the moral justification of her existence; thus she can evade at once both economic risk and the metaphysical risk of a liberty in which ends and aims must be contrived without assistance. Indeed, along with the ethical urge of each individual to affirm his subjective existence, there is also the temptation to forgo liberty and become a thing. This is an inauspicious road, for he who takes it—passive, lost, ruined—becomes henceforth the creature of another's will, frustrated in his transcendence and deprived of every value. But it is an easy road; on it one avoids the strain involved in undertaking an authentic existence. When man makes of woman the *Other,* he may, then, expect her to manifest deep-seated tendencies toward complicity. Thus, woman may fail to lay claim to the status of subject because she lacks definite resources, because she feels the necessary bond that ties her to man regardless of reciprocity, and because she is often very well pleased with her role as the *Other.*

But it will be asked at once: how did all this begin? It is easy to see that the duality of the sexes, like any duality, gives rise to conflict. And doubtless the winner will assume the status of absolute. But why should man have won from the start? It seems possible that women could have won the victory; or that the outcome of the conflict might never have been decided. How is it that this world has always belonged to the men and that things have begun to change only recently? Is this change a good thing? Will it bring about an equal sharing of the world between men and women?

These questions are not new, and they have often been answered. But the very fact that woman *is the Other* tends to cast suspicion upon all the justifications that men have ever been able to provide for it. These have all too evidently been dictated by men's interest. A little-known feminist of the seventeenth century, Poulain de la Barre,[17] put it this way: "All that has been written about women by men should be suspect, for the men are at once judge and party to the lawsuit." Everywhere, at all times, the males have displayed their satisfaction in feeling that they are the lords of creation. "Blessed be God . . . that He did not make me a woman," say the Jews in their morning prayers, while their wives pray on a note of resignation: "Blessed be the Lord, who created me according to His will." The first among the blessings for which Plato thanked the gods was that he had been created free, not enslaved; the second, a man, not a woman. But the males could not enjoy this privilege fully unless they believed it to be founded on the absolute and the eternal; they sought to make the fact of their supremacy into a right. "Being men, those who have made and compiled

[17] Poulain de la Barre: François Poulain de la Barre (1647–1723), feminist cleric and follower of Descartes, and author of *On the Equality of the Two Sexes* (1673).

the laws have favored their own sex, and jurists have elevated these laws into principles," to quote Poulain de la Barre once more.

Legislators, priests, philosophers, writers, and scientists have striven to show that the subordinate position of woman is willed in heaven and advantageous on earth. The religions invented by men reflect this wish for domination. In the legends of Eve and Pandora men have taken up arms against women. They have made use of philosophy and theology, as the quotations from Aristotle and St. Thomas have shown. Since ancient times satirists and moralists have delighted in showing up the weaknesses of women. We are familiar with the savage indictments hurled against women throughout French literature. Montherlant, for example, follows the tradition of Jean de Meung, though with less gusto. This hostility may at times be well founded, often it is gratuitous; but in truth it more or less successfully conceals a desire for self-justification. As Montaigne[18] says, "It is easier to accuse one sex than to excuse the other." Sometimes what is going on is clear enough. For instance, the Roman law limiting the rights of woman cited "the imbecility, the instability of the sex" just when the weakening of family ties seemed to threaten the interests of male heirs. And in the effort to keep the married woman under guardianship, appeal was made in the sixteenth century to the authority of St. Augustine, who declared that "woman is a creature neither decisive nor constant," at a time when the single woman was thought capable of managing her property. Montaigne understood clearly how arbitrary and unjust was woman's appointed lot: "Women are not in the wrong when they decline to accept the rules laid down for them, since the men make these rules without consulting them. No wonder intrigue and strife abound." But he did not go so far as to champion their cause.

It was only later, in the eighteenth century, that genuinely democratic men began to view the matter objectively. Diderot,[19] among others, strove to show that woman is, like man, a human being. Later John Stuart Mill[20] came fervently to her defense. But these philosophers displayed unusual impartiality. In the nineteenth century the feminist quarrel became again a quarrel of partisans. One of the consequences of the industrial revolution was the entrance of women into productive labor, and it was just here that the claims of the feminists emerged from the realm of theory and acquired an economic basis, while their opponents became the more aggressive. Although landed property lost power to some extent, the bourgeoisie clung to the old morality that found the guarantee of private property in the solidity of the family. Woman was ordered back into the home the more harshly as her emancipation became a real menace. Even within the working class the men endeavored to restrain woman's liberation, because they began to see the women as dangerous competitors—the more so because they were accustomed to work for lower wages.

---

[18] Montaigne: Michel de Montaigne (1533–1592), French humanist whose *Essays* launched the modern form.

[19] Diderot: Denis Diderot (1713–1784), prominent figure in the French Enlightenment, who edited the famous *Encyclopedia,* which was to contain all knowledge.

[20] John Stuart Mill: English utilitarian philosopher (1806–1873) who wrote *The Subjection of Women* (1869), the chief feminist text of the nineteenth century.

20 In proving woman's inferiority, the antifeminists then began to draw not only upon religion, philosophy, and theology, as before, but also upon science—biology, experimental psychology, etc. At most they were willing to grant "equality in difference" to the *other* sex. That profitable formula is most significant; it is precisely like the "equal but separate" formula of the Jim Crow laws aimed at the North American Negroes. As is well known, this so-called equalitarian segregation has resulted only in the most extreme discrimination. The similarity just noted is in no way due to chance, for whether it is a race, a caste, a class, or a sex that is reduced to a position of inferiority, the methods of justification are the same. "The eternal feminine" corresponds to "the black soul" and to "the Jewish character." True, the Jewish problem is on the whole very different from the other two—to the anti-Semite the Jew is not so much an inferior as he is an enemy for whom there is to be granted no place on earth, for whom annihilation is the fate desired. But there are deep similarities between the situation of woman and that of the Negro. Both are being emancipated today from a like paternalism, and the former master class wishes to "keep them in their place"—that is, the place chosen for them. In both cases the former masters lavish more or less sincere eulogies, either on the virtues of "the good Negro" with his dormant, childish, merry soul—the submissive Negro—or on the merits of the woman who is "truly feminine"—that is, frivolous, infantile, irresponsible—the submissive woman. In both cases the dominant class bases its argument on a state of affairs that it has itself created. As George Bernard Shaw[21] puts it, in substance, "The American white relegates the black to the rank of shoeshine boy; and he concludes from this that the black is good for nothing but shining shoes." This vicious circle is met with in all analogous circumstances; when an individual (or a group of individuals) is kept in a situation of inferiority, the fact is that he *is* inferior. But the significance of the verb *to be* must be rightly understood here; it is in bad faith to give it a static value when it really has the dynamic Hegelian sense of "to have become." Yes, women on the whole *are* today inferior to men; that is, their situation affords them fewer possibilities. The question is: should that state of affairs continue? . . . The most mediocre of males feels himself a demigod as compared with women. It was much easier for M. de Montherlant[22] to think himself a hero when he faced women (and women chosen for his purpose) than when he was obliged to act the man among men—something many women have done better than he, for that matter. And in September 1948, in one of his articles in the *Figaro littéraire,* Claude Mauriac[23]—whose great originality is admired by all—could write regarding woman: "*We* listen on a tone [*sic!*] of polite indifference . . . to the most brilliant among them, well knowing that her wit reflects more or less luminously ideas that come from *us*." Evidently the speaker

[21] George Bernard Shaw: Irish playwright (1856–1950), winner of the Nobel prize for literature in 1925, freethinker and feminist.

[22] Montherlant: Playwright Henri de Montherlant (1896–1972), best known for his play *La Reine Morte* (*The Dead Queen*).

[23] Mauriac: Claude Mauriac (1914–1996), French novelist.

referred to is not reflecting the ideas of Mauriac himself, for no one knows of his having any. It may be that she reflects ideas originating with men, but then, even among men there are those who have been known to appropriate ideas not their own; and one can well ask whether Claude Mauriac might not find more interesting a conversation reflecting Descartes, Marx, or Gide[24] rather than himself. What is really remarkable is that by using the questionable *we* he identifies himself with St. Paul, Hegel, Lenin, and Nietzsche,[25] and from the lofty eminence of their grandeur looks down disdainfully up on the bevy of women who make bold to converse with him on a footing of equality. In truth, I know of more than one woman who would refuse to suffer with patience Mauriac's "tone of polite indifference."

I have lingered on this example because the masculine attitude is here displayed with disarming ingenuousness. But men profit in many more subtle ways from the otherness, the alterity[26] of woman. Here is miraculous balm for those afflicted with an inferiority complex, and indeed no one is more arrogant toward women, more aggressive or scornful, than the man who is anxious about his virility. Those who are not fear-ridden in the presence of their fellow men are much more disposed to recognize a fellow creature in woman; but even to these the myth of Woman, the Other, is precious for many reasons. They cannot be blamed for not cheerfully relinquishing all the benefits they derive from the myth, for they realize what they would lose in relinquishing woman as they fancy her to be, while they fail to realize what they have to gain from the woman of tomorrow. Refusal to pose oneself as the Subject, unique and absolute, requires great self-denial. Furthermore, the vast majority of men make no such claim explicitly. They do not *postulate* woman as inferior, for today they are too thoroughly imbued with the ideal of democracy not to recognize all human beings as equals.

In the bosom of the family, woman seems in the eyes of childhood and youth to be clothed in the same social dignity as the adult males. Later on, the young man, desiring and loving, experiences the resistance, the independence of the woman desired and loved; in marriage, he respects woman as wife and mother, and in the concrete events of conjugal life she stands there before him as a free being. He can therefore feel that social subordination as between the sexes no longer exists and that on the whole, in spite of differences, woman is an equal. As, however, he observes some points of inferiority—the most important being unfitness for the professions—he attributes these to natural causes. When he is in a co-operative and benevolent relation with woman, his theme is the principle of abstract equality, and he does not base his attitude upon such inequality as may exist. But when he is in conflict with her, the situation is reversed: his theme will be the existing inequality, and he will even take it as justification for denying abstract equality.

[24] Gide: André Gide (1869–1981), French novelist, awarded the Nobel Prise for Literature in 1947.

[25] Nietzsche: Friedrich Nietzsche (1844–1900), radical German philosopher, who famously declared, "God is dead" (see Chapter 2, pp. 109–111).

[26] alterity: otherness.

So it is that many men will affirm as if in good faith that women *are* the equals of man and that they have nothing to clamor for, while *at the same time* they will say that women can never be the equals of man and that their demands are in vain. It is, in point of fact, a difficult matter for man to realize the extreme importance of social discriminations which seem outwardly insignificant but which produce in woman moral and intellectual effects so profound that they appear to spring from her original nature. The most sympathetic of men never fully comprehend woman's concrete situation. And there is no reason to put much trust in the men when they rush to the defense of privileges whose full extent they can hardly measure. We shall not, then, permit ourselves to be intimidated by the number and violence of the attacks launched against women, nor to be entrapped by the self-seeking eulogies bestowed on the "true woman," nor to profit by the enthusiasm for woman's destiny manifested by men who would not for the world have any part of it.

We should consider the arguments of the feminists with no less suspicion, however, for very often their controversial aim deprives them of all real value. If the "woman question" seems trivial, it is because masculine arrogance has made of it a "quarrel"; and when quarreling one no longer reasons well. People have tirelessly sought to prove that woman is superior, inferior, or equal to man. Some say that, having been created after Adam, she is evidently a secondary being; others say on the contrary that Adam was only a rough draft and that God succeeded in producing the human being in perfection when He created Eve. Woman's brain is smaller; yes, but it is relatively larger. Christ was made a man; yes, but perhaps for his greater humility. Each argument at once suggests its opposite, and both are often fallacious. If we are to gain understanding, we must get out of these ruts; we must discard the vague notions of superiority, inferiority, equality which have hitherto corrupted every discussion of the subject and start afresh.

Very well, but just how shall we pose the question? And, to begin with, who are we to propound it at all? Man is at once judge and party to the case; but so is woman. What we need is an angel—neither man nor woman—but where shall we find one? Still, the angel would be poorly qualified to speak, for an angel is ignorant of all the basic facts involved in the problem. With a hermaphrodite we should be no better off, for here the situation is most peculiar; the hermaphrodite is not really the combination of a whole man and a whole woman, but consists of parts of each and thus is neither. It looks to me as if there are, after all, certain women who are best qualified to elucidate the situation of woman. Let us not be misled by the sophism that because Epimenides was a Cretan he was necessarily a liar;[27] it is not a mysterious essence that compels men and women to act in good or in bad faith, it is their situation that inclines them more or less toward the search for truth. Many of today's women, fortunate in the restoration of all the privileges pertaining to the estate of the human being, can afford the luxury of impartiality—we even recognize its necessity.

[27] Epimenides . . . liar: Cretan philosopher Epimenides (fl. 600 BCE) posed one of the great philosophical paradoxes by stating, "All Cretans are liars." Did Epimenides speak the truth?

We are no longer like our partisan elders; by and large we have won the game. In recent debates on the status of women the United Nations has persistently maintained that the equality of the sexes is now becoming a reality, and already some of us have never had to sense in our femininity an inconvenience or an obstacle. Many problems appear to us to be more pressing than those which concern us in particular, and this detachment even allows us to hope that our attitude will be objective. Still, we know the feminine world more intimately than do the men because we have our roots in it, we grasp more immediately than do men what it means to a human being to be feminine; and we are more concerned with such knowledge. I have said that there are more pressing problems, but this does not prevent us from seeing some importance in asking how the fact of being women will affect our lives. What opportunities precisely have been given us and what withheld? What fate awaits our younger sisters, and what directions should they take? It is significant that books by women on women are in general animated in our day less by a wish to demand our rights than by an effort toward clarity and understanding. As we emerge from an era of excessive controversy, this book[28] is offered as one attempt among others to confirm that statement.

But it is doubtless impossible to approach any human problem with a mind free from bias. The way in which questions are put, the points of view assumed, presuppose a relativity of interest; all characteristics imply values, and every objective description, so called, implies an ethical background. Rather than attempt to conceal principles more or less definitely implied, it is better to state them openly at the beginning. This will make it unnecessary to specify on every page in just what sense one uses such words as *superior, inferior, better, worse, progress, reaction,* and the like. If we survey some of the works on woman, we note that one of the points of view most frequently adopted is that of the public good, the general interest; and one always means by this the benefit of society as one wishes it to be maintained or established. For our part, we hold that the only public good is that which assures the private good of the citizens; we shall pass judgment on institutions according to their effectiveness in giving concrete opportunities to individuals. But we do not confuse the idea of private interest with that of happiness, although that is another common point of view. Are not women of the harem more happy than women voters? Is not the housekeeper happier than the working woman? It is not too clear just what the word *happy* really means and still less what true values it may mask. There is no possibility of measuring the happiness of others, and it is always easy to describe as happy the situation in which one wishes to place them.

In particular those who are condemned to stagnation are often pronounced happy on the pretext that happiness consists in being at rest. This notion we reject, for our perspective is that of existentialist ethics. Every subject plays his part as such specifically through exploits or projects that serve as a mode of transcendence; he achieves liberty only through a continual reaching out toward other liberties. There is no justification for present existence other than its

[28] this book: *The Second Sex.*

expansion into an indefinitely open future. Every time transcendence falls back into immanence, stagnation, there is a degradation of existence into the "*en-soi*"—the brutish life of subjection to given conditions—and of liberty into constraint and contingence. This downfall represents a moral fault if the subject consents to it; if it is inflicted upon him, it spells frustration and oppression. In both cases it is an absolute evil. Every individual concerned to justify his existence feels that his existence involves an undefined need to transcend himself, to engage in freely chosen projects.

Now, what peculiarly signalizes the situation of woman is that she—a free and autonomous being like all human creatures—nevertheless finds herself living in a world where men compel her to assume the status of the Other. They propose to stabilize her as object and to doom her to immanence since her transcendence is to be overshadowed and forever transcended by another ego (*conscience*) which is essential and sovereign. The drama of woman lies in this conflict between the fundamental aspirations of every subject (ego)—who always regards the self as the essential—and the compulsions of a situation in which she is the inessential. How can a human being in woman's situation attain fulfillment? What roads are open to her? Which are blocked? How can independence be recovered in a state of dependency? What circumstances limit woman's liberty and how can they be overcome? These are the fundamental questions on which I would fain throw some light. This means that I am interested in the fortunes of the individual as defined not in terms of happiness but in terms of liberty.

Quite evidently this problem would be without significance if we were to believe that woman's destiny is inevitably determined by physiological, psychological, or economic forces. Hence I shall discuss first of all the light in which woman is viewed by biology, psychoanalysis, and historical materialism. Next I shall try to show exactly how the concept of the "truly feminine" has been fashioned—why woman has been defined as the Other—and what have been the consequences from man's point of view. Then from woman's point of view I shall describe the world in which women must live; and thus we shall be able to envisage the difficulties in their way as, endeavoring to make their escape from the sphere hitherto assigned them, they aspire to full membership in the human race.

LEARNING MORE

To read more of *The Second Sex* online, see the *Ideas Across Time* website.

QUESTIONING THE TEXT

1. What is the difference between being female, feminine, and a woman? Why do these differences matter to Beauvoir?
2. How is the role of woman as Other a unique social condition?
3. What aspects of the condition of women have made it difficult for them to achieve an independent identity?

4. Why is it so hard to answer the question of how the subjection of women began?
5. Why does Beauvoir devote so much time to Claude Mauriac (par. 20)?
6. How is the condition of women beginning to change?
7. What are the implications of Beauvoir's existentialist ethics for women's liberation?

ANALYZING THE WRITER'S CRAFT

1. What is the tone of this essay? Is it consistent throughout, or are there places where the tone changes?
2. Give some examples of passages in this essay that might make you hesitate to cross Beauvoir in argument.
3. Some of Beauvoir's terminology comes from the specialized language of philosophy. What is *Mitsein?* What does Beauvoir mean when she refers to someone as a "subject"?
4. Beauvoir's essay is full of references to other writers or of philosophical and literary allusions. Choose two or three of these and show how they help her advance her argument.
5. Although she is a formidable dialectician (arguer), Beauvoir can also be disarmingly down to earth and matter of fact. Cite some instances where Beauvoir punctures fancy arguments by commonsense refutations or counterexamples.
6. The very category of Other implies a world of contrasts. Show how Beauvoir uses the structure of contrasts to arrive at the conclusion of her argument.
7. Does Beauvoir's avowal of existentialist ethics as her guiding credo seems tacked on to the essay at the very close; or are existentialist ethics the foundation on which the essay is built? Explain.

MAKING CONNECTIONS

1. Jean-Jacques Rousseau (pp. 451–456) maintains that inequality is the natural outgrowth of human nature within society. How might Beauvoir respond to Rousseau?
2. Alexas de Tocqueville (pp. 458–462) opposes equality and liberty, but Beauvoir seems to see equality as the precondition of, or the means toward, liberty. What is your view?
3. Is Vaclav Havel (Chapter 5, pp. 404–412) an undeclared proponent of existentialist ethics? Explain.
4. Is Beauvoir's philosophical outlook diametrically opposed to that of the stoic Marcus Aurelius (Chapter 8, pp. 646–648)? Explain.
5. When living in Paris, James Baldwin became part of Beauvoir's intellectual group. Does his essay on his original stay in Paris (Chapter 1, pp. 29–35) show evidence of being influenced by Beauvoir? Explain and illustrate.

FORMULATING IDEAS FOR WRITING

1. This essay was written just after the Second World War, in 1949. Write an essay that explores the extent to which it is dated and reflects a reality that no longer exists, and to what extent it remains relevant.
2. How do the philosophical assumptions of an existentialist ethics reflect the conditions under which Beauvoir lived just before, during, and after the Second World War?
3. Write an essay that explores Beauvoir's point that it is difficult if not impossible to be objective, or to put it differently, unbiased when writing about men and women. Is the male worldview the standard against which thought and behavior are necessarily judged? Can there be an androgynous (male–female) worldview? Have women arrived at an independent identity, Woman?
4. Beauvoir seems to assume a progressive direction in history—today (1949) women are beginning to enjoy greater equality, tomorrow they will enjoy more, and so on. Has history proved her right? Can you imagine a limitation of women's freedom in the future, a return to a more dependent condition? Is the dependent condition of women in many cultures a sign that Beauvoir's progressive assumptions may not be universal?

The Problem That Has No Name (1963)

Betty Friedan

Betty Friedan is commonly credited with launching the modern women's liberation movement in the United States with her book *The Feminine Mystique* (1963), from which this selection is taken. In this landmark study, based on extensive social science research and on her own experience, Friedan argues that the idea that women should find complete satisfaction in the life of family and home is an oppressive myth. In effect, she maintains, this notion masks a variety of actual discriminations against women, depriving them of genuine life choices and therefore of equal opportunities with men, as well as true equality before the law. *The Feminine Mystique* was an immediate best-seller, and it roused a generation of women into widespread political action, fundamentally altering the nature of American life.

Born in Peoria, Illinois, on February 4, 1921, one year after women won the right to vote, Betty Naomi Goldstein was the daughter of a Russian Jewish immigrant and a former newspaperwoman. She was educated at one of the leading women's colleges, Smith College in Massachusetts, where she edited the school paper and graduated Phi Beta Kappa with a degree in psychology in 1942. From 1943 until 1949, Friedan worked as journalist on the left-wing labor press, mainly the *UENews,* the paper of the Communist-led United Electrical, Radio, and Machine Workers of America. In 1947, she married Carl Friedan and followed the expected path of the 1950s woman. She had three children and settled into the role of suburban housewife.

But upon discovering that many of her college classmates were as distressed with their strictly domestic roles as she was, Friedan began to collect the material that led to *The Feminine Mystique.* Publication of the book immediately thrust Friedan into public life. In 1966, she became one of the founders and the first president of the National Organization for Women (NOW), an organization dedicated to achieving equality of opportunity for women. She was also at the forefront of the movement to ratify the proposed Equal Rights Amendment.

Friedan's enormously influential publications include *It Changed My Life: Writings on the Woman's Movement* (1976) and *The Fountain of Age* (1993), a work exploring, and attacking, myths about aging. Her memoir, *Life So Far,* appeared in 2000. She died on her eighty-fifth birthday in 2006.

The problem lay buried, unspoken, for many years in the minds of American women. It was a strange stirring, a sense of dissatisfaction, a yearning that women suffered in the middle of the twentieth century in the United States. Each suburban wife struggled with it alone. As she made the beds, shopped for groceries, matched slipcover material, ate peanut butter sandwiches with her children, chauffeured Cub Scouts and Brownies, lay beside her husband at night—she was afraid to ask even of herself the silent question—"Is this all?"

For over fifteen years there was no word of this yearning in the millions of words written about women, for women, in all the columns, books and articles by experts telling women their role was to seek fulfillment as wives and mothers. Over and over women heard in voices of tradition and of Freudian sophistication that they could desire no greater destiny than to glory in their own femininity. Experts told them how to catch a man and keep him, how to breastfeed children and handle their toilet training, how to cope with sibling rivalry and adolescent rebellion; how to buy a dishwasher, bake bread, cook gourmet snails, and build a swimming pool with their own hands; how to dress, look, and act more feminine and make marriage more exciting; how to keep their husbands from dying young and their sons from growing into delinquents. They were taught to pity the neurotic, unfeminine, unhappy women who wanted to be poets or physicists or presidents. They learned that truly feminine women do not want careers, higher education, political rights—the independence and the opportunities that the old-fashioned feminists fought for. Some women, in their forties and fifties, still remembered painfully giving up those dreams, but most of the younger women no longer even thought about them. A thousand expert voices applauded their femininity, their adjustment, their new maturity. All they had to do was devote their lives from earliest girlhood to finding a husband and bearing children.

By the end of the nineteen-fifties, the average marriage age of women in America dropped to 20, and was still dropping, into the teens. Fourteen million girls were engaged by 17. The proportion of women attending college in comparison with men dropped from 47 per cent in 1920 to 35 per cent in 1958. A century earlier, women had fought for higher education; now girls went to college to get a husband. By the mid-fifties, 60 per cent dropped out of college to marry, or because they were afraid too much education would be a marriage bar. Colleges built dormitories for "married students," but the students were almost always the husbands. A new degree was instituted for the wives—"Ph.T." (Putting Husband Through).

Then American girls began getting married in high school. And the women's magazines, deploring the unhappy statistics about these young marriages, urged that courses on marriage, and marriage counselors, be installed in the high schools. Girls started going steady at twelve and thirteen, in junior high. Manufacturers put out brassieres with false bosoms of foam rubber for little girls of ten. And an advertisement for a child's dress, sizes 3–6x, in the *New York Times* in the fall of 1960, said: "She Too Can Join the Man-Trap Set."

5 By the end of the fifties, the United States birthrate was overtaking India's. The birth-control movement, renamed Planned Parenthood, was asked to find a method whereby women who had been advised that a third or fourth baby would be born dead or defective might have it anyhow. Statisticians were especially astounded at the fantastic increase in the number of babies among college women. Where once they had two children, now they had four, five, six. Women who had once wanted careers were now making careers out of having babies. So rejoiced *Life* magazine in a 1956 paean[1] to the movement of American women back to the home.

In a New York hospital, a woman had a nervous breakdown when she found she could not breastfeed her baby. In other hospitals, women dying of cancer refused a drug which research had proved might save their lives: its side effects were said to be unfeminine. "If I have only one life, let me live it as a blonde," a larger-than-life-sized picture of a pretty, vacuous woman proclaimed from newspaper, magazine, and drugstore ads. And across America, three out of every ten women dyed their hair blonde. They ate a chalk called Metrecal, instead of food, to shrink to the size of the thin young models. Department-store buyers reported that American women, since 1939, had become three and four sizes smaller. "Women are out to fit the clothes, instead of vice-versa," one buyer said.

Interior decorators were designing kitchens with mosaic murals and original paintings, for kitchens were once again the center of women's lives. Home sewing became a million-dollar industry. Many women no longer left their homes, except to shop, chauffeur their children, or attend a social engagement with their husbands. Girls were growing up in America without ever having jobs outside the home. In the late fifties, a sociological phenomenon was suddenly

[1] paean: song of praise.

remarked: a third of American women now worked, but most were no longer young and very few were pursuing careers. They were married women who held part-time jobs, selling or secretarial, to put their husbands through school, their sons through college, or to help pay the mortgage. Or they were widows supporting families. Fewer and fewer women were entering professional work. The shortages in the nursing, social work, and teaching professions caused crises in almost every American city. Concerned over the Soviet Union's lead in the space race, scientists noted that America's greatest source of unused brainpower was women. But girls would not study physics: it was "unfeminine." A girl refused a science fellowship at Johns Hopkins to take a job in a real-estate office. All she wanted, she said, was what every other American girl wanted—to get married, have four children and live in a nice house in a nice suburb.

The suburban housewife—she was the dream image of the young American women and the envy, it was said, of women all over the world. The American housewife—freed by science and labor-saving appliances from the drudgery, the dangers of childbirth and the illnesses of her grandmother. She was healthy, beautiful, educated, concerned only about her husband, her children, her home. She had found true feminine fulfillment. As a housewife and mother, she was respected as a full and equal partner to man in his world. She was free to choose automobiles, clothes, appliances, supermarkets; she had everything that women ever dreamed of.

In the fifteen years after World War II, this mystique of feminine fulfillment became the cherished and self-perpetuating core of contemporary American culture. Millions of women lived their lives in the image of those pretty pictures of the American suburban housewife, kissing their husbands goodbye in front of the picture window, depositing their stationwagonsful of children at school, and smiling as they ran the new electric waxer over the spotless kitchen floor. They baked their own bread, sewed their own and their children's clothes, kept their new washing machines and dryers running all day. They changed the sheets on the beds twice a week instead of once, took the rug-hooking class in adult education, and pitied their poor frustrated mothers, who had dreamed of having a career. Their only dream was to be perfect wives and mothers; their highest ambition to have five children and a beautiful house, their only fight to get and keep their husbands. They had no thought for the unfeminine problems of the world outside the home; they wanted the men to make the major decisions. They gloried in their role as women, and wrote proudly on the census blank: "Occupation: housewife."

10 For over fifteen years, the words written for women, and the words women used when they talked to each other, while their husbands sat on the other side of the room and talked shop or politics or septic tanks, were about problems with their children, or how to keep their husbands happy, or improve their children's school, or cook chicken or make slipcovers. Nobody argued whether women were inferior or superior to men; they were simply different. Words like "emancipation" and "career" sounded strange and embarrassing; no one had used them for years. When a Frenchwoman named Simone de Beauvoir wrote

a book called *The Second Sex,*[2] an American critic commented that she obviously "didn't know what life was all about," and besides, she was talking about French women. The "woman problem" in America no longer existed.

If a woman had a problem in the 1950's and 1960's, she knew that something must be wrong with her marriage, or with herself. Other women were satisfied with their lives, she thought. What kind of a woman was she if she did not feel this mysterious fulfillment waxing the kitchen floor? She was so ashamed to admit her dissatisfaction that she never knew how many other women shared it. If she tried to tell her husband, he didn't understand what she was talking about. She did not really understand it herself. For over fifteen years women in America found it harder to talk about this problem than about sex. Even the psychoanalysts had no name for it. When a woman went to a psychiatrist for help, as many women did, she would say, "I'm so ashamed," or "I must be hopelessly neurotic." "I don't know what's wrong with women today," a suburban psychiatrist said uneasily. "I only know something is wrong because most of my patients happen to be women. And their problem isn't sexual." Most women with this problem did not go to see a psychoanalyst, however. "There's nothing wrong really," they kept telling themselves. "There isn't any problem."

But on an April morning in 1959, I heard a mother of four, having coffee with four other mothers in a suburban development fifteen miles from New York, say in a tone of quiet desperation, "the problem." And the others knew, without words, that she was not talking about a problem with her husband, or her children, or her home. Suddenly they realized they all shared the same problem, the problem that has no name. They began, hesitantly, to talk about it. Later, after they had picked up their children at nursery school and taken them home to nap, two of the women cried, in sheer relief, just to know they were not alone.

Gradually I came to realize that the problem that has no name was shared by countless women in America. As a magazine writer I often interviewed women about problems with their children, or their marriages, or their houses, or their communities. But after a while I began to recognize the telltale signs of this other problem. I saw the same signs in suburban ranch houses and split-levels on Long Island and in New Jersey and Westchester County; in colonial houses in a small Massachusetts town; on patios in Memphis; in suburban and city apartments; in living rooms in the Midwest. Sometimes I sensed the problem, not as a reporter, but as a suburban housewife, for during this time I was also bringing up my own three children in Rockland County, New York. I heard echoes of the problem in college dormitories and semiprivate maternity wards, at PTA meetings and luncheons of the League of Women Voters, at suburban cocktail parties, in station wagons waiting for trains, and in snatches of conversation

[2] *The Second Sex:* French writer and existentialist thinker Simone de Beauvoir (1908–1986; see pp. 481–494), probed the condition of women in her pathbreaking book *The Second Sex* (1949), now considered a foundation document of contemporary feminism.

overheard at Schrafft's. The groping words I heard from other women, on quiet afternoons when children were at school or on quiet evenings when husbands worked late, I think I understood first as a woman long before I understood their larger social and psychological implications.

Just what was this problem that has no name? What were the words women used when they tried to express it? Sometimes a woman would say "I feel empty somehow . . . incomplete." Or she would say, "I feel as if I don't exist." Sometimes she blotted out the feeling with a tranquilizer. Sometimes she thought the problem was with her husband, or her children, or that what she really needed was to redecorate her house, or move to a better neighborhood, or have an affair, or another baby. Sometimes, she went to a doctor with symptoms she could hardly describe: "A tired feeling . . . I get so angry with the children it scares me . . . I feel like crying without any reason." (A Cleveland doctor called it "the housewife's syndrome.") A number of women told me about great bleeding blisters that break out on their hands and arms. "I call it the housewife's blight," said a family doctor in Pennsylvania. "I see it so often lately in these young women with four, five and six children who bury themselves in their dishpans. But it isn't caused by detergent and it isn't cured by cortisone."

15 Sometimes a woman would tell me that the feeling gets so strong she runs out of the house and walks through the streets. Or she stays inside her house and cries. Or her children tell her a joke, and she doesn't laugh because she doesn't hear it. I talked to women who had spent years on the analyst's couch, working out their "adjustment to the feminine role," their blocks to "fulfillment as a wife and mother." But the desperate tone in these women's voices, and the look in their eyes, was the same as the tone and the look of other women, who were sure they had no problem, even though they did have a strange feeling of desperation.

A mother of four who left college at nineteen to get married told me:

> I've tried everything women are supposed to do—hobbies, gardening, pickling, canning, being very social with my neighbors, joining committees, running PTA teas. I can do it all, and I like it, but it doesn't leave you anything to think about—any feeling of who you are. I never had any career ambitions. All I wanted was to get married and have four children. I love the kids and Bob and my home. There's no problem you can even put a name to. But I'm desperate. I begin to feel I have no personality. I'm a server of food and a putter-on of pants and a bedmaker, somebody who can be called on when you want something. But who am I?

A twenty-three-year-old mother in blue jeans said:

> I ask myself why I'm so dissatisfied. I've got my health, fine children, a lovely new home, enough money. My husband has a real future as an electronics engineer. He doesn't have any of these feelings. He says maybe I need a vacation, let's go to New York for a weekend. But that isn't it. I always had this idea we should do everything together. I can't sit down and read a book alone. If the children are napping and I have one hour to myself I just walk through the house waiting for them to wake up. I don't make a move until I know where the rest of the crowd is going. It's as if ever since you were a little girl, there's always been somebody or something that will take care of your life: your parents,

> or college, or falling in love, or having a child, or moving to a new house. Then you wake up one morning and there's nothing to look forward to.

A young wife in a Long Island development said:

> I seem to sleep so much. I don't know why I should be so tired. This house isn't nearly so hard to clean as the cold-water flat we had when I was working. The children are at school all day. It's not the work. I just don't feel alive.

In 1960, the problem that has no name burst like a boil through the image of the happy American housewife. In the television commercials the pretty housewives still beamed over their foaming dishpans and *Time's* cover story on "The Suburban Wife, an American Phenomenon" protested: "Having too good a time . . . to believe that they should be unhappy." But the actual unhappiness of the American housewife was suddenly being reported—from the *New York Times* and *Newsweek* to *Good Housekeeping* and CBS Television ("The Trapped Housewife"), although almost everybody who talked about it found some superficial reason to dismiss it. It was attributed to incompetent appliance repairmen (*New York Times*), or the distances children must be chauffeured in the suburbs (*Time*), or too much PTA (*Redbook*). Some said it was the old problem—education: more and more women had education, which naturally made them unhappy in their role as housewives. "The road from Freud to Frigidaire, from Sophocles to Spock,[3] has turned out to be a bumpy one," reported the *New York Times* (June 28, 1960). "Many young women—certainly not all—whose education plunged them into a world of ideas feel stifled in their homes. They find their routine lives out of joint with their training. Like shut-ins, they feel left out. In the last year, the problem of the educated housewife has provided the meat of dozens of speeches made by troubled presidents of women's colleges who maintain, in the face of complaints, that sixteen years of academic training is realistic preparation for wifehood and motherhood."

20 There was much sympathy for the educated housewife. ("Like a two-headed schizophrenic . . . once she wrote a paper on the Graveyard poets,[4] now she writes notes to the milkman. Once she determined the boiling point of sulphuric acid; now she determines her boiling point with the overdue repairman. . . . The housewife often is reduced to screams and tears. . . . No one, it seems, is appreciative, least of all herself, of the kind of person she becomes in the process of turning from poetess into shrew.")

Home economists suggested more realistic preparation for housewives, such as high-school workshops in home appliances. College educators suggested more discussion groups on home management and the family, to prepare women for the adjustment to domestic life. A spate of articles appeared in the mass magazines offering "Fifty-eight Ways to Make Your Marriage More

---

[3] Sophocles to Spock: Sophocles was a Greek tragedian (496–406 BCE); Benjamin Spock (1903–1988) wrote the most influential childrearing guide for the second half of the twentieth century, *Baby and Child Care*, first published in 1946.

[4] Graveyard poets: Group of eighteenth-century English poets (c. 1740–1780) who used the graveyard as a taking-off point for meditations on the human condition.

Exciting." No month went by without a new book by a psychiatrist or sexologist offering technical advice on finding greater fulfillment through sex.

A male humorist joked in *Harper's Bazaar* (July, 1960) that the problem could be solved by taking away woman's right to vote. ("In the pre-19th Amendment era, the American woman was placid, sheltered and sure of her role in American society. She left all the political decisions to her husband and he, in turn, left all the family decisions to her. Today a woman has to make both the family *and* the political decisions, and it's too much for her.")

A number of educators suggested seriously that women no longer be admitted to the four-year colleges and universities: in the growing college crisis, the education which girls could not use as housewives was more urgently needed than ever by boys to do the work of the atomic age.

The problem was also dismissed with drastic solutions no one could take seriously. (A woman writer proposed in *Harper's* that women be drafted for compulsory service as nurses' aides and baby-sitters.) And it was smoothed over with the age-old panaceas:[5] "love is their answer," "the only answer is inner help," "the secret of completeness—children," "a private means of intellectual fulfillment," "to cure this toothache of the spirit—the simple formula of handing one's self and one's will over to God."

The problem was dismissed by telling the housewife she doesn't realize how lucky she is—her own boss, no time clock, no junior executive gunning for her job. What if she isn't happy—does she think men are happy in this world? Does she really, secretly, still want to be a man? Doesn't she know yet how lucky she is to be a woman?

The problem was also, and finally, dismissed by shrugging that there are no solutions: this is what being a woman means, and what is wrong with American women that they can't accept their role gracefully? As *Newsweek* put it (March 7, 1960):

> She is dissatisfied with a lot that women of other lands can only dream of. Her discontent is deep, pervasive, and impervious[6] to the superficial remedies which are offered at every hand. . . . An army of professional explorers have already charted the major sources of trouble. . . . From the beginning of time, the female cycle has defined and confined woman's role. As Freud was credited with saying: "Anatomy is destiny." Though no group of women has ever pushed these natural restrictions as far as the American wife, it seems that she still cannot accept them with good grace. . . . A young mother with a beautiful family, charm, talent and brains is apt to dismiss her role apologetically. "What do I do?" you hear her say. "Why nothing. I'm just a housewife." A good education, it seems, has given this paragon[7] among women an understanding of the value of everything except her own worth . . .

And so she must accept the fact that "American women's unhappiness is merely the most recently won of women's rights," and adjust and say with the

[5] panaceas: cure-alls.
[6] impervious: impenetrable.
[7] paragon: model.

happy housewife found by *Newsweek:* "We ought to salute the wonderful freedom we all have and be proud of our lives today. I have had college and I've worked, but being a housewife is the most rewarding and satisfying role. . . . My mother was never included in my father's business affairs . . . she couldn't get out of the house and away from us children. But I am an equal to my husband; I can go along with him on business trips and to social business affairs."

The alternative offered was a choice that few women would contemplate. In the sympathetic words of the *New York Times:* "All admit to being deeply frustrated at times by the lack of privacy, the physical burden, the routine of family life, the confinement of it. However, none would give up her home and family if she had the choice to make again." *Redbook* commented: "Few women would want to thumb their noses at husbands, children and community and go off on their own. Those who do may be talented individuals, but they rarely are successful women."

The year American women's discontent boiled over, it was also reported (*Look*) that the more than 21,000,000 American women who are single, widowed, or divorced do not cease even after fifty their frenzied, desperate search for a man. And the search begins early—for 70 per cent of all American women now marry before they are twenty-four. A pretty twenty-five-year-old secretary took thirty-five different jobs in six months in the futile hope of finding a husband. Women were moving from one political club to another, taking evening courses in accounting or sailing, learning to play golf or ski, joining a number of churches in succession, going to bars alone, in their ceaseless search for a man.

30 Of the growing thousands of women currently getting private psychiatric help in the United States, the married ones were reported dissatisfied with their marriages, the unmarried ones suffering from anxiety and, finally, depression. Strangely, a number of psychiatrists stated that, in their experience, unmarried women patients were happier than married ones. So the door of all those pretty suburban houses opened a crack to permit a glimpse of uncounted thousands of American housewives who suffered alone from a problem that suddenly everyone was talking about, and beginning to take for granted, as one of those unreal problems in American life that can never be solved—like the hydrogen bomb. By 1962 the plight of the trapped American housewife had become a national parlor game. Whole issues of magazines, newspaper columns, books learned and frivolous, educational conferences and television panels were devoted to the problem.

Even so, most men, and some women, still did not know that this problem was real. But those who had faced it honestly knew that all the superficial remedies, the sympathetic advice, the scolding words and the cheering words were somehow drowning the problem in unreality. A bitter laugh was beginning to be heard from American women. They were admired, envied, pitied, theorized over until they were sick of it, offered drastic solutions or silly choices that no one could take seriously. They got all kinds of advice from the growing armies of marriage and child-guidance counselors, psychotherapists, and armchair psychologists, on how to adjust to their role as housewives. No other road to fulfillment was offered to American women in the middle of the twentieth century. Most adjusted to their role and suffered or ignored the problem that has no name. It can be less painful, for a woman, not to hear the strange, dissatisfied voice stirring within her.

It is no longer possible to ignore that voice, to dismiss the desperation of so many American women. This is not what being a woman means, no matter what the experts say. For human suffering there is a reason; perhaps the reason has not been found because the right questions have not been asked, or pressed far enough. I do not accept the answer that there is no problem because American women have luxuries that women in other times and lands never dreamed of; part of the strange newness of the problem is that it cannot be understood in terms of the age-old material problems of man: poverty, sickness, hunger, cold. The women who suffer this problem have a hunger that food cannot fill. It persists in women whose husbands are struggling internes and law clerks, or prosperous doctors and lawyers; in wives of workers and executives who make $5,000 a year or $50,000. It is not caused by lack of material advantages; it may not even be felt by women preoccupied with desperate problems of hunger, poverty or illness. And women who think it will be solved by more money, a bigger house, a second car, moving to a better suburb, often discover it gets worse.

It is no longer possible today to blame the problem on loss of femininity: to say that education and independence and equality with men have made American women unfeminine. I have heard so many women try to deny this dissatisfied voice within themselves because it does not fit the pretty picture of femininity the experts have given them. I think, in fact, that this is the first clue to the mystery: the problem cannot be understood in the generally accepted terms by which scientists have studied women, doctors have treated them, counselors have advised them, and writers have written about them. Women who suffer this problem, in whom this voice is stirring, have lived their whole lives in the pursuit of feminine fulfillment. They are not career women (although career women may have other problems); they are women whose greatest ambition has been marriage and children. For the oldest of these women, these daughters of the American middle class, no other dream was possible. The ones in their forties and fifties who once had other dreams gave them up and threw themselves joyously into life as housewives. For the youngest, the new wives and mothers, this was the only dream. They are the ones who quit high school and college to marry, or marked time in some job in which they had no real interest until they married. These women are very "feminine" in the usual sense, and yet they still suffer the problem.

Are the women who finished college, the women who once had dreams beyond housewifery, the ones who suffer the most? According to the experts they are, but listen to these four women:

> My days are all busy, and dull, too. All I ever do is mess around. I get up at eight—I make breakfast, so I do the dishes, have lunch, do some more dishes and some laundry and cleaning in the afternoon. Then it's supper dishes and I get to sit down a few minutes before the children have to be sent to bed. . . . That's all there is to my day. It's just like any other wife's day. Humdrum. The biggest time, I am chasing kids.

> Ye Gods, what do I do with my time? Well, I get up at six. I get my son dressed and then give him breakfast. After that I wash dishes and bathe and feed the baby. Then I get lunch and while the children nap, I sew or mend or iron and do all the other things I can't get done before noon. Then I cook supper for the family and my husband watches TV while I do the dishes. After I get the children to bed, I set my hair and then I go to bed.

> The problem is always being the children's mommy, or the minister's wife and never being myself.

> A film made of any typical morning in my house would look like an old Marx Brothers' comedy. I wash the dishes, rush the older children off to school, dash out in the yard to cultivate the chrysanthemums, run back in to make a phone call about a committee meeting, help the youngest child build a blockhouse, spend fifteen minutes skimming the newspapers so I can be well-informed, then scamper down to the washing machines where my thrice-weekly laundry includes enough clothes to keep a primitive village going for an entire year. By noon I'm ready for a padded cell. Very little of what I've done has been really necessary or important. Outside pressures lash me through the day. Yet I look upon myself as one of the more relaxed housewives in the neighborhood. Many of my friends are even more frantic. In the past sixty years we have come full circle and the American housewife is once again trapped in a squirrel cage. If the cage is now a modern plate-glass-and-broadloom ranch house or a convenient modern apartment, the situation is no less painful than when her grandmother sat over an embroidery hoop in her gilt-and-plush parlor and muttered angrily about women's rights.

35 The first two women never went to college. They live in developments in Levittown, New Jersey, and Tacoma, Washington, and were interviewed by a team of sociologists studying workingmen's wives. The third, a minister's wife, wrote on the fifteenth reunion questionnaire of her college that she never had any career ambitions, but wishes now she had. The fourth, who has a Ph.D. in anthropology, is today a Nebraska housewife with three children. Their words seem to indicate that housewives of all educational levels suffer the same feeling of desperation.

The fact is that no one today is muttering angrily about "women's rights," even though more and more women have gone to college. In a recent study of all the classes that have graduated from Barnard College, a significant minority of earlier graduates blamed their education for making them want "rights," later classes blamed their education for giving them career dreams, but recent graduates blamed the college for making them feel it was not enough simply to be a housewife and mother; they did not want to feel guilty if they did not read books or take part in community activities. But if education is not the cause of the problem, the fact that education somehow festers in these women may be a clue.

If the secret of feminine fulfillment is having children, never have so many women, with the freedom to choose, had so many children, in so few years, so willingly. If the answer is love, never have women searched for love with such determination. And yet there is a growing suspicion that the problem may not be sexual, though it must somehow be related to sex. I have heard from many doctors evidence of new sexual problems between man and wife—sexual hunger in wives so great their husbands cannot satisfy it. "We have made woman a sex creature," said a psychiatrist at the Margaret Sanger marriage counseling clinic. "She has no identity except as a wife and mother. She does not know who she is herself. She waits all day for her husband to come home at night to make her feel alive. And now it is the husband who is not interested. It is terrible for the women, to lie there, night after night, waiting for her husband to make her feel alive." Why is there such a market for books and articles offering sexual advice? The kind of sexual orgasm which Kinsey[8] found in statistical plenitude[9] in the recent generations of American women does not seem to make this problem go away.

On the contrary, new neuroses are being seen among women—and problems as yet unnamed as neuroses—which Freud and his followers did not predict, with physical symptoms, anxieties, and defense mechanisms equal to those caused by sexual repression. And strange new problems are being reported in the growing generations of children whose mothers, were always there, driving them around helping them with their homework—an inability to endure pain or discipline or pursue, any self-sustained goal of any sort, a devastating boredom with life. Educators are increasingly uneasy about the dependence, the lack of self-reliance, of the boys and girls who are entering college today. "We fight a continual battle to make our students assume manhood," said a Columbia dean.

A White House conference was held on the physical and muscular deterioration of American children: were they being overnurtured? Sociologists noted the astounding organization of suburban children's lives: the lessons, parties, entertainments, play and study groups organized for them. A suburban housewife in Portland, Oregon, wondered why the children "need" Brownies and Boy Scouts out here. "This is not the slums. The kids out here have the great outdoors. I think people are so bored, they organize the children, and then try to hook everyone else on it. And the poor kids have no time left just to lie on their beds and daydream."

Can the problem that has no name be somehow related to the domestic routine of the housewife? When a woman tries to put the problem into words, she often merely describes the daily life she leads. What is there in this recital of comfortable domestic detail that could possibly cause such a feeling of desperation? Is she trapped simply by the enormous demands of her role as modern housewife: wife, mistress, mother, nurse, consumer, cook, chauffeur; expert on interior decoration, child care, appliance repair, furniture refinishing, nutrition, and education? Her day is fragmented as she rushes from dishwasher to washing machine to telephone to dryer to station wagon to supermarket, and delivers

[8] Kinsey: Alfred Kinsey (1894–1956), pioneer in the study of sexual behavior. His most famous "Kinsey Reports" were *Sexual Behavior in the Human Male* (1948) and *Sexual Behavior in the Human Female* (1953).

[9] plenitude: plenty.

Johnny to the Little League field, takes Janey to dancing class, gets the lawnmower fixed and meets the 6:45. She can never spend more than 15 minutes on any one thing; she has no time to read books, only magazines; even if she had time, she has lost the power to concentrate. At the end of the day, she is so terribly tired that sometimes her husband has to take over and put the children to bed.

This terrible tiredness took so many women to doctors in the 1950's that one decided to investigate it. He found, surprisingly, that his patients suffering from "housewife's fatigue" slept more than an adult needed to sleep—as much as ten hours a day—and that the actual energy they expended on housework did not tax their capacity. The real problem must be something else, he decided—perhaps boredom. Some doctors told their women patients they must get out of the house for a day, treat themselves to a movie in town. Others prescribed tranquilizers. Many suburban housewives were taking tranquilizers like cough drops. "You wake up in the morning, and you feel as if there's no point in going on another day like this. So you take a tranquilizer because it makes you not care so much that it's pointless."

It is easy to see the concrete details that trap the suburban housewife, the continual demands on her time. But the chains that bind her in her trap are chains in her own mind and spirit. They are chains made up of mistaken ideas and misinterpreted facts, of incomplete truths and unreal choices. They are not easily seen and not easily shaken off.

How can any woman see the whole truth within the bounds of her own life? How can she believe that voice inside herself, when it denies the conventional, accepted truths by which she has been living? And yet the women I have talked to, who are finally listening to that inner voice, seem in some incredible way to be groping through to a truth that has defied the experts.

I think the experts in a great many fields have been holding pieces of that truth under their microscopes for a long time without realizing it. I found pieces of it in certain new research and theoretical developments in psychological, social and biological science whose implications for women seem never to have been examined. I found many clues by talking to suburban doctors, gynecologists, obstetricians, child-guidance clinicians, pediatricians, high-school guidance counselors, college professors, marriage counselors, psychiatrists and ministers—questioning them not on their theories, but on their actual experience in treating American women. I became aware of a growing body of evidence, much of which has not been reported publicly because it does not fit current modes of thought about women—evidence which throws into question the standards of feminine normality, feminine adjustment, feminine fulfillment, and feminine maturity by which most women are still trying to live.

I began to see in a strange new light the American return to early marriage and the large families that are causing the population explosion; the recent movement to natural childbirth and breastfeeding; suburban conformity, and the new neuroses, character pathologies and sexual problems being reported by the doctors. I began to see new dimensions to old problems that have long been taken for granted among women: menstrual difficulties, sexual frigidity, promiscuity, pregnancy fears, childbirth depression, the high incidence of emotional breakdown and suicide among women in their twenties and thirties, the menopause crises, the so-called passivity and immaturity of American men, the discrepancy between women's tested intellectual abilities in childhood and their adult achievement, the changing incidence of adult sexual orgasm in American women, and persistent problems in psychotherapy and in women's education.

If I am right, the problem that has no name stirring in the minds of so many American women today is not a matter of loss of femininity or too much education, or the demands of domesticity. It is far more important than anyone recognizes. It is the key to these other new and old problems which have been torturing women and their husbands and children, and puzzling their doctors and educators for years. It may well be the key to our future as a nation and a culture. We can no longer ignore that voice within women that says: "I want something more than my husband and my children and my home."

LEARNING MORE

1. Friedan quotes from a range of general-interest magazine from the late 1950s. Some of these are still newsstand staples, such as *Time* and *Newsweek.* But it would be useful to examine an issue or two of magazines from that time—such as *Look*—as well as those that remain popular but have evolved—such as *Redbook, Harper's Bazaar,* and *Good Housekeeping.*
2. The Kinsey Report (see par. 37) on American sexual behavior attracted wide attention. Selections can be found on the *Ideas Across Time* website.

QUESTIONING THE TEXT

1. What impression of "the problem" do you have in the first paragraphs of Friedan's essay? Has your understanding of "the problem" changed by the close of the essay? Explain.
2. What fifteen years is Friedan referring to in the first sentence of par. 2?
3. What kinds of things were women told to revel in "for over fifteen years" (par. 2)? What kinds of things are not mentioned?
4. What contrast between the past and the present is implied in par. 3?
5. How was the suburban housewife the model of "true feminine fulfillment" (par. 8)?
6. What is the implied relation between the "mystique of feminine fulfillment" (par. 9) and the "woman problem" (par. 10)?
7. If a woman "had a problem" in the 1950s and 1960s, how did she try to solve it? What did society think about a woman with "a problem"?
8. How does Friedan define "this problem that has no name" (par. 12)?
9. How did this problem "burst like a boil through the image of the happy American housewife" (par. 19)?

10. What was the response to the airing of this problem?
11. How is this problem different from "age-old material problems" (par. 32)?
12. What possible sources of this problem does Friedan examine and reject? Why does she reject these explanations for the problem?
13. What does Friedan think is the source of the problem? Does this problem in the lives of women remain a problem today?

ANALYZING THE WRITER'S CRAFT

1. What is the effect of opening the essay with "the problem," a dilemma with which we can't possibly have any familiarity, at least not at this point (the first two words) in the essay?
2. In general, Friedan has a difficult dilemma of definition to solve in this essay. She wants to bring a hidden problem into the bright light of day. She also wants to define a problem that is not amenable to sharp definition—it's more in the nature of a "yearning" (par. 2). Give two or three examples of how Friedan defines "the problem" that you found especially illuminating or persuasive or powerful.
3. What is the thesis statement of this essay?
4. What kinds of evidence does Friedan use to support her thesis? Which of these kinds of evidence did you find most effective, and why?
5. What is the tone of this essay? Is it consistent throughout, or does it change?
6. Much of Friedan's argument is implied—that is, the evidence she offers suggests an opposite or something else that is, however, not named. One way Friedan does this is to offer details that together paint a picture of a certain kind of life—but she leave "something" out. What is the implied point made, for example, by the statistics in par. 3? Or what is missing, for example, from the list of activities in par. 7?
7. Why does Friedan resort to so much direct quotation—some from unnamed women, some from specifically identified magazines or newspapers?
8. Is Friedan's conclusion a good ending for her essay? Why or why not?

MAKING CONNECTIONS

1. How is "the problem" Friedan identifies the same as and different from the one that plagues bell hooks (pp. 528–539)?
2. It is striking that W. E. B. Du Bois (pp. 472–479) identifies himself as "a problem." Is the use of this word by both Friedan and Du Bois just a coincidence, or is the condition of women and the condition of African-Americans similar?
3. Does Jamaica Kincaid (pp. 552–553) express in fiction what Betty Friedan tried to say in expository prose? Explain.
4. Did Friedan let her girls play with Barbie (see p. 555)?

FORMULATING IDEAS FOR WRITING

1. Write a detailed account of a typical day in the life of a working mother—based on someone you know well (or, if you are a working mother, on your own day), or based on what you imagine.
2. In the opening chapter of *Walden,* Henry David Thoreau's famous account of living alone in the woods, the writer says, "The mass of men lead lives of quiet desperation." Freidan uses Thoreau's phrase and applies it to the condition of women. Write an essay comparing Thoreau's outlook with Freidan's (see the *Ideas Across Time* website for Thoreau's chapter).
3. "A century earlier," Friedan writes in the 1950s, "women had fought for higher education; now girls went to college to get a husband" (par. 3). Write an essay exploring why girls go to college today.
4. Is the suburban world and its values a world that has faded into obscurity? Or does that world and its values persist? Discuss from the point of view of the role of women.
5. Write a letter to Betty Friedan from a housewife and mother who is happy to be able to stay home and mind house and family.

Letter from Birmingham Jail (1963)

Martin Luther King Jr.

Martin Luther King Jr. was born in Atlanta, Georgia, in 1929. The leading figure of the civil rights movement of the late 1950s and 1960s, King was a passionate advocate of nonviolent protest, which he fostered as a form of Christian social activism. His grandfather began the family's tenure as ministers of the Ebenezer Baptist Church in Atlanta in 1914. He was followed by Martin Luther King Sr. in 1931. From 1960 until his death, Martin Luther King Jr. served as copastor. King also followed family tradition by attending Morehouse College in Atlanta, where both his father and grandfather had been educated. He graduated with a degree in sociology in 1948 and later received a Ph.D. in systematic theology from Boston University. He met Coretta Scott in Boston, and the couple were married in 1953.

The following year King became pastor of the Dexter Avenue Baptist Church in Montgomery, Alabama. He was twenty-four years old. In December 1955, Rosa Parks refused to comply with the law that required African-Americans to occupy the rear of the municipality's buses. Her arrest resulted in the 382-day-long Montgomery bus boycott, led by King. The boycott triumphed when on December 21, 1956, the U.S. Supreme Court declared the laws requiring segregation on public buses to be unconstitutional. The Montgomery bus boycott galvanized the African-American community and established King as the leader of the burgeoning movement for civil rights.

King assumed his leadership role as a part of his ministry, tying the fight against injustice to the struggle for brotherhood; in fighting hatred, he eschewed hatred. Although he defined social justice broadly to include the right to fair employment and living conditions, and although he spoke out against the Vietnam War, King resisted the anger of many in his community that translated into calls for violence and armed struggle. King saw himself as a moral teacher. His protest tactics were intended to rouse the conscience of the white majority, even when that majority seemed virulently racist. His writing and his speeches drew noticeably on the Bible both for the cadence of their sentences and for the metaphoric nature of their inspirational rhetoric. King's words are clearly intended to move his audience to action but in a spirit of benevolent righteousness. King sought to avoid separatism and class war, pointing to the deep roots of the African-American people in the history of the United States. He placed his faith in the originating principles of the nation.

In the decade from his election as president of the Southern Christian Leadership Conference in 1957 until his death in 1968, King led countless protests across the country, including the one for which he was arrested in Birmingham, Alabama. That was the occasion for his "Letter from Birmingham Jail," a document that immediately became the manifesto for the movement. During these years, King delivered over 2500 speeches. He led the famous March on Washington in 1963, which attracted 250,000 people and where he delivered his address, "I Have a Dream," now one of the revered pieces of American oratory. In 1964, he became the youngest person ever to receive the Nobel Peace Prize.

On April 4, 1968, Martin Luther King Jr. was assassinated on the balcony of the Lorraine Motel in Memphis, Tennessee, while preparing to lead a local march in support of the Memphis sanitation workers' union. The Lorraine Motel is now the site of the National Civil Rights Museum.

Martin Luther King Jr.
Birmingham City Jail
April 16, 1963

Bishop C. C. J. Carpenter
Bishop Joseph A. Durick
Rabbi Milton L. Grafman
Bishop Paul Hardin
Bishop Nolan B. Harmon
The Rev. George M. Murray
The Rev. Edward V. Ramage
The Rev. Earl Stallings

My dear Fellow Clergymen,

While confined here in the Birmingham City Jail, I came across your recent statement calling our present activities "unwise and untimely." Seldom, if ever, do I pause to answer criticism of my work and ideas. If I sought to answer all of the criticisms that cross my desk, my secretaries would be engaged in little else in the course of the day and I would have no time for constructive work. But since I feel that you are men of genuine good will and your criticisms are sincerely set forth, I would like to answer your statement in what I hope will be patient and reasonable terms.

I think I should give the reason for my being in Birmingham, since you have been influenced by the argument of "outsiders coming in." I have the honor of serving as president of the Southern Christian Leadership Conference, an organization operating in every Southern state with headquarters in Atlanta, Georgia. We have some eighty-five affiliate organizations all across the South—one being the Alabama Christian Movement for Human Rights. Whenever necessary and possible we share staff, educational and financial resources with our affiliates. Several months ago our local affiliate here in Birmingham invited us to be on call to engage in a nonviolent direct action program if such were deemed necessary. We readily consented and when the hour came we lived up to our promises. So I am here, along with several members of my staff, because we were invited here. I am here because I have basic organizational ties here. Beyond this, I am in Birmingham because injustice is here. Just as the eighth century prophets left their little villages and carried their "thus saith the Lord" far beyond the boundaries of their home town, and just as the Apostle Paul left his little village of Tarsus and carried the gospel of Jesus Christ to practically every hamlet and city of the Graeco-Roman world, I too am compelled to carry the gospel of freedom beyond my particular home town. Like Paul, I must constantly respond to the Macedonian call for aid.

Moreover, I am cognizant of the interrelatedness of all communities and states. I cannot sit idly by in Atlanta and not be concerned about what happens in Birmingham. Injustice anywhere is a threat to justice everywhere. We are caught in an inescapable network of mutuality tied in a single garment of destiny. Whatever affects one directly affects all indirectly. Never again can we afford to live with the narrow, provincial "outside agitator" idea. Anyone who lives inside the United States can never be considered an outsider anywhere in this country.

You deplore the demonstrations that are presently taking place in Birmingham. But I am sorry that your statement did not express a similar concern for the conditions that brought the demonstrations into being. I am sure that each of you would want to go beyond the superficial social analyst who looks merely at effects, and does not grapple with underlying causes. I would not hesitate to say that it is unfortunate that so-called demonstrations are taking place in Birmingham at this time, but I would say in more emphatic terms it is even more unfortunate that the white power structure of this city left the Negro community with no other alternative.

5 In any nonviolent campaign there are four basic steps: (1) collection of the facts to determine whether injustices are alive; (2) negotiation; (3) self-purification; and (4) direct action. We have gone through all of these steps in Birmingham. There can be no gainsaying of the fact that racial injustice engulfs this community. Birmingham is probably the most thoroughly segregated city in the United States. Its ugly record of police brutality is known in every section of this country. Its unjust treatment of Negroes in the courts is a notorious

reality. There have been more unsolved bombings of Negro homes and churches in Birmingham than any city in this nation. These are the hard, brutal, and unbelievable facts. On the basis of these conditions Negro leaders sought to negotiate with the city fathers. But the political leaders consistently refused to engage in good faith negotiation.

Then came the opportunity last September to talk with some of the leaders of the economic community. In these negotiating sessions certain promises were made by the merchants—such as the promise to remove the humiliating racial signs from the stores. On the basis of these promises Rev. Shuttlesworth and the leaders of the Alabama Christian Movement for Human Rights agreed to call a moratorium on any type of demonstrations. As the weeks and months unfolded we realized that we were the victims of a broken promise. The signs remained. As in so many experiences of the past we were confronted with blasted hopes, and the dark shadow of a deep disappointment settled upon us. So we had no alternative except that of preparing for direct action, whereby we would present our very bodies as a means of laying our case before the conscience of the local and national community. We were not unmindful of the difficulties involved. So we decided to go through a process of self-purification. We started having workshops on nonviolence and repeatedly asked ourselves the questions, "Are you able to accept blows without retaliating?" "Are you able to endure the ordeals of jail?"

We decided to set our direct action program around the Easter season, realizing that with the exception of Christmas, this was the largest shopping period of the year. Knowing that a strong economic withdrawal program would be the by-product of direct action, we felt that this was the best time to bring pressure on the merchants for the needed changes. Then it occurred to us that the March election was ahead, and so we speedily decided to postpone action until after election day. When we discovered that Mr. Connor[1] was in the run-off, we decided again to postpone so that the demonstrations could not be used to cloud the issues. At this time we agreed to begin our nonviolent witness the day after the run-off.

This reveals that we did not move irresponsibly into direct action. We too wanted to see Mr. Connor defeated; so we went through postponement after postponement to aid in this community need. After this we felt that direct action could be delayed no longer.

You may well ask, "Why direct action? Why sit-ins, marches, etc.? Isn't negotiation a better path?" You are exactly right in your call for negotiation. Indeed, this is the purpose of direct action. Nonviolent direct action seeks to create such a crisis and establish such creative tension that a community that has constantly refused to negotiate is forced to confront the issue. It seeks so to dramatize the issue that it can no longer be ignored. I just referred to the creation of tension as a part of the work of the nonviolent resister. This may sound

[1] Mr. Connor: Eugene "Bull" Connor, the police chief of Birmingham, who refused to leave office after losing his reelection bid. He became notorious for ordering police to use force on demonstrators protesting segregation.

rather shocking. But I must confess that I am not afraid of the word tension. I have earnestly worked and preached against violent tension, but there is a type of constructive nonviolent tension that is necessary for growth. Just as Socrates felt that it was necessary to create a tension in the mind so that individuals could rise from the bondage of myths and half-truths to the unfettered realm of creative analysis and objective appraisal, we must see the need of having nonviolent gadflies to create the kind of tension in society that will help men rise from the dark depths of prejudice and racism to the majestic heights of understanding and brotherhood. So the purpose of the direct action is to create a situation so crisis-packed that it will inevitably open the door to negotiation. We, therefore, concur with you in your call for negotiation. Too long has our beloved Southland been bogged down in the tragic attempt to live in monologue rather than dialogue.

10 One of the basic points in your statement is that our acts are untimely. Some have asked, "Why didn't you give the new administration time to act?" The only answer that I can give to this inquiry is that the new administration must be prodded about as much as the outgoing one before it acts. We will be sadly mistaken if we feel that the election of Mr. Boutwell will bring the millennium to Birmingham. While Mr. Boutwell is much more articulate and gentle than Mr. Connor, they are both segregationists dedicated to the task of maintaining the status quo. The hope I see in Mr. Boutwell is that he will be reasonable enough to see the futility of massive resistance to desegregation. But he will not see this without pressure from the devotees of civil rights. My friends, I must say to you that we have not made a single gain in civil rights without determined legal and nonviolent pressure. History is the long and tragic story of the fact that privileged groups seldom give up their privileges voluntarily. Individuals may see the moral light and voluntarily give up their unjust posture; but as Reinhold Niebuhr[2] has reminded us, groups are more immoral than individuals.

We know through painful experience that freedom is never voluntarily given by the oppressor; it must be demanded by the oppressed. Frankly I have never yet engaged in a direct action movement that was "well timed," according to the timetable of those who have not suffered unduly from the disease of segregation. For years now I have heard the word "Wait!" It rings in the ear of every Negro with a piercing familiarity. This "wait" has almost always meant "never." It has been a tranquilizing thaliodomide, relieving the emotional stress for a moment, only to give birth to an ill-formed infant of frustration. We must come to see with the distinguished jurist of yesterday that "justice too long delayed is justice denied." We have waited for more than three hundred and forty years for our constitutional and God-given rights. The nations of Asia and Africa are moving with jet-like speed toward the goal of political independence, and we still creep at horse and buggy pace toward the gaining of a cup of coffee at a lunch counter.

---

[2] Niebuhr: The prominent theologian Reinhold Niebuhr (1892–1971), known for his effort to relate Christianity to contemporary public life.

I guess it is easy for those who have never felt the stinging darts of segregation to say wait. But when you have seen vicious mobs lynch your mothers and fathers at will and drown your sisters and brothers at whim; when you have seen hate-filled policemen curse, kick, brutalize, and even kill your black brothers and sisters with impunity; when you see the vast majority of your twenty million Negro brothers smothering in an air-tight cage of poverty in the midst of an affluent society; when you suddenly find your tongue twisted and your speech stammering as you seek to explain to your six-year-old daughter why she can't go to the public amusement park that has just been advertised on television, and see tears welling up in her little eyes when she is told that Funtown is closed to colored children, and see the depressing clouds of inferiority begin to form in her little mental sky, and see her begin to distort her little personality by unconsciously developing a bitterness toward white people; when you have to concoct an answer for a five-year-old son asking in agonizing pathos: "Daddy, why do white people treat colored people so mean?"; when you take a cross country drive and find it necessary to sleep night after night in the uncomfortable corners of your automobile because no motel will accept you; when you are humiliated day in and day out by nagging signs reading "white" men and "colored"; when your first name becomes "nigger" and your middle name becomes "boy" (however old you are) and your last name becomes "John," and when your wife and mother are never given the respected title "Mrs."; when you are harried by day and haunted by night by the fact that you are a Negro, living constantly at tip-toe stance never quite knowing what to expect next, and plagued with inner fears and outer resentments; when you are forever fighting a degenerating sense of "nobodiness";—then you will understand why we find it difficult to wait. There comes a time when the cup of endurance runs over, and men are no longer willing to be plunged into an abyss of injustice where they experience the bleakness of corroding despair. I hope, sirs, you can understand our legitimate and unavoidable impatience.

You express a great deal of anxiety over our willingness to break laws. This is certainly a legitimate concern. Since we so diligently urge people to obey the Supreme Court's decision of 1954 outlawing segregation in the public schools, it is rather strange and paradoxical to find us consciously breaking laws. One may well ask, "How can you advocate breaking some laws and obeying others?" The answer is found in the fact that there are two types of laws. There are *just* laws and there are *unjust* laws. I would be the first to advocate obeying just laws. One has not only a legal but moral responsibility to obey just laws. Conversely, one has a moral responsibility to disobey unjust laws. I would agree with Saint Augustine that "An unjust law is no law at all."

Now what is the difference between the two? How does one determine when a law is just or unjust? A just law is a man-made code that squares with the moral law or the law of God. An unjust law is a code that is out of harmony with the moral law. To put it in the terms of Saint Thomas Aquinas, an unjust law is a human law that is not rooted in eternal and natural law. Any law that uplifts human personality is just. Any law that degrades human personality is unjust. All segregation statutes are unjust because segregation distorts the soul and damages the personality. It gives the segregator a false sense of superiority and the segregated a false sense of inferiority. To use the words of Martin Buber, the great Jewish philosopher, segregation substitutes an "I-it" relationship for the "I-thou" relationship, and ends up relegating persons to the status of things. So segregation is not only politically, economically, and sociologically unsound, but it is morally wrong and sinful. Paul Tillich[3] has said that sin is separation. Isn't segregation an existential expression of man's tragic separation, an expression of his awful estrangement, his terrible sinfulness? So I can urge men to obey the 1954 decision of the Supreme Court[4] because it is morally right, and I can urge them to disobey segregation ordinances because they are morally wrong.

15 Let us turn to a more concrete example of just and unjust laws. An unjust law is a code that a majority inflicts on a minority that is not binding on itself. This is *difference* made legal. On the other hand a just law is a code that a majority compels a minority to follow that it is willing to follow itself. This is *sameness* made legal.

Let me give another explanation. An unjust law is a code inflicted upon a minority which that minority had no part in enacting or creating because they did not have the unhampered right to vote. Who can say the legislature of Alabama which set up the segregation laws was democratically elected? Throughout the state of Alabama all types of conniving methods are used to prevent Negroes from becoming registered voters and there are some counties without a single Negro registered to vote despite the fact that the Negro constitutes a majority of the population. Can any law set up in such a state be considered democratically structured?

These are just a few examples of unjust and just laws. There are some instances when a law is just on its face but unjust in its application. For instance, I was arrested Friday on a charge of parading without a permit. Now there is nothing wrong with an ordinance which requires a permit for a parade, but when the ordinance is used to preserve segregation and to deny citizens the First Amendment privilege of peaceful assembly and peaceful protest, then it becomes unjust.

I hope you can see the distinction I am trying to point out. In no sense do I advocate evading or defying the law as the rabid segregationist would do. This would lead to anarchy. One who breaks an unjust law must do it *openly, lovingly* (not hatefully as the white mothers did in New Orleans when they were seen on television screaming "nigger, nigger, nigger") and with a willingness to accept the penalty. I submit that an individual who breaks a law that conscience tells him is unjust, and willingly accepts the penalty by staying in jail to arouse the

---

[3] Tillich: Like Niebuhr, Tillich (1886–1965) was known for a theology aimed at relating Christianity to contemporary life. See Chapter 2, pp. 123–130.

[4] Supreme Court: In the 1954 decision *Brown v. Board of Education*, the Supreme Court ruled against "separate but equal" schools and declared racial discrimination in public education unconstitutional.

conscience of the community over its injustice, is in reality expressing the very highest respect for law.

Of course there is nothing new about this kind of civil disobedience. It was seen sublimely in the refusal of Shadrach, Meshach, and Abednego to obey the laws of Nebuchadnezzar because a higher moral law was involved. It was practiced superbly by the early Christians who were willing to face hungry lions and the excruciating pain of chopping blocks, before submitting to certain unjust laws of the Roman Empire. To a degree academic freedom is a reality today because Socrates practiced civil disobedience.

We can never forget that everything Hitler did in Germany was "legal" and everything the Hungarian freedom fighters[5] did in Hungary was "illegal." It was "illegal" to aid and comfort a Jew in Hitler's Germany. But I am sure that, if I had lived in Germany during that time, I would have aided and comforted my Jewish brothers even though it was illegal. If I lived in a communist country today where certain principles dear to the Christian faith are suppressed, I believe I would openly advocate disobeying those antireligious laws.

I must make two honest confessions to you, my Christian and Jewish brothers. First I must confess that over the last few years I have been gravely disappointed with the white moderate. I have almost reached the regrettable conclusion that the Negroes' great stumbling block in the stride toward freedom is not the White Citizens' "Counciler" or the Ku Klux Klanner, but the white moderate who is more devoted to "order" than to justice; who prefers a negative peace which is the absence of tension to a positive peace which is the presence of justice; who constantly says "I agree with you in the goal you seek, but I can't agree with your methods of direct action"; who paternalistically feels that he can set the timetable for another man's freedom; who lives by the myth of time and who constantly advises the Negro to wait until a "more convenient season." Shallow understanding from people of good will is more frustrating than absolute misunderstanding from people of ill will. Lukewarm acceptance is much more bewildering than outright rejection.

I had hoped that the white moderate would understand that law and order exist for the purpose of establishing justice, and that when they fail to do this they become the dangerously structured dams that block the flow of social progress. I had hoped that the white moderate would understand that the present tension in the South is merely a necessary phase of the transition from an obnoxious negative peace, where the Negro passively accepted his unjust plight, to a substance-filled positive peace, where all men will respect the dignity and worth of human personality. Actually, we who engage in nonviolent direct action are not the creators of tension. We merely bring to the surface the hidden tension that is already alive. We bring it out in the open where it can be seen and dealt with. Like a boil that can never be cured as long as it is covered up but must be opened with all its pus-flowing ugliness to the natural medicines of air and light, injustice must likewise be exposed, with all of the tension its exposing

[5] freedom fighters: In 1956, Hungarian patriots revolted against Soviet-backed rule in their country.

creates, to the light of human conscience and the air of national opinion before it can be cured.

In your statement you asserted that our actions, even though peaceful, must be condemned because they precipitate violence. But can this assertion be logically made? Isn't this like condemning the robbed man because his possession of money precipitated the evil act of robbery? Isn't this like condemning Socrates because his unswerving commitment to truth and his philosophical delvings precipitated the misguided popular mind to make him drink the hemlock? Isn't this like condemning Jesus because His unique God consciousness and never-ceasing devotion to His will precipitated the evil act of crucifixion? We must come to see, as federal courts have consistently affirmed, that it is immoral to urge an individual to withdraw his efforts to gain his basic constitutional rights because the quest precipitates violence. Society must protect the robbed and punish the robber.

I had also hoped that the white moderate would reject the myth of time. I received a letter this morning from a white brother in Texas which said: "All Christians know that the colored people will receive equal rights eventually, but is it possible that you are in too great of a religious hurry? It has taken Christianity almost 2000 years to accomplish what it has. The teachings of Christ take time to come to earth." All that is said here grows out of a tragic misconception of time. It is the strangely irrational notion that there is something in the very flow of time that will inevitably cure all ills. Actually time is neutral. It can be used either destructively or constructively. I am coming to feel that the people of ill will have used time much more effectively than the people of good will. We will have to repent in this generation not merely for the vitriolic words and actions of the bad people, but for the appalling silence of the good people. We must come to see that human progress never rolls in on wheels of inevitability. It comes through the tireless efforts and persistent work of men willing to be co-workers with God, and without this hard work time itself becomes an ally of the forces of social stagnation.

25 We must use time creatively, and forever realize that the time is always ripe to do right. Now is the time to make real the promise of democracy, and transform our pending national elegy into a creative psalm of brotherhood. Now is the time to lift our national policy from the quicksand of racial injustice to the solid rock of human dignity.

You spoke of our activity in Birmingham as extreme. At first I was rather disappointed that fellow clergymen would see my nonviolent efforts as those of the extremist. I started thinking about the fact that I stand in the middle of two opposing forces in the Negro community. One is a force of complacency made up of Negroes who, as a result of long years of oppression, have been so completely drained of self-respect and a sense of "somebodiness" that they have adjusted to segregation, and of a few Negroes in the middle class who, because of a degree of academic and economic security, and because at points they profit by segregation, have unconsciously become insensitive to the problems of the masses. The other force is one of bitterness and hatred and comes perilously close to advocating violence. It is expressed in the various black nationalist groups that are springing up over the nation, the largest and best known being Elijah Muhammad's Muslim movement.[6] This movement is nourished by the contemporary frustration over the continued existence of racial discrimination. It is made up of people who have lost faith in America, who have absolutely repudiated Christianity, and who have concluded that the white man is an incurable "devil." I have tried to stand between these two forces saying that we need not follow the "do-nothing-ism" of the complacent or the hatred and despair of the black nationalist. There is the more excellent way of love and nonviolent protest. I'm grateful to God that, through the Negro church, the dimension of nonviolence entered our struggle. If this philosophy had not emerged I am convinced that by now many streets of the South would be flowing with floods of blood. And I am further convinced that if our white brothers dismiss us as "rabble rousers" and "outside agitators"—those of us who are working through the channels of nonviolent direct action—and refuse to support our nonviolent efforts, millions of Negroes, out of frustration and despair, will seek solace and security in black nationalist ideologies, a development that will lead inevitably to a frightening racial nightmare.

Oppressed people cannot remain oppressed forever. The urge for freedom will eventually come. This is what has happened to the American Negro. Something within has reminded him of his birthright of freedom; something without has reminded him that he can gain it. Consciously and unconsciously, he has been swept in by what the Germans call the *Zeitgeist*,[7] and with his black brothers of Africa, and his brown and yellow brothers of Asia, South America, and the Caribbean, he is moving with a sense of cosmic urgency toward the promised land of racial justice. Recognizing this vital urge that has engulfed the Negro community, one should readily understand public demonstrations. The Negro has many pent-up resentments and latent frustrations. He has to get them out. So let him march sometime; let him have his prayer pilgrimages to the city hall; understand why he must have sit-ins and freedom rides. If his repressed emotions do not come out in these nonviolent ways, they will come out in ominous expressions of violence. This is not a threat; it is a fact of history. So I have not said to my people, "Get rid of your discontent." But I have tried to say that this normal and healthy discontent can be channeled through the creative outlet of nonviolent direct action. Now this approach is being dismissed as extremist. I must admit that I was initially disappointed in being so categorized.

But as I continued to think about the matter I gradually gained a bit of satisfaction from being considered an extremist. Was not Jesus an extremist in love? "Love your enemies, bless them that curse you, pray for them that despitefully use you." Was not Amos[8] an extremist for justice—"Let justice roll down like waters and righteousness like a mighty stream." Was not Paul an

---

[6] movement: The Black Muslims opposed integration and advocated creation of a separate black nation within the United States.

[7] *Zeitgeist:* German for "spirit of the age."

[8] Amos: Biblical prophet who railed against immorality.

extremist for the gospel of Jesus Christ—"I bear in my body the marks of the Lord Jesus." Was not Martin Luther an extremist—"Here I stand; I can do none other so help me God." Was not John Bunyan[9] an extremist—"I will stay in jail to the end of my days before I make a butchery of my conscience." Was not Abraham Lincoln an extremist—"This nation cannot survive half slave and half free." Was not Thomas Jefferson an extremist—"We hold these truths to be self-evident, that all men are created equal." So the question is not whether we will be extremist but what kind of extremist will we be. Will we be extremists for hate or will we be extremists for love? Will we be extremists for the preservation of injustice—or will we be extremists for the cause of justice? In that dramatic scene on Calvary's hill three men were crucified. We must never forget that all three were crucified for the same crime—the crime of extremism. Two were extremists for immorality, and thus fell below their environment. The other, Jesus Christ, was an extremist for love, truth, and goodness, and thereby rose above His environment. So, after all, maybe the South, the nation, and the world are in dire need of creative extremists.

I had hoped that the white moderate would see this. Maybe I was too optimistic. Maybe I expected too much. I guess I should have realized that few members of a race that has oppressed another race can understand or appreciate the deep groans and passionate yearnings of those that have been oppressed, and still fewer have the vision to see that injustice must be rooted out by strong, persistent, and determined action. I am thankful, however, that some of our white brothers have grasped the meaning of this social revolution and committed themselves to it. They are still all too small in quantity, but they are big in quality. Some like Ralph McGill, Lillian Smith, Harry Golden, and James Dabbs have written about our struggle in eloquent, prophetic, and understanding terms. Others have marched with us down nameless streets of the South. They have languished in filthy, roach-infested jails, suffering the abuse and brutality of angry policemen who see them as "dirty nigger lovers." They, unlike so many of their moderate brothers and sisters, have recognized the urgency of the moment and sensed the need for powerful "action" antidotes to combat the disease of segregation.

30 Let me rush on to mention my other disappointment. I have been so greatly disappointed with the white Church and its leadership. Of course there are some notable exceptions. I am not unmindful of the fact that each of you has taken some significant stands on this issue. I commend you, Rev. Stallings, for your Christian stand on this past Sunday, in welcoming Negroes to your worship service on a nonsegregated basis. I commend the Catholic leaders of this state for integrating Springhill College several years ago.

But despite these notable exceptions I must honestly reiterate that I have been disappointed with the Church. I do not say that as one of those negative critics who can always find something wrong with the Church. I say it as a minister of the gospel, who loves the Church; who was nurtured in its bosom; who

---

[9] Bunyan: author (1628–1688) of the widely read Puritan allegory *Pilgrim's Progress* (1678).

has been sustained by its spiritual blessings and who will remain true to it as long as the cord of life shall lengthen.

I had the strange feeling when I was suddenly catapulted into the leadership of the bus protest in Montgomery[10] several years ago that we would have the support of the white Church. I felt that the white ministers, priests, and rabbis of the South would be some of our strongest allies. Instead, some have been outright opponents, refusing to understand the freedom movement and misrepresenting its leaders; all too many others have been more cautious than courageous and have remained silent behind the anesthetizing security of stained glass windows.

In spite of my shattered dreams of the past, I came to Birmingham with the hope that the white religious leadership of the community would see the justice of our cause and, with deep moral concern, serve as the channel through which our just grievances could get to the power structure. I had hoped that each of you would understand. But again I have been disappointed.

I have heard numerous religious leaders of the South call upon their worshippers to comply with a desegregation decision because it is the law, but I have longed to hear white ministers say follow this decree because integration is morally right and the Negro is your brother. In the midst of blatant injustices inflicted upon the Negro, I have watched white churches stand on the sideline and merely mouth pious irrelevancies and sanctimonious trivialities. In the midst of a mighty struggle to rid our nation of racial and economic injustice, I have heard so many ministers say, "Those are social issues with which the Gospel has no real concern," and I have watched so many churches commit themselves to a completely other-worldly religion which made a strange distinction between body and soul, the sacred and the secular.

So here we are moving toward the exit of the twentieth century with a religious community largely adjusted to the status quo, standing as a tail-light behind other community agencies rather than a headlight leading men to higher levels of justice.

I have travelled the length and breadth of Alabama, Mississippi, and all the other Southern states. On sweltering summer days and crisp autumn mornings I have looked at her beautiful churches with their spires pointing heavenward. I have beheld the impressive outlay of her massive religious education buildings. Over and over again I have found myself asking: "Who worships here? Who is their God? Where were their voices when the lips of Governor Barnett[11] dripped with words of interposition and nullification? Where were they when Governor Wallace[12] gave the clarion call for defiance and hatred? Where were their voices of support when tired, bruised, and weary Negro men and women

[10] Montgomery: The famous Montgomery bus boycott, which lasted nearly one year, was sparked by the refusal of Rosa Parks to give up her bus seat to a white man.

[11] Barnett: Ross R. Barnett, governor of Mississippi from 1960 to 1964.

[12] Wallace: George C. Wallace, who served as governor of Alabama in 1963–1966, 1971–1979, and 1983–1987, and who attempted to resist enforcement of the Supreme Court decision in *Brown v. Board of Education*.

decided to rise from the dark dungeons of complacency to the bright hills of creative protest?"

Yes, these questions are still in my mind. In deep disappointment, I have wept over the laxity of the Church. But be assured that my tears have been tears of love. There can be no deep disappointment where there is not deep love. Yes, I love the Church; I love her sacred walls. How could I do otherwise? I am in the rather unique position of being the son, the grandson, and the great grandson of preachers. Yes, I see the Church as the body of Christ. But, oh! How we have blemished and scarred that body through social neglect and fear of being nonconformists.

There was a time when the Church was very powerful. It was during that period when the early Christians rejoiced when they were deemed worthy to suffer for what they believed. In those days the Church was not merely a thermometer that recorded the ideas and principles of popular opinion; it was a thermostat that transformed the mores of society. Wherever the early Christians entered a town the power structure got disturbed and immediately sought to convict them for being "disturbers of the peace" and "outside agitators." But they went on with the conviction that they were a "colony of heaven" and had to obey God rather than man. They were small in number but big in commitment. They were too God-intoxicated to be "astronomically intimidated." They brought an end to such ancient evils as infanticide and gladiatorial contest.

Things are different now. The contemporary Church is so often a weak, ineffectual voice with an uncertain sound. It is so often the arch-supporter of the status quo. Far from being disturbed by the presence of the Church, the power structure of the average community is consoled by the Church's silent and often vocal sanction of things as they are.

40 But the judgment of God is upon the Church as never before. If the Church of today does not recapture the sacrificial spirit of the early Church, it will lose its authentic ring, forfeit the loyalty of millions, and be dismissed as an irrelevant social club with no meaning for the twentieth century. I am meeting young people every day whose disappointment with the Church has risen to outright disgust.

Maybe again I have been too optimistic. Is organized religion too inextricably bound to the status quo to save our nation and the world? Maybe I must turn my faith to the inner spiritual Church, the church within the Church, as the true *ecclesia*[13] and the hope of the world. But again I am thankful to God that some noble souls from the ranks of organized religion have broken loose from the paralyzing chains of conformity and joined us as active partners in the struggle for freedom. They have left their secure congregations and walked the streets of Albany, Georgia, with us. They have gone through the highways of the South on torturous rides for freedom. Yes, they have gone to jail with us. Some have been kicked out of their churches and lost the support of their bishops and fellow ministers. But they have gone with the faith that right defeated

---

[13] *ecclesia:* Latin for "church."

is stronger than evil triumphant. These men have been the leaven in the lump of the race. Their witness has been the spiritual salt that has preserved the true meaning of the Gospel in these troubled times. They have carved a tunnel of hope through the dark mountain of disappointment.

I hope the Church as a whole will meet the challenge of this decisive hour. But even if the Church does not come to the aid of justice, I have no despair about the future. I have no fear about the outcome of our struggle in Birmingham, even if our motives are presently misunderstood. We will reach the goal of freedom in Birmingham and all over the nation, because the goal of America is freedom. Abused and scorned though we may be, our destiny is tied up with the destiny of America. Before the pilgrims landed at Plymouth, we were here. Before the pen of Jefferson etched across the pages of history the majestic words of the Declaration of Independence, we were here. For more than two centuries our foreparents labored in this country without wages; they made cotton "king"; and they built the homes of their masters in the midst of brutal injustice and shameful humiliation—and yet out of a bottomless vitality they continued to thrive and develop. If the inexpressible cruelties of slavery could not stop us, the opposition we now face will surely fail. We will win our freedom because the sacred heritage of our nation and the eternal will of God are embodied in our echoing demands.

I must close now. But before closing I am impelled to mention one other point in your statement that troubled me profoundly. You warmly commended the Birmingham police force for keeping "order" and "preventing violence." I don't believe you would have so warmly commended the police force if you had seen its angry violent dogs literally biting six unarmed, nonviolent Negroes. I don't believe you would so quickly commend the policemen if you would observe their ugly and inhuman treatment of Negroes here in the city jail; if you would watch them push and curse old Negro women and young Negro girls; if you would see them slap and kick old Negro men and young Negro boys; if you will observe them, as they did on two occasions, refuse to give us food because we wanted to sing our grace together. I'm sorry that I can't join you in your praise for the police department.

It is true that they have been rather disciplined in their public handling of the demonstrators. In this sense they have been rather publicly "nonviolent." But for what purpose? To preserve the evil system of segregation. Over the last few years I have consistently preached that nonviolence demands that the means we use must be as pure as the ends we seek. So I have tried to make it clear that it is wrong to use immoral means to attain moral ends. But now I must affirm that it is just as wrong, or even more so, to use moral means to preserve immoral ends. Maybe Mr. Connor and his policemen have been rather publicly nonviolent, as Chief Pritchett[14] was in Albany, Georgia, but they have used the moral means of nonviolence to maintain the immoral end of flagrant

[14] Pritchett: Police chief in Albany, Georgia, in 1961 and 1962, who instructed his officers to treat nonviolent protestors with respect and restraint rather than violence.

racial injustice. T. S. Eliot has said that there is no greater treason than to do the right deed for the wrong reason.

45 I wish you had commended the Negro sit-inners and demonstrators of Birmingham for their sublime courage, their willingness to suffer, and their amazing discipline in the midst of the most inhuman provocation. One day the South will recognize its real heroes. They will be the James Merediths,[15] courageously and with a majestic sense of purpose, facing jeering and hostile mobs and the agonizing loneliness that characterizes the life of the pioneer. They will be old, oppressed, battered Negro women, symbolized in a seventy-two year old woman of Montgomery, Alabama, who rose up with a sense of dignity and with her people decided not to ride the segregated buses, and responded to one who inquired about her tiredness with ungrammatical profundity: "My feets is tired, but my soul is rested." They will be young high school and college students, young ministers of the gospel and a host of the elders, courageously and nonviolently sitting in at lunch counters and willingly going to jail for conscience sake. One day the South will know that when these disinherited children of God sat down at lunch counters they were in reality standing up for the best in the American dream and the most sacred values in our Judeo-Christian heritage, and thus carrying our whole nation back to great wells of democracy which were dug deep by the founding fathers in the formulation of the Constitution and the Declaration of Independence.

Never before have I written a letter this long (or should I say a book?). I'm afraid that it is much too long to take your precious time. I can assure you that it would have been much shorter if I had been writing from a comfortable desk, but what else is there to do when you are alone for days in the dull monotony of a narrow jail cell other than write long letters, think strange thoughts, and pray long prayers?

If I have said anything in this letter that is an overstatement of the truth and is indicative of an unreasonable impatience, I beg you to forgive me. If I have said anything in this letter that is an understatement of the truth and is indicative of my having a patience that makes me patient with anything less than brotherhood, I beg God to forgive me.

I hope this letter finds you strong in the faith. I also hope that circumstances will soon make it possible for me to meet each of you, not as an integrationist or a civil rights leader, but as a fellow clergyman and a Christian brother. Let us all hope that the dark clouds of racial prejudice will soon pass away and the deep fog of misunderstanding will be lifted from our fear-drenched communities and in some not too distant tomorrow the radiant stars of love and brotherhood will shine over our great nation with all of their scintillating beauty.

Yours for the cause of
Peace and Brotherhood
Martin Luther King Jr.

---

[15] Merediths: In 1962, James Meredith, accompanied by federal marshals, became the first African-American to enroll at the University of Mississippi.

LEARNING MORE

The history of the civil rights movement forms the backdrop for Martin Luther King Jr.'s writing. To learn more, see the *Ideas Across Time* website.

QUESTIONING THE TEXT

1. The eight clergymen whom King addresses objected to the protests in Birmingham as the actions of "outside agitators." How does King respond to this accusation? What part of his response do you find most persuasive? Explain.
2. King goes out of his way to stress that there was "no alternative" to the civil disobedience he was leading. What evidence does he offer to support this claim? Are you persuaded that there really was no other alternative? Explain.
3. Why is self-purification a part of King's program of civil disobedience?
4. Why do the eight clergymen think King's protest is "untimely" (par. 10)? Why does King disagree?
5. When does King think it is okay to break the law? Do you agree?
6. What disappointed King about white moderates?
7. What disappointed King about the Church?
8. Why does King say the destiny of the Negro is tied to the destiny of America as a whole?

ANALYZING THE WRITER'S CRAFT

1. What is the tone of this essay? Cite two or three examples to support your answer.
2. How does this essay reflect the fact that it is a public letter from one clergyman to other clergymen?
3. Write an outline indicating the main sections of this essay. How does King organize his essay to achieve maximum effect?
4. King's writing is full of biblical cadences and metaphors. Examine two or three of these closely, and discuss how they both reflect and strengthen King's argument.
5. King spends a good deal of time defining just and unjust laws, a distinction of great importance for someone advocating civil disobedience in a democratic society. Do his definitions stand up to careful examination, or are his definitions morally attractive but hard to apply to real-life cases?
6. King embraces the label "extremist" by comparing his acts with those of others whom he now labels extremists, such as Jesus and Martin Luther. Are these comparisons appropriate? Effective? Explain.
7. Why does King leave his disagreement with the eight clergymen over the behavior of the police to the very end of his essay?

8. Do you think that the clergymen whom King addresses changed their views after reading his letter? Explain.

MAKING CONNECTIONS

1. King emphatically identifies himself with the American political tradition. Compare his view of that tradition with that of James Baldwin (Chapter 1, pp. 29–35), a near contemporary of King's.
2. The writer least like King is Niccolo Machiavelli (Chapter 5, pp. 339–345). Do they simply operate on diametrically opposed assumptions and look in politics for diametrically opposed things, or is there some common ground between them? To what extent are their differences attributable to the differences in their circumstances and in the historical context?
3. The writer closest to King is Henry David Thoreau (Chapter 5, pp. 371–383). Can you find examples of Thoreau's influence on King in this essay? Are there points about which Thoreau and King might disagree?
4. Vaclav Havel (Chapter 5, pp. 404–412) also writes about the relation of the powerless to power. Do you see examples of King's influence on Havel in "The Power of the Powerless"?
5. Do King and bell hooks (pp. 548–539), both fighters against oppression, share a common outlook? Would King understand and approve hooks' analysis and arguments? Why or why not?

FORMULATING IDEAS FOR WRITING

1. Write a reply to King on behalf of one of the eight clergymen he addresses, explaining either why you still find his protest "unwise and untimely" or why you have been moved to reconsider your position.
2. The twentieth century provides many examples of unjust laws, and so we are familiar with the idea that following a law just because it is a law may not be all there is to being a good citizen. But it is notoriously difficult to define unjust laws in the abstract. Write an analysis of King's paragraphs on just and unjust laws (pars. 13–20) that explores the extent to which King succeeds—and that also probes the limitations of his definitions. (Consider, for example, this sentence: "An unjust law is a code that a majority inflicts on a minority that is not binding on itself" [par. 15]. How would this definition apply to laws made by the U.S. government about illegal aliens?)
3. King advocates nonviolent civil disobedience. How powerful a weapon is this tactic for resisting or righting injustice? Like Thoreau (Chapter 5, pp. 371–383), King directs his protest at the conscience of his fellow citizens. Would the civil rights marches have succeeded, however, without the support of the federal courts? Would nonviolence have triumphed over Hitler's SS, who seemed to have no conscience?
4. Equal rights for all have undoubtedly become more attainable since Rosa Parks first refused to step to the back of the bus. But inequalities and

injustices remain. How should we judge Martin Luther King Jr.'s accomplishments in light of the continuing inequalities and injustices of our society? Was his faith in nonviolent protest confirmed by events over time?

Feminism: A Movement to End Sexist Oppression (1984)

bell hooks

bell hooks (who uses lowercase letters for her name to emphasize the importance of her writing over her individual identity) is a social critic and left-wing feminist. Born Gloria Watkins in 1950, she assumed the pen name bell hooks to honor her grandmother. hooks grew up in a working-class African-American community in Hopkinsville, Kentucky, and went on to receive her B.A. from Stanford University in 1973 and her Ph.D. from the University of California at Santa Cruz in 1983. Her doctoral dissertation studied the fiction of the African-American novelist Toni Morrison. hooks's work takes as its vantage point the radically isolated situation of the black working-class woman, burdened by multiple and interconnected discriminations at work, at home, in personal and sexual relations, in politics, in education, in the media, and in social life.

Her first major work, the influential *Ain't I a Woman? Black Women and Feminism* (1981), tackles these issues. Here she traces the impact of both racism and sexism on black women, leading to their particular marginalization. She maintains that the oppression of black women is enforced by the educational system and the media, operating within what she styles "the white supremacist patriarchal capitalist system." Moreover, hooks is critical of mainstream white feminism for paying little genuine attention to issues of race and class. As this selection, taken from *Feminist Theory: From Margin to Center* (1984), shows, hooks views feminism as a force for the overthrow the whole oppressive hierarchical structure. Her more recent writing has taken up the theme of community as a counterforce to racism and sexism. This writing follows the path of the Brazilian educationist Paulo Freire, whose *Pedagogy of the Oppressed* (1972) articulates a liberation pedagogy that can empower the disenfranchised through literacy.

hooks is Distinguished Professor of English at City College in New York and Distinguished Writer-in-Residence at Berea College in her native Kentucky.

A central problem within feminist discourse has been our inability to either arrive at a consensus of opinion about what feminism is or accept definition(s) that could serve as points of unification. Without agreed upon definition(s), we lack a sound foundation on which to construct theory or engage in overall meaningful praxis.[1] Expressing her frustrations with the absence of clear definitions in a recent essay, "Towards a Revolutionary Ethics," Carmen Vasquez comments:

> We can't even agree on what a "Feminist" is, never mind what she would believe in and how she defines the principles that constitute honor among us. In key with the American capitalist obsession for individualism and anything goes so long as it gets you what you want. Feminism in America has come to mean anything you like, honey. There are as many definitions of Feminism as there are feminists, some of my sisters say, with a chuckle. I don't think it's funny.[2]

It is not funny. It indicates a growing disinterest in feminism as a radical political movement. It is a despairing gesture expressive of the belief that solidarity between women is not possible. It is a sign that the political naiveté which has traditionally characterized woman's lot in male-dominated culture abounds.

Most people in the United States think of feminism or the more commonly used term "women's lib" as a movement that aims to make women the social equals of men. This broad definition, popularized by the media and mainstream segments of the movement, raises problematic questions. Since men are not equals in white supremacist, capitalist, patriarchal class structure, which men do women want to be equal to? Do women share a common vision of what equality means? Implicit in this simplistic definition of women's liberation is a dismissal of race and class as factors that, in conjunction with sexism, determine the extent to which an individual will be discriminated against, exploited, or oppressed. Bourgeois white women interested in women's rights issues have been satisfied with simple definitions for obvious reasons. Rhetorically placing themselves in the same social category as oppressed women, they were not anxious to call attention to race and class privilege.

Women in lower class and poor groups, particularly those who are non-white, would not have defined women's liberation as women gaining social equality with men since they are continually reminded in their everyday lives that all women do not share a common social status. Concurrently, they know that many males in their social groups are exploited and oppressed. Knowing that men in their groups do not have social, political, and economic power, they would not deem it liberatory to share their social status. While they are aware that sexism enables men in their respective groups to have privileges denied them, they are more likely to see exaggerated expressions of male chauvinism among their peers as stemming from the male's sense of himself as powerless and ineffectual in relation to ruling male groups, rather than an expression of an overall privileged social status. From the very onset of the women's liberation movement, these women were suspicious of feminism

---

[1] praxis: action, practice.
[2] Carmen Vasquez, "Towards a Revolutionary Ethics," p. 1 [hooks's note].

precisely because they recognized the limitations inherent in its definition. They recognized the possibility that feminism defined as social equality with men might easily become a movement that would primarily affect the social standing of white women in middle and upper class groups while affecting only in a very marginal way the social status of working class and poor women.

Not all the women who were at the forefront of organized women's movement shaping definitions were content with making women's liberation synonymous with women gaining social equality with men. On the opening pages of *Woman Power: The Movement for Women's Liberation,* Cellestine Ware, a black woman active in the movement, wrote under the heading "Goals":

> Radical feminism is working for the eradication of domination and elitism in all human relationships. This would make self-determination the ultimate good and require the downfall of society as we know it today.[3]

5 Individual radical feminists like Charlotte Bunch based their analyses on an informed understanding of the politics of domination and a recognition of the inter-connections between various systems of domination even as they focused primarily on sexism. Their perspectives were not valued by those organizers and participants in women's movement who were more interested in social reforms. The anonymous authors of a pamphlet on feminist issues published in 1976, *Women and the New World,* make the point that many women active in women's liberation movement were far more comfortable with the notion of feminism as a reform that would help women attain social equality with men of their class than feminism defined as a radical movement that would eradicate domination and transform society:

> Whatever the organization, the location or the ethnic composition of the group, all the women's liberation organizations had one thing in common: they all came together based on a biological and sociological fact rather than on a body of ideas. Women came together in the women's liberation movement on the basis that we were women and all women are subject to male domination. We saw all women as being our allies and all men as being the oppressor. We never questioned the extent to which American women accept the same materialistic and individualistic values as American men. We did not stop to think that American women are just as reluctant as American men to struggle for a new society based on new values of mutual respect, cooperation and social responsibility.[4]

It is now evident that many women active in feminist movement were interested in reform as an end in itself, not as a stage in the progression towards revolutionary transformation. Even though Zillah Eisenstein can optimistically point to the potential radicalism of liberal women who work for social reform in *The Radical Future of Liberal Feminism,* the process by which this radicalism will surface is unclear. Eisenstein offers as an example of the radical implications of

[3] Cellestine Ware, *Woman Power,* p. 3 [hooks's note].

[4] *Women and the New World,* p. 33 [hooks's note].

liberal feminist programs the demands made at the government-sponsored Houston conference on women's rights issues which took place in 1978:

> The Houston report demands as a human right a full voice and role for women in determining the destiny of our world, our nation, our families, and our individual lives. It specifically calls for (1) the elimination of violence in the home and the development of shelters for battered women, (2) support for women's business, (3) a solution to child abuse, (4) federally funded nonsexist child care, (5) a policy of full employment so that all women who wish and are able to work may do so, (6) the protection of homemakers so that marriage is a partnership, (7) an end to the sexist portrayal of women in the media, (8) establishment of reproductive freedom and the end to involuntary sterilization, (9) a remedy to the double discrimination against minority women, (10) a revision of criminal codes dealing with rape, (11) elimination of discrimination on the basis of sexual preference, (12) the establishment of nonsexist education, and (13) an examination of all welfare reform proposals for their specific impact on women.[5]

The positive impact of liberal reforms on women's lives should not lead to the assumption that they eradicate systems of domination. Nowhere in these demands is there an emphasis on eradicating the politic of domination, yet it would need to be abolished if any of these demands were to be met. The lack of any emphasis on domination is consistent with the liberal feminist belief that women can achieve equality with men of their class without challenging and changing the cultural basis of group oppression. It is this belief that negates the likelihood that the potential radicalism of liberal feminism will ever be realized. Writing as early as 1967, Brazilian scholar Heleith Saffioti emphasized that bourgeois feminism has always been "fundamentally and unconsciously a feminism of the ruling class," that:

> Whatever revolutionary content there is in petty-bourgeois feminist praxis, it has been put there by the efforts of the middle strata, especially the less well off, to move up socially. To do this, however, they sought merely to expand the existing social structures, and never went so far as to challenge the status quo. Thus, while petty-bourgeois feminism may always have aimed at establishing social equality between the sexes, the consciousness it represented has remained utopian in its desire for and struggle to bring about a partial transformation of society; this it believed could be done without disturbing the foundations on which it rested. . . . In this sense, petty-bourgeois feminism is not feminism at all; indeed it has helped to consolidate class society by giving camouflage to its internal contradictions. . . .[6]

Radical dimensions of liberal women's social protest will continue to serve as an ideological support system providing the necessary critical and analytical impetus for the maintenance of a liberalism that aims to grant women greater equality of opportunity within the present white supremacist capitalist, patriarchal state. Such liberal women's rights activism in its essence diminishes

[5] Zillah Eisenstein, p. 232 [hooks's note].

[6] Heleith Saffioti, *Women in Class Society,* p. 223 [hooks's note].

feminist struggle. Philosopher Mihailo Markovic discusses the limitations of liberalism in his essay "Women's Liberation and Human Emancipation":

> Another basic characteristic of liberalism which constitutes a formidable obstacle to an oppressed social group's emancipation is its conception of human nature. If selfishness, aggressiveness, the drive to conquer and dominate, really are among defining human traits, as every liberal philosopher since Locke tries to convince us, the oppression in civil society—i.e., in the social sphere not regulated by the state—is a fact of life and the basic civil relationship between a man and a woman will always remain a battlefield. Woman, being less aggressive, is then either the less human of the two and doomed to subjugation, or else she must get more power-hungry herself and try to dominate man. Liberation for both is not feasible.[7]

Although liberal perspectives on feminism include reforms that would have radical implications for society, these are the reforms which will be resisted precisely because they would set the stage for revolutionary transformation were they implemented. It is evident that society is more responsive to those "feminist" demands that are not threatening, that may even help maintain the status quo. Jeanne Gross gives an example of this co-optation of feminist strategy in her essay "Feminist Ethics from a Marxist Perspective," published in 1977:

> If we as women want change in all aspects of our lives, we must recognize that capitalism is uniquely capable of co-opting piecemeal change. . . . Capitalism is capable of taking our visionary changes and using them against us. For example, many married women, recognizing their oppression in the family, have divorced. They are thrown, with no preparation or protection, into the labor market. For many women this has meant taking their places at the row of typewriters. Corporations are now recognizing the capacity for exploitation in divorced women. The turnover in such jobs is incredibly high. "If she complains, she can be replaced."[8]

Particularly as regards work, many liberal feminist reforms simply reinforced capitalist, materialist values (illustrating the flexibility of capitalism) without truly liberating women economically.

10 Liberal women have not been alone in drawing upon the dynamism of feminism to further their interests. The great majority of women who have benefited in any way from feminist-generated social reforms do not want to be seen as advocates of feminism. Conferences on issues of relevance to women, that would never have been organized or funded had there not been a feminist movement, take place all over the United States and the participants do not want to be seen as advocates of feminism. They are either reluctant to make a public commitment to feminist movement or sneer at the term. Individual African-American, Native American Indian, Asian-American, and Hispanic—American women find themselves isolated if they support feminist movement. Even women who may achieve fame and notoriety (as well as increased economic income) in response to attention given their work by large numbers of

[7] Mihailo Markovic, "Women's Liberation and Human Emancipation," pp. 145–67 [hooks's note].

[8] Jeanne Gross, "Feminist Ethics from a Marxist Perspective," pp. 52–56 [hooks's note].

women who support feminism may deflect attention away from their engagement with feminist movement. They may even go so far as to create other terms that express their concern with women's issues so as to avoid using the term feminist. The creation of new terms that have no relationship to organized political activity tend to provide women who may already be reluctant to explore feminism with ready excuses to explain their reluctance to participate. This illustrates an uncritical acceptance of distorted definitions of feminism rather than a demand for redefinition. They may support specific issues while divorcing themselves from what they assume is feminist movement.

In a recent article in a San Francisco newspaper, "Sisters—Under the Skin," columnist Bob Greene commented on the aversion many women apparently have to the term feminism. Greene finds it curious that many women "who obviously believe in everything that proud feminists believe in dismiss the term 'feminist' as something unpleasant; something with which they do not wish to be associated." Even though such women often acknowledge that they have benefited from feminist-generated reform measures which have improved the social status of specific groups of women, they do not wish to be seen as participants in feminist movement:

> There is no getting around it. After all this time, the term "feminist" makes many bright, ambitious, intelligent women embarrassed and uncomfortable. They simply don't want to be associated with it.
>
> It's as if it has an unpleasant connotation that they want no connection with. Chances are if you were to present them with every mainstream feminist belief, they would go along with the beliefs to the letter—and even if they consider themselves feminists, they hasten to say no.[9]

Many women are reluctant to advocate feminism because they are uncertain about the meaning of the term. Other women from exploited and oppressed ethnic groups dismiss the term because they do not wish to be perceived as supporting a racist movement; feminism is often equated with white women's rights effort. Large numbers of women see feminism as synonymous with lesbianism; their homophobia leads them to reject association with any group identified as pro-lesbian. Some women fear the word "feminism" because they shun identification with any political movement, especially one perceived as radical. Of course there are women who do not wish to be associated with women's rights movement in any form so they reject and oppose feminist movement. Most women are more familiar with negative perspectives on "women's lib" than the positive significations of feminism. It is this term's positive political significance and power that we must now struggle to recover and maintain.

Currently feminism seems to be a term without any clear significance. The "anything goes" approach to the definition of the word has rendered it practically meaningless. What is meant by "anything goes" is usually that any woman who wants social equality with men regardless of her political perspective (she can be a conservative right-winger or a nationalist communist) can

[9] Bob Greene, "Sisters—Under the Skin," p. 3 [hooks's note].

label herself feminist. Most attempts at defining feminism reflect the class nature of the movement. Definitions are usually liberal in origin and focus on the individual woman's right to freedom and self-determination. In Barbara Berg's *The Remembered Gate: Origins of American Feminism,* she defines feminism as a "broad movement embracing numerous phases of woman's emancipation." However, her emphasis is on women gaining greater individual freedom. Expanding on the above definition, Berg adds:

> It is the freedom to decide her own destiny; freedom from sex-determined role; freedom from society's oppressive restrictions; freedom to express her thoughts fully and to convert them freely into action. Feminism demands the acceptance of woman's right to individual conscience and judgment. It postulates that woman's essential worth stems from her common humanity and does not depend on the other relationships of her life.[10]

This definition of feminism is almost apolitical in tone; yet it is the type of definition many liberal women find appealing. It evokes a very romantic notion of personal freedom which is more acceptable than a definition that emphasizes radical political action.

Many feminist radicals now know that neither a feminism that focuses on woman as an autonomous human being worthy of personal freedom nor one that focuses on the attainment of equality of opportunity with men can rid society of sexism and male domination. Feminism is a struggle to end sexist oppression. Therefore, it is necessarily a struggle to eradicate the ideology of domination that permeates Western culture on various levels as well as a commitment to reorganizing society so that the self-development of people can take precedence over imperialism, economic expansion, and material desires. Defined in this way, it is unlikely that women would join feminist movement simply because we are biologically the same. A commitment to feminism so defined would demand that each individual participant acquire a critical political consciousness based on ideas and beliefs.

All too often the slogan "the personal is political" (which was first used to stress that woman's everyday reality is informed and shaped by politics and is necessarily political) became a means of encouraging women to think that the experience of discrimination, exploitation, or oppression automatically corresponded with an understanding of the ideological and institutional apparatus shaping one's social status. As a consequence, many women who had not fully examined their situation never developed a sophisticated understanding of their political reality and its relationship to that of women as a collective group. They were encouraged to focus on giving voice to personal experience. Like revolutionaries working to change the lot of colonized people globally, it is necessary for feminist activists to stress that the ability to see and describe one's own reality is a significant step in the long process of self-recovery; but it is only a beginning. When women internalized the idea that describing their own woe was synonymous with developing a critical political consciousness, the

---

[10] Barbara Berg, *The Remembered Gate* [hooks's note].

progress of feminist movement was stalled. Starting from such incomplete perspectives, it is not surprising that theories and strategies were developed that were collectively inadequate and misguided. To correct this inadequacy in past analysis, we must now encourage women to develop a keen, comprehensive understanding of women's political reality. Broader perspectives can only emerge as we examine both the personal that is political, the politics of society as a whole, and global revolutionary politics.

15 Feminism defined in political terms that stress collective as well as individual experience challenges women to enter a new domain—to leave behind the apolitical stance sexism decrees is our lot and develop political consciousness. Women know from our everyday lives that many of us rarely discuss politics. Even when women talked about sexist politics in the heyday of contemporary feminism, rather than allow this engagement with serious political matters to lead to complex, in-depth analysis of women's social status, we insisted that men were "the enemy," the cause of all our problems. As a consequence, we examined almost exclusively women's relationship to male supremacy and the ideology of sexism. The focus on "man as enemy" created, as Marlene Dixon emphasizes in her essay "The Rise and Demise of Women's Liberation: A Class Analysis," a "politics of psychological oppression" which evoked world views which "pit individual against individual and mystify the social basis of exploitation."[11] By repudiating the popular notion that the focus of feminist movement should be social equality of the sexes and emphasizing eradicating the cultural basis of group oppression, our own analysis would require an exploration of all aspects of women's political reality. This would mean that race and class oppression would be recognized as feminist issues with as much relevance as sexism.

When feminism is defined in such a way that it calls attention to the diversity of women's social and political reality, it centralizes the experiences of all women, especially the women whose social conditions have been least written about, studied, or changed by political movements. When we cease to focus on the simplistic stance "men are the enemy," we are compelled to examine systems of domination and our role in their maintenance and perpetuation. Lack of adequate definition made it easy for bourgeois women, whether liberal or radical in perspective, to maintain their dominance over the leadership of the movement and its direction. This hegemony continues to exist in most feminist organizations. Exploited and oppressed groups of women are usually encouraged by those in power to feel that their situation is hopeless, that they can do nothing to break the pattern of domination. Given such socialization, these women have often felt that our only response to white, bourgeois, hegemonic dominance of feminist movement is to trash, reject, or dismiss feminism. This reaction is in no way threatening to the women who wish to maintain control over the direction of feminist theory and praxis. They prefer us to be silent, passively accepting their ideas. They prefer us speaking against "them" rather than developing our own ideas about feminist movement.

---

[11] Marlene Dixon, "The Rise and Demise of Woman's Liberation: A Class Analysis," p. 61 [hooks's note].

Feminism is the struggle to end sexist oppression. Its aim is not to benefit solely any specific group of women, any particular race or class of women. It does not privilege women over men. It has the power to transform in a meaningful way all our lives. Most importantly, feminism is neither a lifestyle nor a ready-made identity or role one can step into. Diverting energy from feminist movement that aims to change society, many women concentrate on the development of a counter-culture, a woman-centered world wherein participants have little contact with men. Such attempts do not indicate a respect or concern for the vast majority of women who are unable to integrate their cultural expressions with the visions offered by alternative woman-centered communities. In *Beyond God the Father,* Mary Daly urged women to give up "the securities offered by the patriarchal system" and create new space that would be woman-centered. Responding to Daly, Jeanne Gross pointed to the contradictions that arise when the focus of feminist movement is on the construction of new space:

> Creating a "counterworld" places an incredible amount of pressure on the women who attempt to embark on such a project. The pressure comes from the belief that the only true resources for such an endeavor are ourselves. The past which is totally patriarchal is viewed as irredeemable. . . .
>
> If we go about creating an alternative culture without remaining in dialogue with others (and the historical circumstances that give rise to their identity) we have no reality check for our goals. We run the very real risk that the dominant ideology of the culture is re-duplicated in the feminist movement through cultural imperialism.[12]

Equating feminist struggle with living in a counter-cultural, woman-centered world erected barriers that closed the movement off from most women. Despite sexist discrimination, exploitation, or oppression, many women feel their lives as they live them are important and valuable. Naturally the suggestion that these lives could be simply left or abandoned for an alternative "feminist" lifestyle met with resistance. Feeling their life experiences devalued, deemed solely negative and worthless, many women responded by vehemently attacking feminism. By rejecting the notion of an alternative feminist "lifestyle" that can emerge only when women create a subculture (whether it is living space or even space like women's studies that at many campuses has become exclusive) and insisting that feminist struggle can begin wherever an individual woman is, we create a movement that focuses on our collective experience, a movement that is continually mass-based.

Over the past six years, many separatist-oriented communities have been formed by women so that the focus has shifted from the development of woman-centered space towards an emphasis on identity. Once woman-centered space exists, it can be maintained only if women remain convinced that it is the only place where they can be self-realized and free. After assuming a "feminist" identity, women often seek to live the "feminist" lifestyle. These women do not see that it undermines feminist movement to project the

[12] Gross, p. 54 [hooks's note].

assumption that "feminist" is but another prepackaged role women can now select as they search for identity. The willingness to see feminism as a lifestyle choice rather than a political commitment reflects the class nature of the movement. It is not surprising that the vast majority of women who equate feminism with alternative lifestyle are from middle class backgrounds, unmarried, college-educated, often students who are without many of the social and economic responsibilities that working class and poor women who are laborers, parents, homemakers, and wives confront daily. Sometimes lesbians have sought to equate feminism with lifestyle but for significantly different reasons. Given the prejudice and discrimination against lesbian women in our society, alternative communities that are woman-centered are one means of creating positive, affirming environments. Despite positive reasons for developing woman-centered space (which does not need to be equated with a "feminist" lifestyle), like pleasure, support, and resource-sharing, emphasis on creating a counter-culture has alienated women from feminist movement, for such space can be in churches, kitchens, etc.

20 Longing for community, connection, a sense of shared purpose, many women found support networks in feminist organizations. Satisfied in a personal way by new relationships generated in what was called a "safe," "supportive" context wherein discussion focused on feminist ideology, they did not question whether masses of women shared the same need for community. Certainly many black women as well as women from other ethnic groups do not feel an absence of community among women in their lives despite exploitation and oppression. The focus on feminism as a way to develop shared identity and community has little appeal to women who experience community, who seek ways to end exploitation and oppression in the context of their lives. While they may develop an interest in a feminist politic that works to eradicate sexist oppression, they will probably never feel as intense a need for a "feminist" identity and lifestyle.

Often emphasis on identity and lifestyle is appealing because it creates a false sense that one is engaged in praxis. However, praxis within any political movement that aims to have a radical transformative impact on society cannot be solely focused on creating spaces wherein would-be-radicals experience safety and support. Feminist movement to end sexist oppression actively engages participants in revolutionary struggle. Struggle is rarely safe or pleasurable.

Focusing on feminism as political commitment, we resist the emphasis on individual identity and lifestyle. (This should not be confused with the very real need to unite theory and practice.) Such resistance engages us in revolutionary praxis. The ethics of Western society informed by imperialism and capitalism are personal rather than social. They teach us that the individual good is more important than the collective good and consequently that individual change is of greater significance than collective change. This particular form of cultural imperialism has been reproduced in feminist movement in the form of individual women equating the fact that their lives have been changed in a meaningful way by feminism "as is" with a policy of no change need occur in the theory and praxis even if it has little or no impact on society as a whole, or on masses of women.

To emphasize that engagement with feminist struggle as political commitment we could avoid using the phrase "I am a feminist" (a linguistic structure designed to refer to some personal aspect of identity and self-definition) and could state "I advocate feminism." Because there has been undue emphasis placed on feminism as an identity or lifestyle, people usually resort to stereotyped perspectives on feminism. Deflecting attention away from stereotypes is necessary if we are to revise our strategy and direction. I have found that saying "I am a feminist" usually means I am plugged into preconceived notions of identity, role, or behavior. When I say "I advocate feminism" the response is usually "what is feminism?" A phrase like "I advocate" does not imply the kind of absolutism that is suggested by "I am." It does not engage us in the either/or dualistic thinking that is the central ideological component of all systems of domination in Western society. It implies that a choice has been made, that commitment to feminism is an act of will. It does not suggest that by committing oneself to feminism, the possibility of supporting other political movements is negated.

As a black woman interested in feminist movement, I am often asked whether being black is more important than being a woman; whether feminist struggle to end sexist oppression is more important than the struggle to end racism and vice-versa. All such questions are rooted in competitive either/or thinking, the belief that the self is formed in opposition to an other. Therefore one is a feminist because you are not something else. Most people are socialized to think in terms of opposition rather than compatibility. Rather than see anti-racist work as totally compatible with working to end sexist oppression, they are often seen as two movements competing for first place. When asked "Are you a feminist?" it appears that an affirmative answer is translated to mean that one is concerned with no political issues other than feminism. When one is black, an affirmative response is likely to be heard as a devaluation of struggle to end racism. Given the fear of being misunderstood, it has been difficult for black women and women in exploited and oppressed ethnic groups to give expression to their interest in feminist concerns. They have been wary of saying "I am a feminist." The shift in expression from "I am a feminist" to "I advocate feminism" could serve as a useful strategy for eliminating the focus on identity and lifestyle. It could serve as a way women who are concerned about feminism as well as other political movements could express their support while avoiding linguistic structures that give primacy to one particular group. It would also encourage greater exploration in feminist theory.

25 The shift in definition away from notions of social equality towards an emphasis on ending sexist oppression leads to a shift in attitudes in regard to the development of theory. Given the class nature of feminist movement so far, as well as racial hierarchies, developing theory (the guiding set of beliefs and principles that become the basis for action) has been a task particularly subject to the hegemonic dominance of white academic women. This has led many women outside the privileged race/class group to see the focus on developing theory, even the very use of the term, as a concern that functions only to reinforce the power of the elite group. Such reactions reinforce the sexist/racist/classist notion that developing theory is the domain of the white intellectual. Privileged white women active in feminist movement, whether liberal or radical in

perspective, encourage black women to contribute "experiential" work, personal life stories. Personal experiences are important to feminist movement but they cannot take the place of theory. Charlotte Bunch explains the special significance of theory in her essay "Feminism and Education: Not by Degrees":

> Theory enables us to see immediate needs in terms of long-range goals and an overall perspective on the world. It thus gives us a framework for evaluating various strategies in both the long and the short run and for seeing the types of changes that they are likely to produce. Theory is not just a body of facts or a set of personal opinions. It involves explanations and hypotheses that are based on available knowledge and experience. It is also dependent on conjecture and insight about how to interpret those facts and experiences and their significance.[13]

Since bourgeois white women had defined feminism in such a way as to make it appear that it had no real significance for black women, they could then conclude that black women need not contribute to developing theory. We were to provide the colorful life stories to document and validate the prevailing set of theoretical assumptions.[14] Focus on social equality with men as a definition of feminism led to an emphasis on discrimination, male attitudes, and legalistic reforms. Feminism as a movement to end sexist oppression directs our attention to systems of domination and the inter-relatedness of sex, race, and class oppression. Therefore, it compels us to centralize the experiences and the social predicaments of women who bear the brunt of sexist oppression as a way to understand the collective social status of women in the United States. Defining feminism as a movement to end sexist oppression is crucial for the development of theory because it is a starting point indicating the direction of exploration and analysis.

The foundation of future feminist struggle must be solidly based on a recognition of the need to eradicate the underlying cultural basis and causes of sexism and other forms of group oppression. Without challenging and changing these philosophical structures, no feminist reforms will have a long range impact. Consequently, it is now necessary for advocates of feminism to collectively acknowledge that our struggle cannot be defined as a movement to gain social equality with men; that terms like "liberal feminist" and "bourgeois feminist" represent contradictions that must be resolved so that feminism will not be continually co-opted to serve the opportunistic ends of special interest groups.

WORKS CITED

Berg, Barbara. *The Remembered Gate: Origins of American Feminism.* New York: Oxford University Press, 1979.

Bunch, Charlotte. "Feminism and Education: Not by Degrees," in *Quest*, Vol. V, No. 1 (Summer 1979), pp. 1–7.

---

[13] Charlotte Bunch, "Feminism and Education: Not by Degrees," pp. 7–18 [hooks's note].

[14] An interesting discussion of black women's responses to feminist movement may be found in the essay "Challenging Imperial Feminism" by Valerie Amos and Pratibha Parmar in the Autumn 1984 issue of *Feminist Review* [hooks's note].

Dixon, Marlene. *Women in Class Struggle.* San Francisco: Synthesis Publications, 1980.

Eisenstein, Zillah. *The Radical Future of Liberal Feminism.* New York: Longman, 1981.

Greene, Bob. "Sisters—Under the Skin," in *San Francisco Examiner* (San Francisco), May 15, 1983.

Gross, Jeanne. "Feminist Ethics from a Marxist Perspective," in *Radical Religion,* Vol. III, No. 2 (1977), pp. 52–56.

Markovic, Mihailo. "Women's Liberation and Human Emancipation," in *Women and Philosophy.* Eds. Carol Gould and Mary Wartofsky. New York: G. P. Putnam, 1976, pp. 145–67.

Saffioti, Heleith I. B. *Women in Class Society.* New York: Monthly Review Press, 1978.

Vasquez, Carmen. "Towards a Revolutionary Ethics," in *Coming Up,* January 1983, p. 11.

Ware, Cellestine. *Woman Power: The Movement for Women's Liberation.* New York: Tower Publications, 1970.

Women and the New World. Detroit: Advocators, 1976.

LEARNING MORE

hooks has been outspoken throughout her career, forcefully arguing for her point of view. To learn more of what she thinks, see the *Ideas Across Time* website.

QUESTIONING THE TEXT

1. Why does hooks believe it's important to begin thinking about feminism with agreed-upon definitions of terms?
2. Why does hooks object to the idea that feminism should be defined as movement "to make women the social equals of men" (par. 2)?
3. How does hooks distinguish between a feminist movement for reform and a feminist movement for revolution?
4. Why, according to hooks, are many women "reluctant to advocate feminism" (par. 11)?
5. hooks often adds the word "radical" to her categories—for example, in par. 13, she speaks of "feminist radicals." What do you think she means by a "radical"? What evidence supports your answer?
6. What is the advantage of defining feminism "in political terms that stress collective as well as individual experience" (par. 15)?
7. What is hooks's definition of feminism? Do you find it helpful?
8. How is hooks's definition of feminism aimed at "a shift in attitudes in regard to the development of theory" (par. 25)? What theory is she speaking about?
9. hooks says she is "a black woman interested in feminist movement" (par. 24). How, according to hooks, has her being black helped her in her analysis of feminist thought?

ANALYZING THE WRITER'S CRAFT

1. What is hooks's thesis? Where is it stated?
2. This is an essay one of whose main purposes is to define feminism. How does hooks show that existing definitions are inadequate? How does hooks attempt to improve on these flawed definitions? Do you think hooks succeeds in arriving at a better definition of feminism that the ones she finds inadequate? Explain.
3. hooks quotes many other thinkers in this essay. How do these quotations help hooks in her effort to fashion a stronger definition of feminism?
4. How would you characterize hooks's diction (her word choice)? Does her diction make her work more accessible to the groups she thinks are often left out of feminist discussions, such as poor or black women? Explain.
5. What is the tone of this essay? Illustrate by citing two or three examples.
6. hooks uses analysis and logical argument to try to persuade the reader of the shortcomings of existing definitions of feminism and the strengths of her own definition. Are you persuaded? Cite one or two examples of hooks' analysis and logic to support your answer.
7. hooks writes about "feminist movement" when it would seem she should write "the feminist movement"—see, for example, the first sentence in par. 24 ("As a black woman interested in feminist movement . . ."). How does hooks' preference for "feminist movement" (minus the article "the") reflect her overall point of view?
8. Does hooks base her argument on logically sound assumptions? Explain.

MAKING CONNECTIONS

1. Is hooks a revolutionary in the tradition of American radicals and revolutionaries such as Thomas Jefferson (Chapter 5, pp. 354–360) and Henry David Thoreau (Chapter 5, pp. 371–383), or does she stand apart from them, basing her thinking and fashioning her aims for reasons they would find alien? Discuss.
2. How do you think Mike Lefevre (Chapter 4, pp. 300–307) would respond to hooks' argument? Explain.
3. Vaclav Havel (Chapter 5, pp. 404–412), in his analysis of the power of the powerless, stresses the role of moral choice in politics. In what ways, if any, does hooks see the world like Havel? In what ways does she see the world differently?
4. Imagine a dialogue between hooks and Richard Rodriguez (pp. 542–549). What do you think would be the main points they would want to make to each other?
5. hooks seems explicitly to reject Betty Friedan's (pp. 496–509) view of the problems faced by women in society. How do you think Friedan might respond to hooks' rejection of her own analysis?

6. Should we see hooks's analysis of the reasons behind the lack of clear definition of feminism as evidence for Simone de Beauvoir's (pp. 481–494) explanation of why it is so difficult for women to act as a coherent group?

FORMULATING IDEAS FOR WRITING

1. This is a detailed and closely argued essay strongly advancing a certain point of view. Write a methodical and also closely argued essay that takes issue with hooks. Be sure to analyze several of her supporting quotations. Consider, too, the many assertions and assumptions in the essay. Does hooks proceed logically? Does hooks have sufficient evidence to support her generalizations?
2. hooks wants to expand feminism to include groups she believes are usually left out of the equation, such as poor women and black women. How does her concern with poor and black women affect her political analysis? Is she on sound ground in thinking that she understands the reluctance of poor and/or black women to identify themselves as feminists? If the feminist movement were grounded in hooks's view of "sexist oppression," would that result in many more poor and/or black women identifying themselves as feminists? Discuss.
3. This essay frequently uses the word *theory.* Write an essay that explores the concept and role of theory in political activity, relying largely on hooks's essay. If you are familiar with political or revolutionary theory from other readings, by all means use this outside knowledge. hooks is convinced that "feminist movement" depends on sound theory. Do you agree? Discuss.
4. hooks objects to the idea that the personal is political, maintaining that the dilemma of the oppressed individual should be seen the other way around: the political is what governs the personal. What is your view? To what extent does personal life reflect society as a whole? How important is politics, or what happens in the public arena, to personal fulfillment?

Brown: The Last Discovery of America (2002)

Richard Rodriguez

Born in San Francisco in 1944, Richard Rodriguez came to national attention with his memoir *Hunger of Memory: The Education of Richard Rodriguez* (1982), an iconoclastic, eloquent, impassioned account of growing up in white Sacramento, California, as the son of Mexican immigrants. Rodriguez entered first grade at the Sacred Heart School knowing fifty words of English, but he went on to earn a B.A. in English at Stanford (1967) and an M.A. in philosophy at Columbia (1969). Along the way, Rodriguez became, as he says, "a middle-class American man," something he has sought to define in each of his books, most recently *Brown: The Last Discovery of America* (2002), from which the following selections are taken. For Rodriguez, the essence of American identity is its "impurity." We are, he maintains, a mixture of races and experiences, of black, white, red, yellow, and brown. As a writer of Mexican ancestry who is avowedly Catholic and homosexual, Rodriguez rejects current notions of diversity. "The best metaphor of America," he writes in *Days of Obligation: An Argument with My Mexican Father* (1992), "remains the dreadful metaphor—the Melting Pot."

A regular essayist on PBS's *NewsHour with Jim Lehrer,* Rodriguez is also an editor at the Pacific News Service in San Francisco and a contributing editor for *Harper's* magazine. President Clinton bestowed on Rodriguez the Frankel Award of the National Endowment for the Humanities, the highest national award for achievement in the humanities.

Brown

Brown as impurity.

I write of a color that is not a singular color, not a strict recipe, not an expected result, but a color produced by careless desire, even by accident; by two or several. I write of blood that is blended. I write of brown as complete freedom of substance and narrative. I extol impurity.

I eulogize[1] a literature that is suffused with brown, with allusion, irony, paradox—ha!—pleasure.

I write about race in America in hopes of undermining the notion of race in America.

5 Brown bleeds through the straight line, unstaunchable—the line separating black from white, for example. Brown confuses. Brown forms at the border of contradiction (the ability of language to express two or several things at once, the ability of bodies to experience two or several things at once).

It is that brown faculty I uphold by attempting to write brownly. And I defy anyone who tries to unblend me or to say what is appropriate to my voice.

You will often find brown in this book as the cement between leaves of paradox.

You may not want paradox in a book. In which case, you had better seek a pure author.

Brown is the color most people in the United States associate with Latin America.

10 Apart from stool sample, there is no browner smear in the American imagination than the Rio Grande. No adjective has attached itself more often to the Mexican in America than "dirty"—which I assume gropes toward the simile "dirt-like," indicating dense concentrations of melanin.[2]

---

[1] eulogize: praise.
[2] melanin: dark pigment in human skin.

I am dirty, all right. In Latin America, what makes me brown is that I am made of the conquistador[3] and the Indian. My brown is a reminder of conflict.

And of reconciliation.

In my own mind, what makes me brown in the United States is that I am Richard Rodriguez. My baptismal name and my surname marry England and Spain, Renaissance rivals.

North of the U.S.–Mexico border, brown appears as the color of the future. The adjective accelerates, becomes a verb: "America is browning." South of the border, brown sinks back into time. Brown is time.

15 In middle chapters, I discuss the ways Hispanics brown an America that traditionally has chosen to describe itself as black-and-white. I salute Richard Nixon, the dark father of Hispanicity. But my Hispanic chapters, as I think of them—the chapters I originally supposed were going to appear first in this book—gave way to more elementary considerations. I mean the meeting of the Indian, the African, and the European in colonial America. Red. Black. White. The founding palette.

Some months ago, a renowned American sociologist predicted to me that Hispanics will become "the new Italians" of the United States. (What the Sicilian had been for nineteenth-century America, the Colombian would become for the twenty-first century.)

His prediction seems to me insufficient because it does not account for the influence of Hispanics on the geography of the American imagination. Because of Hispanics, Americans are coming to see the United States in terms of a latitudinal vector, in terms of south-north, hot-cold; a new way of placing ourselves in the twenty-first century.

America has traditionally chosen to describe itself as an east-west country. I grew up on the east-west map of America, facing east. I no longer find myself so easily on that map. In middle age (also brown, its mixture of loss and capture), I end up on the shore where Sir Francis Drake[4] first stepped onto California. I look toward Asia.

As much as I celebrate the browning of America (and I do), I do not propose an easy optimism. The book's last chapter was completed before the events of September 11, 2001, and now will never be complete. The chapter describes the combustible dangers of brown; the chapter annotates the tragedies it anticipated.

20 I think brown marks a reunion of peoples, an end to ancient wanderings. Rival cultures and creeds conspire with Spring to create children of a beauty, perhaps of a harmony, previously unknown. Or long forgotten. Even so, the terrorist and the skinhead dream in solitude of purity and of the straight line because they fear a future that does not isolate them. In a brown future, the most dangerous actor might likely be the cosmopolite, conversant in alternate currents, literatures, computer programs. The cosmopolite may come to hate his

[3] conquistadors: Spanish conquerors of Mexico and Peru in the sixteenth century.

[4] Sir Francis Drake: Explorer (c. 1540–1596) who sailed the world in the *Golden Hind* and landed on the shore of California in 1579.

brownness, his facility, his indistinction, his mixture; the cosmopolite may yearn for a thorough religion, ideology, or tribe.

Many days, I left my book to wander the city,[5] to discover the city outside my book was comically browning. Walking down Fillmore Street one afternoon, I was enjoying the smell of salt, the brindled pigeons, brindled light, when a conversation overtook me, parted around me, just as I passed the birdstore window: Two girls. Perhaps sixteen. White, Anglo, whatever. Tottering on their silly shoes. Talking of boys. The one girl saying to the other: . . . *His complexion is so cool, this sort of light—well, not that light . . .*

I realized my book will never be equal to the play of the young.

. . . *Sort of reddish brown, you know* . . . The other girl nodded, readily indicated that she did know. But still Connoisseur Number One sought to bag her simile. . . . *Like a Sugar Daddy bar—you know that candy bar?*

Two decades ago, I wrote *Hunger of Memory,* the autobiography of a scholarship boy. Ten years later, in *Days of Obligation,* I wrote about the influence of Mexican ethnicity on my American life. This volume completes a trilogy on American public life and my private life. *Brown* returns me to years I have earlier described. I believe it is possible to describe a single life thrice, if from three isolations: *Class. Ethnicity. Race.*

25 When I began this book, I knew some readers would take "race" for a tragic noun, a synonym for conflict and isolation. Race is not such a terrible word for me. Maybe because I am skeptical by nature. Maybe because my nature is already mixed. The word race encourages me to remember the influence of eroticism on history. For that is what race memorializes. Within any discussion of race, there lurks the possibility of romance.

The Triad of Alexis de Tocqueville

Two women and a child in a glade beside a spring. Beyond them, the varnished wilderness wherein bright birds cry. The child is chalk, Europe's daughter. Her dusky attendants, a green Indian and a maroon slave.

The scene, from *Democracy in America,* is discovered by that most famous European traveler to the New World, Alexis de Tocqueville,[6] aristocratic son of the Enlightenment, liberal, sickly, gray, violet, lacking the vigor of the experiment he has set himself to observe.

"I remember . . . I was traveling through the forests which still cover the state of Alabama. . . ."

In a clearing, at some distance, an Indian woman appears first to Monsieur, followed by a "Negress," holding by the hand "a little white girl of five or six years."

30 The Indian: "A sort of barbarous luxury" set off her costume; "rings of metal were hanging from her nostrils and ears, her hair, which was adorned with glass beads, fell loosely upon her shoulders. . . . " The Negress wore "squalid European garments."

[5] the city: San Francisco.

[6] Tocqueville: see pp. 458–463.

Such garments are motifs of de Tocqueville's pathos. His description intends to show the African and the Indian doomed by history in corresponding but opposing ways. (History is a coat cut only to the European.)

"The young Indian, taking the child in her arms, lavished upon her such fond caresses as mothers give, while the Negress endeavored, by various little artifices, to attract the [child's] attention. . . ."

The white child "displayed in her slightest gestures a consciousness of superiority that formed a strange contrast with her infantine weakness; as if she received the attentions of her companions with a sort of condescension."

Thus composed: The Indian. The Negress. The white child.

35 ". . . In the picture that I have just been describing there was something peculiarly touching; a bond of affection here united the oppressors with the oppressed, and the effort of Nature to bring them together rendered still more striking the immense distance placed between them by prejudice and the laws."

At Monsieur's approach, this natural colloquy[7] is broken. He becomes the agent of history. Seeing him, the Indian suddenly rises, "push[es] the child roughly away and, giving [Monsieur] an angry look, plunge[s] into the thicket."

The Negress rests; awaits de Tocqueville's approach.

Neither response satisfies the European. The African, de Tocqueville writes, has lost the memory of ancestors, of custom and tongue; the African has experienced degradation to his very soul, has become a true slave. "Violence made him a slave, and the habit of servitude gives him the thoughts and desires of a slave; he admires his tyrants more than he hates them, and finds his joy and his pride in the servile imitation of those who oppress him."

The bejeweled Indian, alternately, is "condemned . . . to a wandering life, full of inexpressible sufferings," because European interlopers have unbalanced the provender[8] of Nature.

40 And, de Tocqueville remarks (a fondness for fable), whereas the Negro's response to mistreatment is canine, the Indian's is feline. "The Negro makes a thousand fruitless efforts to insinuate himself among men who repulse him. . . ." The Indian is filled with diffidence toward the white, "has his imagination inflated with the pretended nobility of his origin, and lives and dies in the midst of these dreams of pride." The Indian refuses civilization; the African slave is rendered unfit for it.

But cher Monsieur: You saw the Indian sitting beside the African on a drape of baize. They were easy together. The sight of them together does not lead you to wonder about a history in which you are not the narrator?

These women are but parables of your interest in yourself. Rather than consider the nature of their intimacy, you are preoccupied alone with the meaning of your intrusion. You in your dusty leather boots, cobbled on the rue du Faubourg St.-Honoré. Your tarnished silver snuffbox, your saddlebag filled with the more ancient dust of books. You in your soiled cambric. Vous-même.

[7] colloquy: conversation.
[8] provender: food.

La Raza Cosmica

As a young man, I was more a white liberal than I ever tried to put on black. For all that, I ended up a "minority," the beneficiary of affirmative action programs to redress black exclusion. And, harder to say, my brown advantage became a kind of embarrassment. For I never had an adversarial relationship to American culture. I was never at war with the tongue.

Brown was no longer invisible by the time I got to college. In the white appraisal, brown skin became a coat of disadvantage, which was my advantage. Acknowledgment came at a price, then as now. (Three decades later, the price of being a published brown author is that one cannot be shelved near those one has loved. The price is segregation.)

45 I remain at best ambivalent about those Hispanic anthologies where I end up; about those anthologies where I end up the Hispanic; about shelves at the bookstore where I look for myself and find myself. The fact that my books are published at all is the result of the slaphappy strategy of the northern black Civil Rights movement.

Late in the 1960s, the university complied with segregation—the notion that each can only describe and understand her own, that education is a deeper solipsism, that pride is the point of education, that I would prefer to live among my kind at a separate theme-house dormitory; that I would prefer to eat with my kind at the exclusive cafeteria table where all conversation conforms to the implicit: *You Can't Know What I'm Feeling Unless You Are Me.*

In college, I revisited James Baldwin,[9] seeking to forestall what I feared was the disintegration of my reading life, which had been an unquestioned faith in Signet Classics. My rereading of "Stranger in a Village" discovered a heavy hand. In the Swiss Alps, humorless *frauen*[10] with crackled eyes go in and out their humorous houses, while on the twisting streets of the village, towheaded children point to Baldwin and shout after him *Neger! Neger!* ("From all available evidence no black man had ever set foot in this tiny Swiss village before I came.") So what is the point of the essay? It seemed to me Baldwin had traveled rather far to get himself pointed at; to arrange such an outlandish contrast; to describe himself as an outsider. And, too, the Alps seemed to represent Baldwin's obsession, an obsession that now seemed to stand between us.

This was not a generous assessment on my part, not a generous moment in my life. As a young reader, I would never have noticed or objected to Baldwin's preoccupation with White to the exclusion of all other kind. In the 1950s it would have seemed to me that a Negro writer was writing about the nation in which I was a part, regardless of whether my tribe was singled out for mention. But when the American university began to approve, then to enforce fracture, and when blood became the authority to speak, I felt myself rejected by black literature and felt myself rejecting black literature as "theirs."

Neither did I seek brown literature or any other kind. I sought Literature—the deathless impulse to explain and describe. I trusted white literature,

[9] Baldwin: see pp. 29–35.

[10] *frauen:* German for "women."

because I was able to attribute universality to white literature, because it did not seem to be written for me.

50 William Makepeace Thackeray[11] mocks my mother's complexion. And mine. My smell. My fingers. My hair. Cunning little savage. Little Jew. Little milkmaid. Little Cockney. Really, how can I laugh?

By brown I mean love.

The brownest rendition of love I can summon is the Sermon on the Mount, that plein-air[12] toss of ambiguous bread. All paradox is brown and divine paradox is browner than which no browner can be conceived.

The brownest secular essay I know is the one called *La Raza Cósmica* by José Vasconcelos,[13] a Mexican who wrote in 1925:

> The days of pure whites, the victors of today, are as numbered as the days of their predecessors. Having fulfilled their destiny of mechanizing the world, they themselves have set, without knowing it, the basis for the new period: The period of the fusion and mixing of all peoples.

This is not the same as saying "the poor shall inherit the earth" but is possibly related. The poor shall overrun the earth. Or the brown shall.

55 Many Americans opt for a centrifugal view of the future, a black-and-white version—I don't mean skin but cultural intransigence—deduced from history as hatred. A future of real armies ranged on opposing sides of a cultural divide—Muslims and Hindus, say. But in our postmodern, post-everything world, the competing armies—theologies, tribes—I think might as likely assemble within a single breast. The result of love. Can what love has bound together as flesh be reconciled? The traditional task of marriage is to make flesh. The Indian, the ash blond, stir, make flesh.

Perhaps my parents became one by creating my flesh, but I may have a problem with it: It was the grandson of an observant Jew, a young man who feared he was irrelevant to history; who, on the anniversary of Hitler's birthday, pulled on a long dark raincoat, in the style of a comic-book avenger, secreted several rifles beneath his long coat, burst into his high school cafeteria; opened fire. He is dead now. His life is over.

We of the twenty-first century may be headed for a desire for cleansing, of choosing, of being one thing or another. The brown child may grow up to war against himself. To attempt to be singular rather than several. May seek to obliterate a part of himself. May seek to obliterate others.

(I reopen this book in the terrible dusk of September 11, 2001. On that day, several medieval men in the guise of multicultural America and in the manner of American pop culture, rode dreadnoughts through the sky. These were men from a world of certainty, some hours distant—a world where men presume to

---

[11] Thackeray: British novelist (1811–1863).

[12] plein-air: reference to painting outside in daylight.

[13] Jose Vasconcelos: Mexican intellectual and politician (1882–1959) who fostered literacy and defined Latin American identity within a concept of universal culture.

divine, to enforce, to protectively wear the will of God; a world where men wage incessant war against the impurity that lies without [puritans!] and so they mistrust, they wither whatever they touch; they have withered the flower within the carpet they have walked upon. These several inauthentic men, of fake I.D., of brutish sentimentality, went missing from U.S. immigration rolls, were presumed lost and assimilated into brown America, these men of certainty refused to be seduced by modernity, postmodernity; by what I have been at pains to describe as brown, as making.)

The headmaster walking me down a long corridor on that day I spoke at a high school in Los Angeles, admitted, as we drew near the assembly room, that most of his students are bored by talk of "diversity"; are impious toward that word. "It's the parents who are eager for their kids to learn about multiculturalism."

60 The parent's complaint: The working-class father purchased his daughter a computer, because (he told me) he wanted to give his daughter the world. (He believed the television commercial.) Whereupon the daughter logged into chatrooms crowded with people only exactly like herself.

Teachers tell me their students are "beyond race, don't think about it the way we do." Other teachers tell me cafeteria tables sort as reliably as ever and according to every conceivable border: color, jock, slut, nerd, born-again, heavy metal, rap. Both descriptions must be true.

Remember where you came from. Such is not our way. Who can say that anymore in America? As lives meet, chafe, there will be a tendency to retreat. When the line between us is unenforced or seems to disappear, someone will surely be troubled and nostalgic for straight lines and will demand that the future give him the fundamental assurance of a border.

A thought that haunts many African Americans I know is that they are the same distance from the slave owner as from the slave. Both strains have contributed to their bodies, to their waking spirits. I am the same distance from the conquistador as from the Indian. Righteousness should not come easily to any of us.

Perhaps she chose a smile.

65 Perhaps she kept the appointment for an eye examination. Perhaps the examining technician reached to adjust the overhead lamp. He did this in some way so as to suggest the competence of an athlete or the thinness of a matador's waist—he somehow surpassed himself in the gesture—a gesture so thorough that she could seem to inhabit it for the eternity of one moment, rather like the Virgin in the painting of the Annunciation; the overwhelming competence of the angel. It was only one of thousands of involuntary responses to any given moment. Except at that moment he smiled.

She turns from the painting of the Annunciation in tears. Her sinuses have dilated, spoiling the taste of the gum. She locates the rest room. She pauses at the case full of swords. She recoils from her imagination of their sharpness. She looks at her watch. She exits the museum. She needs an abortion. The angel was married.

LEARNING MORE

The preceding selections come from what Rodriguez has described as the third volume of an extended memoir, an effort to understand better both himself and America. It might be helpful to look at some essays from the two earlier volumes of this trilogy, *Hunger of Memory* and *Days of Obligation*. The full text of Alexis de Tocqueville's essay on the relation of Native American, African American, and European peoples in America can be found on the *Ideas Across Time* web site.

QUESTIONING THE TEXT

1. What are some of the contraries that "brown" unites?
2. What in Rodriguez's writing might serve to undermine the notion of race in America?
3. What is the difference in the meaning of brown north and south of the U.S. Mexican border?
4. What do you think Rodriguez means by saying that "the terrorist and the skinhead . . . fear a future that does not isolate them" (par. 21)?
5. In his recounting of Tocqueville, why does Rodriguez refer to a "green" Indian and a "maroon" slave (par. 26)?
6. What does Rodriguez mean when he says of Tocqueville, "He became the agent of history" (par. 36)?
7. Do you agree with Rodriguez's accusation against Tocqueville: *"you are preoccupied alone with the meaning of your intrusion"* (par. 42)?
8. How is the Sermon on the Mount "the brownest rendition of love" (par. 52)?
9. What dangers does Rodriguez see in the mixing that he thinks characterizes America today and will characterize America even more in the future?

ANALYZING THE WRITER'S CRAFT

1. Rodriguez says he wants to "uphold" brown "by attempting to write brownly" (par. 6). What qualities of his writing do you think could be said to be brown? How is writing "brownly" different from writing "whitely" or "redly"?
2. Rodriguez uses brown as an extended metaphor, that is, as a way of making a complex comparison between one thing—the color brown—and a number of other things that have the mixed quality of brown. Give some examples of the mixes in American society that brown, as a metaphor, represents.
3. Rodriguez uses the color/concept brown to suggest both impurity and harmony. Give two or three examples of brown as impurity and of brown as harmony.

4. How does Rodriguez's diction (word choice) in his account of Tocqueville imply a subtle critique of Tocqueville? Consider, for example, words such as "glade" and "wherein" in par. 26 or Rodriguez's quotation of Tocqueville's description of the Indian woman : "a sort of barbarous luxury" (par. 30).
5. What is the thesis of "Brown"? Of "The Triad of Alexis de Tocqueville"?
6. Why does Rodriguez call Tocqueville "Monsieur" instead of simply using Tocqueville's name?
7. What is the tone of Rodriguez's discussion of Tocqueville?
8. "La Raza Cosmica" explores the possible divide in the future between a world of paradox and mixing, and a world of contradictions among "singular" conditions. Give two examples of each (paradoxical mixing versus singularity). How does Rodriguez convey his attitude toward each of these possible futures?

MAKING CONNECTIONS

1. Rodriguez seems to be in dialogue with many in this text—specifically, of course, Tocqueville (pp. 458–463) but as much with St. John de Crevecoeur (Chapter 1, pp. 22–27) and James Baldwin (Chapter 1, pp. 29–35). Is Rodriguez articulating a contemporary version of the original version of the American Dream, or is he in denial about fundamental changes in American life and simply stuck in a reactionary reading of American realities?
2. Jose Vasconcelos, although a champion of Latin American culture for the same reasons Rodriguez is a champion of U.S. culture, was also antidemocratic, a believer in the strong man and in concepts based on race. Look further into *La Raza Cosmica* (1925). How has Vasconcelos helped shape Rodriguez's outlook?
3. Compare Rodriguez's views on the dangers of singularity and isolation with those of Danie J. Boorstin (Chapter 5, pp. 390–402).

FORMULATING IDEAS FOR WRITING

1. Write an essay that considers whether Rodriguez's ideas about brown as love need to be seriously qualified in light of 9/11 (You will of course want to review what he has to say about that event—see par. 58).
2. Offer a critique of Rodriguez's ideas from the point of view of a proud "hyphenated American."
3. Reread Tocqueville (pp. 458–463) and, with Rodriguez's comments in mind, write an analytical account of both essays that reflects on race in America.
4. Write about your own experience of the paradoxes of identity, focusing on the difficult, troubling, sometimes weird relation between private and public selves.

Girl (1978)

Jamaica Kincaid

In a style widely admired for its eloquence and poetic range, Jamaica Kincaid has probed the painful, complex, intricate terrain of postcolonial culture, focusing in particular on the travail of her native Antigua, in the West Indies, where she was born as Elaine Potter Richardson in 1949. Educated in the British system of her native island—Antigua gained independence from Britain only in 1981—Kincaid came to the United States in 1965. In 1973, she adopted the name Jamaica Kincaid so she could write despite the disapproval of her family. Her first three books—*At the Bottom of the River* (1984), a collection of stories; *Annie John* (1985), a novel; and *A Small Place* (1988), a memoir—are set in Antigua, and they chiefly concern both the crippling impact of colonialism and the ways the relations of mothers and daughters shape feminine identity in this charged, corrosive public context. Her judgments of colonialism and of the fitful development of her country free of colonialism are equally angry, and they have attracted both harsh criticism and fulsome praise. The present selection, "Girl" is taken from Kincaid's first book, *At the Bottom of the River.* Her most recent publication, the novel *Mr. Potter* (2003), again set in Antigua, depicts the life of an illiterate taxi driver.

Jamaica Kincaid has worked as a staff writer for *The New Yorker* magazine and received the Morton Dawen Zabel Award from the American Academy and Institute of Arts and Letters for *At the Bottom of the River.* She is married to the composer Allen Shawn, son of *The New Yorker*'s legendary editor William Shawn, with whom she lives in Vermont and New York City.

Wash the white clothes on Monday and put them on the stone heap; wash the color clothes on Tuesday and put them on the clothesline to dry; don't walk barehead in the hot sun; cook pumpkin fritters in very hot sweet oil; soak your little cloths right after you take them off; when buying cotton to make yourself a nice blouse, be sure that it doesn't have gum on it, because that way it won't hold up well after a wash; soak salt fish overnight before you cook it; is it true that you sing benna[1] in Sunday school?; always eat your food in such a way that it won't turn someone else's stomach; on Sundays try to walk like a lady and not like the slut you are so bent on becoming; don't sing benna in Sunday school; you mustn't speak to wharf-rat boys, not even to give directions; don't eat fruits on the street—flies will follow you; *but I don't sing benna on Sundays at*

[1] benna: A kind of calypso that originated in Antigua following the prohibition of slavery. These were usually bawdy songs, featuring scandals and sexual affairs.

all and never in Sunday school; this is how to sew on a button; this is how to make a buttonhole for the button you have just sewed on; this is how to hem a dress when you see the hem coming down and so to prevent yourself from looking like the slut I know you are so bent on becoming; this is how you iron your father's khaki shirt so that it doesn't have a crease; this is how you iron your father's khaki pants so that they don't have a crease; this is how you grow okra—far from the house, because okra tree harbors red ants; when you are growing dasheen, make sure it gets plenty of water or else it makes your throat itch when you are eating it; this is how you sweep a corner; this is how you sweep a whole house; this is how you sweep a yard; this how you smile to someone you don't like too much; this is how you smile to someone you don't like at all; this is how you smile to someone you like completely; this is how you set a table for tea; this is how you set a table for dinner; this is how you set a table for dinner with an important guest; this is how you set a table for lunch; this is how you set a table for breakfast; this is how to behave in the presence of men who don't know you very well, and this way they won't recognize immediately the slut I have warned you against becoming; be sure to wash every day, even if it is with your own spit; don't squat down to play marbles—you are not a boy, you know; don't pick people's flowers—you might catch something; don't throw stones at blackbirds, because it might not be a blackbird at all; this is how to make a bread pudding; this is how to make doukona[2]; this is how to make pepper pot; this is how to make a good medicine for a cold; this is how to make a good medicine to throw away a child before it even becomes a child; this is how to catch a fish; this is how to throw back a fish you don't like, and that way something bad won't fall on you; this is how to bully a man; this is how a man bullies you; this is how to love a man, and if this doesn't work there are other ways, and if they don't work don't feel too bad about giving up; this is how to spit up in the air if you feel like it, and this is how to move quick so that it doesn't fall on you; this is how to make ends meet; always squeeze bread to make sure it's fresh, *but what if the baker won't let me feel the bread?;* you mean to say that after all you are really going to be the kind of woman who the baker won't let near the bread?

LEARNING MORE

If you are intrigued by "Girl," you can learn more about Jamaica Kincaid on the *Ideas Across Time* website.

QUESTIONING THE TEXT

1. Who is speaking to whom in this story? How do you know?
2. What do the things the person addressed in this story is advised to do tell you about the speaker and the listener?
3. What is the attitude of the speaker toward the person addressed? How do you know?

[2] doukona: a sweet, spicy pudding.

4. What is the attitude of the person addressed toward the speaker? How do you know?
5. How old is the girl in this story? How do you know?
6. Why does the speaker think the girl is or may become a slut? Why is it important not to be a slut?
7. How are we to understand the speaker's final words—is it a good thing or not to be allowed to feel the bread? Explain.
8. What is the speaker's view of the relations between men and women?
9. What does this story say about the roles of women in society? What are the expectations it assumes about the life of a girl? Does the story imply any other way of being than the one the speaker portrays?

ANALYZING THE WRITER'S CRAFT

1. Why do you think Kincaid chose to tell this story in one sentence? How would it be different if it were set out in more conventional ways?
2. Kincaid does not identify or name either the speaker or the person on whom the speaker showers advice. What is the effect of this formal choice?
3. Classify the advice given. Explain your classification, and then think about how the various categories of advice may be related.
4. Is there any order to the advice being given?
5. What is the tone of this story—the tone of the dominant voice and the tone of the person addressed when, on two occasions, she speaks? Does the speaker, the advice giver and judge, care for the girl being addressed? Explain.
6. Why is the story called "Girl"?
7. Choose two or three details from this story, and discuss what they say about the role of women in society.
8. How do the details in this story identify the things that are most important in the coming of age of a girl? What, according to the story, are these things?
9. How does the story convey a sense of how much room the girl has to carve out a life of her own choosing? Explain.

MAKING CONNECTIONS

1. Kincaid's title calls up a whole literature, including such works as Harriet Jacobs's *Incidents in the Life of a Slave Girl* (pp. 464–469). Compare and contrast these works. Do you think Kincaid had books such as Jacobs's in mind when she wrote her story? Explain.
2. Is the situation of the girl in this story similar to the situation of the women in Betty Friedan's *The Feminine Mystique* (pp. 496–509)?
3. Would the advice in this story have been useful to Louisa May Alcott when she went to work as a servant (Chapter 4, pp. 275–286)? How is Alcott like and unlike the girl in this story?

FORMULATING IDEAS FOR WRITING

1. Is the mother in this story motivated by love of her daughter? Write an analysis of the mother–daughter relationship in this story that aims to answer this question.
2. Write a present-day American version of this story, but title it "Boy."
3. Rewrite this story in an explicitly affectionate, forthcoming mode. Allow the girl to have more say, too.
4. What is the best way to raise adolescents in a treacherous world? Strict discipline? Treating the child as a buddy? Letting the child learn from her or his own mistakes? Discuss. Use the story for support, evidence, and/or contrast.

Nostalgic Barbie

Barbie is a world-wide best-selling doll, introduced in 1959. Her appearance has been the source of her enormous popularity as well as of criticism of the doll as promoting an unrealistic body image for girls to emulate. The Barbie pictured here is from the "Cabin Crew" edition of the early 1960s.

LEARNING MORE

Ideas Across Time website.

QUESTIONING THE TEXT

1. Why is Barbie wearing a bathing suit while the other dolls are in airline costumes?
2. What "shape" does the image of Barbie suggest women should aspire to?
3. What do Barbie's accessories add to her appearance?
4. What is the effect of Barbie's lipstick?

ANALYZING THE ARTIST'S CRAFT

1. What does the presentation of Barbie in a group stewardesses and a pilot suggest about her life-style?
2. Does the photo use contrasts to make a satirical point? What is its satirical point?
3. Why does Barbie lend herself so well to satire?
4. What is the eye most drawn to in this composition? Explain.
5. What makes Barbie's appearance so attractive to young girls?
6. Barbie is immediately recognizable. What makes her so strongly herself?

MAKING CONNECTIONS

1. Is Barbie representative of American identity (see Chapter 1)? Explain.
2. Does Barbie support or question the views of America expressed by artists outside the United States in "The American Effect" (Chapter 1, pp. 11–19)?
3. Does Barbie support or undermine Betty Friedan's analysis of the condition of the American woman in the 1950s (pp. 496–509)?
4. Would bell hooks (pp. 528–540) see this photo as supporting or combating what she calls "sexist oppression"?
5. Imagine a dialogue between Jamaica Kincaid's protagonist (pp. 552–553) and Barbie. What would they say to each other? Could they understand each other in any way?

FORMULATING IDEAS FOR WRITING

1. Barbie is a creation of the early 1960s and has been hugely popular with young girls world-wide ever since. Yet the very qualities that make Barbie immediately recognizable have also attracted considerable criticism. Barbie is said to promote a distorted and even harmful image of the shape of a woman's body and a glamorized picture of the nature of women's daily

lives. What is your view? Is it credible that playing with one doll rather than another can profoundly affect a child's self-image? Should playing with dolls be discouraged?

2. Write an essay praising Barbie as a brilliant piece of design.
3. Do a bit of research on Mattel, the company that makes Barbie, and write an essay arguing that Barbie's success depends not on her appearance but on how she has been marketed.
4. In the early 1960s, when the doll pictured here was first produced, airline travel was more glamorous and luxurious than it is today. Moreover, stewardesses had to meet certain criteria of age and appearance that are no longer considered proper and in some cases would today constitute illegal job discrimination. Even so, what makes working for an airline, even today, a great job for Barbie? But, is it right that Barbie should have to get a job? Is nothing sacred?

chapter 7

Art

At the end of the twentieth century, the mayor of New York City threatened to cut off funding from one of the city's chief art museums because he found a major exhibition of contemporary paintings and sculpture deeply offensive. The exhibit included a portrait of the Virgin Mary done with elephant dung. "You can't desecrate the most personal and deeply held views of people in society," Mayor Rudolf Giuliani said. This quotation comes from the Keynote reading, "Giuliani Vows to Cut Subsidy over 'Sick' Art."

The mayor's outrage attests both to the abiding power of art and to the persistence of what Socrates, 2500 years before, had already identified as "an ancient quarrel between philosophy and poetry." For Socrates, this is a quarrel about the nature of "truth." Socrates, like his pupil and scribe Plato, is an idealist. He believes that each table in the world is no more than an approximation of the idea of a table. It is the *idea* of the table that God has created, and it is the idea "table" that is consequently real. God is the maker of this ideal reality; each actual table, in contrast, is no more than one imperfect object in the world of appearances, by definition a false and "untrue" realm. The artist imitates the world of appearances and propagates untruth. Each work of art, whether in colors or materials or words, is merely a copy of a copy, as in a painting of a table. Far from improving human understanding and helping us see what is real, art is impelled by "rebellious" impulses that are not "healthy"—both quoted words are those of Socrates. Art therefore is a power for evil, somewhat as Mayor Guiliani seems to have seen in the art at the Brooklyn Museum, and is banned from Socrates'and Plato's utopian Republic (see pp. 565–574).

But Plato's pupil Aristotle (see pp. 575–579) sees things differently. Poetry is the expression our deepest instincts, "implanted" in us from birth. These instincts distinguish us from the animals. They are the instincts of "imitation" and "harmony." Aristotle affirms his outlook not by a course of reasoning or abstract deductive logic but rather by reference to experience. He notes, for example, that "objects which in themselves we view with pain [such as dead bodies], we delight to contemplate when reproduced with minute fidelity." Aristotle says, the reproduction of reality is a form of teaching and "to learn gives the liveliest pleasure." This pleasure is enhanced when the imitation is harmonious. Art, expressing our deepest instincts, takes the form of harmonious imitation of the very world of appearances denounced by Socrates as "untrue."

The lines are drawn. On one side stand those who believe that the aim of a reflective life is to discover truth and that truth is to be discovered by reason. For these thinkers, pleasure and pain are corrupt guides, sure to lead to chaos in the republic. This view of art logically leads to various arguments for censorship, and although some holders of this view may enjoy art, they value truth more than art. On the other side stand those for whom pleasure in artful things is instinctual and quintessentially human. This view of art logically leads to advocacy of unlimited freedom of expression for the artist. The holders of this view see art as one of the highest human achievements.

Several millennia after the death of Aristotle, the American Transcendentalist Ralph Waldo Emerson attempted to bypass these dichotomies in his influential essay "Art" (see pp. 581–585). The artist, Emerson says, should aim not at imitation but at creation. What this seems to mean is a synthesis of the apparently contradictory views of Plato and Aristotle. Through art the artist conveys to us the God in nature, in the world of appearances. Far from being an imperfect copy of God's reality, art is both a window onto the soul of creation and a view from "the height of the human soul." For Emerson, art reveals the deepest truths both of history and of nature.

By the end of the nineteenth century, however, artists seem no longer persuaded that art can be a special instrument for the exposure of truth in nature. Oscar Wilde declares irreverently, "All art is quite useless" (see pp. 587–588). For whatever reasons, the idealist (Plato), realist (Aristotle), and Romantic (Emerson) traditions seem to fail in the encounter with mass industrial and later postindustrial society—what we can call "our world." In writing about the Armory Show (1911), the event that introduced "modern art" to the United States, Meyer Schapiro (see pp. 590–602) says that in the paintings of Matisse, Picasso, Braque, and the other "modernists," centuries of artistic practice rooted in the notion of "image making" came to an end. The painting in the show that attracted the most attention, good and bad, was Marcel Duchamp's "Nude Descending a Staircase." At first glance, the painting reveals neither a nude nor a staircase. Instead of image making, Schapiro says that the Armory Show inaugurated the era of "imageless art," an era more about the artist as "personality" or creator than about anything being imitated.

Indeed, the ongoing revolutions of the nineteenth and twentieth centuries seem to have accumulated into a historical force so powerful as to have overturned many established ways and norms. At the same time, the possibilities of new technologies have resulted in whole new art forms, none more representative of the twentieth century than movies. As Susan Sontag says, the advent of movies brought into the culture not only a new visual experience but also a big business. Sontag traces the century-long tension between art and money in the cinema (see pp. 604–610).

The explosion of new possibilities in art opened the way for a return to consideration of the most basic features of human communication, a return journey to previous times and practices to discover anew the essential qualities, purposes, and pleasures of human visual and verbal sign making. Without doubt this broad cultural revisiting among artists of cultures that thrived before reading and writing has something religious about it, an effort through art to make the worldly once again sacred. N. Scott Momaday in this chapter recounts the American Indian tale of "The Arrowmaker," whom Momaday styles as "the man made of words" (see pp. 612–616). In one sense, this story accentuates the precariousness of oral tradition since every telling is "but one generation removed from extinction." In another sense, the arrowmaker clarifies the crucial connection between art and survival because this is a story about the nature of stories. Finally, Sandra Cisneros also explores the relation between words and mortality in her formally inventive and spiritually deft study of the words of prayer, which Cisneros suggests partake of "Little Miracles" and "Kept Promises" (pp. 618–626).

KEYNOTE

Giuliani Vows to Cut Subsidy over "Sick" Art (1999)

Dan Barry and Carol Vogel

Dan Barry and Carol Vogel are reporters for *The New York Times,* where this story appeared on September 23, 1999. Barry, winner of a Pulitzer Prize in 1994 for his work on the *Providence Journal-Bulletin,* writes the "About New York" column. Vogel frequently writes the paper's stories about art.

Mayor Rudolph W. Giuliani threatened yesterday to cut off all city subsidies to the Brooklyn Museum of Art unless it cancels next week's opening of a British art exhibition that features, among other works, a shark suspended in a tank of formaldehyde, a bust of a man made from his own frozen blood and a portrait of the Virgin Mary stained with a clump of elephant dung.

The Mayor, who has seen the show's catalogue but not the exhibition itself, derided the works of art generally as "sick stuff." But he singled out the portrait of the Virgin Mary as particularly offensive.

"You don't have a right to government subsidy for desecrating somebody else's religion," he said. "And therefore we will do everything that we can to remove funding for the Brooklyn Museum until the director comes to his senses and realizes that if you are a government-subsidized enterprise, then you can't do things that desecrate the most personal and deeply held views of people in society. I mean, this is an outrageous thing to do."

If the Mayor follows through on his threat, it could severely hamper the museum's operations. The city gives the museum nearly $7 million a year in operating expenses—nearly one-third of its $23 million budget—and has reserved another $20 million in the budget for capital improvements. The museum is the second largest in New York, after the Metropolitan, and has a permanent collection of more than 1.5 million objects.

5 But if Arnold L. Lehman, the director, was intimidated by Mr. Giuliani's expression of outrage, he did not let on yesterday. He said he hoped to meet with him "to encourage him not to take such an action," and added "it is part of a museum's job to support the right of artists to express themselves freely."

The Mayor's angry reaction—"I'm offended," he said—is typical of the visceral response that the show, called "Sensation: Young British Artists From the Saatchi Collection," has generated in the United States and Europe, where it opened to raves and criticism at the Royal Academy of Arts in London two years ago. Featuring the work of young artists whose works are displayed in museums around the world, the show is intended to disturb, perturb and provoke thought.

Mounted at a cost of $1 million, it is the largest ever held by the Brooklyn Museum, which is in a landmark McKim, Mead & White building owned by the city. The show is financed in part by Christie's, the auction house.

Some viewers in London asserted that the content of the show was offensive and intended to shock for shock's sake. A few wryly suggested that it existed primarily to increase the value of the works amassed by Charles Saatchi, the advertising executive who is London's most important contemporary art collector.

The most extreme reaction was to the artist Marcus Harvey's depictions of Myra Hindley, who was convicted in the macabre "moors murders" of children in western England in the 1960's. Protesters splattered ink and raw eggs on the painting, saying it trivialized her victims' suffering and glorified her crimes.

10 The exhibition attracted record crowds in London and at the Hamburger Bahnhof in Berlin.

The Brooklyn Museum sought to create the same excitement for the show's only North American engagement, which opens Oct. 2. It announced that children under 17 would have to be accompanied by an adult. Even its promotions read like health warnings on a cigarette pack: "The contents of this exhibition may cause shock, vomiting, confusion, panic, euphoria and anxiety. If you suffer from high blood pressure, a nervous disorder or palpitations, you should consult your doctor."

But it was the show's catalogue that sparked the charged emotions publicity-hungry museums crave.

Damien Hirst is perhaps the show's best-known artist. His work depicting a pair of cows sliced and suspended in a tank of formaldehyde caused a stir at a London gallery three years ago. His shark-in-a-tank piece immediately attracted the ire of People for the Ethical Treatment of Animals. Ingrid Newkirk, the group's president, dismissed Mr. Hirst as a "shock jock" who "is contributing to the slaughter of animals for no other reason than his own aggrandizement." (Mr. Hirst denies killing animals, saying they are already dead.)

Meanwhile, William A. Donohue, the president of the Catholic League for Religious and Civil Rights, said a review of the catalogue turned his stomach. "I think the whole city should picket the show," he said. "This exhibition is designed to shock, but instead it induces revulsion."

15 But it was the reaction of Mayor Giuliani that signaled both a publicity coup for the museum and a threat to its own finances.

"If somebody wants to do that privately and pay for that privately, well, that's what the First Amendment is all about," he said. "I mean, you can be offended by it and upset by it, and you don't have to go see it, if somebody else is paying for it. But to have the government subsidize something like that is outrageous."

He added a quick critique of Mr. Hirst's work. "I thought that's what they did in biology laboratories," he said, "not in museums of art."

Deputy Mayor Randy Levine later explained the mechanics of the Mayor's threat to cut off city money. "They get their checks on a first-of-the-month basis," Mr. Levine said. "Those checks will be suspended unless this exhibit is canceled."

When asked what would happen if the museum did not cancel the show, Mr. Levine said, "Then they're not going to get any more city funds."

20 The Mayor's threat may set up another confrontation with the City Council. Speaker Peter F. Vallone also said he was offended by the artworks, and urged New Yorkers not to see the show, but said he would oppose the Mayor's withholding of the museum subsidy. The Council has final authority over the budget.

Floyd Abrams, a lawyer specializing in the First Amendment, said the Mayor understood the amendment "precisely backward."

"Punishing the Brooklyn Museum by seeking to remove its funding because the Mayor disapproves of what he perceives is the message of its art is at war with the First Amendment," Mr. Abrams said. "The Mayor has every right to denounce the exhibition. He should understand, however, that the First Amendment limits what he can do to retaliate against art of which he disapproves."

The struggle between artists who are trying to express themselves and the government's attempt to define what it considers acceptable has intensified in recent years with disputes over several exhibits.

In 1989, the Corcoran Gallery in Washington backed down and canceled an exhibition featuring the homoerotic art of Robert Mapplethorpe and financed by the National Endowment for the Arts.

25 In June 1998, the Supreme Court upheld a Congressional decency test for awarding Federal arts grants, but only after a majority interpreted a 1990 law as containing only "advisory language" that did not actually prohibit Federal subsidies for indecent art. In a majority opinion by Justice Sandra Day O'Connor, the Court suggested that if the law was invoked to impose "a penalty on disfavored viewpoints," it would violate the First Amendment.

The decision came in a case brought against the N.E.A. by the performance artist Karen Finley and three other artists. Two N.E.A. grants in 1989, to Mr. Mapplethorpe for a retrospective of sexually explicit photographs and to the artist Andres Serrano, who photographed a crucifix immersed in his own urine, had ignited a furor that has never completely died down.

Some museum directors were taken aback by Mayor Giuliani's decision. "I'm appalled," Mimi Gaudieri, the director of the Association of Art Museum Directors, said of Mr. Giuliani's threat. "We've been through this war before, not only with Mapplethorpe but with Serrano and others, and we've won. It just doesn't play in the political arena."

Meanwhile, Chris Ofili, a Roman Catholic whose portrait of the Virgin Mary so offended the Mayor and whose work often features clumps of elephant dung, defended his work.

"As an altar boy, I was confused by the idea of a holy Virgin Mary giving birth to a young boy," he said. "Now when I go to the National Gallery and see paintings of the Virgin Mary, I see how sexually charged they are. Mine is simply a hip-hop version."

LEADING QUESTIONS

The works of art that Plato and Aristotle refer to in their writing were part of the central religious rituals of their society. These works engaged the attention of the citizens of Athens, therefore, in a way that seems unthinkable today. But Mayor Giuliani's anger seems to suggest that art still has something of the religious role it once had. The theologian Paul Tillich (Chapter 2, pp. 123–130) also finds a religious dimension in modern art—precisely in its struggle, in its provocative expression, in its exhibition of spiritual disturbance. In a secular age, should art serve the role of solace and inspiration, as Mayor Giuliani seems to want, or should art probe what we fear and ask what we don't dare ask? And when the artist asks disturbing questions, do we under any circumstances have the right to order him or her to keep mum? What is the role of art today, and why?

LEARNING MORE

1. You may want to find out what happened next, in the days and months following this story. Visit *The New York Times* online (www.nytimes.com).
2. It would be useful to have a look at the work of Robert Mapplethorpe, Karen Finley, and Andres Serrano. See the *Ideas Across Time* website for links.
3. You may want to learn more about the Catholic League for Religious and Civil Rights. (Compare William A. Donohue's view of the First Amendment [par. 16] and what the Constitution actually says—see the *Ideas Across Time* website.)

QUESTIONING THE TEXT

1. What is Mayor Giuliani's objection to the show at the Brooklyn Museum?
2. What does he threaten to do?
3. How can he harm the museum?
4. What is the view of the museum's director about the mayor's threats?
5. How did the museum contribute to the emotional expectations for its show?
6. What views of the First Amendment are held by the various actors in this controversy?
7. How has the Supreme Court viewed censorship of art by the government?

ANALYZING THE WRITER'S CRAFT

1. How does the fact that this is a news story affect the way it is written and organized? Consider, for example, the information chosen for inclusion in the opening paragraph; or consider, to take another example, the length of the paragraphs.
2. What kinds of people are quoted in this story? What guides the choice of people to be quoted? How do these quotations contribute to the story?
3. In your own words, state the position of the two sides in this dispute.
4. What do you make of the fact that none of those outraged by the show had seen it?
5. Choose two or three especially effective transitions in this story, and explain your choices.
6. Is the conclusion a good way to end the story? Explain.

MAKING CONNECTIONS

1. Have a look at Christ Ofili's *Madonna* on the *Ideas Across Time* website. What is your view of this painting in light of the controversy over it?
2. What do you think would be Plato's view of this controversy (see pp. 565–574)?
3. Which side would the theologian Paul Tillich (see Chapter 2, pp. 127–130) take in this dispute, and why?
4. How does what you know about the art in this exhibition confirm or depart from the definition of modern art offered by Meyer Schapiro (see pp. 590–602)?

FORMULATING IDEAS FOR WRITING

1. In this controversy, which side are you on, and why?
2. Our society is full of provocative visual material—from pop singers baring their breasts on national television to outright pornography that can be bought at every newsstand. Why do you think the mayor became so incensed by this visual material in particular? Do you think he's got a point?

3. What is the responsibility of the artist to society? Should artists pay no attention to the sensibilities of their communities? Why is it valid, from the artist's point of view, to show disrespect to the most sacred feelings of others? Shouldn't the artist elevate the community and human nobility rather than besmirch his or her neighbors? (In answering this question, do not address the question of what society ought to allow or permit by law—write about the artist's own responsibility.)

The Republic (360 BCE)

Plato

When we speak of "classical Greece" what we refer to is an amazingly rich and relatively brief span of time in the city-state of Athens, concentrated in the years 461–429 BCE when Pericles led the city. This was Athens' Golden Age, the triumphant era of classical Greek culture and Greek democracy. But this entire edifice, upon which so much of the history of the West is founded, collapsed in the Peloponnesian War (431–404 BCE) between Athens and Sparta, which ended in the defeat of Athens.

Greek philosophy was developed against the background of Athens' Golden Age and its collapse. Socrates was born around 470 BCE, Plato around 427 BCE, and Aristotle in 384 BCE. These great men were closely associated. Socrates, a "street teacher" eventually executed for "impiety," taught Plato, and Plato in turn taught Aristotle (see pp. 575–579). Moreover, Socrates himself wrote nothing. What we know of his thought we know mainly through Plato's writing. Brought up in an aristocratic Athenian family, Plato considered going into politics until he was revolted by the execution of Socrates by the courts of democratic Athens. He founded a philosophical school, the Academy, in a grove called Academus in Athens in 385 BCE. For the remainder of his life, he taught and wrote. His books cast Socrates as the main character in wide-ranging dialogues that explore fundamental questions of justice, ethics, and the nature of reality. These dialogues, of which *The Republic* is perhaps the most famous, are question-and-answer exchanges between Socrates and one or another of his students or some hapless young man of Athens who happens by. They exemplify Socrates' central maxim that "the unexamined life is not worth living" and seek truth through a process of relentless logical questioning. In *The Republic,* this questioning aims to establish the parameters of the best possible form of political organization. In Plato's ideal republic, philosophy is king because the philosophical method educates men in truth. Since for Plato truth is absolute and ideal, the very rootedness of art in *this* world diminishes its value. By definition, art (he uses "poetry" to represent all art) is an "imitation" or "representation" of life and proposes a lie—the concrete example versus the absolute Ideal. Art, therefore, can lead men astray and harm rather than aid society.

The famous passages below are from Book X of *The Republic*.

Of the many excellences which I perceive in the order of our State, there is none which upon reflection pleases me better than the rule about poetry.[1]

To what do you refer?

To the rejection of imitative poetry, which certainly ought not to be received; as I see far more clearly now that the parts of the soul have been distinguished.

What do you mean?

Speaking in confidence, for I should not like to have my words repeated to the tragedians and the rest of the imitative tribe—but I do not mind saying to you, that all poetical imitations are ruinous to the understanding of the hearers, and that the knowledge of their true nature is the only antidote[2] to them.

Explain the purport of your remark.

Well, I will tell you, although I have always from my earliest youth had an awe and love of Homer, which even now makes the words falter on my lips, for he is the great captain and teacher of the whole of that charming tragic company; but a man is not to be reverenced more than the truth, and therefore I will speak out.

Very good, he said.

Listen to me then, or rather, answer me.

Put your question.

Can you tell me what imitation is? for I really do not know.

A likely thing, then, that I should know.

Why not? for the duller eye may often see a thing sooner than the keener.

Very true, he said; but in your presence, even if I had any faint notion, I could not muster courage to utter it. Will you enquire yourself?

Well then, shall we begin the enquiry in our usual manner: Whenever a number of individuals have a common name, we assume them to have also a corresponding idea or form:—do you understand me?

I do.

Let us take any common instance; there are beds and tables in the world—plenty of them, are there not?

Yes.

But there are only two ideas or forms of them—one the idea of a bed, the other of a table.

True.

And the maker of either of them makes a bed or he makes a table for our use, in accordance with the idea—that is our way of speaking in this and similar instances—but no artificer makes the ideas themselves: how could he?

Impossible.

---

[1] poetry: In this dialogue, Socrates is talking to Glaucon.

[2] antidote: medicine given to counteract an infection or disease.

And there is another artist,—I should like to know what you would say of him.

Who is he?

25 One who is the maker of all the works of all other workmen.

What an extraordinary man!

Wait a little, and there will be more reason for your saying so. For this is he who is able to make not only vessels of every kind, but plants and animals, himself and all other things—the earth and heaven, and the things which are in heaven or under the earth; he makes the gods also.

He must be a wizard and no mistake.

Oh! you are incredulous, are you? Do you mean that there is no such maker or creator, or that in one sense there might be a maker of all these things but in another not? Do you see that there is a way in which you could make them all yourself?

30 What way?

An easy way enough; or rather, there are many ways in which the feat might be quickly and easily accomplished, none quicker than that of turning a mirror round and round—you would soon enough make the sun and the heavens, and the earth and yourself, and other animals and plants, and all the other things of which we were just now speaking, in the mirror.

Yes, he said; but they would be appearances only.

Very good, I said, you are coming to the point now. And the painter too is, as I conceive, just such another—a creator of appearances, is he not?

Of course.

35 But then I suppose you will say that what he creates is untrue. And yet there is a sense in which the painter also creates a bed?

Yes, he said, but not a real bed.

And what of the maker of the bed? were you not saying that he too makes, not the idea which, according to our view, is the essence of the bed, but only a particular bed?

Yes, I did.

Then if he does not make that which exists he cannot make true existence, but only some semblance of existence; and if any one were to say that the work of the maker of the bed, or of any other workman, has real existence, he could hardly be supposed to be speaking the truth.

40 At any rate, he replied, philosophers would say that he was not speaking the truth.

No wonder, then, that his work too is an indistinct expression of truth.

No wonder.

Suppose now that by the light of the examples just offered we enquire who this imitator is?

If you please.

45 Well, then, here are three beds: one existing in nature, which is made by God, as I think that we may say—for no one else can be the maker?

No.

There is another which is the work of the carpenter?

Yes.

And the work of the painter is a third?

50 Yes.

Beds, then, are of three kinds, and there are three artists who superintend them: God, the maker of the bed, and the painter?

Yes, there are three of them.

God, whether from choice or from necessity, made one bed in nature and one only; two or more such ideal beds neither ever have been nor ever will be made by God.

Why is that?

55 Because even if He had made but two, a third would still appear behind them which both of them would have for their idea, and that would be the ideal bed and not the two others.

Very true, he said.

God knew this, and He desired to be the real maker of a real bed, not a particular maker of a particular bed, and therefore He created a bed which is essentially and by nature one only.

So we believe.

Shall we, then, speak of Him as the natural author or maker of the bed?

60 Yes, he replied; inasmuch as by the natural process of creation He is the author of this and of all other things.

And what shall we say of the carpenter—is not he also the maker of the bed?

Yes.

But would you call the painter a creator and maker?

Certainly not.

65 Yet if he is not the maker, what is he in relation to the bed?

I think, he said, that we may fairly designate him as the imitator of that which the others make.

Good, I said; then you call him who is third in the descent from nature an imitator?

Certainly, he said.

And the tragic poet is an imitator, and therefore, like all other imitators, he is thrice removed from the king and from the truth?

70 That appears to be so.

Then about the imitator we are agreed. And what about the painter?—I would like to know whether he may be thought to imitate that which originally exists in nature, or only the creations of artists?

The latter.

As they are or as they appear? you have still to determine this.

What do you mean?

75 I mean, that you may look at a bed from different points of view, obliquely or directly or from any other point of view, and the bed will appear different, but there is no difference in reality. And the same of all things.

Yes, he said, the difference is only apparent.

Now let me ask you another question: Which is the art of painting designed to be—an imitation of things as they are, or as they appear—of appearance or of reality?

Of appearance.

Then the imitator, I said, is a long way off the truth, and can do all things because he lightly touches on a small part of them, and that part an image. For example: A painter will paint a cobbler, carpenter, or any other artist, though he knows nothing of their arts; and, if he is a good artist, he may deceive children or simple persons, when he shows them his picture of a carpenter from a distance, and they will fancy that they are looking at a real carpenter.

Certainly.

And whenever any one informs us that he has found a man who knows all the arts, and all things else that anybody knows, and every single thing with a higher degree of accuracy than any other man—whoever tells us this, I think that we can only imagine him to be a simple creature who is likely to have been deceived by some wizard or actor whom he met, and whom he thought all-knowing, because he himself was unable to analyse the nature of knowledge and ignorance and imitation.

Most true.

And so, when we hear persons saying that the tragedians, and Homer, who is at their head, know all the arts and all things human, virtue as well as vice, and divine things too, for that the good poet cannot compose well unless he knows his subject, and that he who has not this knowledge can never be a poet, we ought to consider whether here also there may not be a similar illusion. Perhaps they may have come across imitators and been deceived by them; they may not have remembered when they saw their works that these were but imitations thrice removed from the truth, and could easily be made without any knowledge of the truth, because they are appearances only and not realities? Or, after all, they may be in the right, and poets do really know the things about which they seem to the many to speak so well?

The question, he said, should by all means be considered.

Now do you suppose that if a person were able to make the original as well as the image, he would seriously devote himself to the image-making branch? Would he allow imitation to be the ruling principle of his life, as if he had nothing higher in him?

I should say not.

The real artist, who knew what he was imitating, would be interested in realities and not in imitations; and would desire to leave as memorials of himself works many and fair; and, instead of being the author of encomiums,[3] he would prefer to be the theme of them.

Yes, he said, that would be to him a source of much greater honour and profit.

Then, I said, we must put a question to Homer; not about medicine, or any of the arts to which his poems only incidentally refer: we are not going to ask him, or any other poet, whether he has cured patients like Asclepius,[4] or left

[3] encomiums: praises.

[4] Asclepius: Legendary physician, made immortal upon his death and known as the god of medicine.

behind him a school of medicine such as the Asclepiads were, or whether he only talks about medicine and other arts at second-hand; but we have a right to know respecting military tactics, politics, education, which are the chiefest and noblest subjects of his poems, and we may fairly ask him about them. "Friend Homer," then we say to him, "if you are only in the second remove from truth in what you say of virtue, and not in the third—not an image maker or imitator—and if you are able to discern what pursuits make men better or worse in private or public life, tell us what State was ever better governed by your help? The good order of Lacedaemon is due to Lycurgus,[5] and many other cities great and small have been similarly benefited by others; but who says that you have been a good legislator to them and have done them any good? Italy and Sicily boast of Charondas,[6] and there is Solon[7] who is renowned among us; but what city has anything to say about you?" Is there any city which he might name?

I think not, said Glaucon; not even the Homerids themselves pretend that he was a legislator.

Well, but is there any war on record which was carried on successfully by him, or aided by his counsels, when he was alive?

There is not.

Or is there any invention of his, applicable to the arts or to human life, such as Thales the Milesian or Anacharsis the Scythian,[8] and other ingenious men have conceived, which is attributed to him?

There is absolutely nothing of the kind. . . .

Thus far we are pretty well agreed that the imitator has no knowledge worth mentioning of what he imitates. Imitation is only a kind of play or sport, and the tragic poets, whether they write in Iambic or in Heroic verse, are imitators in the highest degree?

Very true.

And now tell me, I conjure you, has not imitation been shown by us to be concerned with that which is thrice removed from the truth?

Certainly.

And what is the faculty in man to which imitation is addressed?

What do you mean?

I will explain: The body which is large when seen near, appears small when seen at a distance?

True.

And the same objects appear straight when looked at out of the water, and crooked when in the water; and the concave becomes convex, owing to the

---

[5] Lycurgus: Lawgiver of Sparta (700–630 BCE).

[6] Charondas: Sixth-century-BCE Sicilian lawgiver, admired by Aristotle for his clarity of expression.

[7] Solon: Lived 638–558 BCE; wrote the Athenian constitution that incorporated the first democratic elements in world history.

[8] Thales the Milesian or Anacharsis the Scythian: two of the Seven Sages of Greece. Thales (635–543 BCE) is the father of Greek philosophy; the sixth-century-BCE prince and philosopher Anacharsis was so admired for his thought that he became the first outsider to receive the privilege of Athenian citizenship.

illusion about colours to which the sight is liable. Thus every sort of confusion is revealed within us; and this is that weakness of the human mind on which the art of conjuring and of deceiving by light and shadow and other ingenious devices imposes, having an effect upon us like magic.

True.

And the arts of measuring and numbering and weighing come to the rescue of the human understanding—there is the beauty of them—and the apparent greater or less, or more or heavier, no longer have the mastery over us, but give way before calculation and measure and weight?

Most true.

And this, surely, must be the work of the calculating and rational principle in the soul?

To be sure.

And when this principle measures and certifies that some things are equal, or that some are greater or less than others, there occurs an apparent contradiction?

True.

But were we not saying that such a contradiction is impossible—the same faculty cannot have contrary opinions at the same time about the same thing?

Very true.

Then that part of the soul which has an opinion contrary to measure is not the same with that which has an opinion in accordance with measure?

True.

And the better part of the soul is likely to be that which trusts to measure and calculation?

Certainly.

And that which is opposed to them is one of the inferior principles of the soul?

No doubt.

This was the conclusion at which I was seeking to arrive when I said that painting or drawing, and imitation in general, when doing their own proper work, are far removed from truth, and the companions and friends and associates of a principle within us which is equally removed from reason, and that they have no true or healthy aim. . . .

But when a man is drawn in two opposite directions, to and from the same object, this, as we affirm, necessarily implies two distinct principles in him?

Certainly.

One of them is ready to follow the guidance of the law?

How do you mean?

The law would say that to be patient under suffering is best, and that we should not give way to impatience, as there is no knowing whether such things are good or evil; and nothing is gained by impatience; also, because no human thing is of serious importance, and grief stands in the way of that which at the moment is most required.

What is most required? he asked.

That we should take counsel about what has happened, and when the dice have been thrown order our affairs in the way which reason deems best; not, like children who have had a fall, keeping hold of the part struck and wasting time in setting up a howl, but always accustoming the soul forthwith to apply a remedy, raising up that which is sickly and fallen, banishing the cry of sorrow by the healing art.

Yes, he said, that is the true way of meeting the attacks of fortune.

Yes, I said; and the higher principle is ready to follow this suggestion of reason?

Clearly.

130 And the other principle, which inclines us to recollection of our troubles and to lamentation, and can never have enough of them, we may call irrational, useless, and cowardly?

Indeed, we may.

And does not the latter—I mean the rebellious principle—furnish a great variety of materials for imitation? Whereas the wise and calm temperament, being always nearly equable, is not easy to imitate or to appreciate when imitated, especially at a public festival when a promiscuous crowd is assembled in a theatre. For the feeling represented is one to which they are strangers.

Certainly.

Then the imitative poet who aims at being popular is not by nature made, nor is his art intended, to please or to affect the rational principle in the soul; but he will prefer the passionate and fitful temper, which is easily imitated?

135 Clearly.

And now we may fairly take him and place him by the side of the painter, for he is like him in two ways: first, inasmuch as his creations have an inferior degree of truth—in this, I say, he is like him; and he is also like him in being concerned with an inferior part of the soul; and therefore we shall be right in refusing to admit him into a well-ordered State, because he awakens and nourishes and strengthens the feelings and impairs the reason. As in a city when the evil are permitted to have authority and the good are put out of the way, so in the soul of man, as we maintain, the imitative poet implants an evil constitution, for he indulges the irrational nature which has no discernment of greater and less, but thinks the same thing at one time great and at another small—he is a manufacturer of images and is very far removed from the truth.

Exactly.

But we have not yet brought forward the heaviest count in our accusation:—the power which poetry has of harming even the good (and there are very few who are not harmed), is surely an awful thing?

Yes, certainly, if the effect is what you say.

140 Hear and judge: The best of us, as I conceive, when we listen to a passage of Homer, or one of the tragedians, in which he represents some pitiful hero who is drawling out his sorrows in a long oration, or weeping, and smiting his breast—the best of us, you know, delight in giving way to sympathy, and are in raptures at the excellence of the poet who stirs our feelings most.

Yes, of course I know.

But when any sorrow of our own happens to us, then you may observe that we pride ourselves on the opposite quality—we would fain be quiet and patient; this is the manly part, and the other which delighted us in the recitation is now deemed to be the part of a woman.

Very true, he said.

Now can we be right in praising and admiring another who is doing that which any one of us would abominate and be ashamed of in his own person?

No, he said, that is certainly not reasonable.

Nay, I said, quite reasonable from one point of view.

What point of view?

If you consider, I said, that when in misfortune we feel a natural hunger and desire to relieve our sorrow by weeping and lamentation, and that this feeling which is kept under control in our own calamities is satisfied and delighted by the poets;—the better nature in each of us, not having been sufficiently trained by reason or habit, allows the sympathetic element to break loose because the sorrow is another's; and the spectator fancies that there can be no disgrace to himself in praising and pitying any one who comes telling him what a good man he is, and making a fuss about his troubles; he thinks that the pleasure is a gain, and why should he be supercilious[9] and lose this and the poem too? Few persons ever reflect, as I should imagine, that from the evil of other men something of evil is communicated to themselves. And so the feeling of sorrow which has gathered strength at the sight of the misfortunes of others is with difficulty repressed in our own.

How very true!

And does not the same hold also of the ridiculous? There are jests which you would be ashamed to make yourself, and yet on the comic stage, or indeed in private, when you hear them, you are greatly amused by them, and are not at all disgusted at their unseemliness;—the case of pity is repeated;—there is a principle in human nature which is disposed to raise a laugh, and this which you once restrained by reason, because you were afraid of being thought a buffoon, is now let out again; and having stimulated the risible[10] faculty at the theatre, you are betrayed unconsciously to yourself into playing the comic poet at home.

Quite true, he said.

And the same may be said of lust and anger and all the other affections, of desire and pain and pleasure, which are held to be inseparable from every action—in all of them poetry feeds and waters the passions instead of drying them up; she lets them rule, although they ought to be controlled, if mankind are ever to increase in happiness and virtue.

I cannot deny it.

Therefore, Glaucon, I said, whenever you meet with any of the eulogists[11] of Homer declaring that he has been the educator of Hellas,[12] and that he is

---

[9] supercilious: condescending.
[10] risible: laughable.
[11] eulogists: praise givers.
[12] Hellas: Greece.

profitable for education and for the ordering of human things, and that you should take him up again and again and get to know him and regulate your whole life according to him, we may love and honour those who say these things—they are excellent people, as far as their lights extend; and we are ready to acknowledge that Homer is the greatest of poets and first of tragedy writers; but we must remain firm in our conviction that hymns to the gods and praises of famous men are the only poetry which ought to be admitted into our State. For if you go beyond this and allow the honeyed muse to enter, either in epic or lyric verse, not law and the reason of mankind, which by common consent have ever been deemed best, but pleasure and pain will be the rulers in our State.

155 That is most true, he said. . . .

LEARNING MORE

You can access the rest of *The Republic* on the *Ideas Across Time* website.

QUESTIONING THE TEXT

1. Why does Socrates speak of poetry (or art) as "imitative poetry" or "practical imitation"?
2. What in general is Socrates' view of poetry?
3. What for Socrates is "the essence" (par. 37) or "true existence" (par. 39) of anything in the world—say, to use his examples, a bed or a chair?
4. Even if art is "only" imitation, Socrates concedes it *might* be of some use (par. 89). How might art be useful? Does Socrates believe that in fact it *is* useful? Why or why not?
5. How do the tastes of the "promiscuous crowd" (par. 132) affect what the artist chooses to imitate?
6. Why is the "imitative poet" banned from Socrates' "well-ordered State" (pars. 134–136)?
7. What, according to Socrates, is "the heaviest count" (par. 139) in his accusations against poetry?

ANALYZING THE WRITER'S CRAFT

1. This is a typical, and indeed famous, example of the Socratic or questioning method—as a form of teaching and of critical thinking. What are the main characteristics of this method that you observe? What must pertain in order for this method to be rigorous and reliable? From the point of view of teaching and learning, what are the advantages of this method? The disadvantages? From the point of view of critical thinking, what are the strengths of this method? The weaknesses? Would you recommend this method to every teacher? Why or why not?
2. This passage is, of course, not a literal transcription of a conversation between Socrates and Glaucon but rather Plato's reconstruction of a

conversation. How might this exchange have been different in real life from how it appears in writing?

3. If you were Glaucon, would you have responded differently to Socrates at any point? Why or why not?
4. Are you persuaded by Socrates? If so, what makes him persuasive? If not, why not?

MAKING CONNECTIONS

1. How do Plato and Aristotle differ in method? In outlook?
2. Do you think Ralph Waldo Emerson (see pp. 581–585) is indebted to Plato?
3. N. Scott Momaday (pp. 612–616) sees the artist, the man made of words, as engaged in a life-and-death activity. Do you think Socrates would have thought differently about the usefulness of poetry had he read Momaday? Explain.
4. How does Plato/Socrates' view of what's real, and therefore of God (see also what Socrates said on his deathbed, Chapter 8, pp. 640–644), compare and contrast with the views of another rationalist, Tom Paine (Chapter 2, pp. 98–103)?

FORMULATING IDEAS FOR WRITING

1. Write a dialogue proving some proposition you strongly believe in, such as, "Freedom of thought depends on separation of church and state" or "Experiment is the best route to truth."
2. Support Socrates by amplifying his argument—in other words, don't bring in new arguments but deepen and expand the ones he has already used.
3. Write an essay that takes issue with Socrates' expulsion of the poets. Be sure that you refute and rebut Socrates' argument and main points.

Poetics (350 BCE)

Aristotle

Unlike Socrates and Plato, Aristotle (384–322 BCE) was a native not of Athens but of the town of Stagira near Macedonia. Aristotle enrolled in Plato's Academy at age seventeen and remained there until Plato died (347 BCE). Soon thereafter, Aristotle became tutor of the son of the Macedonian ruler Philip II. This son, who later established the greatest of the classical empires, is known to us as Alexander the Great. Aristotle returned to Athens in 335 BCE and founded the Lyceum, a research center for the study of every branch of knowledge. Aristotle wrote around four hundred works, ranging over such fields of classical knowledge as mathematics, zoology, botany, biology, physics, politics, ethics, logic, and the arts. After Alexander's death in 323 BCE, the Athenians gave vent to their resentment of his domination, and Aristotle left the city for the Chalcidian peninsula in Macedonia, where he died in 322 BCE.

Aristotle studied the world as we know and perceive it. Unlike Socrates and Plato, he did not attempt to derive ideal truth from abstract reasoning but rather applied logic to experience. Often—as in the *Poetics*—he was interested in accurate classification and codification as itself a meaningful form of knowledge. He does not say what poetry *ought* to be but rather analyzes it to discover what it *is*. This methodology laid the ground for the ultimate development of science as we know it today.

The differences in worldview between Plato and Aristotle account for the two men's different assessments of art. Plato through Socrates derides the inauthenticity of art, a mere imitation of an imitation, a lie, whereas Aristotle observes that art seems to emerge from our deepest instincts, including our pleasure in beauty, and that it engages our deepest human emotions. This difference of perspective and emphasis foreshadows centuries of quarrel over the function, value, and morality of art.

I propose to treat of Poetry in itself and of its various kinds, noting the essential quality of each; to inquire into the structure of the plot as requisite to a good poem; into the number and nature of the parts of which a poem is composed; and similarly into whatever else falls within the same inquiry. Following, then, the order of nature, let us begin with the principles which come first.

2. Epic poetry and Tragedy, Comedy also and Dithyrambic poetry,[1] and the music of the flute and of the lyre in most of their forms, are all in their general conception modes of imitation. 3. They differ, however, from one another in three respects,—the medium, the objects, the manner or mode of imitation, being in each case distinct.

4. For as there are persons who, by conscious art or mere habit, imitate and represent various objects through the medium of colour and form, or again by the voice; so in the arts above mentioned, taken as a whole, the imitation is produced by rhythm, language, and "harmony," either single, or combined.

II

Since the objects of imitation are men in action, and these men must be either of a higher or a lower type (for moral character mainly answers to these divisions, goodness and badness being the distinguishing marks of moral differences), it follows that we must represent men either as better than in real life, or as worse,

[1] Dithyrambic poetry: impassioned hymns in honor of Dionysus.

or as they are. It is the same in painting. Polygnotus depicted men as nobler than they are, Pauson as less noble, Dionysius[2] drew them true to life.

2. Now it is evident that each of the modes of imitation above mentioned will exhibit these differences, and become a distinct kind in imitating objects that are thus distinct. 3. Such diversities may be found even in dancing, flute-playing, and lyre-playing. So again in language, whether prose or verse unaccompanied by music. Homer, for example, makes men better than they are; Cleophon as they are; Hegemon the Thasian, the inventor of parodies, and Nicochares,[3] the author of the Deiliad, worse than they are.

III

There is still a third difference—the manner in which each of these objects may be imitated. For the medium being the same, and the objects the same, the poet may imitate by narration—in which case he can either take another personality as Homer does, or speak in his own person, unchanged—or he may present all his characters as living and moving before us.

2. These, then, as we said at the beginning, are the three differences which distinguish artistic imitation—the medium, the objects and the manner.

IV

Poetry in general seems to have sprung from two causes, each of them lying deep in our nature. 2. First, the instinct of imitation is implanted in man from childhood, one difference between him and other animals being that he is the most imitative of living creatures; and through imitation he learns his earliest lessons; and no less universal is the pleasure felt in things imitated. 3. We have evidence of this in the facts of experience. Objects which in themselves we view with pain, we delight to contemplate when reproduced with minute fidelity: such as the forms of the most ignoble animals and of dead bodies. 4. The cause of this again is, that to learn gives the liveliest pleasure, not only to philosophers but to men in general; whose capacity, however, of learning is more limited. 5. Thus the reason why men enjoy seeing a likeness is, that in contemplating it they find themselves learning or inferring, and saying perhaps, "Ah, that is he." For if you happen not to have seen the original, the pleasure will be due not to the imitation as such, but to the execution, the colouring, or some such other cause.

6. Imitation, then, is one instinct of our nature. Next, there is the instinct for "harmony" and rhythm, metres being manifestly sections of rhythm. Persons, therefore, starting with this natural gift developed by degrees their special aptitudes, till their rude improvisations gave birth to Poetry.

---

[2] Polygnotus . . . Pauson . . . Dionysius: Of these we have information about Polygnotus, who flourished c. 460–447 BCE and painted the *Capture of Troy,* but none of his work survives.

[3] Celophon . . . Hegemon . . . Nichochares: Cleophon was a fourth-century-BCE Athenian tragedian; Hegemon was a contemporary of Pericles who some scholars say introduced parodies; and Nichochares was a Greek comic poet of the fifth century BCE.

7. Poetry now diverged in two directions, according to the individual character of the writers. The graver spirits imitated noble actions, and the actions of good men. The more trivial sort imitated the actions of meaner persons, at first composing satires, as the former did hymns to the gods and the praises of famous men. 8. A poem of the satirical kind cannot indeed be put down to any author earlier than Homer; though many such writers probably there were. But from Homer onward, instances can be cited,—his own Margites,[4] for example, and other similar compositions. The appropriate metre was also here introduced; hence the measure is still called the iambic or lampooning measure, being that in which people lampooned one another. 9. Thus the older poets were distinguished as writers of heroic or of lampooning verse.

Let us now discuss Tragedy, resuming its formal definition, as resulting from what has been already said.

Tragedy then, is an imitation of an action that is serious, complete, and of a certain magnitude; in language embellished with each kind of artistic ornament, the several kinds being found in separate parts of the play; in the form of action, not of narrative; through pity and fear effecting the proper purgation of these emotions. 3. By "language embellished," I mean language into which rhythm, "harmony," and song enter. By "the several kinds in separate parts," I mean, that some parts are rendered through the medium of verse alone, others again with the aid of song.

Now as tragic imitation implies persons acting, it necessarily follows, in the first place, that Spectacular equipment will be a part of Tragedy. Next, Song and Diction, for these are the medium of imitation. By "Diction" I mean the mere metrical arrangement of the words: as for "Song," it is a term whose sense every one understands.

Again, Tragedy is the imitation of an action; and an action implies personal agents, who necessarily possess certain distinctive qualities both of character and thought; for it is by these that we qualify actions themselves, and these—thought and character—are the two natural causes from which actions spring, and on actions again all success or failure depends. Hence, the Plot is the imitation of the action:—for by plot I here mean the arrangement of the incidents. By Character I mean that in virtue of which we ascribe certain qualities to the agents. Thought is required wherever a statement is proved, or, it may be, a general truth enunciated. Every Tragedy, therefore, must have six parts, which parts determine its quality—namely, Plot, Character, Diction, Thought, Spectacle, Song. Two of the parts constitute the medium of imitation, one the manner, and three the objects of imitation. And these complete the list. These elements have been employed, we may say, by the poets to a man; in fact, every play contains Spectacular elements as well as Character, Plot, Diction, Song, and Thought.

[4] Margites: Comic epic about a dunce so foolish he did not know which of his parents gave birth to him, attributed perhaps erroneously to Homer.

15 But most important of all is the structure of the incidents. For Tragedy is an imitation, not of men, but of an action and of life, and life consists in action, and its end is a mode of action, not a quality. Now character determines men's qualities, but it is by their actions that they are happy or the reverse. Dramatic action, therefore, is not with a view to the representation of character: character comes in as subsidiary to the actions. Hence the incidents and the plot are the end of a tragedy; and the end is the chief thing of all. Again, without action there cannot be a tragedy; there may be without character. . . . Again, if you string together a set of speeches expressive of character, and well finished in point of diction and thought, you will not produce the essential tragic effect nearly so well as with a play which, however deficient in these respects, yet has a plot and artistically constructed incidents. 13. Besides which, the most powerful elements of emotional interest in Tragedy—Peripeteia or Reversal of Intention, and Recognition scenes—are parts of the plot. 14. A further proof is, that novices in the art attain to finish of diction and precision of portraiture before they can construct the plot. It is the same with almost all the early poets.

The Plot, then, is the first principle, and, as it were, the soul of a tragedy: Character holds the second place. 15. A similar fact is seen in painting. The most beautiful colours, laid on confusedly, will not give as much pleasure as the chalk outline of a portrait. Thus Tragedy is the imitation of an action, and of the agents, mainly with a view to the action.

16. Third in order is Thought,—that is, the faculty of saying what is possible and pertinent in given circumstances. In the case of oratory, this is the function of the political art and of the art of rhetoric: and so indeed the older poets make their characters speak the language of civic life; the poets of our time, the language of the rhetoricians.

17. Character is that which reveals moral purpose, showing what kind of things a man chooses or avoids. Speeches, therefore, which do not make this manifest, or in which the speaker does not choose or avoid anything whatever, are not expressive of character. Thought, on the other hand, is found where something is proved to be or not to be, or a general maxim is enunciated.

LEARNING MORE

From Aristotle's time onward, tragedy has stood high as a grand, maybe the grandest of all, literary forms. The *Ideas Across Time* website offers links to useful information about tragedy and writers about tragedy, as well as to the rest of *Poetics.*

QUESTIONING THE TEXT

1. What does Aristotle say is his purpose in writing?
2. What do epic poetry, tragedy, comedy, and music have in common? How do they differ?
3. What, according to Aristotle, does literature imitate?

4. What for Aristotle are "the distinguishing marks of moral differences" (par. 4)?
5. What for Aristotle are the roots of poetry?
6. How does Aristotle explain our enjoyment of an imitation or likeness?
7. What, for Aristotle, are the two main kinds of poetry?
8. What are the key points of Aristotle's definition of tragedy?
9. Why is "the structure of the incidents" (par. 15) the most important feature of tragedy?
10. How does Aristotle distinguish between writing that depicts character and writing that depicts thought?

ANALYZING THE WRITER'S CRAFT

1. On the basis of this classic and enormously influential passage, what would you say are the main elements of classification? Of definition? Give one or two examples of each.
2. Is Aristotle's account of tragedy based on more or less objective observation, or does he *impose* an order on what he sees?
3. Cite two or three examples of logical reasoning in this passage, and explain Aristotle's purpose in each example.
4. Aristotle laces his paragraphs with allusions—to writers, to works of literature. What is Aristotle's purpose in making these references? How are his allusions determined by his goals in the *Poetics*.
5. What means does Aristotle use to persuade readers that his definitions and classifications are correct?

MAKING CONNECTIONS

1. How does Aristotle's approach to poetry compare and contrast with that of Plato (pp. 565–574)?
2. How does Aristotle influence Ralph Waldo Emerson (pp. 581–585)?
3. Aristotle's account of poetry rests on two main propositions: first, that art is "imitation"; and second, that tragedy in particular imitates action. Do you see echoes of Aristotle's views—or rejections of it—in the writing of more contemporary writers such as N. Scott Momaday (pp. 612–616) and Gish Jen (Chapter 5, pp. 427–438)?

FORMULATING IDEAS FOR WRITING

1. Using Aristotle as a model, attempt a definition of a literary form—say, lyric poetry or the novel.
2. Does Aristotle's definition of tragedy help you understand tragic drama? Answer with respect to a work generally classified as a tragedy that you have read and especially enjoyed.

3. In what respects is Aristotle's thinking about literature dated, and therefore no longer useful? In what respects is Aristotle's work still pertinent?
4. Write an essay explaining why your view of the nature and role of art is best stated by Plato or by Aristotle. Imagine how they might regard a famous contemporary work of art, such as a painting by Picasso or a play by Arthur Miller.

Art (1841)

Ralph Waldo Emerson

Probably no one better exemplifies America in the mid-nineteenth century than Ralph Waldo Emerson. A thoroughgoing Yankee, Emerson was born in Boston on May 25, 1803, into a family of preachers able to trace their American roots to 1634. "The Sage of Concord," as he came to be known, Emerson preached an inspirational philosophy that found in nature an abiding resonance with the inner soul and that optimistically affirmed the perfectibility of human beings. He stands as one of our finest examples of American individualism by espousing the virtues of nonconformity, independence of thought, and self-reliance. He fought against slavery, for the rights of Native Americans, and for educational reform. These were causes that he advanced not only in his public lectures but also through the journal *The Dial,* which he founded in 1840 with Margaret Fuller.

Emerson's father, minister at Boston's First Church, died when he was eight, and as a result, Emerson's childhood passed in difficult circumstances. He followed the family tradition and went to Harvard, becoming a Unitarian minister in 1826. Six years later, following the death from tuberculosis of his nineteen-year-old bride after only eighteen months of marriage, Emerson resigned from his post as pastor of the Second Church, saying he could no longer in good conscience administer communion. He remained a fervent believer for the rest of his life, but he did not affirm his belief through the practices of any particular church.

The death of his first wife had two profound consequences for Emerson: the settlement of her estate left him independently wealthy, and his resignation from the ministry launched him on a new career as a lecturer and writer. He remarried in 1834 and settled in rural Concord, where his family had lived for generations. He became the center of a remarkable group of men and women who profoundly influenced American life, including Henry David Thoreau, the Alcott family, Nathaniel Hawthorne, and—across the Atlantic—Thomas Carlyle, with whom he shared a special bond.

Like Carlyle, Emerson spoke a fervent language that takes some adjustment for the contemporary reader. By turns eloquent, wordy, profound, preachy, obscure, and inspiring, Emerson's posture is bardic and public. In his prose, the diction and the cadences are similar to the oratory from pulpit. Unlike the intimate tone of contemporary writing, Emerson's language projects across large public spaces, sometimes across the lecture hall or the whole American landscape. His view of art is similar to his view of human psychology, politics, and religion: the aim of art is "not imitation, but creation." The artist denotes "the height of the human soul" at any given moment of time, and art at once reveals the "aboriginal Power" and makes or creates the individual and society.

Among the essays that shaped the American outlook are his "Nature," "The American Scholar," "Self-Reliance," "The Divinity School Address," and "The Over-Soul." Emerson died of pneumonia in Concord on April 27, 1882. This selection originally appeared in his *Essays* of 1841.

Because the soul is progressive, it never quite repeats itself, but in every act attempts the production of a new and fairer whole. This appears in works both of the useful and the fine arts, if we employ the popular distinction of works according to their aim, either at use or beauty. Thus in our fine arts, not imitation, but creation is the aim. In landscapes, the painter should give the suggestion of a fairer creation than we know. The details, the prose of nature he should omit, and give us only the spirit and splendor. He should know that the landscape has beauty for his eye, because it expresses a thought which is to him good: and this, because the same power which sees through his eyes, is seen in that spectacle; and he will come to value the expression of nature, and not nature itself, and so exalt in his copy, the features that please him. He will give the gloom of gloom, and the sunshine of sunshine. In a portrait, he must inscribe the character, and not the features, and must esteem the man who sits to him as himself only an imperfect picture or likeness of the aspiring original within. . . .

. . . The artist must employ the symbols in use in his day and nation, to convey his enlarged sense to his fellow-men. Thus the new in art is always formed out of the old. The Genius of the Hour sets his ineffaceable seal on the work, and gives it an inexpressible charm for the imagination. As far as the spiritual character of the period overpowers the artist, and finds expression in his work, so far it will retain a certain grandeur, and will represent to future beholders the Unknown, the Inevitable, the Divine. No man can quite exclude this element of Necessity from his labor. No man can quite emancipate himself from his age and country, or produce a model in which the education, the religion, the politics, usages, and arts, of his times shall have no share. Though he were never so original, never so wilful and fantastic, he cannot wipe out of his work every trace of the thoughts amidst which it grew. The very avoidance betrays the usage he avoids. Above his will, and out of his sight, he is necessitated, by the air he breathes, and the idea on which he and his contemporaries live and toil, to share the manner of his times, without knowing what that manner is. Now that which is inevitable in the work has a higher charm than individual talent can ever give, inasmuch as the artist's pen or chisel seems to have been held and guided by a gigantic hand to inscribe a line in the history of the human race. This circumstance gives a value to the Egyptian hieroglyphics, to the Indian, Chinese, and Mexican idols, however gross and shapeless. They denote the height of the human soul in that hour, and were not fantastic, but sprung from a necessity as deep as the world. Shall I now add, that the whole extant product of the plastic arts has herein its highest value, as history; as a stroke drawn in the portrait of that fate, perfect and beautiful, according to whose ordinations all beings advance to their beatitude?

Thus, historically viewed, it has been the office of art to educate the perception of beauty. We are immersed in beauty, but our eyes have no clear vision. It needs, by the exhibition of single traits, to assist and lead the dormant taste. We carve and paint, or we behold what is carved and painted, as students of the mystery of Form. The virtue of art lies in detachment, in sequestering one object from the embarrassing variety. Until one thing comes out from the connection of things, there can be enjoyment, contemplation, but no thought. . . .

The office of painting and sculpture seems to be merely initial. The best pictures can easily tell us their last secret. The best pictures are rude draughts of a few of the miraculous dots and lines and dyes which make up the ever-changing "landscape with figures" amidst which we dwell. Painting seems to be to the eye what dancing is to the limbs. When that has educated the frame to self-possession, to nimbleness, to grace, the steps of the dancing-master are better forgotten; so painting teaches me the splendor of color and the expression of form, and, as I see many pictures and higher genius in the art, I see the boundless opulence of the pencil, the indifferency in which the artist stands free to choose out of the possible forms. If he can draw every thing, why draw any thing? and then is my eye opened to the eternal picture which nature paints in the street with moving men and children, beggars, and fine ladies, draped in red, and green, and blue, and gray; long-haired, grizzled, white-faced, black-faced, wrinkled, giant, dwarf, expanded, elfish,—capped and based by heaven, earth, and sea. . . .

5 The reference of all production at last to an aboriginal Power explains the traits common to all works of the highest art,—that they are universally intelligible; that they restore to us the simplest states of mind; and are religious. Since what skill is therein shown is the reappearance of the original soul, a jet of pure light, it should produce a similar impression to that made by natural objects. In happy hours, nature appears to us one with art; art perfected,—the work of genius. And the individual, in whom simple tastes and susceptibility to all the great human influences overpower the accidents of a local and special culture, is the best critic of art. Though we travel the world over to find the beautiful, we must carry it with us, or we find it not. The best of beauty is a finer charm than skill in surfaces, in outlines, or rules of art can ever teach, namely, a radiation from the work of art of human character,—a wonderful expression through stone, or canvas, or musical sound, of the deepest and simplest attributes of our nature, and therefore most intelligible at last to those souls which have these attributes. In the sculptures of the Greeks, in the masonry of the Romans, and in

the pictures of the Tuscan and Venetian masters, the highest charm is the universal language they speak. A confession of moral nature, of purity, love, and hope, breathes from them all. That which we carry to them, the same we bring back more fairly illustrated in the memory. The traveller who visits the Vatican, and passes from chamber to chamber through galleries of statues, vases, sarcophagi,[1] and candelabra, through all forms of beauty, cut in the richest materials, is in danger of forgetting the simplicity of the principles out of which they all sprung, and that they had their origin from thoughts and laws in his own breast. He studies the technical rules on these wonderful remains, but forgets that these works were not always thus constellated, [2] that they are the contributions of many ages and many countries; that each came out of the solitary workshop of one artist, who toiled perhaps in ignorance of the existence of other sculpture, created his work without other model, save life, household life, and the sweet and smart of personal relations, of beating hearts, and meeting eyes, of poverty, and necessity, and hope, and fear. These were his inspirations, and these are the effects he carries home to your heart and mind. In proportion to his force, the artist will find in his work an outlet for his proper character. He must not be in any manner pinched or hindered by his material, but through his necessity of imparting himself the adamant[3] will be wax in his hands, and will allow an adequate communication of himself, in his full stature and proportion. He need not cumber himself with a conventional nature and culture, nor ask what is the mode in Rome or in Paris, but that house, and weather, and manner of living which poverty and the fate of birth have made at once so odious and so dear, in the gray, unpainted wood cabin, on the corner of a New Hampshire farm, or in the log-hut of the backwoods, or in the narrow lodging where he has endured the constraints and seeming of a city poverty, will serve as well as any other condition as the symbol of a thought which pours itself indifferently through all.

I remember, when in my younger days I had heard of the wonders of Italian painting, I fancied the great pictures would be great strangers; some surprising combination of color and form; a foreign wonder, barbaric pearl and gold, like the spontoons[4] and standards of the militia, which play such pranks in the eyes and imaginations of school-boys. I was to see and acquire I knew not what. When I came at last to Rome, and saw with eyes the pictures, I found that genius left to novices the gay and fantastic and ostentatious, and itself pierced directly to the simple and true; that it was familiar and sincere; that it was the old, eternal fact I had met already in so many forms,—unto which I lived; that it was the plain you and me I knew so well,—had left at home in so many conversations. . . . All great actions have been simple, and all great pictures are.

The Transfiguration, by Raphael, is an eminent example of this peculiar merit. A calm, benignant beauty shines over all this picture, and goes directly to

---

[1] sarcophagi: stone coffins, usually with sculpture and inscriptions.
[2] constellated: clustered together.
[3] the adamant: legendary stone, said to be hard as diamond.
[4] spontoons: half-pikes carried by infantry officers.

the heart. It seems almost to call you by name. The sweet and sublime face of Jesus is beyond praise, yet how it disappoints all florid expectations! This familiar, simple, home-speaking countenance is as if one should meet a friend. The knowledge of picture-dealers has its value, but listen not to their criticism when your heart is touched by genius. It was not painted for them, it was painted for you; for such as had eyes capable of being touched by simplicity and lofty emotions.

Yet when we have said all our fine things about the arts, we must end with a frank confession, that the arts, as we know them, are but initial. Our best praise is given to what they aimed and promised, not to the actual result. He has conceived meanly of the resources of man, who believes that the best age of production is past. The real value of the Iliad, or the Transfiguration, is as signs of power; billows or ripples they are of the stream of tendency; tokens of the everlasting effort to produce, which even in its worst estate the soul betrays. Art has not yet come to its maturity, if it do not put itself abreast with the most potent influences of the world, if it is not practical and moral, if it do not stand in connection with the conscience, if it do not make the poor and uncultivated feel that it addresses them with a voice of lofty cheer. There is higher work for Art than the arts. They are abortive births of an imperfect or vitiated[5] instinct. Art is the need to create; but in its essence, immense and universal, it is impatient of working with lame or tied hands, and of making cripples and monsters, such as all pictures and statues are. Nothing less than the creation of man and nature is its end. A man should find in it an outlet for his whole energy. He may paint and carve only as long as he can do that. Art should exhilarate, and throw down the walls of circumstance on every side, awakening in the beholder the same sense of universal relation and power which the work evinced in the artist, and its highest effect is to make new artists. . . .

LEARNING MORE

1. See the *Ideas Across Time* website for links to information about transcendentalism.
2. In his discussion, Emerson relies heavily on the example of Raphael's painting *The Transfiguration.* It will be useful to have a look at the painting (or a reproduction of it) in color and learn something about the better to appreciate Emerson's point. See the *Ideas Across Time* website.

QUESTIONING THE TEXT

1. State in your own words what you think Emerson means when he says, "Thus in our fine arts, not imitation, but creation is the aim" (par. 1).
2. What is Emerson's view about the use that an artist ought to make of the common references of his time and place?

[5] vitiated: spoiled or corrupted.

3. How, according to Emerson, does the society in which the artist finds him- or herself manifest itself in the artist's work?
4. State in your own words what you think Emerson means when he says that "it has been the office of art to educate the perception of beauty" (par. 3).
5. To whom does art speak best?
6. What general aesthetic principle does Emerson say Raphael's *Transfiguration* exemplifies?
7. How is even the greatest art just a reaching rather than an achieving?

ANALYZING THE WRITER'S CRAFT

1. How does Emerson's style reinforce his message? What are the main rhetorical features of that style?
2. Is Emerson's method of argument logical? Offer one or two illustrative examples, and explain.
3. How would you characterize Emerson's diction (his word choice)?
4. Do you find Emerson's extensive use of aphorism effective? Explain.
5. Write an outline of Emerson's essay.
6. Discuss Emerson's introduction and conclusion. Are they fairly conventional? Effective? Explain.
7. Look up the work "bardic," and discuss its applicability to Emerson's style and method.

MAKING CONNECTIONS

1. Emerson was known as "the Socrates of Concord [his hometown in Massachusetts]." Do you see a strong relation between him and the Socrates who appears in Plato's *Republic* (pp. 565–574)?
2. What would Aristotle (pp. 575–579) find familiar in this essay? What would he find to be new, or even strange?
3. Compare and contrast Emerson's view of creativity with Plato's (pp. 565–574) and Aristotle's (pp. 575–579).
4. Do you think N. Scott Momaday (pp. 612–616) was influenced by Emerson?
5. Compare Emerson's view of art and religion and that of Paul Tillich (Chapter 2, pp. 123–130).
6. Compare and contrast Emerson's view of history and historical forces with Karl Marx's (Chapter 4, pp. 264–273).

FORMULATING IDEAS FOR WRITING

1. Explicate par. 2, 3, and 7.
2. Discuss how Emerson seems to both incorporate and then try to move beyond Plato's and Aristotle's views of art.
3. Use the links on the *Ideas Across Time* website and consider whether this essay is helpfully illuminated by the tenets of transcendentalism? Discuss your findings in a brief essay.

4. Emerson implies a philosophy of history that is teasingly like as well as unlike that of Karl Marx (Chapter 4, pp. 264–273). Emerson, for example, insists on the permeating impact of time and place; and he sees history not as fixed but as evolving as a consequence of human striving. Discuss the similarities and differences in Emerson's and Marx's views of the human record.

Preface to *The Picture of Dorian Gray* (1891)

Oscar Wilde

Oscar Fingal O'Flahertie Wills Wilde was born into an illustrious Anglo-Irish family in 1854. His father was the leading ear and eye surgeon in Ireland, and his mother was a colorful author and nationalist. In 1874, Wilde won a scholarship to Oxford and was immediately launched on his flamboyant, brilliant, and tragic career. At Oxford, he displayed his considerable talents by winning the coveted Newdigate Prize for poetry and graduating with a double first—highest honors. Beyond his intellect, Wilde was also well known for his flamboyant aestheticism, dandyism, and wayward sex life. Soon after graduation, he was dazzling London society with his sparkling conversation. Wilde was later to remark, "I have put only my talent into my works. I have put my genius into my life." In his writing, he was a witty, resourceful, and socially progressive proponent of Art for Art's Sake. The point of art is to be beautiful and pleasing; the point of life is to imitate art.

Wilde's only novel, *The Portrait of Dorian Gray,* was published in 1890. A year later Wilde added the Preface as a response to criticism of the book as immoral. *Dorian Gray* tells the story of a hedonistic young man, beautiful and thinly disguised by Wilde as homosexual, who makes a Faustian bargain: in life he will keep his good looks, but his portrait will decay. The book was hugely successful, its notorious reputation for decadence fueling sales. But Wilde's greatest successes came on the stage, in particular the comedy-of-manners *Lady Windermere's Fan* (1892) and his masterpiece, *The Importance of Being Earnest* (1895).

At the height of his career, Wilde fell into a dreadful, sordid chastisement on account of his homosexuality that landed him in jail under harsh conditions for two years, and from which his health, his reputation, and his finances never recovered. Wilde in fact was married and the father of two sons. His wife, Constance Lloyd, was a wealthy and educated woman. But Wilde soon tired of married life. He fell in love with Lord Alfred Douglas, the mercurial, wastrel son of the Marquess of Queensberry. Homosexuality, however, was illegal under British criminal law, and the Marquess pursued Wilde until he succeeded in having him arrested and sent to jail. Wilde emerged from jail degraded, forbidden to see his sons, his plays shut down, and shunned by his former friends.

Wilde left for Paris and never returned. On his deathbed, in the Hotel d'Alsace in Paris, he converted to Catholicism. He succumbed to cerebral meningitis on November 30, 1900.

The artist is the creator of beautiful things.

To reveal art and conceal the artist is art's aim.

The critic is he who can translate into another manner or a new material his impression of beautiful things.

The highest as the lowest form of criticism is a mode of autobiography.

Those who find ugly meanings in beautiful things are corrupt without being charming. This is a fault.

Those who find beautiful meanings in beautiful things are the cultivated. For these there is hope.

They are the elect to whom beautiful things mean only Beauty.

There is no such thing as a moral or an immoral book.

Books are well written, or badly written. That is all.

The nineteenth century dislike of Realism[1] is the rage of Caliban[2] seeing his own face in a glass.

The nineteenth century dislike of Romanticism[3] is the rage of Caliban not seeing his own face in a glass.

The moral life of man forms part of the subject-matter of the artist, but the morality of art consists in the perfect use of an imperfect medium.

No artist desires to prove anything. Even things that are true can be proved.

No artist has ethical sympathies. An ethical sympathy in an artist is an unpardonable mannerism of style.

No artist is ever morbid. The artist can express everything.

Thought and language are to the artist instruments of an art.

Vice and virtue are to the artist materials for an art.

From the point of view of form, the type of all the arts is the art of the musician. From the point of view of feeling, the actor's craft is the type.

All art is at once surface and symbol.

Those who go beneath the surface do so at their peril.

Those who read the symbol do so at their peril.

It is the spectator, and not life, that art really mirrors.

Diversity of opinion about a work of art shows that the work is new, complex, and vital.

When critics disagree the artist is in accord with himself.

We can forgive a man for making a useful thing as long as he does not admire it. The only excuse for making a useless thing is that one admires it intensely.

All art is quite useless.

---

[1] Realism: Mid-nineteenth-century movement, reacting to Romanticism (see note 3), which sought to render everyday life and recognizable, ordinary experience.

[2] Caliban: Character from Shakespeare's *The Tempest* (1611). Caliban, the son of the witch Sycorax, is a half-deformed monster, enslaved by the sorcerer Prospero.

[3] Romanticism: Early-nineteenth-century movement that stressed strong emotion and imagination in art and reacted against the rationalism of the eighteenth-century Enlightenment.

LEARNING MORE

To learn more about the end-of-the-century Art for Art's Sake movement, and to read more of Wilde's work, see the *Ideas Across Time* website.

QUESTIONING THE TEXT

1. What is a "beautiful thing" (par. 1)? Is a poem a "thing"?
2. Do you think Wilde would find any work of art "ugly"? Explain.
3. Can we speak of morality with respect to, say, a vase? In Wilde's view? In your view?
4. Can we speak of morality with respect to a poem? If a poem makes a statement, can we divorce what's said from what's right and wrong? In Wilde's view? In your view?
5. Is the subject matter of a work of art irrelevant to our appreciation of the work? In Wilde's view? In your view?
6. What is the artist's obligation to his audience? In Wilde's view? In your view?
7. How do you interpret par. 22 ("It is the spectator . . .")?
8. If art is useless, why would anyone want to create art? If art is useless, what is its reason for being?

ANALYZING THE WRITER'S CRAFT

1. What is gained and what is lost by Wilde's epigrammatic approach in this selection?
2. Is there a logical order to Wilde's declarative sentences here, a beginning, a middle, and an end? Explain.
3. Wilde is the master of paradox and reversal. How is his paradoxical wit appropriate to what appear to be his aims in this essay?
4. Who is the audience for this selection? Explain.
5. What is the tone of this selection? Explain.
6. Wilde is at once being highly judgmental in his approach and subtly proselytizing for a certain aesthetic. How effective is his explicit assumption of the role of judge (as in his use of "a fault" in par. 5 or "unpardonable" par. 13)? What kind of outlook is implicit in his use of the words "charming" (par. 5) or "the elect" (par. 7)?
7. Does Wilde's focus on morality convey a moral outlook?

MAKING CONNECTIONS

1. Does Wilde confirm Socrates' reasons for excluding poets from *The Republic* (pp. 565–574)?
2. What would Wilde say to Rudy Giuliani about his condemnation of "sick" art (pp. 560–563)?

3. N. Scott Momaday (pp. 612–616) seems to see a profound usefulness in art. Imagine a dialogue between Momaday and Wilde. Would they be sympathetic to each other's outlook? Could one persuade the other to see things differently?
4. Was Wilde's view of art vindicated in the abstractions of modernist art (see Meyer Schapiro, pp. 590–602)?

FORMULATING IDEAS FOR WRITING

1. Write an essay that demonstrates the moral influence of a work of art. Choose a poem, novel, story, or painting that has had a significant impact on your outlook on life or on your understanding of yourself.
2. Many artists create art that they believe has an explicit moral purpose, such as antiwar poetry, to take one obvious example. Are these artists misguided? Is Wilde right that there are only well written and badly written poems, books, and so on? Are style and form all that really matters regardless of what the artist intends?
3. Choose a work of art that has been judged offensive—such as the work from the Brooklyn exhibition that angered Rudy Giuliani, or a famous book that was banned for being obscene—and defend the view that this work should not be judged on the usual moral standards but rather aesthetically, as art. If works of art are not to be judged for how effective they are as aesthetic creations, then what makes them art?
4. Is the category "beautiful" useful insofar as a discussion of art goes? Can art be "ugly"? Is the goal of the artist to create beauty or to express a vision in aesthetic form, regardless of beauty?

The Introduction of Modern Art in America: The Armory Show (1952)

Meyer Schapiro

No American critic is more identified with the celebration of modern art than Meyer Schapiro. Viewed universally during his long career at Columbia University as one of greatest teachers of his time, he was a rhapsodic presence and an essential resource for the comprehension and appreciation of twentieth-century art. "It was in order to study with Meyer Schapiro that I came to New York," said the painter Robert Motherwell. His studies with Schapiro, Motherwell continued, were "the single most decisive factor in [his] development."

Motherwell's words echo those of many major American artists of the century, including such leading figures as Jasper Johns, Roy Lichtenstein, Claes Oldenburg, Frank Stella, and Andy Warhol.

Meyer Schapiro was born in Lithuania in 1904, and he arrived in New York with his family at the age of three. From Boys High School in Brooklyn, he gained entry to Columbia, where he remained for the rest of his life. Schapiro died professor emeritus in 1996; he was ninety-one years old. Raised in the vivid political environment of the Yiddish communities of New York in the early years of the twentieth century, Schapiro tirelessly promoted radical and socialist causes. But he was known internationally as the foremost champion of modern art, which he succinctly introduces in the present selection.

For Schapiro, the key breakthrough of the moderns was to express the theater of the unconscious in new forms. This art demanded of artist and audience a brave leap into experience, unguided by the academic tutelage of the late-Victorian artistic establishment. Modern art is the art of the untrammeled, free individual, searching for meaning from a dispassionate vantage point on the periphery of society. This individualistic art opened "fresh possibilities" for aesthetic expression, challenging received truths with respect to both art and society. This radicalism wholly suited Schapiro.

Schapiro's influence derived far more from his lectures and his presence than from his writings, which tended to be few and far between. His main ideas are collected in a four-volume series published by George Braziller: *Romanesque Art* (1977), *Modern Art: 19th and 20th Centuries* (1978), *Late Antique, Early Christian and Medieval Art* (1979), and *Theory and Philosophy of Art: Style, Artist and Society* (1994). The essay "The Introduction of Modern Art in America: The Armory Show" originally appeared under the title "Rebellion in Art" in *America in Crisis: Fourteen Crucial Episodes in American History* (1952), edited by Daniel Aron.

The great event, the turning-point in American art called the Armory Show, was briefly this. In December 1911, some American artists who were dissatisfied with the restricted exhibitions of the National Academy of Design formed a new society, the American Association of Painters and Sculptors, in order to exhibit on a broader basis, without jury or prizes. The members did not belong to a particular school of art; several of them had shown at the National Academy itself. They came together not simply from opposition to the aesthetic of the Academy (although there was a stirring towards modernity among them) but from a collective professional need: to create a more open market, so to speak, a means of exhibition accessible to the unacademic and not yet established men. The most active elements in the new society were the younger and more advanced artists; but not the most advanced ones, who seem to have been less concerned about exhibitions or societies at that moment.

This aim of the Association was soon overlaid by another, which none of the members perhaps foresaw. Their first exhibition, planned as a great show of American painting and sculpture at the Sixty-ninth Regiment Armory in

New York—a show inspired by a new confidence of American artists in the importance of their work and of art in general—became an international show in which European paintings and sculpture far surpassed in interest and overshadowed the American. The change in the intention of the Show was due to the idea of the president, Arthur B. Davies,[1] to exhibit as well some recent European work. But while traveling abroad for this purpose, Davies and his collaborator, Walt Kuhn, were so impressed by the new European art, which they had known only slightly, and by the great national and international shows of the newest movements in art, held in 1912 in London, Cologne, and Munich, that they borrowed much more than they had first intended. They were caught up by the tide of advancing art and carried beyond their original aims into a field where they could not maintain themselves; their own work, while unacademic, was submerged by the new art. In the great public that attended the Show in New York, Chicago, and Boston in the spring of 1913, this foreign painting and sculpture called out an extraordinary range of feelings, from enthusiasm for the new to curiosity, bewilderment, disgust, and rage. For months the newspapers and magazines were filled with caricatures, lampoons, photographs, articles, and interviews about the radical European art. Art students burned the painter Matisse in effigy, violent episodes occurred in the schools, and in Chicago the Show was investigated by the Vice Commission upon the complaint of an outraged guardian of morals. So disturbing was the exhibition to the society of artists that had sponsored it that many members repudiated the vanguard and resigned; among them were painters like Sloan and Luks, who the day before had been considered the rebels of American art. Because of the strong feelings aroused within the Association, it broke up soon after, in 1914. The Armory Show was its only exhibition. For years afterwards the Show was remembered as a historic event, a momentous example of artistic insurgence. It excited the young painters and sculptors, awakened them to fresh possibilities, and created in the public at large a new image of modernity. It forced on many an awareness that art had just undergone a revolution and that much they had admired in contemporary art during the last decades was problematic, old-fashioned, destined to die. In time the new European art disclosed at the Armory Show became the model of art in the United States.

Because of the immense excitement provoked by the foreign works, it is easy to exaggerate the effect of the Armory Show upon American art. The later course of art and public taste was undoubtedly the result of other factors besides this exhibition, although we can hardly estimate precisely how much any one of them counted in the end. It may be that, without the Armory Show, art today and our ideas about art would be much as they are. For some years before, there had been in New York a growing interest in advanced European

[1] Davies: Schapiro incorporates references to a great many artists and artistic movements in this essay. To provide adequate comment on each allusion would amount to writing a brief history of Western art. But a workable set of references is accessible on the *Ideas Across Time* website. See Learning More, p. 602. The most notorious painting of the exhibition, Duchamp's *Nude Descending a Staircase,* is reproduced on the website as well.

art, supported and stimulated mainly by Alfred Stieglitz, the pioneer artist-photographer, at his gallery "291"; here were shown works by Rodin, Lautrec, Matisse, and Picasso, and by young Americans (Weber, Maurer, Marin, and Hartley) who had been abroad and absorbed the new art. American painters and sculptors had been going to Europe to study all through the last century, and the best of them had brought back the lessons of the latest European work. Paintings by several who belonged to the current of European modernism could be seen at the Armory Show. Since 1908 there had been a number of exhibitions in New York of artists who had banded together as "independents"; their work was hardly as advanced as what Stieglitz was showing, but it helped to prepare the public and the young painters for the newest art. Most important of all—although not easy to prove—the conditions that had disposed men to create a new kind of art in Europe were becoming more evident in the United States. The appeal of the new art coincided with a trend towards greater freedom in many fields. Modern art eventually came to satisfy a demand that was felt also in architecture, literature, music, and dance.

In this continuous process the Armory Show marks a point of acceleration, and it is instructive for the student of social life as well as of art to observe how a single event in a long series may acquire a crucial importance because it dramatizes or brings into the open before a greater public what is ordinarily the affair of a small group. The very scope and suddenness of this manifestation of the new art were a shock that stirred the sensitive more effectively than a dozen small exhibitions could have done. The Show, coming at a moment of intense ferment in European art, lifted people out of the narrowness of a complacent provincial taste and compelled them to judge American art by a world standard. The years 1910 to 1913 were the heroic period in which the most astonishing innovations had occurred; it was then that the basic types of the art of the next forty years were created. Compared to the movement of art at that time, today's modernism seems a slackening or stagnation. About 1913 painters, writers, musicians, and architects felt themselves to be at an epochal turning-point corresponding to an equally decisive transition in philosophical thought and social life. This sentiment of imminent change inspired a general insurgence, a readiness for great events. The years just before the first World War were rich in new associations of artists, vast projects, and daring manifestos. The world of art had never known so keen an appetite for action, a kind of militancy that gave to cultural life the quality of a revolutionary movement or the beginnings of a new religion. The convictions of the artists were transmitted to an ever larger public, and won converts for whom interest in the new art became a governing passion.

5 As a type of exhibition, the Armory Show was a challenging experience for the public which was placed here in a new role. It had to consider more than ever before an unfamiliar and difficult art. Its judgments were unprepared by the selections of an authoritative jury, nor could it rely on established criteria of its own. Through the Armory Show modern art burst upon the public like a problematic political issue that called for a definite choice. Taste as a personal decision assumed a new significance which was to affect the meaning of art as

such. Until then the idea of great art had been embodied mainly in those solemn, well certified, old European works of fabulous price, transported from the palaces of the declining European aristocracy, together with objects from the treasure chambers of kings, to the homes of the American rich. After the Armory Show—for more than one reason, but especially because of the growth of modern art—the collecting of old masters began to lose its former prestige, just as the reproduction of Renaissance villas and chateaux gave way to the design of modern homes. The cultural dignity of modern painting and sculpture was also recognized by the law; within a year of the Show, one of its most enthusiastic supporters, the collector John Quinn,[2] persuaded the government to remove the import duty on foreign works of contemporary art.

The three hundred thousand or more visitors who saw the exhibition in the three cities were a far greater number than had attended the annual salons of the National Academy, although smaller than the public that wandered through the picture galleries at the World's Fairs. But the 1913 show was of art alone, unlike the Fairs where art was one spectacle among many, beside machines, manufactured goods, and popular amusements. Here one came for art itself, whether one took it seriously or to satisfy curiosity about a widely advertised sensational matter. And as art it was more pointedly contemporary, in a new and radical sense—unknown to previous exhibitions, and standard from then on for shows of independent art—namely, that modernity as such was a quality, so that people looking at these works were led to consider them as belonging to the moment, to the year 1913, like the new airplanes and automobiles and the current ideas of science or the aims of the advanced political groups. Indeed, the Armory Show had something of the role in art that the Halls of Machines, with their exciting display of new inventions, had for the public feeling about technology at the World's Fairs. The contemporary in art—or living art, as it was called—did not mean simply whatever was done at the time, since the old styles and the new, the imitative and inventive, were on view together, side by side. It meant rather the progressively contemporary, that which modified the acquired past and opened the way to a still newer future. And this sense of the growing present led to a revision of the image of the past, so that one could single out in history a family of the great moderns of the past, those artists whose independence had transformed art. For them, a room had been reserved at the Armory Show; Ingres, Delacroix, Corot, Courbet and the Impressionists, artists whom the academicians acknowledged as masters, were presented beside the modern insurgents as their ancestors, a line of great innovating spirits. The plan of the Show contained then a lesson and a program of modernity. It was also a lesson of internationalism, although the emblem of the Show was the native pine, a reminder of the American revolution as well as of the eternal greenness of the tree of art. Since the awareness of modernity as the advancing historical present was forced upon the spectator by the art of Spaniards, Frenchmen, Russians, Germans, Englishmen, and Americans, of whom many were working in Paris,

[2] John Quinn: Irish-American attorney (1870–1942) who was a patron of leading figures of modern art and especially literature, including W. B. Yeats and James Joyce.

away from their native lands, this concept of the time was universalized; the moment belonged to the whole world; Europe and America were now united in a common cultural destiny, and people here and abroad were experiencing the same modern art that surmounted local traditions.

II

What was the nature of this new art? In what lay its novelty and its challenge to the art it came to supplant? . . .

1. In only a few works had representation been abandoned entirely. But in many that preserved recognizable object-forms, these were strangely distorted. It is not easy to say which was more disturbing, nature deformed or the canvas without nature. Both seemed to announce the end of painting as an art.

For millennia, painting had been an art of image-making. The painter represented imaginary religious, mythical, or historical subjects, or he imaged the world before him in landscapes, portraits, and still-lifes. The word, "picture," which literally means: "what is painted," had come to stand for any representation, even a verbal or mental one. All through the nineteenth century, however, artists and writers had proposed that the true aim of painting should not be to tell a story or to imitate a natural appearance, but to express a state of feeling, an idea, a fancy, or, aspiring to the condition of music, to create a harmony of colors and forms. Yet the image remained the indispensable foundation of painting. The coming of photography about 1840 strengthened the conviction of artists that the purely aesthetic or expressive was the goal of art; but for sixty years afterwards image-painting continued and even became more realistic, exploring new aspects of appearance, light, atmosphere, and movement—a fact that speaks against the view that modern art arose as an answer to photography. In the twentieth century the ideal of an imageless art of painting was realized for the first time, and the result was shocking—an arbitrary play with forms and colors that had only a vague connection with visible nature. Some painters had discovered that by accenting the operative elements of art—the stroke, the line, the patch, the surface of the canvas—and by disengaging these from the familiar forms of objects, and even by eliminating objects altogether, the painting assumed a more actively processed appearance, the aspect of a thing made rather than a scene represented, a highly ordered creation referring more to the artist than to the world of external things. The picture also became in this way a more powerful, direct means of conveying feeling or, at least, the interior patterns of feeling; the strokes and spots, in their degree of contrast, in their lightness or weight, their energy or passivity, were unmistakably "physiognomic." And in paintings that still preserved some representation, beside the new self-evidence of the painter's marks with their vague intimations and tendencies of feeling, the image acquired an aspect of fantasy or of some obscure region of thought. It was such positive effects rather than a search for some presumed absolute or long-lost ideal essence of art that guided the artists in their approach to abstraction. They were neither geometers nor logicians nor philosophers, but painters who had discovered new possibilities in the processes of their art. Much was said about purity or form in itself, but in practice this meant a particular economy and rigor in employing the new means.

The visitors at the Show had all seen nonrepresentational works of art before—geometric ornament is an example—and many who enjoyed the new art tried to justify it by the analogy of rugs and textiles. (To which Theodore Roosevelt in a critical, though not unfriendly review of the Show, answered that he preferred the Navajo rug in his bathroom.) But this explanation was unconvincing and obscured the nature of the new art. Decoration, even in its freer forms, is servile, bound to some practical object, and bears within its patterns the trace of adaptation. Ornament embellishes its object, makes it richer, more charming or prominent; it accents the marginal or terminal parts of its carrier—the surface, the base, the border, or crown—but has no intensity and rarely invites us into itself. We can imagine the pattern of a rug continued indefinitely or enlarged, without much loss of effect; but how would we respond to a Rembrandt portrait exactly repeated several times on the same wall? In past arts of ornament, the whole was legible at once as a simple structure; a particular unit was expanded in a fairly regular way; given a part of the work, one could easily reconstruct the whole. In the new art of "abstract" painting there is no obvious nuclear motif or simple rule of design. No less than in the latest image-painting, something intimate, close to the artist himself, was projected, which required of the spectator an active engagement and response. The unpredictable character of the whole and of the details of form reflected the contingencies of life itself, with its changing complication, conflicts and occasions of freedom. (Not by chance had modern architects, who admired the new painting and sculpture, eliminated all ornament from their buildings.) Only weak imitators who failed to grasp the organic complexity of the new works, passive personalities who preferred the "decorative" in image-painting as well, interpreted Cubism or abstract art as a kind of ornament of the canvas. But for the unprepared or prejudiced observer the strongest works were chaotic and illegible, without the obvious course of an ornament; they possessed an intricacy very close to the formless, hence requiring a most tense control by the artist. A protest against formlessness and unintelligibility had been addressed in the 1870s to the Impressionist masters whose pictures of landscapes were also informal in design, offering to the spectator a turbulent surface of little brushstrokes, many of which could not be matched with a represented object. The "impression" struck people then as something arbitrary, and several decades passed before it came to be widely recognized and enjoyed as the artist's elaboration of a common experience. Impressionism was in fact the true forerunner of this art in so far as it translated on the canvas the "subjective" moment in vision (including the induced complementary colors), as well as the shapeless, diffused, unlocalized components of the landscape due to the light and atmosphere, giving at the same time a new tangibility and independence to the crust of pigment. But while the vision of an Impressionist painter was tied to a moment and place that could still be recaptured through the image of the subject (however much this subject had been transformed by the brushwork—and the image was often most faithful through this vagueness), in the new art the transformation was more radical and complete, and the starting-point often something more distinctly personal than the impression of a landscape.

Imageless painting of this kind—without objects, yet with a syntax as complex as that of an art of representation—was a revolution in the concept of art. The image had pointed to something external to the artist, an outer world to which he conformed or from which he took his most cherished values. It had not mattered whether the image was symbolical or accurate or free; whatever its style, it carried the spectator to a common sphere beyond art in nature, religion, myth, history, or everyday life. The represented objects possessed qualities that often provided a bridge to the qualities of the painting. But in the new art this kind of organizer of the observer's attention had largely disappeared. Now for the first time the content of the art was constituted by the special world of the artist, whether as personality or painter. His feelings, his operations, his most specialized and subtle perceptions, furnished the primary themes of his art. And he trained himself to perceive, feel, and design in such a way as to realize to the highest degree the freedom and self-sufficiency of his work, seeking for means that would contribute most to the desired independence and fertility of the artistic act.

The artists who abandoned the image completed a long process of dethronement of an ancient hierarchy within the subject-matter of art. In the Western tradition, the greatest works had been judged to be those with the noblest subjects. Art with themes of religion, history, and myth was conceded an intrinsic superiority. By the middle of the nineteenth century, with the decline of aristocratic and religious institutions, the more intimate themes of persons, places, and things had come to be regarded as no less valid than the others; only the personal and the artistic mattered in judging a work of art. From the viewpoint of the artists who were aware of this development of the subjects, the new art was the most emancipated of all, the most advanced in the humanizing of culture, indeed the most spiritual too, since only what was immediately given in feeling and thought, unfettered by exterior objects, was admitted to the work of art.

It was objected that such an art would cut off the artist from others, that he would end by communicating only with himself. But the fact that so many painters and sculptors adopted this art and created freely within it, learning from one another and producing an astonishing variety of work, showed that abstraction had a common human basis; it was not so arbitrary and private as had seemed.

But even the artists who retained some links with the world of objects, without submitting to the strict requirement of likeness, were criticized as eccentrics; they were told that if one accepted some natural forms, a consistent representation was necessary. In time it became clear that precisely this free play of object-forms and invented forms gave to such works their peculiar expressiveness; here too the active presence of the artist was felt in the power of the operative elements of stroke, spot, and surface, and in the transformation of the world of objects.

2. Besides taking the observer into a no-man's land of imageless painting, where he had great trouble in finding his way, the new art disturbed him by the intensity of its colors and forms. To many cultivated eyes, brought up on the old masters, these works were not only meaningless, but altogether without taste. An artist like Matisse, who represented objects and was respected for the skill of his drawings, employed shockingly strong tones and abrupt contrasts, and scored his outlines emphatically in black. The brush-strokes of a Kandinsky, a Rouault, or a Vlaminck were a violent assault on the canvas. The normally courteous critic, Royal Cortissoz,[3] described a Kandinsky "improvisation" as "fragments of refuse thrown out of a butcher's shop upon a bit of canvas"; and another, more liberal writer spoke of Matisse's art as "blatantly inept" and "essentially epileptic." It is true that the qualities of intense works of art seem more drastic when first shown and in time lose their flagrancy; Romantic and Impressionist paintings that had appeared outrageous in their relative formlessness and high color today look obvious in composition and even subdued in tone. But in the art of the last sixty or seventy years, especially since Van Gogh, there has been a mounting intensity, of which the effect is not reduced by long acquaintance with the works. (At the other end of the spectrum of modern expressiveness is a kind of negative intensity, not always less difficult than the positive kind and no less striking, a search for faint nuances, for an ultimate in delicacy and bareness, that still surprises us; it appeared in Whistler, Monet, and Redon, and more recently in works of Malevich and Klee, among others.)

In the painting of the seventeenth to the nineteenth century the elements were graded and tempered, and brought into a smooth harmony dominated by a particular color or key; the whole lay within a middle range and extremes were avoided. Light and shade softened the colors, the edges of objects were finely blurred in atmosphere and shadows, contrasts were mitigated by many qualifying tones, and objects were set back at some distance from the picture plane. Nothing was stated brusquely or loudly. The high examples of intensity of color were Titian, Rubens, and Delacroix, artists of mellowed aspect who subdued their strongest tones by light and shadow.

Beside this measured art, the new painters seem to be coarse ruffians, and their art a reversion to barbarism. These artists were aware of their own savagery and admired the works in the ethnological museums, the most primitive remains of the Middle Ages, folk art and children's art, all that looked bold and näive. In this love of the primitive as a stronger, purer humanity, the moderns built upon a novel taste of the nineteenth century; the realists of the 1840s and 1850s—lovers of the sincere in art and life—had discovered the beauty of children's drawings and popular imagery and the carvings of savages. But now for the first time the intensity and simplicity of primitive color and drawing were emulated seriously. Before that, even in Gauguin's art, the primitive qualities were still subject to the naturalism and tempering devices, the atmosphere, depth, and light and shade of civilized European art. These sophisticated means were not abandoned in the twentieth century, but they were no longer a rule.

[3] Royal Cortissoz: (1869–1948); art critic for the New York *Herald* from 1891 on.

The primitive aspect was hardly a return to a savage or archaic art, as inattentive critics supposed. Comparing a Matisse or Picasso with a primitive painting, one recognizes in the moderns the sensibility of a thoughtful disciplined artist, always alert to new possibilities. The simplicity of the primitive is a fixed, often rigid style with a limited range of elements, and pervades his entire work; in the modern it is only a quality of certain aspects. Like the intricacy of composition already mentioned, which is not less complex than that of the most realistic art of the nineteenth century, the color includes besides the new intensities rare chords, off-tones, and subtle combinations—the heritage of the post-Renaissance palette applied with a new freedom. For the moderns the saturated colors, the forceful outlines, and geometric forms were a rediscovery of elementary potencies of the medium. They were more than aesthetic, for through them one affirmed the value of the feelings as essential human forces unwisely neglected or suppressed by a utilitarian or hypocritically puritanic society. Together with this corrective simplicity and intensity, which seemed to revive a primitive layer of the self, like the child's and the savage's, and which gave a new vitality to art, the painters admitted to their canvases, with much wonder, gaiety and courage, uncensored fancies and associations of thought akin to the world of dreams; and in this double primitivism of the poetic image and the style they joined hands with the moralists, philosophers, and medical psychologists who were exploring hidden regions and resources of human nature in a critical, reforming spirit. The artists' search for a more intense expression corresponded to new values of forthrightness, simplicity, and openness, to a joyous vitality in everyday life.

3. A third disturbing innovation, related to the others, was the loosening of technique. It had begun even before Impressionism, which was attacked in the 1870s and '80s for its frightful daubing of paint. The later artists outdid this freedom, enlarging and weighting the brush-strokes and painting more sketchily, sometimes with an unconstrained fury. The old conception of painting as a magic art, the source of a jeweled, mysteriously luminous surface of impastos[4] and glazes, was abandoned for simpler, franker means. The new painters were no less sensitive to the fabric of their work, but, concerned with immediacy of effect and with the elementary expressiveness of colors and forms, they found the inherited standards of *facture*[5] an obstacle to their aims. As practiced by conservative contemporaries, the old craftsmanship had become an empty, useless skill, an elaborate cookery, that had lost its original savor. Some of the moderns adopted instead the bare coat of flat color, the house-painter's method, as better suited to their ends; or they devised still other sketchy techniques and new textures with a greater range of expression than the old. Just before the Armory Show, the Cubists, with a sublime daring or impudence, had begun to replace the sacred substance of oil paint by pasted paper, newsprint, sand, and other

[4] impastos: Painting technique in which the paint is laid on the surface very thickly, so that the brush or painting knife strokes are visible.

[5] *facture:* French for the way in which a work of art is made; literally, "the making" of something.

vulgar materials, which were applied to the canvas with a playful humor. Among the sculptors, too, the traditional marble and bronze were losing their aura of intrinsic beauty; roughly finished stone and plaster, cast stone, wood, brass, and new alloys became more frequent in this art. Most astonishing of all were the open sculptures of metal without pedestal or frame, pure constructions like industrial objects, suspended from the wall or ceiling; these first appeared shortly after the Armory Show and have transformed the character of sculpture in our time. Just as there was no longer a superior subject-matter in art, the privileged techniques and materials were brought down to a common level of substances and means, including those of modern industry and everyday use. The new materials and processes of sculpture possess within their commonplaceness a poetic appeal, like that of the vernacular in modern verse; they have also awakened the observer to the qualities of materials in their native and processed states, and to the beauty of the technical as an inventive manipulation of forms.

III

It would be surprising if such an art, introduced full-grown to an unprepared public and to artists who were bound to tradition, met with no resistance.

20 The modernists took this for granted; they knew that all the advanced movements of the nineteenth century, since the Romantic, had been violently attacked, and it had become a platitude of criticism that in every age innovators have had to fight against misunderstanding. This view of the original artist as a martyr, and of the development of art as a bitter struggle between partisans of opposed styles, is hardly borne out by history. The great artists of the Renaissance who created the new forms were recognized early in their careers and received important commissions—Masaccio, van Eyck, Donatello, Leonardo, Raphael, and Titian are examples. Conflicts had indeed occurred in the sixteenth century, but at no time in the past were they as acute as in the last hundred years, except perhaps in the medieval iconoclastic controversy that arose from factions in church and state, more than from artists or new styles of painting and sculpture. The hostility to novel contemporary art, the long-delayed public recognition of the most original recent artists, point rather to singularities of modern culture. Among these are the great span in the cultural levels of those who support art; the ideological value of competing styles as representative of conflicting social viewpoints; and the extraordinary variability of modern art, which requires from its audience a greater inner freedom and openness to others and to unusual feelings and perceptions than most people can achieve under modern conditions, in spite of the common desire for wider experience. But most important of all perhaps is the changed relation of culture to institutional life. Past art, attached to highly organized systems of church, aristocracy, and state, or to the relatively closed, stable world of the family, remained in all its innovations within the bounds of widely accepted values, and continued to express feelings and ideas that had emerged or were emerging within these institutions; while

independent modern art, which constructs a more personal, yet unconfined world, often critical of common ideas, receives little or no support from organized groups and must find its first backers among private individuals—many of them artists and amateurs—for whom art is an altogether personal affair. The original modern art is usually far in advance of the public, which shares the artist's freedom and feeling of isolation (in both their agreeable and negative aspects), but has not discovered the sense of its new experience and aspirations still vaguely formulated within the framework of inherited and often contradictory beliefs, and must assimilate gradually—if it does so at all—and most often in a weakened, vulgarized form, the serious artistic expressions emanating from its own world. The inventions of the artist are in this respect unlike the novelties of physical science and technology. These make little claim on the feelings of lay individuals and are accepted at once as gadgets or ideas that can be utilized without personal involvement or shift in general outlook.

At the same time, the very mobility of our culture, the frequent changes of art in the nineteenth century, have weakened the resistance to new styles, although a generation or more is required for the modern forms to penetrate the originally hostile groups. In our day what is defended against the advanced art is itself something fairly recent that was at first equally difficult. . . . The necessary conclusion that all periods are equal in the eyes of God, provided they have their own style, dismayed many who could not easily give up in practice so much that they cherished in past art, and who found nothing of comparable nobility in their own time. What seemed to be a hopeless relativism in this eternal treadmill of stylistic invention—which appeared to some writers a cyclical motion, bringing art back to its primitive states—was surmounted, however, in the modernist's vision of the art of the last few centuries, and even of older art, as a process pointing to a goal: the progressive emancipation of the individual from authority, and the increasing depth of self-knowledge and creativeness through art. While few artists believed that there was progress in art as in science and industry or in social institutions, many were certain that there was, relative to the possibilities of the time, a reactionary and a progressive art, the latter being engaged in a constant effort of discovery, as in science, although the genius of the old painters, like that of Newton and Galileo, was not surpassed. The great artist, in this view, is essentially a revolutionary spirit who remakes his art, disclosing ever new forms. The accomplishment of the past ceases to be a closed tradition of noble content or absolute perfection, but a model of individuality, of history-making effort through continual self-transformation. Far from being the destroyers of eternal values, as their opponents said, the new artists believed themselves to be the true bearers of a great tradition of creativeness. . . . The movement of modern art had therefore an ethical content; artistic integrity required a permanent concern with self-development and the evolution of art. This belief in a common historical role, dramatized by the opposition of a static, conservative art, gave the artists a solidarity and collective faith, a creative morale, that sustained them at a time when they were most cut off from the public and institutional life.

The issues at stake in the Armory Show were not simply aesthetic problems isolated from all others. To accept the new art meant to further the outlook of modern culture as a whole. The rejection of the new art was for many an expression of an attitude to all modernism. The revolt of students against academic art was not only a break with the art of their elders, but also part of a more general desire for emancipation. People in 1913 overestimated the spiritual unity of the different examples of freedom or progress; they felt that all innovations belonged together, and made up one great advancing cause. Fewer thought, as we do today, that modernity is problematic and includes conflicting, irreconcilable elements.

LEARNING MORE

Inevitably, an essay about a seminal art show refers to any number of artists and artistic movements. The *Ideas Across Time* website has organized these for useful reference. You will find entries or links for the art of the Middle Ages and Renaissance, as well as Impressionism and Cubism. Among those mentioned in this essay, you will find entries or links for Arthur B. Davies, Walter Kuhn, Alfred Stieglitz, Sloan, Rodin, Lautrec, Weber, Maurer, Marin, Hartley, Whistler, Monet, Titian, Rubens, Raphael, Delacroix, Matisse, Picasso, Kandinsky, Rouault, Gaugin, Vlaminck, Klee, Redon, and Malevich.

QUESTIONING THE TEXT

1. How did it happen that an art exhibit intended to showcase nonacademic American artists ended up being dominated by Europeans?
2. Why was the Armory Show especially important?
3. What made the Armory Show "a challenging experience for the public" (par. 5)?
4. How did the Armory Show alter the valuation of contemporary as against older art?
5. What was the major break with the past evidenced in the new art?
6. What was the forerunner of the new art, and why?
7. What constituted the new subject of the new art?
8. In addition to its break with image making, what else distinguishes the new art?
9. Why was the new art misunderstood?

ANALYZING THE WRITER'S CRAFT

1. What is the tone of this essay? Give one or two illustrative examples.
2. How is Schapiro's attitude toward the new art evident in his writing?
3. Why do you think Schapiro formally divides this essay into three parts?

4. Is this essay an example of narrative? Definition? Analysis? Explain and offer examples to support your answer.
5. This is a relatively long essay. How does Schapiro guide the reader from one point to the next?
6. Schapiro offers a large number of judgments in this essay without once using the word "I." What is the effect of the relatively impersonal approach employed in the essay?
7. Schapiro was well known as a remarkable teacher and lecturer. Does this essay have any of the qualities of a lecture?

MAKING CONNECTIONS

1. Would Plato (pp. 565–574) have been thrilled or horrified by modern art? What about Aristotle (pp. 575–579) or Ralph Waldo Emerson (pp. 581–585)?
2. Is there a spiritual dimension to modern art that Schapiro neglects? See, for comparison, Paul Tillich (Chapter 2, pp. 123–130).
3. Compare and contrast Schapiro's understanding of the role of the artist with N. Scott Momaday's (pp. 612–626).

FORMULATING IDEAS FOR WRITING

1. Take one of the main paintings in the Armory Show—say, Duchamp's *Nude Descending a Staircase* (see the *Ideas Across Time* website)—and discuss whether Schapiro's account is confirmed by your experience of viewing this painting.
2. Schapiro downplays the importance of abstract elements in decoration or ornament—that is, the "artfulness" of design. Since his time, decorative arts have gained greater prominence, and are in fact displayed at the Museum of Modern Art in New York. Write an essay that explores the similarities and differences between painting and design.
3. There have been periodic revolts against abstraction by contemporary artists. These artists argue that representation has never lost its validity and ought to be at the center of any artistic practice in any era. This is a view often applauded by a public that is still wary of abstraction and other "excesses" of art in the second half of the twentieth century, when the rigor of the early moderns seems to have been supplanted by an indulgent exhibitionism or apparent neglect of formal discipline. Write an essay that explores the conflicting claims to artistic integrity made by abstract and representational art.
4. Visit your local art museum and write a personal account of your experience of viewing one work from before the modern era and one contemporary work. Include a more or less neutral description of both works in your essay, assuming the reader has not seen either work.

A Century of Cinema (1995)

Susan Sontag

Highly acclaimed as an essayist, novelist, and intellectual, Susan Sontag (1933–2004) is hard to identify either with a particular piece of writing or a school of thought. Many of her best-known works are self-consciously provocative, and she often changed her mind. Born in New York City, she said, "What I like about Manhattan is that it's full of foreigners. The America I live in is the America of the cities. The rest is drive-through." She could be elitist, and as easily, she could embrace popular art. Her breakthrough book of essays, *Against Interpretation* (1966), dismissed the theoretical bent of criticism as reactionary, a usurpation of the work of art for alien purposes. She advocated instead a form of radical aestheticism, a kind of updated art for art's sake (see Oscar Wilde, pp. 587–588). At the same time, she often wrote about politics, usually from moral perspective.

Susan Sontag was raised in Arizona and Los Angeles, and she studied as an undergraduate at the University of Chicago. At the age of seventeen, she married one of her professors, the social thinker Philip Rieff, whom she divorced eight years later. In the late 1950s, she settled in Paris and immersed herself in French films and French philosophy. Her work subsequently bore the mark of French experimental fiction. In 1958, she returned to New York, where she became an important presence in the circle of New York intellectuals.

In the late 1970s, she was diagnosed with breast cancer, an experience that resulted in her book *Illness as Metaphor* (1978). At this time, she had also turned her attention increasingly to visual art, publishing *On Photography* in 1977. The present selection reflects her life-long love of the movies. It first appeared in 1995 in the German newspaper *Frankfurter Rundschau* and was republished in *The New York Times Magazine* in February 1996.

Cinema's hundred years appear to have the shape of a life cycle: an inevitable birth, the steady accumulation of glories, and the onset in the last decade of an ignominious,[1] irreversible decline. This doesn't mean that there won't be any more new films one can admire. But such films will not simply be exceptions; that's true of great achievement in any art. They will have to be heroic violations of the norms and practices which now govern moviemaking everywhere in the capitalist and would-be capitalist world—which is to say, everywhere. And ordinary films, films made purely for entertainment (that is, commercial)

[1] ignominious: involving disgrace.

purposes, will continue to be astonishingly witless; already the vast majority fail resoundingly to appeal to their cynically targeted audiences. While the point of a great film is now, more than ever, to be a one-of-a-kind achievement, the commercial cinema has settled for a policy of bloated, derivative filmmaking, a brazen combinatory or recombinatory art, in the hope of reproducing past successes. Every film that hopes to reach the largest possible audience is designed as some kind of remake. Cinema, once heralded as *the* art of the twentieth century, seems now, as the century closes numerically, to be a decadent art.

Perhaps it is not cinema which has ended but only cinephilia—the name of the distinctive kind of love that cinema inspired. Each art breeds its fanatics. The love movies aroused was more imperial. It was born of the conviction that cinema was an art unlike any other: quintessentially modern; distinctively accessible; poetic and mysterious and erotic and moral—all at the same time. Cinema had apostles (it was like religion). Cinema was a crusade. Cinema was a world view. Lovers of poetry or opera or dance don't think there is *only* poetry or opera or dance. But lovers of cinema could think there was only cinema. That the movies encapsulated everything—and they did. It was both the book of art and the book of life.

As many have noted, the start of moviemaking a hundred years ago was, conveniently, a double start. In that first year, 1895, two kinds of films were made, proposing two modes of what cinema could be: cinema as the transcription of real, unstaged life (the Lumière brothers) and cinema as invention, artifice, illusion, fantasy (Méliès).[2] But this was never a true opposition. For those first audiences watching the Lumière brothers' *The Arrival of a Train at La Ciotat Station,* the camera's transmission of a banal sight was a fantastic experience. Cinema began in wonder, the wonder that reality can be transcribed with such magical immediacy. All of cinema is an attempt to perpetuate and to reinvent that sense of wonder.

Everything begins with that moment, one hundred years ago, when the train pulled into the station. People took movies into themselves, just as the public cried out with excitement, actually ducked, as the train seemed to move toward *them.* Until the advent of television emptied the movie theatres, it was from a weekly visit to the cinema that you learned (or tried to learn) how to strut, to smoke, to kiss, to fight, to grieve. Movies gave you tips about how to be attractive, such as . . . it looks good to wear a raincoat even when it isn't raining. But whatever you took home from the movies was only a part of the larger experience of losing yourself in faces, in lives that were *not* yours—which is the more inclusive form of desire embodied in the movie experience. The strongest experience was simply to surrender to, to be transported by, what was on the screen. You wanted to be kidnapped by the movie.

5 The prerequisite of being kidnapped was to be overwhelmed by the physical presence of the image. And the conditions of "going to the movies" secured

[2] In 1895, Auguste and Louis Jean Lumiere perfected the Cinematographe—in effect, the first movie camera. Georges Melies (1861–1938) filmed the first nondocumentary films.

that experience. To see a great film only on television isn't to have really seen that film. (This is equally true of those made for TV, like Fassbinder's *Berlin Alexanderplatz* and the two *Heimat* films of Edgar Reitz.)[3] It's not only the difference of dimensions: the superiority of the larger-than-you image in the theatre to the little image on the box at home. The conditions of paying attention in a domestic space are radically disrespectful of film. Since film no longer has a standard size, home screens can be as big as living room or bedroom walls. But you are still in a living room or a bedroom, alone or with familiars. To be kidnapped, you have to be in a movie theatre, seated in the dark among anonymous strangers.

No amount of mourning will revive the vanished rituals—erotic, ruminative[4]—of the darkened theatre. The reduction of cinema to assaultive images, and the unprincipled manipulation of images (faster and faster cutting) to be more attention-grabbing, have produced a disincarnated, lightweight cinema that doesn't demand anyone's full attention. Images now appear in any size and on a variety of surfaces: on a screen in a theatre, on home screens as small as the palm of your hand or as big as a wall, on disco walls and megascreens hanging above sports arenas and the outsides of tall public buildings. The sheer ubiquity of moving images has steadily undermined the standards people once had both for cinema as art at its most serious and for cinema as popular entertainment.

In the first years there was, essentially, no difference between cinema as art and cinema as entertainment. And *all* films of the silent era—from the masterpieces of Feuillade, D. W. Griffith, Dziga Vertov, Pabst, Murnau, King Vidor[5] to the most formula-ridden melodramas and comedies—look, are, better than most of what was to follow. With the coming of sound, the image-making lost much of its brilliance and poetry, and commercial standards tightened. This way of making movies—the Hollywood system—dominated filmmaking for about twenty-five years (roughly from 1930 to 1955). The most original directors, like Erich von Stroheim and Orson Welles,[6] were defeated by the system and eventually went into artistic exile in Europe—where more or less the same quality-defeating system was in place with lower budgets;

[3] Rainer Werner Fassbinder (1946–1982) and Edgard Reitz (b. 1932) are German film directors.

[4] ruminative: contemplative.

[5] Louis Feuillade (1873–1925) launched pulp fantasy serials as a movie genre; David Wark Griffith (1875–1948), the greatest American silent film director, is best known for his epic film *The Birth of a Nation* (1915); Dziga Vertov (Denis Arkadyevich Kaufman, 1896–1954), Soviet filmmaker, used his camera as if it were the human eye; Georg Wilhelm Pabst (1885–1967) created montage; Friedrich Wilhlem Murnau (1889–1931), one of the poets of the early cinema, is considered to have made three of the greatest movies ever made—*Nosferatu* (1922), *The Last Laugh* (1924), and *Sunrise* (1927); King Vidor (1894–1982) directed the black-and-white Kansas sequences in *The Wizard of Oz* (1939).

[6] The German director Eric Von Stroheim (1885–1957) is best known for *Greed* (1925). The legendary American actor and director Orson Welles (1915–1985) is identified with his film about a monomaniacal newspaper magnate, *Citizen Kane* (1941).

Napoleon, 1927.

only in France were a large number of superb films produced throughout this period. Then, in the mid-1950s, vanguard ideas took hold again, rooted in the idea of cinema as a craft pioneered by the Italian films of the early postwar era. A dazzling number of original, passionate films of the highest seriousness got made with new actors and tiny crews, went to film festivals (of which there were more and more), and from there, garlanded with festival prizes, into movie theatres around the world. This golden age actually lasted as long as twenty years.

It was at this specific moment in the hundred-year history of cinema that going to movies, thinking about movies, talking about movies became a passion among university students and other young people. You fell in love not just with actors but with cinema itself. Cinephilia had first become visible in the 1950s in France: its forum was the legendary film magazine *Cahiers du Cinéma* (followed by similarly fervent magazines in Germany, Italy, Great Britain, Sweden, the United States, Canada). Its temples, as it spread throughout Europe and the Americas, were the cinematheques and film clubs specializing in films from the past and directors' retrospectives. The 1960s and early 1970s were the age of feverish moviegoing, with the full-time cinephile always hoping to find a seat as close as possible to the big screen, ideally the third row center. "One can't live without Rossellini," declares a character in Bertolucci's *Before the Revolution* (1964)—and means it.

The 400 Blows, 1959.

Cinephilia—a source of exultation in the films of Godard and Truffaut and the early Bertolucci and Syberberg;[7] a morose lament in the recent films of Nanni Moretti[8]—was mostly a Western European affair. The great directors of "the other Europe" (Zanussi in Poland, Angelopoulos in Greece, Tarkovsky and Sokurov in Russia, Jancsó and Tarr in Hungary) and the great Japanese directors (Ozu, Mizoguchi, Kurosawa, Naruse, Oshima, Imamura) have tended not to be cinephiles, perhaps because in Budapest or Moscow or Tokyo or Warsaw or Athens there wasn't a chance to get a cinematheque education. The distinctive thing about cinephile taste was that it embraced both "art" films and popular films. Thus, European cinephilia had a romantic relation to the films of certain directors in Hollywood at the apogee of the studio system: Godard for Howard Hawks, Fassbinder for Douglas Sirk. Of course, this moment—when cinephilia emerged—was also the moment when the Hollywood studio system was breaking up. It seemed that moviemaking had re-won the right to experiment; cinephiles could *afford* to be passionate (or sentimental) about the old

[7] The leading directors of the French New Wave of the late 1950s and 1960s are Jean-Luc Godard (b. 1930), known for *Breathless* (1959), and François Truffaut (1932–1984), whose films include *The 400 Blows* (1959) and *Jules and Jim* (1962). The Italian director Bernardo Berolucci's (b. 1940) work includes the Marlon Brando movie *Last Tango in Paris* (1973). Hans-Jürgen Syberberg (b. 1935) is a German director, best known for his *Parsifal* (1988).

[8] The Italian director Nanni Moretti (b. 1953) is best known for *Caro Diario* (*Dear Diary*, 1993).

Hollywood genre films. A host of new people came into cinema, including a generation of young film critics from *Cahiers du Cinéma*; the towering figure of that generation, indeed of several decades of filmmaking anywhere, was Jean-Luc Godard. A few writers turned out to be wildly talented filmmakers: Alexander Kluge in Germany, Pier Paolo Pasolini in Italy. (The model for the writer who turns to filmmaking actually emerged earlier, in France, with Pagnol in the 1930s and Cocteau in the 1940s; but it was not until the 1960s that this seemed, at least in Europe, normal.) Cinema appeared to be reborn.

For some fifteen years there was a profusion of masterpieces, and one allowed oneself to imagine that this would go on forever. To be sure, there was always a conflict between cinema as an industry and cinema as an art, cinema as routine and cinema as experiment. But the conflict was not such as to make impossible the making of wonderful films, sometimes within and sometimes outside of mainstream cinema. Now the balance has tipped decisively in favor of cinema as an industry. The great cinema of the 1960s and 1970s has been thoroughly repudiated. Already in the 1970s Hollywood was plagiarizing and banalizing the innovations in narrative method and editing of successful new European and ever-marginal independent American films. Then came the catastrophic rise in production costs in the 1980s, which secured the worldwide reimposition of industry standards of making and distributing films on a far more coercive, this time truly global, scale. The result can be seen in the melancholy fate of some of the greatest directors of the last decades. What place is there today for a maverick like Hans Jürgen Syberberg, who has stopped making films altogether, or for the great Godard, who now makes films about the history of film on video? Consider some other cases. The internationalizing of financing and therefore of casts was a disaster for Andrei Tarkovsky[9] in the last two films of his stupendous, tragically abbreviated career. And these conditions for making films have proved to be as much an artistic disaster for two of the most valuable directors still working: Krzysztof Zanussi (*The Structure of Crystals, Illumination, Spiral, Contract*) and Theo Angelopoulos (*Reconstruction, Days of '36, The Travelling Players*). And what will happen now to Béla Tarr (*Damnation, Satantango*)? And how will Aleksandr Sokurov (*Save and Protect, Days of Eclipse, The Second Circle, Stone, Whispering Pages*) find the money to go on making films, his sublime films, under the rude conditions of Russian capitalism?

Predictably, the love of cinema has waned. People still like going to the movies, and some people still care about and expect something special, necessary from a film. And wonderful films are still being made: Mike Leigh's *Naked,* Gianni Amelio's *Lamerica,* Hou Hsiao-hsien's *Goodbye South, Goodbye,* and Abbas Kiarostami's *Close-Up* and Koker trilogy. But one hardly finds anymore, at least among the young, the distinctive cinephilic love of movies, which is not simply love of but a certain *taste* in films (grounded in a vast appetite for seeing and reseeing as much as possible of cinema's glorious past). Cinephilia itself has come

[9] Andrei Tarkovsky's (1932–1986) work was censored in his native Soviet Union but gained him an international reputation.

Breathless, 1959.

under attack, as something quaint, outmoded, snobbish. For cinephilia implies that films are unique, unrepeatable, magic experiences. Cinephilia tells us that the Hollywood remake of Godard's *Breathless* cannot be as good as the original. Cinephilia has no role in the era of hyperindustrial films. For by the very range and eclecticism of its passions, cinephilia cannot help but sponsor the idea of the film as, first of all, a poetic object; and cannot help but incite those outside the movie industry, like painters and writers, to want to make films, too. It is precisely this that must be defeated. That has been defeated.

If cinephilia is dead, then movies are dead . . . no matter how many movies, even very good ones, go on being made. If cinema can be resurrected, it will only be through the birth of a new kind of cine-love.

LEARNING MORE

Sontag's death in 2004 produced a spate of illuminating reminiscences and reassessments of her work. You can access some of these comments on the *Ideas Across Time* website.

QUESTIONING THE TEXT

1. Why does Sontag use the word "cinema" instead of "movies"?
2. Why are the great days of the cinema over?

3. What made moviegoing in its early days—the days of silent movies—so enthralling?
4. How has the "ubiquity of moving images" (par. 5) ruined the experience of moviegoing?
5. What is cinephilia? Why did it arise in France in the 1950s?
6. How has the conflict between art and business in the cinema ended the era of cinephilia?

ANALYZING THE WRITER'S CRAFT

1. For whom is Sontag writing? Why do you think so?
2. Sontag makes many allusions to foreign filmmakers whose work is unlikely ever to have reached the nation's cineplexes. What is the effect of these necessarily obscure allusions on the average reader—can we get her point anyway? Are we put off? Does Sontag know most of her readers will never have seen many of the films she names? Or does she assume no one uninterested in cinema will read her? Or does she want to get these names out so they may gain a wider audience?
3. Discuss the impact of two or three of Sontag's aphoristic statements ("All of cinema is an attempt to perpetuate and reinvent that sense of wonder," par. 3). Do her aphorisms convey complex ideas in a powerfully compact form? Or is Sontag just showing off in catchy sentences?
4. Sontag places at the center of the history of the cinema that age of the cinephile—in fact, the age of her young adulthood. Does the essay reflect a nostalgic look backward to the era of her lost youth? Explain.
5. Nostalgic or not, the essay depends on numerous contrasts between then and now. Choose two examples that especially capture the difference between today's commercialization and the earlier eras of film.
6. Sontag says that first of all film needs to be seen as "a poetic object" (par. 11). Show how her writing tries to convey this sense of film as poetic object.

MAKING CONNECTIONS

1. More than other writers in this book, Sontag identifies herself as a world citizen, a cosmopolitan. Is her outlook an implicit critique of those writers who seem obsessed with their experiences as Americans, even when, as in the case of James Baldwin (Chapter 1, pp. 29–35), they find themselves in Paris?
2. Paul Tillich (Chapter 2, pp. 123–130) took Sontag under his wing when she studied briefly as a graduate student at Harvard. Does their work show any affinities? Explain.
3. Is Sontag's account of the inevitable evolution in the life of the cinema—birth, glory, decline—similar to the attenuating impact of technology, such as photography, discussed by Daniel J. Boorstin (Chapter 5, pp. 390–402)?
4. What debt does Sontag owe to Oscar Wilde (pp. 587–588)?

FORMULATING IDEAS FOR WRITING

1. Sontag is not kind about contemporary movies. They are "astonishingly witless," "bloated," "derivative," and so forth. Choose two movies you have seen recently, and show how they confirm, or refute, or modify her assessment.
2. Increasingly, people watch movies on tiny screens on their phones or as DVDs on their TV screens at home. Films are now often released to the movie houses at the same time that they are issued on DVD. Sontag says you just can't appreciate a movie if you're not sitting in a darkened theater looking at a huge screen. Write an essay that agrees or takes issue with her view.
3. Once sound came in, cinema "lost much of its brilliance and poetry," Sontag says. Write an essay exploring the strengths and drawbacks of silent versus sound movies. Alternatively, write about the strengths and drawbacks of black-and-white versus color movies.
4. Write an essay that explores the meanings and connotations of the words *cinema*, *film*, and *movie*.

The Arrowmaker (1997)

N. Scott Momaday

There can be few people who appreciate the multiplex story of the American West more than Navarre Scott Momaday. Born at the Kiowa Indian Hospital in Lawton, Oklahoma, on February 7, 1934, Momaday was the son of a Kiowa Indian father and an English/Cherokee mother. He grew up in a Pan-Indian environment that early roused in him a love for the words of a great range of languages, among them Kiowa, Navajo, Jemez Pueblo, Spanish, and English. Educated in reservation schools—where both his parents worked as teachers—Momaday chose in his senior year of high school to attend a military academy in Virginia because of his attraction to the ancestral world of his mother, who was born in Kentucky. The pivotal event in his education, occurred when, after receiving his B.A. from the University of New Mexico, he was selected by the poet and critic Yvor Winters to be the recipient of a poetry fellowship at Stanford University. Under Winters' tutelage, Momaday went on to complete a doctorate in literature at Stanford in 1963.

In 1969, Momaday's first novel, *House Made of Dawn*, won the Pulitzer Prize for fiction. Also in that year, he published a collection of Kiowa tales, *The Way to Rainy Mountain*, illustrated by his father. Since then he has not only published celebrated collections of poems, essays, and memoirs but also produced paintings and designs. His more recent books are illustrated by his own paintings and etchings. Among his major publications are the poetry collections *The Gourd Dancer* (1976) and *In the Presence of the Sun* (1992), the memoir *The Names* (1976), and a book of poetry and prose, *In the Bear's House* (1999). Momaday is the Regents' Professor of the Humanities at the University of Arizona.

The present selection comes from Momaday's influential collection of essays and stories *The Man Made of Words* (1997), which is dedicated to Yvor Winters and his wife, the writer Janet Lewis. In this essay, Momaday explores the nature of oral tradition, the relation between warriorlike actions and story, and the meaning of what he considers to be the ultimate story about stories. Momaday's account is an especially resonant illustration of how to read.

The story of the arrowmaker, the "man made of words," is perhaps the first story I was told. My father loved to tell it to me, and I loved to hear it. It remains for me one of the most intensely vital stories in my experience, not only because it is a supernal[1] example of the warrior idea—an adventure story in the best sense—but because it is a story about story, about the efficacy of language and the power of words. One does not come to the end of such a story. I have lived with the story of the arrowmaker for many years, and I am sure that I do not yet understand it in all of its consequent meanings. Nor do I expect to understand it so. The stories I keep close to me, day by day, are those that yield more and more of their spirit in time.

If an arrow is well made, it will have tooth marks upon it. That is how you know. The Kiowas made fine arrows and straightened them in their teeth. Then they drew them to the bow to see that they were straight.

Once there was a man and his wife. They were alone at night in their tepee. By the light of a fire the man was making arrows. After a while he caught sight of something. There was a small opening in the tepee where two hides had been sewn together. Someone was there on the outside, looking in. The man went on with his work, but he said to his wife, "Someone is standing outside. Do not be afraid. Let us talk easily, as of ordinary things." He took up an arrow and straightened it in his teeth; then, as it was right for him to do, he drew it to the bow and took aim, first in this direction and then in that. And all the while he was talking, as if to his wife. But this is how he spoke: "I know that you are there on the outside, for I can feel your eyes upon me. If you are a Kiowa, you will understand what I am saying, and you will speak your name." But there was no answer, and the man went on in the same way, pointing the arrow all around. At last his aim fell upon the place where his enemy stood, and he let go of the string. The arrow went straight to the enemy's heart.

Until very recently the story of the arrowmaker has been the private possession of a few, a tenuous[2] link in that most ancient chain of language which we call the oral tradition; tenuous because the tradition itself appears to be so,

[1] supernal: heavenly.

[2] tenuous: flimsy, weak.

for as many times as the story has been told, it has always been but one generation removed from extinction. That is to say, it has been neither more nor less durable than the human voice, and neither more nor less concerned to express the meaning of the human condition.

5 A comparison of the written and oral traditions is of course a matter of the greatest complexity. Those who make this comparison are irrevocably committed to the written tradition. Writing defines the very terms of our existence. We cannot know what it is to exist within an oral tradition, or we cannot know entirely. But we can know more than we do, and it behooves us to learn as much as we can, if for no other reason than to gain possession of invaluable resources that are rightfully ours, to discover, that is, a great and legitimate part of our literary heritage.[3]

Writing engenders in us certain attitudes toward language. It encourages us to take words for granted. Writing has enabled us to store vast quantities of words indefinitely. This is advantageous on the one hand but dangerous on the other. The result is that we have developed a kind of false security where language is concerned, and our sensitivity to language has deteriorated. And we have become in proportion insensitive to silence.

But in the oral tradition one stands in a different relation to language. Words are rare and therefore dear. They are jealously preserved in the ear and in the mind. Words are spoken with great care, and they are heard. They matter, and they must not be taken for granted; they must be taken seriously and they must be remembered.

With respect to the oral tradition of the American Indian, these attitudes are reflected in the character of the songs and stories themselves. Perhaps the most distinctive and important aspect of that tradition is the way in which it reveals the singer's and the storyteller's respect for and belief in language.

At the heart of the American Indian oral tradition is a deep and unconditional belief in the efficacy of language. Words are intrinsically powerful. They are magical. By means of words can one bring about physical change in the universe. By means of words can one quiet the raging weather, bring forth the harvest, ward off evil, rid the body of sickness and pain, subdue an enemy, capture the heart of a lover, live in the proper way, and venture beyond death. Indeed, there is nothing more powerful. When one ventures to speak, when he utters a prayer or tells a story, he is dealing with forces that are supernatural and irresistible. He assumes great risks and responsibilities. He is clear and deliberate in his mind and in his speech; he will be taken at his word. Even so, he knows that he stands the chance of speaking indirectly or inappropriately, or of being mistaken by his hearers, or of not being heard at all. To be careless in the presence of words, on the inside of language, is to violate a fundamental morality.

---

[3] heritage: Pars. 5–9 originally appeared in Momaday's essay "The Native American Voice in American Literature," also found in the collection *The Man Made of Words*.

10 The story of the arrowmaker is a remarkable act of the imagination, a realization of words and meanings that is altogether simple and direct, yet nonetheless rare and profound, and it illustrates more clearly than anything else in my own experience something of the essential character of the imagination—and in particular of that personification which in this instance emerges from it: the man made of words.

It is important that the story of the arrowmaker returns in a special way upon itself. It is about language, after all, and it is therefore part and parcel of its own subject. Virtually, there is no difference between the telling and that which is told. The point of the story lies not so much in what the arrowmaker does, but in what he says—and, indeed, *that* he says it. The principal fact is that he speaks, and in so doing he places his very life in the balance.

It is this aspect of the story which interests me most, for it is here that the language becomes most conscious of itself; here we are very close to the origin and object of literature; here our sense of the verbal dimension is very keen, and we are aware of something in the nature of language that is at once perilous and compelling. "If you are a Kiowa, you will understand what I am saying, and you will speak your name." Everything is ventured in this simple declaration, which is also a question and a plea.

Precisely at this moment is the arrowmaker realized completely, and his reality consists in language. Implicit in his simple speech is all of his definition and all of his destiny, and by implication all of ours. He ventures to speak because he must; language is the repository of his whole knowledge, and it represents the only chance he has for survival. Instinctively and with great care he deals in the most honest and basic way with words. "Let us talk easily, as of ordinary things," he says. And of the ominous unknown he asks only the utterance of a name, only the most nominal[4] sign that he is understood, that a word or a syllable is returned to him on the sheer edge of meaning. But there is no answer, and the arrowmaker knows at once what he has not known before: that his enemy is, and is present, and that he, the arrowmaker, has gained a crucial advantage over him. Make no mistake, the words of the arrowmaker reveal his peril clearly. The presence outside is decidedly an enemy; twice the storyteller tells us so. The venture is complete and irrevocable, and it ends in the restoration of order and well-being.

The story is meaningful. It is so because it is in the nature of language that it proceeds to the formulation of meaning. Moreover, the story of the arrowmaker especially centers upon this procession of words toward meaning. It seems in fact to turn upon the very idea that language involves the elements of risk and responsibility; and in this it seeks to confirm itself. In a word, it seems to say, everything is a risk. That may well be true, and it may also be that the whole of literature rests upon that truth.

15 The story of the arrowmaker is supremely metaphorical; indeed it is acutely and incisively a story about story; it is both an example and a definition of literature. It is complex, and yet it is clear; it seems to give more and more of itself

---

[4] nominal: literally, relating to a name; or, being something in name only.

in time. Clear it is, and yet there is a kind of resistance in it, as in a riddle; it is the richer for that. It is a kind of prism.

The arrowmaker is preeminently the man made of words. He has consummate[5] being in language; it is the world of his origin and of his posterity, and there is no other. But it is a world of definite reality and of infinite possibility. I have come to believe that there is a sense in which the arrowmaker has a quality of being that is more viable than that of men in general—he has nearly a perfect right to be. We can imagine him, and he imagines himself, whole and vital, going on into the unknown darkness and beyond.

And yet the story has it that he is cautious and alone, and we are given to understand that his peril is great and immediate, and that he confronts it in the only way he can. I have no doubt that this is true. Language determines the arrowmaker, and his story determines our literary experience.

A word, then, on an essential irony which marks the story and gives peculiar substance to the man made of words. The storyteller is nameless and unlettered. We know very little about him, except that in the story is his presence and his mask. And that is enough. He tells of his life in language, and of the risk involved. It occurs to us that he is one with the arrowmaker, and that he has survived, by word of mouth, beyond other men. For the storyteller, for the arrowmaker, language does indeed represent the only chance for survival. It is appropriate that he survives in our time and that he has survived over a period of untold generations.

LEARNING MORE

To read more of N. Scott Momaday's work, see the *Ideas Across Time* website.

QUESTIONING THE TEXT

1. Why does Momaday think of the story of the arrowmaker as "one of the most intensely vital stories in my experience" (par. 1)?
2. How was the "existence" of the story "tenuous" until very recently? What changed to make its existence less tenuous?
3. What is the main difference between written and oral literature?
4. How does "the point of the story" lie not in what the arrowmaker does but in what he says?
5. How does this story illustrate "the origin and object of literature" (par. 11)?
6. What is the effect or meaning of the killing of the warrior's enemy in the Kiowa story?
7. How does this story illustrate that "language involves elements of risk and responsibility" (par. 14)?
8. Why does Momaday end his discussion by reference to the storyteller, the narrator?

[5] consummate: perfect.

ANALYZING THE WRITER'S CRAFT

1. What is the effect of Momaday's telling us, in his first sentence, that the story of the arrowmaker is the first story he was ever told?
2. Why does Momaday give us the story entire?
3. Is the story as Momaday presents it "a version" of the story, or the authentic story itself? For example, when this story is told, does it always have the same beginning? What difference would it make if the story simply began with the second paragraph?
4. Upon reading the story, did you find it engrossing? Profound? A story about stories?
5. Why does Momaday tell us that until very recently this story was part of the oral tradition? How does its being put on paper change the story?
6. Write a rough outline of Momaday's interpretive argument. What guides the organization of Momaday's essay? By what steps does he move from opening to closing?
7. By what rhetorical means does Momaday link the act of speaking—language—and survival?
8. How does Momaday establish the connection between the arrowmaker and us?
9. How does Momaday's account alter, amplify, or qualify your original reading of the story?
10. What is the connection between the essay's opening and its closing?

MAKING CONNECTIONS

1. How does Momaday's sense of literature as an act of salvation, literally and figuratively, compare and contrast with the view of Sandra Cisneros (pp. 618–626)? Of Cisneros' note writers?
2. Compare and contrast Momaday's essay with those of Luther Standing Bear (Chapter 3, pp. 187–191) and Leslie Marmon Silko (Chapter 8, pp. 693–694). Are these essays recognizably part of a single national tradition? Explain

FORMULATING IDEAS FOR WRITING

1. Write your own interpretation of the story of the arrowmaker. (Momaday seems to ignore the story's opening. Consider an interpretation that takes the opening to be the key to the story.)
2. In two paragraphs, write down a story that means a lot to you that was told to you when you were a child (or that you read in an illustrated children's book; no fairy tales).
3. Read Momaday's "The American West and the Burden of Belief" (like "The Arrowmaker," also to be found in the collection *The Man Made of Words*),

and discuss Momaday's understanding of the differences between oral and written literature.

4. Discuss Momaday's essay by exploring the connections between, and implications of, his opening and closing paragraphs.

Little Miracles, Kept Promises (1991)

Sandra Cisneros

The only daughter among the seven children of a Mexican father and a Chicana mother, Sandra Cisneros is among the literary pioneers charting new terrain in the ethnically diverse United States of the late twentieth and early twenty-first centuries. In a voice vivid with the accents of crossed-cultures—Spanish and English, Mexican and American—Cisneros writes of the struggle for self-realization of Latina and Latino characters living in, but isolated from, contemporary Middle America by poverty, culture, and prejudice. She has also championed the right of women to an independent sexuality, proudly asserting that she is "nobody's mother and nobody's wife."

Born in Chicago in 1954, Cisneros graduated from Loyola University of Chicago in 1976 and received an M.F.A. from the Iowa Writers' Workshop in 1978. Her widely acclaimed book *The House on Mango Street* was published by the Arte Publico Press of Houston in 1984 and has been translated worldwide. *My Wicked, Wicked Ways*, her first book of poems, appeared in 1987. The present selection first appeared in Cisneros's short story collection *Woman Hollering Creek* (1991), which won the PEN Center West Award for Best Fiction of 1991. In 1995, she received the prestigious MacArthur Foundation Fellowship.

Exvoto Donated as Promised

On the 20th of December of 1988 we suffered a terrible disaster on the road to Corpus Christi. The bus we were riding skidded and overturned near Robstown and a lady and her little girl were killed. Thanks to La Virgen de Guadalupe we are alive, all of us miraculously unharmed, and with no visible scars, except we are afraid to ride buses. We dedicate this retablo to La Virgencita with our affection and gratitude and our everlasting faith.

Familia Arteaga
Alice, Texas
G.R. (Gracias Recibido/Thanks Given)

Blessed Santo Niño de Atocha,

Thank you for helping us when Chapa's truck got stolen. We didn't know how we was going to make it. He needs it to get to work, and this job, well, he's been on probation since we got him to quit drinking. Raquel and the kids are hardly ever afraid of him anymore, and we are proud parents. We don't know how we can repay you for everything you have done for our family. We will light a candle to you every Sunday and never forget you.

Sidronio Tijerina
Brenda A. Camacho de Tijerina
San Angelo, Texas

Dear San Martín de Porres,

Please send us clothes, furniture, shoes, dishes. We need anything that don't eat. Since the fire we have to start all over again and Lalo's disability check ain't much and don't go far. Zulema would like to finish school but I says she can just forget about it now. She's our oldest and her place is at home helping us out I told her. Please make her see some sense. She's all we got.

Thanking you,
Adelfa Vásquez
Escobas, Texas

Dear San Antonio de Padua,

Can you please help me find a man who isn't a pain in the nalgas. There aren't any in Texas, I swear. Especially not in San Antonio.

Can you do something about all the educated Chicanos who have to go to California to find a job. I guess what my sister Irma says is true: "If you didn't get a husband when you were in college, you don't get one."

I would appreciate it very much if you sent me a man who speaks Spanish, who at least can pronounce his name the way it's supposed to be pronounced. Someone please who never calls himself "Hispanic" unless he's applying for a grant from Washington, D.C.

Can you send me a man man. I mean someone who's not ashamed to be seen cooking or cleaning or looking after himself. In other words, a man who acts like an adult. Not one who's never lived alone, never bought his own underwear, never ironed his own shirts, never even heated his own tortillas. In other words, don't send me someone like my brothers who my mother ruined with too much chichi, or I'll throw him back.

I'll turn your statue upside down until you send him to me. I've put up with too much too long, and now I'm just too intelligent, too powerful, too beautiful, too sure of who I am finally to deserve anything less.

Ms. Barbara Ybañez
San Antonio, TX

Dear Niño Fidencio,

I would like for you to help me get a job with good pay, benefits, and retirement plan. I promise you if you help me I will make a pilgrimage to your tomb in Espinazo and bring you flowers. Many thanks.

César Escandón
Pharr, Tejas

DEAR DON PEDRITO JARAMILLO HEALER OF LOS OLMOS

MY NAME IS ENRIQUETA ANTONIA SANDOVAL I LIVE IN SAN MARCOS TX I AM SICK THEY OPERATED ME FROM A KIDNEY AND A TUMOR OF CANCER BUT THANKS TO GOD I AM ALIVE BUT I HAVE TO GET TREATMENTS FOR A YEAR THE KIMO I AM 2½ YEARS OLD BUT MY GRANDMA BROUGHT ME THAT YOU AND OUR LORD WHO IS IN THE HEAVENS WILL CURE ME WITH THIS LETTER THAT I AM DEPOSITING HERE ITS MY GRANDMA WHO IS WRITING THIS I HOPE EVERYBODY WHO SEES THIS LETTER WILL TAKE A MINUTE TO ASK FOR MY HEALTH

ENRIQUETA ANTONIA SANDOVAL
2 AND A HALF YEARS OLD

I LEOCADIA DIMAS VDA DE CORDERO OF SAN MARCOS TX HAVE COME TO PAY THIS REQUEST TO DON PEDRITO THAT MY GRAND-DAUGHTER WILL COME OUT FINE FROM HER OPERATION THANKS TO GOD AND THOSE WHO HELPED SUCH GOOD DOCTORS THAT DID THEIR JOB WELL THE REST IS IN GODS HANDS THAT HE DO HIS WILL MANY THANKS WITH ALL MY HEART.

YOUR VERY RESPECTFUL SERVANT
LEOCADIA

Oh Mighty Poderosos, Blessed Powerful Ones,

You who are crowned in heaven and who are so close to our Divine Savior, I implore your intercession before the Almighty on my behalf. I ask for peace of spirit and prosperity, and that the demons in my path that are the cause of all my woes be removed so that they no longer torment me. Look favorably on this petition and bless me, that I may continue to glorify your deeds with all my heart—santísimo Niño Fidencio, gran General Pancho Villa, bendito Don Pedrito Jaramillo, virtuoso John F. Kennedy, and blessed Pope John Paul. Amen.

Gertrudis Parra
Uvalde, Tejas

Father Almighty,

Teach me to love my husband again. Forgive me.

S. Corpus Christi

Seven African Powers that surround our Savíor—Obatala, Yemaya, Ochún, Orunla, Ogun, Elegua, and Shango—why don't you behave and be good to me? Oh Seven African Powers, come on, don't be bad. Let my Illinois lottery ticket win, and if it does, don't let my cousin Cirilo in Chicago cheat me out of my winnings, since I'm the one who pays for the ticket and all he does is buy it for me each week—if he does even that. He's my cousin, but like the Bible says, better to say nothing than to say nothing nice.

Protect me from the evil eye of the envious and don't let my enemies do me harm, because I've never done a thing wrong to anyone first. Save this good Christian who the wicked have taken advantage of.

Seven Powers, reward my devotion with good luck. Look after me, why don't you? And don't forget me because I never forget you.

Moises Ildefonso Mata
San Antonio, Texas

Virgencita de Guadalupe,

I promise to walk to your shrine on my knees the very first day I get back, I swear, if you will only get the Tortillería la Casa de la Masa to pay me the $253.72 they owe me for two weeks work. I put in 67½ hours that first week and 79 hours the second, and I don't have anything to show for it yet. I calculated with the taxes deducted, I have $253.72 coming to me. That's all I'm asking for. The $253.72 I have coming to me.

I have asked the proprietors Blanquita and Rudy Mondragón, and they keep telling me next week, next week, next week. And it's almost the middle of the third week already and I don't know how I'm going to do it to pay this week's rent, since I'm already behind, and the other guys have loaned me as much as they're able, and I don't know what I'm going to do, I don't know what I'm going to do.

My wife and the kids and my in-laws all depend on what I send home. We are humble people, Virgencita. You know I'm not full of vices. That's how I am. It's been hard for me to live here so far away without seeing my wife, you know. And sometimes one gets tempted, but no, and no, and no. I'm not like that. Please, Virgencita, all I'm asking for is my $253.72. There is no one else I can turn to here in this country, and well, if you can't help me, well, I just don't know.

Arnulfo Contreras
San Antonio, Tejas

Saint Sebastian who was persecuted with arrows and then survived, thank you for answering my prayers! All them arrows that had persecuted me—my brother-in-law Ernie and my sister Alba and their kids—el Junior, la Gloria, and el Skyler—all gone. And now my home sweet home is mine again, and my Dianita bien lovey-dovey, and my kids got something to say to me besides who hit who.

Here is the little gold milagrito I promised you, a little house, see? And it ain't that cheap gold-plate shit either. So now that I paid you back, we're even, right? Cause I don't like for no one to say Victor Lozano don't pay his debts. I pays cash on the line, bro. And Victor Lozano's word like his deeds is solid gold.

Victor A. Lozano
Houston, TX

Dear San Lázaro,

My mother's comadre Demetria said if I prayed to you that like maybe you could help me because you were raised from the dead and did a lot of miracles and maybe if I lit a candle every night for seven days and prayed, you might maybe could help me with my face breaking out with so many pimples. Thank you.

Rubén Ledesma
Hebbronville, Texas

Santísima Señora de San Juan de los Lagos,

We came to see you twice when they brought you to San Antonio, my mother and my sister Yolanda and two of my aunts, Tía Enedina and my Tía Perla, and we drove all the way from Beeville just to visit you and make our requests.

I don't know what my Tía Enedina asked for, she's always so secretive, but probably it had to do with her son Beto who doesn't do anything but hang around the house and get into trouble. And my Tía Perla no doubt complained about her ladies' problems—her ovaries that itch, her tangled fallopians, her uterus that makes her seasick with all its flipping and flopping. And Mami who said she only came along for the ride, lit three candles so you would bless us all and sweep jealousy and bitterness from our hearts because that's what she says every day and every night. And my sister Yoli asked that you help her lose weight because I don't want to wind up like Tía Perla, embroidering altar cloths and dressing saints.

But that was a year ago, Virgencita, and since then my cousin Beto was fined for killing the neighbor's rooster with a flying Big Red bottle, and my Tía Perla is convinced her uterus has fallen because when she walks something inside her rattles like a maraca, and my mother and my aunts are arguing and yelling at each other same as always. And my stupid sister Yoli is still sending away for even stupider products like the Grasa Fantástica, guaranteed to burn away fat—It really works, Tere, just rub some on while you're watching TV—only she's fatter than ever and just as sad.

What I realize is that we all made the trip to San Antonio to ask something of you, Virgencita, we all needed you to listen to us. And of all of us, my mama and sister Yoli, and my aunts Enedina and Perla, of all of us, you granted me my petition and sent, just like I asked, a guy who would love only me because I was tired of looking at girls younger than me walking along the street or riding in cars or standing in front of the school with a guy's arm hooked around their neck.

So what is it I'm asking for? Please, Virgencita. Lift this heavy cross from my shoulders and leave me like I was before, wind on my neck, my arms swinging free, and no one telling me how I ought to be.

Teresa Galindo
Beeville, Texas

Miraculous Black Christ of Esquipulas,

Please make our grandson to be nice to us and stay away from drugs. Save him to find a job and move away from us. Thank you.

Grandma y Grandfather
Harlingen

M3r1c5l45s Bl1ck Chr3st 4f 2sq53p5l1s,

3 1sk y45, L4rd, w3th 1ll my h21rt pl21s2 w1tch 4v2r M1nny B2n1v3d2s wh4 3s 4v2rs21s. 3 l4v2 h3m 1nd 3 d4n't kn4w wh1t t4 d4 1b45t 1ll th3s l4v2 s1dn2ss 1nd sh1m2 th1t f3lls m2.

B2nj1m3n T.
D21 R34 TX

Milagroso Cristo Negro de Esquipulas,

Te ofrezco este retrato de mis niños. Wáchelos, Dios Santo, y si le quitas el trago a mi hijo te prometo prender velitas. Ayúdanos con nuestras cuentas, Señor, y que el cheque del income tax nos llegue pronto para pagar los biles. Danos una buena vida y que les ayudes a mis hijos a cambiar sus modos. Tú que eres tan bondadoso escucha estas peticiones que te pido con todo mi corazón y con toda la fe de mi alma. Ten piedad, Padre mio. Mi nombre es Adela O.

Elizondo
Cotulla TX

Milagroso Cristo Negro,

Thank you por el milagro de haber graduado de high school. Aquí le regalo mi retrato de graduation.

Fito Moroles
Rockport, Texas

Cristo Negro,

Venimos desde muy lejos. Infinitas gracias, Señor. Gracias por habernos escuchado.

Familia Armendáriz G.
Matamoros, Tamps. México

Jesus Christ,

Please keep Deborah Abrego and Ralph S. Urrea together forever.

Love,
Deborah Abrego
Sabinal, Texas

Blessed Virgen de los Remedios,

Señora Dolores Alcalá de Corchado finds herself gravely ill from a complication that resulted after a delicate operation she underwent Thursday last, and from which she was recovering satisfactorily until suffering a hemmorhage Tuesday morning. Please intercede on her behalf. We leave her in the hands of God, that His will be done, now that we have witnessed her suffering and don't know whether she should die or continue this life. Her husband of forty-eight years offers this request with all his heart.

Señor Gustavo Corchado B.
Laredo, Tejas

Madrecita de Dios,

Thank you. Our child is born healthy!

Rene y Janie Garza
Hondo, TX

Saint Jude, patron saint of lost causes,

Help me pass my English 320, British Restoration Literature class and everything to turn out ok.

Eliberto González
Dallas

Virgencita

I've cut off my hair just like I promised I would and pinned my braid here by your statue. Above a Toys "Я" Us name tag that says IZAURA. Along several hospital bracelets. Next to a business card for Sergio's Casa de la Belleza Beauty College. Domingo Reyna's driver's license. Notes printed on the flaps of envelopes. Silk roses, plastic roses, paper roses, roses crocheted out of fluorescent orange yarn. Photo button of a baby in a *charro* hat. Caramel-skinned woman in a white graduation cap and gown. Mean dude in bandanna and tattoos. Oval black and white passport portrait of the sad uncle who never married. A mama in a sleeveless dress watering the porch plants. Sweet boy with new mustache and new soldier uniform. Teenager with a little bit of herself sitting on her lap. Blurred husband and wife leaning one into the other as if joined at the hip. Black-and-white photo of the cousins *la* Josie *y la* Mary Helen, circa 1942. Polaroid of Sylvia Rios, First Holy Communion, age nine years.

So many *milagritos* safety-pinned here, so many little miracles dangling from red thread—a gold Sacred Heart, a tiny copper arm, a kneeling man in silver, a bottle, a brass truck, a foot, a house, a hand, a baby, a cat, a breast, a tooth, a belly button, an evil eye. So many petitions, so many promises made and kept. And there is nothing I can give you except this braid of hair the color of coffee in a glass.

Chayo, what have you done! All that beautiful hair.
Chayito, how could you ruin in one second what your mother took years to create? You might as well've plucked out your eyes like Saint Lucy. All that hair!

My mother cried, did I tell you? All that beautiful hair . . .

I've cut off my hair. Which I've never cut since the day I was born. The donkey tail in a birthday game. Something shed like a snakeskin.

My head as light as if I'd raised it from water. My heart buoyant again, as if before I'd worn *el* Sagrado Corazón in my open chest. I could've lit this entire church with my grief.

I'm a bell without a clapper. A woman with one foot in this world and one foot in that. A woman straddling both. This thing between my legs, this unmentionable.

I'm a snake swallowing its tail. I'm my history and my future. All my ancestors' ancestors inside my own belly. All my futures and all my pasts.

I've had to steel and hoard and hone myself. I've had to push the furniture against the door and not let you in.

What you doing sitting in there in the dark?

I'm thinking.

Thinking of what?

Just . . . thinking.

You're nuts. Chayo, ven a saludar. *All the relatives are here. You come out of there and be sociable.*

Do boys think, and girls daydream? Do only girls have to come out and greet the relatives and smile and be nice and *quedar bien?*

It's not good to spend so much time alone.
What she do in there all by herself? It don't look right.
Chayito, when you getting married? Look at your cousin Leticia. She's younger than you.
How many kids you want when you grow up?
When I become a mommy . . .
You'll change. You'll see. Wait till you meet Mr. Right.
Chayo, tell everybody what it is you're studying again.
Look at our Chayito. She likes making her little pictures. She's gonna be a painter.
A painter! Tell her I got five rooms that need painting.
When you become a mother . . .

Thank you for making all those months I held my breath not a child in my belly, but a thyroid problem in my throat.

I can't be a mother. Not now. Maybe never. Not for me to choose, like I didn't choose being female. Like I didn't choose being artist—it isn't something you choose. It's something you are, only I can't explain it.

I don't want to be a mother.

I wouldn't mind being a father. At least a father could still be artist, could love some*thing* instead of some*one,* and no one would call that selfish.

I leave my braid here and thank you for believing what I do is important. Though no one else in my family, no other woman, neither friend nor relative, no one I know, not even the heroine in the *telenovelas,* no woman wants to live alone.

I do.

Virgencita de Guadalupe. For a long time I wouldn't let you in my house. I couldn't see you without seeing my ma each time my father came home drunk and yelling, blaming everything that ever went wrong in his life on her.

I couldn't look at your folded hands without seeing my *abuela* mumbling. "My son, my son, my son . . . " Couldn't look at you without blaming you for all the pain my mother and her mother and all our mothers' mothers have put up with in the name of God. Couldn't let you in my house.

I wanted you bare-breasted, snakes in your hands. I wanted you leaping and somersaulting the backs of bulls. I wanted you swallowing raw hearts and rattling volcanic ash. I wasn't going to be my mother or my grandma. All that self-sacrifice, all that silent suffering. Hell no. Not here. Not me.

Don't think it was easy going without you. Don't think I didn't get my share of it from everyone. Heretic. Atheist. *Malinchista. Hocicona.* But I wouldn't shut my yap. My mouth always getting me in trouble. *Is* that *what they teach you at the university? Miss High-and-Mighty. Miss Thinks-She's-Too-Good-for-Us.* Acting like a *bolilla,* a white girl. *Malinche.* Don't think it didn't hurt being called a traitor. Trying to explain to my ma, to my *abuela,* why I didn't want to be like them.

I don't know how it all fell in place. How I finally understood who you are. No longer Mary the mild, but our mother Tonantzín. Your church at Tepeyac built on the site of her temple. Sacred ground no matter whose goddess claims it.

That you could have the power to rally a people when a country was born, and again during civil war, and during a farmworkers' strike in California made me think maybe there is power in my mother's patience, strength in my grandmother's endurance. Because those who suffer have a special power, don't they? The power of understanding someone else's pain. And understanding is the beginning of healing.

When I learned your real name is Coatlaxopeuh, She Who Has Dominion over Serpents, when I recognized you as Tonantzín, and learned your names are Teteoinnan, Toci, Xochiquetzal, Tlazolteotl, Coatlicue, Chalchiuhtlicue, Coyolxauhqui, Huixtocihuatl, Chicomecoatl, Cihuacoatl, when I could see you as Nuestra Señora de la Soledad, Nuestra Señora de los Remedios, Nuestra Señora del Perpetuo Socorro, Nuestra Señora de San Juan de los Lagos, Our Lady of Lourdes, Our Lady of Mount Carmel, Our Lady of the Rosary, Our Lady of Sorrows, I wasn't ashamed, then, to be my mother's daughter, my grandmother's granddaughter, my ancestors' child.

When I could see you in all your facets, all at once the Buddha, the Tao, the true Messiah, Yahweh, Allah, the Heart of the Sky, the Heart of the Earth, the Lord of the Near and Far, the Spirit, the Light, the Universe, I could love you, and, finally, learn to love me.

Mighty Guadalupana Coatlaxopeuh Tonantzín,

What "little miracle" could I pin here? Braid of hair in its place and know that I thank you.

Rosario (Chayo) De Leon
Austin, Tejas

LEARNING MORE

Links to interviews with Sandra Cisneros be can be found on the *Ideas Across Time* website.

QUESTIONING THE TEXT

1. How would you describe the people who have written these notes?
2. What motivates people to write the notes in these stories?
3. What picture do these notes paint of the life of Chicanos in Texas?

4. How would you characterize the saints or deities to whom these notes are written?
5. What picture do these notes paint of the life of the women in the Chicano community? To what extent is the condition of the women universal and true of women everywhere, and to what extent is it particular to this community?
6. List the miracles and promises of the title. What makes these "miracles" miracles? Have the promises actually been kept?
7. How do you think the Cisneros wants us to feel about the writers of these notes? Compassionate? Judgmental? Explain and offer examples to support your point of view.
8. What relationship do the writers of these notes have with the saints and with God? Would you describe the writers of these notes as religious people? Are these people Christian? Explain.
9. How is the long final note different from the others? Is the name of the Virgin of Guadalupe Coatlaxopeuh? Why does Rosario attribute the long list of names to the Virgin? What is the little miracle in Rosario's life that brings her to the Virgin? Does Rosario make any promise?

ANALYZING THE WRITER'S CRAFT

1. Is this a story? Why or why not? How does the form of this story suggest a certain view of the role of fiction and of writing?
2. What does the language used in these notes tell you about the writers? Specify and explain.
3. What does this story achieve that a traditional narrative might not? How might this story have benefited from the conventions of traditional narrative?
4. These notes often communicate by what is not said as much as by what is. Choose a few examples and illustrate.
5. What is the effect of the mixing of languages in this story? Why do you think one of the notes is written in code? What is the code?
6. Is there a narrative in this story? If so, what is it? If not, how does the story develop its themes?
7. How is the final note a summation of and a commentary on the rest of the story?

MAKING CONNECTIONS

1. Compare Cisneros's cumulative portrait of the lives of Chicano women with Jamaica Kincaid's picture of the female condition in "Girl" (Chapter 6, pp. 552–553).
2. Cisneros's devotees have an immediate, even intimate relation with God, gods, and the saints. Compare and contrast this vivid immediacy with

the religious rationality of Socrates (Chapter 8, pp. 565–574) and Marcus Aurelius (Chapter 8, pp. 646–648).

3. The story of the Arrowmaker, N. Scott Momaday says (pp. 612–616), is about life and death; in this way, the story serves as a kind of vital resource for a people. Does Cisneros imply a similar role for her work in relation to her people?

FORMULATING IDEAS FOR WRITING

1. Write a letter to the Virgin of Guadalupe.
2. Using Cisneros's story as a model, write a story in letters—but provide only one side of the correspondence. These can be letters between friends, lovers, children and parents, a woman and her God, and so on.
3. How does this story comment on the efficacy of traditional narrative? What does it achieve that a traditional narrative could not? What qualities of traditional narrative might have been useful in this story?
4. What is the responsibility of the writer to his or her community? Discuss in relation to "Little Miracle, Kept Promises."

Death and Dying

Every society has its fixations and its taboos. For the Victorians, it is said that sex was taboo but death was commonplace, whereas for us today sex is everywhere and death is taboo. But as Studs Terkel reports in the Keynote essay of this chapter, the more he interviewed people about death and dying for his book *Will the Circle Be Unbroken?* the more he found that "we reflect on death like crazy much of our lives." Death may be taboo, but it is certain, and each of us know it. Paradoxically, Terkel discovers that reflecting about death, "the one experience none of us has had," leads him not to fear his demise but rather to appreciate "life and its pricelessness." The essays in this chapter open a small window onto the vast library of writing about death across time and across cultures.

After Terkel's Keynote, the first to have his say is Socrates, arguably the single most important figure in Western philosophy. An irrepressible nonconformist, who always wanted to know why he should do something before doing it, Socrates was an irritant to the powerful men of his time. In the end, they tried him for corrupting the youth of Athens and condemned him to death. Socrates accepted his verdict and the prospect of death with equanimity. Via Plato's account, he subjects his own death to the same rational analysis that he focused on all other topics during his lifetime, and he concludes that death is either total annihilation or a journey of the soul to another realm. In either case, there can be nothing to fear in death. Socrates' final address to the jurists who tried him is plain-spoken and often amusing. He concludes by saying, "Now it is time that we were going, I to die and you to live, but which of us has the happier prospect is unknown to anyone but God."

The Roman Emperor Marcus Aurelius (121–180 CE) died almost six hundred years after Socrates. One of the so-called good Roman emperors, he was a profoundly civilized man forced by circumstances to spend much of his life in war. During his life, he wrote down his views in his famous *Meditations*, a sort of philosophical diary. Here he eloquently expresses the tenets of Stoic philosophy, which emphasizes moderation and reflectiveness as keys to virtue in a dangerous and unpredictable world. "All things," he writes, "take place by change." Life and death are constantly changing one into the other. We have no choice but to accept things as they are. "Do not despise death but be well content with it," he says, "since this too is one of those things which nature wills."

These reasonable, equable views of death from classical times, however, are hardly the last word on the subject, nor do they exhaust our perplexity and fascination with death. What is death? The modernist English writer Virginia Woolf, watching the death of a moth on her windowpane, sees death as an enormous, overpowering force, a counterforce to the dynamic power of being. She admires and identifies with the moth, bravely but vainly beating its frail wings against death. The life force in us, she seems to say, is one with the vitality of nature; but death is also natural and so much stronger than any creature, be it a moth or a person.

After the selection by Virginia Woolf, there follows an album of poems and interviews on death, including "The Last Night That She Lived," a poem written by Emily Dickinson in Amherst, Massachusetts, in the 1860s. As the selections in this chapter already discussed demonstrate, all cultures and all religions offer an account of death, most asserting some kind of life for the individual after death. In Christianity, the religion of all the poets and speakers in this album, death is the occasion of an eternal judgment. It is sometimes portrayed as portending doom and eternal damnation, and it is sometimes portrayed as promising salvation and eternal life, a redemption emanating from God's love. Living in the center of a region originally conceived as the Puritan Commonwealth, Dickinson narrates the last moments of an unnamed woman. The implicit context for the poem is naturally Christian. At one point, the poet says that those tending to the dying woman are "jealous" of her, "So nearly infinite." But the direct confrontation with death challenges all preconceptions. Her poem ends:

> And We—We placed the Hair—
>
> And drew the Head erect—
>
> And then an awful leisure was
>
> Belief to regulate—

How to regulate belief in the face of death is the concern of each selection in this album.

In the last selection in the album, "Day of the Dead," Carlos Cortez introduces a new theme—the attitude toward death in different cultures. Of Mexican ancestry, Cortez speaks of the Mexican celebration of death on the Day of the Dead. Death, Cortez says, should be honored. "Without death, there is no life." On the Day of the Dead, children are given as toys little pushcarts with skeletons in them. The message to the children, Cortez says, is "Don't be afraid of death. What's more important: *Don't Be Afraid of Life*." The noted physician and psychoanalyst Elisabeth Kübler-Ross, who is credited with inspiring the hospice movement, similarly draws on ancient practices to draw our attention to the person within the dying body. Quarantining the dying in hospitals raises our fear of death and makes us less able to cope with it as part of life, she says.

Studs Terkel titles his book of interviews on the subject of death *Will the Circle Be Unbroken?* Not only does Terkel ask a question rather than offer an answer, but his question also invokes an ancient conception of life and death as one continuous cycle. This conception resembles that of Marcus Aurelius; it views the universe as continually in the process of change. Leslie Marmon Silko provides a magisterial rendition of this conception of things in her account of the customs and beliefs concerning death of the Pueblo people. Raised on Laguna Pueblo near Albuquerque, New Mexico, Marmon Silko tells us that the Pueblo people "buried the dead in vacant rooms or partially collapsed rooms adjacent to the main living quarters." For the Pueblo, the decay of the body into dust is a generous process, in the first instance feeding small rodents and insects, and finally, when the dead at last become dust, returning briefly to the fecund essence of things, the rocks and clay that are part of the Mother Creator. The dead participate in a cycle that is deathless. "In the end we all originate from the depths of the earth."

A different understanding of death is advanced by the Japanese novelist Yukio Mishima. Writing in the years after Japan's defeat in World War II, Mishima discovers in the samurai code an enriching philosophy of living. In this philosophy, the goal of living is not long life but a fulfilled life, a life of honor. "The way of the samurai," Mishima says, "is death." The samurai must be ready to die for his lord at every moment, whether it is right now or ten or twenty years from now. This traditional warrior code is, for Mishima, the antidote to modern fecklessness. Rather than wait for death, death should be chosen, either in battle or by ritual suicide. In this way, the principle of life is fulfilled at the height of the person's achievement rather than wasted in the decrepitude of feeble old age.

The physician Sherman B. Nuland, in contrast, says that "taking one's own life is almost always the wrong thing to do." But he allows two exceptions to this statement. The first exception he grants is when the individual faces "the unendurable infirmities of a crippling old age"; the second is when the individual suffers "the final devastations of terminal disease." From his perspective as a physician sworn to curing illness, saving life, and alleviating suffering, Nuland offers an informed, balanced, and sensitively nuanced deliberation on the agonizing decisions individuals, families, and professionals confront in the present-day struggle with death.

KEYNOTE

Will the Circle Be Unbroken? (2001)

Studs Terkel

For more than half a century, Louis (Studs) Terkel has devoted himself to recording the lives of ordinary Americans of every class, age, and race. "What's it like," Terkel asks, "to be that goofy little soldier, scared stiff, with his bayonet pointed at Christ? What's it like to have been a woman in a defense-plant job during World War II? What's it like to be a kid at the front lines?" The tapes of his famous radio program on Chicago station WFMT, *The Studs Terkel Program,* which ran from 1952 to 1997, and his many books of interviews, form an unparalleled record of the personal stories of Americans from all walks of life in the twentieth century.

Born in Brooklyn, New York, in 1912, Terkel was the third son of Russian-Jewish immigrants. His father was a tailor and his mother a seamstress; when Terkel was ten, the family moved to Chicago and opened first a boarding house and later a small hotel near Bughouse Square. Terkel says his fascination with all kinds of people can be traced to the diverse crowds that gathered in that square, including religious fanatics, labor organizers, and the spectrum of employed and unemployed people. Terkel received a law degree in 1934 but never practiced law, following instead a varied career in radio and writing. He proved to have an unusual gift for getting people to talk. His first book of oral history was *Division Street: America* (1967), for which he spoke to seventy people who had lived in Chicago. His next book recorded the experience of the Depression (*Hard Times,* 1967), followed by his interviews with people about work (*Working,* 1974), from which the selection reprinted in Chapter 4, "Mike Lefevre, Steelworker" (pp. 300–307), is taken. His interviews about people's experiences during World War II, contained in *The Good War* (1985), won him the Pulitzer Prize. His most recent publications are *Will the Circle Be Unbroken? Reflections on Death, Rebirth, and the Hunger for Faith* (2001) and *All They Sang: Adventures of an Electric Disc Jockey* (2005). Terkel, who is Distinguished Scholar-in-Residence at the Chicago Historical Society, says *Will the Circle Be Unbroken?* is about redemption. "Anybody can be redeemed," he says, pointing to his interview with C. P. Ellis, a former Ku Klux Klan leader who ended up fighting for the rights of black janitors, accompanied by his partner, an African-American woman. Following is a part of Terkel's introduction to *Will the Circle Be Unbroken?* Three of the interviews that appear in the book are reprinted in the album section of this chapter (pp. 661–670).

I've courted death ever since I was six. I was an asthmatic child. With each labored breath, each wheeze, came a toy whistle obbligato. At my bedside, my eldest brother, to comfort me, would whistle back "I'm Forever Blowing Bubbles," in cadence with my breathing. It was funny, and pleasing, but not much help.

That plus a couple of bouts with mastoiditis, head swathed in bandages, made my awakening the next morning a matter of touch and go. What troubled me was not that I wouldn't make it, but that I would no longer enjoy the whimsical care of my father and my two brothers. My mother was another matter; her hypertense attention more often than not added to my discomfort.

Death itself was too abstract an idea for me then, though I had, in a cursory fashion, become acquainted with the *fact* of death. For a week or so, there had been a warning sign on the door of the adjacent house: SCARLET FEVER CONTAGIOUS. It was taken down the day after the girl inside died. She was my contemporary. Still, near as she was, I felt somewhat detached, only vaguely saddened. My ailments, though serious, were not of epidemic proportions. Nor did the unfortunate girl have two brothers and a gentle father who brought forth phlegmy laughter.

Of course, I had some difficulty, a fear really, of falling asleep. The idea of counting sheep might have worked had I been the child of a Basque shepherd in Idaho. I really knew nothing about sheep, not that I had anything against them. I was living in Chicago, where a fair south wind blowing in from the stockyards wafted the aroma of slaughtered cattle toward our rooming house on Flournoy Street. No, there was really nothing soporific in counting cows.

5 My brother, an assiduous newspaper bug, suggested counting celebrated names, names that made headlines. Charlie Chaplin. Caruso. The Bambino. Clara Bow, the "It" Girl. Peggy Hopkins Joyce.[1] In an inspired moment, he dropped the names of the celebrated lovers Ruth Snyder and Judd Gray, who had just been executed for bopping her husband on the head with a heavy, leaden window sash. Nah. It did nothing for my sleeplessness.

Astonishingly, it was my first awareness of baseball that turned the trick; at least, for a year or two. The Cleveland Indians had beaten the Brooklyn Dodgers in the World Series of 1920. Each night, the names of these new celebrities rolled from my tongue as I signed off. Stanley Coveleski, the Indians' pitcher, who had won three games. Stan-ley Cov-el-es-ki. Six salubrious[2] syllables. The peerless Tris Speaker, who covered center field like a *comfortable quilt*. (A sports writer's apt phrase, my brother informed me.) Bill Wambsganns, the second baseman, who pulled off that unassisted triple play. Wambsganns. The name's slow pronunciation had the pleasant, slumberous effect of a Dutch hot chocolate.

After a few years, when I had recovered from my childhood ailments, the effects of this nocturnal ritual wore off. Once again, I was in the thrall of sleeplessness. Now, a touch of fear that I might indeed die in my sleep distinctly possessed me. It brought forth a habit that still obsesses me. Whenever I'm about to doze off, I deliberately unclasp my hands and remove them from my breast. Every night. Even now.

Was it that photograph I saw on the front page of the morning Hearst newspaper seventy-eight years ago? The late Pope Benedict XV lay in state. On the catafalque,[3] the pontiff's hands were clasped across his breast. It was the first image I remember of a dead person in a casket. From time to time, my young Catholic friends suggested a prayer. "If I should die before I wake. . . ." No soap. I didn't want any Lord my soul to take because I obstinately insisted on waking up the next morning.

Fortunately, at the age of thirteen, I had a young English teacher in my freshman class at McKinley High School. With his scraggly mustache and tubercular mien, he bore a remarkable resemblance to Robert Louis Stevenson.[4]

---

[1] Charlie Chaplin . . . Peggy Hopkins Joyce: Chaplin (1889–1977) was a comedian in silent films. Ernest Caruso (1873–1921) was one of the most famous tenors in the history of opera. Clara Bow (1906–1965), the "It" girl, was the sex idol of the silent movies. Peggy Hopkins Joyce (1893–1957) was a glamorous ex-Ziegfield showgirl, notorious for her many marriages.

[2] salubrious: health-promoting.

[3] catafalque: platform on which the coffin is placed in formal funerals.

[4] Robert Louis Stevenson: Scottish author (1850–1894) of such popular adventure books as *Treasure Island* (1883) and *The Strange Case of Dr. Jekyll and Mr. Hyde* (1886).

He had assigned us Coleridge's "The Rime of the Ancient Mariner."[5] And—bingo!—there was a five-line stanza that did the trick.

Oh sleep, thou art a gentle thing
Beloved from pole to pole!
To Mary Queen, the praise be given,
She sent the gentle sleep from Heaven,
That slid into my soul.

10 For years, I mumbled those lines before sacking out. And it worked—after a fashion. (Ironically, my young Catholic friends had scored a point. They knew who Mary Queen was; I didn't.)

Now, at eighty-eight, after a quintuple bypass among other medical adventures, those words have lost their charm. Too many of my old friends, contemporaries, have died. Fortunately, I've discovered a new way of popping off to sleep. I count down the names of those departed buddies. Unfortunately, the list has grown exponentially during these last few years. Amend that: every month, every week, I spot more familiar names in the obituary columns.

Mordant[6] though it may sound, it's not an unpleasant way of sacking out. I recall funny stories, jokes, and even imagined amours, especially after a few drinks, say, at Riccardo's, a favorite watering hole in Chicago, but now transmogrified into an "in" place for Generation X. I have a good number of young friends, who are delightful company, generous-hearted, witty, and all that. Yet, there is that slight ache—*heimweh,* as Bill Wambsganns put it.

My fellow octogenarian Charlie Andrews explains: "Have you heard the one about the old sport who married a much younger woman? It worked for a couple of years. One day, a mutual friend encounters him. The old boy informs him that they've split up. 'She didn't know the songs.'" My young friends do my heart good every time I see them, but they don't know the songs. . . .

My father and two brothers died in their mid-fifties. Angina. Bad tickers. I had a touch of it, too. It was in our genes, I guess. My mother, a tough little sparrow, fought out her last days in a nursing home. She hung up her gloves at eighty-seven.

15 From my fifties into my mid-eighties, the sublingual nitro pills were mother's milk to me. Whenever that tight fist would punch or grab at my left side, I'd slip a nitro under my tongue and all would be well. For a time. I still carry that tiny bottle in my side pocket. In 1996, while I was watching the Chicago Bulls and the Seattle Sonics in the NBA finals, a sharp zing stabbed me. It ran crazily up and down my left arm. I was perspiring freely and coldly.

The next day's angiogram was not that great. My arteries were a mess. My doctors were of one mind: unless something was immediately done, I had maybe six months to live. A quintuple bypass was suggested. *Quintuple!* I was

[5] Coleridge . . . didn't: Samuel Taylor Coleridge (1772–1834), a major English Romantic poet.
[6] mordant: caustic.

impressed, though somewhat disturbed because I was in the middle of work on a new book.

"What are the odds?" Very good, the surgeon assured me. He had performed this one a number of times. He said something about ten-to-one in my favor. I liked those odds, and the procedure worked. Since 1996 there has been no sign of the fist, let alone the zing, and I've yet to touch the tiny nitro bottle. Of course, I'm aware that mortality is lurking just around the corner, waiting to pounce. One of my carotid arteries is shot, the other hangs in there barely, if obstinately. Stroke, stay away from my door—at least for now.

All in all, it's been a good run. Going on eighty-nine, I was born the year the *Titanic* went down. Who would want to live to be ninety? Churchill is reputed to have replied: "Everyone who is eighty-nine." We are a greedy lot, aren't we? We old ones secretly sing the words of a little-known bard, Ralph Hodgson:

Time, you old gipsy man,
Will you not stay,
Put up your caravan
Just for one day?[7]

These days I think constantly of my father and brothers. They died in what should have been their prime. I, the favored, sickly little child they loved (as did my mother in her own wild way), have had so much the better of it. Though I grieved when each of my brothers died, my father's death, the first in our family, brought upon me a heartache that was too much to bear.

20 At the rooming house my mother ran, my father was the invalid, bedridden much of the time. I shared that bed with him all of my preadolescent years. In New York, before he was stricken, my father had been a fine tailor. My mother, always nimble with her fingers and more so with her mind, was a magnificent seamstress. I still see her on her knee, pins in her mouth, fitting a neighbor woman into a new gown. I still see my father coming home from the sanitarium, wan, fatigued, gallant, insisting on going back to work. It was not in the cards.

In 1920, we headed out for the territories. Chicago. A fairly well-off uncle funded us into leasing a rooming house on the city's near West Side. It was in the heart of Chicago's huge hospital complex. Among our guests were student nurses, interns, a barber, and a hooker. She was a kid from Terre Haute. She was prohibited from having gentlemen callers. No tricks on these premises.

My mother was a cross between a harried Ruth Gordon and Eliza Gant, the mother in *Look Homeward, Angel.*[8] I was bowled over reading it. Thomas Wolfe's mother, Eliza, was a dead ringer for mine, Annie. Eliza's boardinghouse in Asheville was Annie's rooming house in Chicago. They were both sparrowy, tough, and prevailing: living life at its flood tide. Too excessively, perhaps.

---

[7] Ralph Hodgson: English poet (1871–1962). Terkel quotes the first four lines of "Time, You Old Gypsy Man."

[8] *Look Homeward Angel:* Novel by the celebrated writer Thomas Wolfe (1900–1938), native of North Carolina and author of autobiographical novels, of which *Look Homeward, Angel* (1929) is the best known.

We had a crystal radio set, my father and I. It was at our bedside. Fooling around with that cat's-whisker wire scratched against the lump of silvery mineral, we caught Wendell Hall, the Red-Headed Music Maker, on KYW, singing "It Ain't Gonna Rain No More." He played the ukulele.

We heard Hal Totten, on WGN, coming at us from Dayton, Tennessee; we caught fragments of the Monkey Trial. I swear we heard the voices of Clarence Darrow and William Jennings Bryan.[9] Day after day after day, we followed the ordeal of Floyd Collins, the unlucky guide who was freakily trapped in Kentucky's Mammoth Caves. Sharing the earphones, my father one and I the other, we were radio-hip to all that was going on. In 1925, the rooming house was sold. After a brief family breakup, my father refused to play the invalid any further, ailing heart or no. He leased a men's hotel on the near North Side, the Wells-Grand. For five years, even into the Crash of '29, he gallantly made a go of it. With considerations from our McKinley-Republican landlord, Henry L. Flentye, a fair man who admired my father's stick-to-it-iveness, we were making it toughly. Suddenly, in 1931, my father died.

It was I who found him in bed, his spectacles askew. It was the day we had planned to visit Mr. Flentye's three-step-down bare office on North LaSalle. "H.F." was feelingly fond of my old man. He was to offer more concessions. The new contract had already been written in Palmer penmanship longhand and was only waiting to be signed.

I was remarkably calm until, seated on the Grand Avenue streetcar the next day, heading nowhere in particular, I surprised myself by breaking into uncontrollable sobs. Embarrassed, seeking to stifle them, blubbering despite myself, I hurried toward the rear of the car, ready to hop off anywhere, just to escape my show of grief.

It was not until sixty-eight years later—after up-and-down experiences as actor, disc jockey, radio commentator, book writer—that I was to experience a grief far deeper, though my manifestation of it was more muted.

Those memories of streetcar grief came back to me when Antoinette Korotko-Hatch, a woman I was interviewing for this book, described an incident on a bus in which she came to the aid of a man having a heart attack. "People on the bus," she said, "were mumbling about being late to work. I told the driver, 'Get these people off the bus, tell them to take another one.'" The man, she told me, though in pain, "didn't want to be trouble." He was embarrassed that he was "holding up the whole bus."

That man's embarrassment touched off the memory of that nineteen-year-old boy so uncomfortable at daring to grieve out loud for his father. Everything about this book became, unexpectedly for me, a journey into long-suppressed memories and all sorts of ambivalences in feeling of which I wasn't aware.

---

[9] Monkey Trial . . . Bryan: the trial of John Scopes for violating the Tennessee statue against teaching evolution (1925) became known as the Monkey Trial. The famous defense attorney Clarence Darrow (1857–1938) defended Scopes, and the great populist leader William Jennings Bryan (1860–1925) prosecuted him. Bryan won.

30 In her memoir of her mother's death, Myra MacPherson refers to "disenfranchised grief." During an interview, she said, "I fell in this category. It means you're not supposed to feel it, certainly not supposed to show it. I was in my late fifties when my mother died. She was eighty-one. People came up with the usual platitudes. 'After all, she lived a good life,' 'You shouldn't feel so full of grief.'

"That's bullshit. That's why we really can't handle death very well. We want sort of drive-by grieving. Nobody wants you to carry on about it. They want you to deposit it like you do in a bank."[10]

On December, 23, 1999, as I was beginning work on this book, my wife, Ida, died. She had been my companion for sixty years. She was eighty-seven. A few months later, a friend of mine, disturbed by my occasional despondency, burst out: "For chrissake, you've had sixty great years with her!" Myra MacPherson was on the button.

Ida was seventeen years beyond her traditionally allotted time of three score and ten. On occasion, I'd hear her murmur in surprise, "Why do I still feel like a girl?"

They were roller-coaster years we shared, since I first spotted her in a maroon smock in 1937. She had been a social worker during most of those tumultuous years: the Great Depression, World War II, the Cold War, Joe McCarthy, the sixties, the civil rights and peace movements. She had been, as they say, "involved." Garry Wills[11] remembers her greeting him, years after the Vietnam War had ended: "Oh, we were arrested together in Washington."

35 A year or so before her death, Laura Watson, a neighbor, "looked out the window and saw this slim young girl in jeans, with a flower in her hair, plucking out weeds in her garden." The girl looked up. "It was Ida, of course." Gwendolyn Brooks's bet: "She could dance on a moonbeam."[12]

Yeah, she did live to the ripe old age of eighty-seven, but it doesn't cut the mustard, Charlie. I still see that girl in the maroon smock who liked yellow daisies.

Each week, there is a fresh bunch of yellow daisies near the windowsill. On the sill is the urn with her ashes. On occasion, either indignant about something or somewhat enthused, I mumble toward it (her): "Whaddya think of that, kid?" Her way of seeing things had always been so clear-eyed. . . .

We've had one child, a son Dan has become the good companion, the troubleshooter, the rock. There's a *lied* Lotte Lehmann[13] sang, of a mountainside against which you lean when weary or bereft. My son is that mountainside.

One last personal note: The sixty-three heroes of this book, in offering me their bone-deep, honest testimonies, have been a palliative beyond prescription.

---

[10] Myra MacPherson, *She Came to Live Out Loud: An Intimate Family Journey Through Illness, Loss, and Grief* (New York: Scribner, 1999) [Terkel's note].

[11] Gary Wills: Pulitzer Prize–wining author and historian, born 1934.

[12] Gwendolyn Brooks: African–American poet (1917–2000), the first African-American to win the Pulitzer Prize. The line is from Act 2 of Henrik Ibsen's play *A Doll's House* (1879).

[13] *lied* . . . Lehmann: a *lied* is a German high-art song. Lehmann was a famous German soprano (1888–1976).

40 There was something of a "poem" fraudulently attributed to Gabriel García Márquez.[14] The novelist was understandably indignant. Nonetheless, the words of some ersatz[15] philosophe, coffee-house pundit, or practical joker suit me fine at this moment:

> I would teach the old that death does not come with old age, but with forgetting. . . . I would walk when others hold back, I would wake when others sleep, I would listen when others talk, and how I would enjoy good chocolate ice cream.

Hopefully, that's what this book is about: death, of course, but only by living to the full its long prelude, life.

LEADING QUESTIONS

The mystery of life, and so of death, evokes wonder and fear. Terkel interviews many people, few of them overtly religious, and yet all resorting to the language or the outlook of religion when thinking of, or anticipating, death. Is that because, deep inside, we all believe in God? Is it because death is so unthinkable that we must reach for something beyond ourselves when its shadow crosses our path?

Many of the writers in this chapter invoke old traditions as a rebuke to our modern, hospital-dominated way of dying, as if death were a disease. Is the dreadfully impersonal death that Elisabeth Kübler-Ross describes (pp. 677–683) as being what's in store for most of us in the United States the product of science and technology, or is there some other explanation. Why can't people die in peace at home?

Is our disconnection from death just one part of our disconnection from the rhythms of nature? Would it be better if we let death once more enter everyday life, as a part of life rather than a taboo?

LEARNING MORE

For decades, Studs Terkel has been one of the most original chroniclers of everyday life in America. To learn more about his work, see the *Ideas Across Time* website.

QUESTIONING THE TEXT

1. What have most of Terkel's books been about? Whom has he been interested in interviewing?
2. Why did Terkel think this was one book he would never write?

[14] Gabriel García Márquez: Colombian writer, born 1928, winner of the 1982 Nobel Prize for Literature.

[15] ersatz: imitation.

3. What most astonished him in writing it?
4. What group of people in particular urged Terkel to write the book? Why?
5. Why does Terkel think so much now about his father and brothers?
6. What memory did Antoinette Korotko-Hatch rouse in Terkel?
7. What insight of Myra MacPherson's seemed especially apt to Terkel at the time of his wife's death?
8. State in your own words what Terkel says his book is about.

ANALYZING THE WRITER'S CRAFT

1. How would you characterize Terkel's diction? Offer some representative quotations and discuss them.
2. Terkel seems purposely, or by nature, to depart from the conventions of the well-made essay. How is his approach unconventional? How does his approach nevertheless fulfill the necessities of expository composition?
3. Discuss Terkel's transitions: how does he get from point a to point b?
4. What sort of personality does Terkel project in this essay? Offer a few quotations to support your answer.
5. This selection forms most of Terkel's introduction to his book of interviews. Why do you think he chooses to write so personally here? Do you find the up-close-and-personal quality of this introduction effective? Why or why not?
6. What do you learn about Terkel from his literary allusions?
7. Is there a philosophy of living conveyed in this introduction? If so, what is it, and what evidence can you cite to support your view of it? If not, ought there to have been—that is, does the subject "require" of the writer what he required of the people he interviewed?

MAKING CONNECTIONS

1. How does Terkel's interview with the steelworker Mike Lefevre (Chapter 4, pp. 300–307) compare to the interviews in this chapter with Angelina Rossi, Rick Rundle, and Carlos Cortez? What do all of these people have in common? Are there differences?
2. Is how we view death actually an expression of how we view life? What do the writers in the selections on belief in Chapter 2 have to contribute to Terkel's challenge in his essay? Or to the views of the people Terkel interviews that appear in this chapter?
3. How does Terkel—and Angelina Rossi, Rick Rundle, and Carlos Cortez—think about the after life? What evidence might tilt the scales in one direction or another? How does science come into the picture—for example, with respect to "truth"? Consider how Charles Darwin (Chapter 3, pp. 167–180), Albert Einstein (Chapter 3, pp. 193–200), and Richard Feynman (Chapter 3, pp. 201–207) might inform the question that vexes Terkel and his friends.

FORMULATING IDEAS FOR WRITING

1. For the most part, those who overtly identify themselves as religious—see the interviews with Angelina Rossi and Rick Rundle, for example (pp. 661–664 and pp. 664–668)—identify religion with an institution, in this case the Catholic Church. Religion is a matter of an institution and a doctrine. But Terkel says that, over and over again, people expressed religious views by dissociating themselves from religion, opting instead to claim that they are "spiritual." Probe the implications of these two different forms of identifying one's views. Are they sharply distinct? Do they mean, or imply, distinctly different philosophies? Do they merge and separate depending on what you're talking about?
2. Conduct an interview (or interviews) of your own on the subject of death. (It might be interesting to reverse Terkel's practice and to interview young people, or even children.)
3. Why do people live out their days, passively awaiting death, rather than purposely choosing an appropriate time to die?
4. Does the experience of losing a loved one, or the imminence of death, strengthen or weaken life-long religious belief?
5. Is it an is or is it an ain't? Can science answer this question?

Socrates's Defense (*Apology*) (399 BCE)

Plato

Greek philosophy developed against the background of Athens' Golden Age, the Age of Pericles (461–429 BCE), and its collapse. Socrates was born around 470 BCE, Plato around 427 BCE, and Aristotle in 384 BCE. These influential philosophers were closely associated. Socrates, a "street teacher," taught Plato, and Plato taught Aristotle. Moreover, Socrates himself wrote nothing. What we know of his thought we know mainly through Plato's writing, known as *Dialogues* because of the method of inquiry they express. We don't know in what order Plato wrote *Dialogues*, but collections usually begin with the trial and death of Socrates. In *Apology*, Plato records Socrates' speech in his defense against the charges against him—"Socrates is guilty of corrupting the minds of the young, and of believing in deities of his own invention instead of the gods recognized by the state." The selection that follows is taken from the very close of *Apology*, where Socrates discusses the death that awaits him. In *Crito*, Socrates' friends inform him that they want to make arrangements for his escape from prison, and they urge him to flee. Socrates asks whether it can ever be right to defend oneself against an injustice by committing an injustice oneself. He concludes that it can never be right. What would happen if individuals could simply set aside the laws? A person must always follow the law of the land.

The son of the sculptor Sophroniscus, Socrates served as a soldier in the Peloponnesian War (431–404 BCE), the war that brought Athens' Golden Age to an end. Upon his return, he worked as a stonemason until he inherited a small competence from his father. For the rest of his life, Socrates roamed the streets of Athens engaging the aristocratic young men of the city in critical examination of their core values and beliefs. Socrates' goal was to understand and achieve virtue through a dialectical method, what we might today call critical reasoning. He accepted no money from his students. But he roused the enmity of their parents, and eventually he was tried on the charges mentioned earlier. As this selection shows, he accepted his unjust sentence with grace and humor, and refused the easy escape to exile offered him by his friends. He died in 399 BCE after drinking hemlock.

Well, gentlemen, for the sake of a very small gain in time you are going to earn the reputation—and the blame from those who wish to disparage our city—of having put Socrates to death, "that wise man"—because they will say I am wise even if I am not, these people who want to find fault with you. If you had waited just a little while, you would have had your way in the course of nature. You can see that I am well on in life and near to death. I am saying this not to all of you but to those who voted for my execution, and I have something else to say to them as well.

No doubt you think, gentlemen, that I have been condemned for lack of the arguments which I could have used if I had thought it right to leave nothing unsaid or undone to secure my acquittal. But that is very far from the truth. It is not a lack of arguments that has caused my condemnation, but a lack of effrontery and impudence, and the fact that I have refused to address you in the way which would give you most pleasure. You would have liked to hear me weep and wail, doing and saying all sorts of things which I regard as unworthy of myself, but which you are used to hearing from other people. But I did not think then that I ought to stoop to servility because I was in danger, and I do not regret now the way in which I pleaded my case. I would much rather die as the result of this defense than live as the result of the other sort. In a court of law, just as in warfare, neither I nor any other ought to use his wits to escape death by any means. In battle it is often obvious that you could escape being killed by giving up your arms and throwing yourself upon the mercy of your pursuers, and in every kind of danger there are plenty of devices for avoiding death if you are unscrupulous enough to stick at nothing. But I suggest, gentlemen, that the difficulty is not so much to escape death; the real difficulty is to escape from doing wrong, which is far more fleet of foot. In this present instance I, the slow old man, have been overtaken by the slower of the two, but my accusers, who are clever and quick, have been overtaken by the faster—by iniquity.[1] When I

---

[1] iniquity: gross injustice.

leave this court I shall go away condemned by you to death, but they will go away convicted by truth herself of depravity and wickedness. And they accept their sentence even as I accept mine. No doubt it was bound to be so, and I think that the result is fair enough.

Having said so much, I feel moved to prophesy to you who have given your vote against me, for I am now at that point where the gift of prophecy comes most readily to men—at the point of death. I tell you, my executioners, that as soon as I am dead, vengeance shall fall upon you with a punishment far more painful than your killing of me. You have brought about my death in the belief that through it you will be delivered from submitting your conduct to criticism, but I say that the result will be just the opposite. You will have more critics, whom up till now I have restrained without your knowing it, and being younger they will be harsher to you and will cause you more annoyance. If you expect to stop denunciation of your wrong way of life by putting people to death, there is something amiss with your reasoning. This way of escape is neither possible nor creditable. The best and easiest way is not to stop the mouths of others, but to make yourselves as good men as you can. This is my last message to you who voted for my condemnation.

As for you who voted for my acquittal, I should very much like to say a few words to reconcile you to the result, while the officials are busy and I am not yet on my way to the place where I must die. I ask you, gentlemen, to spare me these few moments. There is no reason why we should not exchange fancies while the law permits. I look upon you as my friends, and I want you to understand the right way of regarding my present position.

5 Gentlemen of the jury—for *you* deserve to be so called—I have had a remarkable experience. In the past the prophetic voice to which I have become accustomed has always been my constant companion, opposing me even in quite trivial things if I was going to take the wrong course. Now something has happened to me, as you can see, which might be thought and is commonly considered to be a supreme calamity; yet neither when I left home this morning, nor when I was taking my place here in the court, nor at any point in any part of my speech did the divine sign oppose me. In other discussions it has often checked me in the middle of a sentence, but this time it has never opposed me in any part of this business in anything that I have said or done. What do I suppose to be the explanation? I will tell you. I suspect that this thing that has happened to me is a blessing, and we are quite mistaken in supposing death to be an evil. I have good grounds for thinking this, because my accustomed sign could not have failed to oppose me if what I was doing had not been sure to bring some good result.

We should reflect that there is much reason to hope for a good result on other grounds as well. Death is one of two things. Either it is annihilation, and the dead have no consciousness of anything, or, as we are told, it is really a change—a migration of the soul from this place to another. Now if there is no consciousness but only a dreamless sleep, death must be a marvelous gain. I suppose that if anyone were told to pick out the night on which he slept so soundly as not even to dream, and then to compare it with all the other nights and days of his life, and then were told to say, after due consideration, how many better and happier days and nights than this he had spent in the course of his life—well, I think that the Great King himself, to say nothing of any private person, would find these days and nights easy to count in comparison with the rest. If death is like this, then, I call it gain, because the whole of time, if you look at it in this way, can be regarded as no more than one single night. If on the other hand death is a removal from here to some other place, and if what we are told is true, that all the dead are there, what greater blessing could there be than this, gentlemen? If on arrival in the other world, beyond the reach of our so-called justice, one will find there the true judges who are said to preside in those courts, Minos and Rhadamanthus and Aeacus and Triptolemus[2] and all those other half-divinities who were upright in their earthly life, would that be an unrewarding journey? Put it in this way. How much would one of you give to meet Orpheus and Musaeus, Hesiod and Homer?[3] I am willing to die ten times over if this account is true. It would be an especially interesting experience for me to join them there, to meet Palamedes and Ajax, the son of Telamon,[4] and any other heroes of the old days who met their death through an unfair trial, and to compare my fortunes with theirs—it would be rather amusing, I think. And above all I should like to spend my time there, as here, in examining and searching people's minds, to find out who is really wise among them, and who only thinks that he is. What would one not give, gentlemen, to be able to question the leader of that great host against Troy, or Odysseus, or Sisyphus,[5] or the thousands of other men and women whom one could mention, to talk and mix and argue with whom would be unimaginable happiness? At any rate I presume that they do not put one to death there for such conduct, because apart from the other happiness in which their world surpasses ours, they are now immortal for the rest of time, if what we are told is true.

You too, gentlemen of the jury, must look forward to death with confidence, and fix your minds on this one belief, which is certain—that nothing can harm a good man either in life or after death, and his fortunes are not a matter of

---

[2] Minos . . . Triptolemus: Minos, king of Crete, became after his death judge of the shades in the Underworld. Rhadamanthus and Aecus are the other two judges. Triptolemus was one of the original priests of Demeter, who taught the Greeks agriculture.

[3] Orpheus . . . Homer: Orpheus was the greatest musician and poet of Greek myth. Musaeus, his son, is the founder of Attic (Classical Greek) poetry. Hesiod was an early Greek poet (c. 800 BCE) and major source of Greek myth. The greatest ancient Greek poet, Homer is thought to have lived shortly after Hesiod and is the author of *The Iliad* and *The Odyssey,* which tell the story of the sacking of Troy and the return of Odysseus from the Trojan War.

[4] Palamedes . . . Telamon: Palamedes discovered counting and measures; he was falsely accused by Odysseus and stoned to death. Ajax was one of Helen of Troy's suitors and a great Greek warrior. Telamon was one of the Argonauts who accompanied Jason in his quest for the Golden Fleece.

[5] Troy . . . Sisyphus: Troy, the city where Paris took Helen, and the site of the Trojan War. The leader of the Greeks was Agamemnon. Odysseus, a wily Greek hero, is memorialized in Homer's epic *The Odyssey.* Sisyphus betrayed the secrets of the gods and was punished by being forced to roll a boulder up a steep hill. Whenever he reached the top, the boulder rolled back down and he had to start again—and so on for eternity.

indifference to the gods. This present experience of mine has not come about mechanically. I am quite clear that the time had come when it was better for me to die and be released from my distractions. That is why my sign never turned me back. For my own part I bear no grudge at all against those who condemned me and accused me, although it was not with this kind intention that they did so, but because they thought that they were hurting me; and that is culpable of them. However, I ask them to grant me one favor. When my sons grow up, gentlemen, if you think that they are putting money or anything else before goodness, take your revenge by plaguing them as I plagued you; and if they fancy themselves for no reason, you must scold them just as I scolded you, for neglecting the important things and thinking that they are good for something when they are good for nothing. If you do this, I shall have had justice at your hands, both I myself and my children.

Now it is time that we were going, I to die and you to live, but which of us has the happier prospect is unknown to anyone but God.

LEARNING MORE

If your interest is piqued and you want to read the entire *Apology,* as well as *Crito,* you can find the full texts on the *Ideas Across Time* website.

QUESTIONING THE TEXT

1. Having just been condemned to death, Socrates seems to turn the tables on his accusers. What does he predict for them? Of what does he accuse them? Do you find Socrates's predictions and accusations credible?
2. What is the main reason that Socrates thinks the jury has voted against him? Do you think his advice to them is good advice?
3. How can what has happened to Socrates be, as he says, "a blessing" (par. 5)?
4. Are there ways of understanding death other than the two alternatives Socrates presents? If so, why has Socrates not examined them, too?
5. Why can no harm come to "a good man in life or in death" (par. 7)? Explain why you agree or disagree with Socrates on this point.

ANALYZING THE WRITER'S CRAFT

1. How would you characterize Socrates's tone in his speech? Does the tone change? Offer examples to support your answers.
2. Socrates is considered one of the greatest reasoners of all time. His speech is full of reasoning, and his address to those who condemned him and those who voted for his acquittal is also full of appeals to rational positions. Quote two or three examples, and explain whether you think Socrates's points hold up to logical scrutiny.

3. How can a person so committed to reason speak about being guided by a "prophetic voice"? Is this appeal to prophecy a contradiction of the Socratic method?
4. Socrates's analysis of death (par. 6) is an excellent example of argument. Explain why.
5. Socrates gives a number of examples of people whom he would love to meet among the dead (par. 6). What do you learn about Socrates from this list?
6. What do you make of Socrates's request of a "favor" from the jurists? Is he being serious? Is he making fun of them? Is he making a subtle point? Explain.
7. Is Socrates's closing paragraph a good conclusion for his speech (see Introduction, pp. 1–8)?

MAKING CONNECTIONS

1. Compare and contrast Socrates's view of death with that found in holy books (see Chapter 2, pp. 68–96).
2. Do you think Paul Tillich (Chapter 2, pp. 123–130) would say that Socrates's confrontation of death reveals a true religious concern?
3. Since this chapter contains many well-known (and some not-so-well-known) views of death, you will have many opportunities to find connections among them. Looking ahead to the next reading, by the Roman Emperor Marcus Aurelius, speculate about what these two men might say to each other upon meeting in the Underworld.

FORMULATING IDEAS FOR WRITING

1. Write an essay explaining why you find Socrates's attitude toward death admirable or unsatisfying.
2. History offers us many examples of people in power who seek to silence those who criticize them. Socrates says to his accusers, "If you expect to stop denunciation of your wrong way of life by putting people to death, there is something amiss with your reasoning" (par. 3). Draw out Socrates's full meaning from this terse sentence. Give some attention to "denunciation," "wrong way of life," "putting people to death," and "amiss with your reasoning." *Is* there something amiss with their reasoning? Does Socrates's advice about how "to stop the mouths of others" show a good understanding of human nature?
3. Socrates is a great reasoner. But is he also a good student of human nature? Can he be right in thinking but wrong in practice?
4. "Nothing can harm a good man either in life or after death," says Socrates. Do you agree or disagree?
5. Should Socrates have followed the entreaties of his friends, bribed the guards, and lived out his life in honorable exile? Discuss.

Meditations (167 CE)

Marcus Aurelius

Marcus Aurelius (121–180 CE), born into an aristocratic Roman family, attracted the attention of the Emperor Hadrian while still a boy. Under Hadrian's patronage, he received an outstanding education. When Hadrian named Antoninus Pius his successor, he did so under the condition that Antoninus in turn should name as successors Marcus Aurelius and Lucius Verus, the son of Hadrian's adopted son Aelius. Marcus in due course ascended to the throne along with Lucius in the role of subordinate emperor in 161, when he was forty years old.

Marcus Aurelius was hounded throughout his reign by military threats to Rome from the north by the Germanic tribes and from the east by the Parthians. Internally, Rome suffered from plague and financial crisis. Marcus Aurelius dealt with these challenges firmly and effectively but was forced to spend much time abroad on military campaigns. Before and after battle he wrote *Meditations,* literally "Writings to Himself."

Meditations, which is a diarylike journal rather than a continuous discourse, reveals that Marcus found in Stoic philosophy the support and solace to overcome the formidable difficulties of his position. Stoicism is named after the Stoa Poikile, a hall in Athens where Zeno, the first Stoic philosopher, taught. Marcus was probably more familiar, though, with the work of Epictetus (c. 55–135 CE), whose guiding principles were endurance and abstainance. Happiness is to be found by living in harmony with nature and reason. Since the world is in constant flux, reason teaches us to accept what comes (endure). Wisdom lies in disciplined distance (abstain) from vicissitudes, which are both inescapable and merely external to the spirit. *Meditations* was first printed in 1559 in Zurich and appeared for the first time in English in 1634.

Marcus Aurelius died at his camp on the Danube, near Vienna, on March 17, 180. He was succeeded by one of his thirteen children, Commodus.

IV

35. Everything is only for a day, both that which remembers and that which is remembered.

36. Observe constantly that all things take place by change, and accustom thyself to consider that the nature of the universe loves nothing so much as to change the things which are and to make new things like them. For everything that exists is in a manner the seed of that which will be. . . .

40. Constantly regard the universe as one living being, having one substance and one soul; and observe how all things have reference to one perception, the

perception of this one living being; and how all things act with one movement; and how all things are the co-operating causes of all things which exist; observe too the continuous spinning of the thread and the contexture of the web.

41. Thou art a little soul bearing about a corpse, as Epictetus[1] used to say.

42. It is no evil for things to undergo change, and no good for things to subsist in consequence of change.

43. Time is like a river made up of the events which happen, and a violent stream; for as soon as a thing has been seen, it is carried away, and another comes in its place, and this will be carried away too. . . .

46. Always remember the sayings of Heraclitus,[2] that the death of earth is to become water, and the death of water is to become air, and the death of air is to become fire, and reversely. And think too of him who forgets whither the way leads, and that men quarrel with that with which they are most constantly in communion, the reason which governs the universe; and the things which they daily meet with seem to them strange: and consider that we ought not to act and speak as if we were asleep, for even in sleep we seem to act and speak; and that we ought not, like children who learn from their parents, simply to act and speak as we have been taught.

47. If any god told thee that thou shalt die to-morrow, or certainly on the day after to-morrow, thou wouldst not care much whether it was on the third day or on the morrow, unless thou wast in the highest degree mean-spirited—for how small is the difference?—so think it no great thing to die after as many years as thou canst name rather than tomorrow.

48. Think continually how many physicians are dead after often contracting their eyebrows over the sick; and how many astrologers after predicting with great pretensions the deaths of others; and how many philosophers after endless discourses on death or immortality; how many heroes after killing thousands; and how many tyrants who have used their power over men's lives with terrible insolence as if they were immortal; and how many cities are entirely dead, so to speak, Helice and Pompeii and Herculaneum,[3] and others innumerable. Add to the reckoning all whom thou hast known, one after another. One man after burying another has been laid out dead, and another buries him; and all this in a short time. To conclude, always observe how ephemeral[4] and worthless human things are, and what was yesterday a little mucus, to-morrow will be a mummy or ashes. Pass then through this little space of time conformably to nature, and end thy journey in content, just as an olive falls off when it is ripe, blessing nature who produced it, and thanking the tree on which it grew. . . .

50. It is a vulgar but still a useful help towards contempt of death, to pass in review those who have tenaciously stuck to life. What more then have they

---

[1] Epictetus: Stoic philosopher (55–135); he was born a slave.

[2] Heraclitus: Important Greek philosopher (540–480 BCE) before Socrates who thought only change was constant.

[3] Helice . . . Herculaneum: Helice was destroyed by a tsunami in 373 BCE. Both Pompeii and Herculaneum were destroyed by the eruption of Mount Vesuvius in 79 CE.

[4] ephemeral: temporary.

gained than those who have died early? Certainly they lie in their tombs somewhere at last, Cadicianus, Fabius, Julianus, Lepidus,[5] or any one else like them, who have carried out many to be buried, and then were carried out themselves. Altogether the interval is small [between birth and death]; and consider with how much trouble, and in company with what sort of people, and in what a feeble body this interval is laboriously passed. Do not then consider life a thing of any value. For look to the immensity of time behind thee, and to the time which is before thee, another boundless space. In this infinity then what is the difference between him who lives three days and him who lives three generations?

51. Always run to the short way; and the short way is the natural: accordingly say and do everything in conformity with the soundest reason. For such a purpose frees a man from trouble, and warfare, and all artifice and ostentatious display.

V

3. Do not despise death, but be well content with it, since this too is one of those things which nature wills. For such as it is to be young and to grow old, and to increase and to reach maturity, and to have teeth and beard and gray hairs, and to beget, and to be pregnant, and to bring forth, and all the other natural operations which the seasons of thy life bring, such also is dissolution. This, then, is consistent with the character of a reflecting man, to be neither careless nor impatient nor contemptuous with respect to death, but to wait for it as one of the operations of nature. As thou now waitest for the time when the child shall come out of thy wife's womb, so be ready for the time when thy soul shall fall out of this envelope. But if thou requirest also a vulgar kind of comfort which shall reach thy heart, thou wilt be made best reconciled to death by observing the objects from which thou art going to be removed, and the morals of those with whom thy soul will no longer be mingled. For it is no way right to be offended with men, but it is thy duty to care for them and to bear with them gently; and yet to remember that thy departure will be not from men who have the same principles as thyself. For this is the only thing, if there be any, which could draw us the contrary way and attach us to life, to be permitted to live with those who have the same principles as ourselves. But now thou seest how great is the trouble arising from the discordance of those who live together, so that thou mayst say, Come quick, O death, lest perchance I, too, should forget myself.

LEARNING MORE

Further readings from the *Meditations* and about Marcus Aurelius's life and philosophy can be found on the *Ideas Across Time* website.

---

[5] Cadicianus . . . Lepidus: Aurelius lists famous Roman leaders, of whom Fabius was the mythical founder of the illustrious Roman family of that name; Julianus (133–193) was emperor; and Lepidus, the name of another illustrious Roman family, likely was the ally of Julius Caesar.

QUESTIONING THE TEXT

1. What does Marcus Aurelius mean, in par. 1, by "that which remembers and that which is remembered"? What are the implications of putting his idea in these words?
2. Par. 3 is an often-quoted passage from Marcus Aurelius, said to contain his understanding of the universe. Some have read this passage as a kind of Pantheism: God is Nature, and Nature is God. But in par. 7, Marcus talks about "the reason which governs the universe." Does Marcus Aurelius believe in an animating Creator, or is the universe itself order and reason?
3. How does Marcus Aurelius explain the apparent contradiction between never-ending flux, which seems random, and reason or meaning in nature?
4. In Marcus Aurelius's view, is human life meaningful and important?
5. What do you think Marcus Aurelius means by "vulgar" in par. 10? If everything changes into something else, and nothing much matters in the stretch of infinity, why does Marcus bother with dismissing a certain sentiment as "vulgar"?
6. Does Marcus's hunger for like-minded company (par. 12) contradict the rest of his philosophy?
7. Why does Marcus Aurelius say we should be content with death? Do you agree?
8. What do the concluding words of par. 12 ("Come quick, O death . . .") suggest about Marcus's recourse to Stoic philosophy for guidance?

ANALYZING THE WRITER'S CRAFT

1. To whom are *Meditations* addressed (see "Conventions of Address," in the Appendix, pp. 705–706)? Explain your answer and use supporting quotations to illustrate it.
2. What is the effect of Marcus's use of similar phrases like "Observe constantly" (par. 2), "Constantly regard" (par. 3), "Always remember" (par. 7) and "Think continually" (par. 9)?
3. How would you characterize Marcus's language? Do you find it plain and direct? Highly metaphorical? Abstract? How does his language reflect his purpose in writing? Discuss.
4. Marcus constantly moves from the general and the vast (the universe) to the specific and minute (himself). How does Marcus bring his view of the nature of the universe to bear on the way we should think and live?
5. Marcus employs a range of rhetorical devices to make his point, from metaphors and analogies to illustrations and examples. Discuss at least one instance of each, and show how Marcus's use of the "Conventions of Rhetoric" (see the Appendix, pp. 714–719) effectively conveys his central idea.
6. What impression of Marcus the man does his tone and diction convey? Specify and explain.

MAKING CONNECTIONS

1. Would Marcus Aurelius consider Charles Darwin's theory of natural selection (Chapter 3, pp. 167–180) as compatible with his Stoic philosophy?
2. Would Richard Feynman (Chapter 3, pp. 201–207) consider Marcus's Stoicism as reflecting a scientific way of thought?
3. What are the similarities and differences between Socrates' (pp. 640–644) and Marcus's understanding of death?
4. What do you think Marcus would contribute to a dialogue about suicide between Yukio Mishima (pp. 685–691) and Sherwin B. Nuland (pp. 696–701)?

FORMULATING IDEAS FOR WRITING

1. Marcus Aurelius assumes that because the universe is "one living being," what applies to the vast (the universe) applies to the small (human life). Write an essay that explores the ways in which the laws of nature can (or perhaps cannot) be a guide for how we should govern human life.
2. Marcus is clearly right that "all things take place by change." Do you share the conclusions he draws from this fact ("how ephemeral and worthless human things are")? If you do, explain whether Marcus expresses a view you have always held, or whether he has helped you clarify your own thoughts. If you do not, explain both why you do not and what your own view is. Does Marcus make an error in reasoning in concluding that because all things change and all things are ephemeral, human things are therefore worthless?
3. Discuss Marcus's notion of the "vulgar." What does he think is vulgar, and why? Consider why he seems concerned to distinguish between a vulgar and a more refined attitude toward life.
4. Discuss the indications in Marcus's writing that even in him we can find tensions between theory and practice.

The Death of the Moth (1942)

Virginia Woolf

Virginia Woolf (1882–1941), the chief figure of English literary modernism, was profoundly affected by death. When she was young, many of those closest to her passed away in succession. Her mother, whom she adored, died when Woolf was thirteen, leading to her first nervous breakdown. Her half-sister

Stella died two years later. Her father died after a long bout with cancer in 1904, and her favorite brother, Thoby, died of typhoid fever in 1906, at the age of twenty-six. After that, Woolf, now twenty-four, again suffered a mental breakdown, and she passed the rest of her life in a constant struggle to ward off madness.

Woolf's writing, however, is not dark but rather vivacious, inventive, and intensely receptive to sensuous impressions, evoked in often dazzling prose. She shows us human life as only one feature of a densely populated world teeming with other creatures, as well as plants, flowers, and clouds. Although death is frequently a presence in her fiction and essays, it forms one part of a complex whole that is powerful, mysterious, and inescapable.

Woolf was the third of her parents' four children, but there were four other siblings from previous marriages. She received no formal education and did not attend college, something she resented all her life. However, she did have the free run of her father's considerable library. Her father, Sir Leslie Stephen, was an eminent Victorian, a prominent literary editor and friend of such great writers as George Eliot, Henry James, Matthew Arnold, and Alfred, Lord Tennyson. Woolf grew up as part of an intellectual aristocracy. But the Stephen children—Woolf had one sister, Vanessa, who became a painter, and two brothers, Thoby and Adrian—resented their imperious father. Upon his death, they moved from their fashionable family home to Bloomsbury, less a residential than a commercial district, near the British Museum. A law firm occupied the ground floor of their house. Here the young Stephens established regular "evenings," attended by many of the major figures in cultural and public life, such as the writers Lytton Strachey and E. M. Forster, the poet T. S. Eliot, the art critic Roger Fry, and the economist John Maynard Keynes. Virginia married one of these regulars, a friend of her brothers at Cambridge, Leonard Woolf. This loose group of friends became known as "the Bloomsbury Group," and their bohemian intellectualism, their iconoclasm, their egalitarian sexual and political views, and their taste in furniture, summer houses, and art all became a model of how to live for the Anglo-American intelligentsia of the mid-twentieth century.

Among Woolf's most important works are the novels *Mrs. Dalloway* (1925) and *To the Lighthouse* (1927), which aimed to establish a sharp break with late-Victorian realism. Her feminist essays *A Room of One's Own* (1929) and *Three Guineas* (1938) are formative statements of the twentieth-century movement for equality for women. Woolf's diaries, letters, and essays have appeared posthumously in multivolume collections. The present selection is the title essay of the posthumously published *Death of the Moth and Other Essays* (1942).

As the Second World War intensified and the British anticipated a Nazi invasion, Woolf feared another attack of mental illness and drowned herself on March 28, 1941, in the river Ouse near her house in Sussex, south of London.

Moths that fly by day are not properly to be called moths; they do not excite that pleasant sense of dark autumn nights and ivy-blossom which the commonest yellow-underwing asleep in the shadow of the curtain never fails to rouse in us.

They are hybrid creatures, neither gay like butterflies nor sombre like their own species. Nevertheless the present specimen, with his narrow hay-colored wings, fringed with a tassel of the same color, seemed to be content with life. It was a pleasant morning, mid-September, mild, benignant, yet with a keener breath than that of the summer months. The plough was already scoring the field opposite the window, and where the share[1] had been, the earth was pressed flat and gleamed with moisture. Such vigor came rolling in from the fields and the down[2] beyond that it was difficult to keep the eyes strictly turned upon the book. The rooks[3] too were keeping one of their annual festivities; soaring round the tree tops until it looked as if a vast net with thousands of black knots in it had been cast up into the air; which, after a few moments sank slowly down upon the trees until every twig seemed to have a knot at the end of it. Then, suddenly, the net would be thrown into the air again in a wider circle this time, with the utmost clamor and vociferation, as though to be thrown into the air and settle down upon the tree tops were a tremendously exciting experience.

The same energy which inspired the rooks, the ploughmen, the horses, and even, it seemed, the lean bare-backed downs, sent the moth fluttering from side to side of his square of the windowpane. One could not help watching him. One was, indeed, conscious of a queer feeling of pity for him. The possibilities of pleasure seemed that morning so enormous and so various that to have only a moth's part in life, and a day moth's at that, appeared a hard fate, and his zest in enjoying his meagre opportunities to the full, pathetic. He flew vigorously to one corner of his compartment, and, after waiting there a second, flew across to the other. What remained for him but to fly to a third corner and then to a fourth? That was all he could do, in spite of the size of the downs, the width of the sky, the far-off smoke of houses, and the romantic voice, now and then, of a steamer out at sea. What he could do he did. Watching him, it seemed as if a fibre, very thin but pure, of the enormous energy of the world had been thrust into his frail and diminutive body. As often as he crossed the pane, I could fancy that a thread of vital light became visible. He was little or nothing but life.

Yet, because he was so small, and so simple a form of the energy that was rolling in at the open window and driving its way through so many narrow and intricate corridors in my own brain and in those of other human beings, there was something marvellous as well as pathetic about him. It was as if someone had taken a tiny bead of pure life and decking it as lightly as possible with down and feathers, had set it dancing and zigzagging to show us the true nature of life. Thus displayed one could not get over the strangeness of it. One is apt to forget all about life, seeing it humped and bossed and garnished and cumbered so that it has to move with the greatest circumspection and dignity. Again, the thought of all that life might have been had he been born in any other shape caused one to view his simple activities with a kind of pity.

[1] share: ploughshare, the blade in a plough that cuts the soil at the bottom of a furrow.
[2] down: open expanse of undulating land.
[3] rooks: noisy English crows.

After a time, tired by his dancing apparently, he settled on the window ledge in the sun, and, the queer spectacle being at an end, I forgot about him. Then, looking up, my eye was caught by him. He was trying to resume his dancing, but seemed either so stiff or so awkward that he could only flutter to the bottom of the windowpane; and when he tried to fly across it he failed. Being intent on other matters I watched these futile attempts for a time without thinking, unconsciously waiting for him to resume his flight, as one waits for a machine, that has stopped momentarily, to start again without considering the reason of its failure. After perhaps a seventh attempt he slipped from the wooden ledge and fell, fluttering his wings, on to his back on the window sill. The helplessness of his attitude roused me. It flashed upon me that he was in difficulties; he could no longer raise himself; his legs struggled vainly. But, as I stretched out a pencil, meaning to help him to right himself, it came over me that the failure and awkwardness were the approach of death. I laid the pencil down again.

5 The legs agitated themselves once more. I looked as if for the enemy against which he struggled. I looked out of doors. What had happened there? Presumably it was midday, and work in the fields had stopped. Stillness and quiet had replaced the previous animation. The birds had taken themselves off to feed in the brooks. The horses stood still. Yet the power was there all the same, massed outside, indifferent, impersonal, not attending to anything in particular. Somehow it was opposed to the little hay-colored moth. It was useless to try to do anything. One could only watch the extraordinary efforts made by those tiny legs against an oncoming doom which could, had it chosen, have submerged an entire city, not merely a city, but masses of human beings; nothing, I knew, had any chance against death. Nevertheless after a pause of exhaustion the legs fluttered again. It was superb this last protest, and so frantic that he succeeded at last in righting himself. One's sympathies, of course, were all on the side of life. Also, when there was nobody to care or to know, this gigantic effort on the part of an insignificant little moth, against a power of such magnitude, to retain what no one else valued or desired to keep, moved one strangely. Again, somehow, one saw life, a pure bead. I lifted the pencil again, useless though I knew it to be. But even as I did so, the unmistakable tokens of death showed themselves. The body relaxed, and instantly grew stiff. The struggle was over. The insignificant little creature now knew death. As I looked at the dead moth, this minute wayside triumph of so great a force over so mean an antagonist filled me with wonder. Just as life had been strange a few minutes before, so death was now as strange. The moth having righted himself now lay most decently and uncomplainingly composed. O yes, he seemed to say, death is stronger than I am.

LEARNING MORE

A great deal has been written about Virginia Woolf and her circle. Useful links to more information about Woolf and the Bloomsbury Group can be found on the *Ideas Across Time* website.

QUESTIONING THE TEXT

1. Why do you think Woolf bothers to distinguish between night moths and day moths?
2. What impression of the day does Woolf establish?
3. Does it matter that the essay is set in mid-September?
4. How does the moth, stuck indoors, reflect the outdoors?
5. How does Woolf's view of the moth shift and change during the course of the essay?
6. How is the moth like a human being?
7. In your own words, explain what Woolf means when she says, at the very close of par. 2, "He was little or nothing but life."
8. Woolf says life is "strange" (par. 3). Explain.
9. Why is Woolf holding a pencil? What do you think the pencil could be said to represent?
10. The moth is indoors. How does this affect the essay?
11. Is life here intentionally purposeful? Is death intentionally wicked? Which is stronger—life, or death?
12. What is the final impression the moth makes on Woolf?
13. How do you think we ought to interpret the essay's final sentence?

ANALYZING THE WRITER'S CRAFT

1. This essay is full of comparisons and contrasts. Explore the significance of the contrast between the world outside the window and on the inside, for example, or between the vast and the tiny.
2. Clearly, this essay offers very evocative descriptions that can be appreciated for themselves, and at the same time, the essay intends concrete details—the pencil, the moth—to stand for ideas larger than themselves. How does Woolf establish that one thing in her essay may stand for something else, too?
3. How would you characterize the tone of this essay?
4. How would you characterize the diction of this essay?
5. Trace the changes in Woolf's view of the moth.
6. Woolf develops an accumulation of meanings around the word "energy." Look at each instance of Woolf's use of this word, and discuss the cumulative effect of her repeated use of it.
7. Although Woolf is often precise and detailed in her descriptions here, she is also often very abstract ("He was little or nothing but life," par. 2). How does Woolf aim to make abstract ideas concrete? Does she succeed?
8. Is there a thesis in this essay? If so, where is it and what is it? If not, what holds the essay together?
9. Is Woolf's conclusion effective? Explain.

MAKING CONNECTIONS

1. What is Woolf's understanding of nature? How does it compare and contrast with the views of Luther Standing Bear (Chapter 3, pp. 187–191)?

2. How does Woolf's view of death as a power compare and contrast with Leslie Marmon Silko's account of the Pueblo view of death (pp. 693–694)?
3. Is it conceivable, from what you read in this essay, that a living thing might *choose* death? On the basis of this essay, what do you think Woolf would say to Yukio Mishima (pp. 685–691)? And yet, Woolf committed suicide. Is there any indication in this essay that suicide might be a possibility for the author?

FORMULATING IDEAS FOR WRITING

1. Write an essay that explores whether Woolf depicts life or death as being the stronger force. Do you agree with her?
2. Write an essay that explores Woolf's use of the window and the pencil.
3. Is this an optimistic or pessimistic essay? Use quotations carefully to support your answer.
4. How is the moth like us?
5. What view of nature does this essay convey?

"Where Are the Snows of Yesteryear?" Thoughts on Death and Dying (1450–2001)

François Villon, Emily Dickinson, Dylan Thomas, Anne Sexton, Angelina Rossi, Rick Rundle, and Carlos Cortez

This album of reflections on death is composed of famous poems about death and prose by some of the everyday people interviewed by Studs Terkel for *Will the Circle Be Unbroken?* It opens with François Villon's celebrated "The Ballad of Dead Ladies," written in Paris in the mid-fifteenth century. Although educated to enter the priesthood, Villon killed a priest in a tavern brawl in 1455 and thereafter lived as a vagabond and thief, continually in and out of jail. In 1463, he was condemned to hang but was reprieved and instead banished from Paris. He was thirty-four years old, and no record of him exists after that date. His vivid and iconoclastic writing, composed in his decade of outlaw life in Paris, saucily confronts human pretentiousness and death. "The Ballad of Dead Ladies" memorably expresses one of the great Renaissance literary themes: that fame and beauty are negated by time. Villon's famous line—"But where are the snows of yesteryear?"—conveys at once the inexorable sense of life's passing and a nostalgia and longing for the brilliant days of life, always about to vanish into the mystery of death. Villon's formal brilliance laid the foundations of modern French poetry.

Unlike Villon, Emily Dickinson (1830–1886), the greatest American lyric poet, lived a life of uncommon, even eccentric seclusion. Born to a prominent educational and political family in Amherst, Massachusetts, Dickinson never left Amherst, or for that matter her own room, after she reached the age of thirty. Although she wrote around 1800 poems, only 7 were published in her lifetime. She appears to have read widely, and she was an avid correspondent. Her work is radically original and anticipates the manner and techniques of twentieth-century poetry, such as off-rhymes and broken meter. Her punctuation, with its reliance on the dash for almost all breaks and transitions, also anticipates the modern stress on the breath as a basis for meter. Many of her greatest poems, like the ones in this album, concern death. Dickinson stopped attending religious services in her late twenties, but her attention to human mortality was profound. She registered with unique force an extraordinary range of responses to death, including terror, wry amusement, sisterly familiarity, and affection.

Affection is far from the attitude toward death expressed by the Welsh poet Dylan Thomas (1914–1953) in his much-loved "Do Not Go Gentle into That Good Night," a poem written near the end of his life. A poet whose work seems always written in the shadow of lost innocence, whose effort to rekindle childhood joys often results in extreme dislocations of language and buoyant wordplay, Dylan evinces a pugilistic anger at death as the thief of time. Disorderly in his everyday affairs, personal and professional, Dylan embraced the Romantic life of the drunken poet, too bitten by life's joys and pains to function without the balm of liquor. Drink ruined Dylan's health and cut his life short. But in his work, the brilliance of life is what matters; death is the outrageous enemy.

In the last poem of this album, "Imitations of Drowning," by the twentieth-century American poet Anne Sexton (1928–1974), death exerts an enormous pull, sucking the writer under like a strong undertow, irresistible and terrifying. Indeed Sexton, raised in a flamboyantly dysfunctional family (her father, like Dylan, was an alcoholic), was troubled by repeated mental breakdowns and finally committed suicide. She sought to contain her personal trauma through art, giving her poems an intense connection with the traumas of her time. Her success in turning personal anguish into a vehicle for cultural distress earned her the Pulitzer Prize in 1967. "The soul," she wrote in a letter, "is a human being who speaks with the pressure of death at his head." That pressure is palpable in "Imitations of Drowning."

The responses to death of great writers emerge in the lives of Angelina Rossi, Rick Rundle, and Carlos Cortez as inescapable challenges to living. Angelina Rossi measures her Catholic faith against the huge changes in society and in her own life as these appear to her in the shadow of oncoming death. She confronts uncertainty with skepticism and calm, thinking unselfishly of what will be best for her family. Rick Rundle donated a part of his liver to a stranger, John Husar, on an impulse rooted in the depth of his faith and religious practice. Why did he do it? Because he had the chance "to give life" and to make a small gesture in the light of God's love. Rundle says that for him "God is unconditional love." In an afterword to the interview, Rundle tells Studs Terkel how he reacted when John Husar died despite his liver donation. Finally, Carlos Cortez, a seventy-six-year-old painter, says that at his age "there's no time to be afraid of death—you know it's coming." Of Mexican ancestry, Cortez finds that the feast of the Dead, with its *calverismo,* or skull imagery, and its exaggerated embrace of death, not only is a lucid confrontation with the inevitable but through its traditional celebration of death achieves a vigorous celebration of life. The album ends then in a paradox often confronted in this chapter, namely, that the gaze we cast on death reveals less about what lies beyond than about the life we continue so avidly to pursue.

The Ballad of Dead Ladies

François Villon

Tell me now in what hidden way is
    Lady Flora the lovely Roman?[1]
Where's Hipparchia, and where is Thaïs,[2]
    Neither of them the fairer woman?
    Where is Echo,[3] beheld of no man,
Only heard on river and mere—
    She whose beauty was more than human? . . .
But where are the snows of yesteryear?

Where's Héloise, the learned nun,
    For whose sake Abeillard, I ween,
Lost manhood and put priesthood on?[4]
    (From Love he won such dule and teen!)
    And where, I pray you, is the queen[5]
Who willed that Buridan should steer
    Sewed in a sack's mouth down the Seine? . . .
But where are the snows of yesteryear?

White Queen Blanche, like a queen of lilies,
    With a voice like any mermaidén[6]—
Bertha Broadfoot, Beatrice, Alice,
    And Ermengarde, the lady of Maine[7]—
    And that good Joan whom Englishmen

---

[1] Roman: Flora is the goddess of flowers and spring.
[2] Hipparchia . . . Thais: Hipparchia (c. third century BCE) was wife of Crates, the Greek Cynic philosopher. Thais was mistress of Alexander the Great.
[3] Echo: Nymph who pined after Narcissus until she became merely a voice.
[4] Héloise . . . priesthood on?: Héloise fell in love with her teacher, the churchman Abelard (1079–1142). They were secretly married in order to protect his career in the church. Héloise's uncle, in revenge, had Abelard castrated. As a result, Abelard became a monk and Héloise a nun.
[5] queen: Marguerite de Bourgogne, heroine of the legend of the Tour de Nesle; she had her numerous lovers slain and thrown into the river Seine. Only Jean Buridan escaped.
[6] mermaiden: thought to refer to the mother of Louis IX of France (1226–1270), Blanche of Castille.
[7] Maine: list of famous medieval ladies, of whom Bertha Broadfoot was mother of Charlemagne.

At Rouen doomed and burned her there[8]—
Mother of God, where are they then? . . .
But where are the snows of yesteryear?

Nay, never ask this week, fair lord,
Where they are gone, nor yet this year,
Except with this for an overword—
"But where are the snows of yesteryear?"

The Last Night She Lived

Emily Dickinson

The last Night that She lived
It was a Common Night
Except the Dying—this to Us
Made Nature different

We noticed smallest things—
Things overlooked before
By this great light upon our Minds
Italicized—as 'twere.

As We went out and in
Between Her final Room
And Rooms where Those to be alive
Tomorrow were, a Blame

That Others could exist
While She must finish quite
A Jealousy for Her arose
So nearly infinite—

We waited while She passed—
It was a narrow time—
Too jostled were Our Souls to speak
At length the notice came.
She mentioned, and forgot—
Then lightly as a Reed
Bent to the Water, struggled scarce—
Consented, and was dead—

And We—We placed the Hair—
And drew the Head erect—

[8] there: Joan of Arc, who was burned at the stake in 1431.

And then an awful leisure was
Belief to regulate—

Because I Could Not Stop for Death

Emily Dickinson

Because I could not stop for Death,
He kindly stopped for me;
The carriage held but just ourselves
And Immortality.

We slowly drove, he knew no haste,
And I had put away
My labor, and my leisure too,
For his civility.

We passed the school, where children strove
At recess, in the ring;
We passed the fields of gazing grain,
We passed the setting sun.

Or rather, he passed us;
The dews grew quivering and chill,
For only gossamer my gown,
My tippet only tulle.[1]

We paused before a house that seemed
A swelling of the ground;
The roof was scarcely visible,
The cornice in the ground.

Since then 'tis centuries, and yet
Feels shorter than the day
I first surmised the horses' heads
Were toward eternity.

Do Not Go Gentle into That Good Night

Dylan Thomas

Do not go gentle into that good night,
Old age should burn and rave at close of day;
Rage, rage against the dying of the light.

---

[1] tippet . . . tulle: A tippet is a narrow strip of cloth, usually attached to a head-dress or sleeve; tulle is fine silk.

Though wise men at their end know dark is right,
Because their words had forked no lightning they
Do not go gentle into that good night.

Good men, the last wave by, crying how bright
Their frail deeds might have danced in a green bay,
Rage, rage against the dying of the light.

Wild men who caught and sang the sun in flight,
And learn, too late, they grieved it on its way,
Do not go gentle into that good night.

Grave men, near death, who see with blinding sight
Blind eyes could blaze like meteors and be gay,
Rage, rage against the dying of the light.

And you, my father, there on the sad height,
Curse, bless, me now with your fierce tears, I pray.
Do not go gentle into that good night.
Rage, rage against the dying of the light.

Imitations of Drowning

Anne Sexton

Fear
of drowning,
fear of being that alone,
kept me busy making a deal
as if I could buy
my way out of it
and it worked for two years
and all of July.

This August I began to dream of drowning. The dying
went on and on in water as white and clear
as the gin I drink each day at half-past five.
Going down for the last time, the last breath lying,
I grapple with eels like ropes—it's ether, it's queer
and then, at last, it's done. Now the scavengers arrive,
the hard crawlers who come to clean up the ocean floor.
And death, that old butcher, will bother me no more.

I
had never
had this dream before
except twice when my parents
clung to rafts

and sat together for death,
frozen
like lewd photographs.

Who listens to dreams? Only symbols for something—
like money for the analyst or your mother's wig,
the arm I almost lost in the washroom wringer,
following fear to its core, tugging the old string.
But real drowning is for someone else. It's too big
to put in your mouth on purpose, it puts hot stingers
in your tongue and vomit in your nose as your lungs break.
Tossed like a wet dog by that juggler, you die awake.

Fear,
a motor,
pumps me around and around
until I fade slowly
and the crowd laughs.
I fade out, an old bicycle rider
whose odds are measured
in actuary graphs.

This weekend the papers were black with the new highway
fatalities and in Boston the strangler found another victim
and we were all in Truro drinking beer and writing checks.
The others rode the surf, commanding rafts like sleighs.
I swam—but the tide came in like ten thousand orgasms.
I swam—but the waves were higher than horses' necks.
I was shut up in that closet, until, biting the door,
they dragged me out, dribbling urine on the gritty shore.

Breathe!
And you'll know . . .
an ant in a pot of chocolate,
it boils
and surrounds you.
There is no news in fear
but in the end it's fear
that drowns you.

Mothers and Sons

Angelina Rossi

She is the mother of V.I.M., Victor Israel Marquez. She is seventy. I have known her for many years; a strong, independent-minded woman. She has worked as a bailiff in Chicago courts and as an investigator for the Internal Revenue Service (IRS). She is now retired.

Victor was a very sweet young boy, helpful—the neighbors all loved him. He was the type of kid that would carry the groceries home for the neighbors, sweep their yards or pick up their trash or dump their garbage for them. He was the sweetest kid in the world. And then he went to Vietnam.

He came back completely changed, an altogether different person. Sometimes it's very difficult to take . . . for me. I'm his mother, I knew what he was before. It's very difficult for me to see him the way he is today. It's very sad for me. [*A long pause*]

I've had six children. One of them, his younger brother, was the baby of the family. The other four girls were bossy, as most girls are. They take after their mother, I'm pretty bossy too. I think he got to the point where he just couldn't take so many females around him, and he felt maybe he was missing something not having a man in the house. And so he decided he was going to Vietnam. I'd been divorced for quite some time. I never remarried. I'm not sure what it was, but I think he just felt that he had to break out of where he was and be in a more manly society. So he picked what he thought was the greatest military service in the world, the U.S. Marines.

He's an alcoholic today. He does things that . . . I've never seen him doing these things, but I've heard from others. He's one of the people who has road rage or mall rage or restaurant rage or something. He doesn't seem to care about having any self-control. I am completely confused. I have been very religious, up until five or six years ago. Then all of a sudden, science, technology, the furtherance of our minds has all hit me, and I think to myself, *How could this be?* How could there be a Heaven? When we die, our bodies turn into, the nice way to say it is, dust. We turn into nutrients for worms, for other plant life. We evolve and we come back into a sprig of grass or a flower or a tree. And I think that's how we live on. [*She chokes up.*] I can't believe anymore that there is a Heaven. Am I going to see my mother? I don't think so . . . I am totally confused and scared. I'm scared because I think to myself, *What if I'm denying my religious beliefs?* What if I, for whatever reason, my age, the time of life, my thinking . . .

5 Maybe I want to be back as a six-year-old child. I want to just have my belief that there's a God, that there's a Trinity, that there's Heaven, that there's Hell. I think my Catholic faith has also got a lot to do with it, with my confusion. We have changes in what used to be laws: you couldn't eat meat on Friday night. Now you can eat meat on Friday. You couldn't be cremated. Would you believe I've already paid for my cremation because it's approved now by the Catholic Church. If the Catholic Church, or any Church I would guess, is that correct and that right, then how can they change their rules in the middle of things? So I think to myself, *I've lived through so much life, I've seen things change, I'm realistic, I know what really happens, and I just don't know* . . . Is there a spirit that lives on? According to the Bible, we're all going to meet our maker, we're all going to be judged. Well, I don't have to worry about that. I don't think I'm going to be judged too badly. But I think to myself, how in the world can your entity, your human person come before a governing body, and they're going to decide whether you've been a good person all your life or a bad person all your life?

There's so many differences in people. Some people believe in having multiple wives. Our society believes, no, you only have one wife. Today our society believes you not only have one commitment to a person, but it could be a person of the same sex. You could marry another woman, you could marry another man if you're a man. I'm confused. Am I alone? Am I the only one? I find it very difficult to have any straight thoughts about anything because even though I say things, in my head is something else, something opposite is coming through.

We found that there are as many things beneath the ocean as up in the sky. How do we know what's there until we're there? The floor of the ocean is breaking up on the Eastern Seaboard. They don't know what's going to happen—might be horrible tidal waves that hit the shore. What if there's some kind of a living entity that comes out of that? Now we've got something else to worry about, something else to digest, something else to understand. Are we going to be the same like we are now with the crazy alien things? We're going to go out and kill them? They're human beings, or they're beings, whatever they might be. What if they have a religious background? What if they think there's life hereafter? As a child, there was no question—no question where I came from, where I was going to be, and where I was going to be when I died, I knew. When I died, I was going to Heaven, I was going to be in the arms of God.

I'm of the old school. Another thing that's changed with the Catholic religion is there's no longer a burning Inferno, there's no longer "you're going to burn forever." Today, the word is that Hell is you're just not in the presence of God—so that too has changed.

I grew up when the nuns used to hit your hand with the ruler or stick gum in your hair if you misbehaved. They did that to me for chewing gum in school. They didn't just make you throw it out, but me, they stuck it in my *hair*—and my mother had to cut it out. Of course, my hair was real long so that was *terrible.* But you believed everything the nuns and the priests told you.

10 I regret my innocence, I regret the absolute belief that I had, because it's making me nuts. I don't know what to think anymore. And this scares me—I'm very fearful that my whole life has been a sort of living—believing a fairy tale. And, I'm wondering: *Is there a supreme being?* And I have to cross myself . . . [*She crosses herself.*] Because there's the part of me that says, "You'd better not be too sure about that, because what if there is a God?" What if all my life my beliefs *are* right? What if something has happened as I've grown older? An arrogance about myself that I think, *Oh, I know a heck of a lot more than the person on the street* . . . And then I think God can't hold that against me if He's for real. Because God made me. He knew what I was going to evolve into. He knew the person I was going to become. So if there is a God, then I have nothing to worry about. I think that's only because I'm as old as I am, and for me God has always been a male, a man. The pictures, the host, everything has always been he, he, he. Now, as far as I'm concerned, I don't care if it's a he, a she, or an it—it doesn't matter to me. If it's just a spirit, that's OK. If it's a force, that's OK too. Whatever it is . . .

I know I'm going to die. The only thing I hope and pray for is that I die quietly, that I don't die with pain and anxiety, fear. But I don't fear dying. I've lived.

My goodness, have I *lived*. I have lived a life: I've raised six children. I've had a law enforcement career . . . I've been very happy, I've got very good friends. I can go at any time, it doesn't matter. And I'm all set for it. I'm all prepared for my death. I've got my funeral arrangements made. What little money I have is going where it's supposed to go. I hate to be very, very human right now, but I've got to tell you: I just cannot stand the idea of my body being infested with worms and maggots. I would rather be burned. After all, we go to dust anyway, according to the Bible: dust to dust. So I'm happy about all that.

I'm going to be seventy years old. Most people call this the golden years. I don't. For me, they're the rust years. Everything is rusting up—especially the knees.

When I go, I'd like some kind of closure for my family. I would like them to have a little memorial service with any friends that might want to come. A lot of my contemporaries are deceased now, so it doesn't much matter. [*Laughs*] I'm not a famous person, so there might not be that many people to come to my wake. If you're around and you've got the time, come on over and just say a few prayers for me. Because still I keep thinking, *OK, the person says a prayer for me, it works for me, so* . . . I would like to be remembered as a person who always did the best she could do, but who had a lot of faults. And forgive me for the faults that I had. For the most part, I tried to do the best I could do.

I find that the majority of people don't want to discuss death. I tried to speak to my family about what I want done when I die. I can't find anybody that wants to talk to me about it. I had to talk to my son-in-law . . . [*Laughs*] It's like it's never going to happen. It's like they're ostriches with their heads in the sand. It happens to everybody else, but it's not going to happen to us. See, that's not the way I think: I know it's going to happen. And I want to be prepared.

The Stranger

Rick Rundle

He arrives by bike. He is a forty-five-year-old "hoisting engineer" for the Streets and Sanitation Department; he works in graffiti removal. He lives with his mother and a younger brother, John, who has Down's syndrome. Just the previous month he had donated part of his liver to John Husar, a columnist on the outdoors for the Chicago Tribune *and a member of his parish congregation. Theirs is the only white family in a black community on the south side of the city.*

My family was always religious, but I think anyone's faith, it ebbs and flows. For a true seeker of answers, it ebbs and flows. So I can't say I always had strong faith—I'd be lying. But it's not the hour you're in church, it's all the other hours you're not in church that truly show who you are.

I went searching for different parishes to get what I needed. The parish that I settled on is Old St. Pat's, down on the near West Side of downtown Chicago. It's the oldest public building in the city of Chicago. I had slowly become a Eucharist minister, a liturgical minister, one that does the readings and passes out the bulletins. About three months ago, at the end of the mass, the priest made an announcement that there was a parishioner who was looking for a liver transplant. Five of my close friends have come down with hepatitis C, which is a chronic liver disease—lifelong friends that I've known for years. So I was somewhat familiar with liver disease. The odd thing about hepatitis C, it's pandemic. Probably more people are going to die of hepatitis C this year than will die of HIV in this country. Because it's a silent disease, it's a disease that takes fifteen to twenty years to incubate and once it does, it affects different people in different ways. The only known cure, and it's not even a cure, is a liver transplant.

John Husar wasn't a friend. I'd see him at church and, of course, I enjoyed reading his column.

I wanted to see him live. I wanted to give him a chance at a life that was being denied him. I knew my friends who had hepatitis C, and it's not a good existence. It's a lot of sleeping, it's a lot of times you don't even feel good enough to get out of bed. And I met a priest who got the last liver in the previous millennium, 1999. He talked about how much it did for him and how good he felt.

5 Everything has a purpose. By meeting people, you make an equation and make your own decision. So I met this Carmelite priest, oh, he's got to be close to seventy or older. And he said to me, he goes, "I don't know why they decided a person like me should get the liver. They should give it to a person who was thirty years old. But I guess they see that I have a purpose in life, that I can do something with this life of mine." I saw that without a liver, John Husar had no hope, that he was going to die. There was no ands, ifs, or buts about it.

I felt it didn't have a risk to it, but the doctors told me it had a big risk to it because there's a number of complications that could have happened besides me dying on the table. I gave one pint of blood in case they needed it during the operation, which I was told would take six hours. Then the nurses told me the operation would take nine hours. Then it took twelve hours. So it's a very long, complicated, sophisticated operation. Because of all the bile ducts and arteries and veins going into the liver, because of filtering properties of the liver—it's a more complicated transplant than the heart or the kidney. What happens is, they take the right lobe of your liver—they take over fifty percent of it. But the unique thing about the liver is, it regenerates itself. The liver you have right now will not be the same liver you have three weeks from now—it'll totally disintegrate, let's say—and replace itself within three weeks as long as you're healthy and there's no fevers. So my liver is back to full strength, though the scar is still there.

It was about a month ago, but it still feels like somebody whacked me with a paddle or a cane right across my abdominals. As soon as you get out of the hospital they tell you . . . Well, I like to golf: so no golf, no sailing, no strenuous exercise. And, of course, no drinking. So all I've been doing is reading, listening to music, and taking naps.

I did it because it would only be a couple months of me not being able to work or do what I want, and this is something I could do in my life. I could give life to someone else, give them hope, give them the chance. I minimized the risk in my mind. For years I used to race a sailboat and not be a good swimmer. I rode a motorcycle for years and was in a lot of close accidents. You take a chance any time you get on a bus or an airplane or a train or a car—so everything is risk. But if you're not willing to risk, you truly don't own it, do you? So I thought: *It's my life.* You have to risk your life, and especially for someone else, to give life. We're all part of this human community, and if you're not willing to give of yourself, then you're held captive. To me, God is unconditional love. That means to love someone, no matter what they do, how they are, how little you know them, but to help someone with all they have.

I got this belief through years of listening to the sermons at Old St. Pat's. And also from my mother. She's eighty-two years old. She went to work for the city in the Health Department, in the Water Department. She met my father in the late forties and had five children; then as my younger brother, John, was old enough to be put in day care, she wanted to go back to work and make money. So then she taught high school for twenty years in the Catholic high school system. So I get a lot of this doing from her.

10 She believes in people. If she didn't believe in life, in the dignity of life, whatever life there is, she wouldn't be that way to my brother, Johnny, who has Down's syndrome.

Life is sacred. And if you can help someone in a time of need, you would not even think twice about it. It's what they call a no-brainer. I got it, I don't need it. You get by with forty percent of your liver. Right now my liver is back to full strength. The right lobe was taken out and now it's back to a hundred-percent volume.

The surgeon came to me right before they were going to put me under and said, "If you die on the operating table, you're not going to come back and haunt me?" He says, "If you want to get out, get out now." He wanted to make sure that I knew the consequences, or the ultimate risk, and that I was doing this of my free will. He wanted to challenge me one more time and tell me that I could get out. I said, "I've had a good life these forty-five years. And if I die, I'm at peace with myself. But if I don't take the risk to help this person, I'll forever look back at myself and say, 'Why didn't I?'" So I told him, "I do this of my own free will, I'm at peace, and I wouldn't haunt you. Don't worry about me." This is one thing that I could do and would do and feel good about doing it.

My mother said, "Well, Rick, I think it's OK because you're going to do whatever you want anyway. You've made up your mind." It wasn't until my mother met Laura, who is John Husar's daughter, that she actually understood what it meant to John's family. John had been on a transplant list for the last two years and gone to the hospital as a standby, but never got it. Five times he was prepped for an operation. I'll never forget: we were at a meeting a couple of months before the operation and the doctor looked at him and said, "I give you six weeks on the inside and six months on the outside. If you don't get a liver by then, you'll be dead." That's really looking down the barrel of a gun.

I didn't really make a will. I contacted a lot of people that I thought would be upset, through e-mail and telephone, to let them know that I was doing this and there was a small amount of risk there. A lot of times in life we try to play down our own risk, you know what I mean? More people told me there was a risk than I believed there was. I don't know if it was my strong faith or my vitality.

Now, from what I learned there's a ninety- to ninety-five-percent success rate for the recipient. The donor—they've only lost I think two, three donors. There's always complications of bleeding, of bile, and infection. But I didn't see it coming my way. Of course, I have a scapular on. It's a thing that was given to St. Simon Stock, who was the head of the Carmelite Order, by the Virgin Mary. Basically, it says whoever wears my scapular will never suffer the flames of Hell.

To me, Heaven is no pain, seeing the people you want, having the questions in your mind answered. People are always nice, they're always altruistic, you only have rainy days if you want them. You see the people that you haven't seen that are in the other world. To me, it'd be like a big picnic. Whatever you're missing in this life, you're made whole. My brother, who has Down's syndrome—I would probably not even recognize him. He'd be able to talk and we'd converse more than we would now. Johnny as a whole person—not handicapped, no wheelchairs.

When it's time for you to go, when you're near there, they say it's usually someone from the other world who you know who will come and get you. And not that I wouldn't mind seeing my sister, who's been dead for twenty years or so—in that automobile accident. Or my father. But I see now that it'll probably be someone like John Husar. And in your mind, Studs, you would be at a radio station, doing a radio show of fifty years ago. And you would see someone that you haven't seen in a long time. And they'd say, "Studs, where have you been? I've been looking for you. We've got another show to do on the other side of the river." I see myself, I'd be in the St. Patrick's Day Parade, either on the South Side, on Western Avenue, or downtown on Dearborn. And this guy will come up all dressed in white, and it'll be John Husar. And he'll have the torch—he ran with the torch in the Olympics one time—and he'll say, "Rick, I've been looking all over for you. It's time for you to run with the torch. We've got somewhere to go!" Or I'll be sailing my boat and out of the corner of my eye I'll see this rowboat will be trying to catch me. I'll try to get the boat to go faster because rowboats aren't supposed to catch my sailboat. And I'll see it's John. John will say, "Rick, I've been looking for you. Come on, get in the boat. We gotta go rowing."

Postscript

When John Husar died, it's not that I was mad at God. I was just like: *How could this be?* How could this be? Because here was a person, although I'm sure he looked at death, he wasn't ready to die. He didn't write his final column. The day he died, the bass came into Chicago, the fish—that's something he worked at. So I'm thinking to myself, he has to live so he can cover the Bass Masters Tournament—it was where they came from all over the country to fish for bass in Lake Michigan, around Chicago. He always had a Sunday and Thursday column and I went out to buy the newspaper, like I had expected to see his column there. *Can't be.* Couldn't be. Can't be. 'Cause I tried to give this person life . . . If you put a new set of tires on your car, you figure you get another fifty thousand miles out of it. You put your money in the tollbooth, you figure you can at least drive to the end of the road. But see, that's the odd thing. Life is so precious. Life is not the given. Death is the given. Death is the certainty. Life is this gift. Life is kind of . . . we make it as we go along. For every birth there is a death. The real thing in life is the journey. Now that's an odd thing in America where you think the goal is how much money we make, or the car we drive, or the position we have. We're getting away from what life is actually about. A lot of times I see the person selling *Streetwise,* the magazine put out by the homeless, and I talk to them. You have to give people dignity. The dignity you give is the dignity you see in yourself and you carry yourself.

I usually pray in the morning—usually a Hail Mary, like that. But there's this one website I go to, the website for Henri Nouwen. He was a Dutch priest, a theologian. He taught at Notre Dame University, Harvard, and Yale. At the last part of his life he was with people with Down's syndrome. I met him once, and his books are just phenomenal for me. You look at the computer and there's a thought of the day, a prayer of the day. He would write whatever thought was in his head for that day. A lot of times, even in this past struggle that I've had in the last month, they really spoke to me. I'll never forget the day that John Husar died, Henri Nouwen's thought of the day was about the Good Samaritan. The person that crosses the road to try to help the other individual. They say that my kind of transplant was a Good Samaritan transplant because it wasn't within the family and it wasn't a close friend. So it spoke very profoundly to me for that day.

Day of the Dead

Carlos Cortez

He is a painter and poet living in Chicago. "I'm seventy-six, going on seventy-seven."

I remember when I was a little kid, it bugged me, the idea of death. My mother said to me, "Hey, just think if you never did die, if you lived forever, that would be worse!" After all, nothing lasts forever—and it's a good thing too. I remember my wife grieving over the death of her mother. An old friend said, "We have to make room for the next generations." I've said to people, "Hey, don't be afraid of death. If you're afraid of death, you shouldn't have been born." I was somewhere between five and seven years old when I first realized what it was. People don't like to accept the finality, but nothing is infinite.

I spent some time with the Jehovah's Witnesses during the war when I was incarcerated for my draft refusal—this was World War II. They would say, "How would you like to live forever, never die?" I said, "No, I don't think I would care for it." To see everything there is to see, know everything there is to know, and have nothing new, that would be terrible. I hope to be conscious when the time comes, because I've had a good life. I'm going to hate to leave it, but I think I'm better being sorry to leave it than saying, "Oh, at last it's come, it's over with." I want to feel that there's still more. If we live a good life, we will live on with those who remember us.

Mozart had a short life, what, thirty-two years? As an old conductor said—it was on your radio program—"He was but a moment in eternity." Well, that's what all of us are. We're but moments in eternity. But we've been a part of it. People have many ways of facing the prospect of death. Some don't want to think about it. When you get to be in your upper seventies, you realize you got more behind you than you got ahead of you. There's no time to be afraid of death anymore—you know it's coming.

Among the Mexicans—my father was a Mexican Indian—they sort of celebrate death. It's a way of honoring the recently departed and honoring one's roots. Without death, there's no life: they're mutually dependent. It's just a process of the circle. The great printmaker José Guadalupe Posada used the death image a lot as a matter of caricature. He would depict the politicians and big people of his day as skeletons, which underneath they are. There's a date now, the second of November, which is called *el día de los muertos,* the Day of the Dead. When the Spanish priests came over, it happened to coincide with All Souls' Day, just the way it coincides with the Anglo-Saxon Halloween. It happens at a time of year when the last green has disappeared, and people are reminded of the impermanences of existence. At the same time, there's a continuity to it. It's a celebration that we've lived and that we've had a good life, that we've done our part. I would not know about the hereafter. The idea of the Heaven, the garden of Allah, the Happy Hunting Ground, is a reluctance to accept the finality of things. Everything has its limitation. As we say: even the mountains fade away. For the better, for the worse, life is what we make of it. Personally, I would not like to spend eternity on a cloud plucking away at a harp. I think I'd rather be where the gang is.

5 Bliss you can't understand unless you've had a little rough bumps. The person who says, "Oh, I've always been happy." *B.S.!* If you haven't known the opposite, how can you know what happiness is? I think I have paradise right now. Despite this messed-up human world that we live in, I think it's a very interesting world. Remember old Cholly Wendorf, the one-armed soapbox orator? He was saying he died once and was sent up to Heaven. St. Peter said, "Oh, you're an *agitator,*" he sent him down to Hell. The Devil says, "I don't want you!" He says, "You only got one arm. You have to shovel souls into that fire there and you have to toss Christians around in the fire. So I'm going to send you to purgatory." *So here I am, back in purgatory!* Existence is a great thing. We hang on to it as much as possible, no matter how rough things are.

When they celebrate the Day of the Dead, they build their home altars and put offerings for the departed there, and photographs of the recently departed. And on that night they go to the cemetery. First they clean off the tombstone and whitewash it, decorate it with flowers. Decorate it with the marigold, because that's the one flower that still grows at that time of year. And then they sit down and have lunch with their departed, and spend the night with them. Sometimes you'll see musical groups out there, mariachi bands. And they spend the night with their departed. This is not only Mexico. I know the cemetery where my wife's mother is buried here on the northwest side of Chicago, a lot of Greek Orthodox people are there, Russian, Serbians, and what have you. And people will come out and have their lunches with them, sit down by the grave site and have lunch with their departed. Or they'll be carrying a case of soda—Coke, Pepsi, or whatever—everybody he sees goes and gives them a can of soda because it's a part of remembering their departed. In Mexico it's become an annual holiday.

You see dry twigs and dry branches, and you're reminded of the impermanence of existence. The Protestants, who settled the northern part of the hemisphere, when they saw the old practices, they said, "Oh, that's stuff of the Devil. We have to stamp this out." The Spanish padres said, "Well, wait a minute, this is *el día de*—the day of St. Gerónimo. From now on this will be the Fiesta of St. Gerónimo." St. Jerome—Gerónimo, the way the Apache chief was named . . .

I recently returned from California, where I picked up a lot of silkscreen posters and a lot of these used the image of death. The image of the *calaverismo. Calavera* means skull or skeleton. It was the practice for thousands of years. You have to consider that in Mexico, people lived next door to earthquakes, volcanoes, pestilences, and bad economic conditions, so death was no stranger. It was something that was accepted philosophically. The poet Octavio Paz says that in the capitals of Paris and London the word "death" gets caught on the tongue, burns the tongue, but in Mexico they embrace it, they play with it, and they celebrate it. It's illustrated in the toys that are found around the Day of the Dead. Skeletons, little pushcarts with skeletons are given to the children: *This is what you'll become someday.* Don't be afraid of death. What's more important: *Don't be afraid of life.* There's a verse from a traditional Mexican song. *"Nadie debe lamentarse por muerte de sus amores,"* "Nobody should lament the passing of one's loves."

I build an altar for my parents or my wife's parents and for recently departed friends. And of course what interests you is the composition of this altar. You put on things that you associate with the departed's life, be they cigarettes or a can of beer or a bottle of wine, but always there's a glass of water. And the idea behind that is the souls, after making the long journey to visit the altar, are thirsty, so they have the water. And of course the water stays there, it evaporates—and so, you know, the souls are drinking it.

10 The altar is made out of many things. It's usually a platform or a table in a corner of the room that you decorate with flowers, candles, and such. I decorate my altar with skulls made out of sugar candy, besides the toys and such. And there are the various breads they make to represent dead people. And pictures of the departed. Friends come over and add their bit to it. I go over to friends and add my bit to their altars. I'll take a drink and raise it up to them, to the altar, to salute them. Life is a celebration, and death means you're reminded of the life you no longer have.

LEARNING MORE

The *Ideas Across Time* website contains useful links to additional information about François Villon, Emily Dickinson, Dylan Thomas, and Anne Sexton.

QUESTIONING THE TEXT

The Ballad of Dead Ladies

1. Villon employs a medieval poetic convention, the list, to convey his point. What characterizes those whom Villon chooses to list? What criteria do you think he used for his selection?
2. Why does he list women exclusively? Does it matter that some of these women are mythical and some actual women?
3. Restate Villon's refrain—"But where are the snows of yesteryear?"—in your own words.

The Last Night That She Lived

1. Who are "us" in this poem?
2. How does the woman's dying make Nature different?
3. Attendance on the dying woman rouses "Blame" and "Jealousy" in the living. Explain. Do those who are attending on the woman want to die?
4. Why do you think the woman's dying is described as "a narrow time"?
5. Describe the moment of the woman's passing in your own words.
6. How would you interpret the poem's closing stanza?

Because I Could Not Stop for Death

1. Death is personified in this poem as a man. What kind of man is he?
2. Why does Dickinson want to differentiate between passing the sun and being passed by the sun?
3. What is the literal and metaphorical effect of the sun's passing?
4. What would you say is the chief characteristic of death that this poem wishes to convey? Specify and explain.
5. The poem employs a number of formidable abstractions—"Death" (l. 1), "Immortality" (l. 4), and "eternity" (l. 24). How does the poem alter our understanding of these abstractions?
6. Dickinson wrote in the heart of an emphatically Christian region. Is the poem an expression of Christian faith?

Do Not Go Gentle into That Good Night

1. If death is a "good night," then why should we rage against it?
2. What do you think Thomas means by the phrase "forked no lightning" (l. 5)?
3. Thomas includes four broad categories of men in the poem: wise men, good men, wild men, and grave men. How does the poem distinguish among these groups?
4. What is the effect of "father" in the last stanza? Is this actually Thomas's father? What is he asking of "my father"?
5. The poem opens as though it is offering advice and closes with a request. How do these two viewpoints hang together in the poem?

Imitations of Drowning

1. What "deal" do you think Sexton is talking about in her opening stanza? What happened in August that seems to have affected her deal?
2. What is Sexton's frame of mind as depicted in this poem? Specify and explain.
3. What is the role of dreaming in the poem? How do Sexton's waking and dreaming fears interact?
4. What is Sexton's attitude toward her dreams?
5. What do you think Sexton means when she says that "real drowning is for someone else" (l. 29)?
6. Why do you think Sexton introduces highway fatalities and the Boston strangler in stanza 6?
7. What "closet" is Sexton referring to in l. 47?
8. The final lines of the poem unite its two closely connected themes—fear and drowning. How do you think we should understand these last lines?

Mothers and Sons

1. Why does Angelina want to be a six-year-old child again (par. 5)?
2. She says, "I am confused" (par. 6) About what is she confused?
3. How might Angelina's belated loss of innocence cast a whole new light on her entire life?
4. How does Angelina's musing about her son Victor lead her to thoughts of death?
5. Why does Angelina wish to be cremated?

The Stranger

1. How has the change in the family's neighborhood been a boon for Rick's brother John?
2. Rick defines himself as a religious person. What does that mean to him?
3. Why did Rick volunteer his liver to a stranger ill with hepatitis C?
4. How did Rick deal with the possibility that he might die during the operation?
5. What is Rick's attitude toward risk?
6. What does Rick look forward to in Heaven? What is your response to his view of Heaven?
7. What was Rick's reaction to John Husar's death?
8. How was the Web site for Henri Nouwen (par. 19) important to Rick on the day of John Husar's death?
9. Why does Rick think that "We're getting away from what life is actually about" (par. 18)?

Day of the Dead

1. What did Carlos learn about death from an early age?
2. How does Carlos view the brevity of life?
3. Why do the Mexicans celebrate death?

4. Why is Carlos skeptical about the idea of Heaven, the garden of Allah, and other views of the hereafter?
5. How do skeletons feature in Mexican art and culture?
6. What is the significance of the glass of water left on the home altar on the Day of the Dead?
7. Why do you think skulls made of sugar candy or of bread are placed on the home altar on the Day of the Dead?

ANALYZING THE WRITER'S CRAFT

The Ballad of Dead Ladies

1. What are the main formal features that stand out in this poem? For example, is there a rhyme scheme? What is distinctive about the poem's diction? Is there a controlling image or metaphor? Is the poem written in any particular meter, or is it written in free verse or in a combination of the two (for a brief discussion of meter, see the *Ideas Across Time* website)? How does the poem's form affect its meaning?
2. Who is the audience for this poem?
3. This version of Villon's original poem was translated by the English poet Dante Gabriel Rossetti in the mid-nineteenth century. What does Rossetti's diction tell you about his attitude toward the Middle Ages? How does Rossetti's diction affect the tone of the poem?
4. What is the effect of Rossetti's frequent repetition of vowel and consonant sounds in his line—for example, "*S*ewed in a *s*ack's mouth down the *S*eine" (l. 15)?
5. Is there a development in the argument of the poem?
6. Is the poem's ending effective?

The Last Night That She Lived

1. What are the main formal features that stand out in this poem? For example, is there a rhyme scheme? What is distinctive about the poem's diction? Is there a controlling image or metaphor? Is the poem written in any particular meter, or is it written in free verse or in a combination of the two (for a brief discussion of meter, see the *Ideas Across Time* website)? How does the poem's form affect its meaning?
2. Dickinson employs her own conventions in her writing, and these are faithfully reproduced here. Can you explain why she chooses to capitalize?
3. Discuss Dickinson's use of comparisons and contrasts in this poem.
4. What is the tone of this poem? Specify and explain.
5. Discuss the metaphors Dickinson uses in stanzas 6 and 7.
6. The words Dickinson employs in the final stanza are very precise. Consider, for example, "placed," "drew . . . erect," "awful leisure," and "regulate." Concentrating on these words, interpret the poem's final stanza, exploring the various possible ways in which these words could be understood.

Because I Could Not Stop for Death

1. What are the main formal features that stand out in this poem? For example, is there a rhyme scheme? What is distinctive about the poem's diction? Is there a controlling image or metaphor? Is the poem written in any particular meter, or is it written in free verse or in a combination of the two (for a brief discussion of meter, see the *Ideas Across Time* website)? How does the poem's form affect its meaning?
2. What is the tone of this poem? Specify and explain.
3. What is the controlling metaphor of this poem?
4. Discuss Dickinson's use of the varieties of motion in the poem—speed (slowness and quickness), passing, pausing, and stopping.
5. How does the poem's tone and argument shift in stanza 4?
6. What does the poem observe about the relation between mortality and eternity?

Do Not Go Gentle into That Good Night

1. What are the main formal features that stand out in this poem? For example, is there a rhyme scheme? What is distinctive about the poem's diction? Is there a controlling image or metaphor? Is the poem written in any particular meter, or is it written in free verse or in a combination of the two (for a brief discussion of meter, see the *Ideas Across Time* website)? How does the poem's form affect its meaning?
2. Who is the audience for this poem? Specify and explain.
3. Discuss Thomas's use of comparisons and contrasts in this poem.
4. What is the effect of the pattern of organization in this poem—for example, the repetitive functions in stanzas 2–5 of each of the three lines?
5. Is the extra line in the final stanza obtrusive, or does it make for a more emphatic ending?
6. How would you characterize Thomas's language? How does his stretching of the language ("sang the sun in flight," l. 10) contribute to the tone and meaning of the poem?
7. Interpret the closing stanza. Who is "my father"? What is suggested by "the sad height"? How can it make sense to ask to be blessed and cursed? What is the effect of "I pray"? How do the final two lines relate to the opening two lines? Is the impact and meaning of the final two lines, lines that have appeared repeatedly in the poem from the outset, changed by the close of the poem?

Imitations of Drowning

1. What are the main formal features that stand out in this poem? For example, is there a rhyme scheme? What is distinctive about the poem's diction? Is there a controlling image or metaphor? Is the poem written in any particular meter, or is it written in free verse or in a combination of the two (for a brief discussion of meter, see the *Ideas Across Time* website)? How does the poem's form affect its meaning?

2. What is the tone of this poem? Specify and explain. Does the tone change? If so, where?
3. Discuss the effect of Sexton's comparisons—for example, ". . . as the gin I drink each day" (l. 11).
4. Explain the title.
5. What relation does the poem expose between Sexton and other people (see, for example, l. 37 or l. 44)?
6. Are Sexton's images heightened to shock the reader, or are they expressions of her frame of mind?
7. Does the poem anticipate death by drowning?
8. Interpret the closing stanza.

Mothers and Sons

1. It's not clear how much Studs Terkel edits his interviews. But assuming the selection you've just read is a faithful transcription of a person talking, what would you say distinguishes talk from writing? Offer two or three examples.
2. Analyze par. 5. Do you think it is coherent? What is the relation between how it begins and how it ends?
3. Angelina says the sign of her confusion is that she says one thing and means another (par. 6). Do you find suggestions of that in the interview?
4. Is Angelina a logical thinker?
5. Does this essay have a thesis statement? Or the equivalent of a thesis statement? If so, what is it and where is it located? If not, what holds the essay/interview together?

The Stranger

1. Assuming the selection you've just read is a faithful transcription of a person talking, what would you say distinguishes talk from writing? Offer two or three examples.
2. Does this essay have a thesis statement? Or the equivalent of a thesis statement? If so, what is it and where is it located? If not, what holds the essay/interview together?
3. Does the fact that Rick wears a scapular (the cloth worn over the torso, with a hole cut through so it can be put on over the head, that serves as a sacramental insignia, for example by monks) come as a surprise? Does it cast a different light on his discussion of risk?

Day of the Dead

1. Assuming the selection you've just read is a faithful transcription of a person talking, what would you say distinguishes talk from writing? Offer two or three examples.
2. Does this essay have a thesis statement? Or the equivalent of a thesis statement? If so, what is it and where is it located? If not, what holds the essay/interview together?

3. Carlos describes a religious practice or ritual celebration that seems to have no sense of afterlife. The Day of the Dead seems grounded in the sense of necessary finality. How does Carlos convey this difference?
4. This essay/interview uses many concrete details to make its point. Choose two or three of Carlos's especially effective concrete examples, and explain their function in the essay.
5. What is the effect of Carlos's use of the word "departed" (pars. 4, 6, 9, 10)? Does his reference to the "departed" support, undermine, or qualify his general outlook on death? Explain.

MAKING CONNECTIONS

1. How do these views of death compare? What common themes or emphases do they share? How are they different? Which do you find most interesting? Most attractive?
2. Paul Tillich (Chapter 2, pp. 123–130) argues that in recent history we have lost the dimension of depth in religion, that we are no longer gripped with an earnest desire to fathom the meaning of existence. How do these poems and essays confirm or question that view?
3. Friedrich Nietzsche proclaims the death of God; he sees this, moreover, as liberating: at last humans are free to celebrate life as it is and to make of life what they wish (Chapter 2, pp. 109–111). Do these poems and essays confirm his view of religion?
4. Why is science so little mentioned in these reflections on death (see Chapter 3)?
5. Studs Terkel makes a number of references to literature in his thoughts on death. Clearly, many artists see their work as religious (or should the word be "spiritual"?) in its concern. But these poems and essays barely touch on art as helpful to understanding, as solace, as insight into life's meaning or purpose. Why do think that's so, and what do you make of it?
6. Are there things that stick out in a comparison of the poems as a whole and the essays as a whole? Can poetry achieve effects unavailable in prose, and vice versa?

FORMULATING IDEAS FOR WRITING

1. Conduct a series of interviews—of your classmates, neighbors, or family—to discover what role science plays in people's thinking about death. Write an essay in which you present your findings and your response to your findings.
2. Write an essay on the topic "Today the meaning of life is found in art." Have a look at what Paul Tillich (Chapter 2, pp. 123–130) has to say on this subject before you write.
3. Write an essay explaining why you would prefer to be buried rather than cremated, or vice versa. Discuss the nature of the ceremony you might

appreciate at your death, and any other requests you might make of your surviving family and friends (For example, should there be a religious service? Should there be a memorial service? Should there be a wake?).

4. Carlos Cortez says a number of evocative things you might choose as topics for an essay—such as, "We're but moments in eternity. But we've been part of it"; or, "Personally, I would not like to spend eternity on a cloud plucking away at a harp. I think I'd rather be where the gang is"; or, "Without death, there's no life."
5. These essayists say that life is a precious gift. How is their view of this gift affected by their religious convictions? Do you think the gift is more poignant to the person who believes in an afterlife or to the person who sees death as final? Explain.
6. Choose one or two poems from this album, and discuss how they illuminate the intellectual and emotional character of the gap between belief and the actuality of death.

On the Fear of Death (1969)

Elisabeth Kübler-Ross

The psychiatrist and physician Elisabeth Kübler-Ross (1926–2004) was best known for her groundbreaking work with dying patients and their families, work that led to a revolution in medical care and inspired the hospice movement. As a young doctor, she was appalled by the hospital treatment of dying persons. Her work with the dying resulted in her revolutionary book *On Death and Dying* (1969), from which the present selection is taken. At the University of Chicago, Kübler-Ross established a seminar in 1965 on the care of the terminally ill, and from 1987 to 1995, she headed a facility for dying patients in Head Waters, Virginia. She developed what is known as the Kübler-Ross model delineating the five stages of grief, applicable both to one's own impending death and to the death of a loved one. These stages are, in sequence, denial, anger, bargaining, depression, and acceptance. "It is only when we truly know and understand that we have a limited time on Earth," she said, "and that we have no way of knowing when our time is up—that we will begin to live each day to the fullest, as if it was the only one we had."

Kübler-Ross was born in Zurich, Switzerland, and graduated with a degree in medicine from the University of Zurich in 1957. She moved to the United States in 1958 and received her degree in psychiatry from the University of Colorado in 1963. Her works include *Death: The Final Stage of Growth* (1974), *On Children and Death* (1985), and *The Wheel of Life: A Memoir of Living and Dying*

(1997). She suffered a series of strokes in 1995 and died at her home in Scottsdale, Arizona, in 2004.

Let me not pray to be sheltered from dangers but to be fearless in facing them.

Let me not beg for the stilling of my pain but for the heart to conquer it.

Let me not look for allies in life's battlefield but to my own strength.

Let me not crave in anxious fear to be saved but hope for the patience to win my freedom.

Grant me that I may not be a coward, feeling your mercy in my success alone; but let me find the grasp of your hand in my failure.

—*Rabindranath Tagore,* Fruit-Gathering[1]

Epidemics have taken a great toll of lives in past generations. Death in infancy and early childhood was frequent and there were few families who didn't lose a member of the family at an early age. Medicine has changed greatly in the last decades. Widespread vaccinations have practically eradicated many illnesses, at least in western Europe and the United States. The use of chemotherapy, especially the antibiotics, has contributed to an ever decreasing number of fatalities in infectious diseases. Better child care and education have effected a low morbidity and mortality among children. The many diseases that have taken an impressive toll among the young and middle-aged have been conquered. The number of old people is on the rise, and with this fact come the number of people with malignancies and chronic diseases associated more with old age.

Pediatricians have less work with acute and life-threatening situations as they have an ever increasing number of patients with psychosomatic disturbances and adjustment and behavior problems. Physicians have more people in their waiting rooms with emotional problems than they have ever had before, but they also have more elderly patients who not only try to live with their decreased physical abilities and limitations but who also face loneliness and isolation with all its pains and anguish. The majority of these people are not seen by a psychiatrist. Their needs have to be elicited and gratified by other professional people, for instance, chaplains and social workers. It is for them that I am trying to outline the changes that have taken place in the last few decades, changes that are ultimately responsible for the increased fear of death, the rising number of emotional problems, and the greater need for understanding of and coping with the problems of death and dying.

When we look back in time and study old cultures and people, we are impressed that death has always been distasteful to man and will probably always be. From a psychiatrist's point of view this is very understandable and can perhaps best be explained by our basic knowledge that, in our unconscious, death

[1] Rabindranath Tagore: considered one of the greatest writers (1861–1941) of modern Indian literature.

is never possible in regard to ourselves. It is inconceivable for our unconscious to imagine an actual ending of our own life here on earth, and if this life of ours had to end, the ending is always attributed to a malicious intervention from the outside by someone else. In simple terms, in our unconscious mind we can only be killed; it is inconceivable to die of a natural cause or of old age. Therefore death in itself is associated with a bad act, a frightening happening, something that in itself calls for retribution and punishment.

One is wise to remember these fundamental facts as they are essential in understanding some of the most important, otherwise unintelligible communications of our patients.

5 The second fact that we have to comprehend is that in our unconscious mind we cannot distinguish between a wish and a deed. We are all aware of some of our illogical dreams in which two completely opposite statements can exist side by side—very acceptable in our dreams but unthinkable and illogical in our wakening state. Just as our unconscious mind cannot differentiate between the wish to kill somebody in anger and the act of having done so, the young child is unable to make this distinction. The child who angrily wishes his mother to drop dead for not having gratified his needs will be traumatized greatly by the actual death of his mother—even if this event is not linked closely in time with his destructive wishes. He will always take part or the whole blame for the loss of his mother. He will always say to himself—rarely to others—"I did it, I am responsible, I was bad, therefore Mommy left me." It is well to remember that the child will react in the same manner if he loses a parent by divorce, separation, or desertion. Death is often seen by a child as an impermanent thing and has therefore little distinction from a divorce in which he may have an opportunity to see a parent again.

Many a parent will remember remarks of their children such as, "I will bury my doggy now and next spring when the flowers come up again, he will get up." Maybe it was the same wish that motivated the ancient Egyptians to supply their dead with food and goods to keep them happy and the old American Indians to bury their relatives with their belongings.

When we grow older and begin to realize that our omnipotence is really not so omnipotent, that our strongest wishes are not powerful enough to make the impossible possible, the fear that we have contributed to the death of a loved one diminishes—and with it the guilt. The fear remains diminished, however, only so long as it is not challenged too strongly. Its vestiges can be seen daily in hospital corridors and in people associated with the bereaved.

A husband and wife may have been fighting for years, but when the partner dies, the survivor will pull his hair, whine and cry louder and beat his chest in regret, fear and anguish, and will hence fear his own death more than before, still believing in the law of talion—an eye for an eye, a tooth for a tooth—"I am responsible for her death, I will have to die a pitiful death in retribution."

Maybe this knowledge will help us understand many of the old customs and rituals which have lasted over the centuries and whose purpose is to diminish the anger of the gods or the people as the case may be, thus decreasing the anticipated punishment. I am thinking of the ashes, the torn clothes, the veil, the *Klage Weiber*[2] of the old days—they are all means to ask you to take pity on them, the mourners, and are expressions of sorrow, grief, and shame. If someone grieves, beats his chest, tears his hair, or refuses to eat, it is an attempt at self-punishment to avoid or reduce the anticipated punishment for the blame that he takes on the death of a loved one.

10 This grief, shame, and guilt are not very far removed from feelings of anger and rage. The process of grief always includes some qualities of anger. Since none of us likes to admit anger at a deceased person, these emotions are often disguised or repressed and prolong the period of grief or show up in other ways. It is well to remember that it is not up to us to judge such feelings as bad or shameful but to understand their true meaning and origin as something very human. In order to illustrate this I will again use the example of the child—and the child in us. The five-year-old who loses his mother is both blaming himself for her disappearance and being angry at her for having deserted him and for no longer gratifying his needs. The dead person then turns into something the child loves and wants very much but also hates with equal intensity for this severe deprivation.

The ancient Hebrews regarded the body of a dead person as something unclean and not to be touched. The early American Indians talked about the evil spirits and shot arrows in the air to drive the spirits away. Many other cultures have rituals to take care of the "bad" dead person, and they all originate in this feeling of anger which still exists in all of us, though we dislike admitting it. The tradition of the tombstone may originate in this wish to keep the bad spirits deep down in the ground, and the pebbles that many mourners put on the grave are left-over symbols of the same wish. Though we call the firing of guns at military funerals a last salute, it is the same symbolic ritual as the Indian used when he shot his spears and arrows into the skies.

I give these examples to emphasize that man has not basically changed. Death is still a fearful, frightening happening, and the fear of death is a universal fear even if we think we have mastered it on many levels.

What has changed is our way of coping and dealing with death and dying and our dying patients.

Having been raised in a country in Europe where science is not so advanced, where modern techniques have just started to find their way into medicine, and where people still live as they did in this country half a century ago, I may have had an opportunity to study a part of the evolution of mankind in a shorter period.

15 I remember as a child the death of a farmer. He fell from a tree and was not expected to live. He asked simply to die at home, a wish that was granted without questioning. He called his daughters into the bedroom and spoke with each one of them alone for a few moments. He arranged his affairs quietly, though he was in great pain, and distributed his belongings and his land, none of which was to be split until his wife should follow him in death. He also asked each of his children to share in the work, duties, and tasks that he had carried on until

[2] *Klage Weiber:* wailing wives.

the time of the accident. He asked his friends to visit him once more, to bid good-bye to them. Although I was a small child at the time, he did not exclude me or my siblings. We were allowed to share in the preparations of the family just as we were permitted to grieve with them until he died. When he did die, he was left at home, in his own beloved home which he had built, and among his friends and neighbors who went to take a last look at him where he lay in the midst of flowers in the place he had lived in and loved so much. In that country today there is still no make-believe slumber room, no embalming, no false makeup to pretend sleep. Only the signs of very disfiguring illnesses are covered up with bandages and only infectious cases are removed from the home prior to the burial.

Why do I describe such "old-fashioned" customs? I think they are an indication of our acceptance of a fatal outcome, and they help the dying patient as well as his family to accept the loss of a loved one. If a patient is allowed to terminate his life in the familiar and beloved environment, it requires less adjustment for him. His own family knows him well enough to replace a sedative with a glass of his favorite wine; or the smell of a home-cooked soup may give him the appetite to sip a few spoons of fluid which, I think, is still more enjoyable than an infusion. I will not minimize the need for sedatives and infusions and realize full well from my own experience as a country doctor that they are sometimes life-saving and often unavoidable. But I also know that patience and familiar people and foods could replace many a bottle of intravenous fluids given for the simple reason that it fulfills the physiological need without involving too many people and/or individual nursing care.

The fact that children are allowed to stay at home where a fatality has stricken and are included in the talk, discussions, and fears gives them the feeling that they are not alone in the grief and gives them the comfort of shared responsibility and shared mourning. It prepares them gradually and helps them view death as part of life, an experience which may help them grow and mature.

This is in great contrast to a society in which death is viewed as taboo, discussion of it is regarded as morbid, and children are excluded with the presumption and pretext that it would be "too much" for them. They are then sent off to relatives, often accompanied with some unconvincing lies of "Mother has gone on a long trip" or other unbelievable stories. The child senses that something is wrong, and his distrust in adults will only multiply if other relatives add new variations of the story, avoid his questions or suspicions, shower him with gifts as a meager substitute for a loss he is not permitted to deal with. Sooner or later the child will become aware of the changed family situation and, depending on the age and personality of the child, will have an unresolved grief and regard this incident as a frightening, mysterious, in any case very traumatic experience with untrustworthy grownups, which he has no way to cope with.

It is equally unwise to tell a little child who lost her brother that God loved little boys so much that he took little Johnny to heaven. When this little girl grew up to be a woman she never solved her anger at God, which resulted in a psychotic depression when she lost her own little son three decades later.

20 We would think that our great emancipation, our knowledge of science and of man, has given us better ways and means to prepare ourselves and our families for this inevitable happening. Instead the days are gone when a man was allowed to die in peace and dignity in his own home.

The more we are making advancements in science, the more we seem to fear and deny the reality of death. How is this possible?

We use euphemisms,[3] we make the dead look as if they were asleep, we ship the children off to protect them from the anxiety and turmoil around the house if the patient is fortunate enough to die at home, we don't allow children to visit their dying parents in the hospitals, we have long and controversial discussions about whether patients should be told the truth—a question that rarely arises when the dying person is tended by the family physician who has known him from delivery to death and who knows the weaknesses and strengths of each member of the family.

I think there are many reasons for this flight away from facing death calmly. One of the most important facts is that dying nowadays is more gruesome in many ways, namely, more lonely, mechanical, and dehumanized; at times it is even difficult to determine technically when the time of death has occurred.

Dying becomes lonely and impersonal because the patient is often taken out of his familiar environment and rushed to an emergency room. Whoever has been very sick and has required rest and comfort especially may recall his experience of being put on a stretcher and enduring the noise of the ambulance siren and hectic rush until the hospital gates open. Only those who have lived through this may appreciate the discomfort and cold necessity of such transportation which is only the beginning of a long ordeal—hard to endure when you are well, difficult to express in words when noise, light, pumps, and voices are all too much to put up with. It may well be that we might consider more the patient under the sheets and blankets and perhaps stop our well-meant efficiency and rush in order to hold the patient's hand, to smile, or to listen to a question. I include the trip to the hospital as the first episode in dying, as it is for many. I am putting it exaggeratedly in contrast to the sick man who is left at home—not to say that lives should not be saved if they can be saved by a hospitalization but to keep the focus on the patient's experience, his needs and his reactions.

25 When a patient is severely ill, he is often treated like a person with no right to an opinion. It is often someone else who makes the decision if and when and where a patient should be hospitalized. It would take so little to remember that the sick person too has feelings, has wishes and opinions, and has—most important of all—the right to be heard.

Well, our presumed patient has now reached the emergency room. He will be surrounded by busy nurses, orderlies, interns, residents, a lab technician perhaps who will take some blood, an electrocardiogram technician who takes the cardiogram. He may be moved to X ray and he will overhear opinions of his condition and discussions and questions to members of the family. He slowly

[3] euphemisms: pleasantries used instead of expressions that might be offensive or unpleasant.

but surely is beginning to be treated like a thing. He is no longer a person. Decisions are made often without his opinion. If he tries to rebel he will be sedated and after hours of waiting and wondering whether he has the strength, he will be wheeled into the operating room or intensive treatment unit and become an object of great concern and great financial investment.

He may cry for rest, peace, and dignity, but he will get infusions, transfusions, a heart machine, or tracheotomy[4] if necessary. He may want one single person to stop for one single minute so that he can ask one single question—but he will get a dozen people around the clock, all busily preoccupied with his heart rate, pulse, electrocardiogram or pulmonary functions, his secretions or excretions but not with him as a human being. He may wish to fight it all but it is going to be a useless fight since all this is done in the fight for his life, and if they can save his life they can consider the person afterwards. Those who consider the person first may lose precious time to save his life! At least this seems to be the rationale or justification behind all this—or is it? Is the reason for this increasingly mechanical, depersonalized approach our own defensiveness? Is this approach our own way to cope with and repress the anxieties that a terminally or critically ill patient evokes in us? Is our concentration on equipment, on blood pressure, our desperate attempt to deny the impending death which is so frightening and discomforting to us that we displace all our knowledge onto machines, since they are less close to us than the suffering face of another human being which would remind us once more of our lack of omnipotence, our own limits and failures, and last but not least perhaps our own mortality?

Maybe the question has to be raised: Are we becoming less human or more human? . . . It is clear that whatever the answer may be, the patient is suffering more—not physically, perhaps, but emotionally. And his needs have not changed over the centuries, only our ability to gratify them.

LEARNING MORE

Additional information about the Kübler-Ross model can be found on the *Ideas Across Time* website.

QUESTIONING THE TEXT

1. For whom does Kübler-Ross say she has written this essay? What are the implications of this focus?
2. Why does Kübler-Ross spend so much time talking about the minds of children?
3. What is the relation between the old customs and rituals of death and the experience of children?
4. Why does Kübler-Ross dwell on the death of a farmer when she was young (par. 15)?

[4] tracheotomy: an incision in trachea—the air tube—in the neck to aid in breathing.

5. What are the signs of our view that death is taboo?
6. What has been the impact of advanced medical knowledge and advanced medical technology on dying patients?
7. How would Kübler-Ross change the American way of treating terminally ill patients?

ANALYZING THE WRITER'S CRAFT

1. Where does Kübler-Ross's introduction end? What is the purpose of her introduction?
2. What is the tone of this essay? Offer two or three examples to support your answer.
3. How does Kübler-Ross establish the contrast between how the dying were treated in the past and how we treat them now?
4. Kübler-Ross makes careful use of details to get her message across. What details in her account did you find especially convincing or moving?
5. Kübler-Ross sets out here to show us how the dying are treated today. Does she also reveal her own view of how they might be treated better?
6. How do the lines by Tagore at the opening of the essay express Kübler-Ross' philosophy?
7. How has Kübler-Ross affected your view of death?
8. How does this essay reflect the Kübler-Ross model (see introduction)?

MAKING CONNECTIONS

1. Consider how Kübler-Ross's explanation of our attitudes toward death—fear, anger, acceptance—might offer an illuminating perspective through which to read the album of selections on death in this chapter (pp. 657–670)?
2. Compare and contrast this essay on death with that by the other physician in this chapter, Sherwin Nuland (pp. 696–701).
3. Do you think Walt Whitman's embrace (Chapter 1, pp. 55–59) of all kinds of Americans, living and dead, expresses an acceptance of life similar to that which Kübler-Ross advocates? Explain.
4. Compare and contrast Kübler-Ross's philosophy and that of the Dalai Lama (Chapter 2, pp. 132–135).
5. Does Frankenstein's view of death and life (Chapter 3, pp. 157–165) foreshadow our own technological evasion of the facts of existence? Explain.
6. How does Annie Dillard's view of us as "life on the rocks" (Chapter 3, pp. 209–217) compare and contrast with Kübler-Ross's?

FORMULATING IDEAS FOR WRITING

1. Write an essay that discusses the impact of Kübler-Ross's writing on your view of death.

2. Kübler-Ross advocates including children in the experience of illness and death. Do you agree? Have you had any experience of being in the presence of a dying relative? How did that experience compare with Kübler-Ross's description of the experience a dying patient is likely to have in today's America?
3. Kübler-Ross says that dying at home and avoiding prettifying the dead body is preferable to our practice of getting the terminally ill to the hospital and then embalming and otherwise beautifying them. What is your view?
4. If you were assigned the task of giving this essay to one person to read, who would that person be? Write an essay explaining your choice.

The Way of the Samurai (1977)

Yukio Mishima

Yukio Mishima was the pen name of Kimitake Hiraoka (1925–1970), one of the most significant Japanese writers of the twentieth century. Raised by his grandmother, who traced her lineage to the lower aristocracy of the Tokugawa period (the period of Japan's several centuries of isolation, prior to its mid-nineteenth-century opening to the West), Mishima focused his talent—in novels, poems, essays, and plays—on the moral drift caused by the chasm between premodern Japanese values and what he considered the emptiness of life in his country after World War II. His fascination with *Hagakure (The Way of the Samurai),* the classic statement of the warrior code, reflects Mishima's quest for an attainment beyond temporal decay. Becoming an expert in karate and kendo, Mishima worked to create a perfect body and mode of living that could not be eroded by age and death. In this way, his personal life was a conscious complement to his art. His greatest work, the four-volume epic *The Sea of Fertility* (1965–1970), poignantly chronicles the entry of Japan into the modern era. For Mishima, this process came at a huge price: an ancient and fulfilling tradition was abandoned for a barren contemporaneity. Japanese culture, he believed, had lost its way.

Three times nominated for the Nobel Prize, Mishima first gained literary success with the semi-autobiographical *Confessions of a Mask* (1949). His notable books include *The Temple of the Golden Pavilion* (1956), *The Sailor Who Fell from Grace with the Sea* (1965), and the aforementioned tetralogy *The Sea of Fertility.*

On November 25, 1970, Mishima and some of his followers seized the headquarters of the Eastern Command of the Japanese army to deliver a patriotic call to arms. This was followed by Mishima's ritual suicide and beheading. He was forty-five years old.

Hagakure, the Book That Teaches Freedom and Passion

It was now that what I had recognized during the war in *Hagakure* began to manifest its true meaning. Here was a book that preached freedom, that taught passion. Those who have read carefully only the most famous line from *Hagakure* still retain an image of it as a book of odious fanaticism. In that one line, "I found that the Way of the Samurai is death," may be seen the paradox that symbolizes the book as a whole. It was this sentence, however, that gave me the strength to live.

My Testimony

I first confessed my devotion to *Hagakure* after the war, in an article published in 1955 called "Writer's Holiday." The statement was as follows:

> I began reading *Hagakure* during the war, and even now I read it from time to time. It is a strange book of peerless morality; its irony is not the deliberate irony of a cynic but irony that arises naturally from the discrepancy between knowledge of proper conduct and decision to act. What an energetic, soul-refreshing, what a human book.
>
> Those who read *Hagakure* from the point of view of established convention, feudal morality for instance, are almost totally insensitive to its exhilaration. This book is brimming with the exuberance and freedom of people who lived under the restrictions of a rigid social morality. This morality lived in the very fabric of the society and its economic system. It was the one premise to their existence, and under this premise all was a glorification of energy and passion. Energy is good; lethargy is evil. An astonishing understanding of the world is unfolded in *Hagakure* without the slightest tinge of cynicism. Its effect is the direct opposite of the unpleasant aftertaste of La Rochefoucauld, for instance.
>
> 5 One rarely finds a book that liberates self-respect in ethical terms as much as does *Hagakure.* It is impossible to value energy while rejecting self-respect. Here there can be no such thing as going too far. Even arrogance is ethical (*Hagakure* does not, however, deal with arrogance in the abstract). "A samurai must have confidence that he is the best and bravest warrior in all Japan." "A samurai must take great pride in his military valor; he must have the supreme resolution to die a fanatic's death." There is no such thing as correctness or propriety in fanaticism.
>
> The practical ethics for daily living taught by *Hagakure* might be called a man of action's belief in expediency. On fashion, Jōchō remarks nonchalantly, "Thus it is essential to do things properly in every age." Expediency is nothing more than an ethically fastidious rejection of extreme refinement of any kind. One must be stubborn, and eccentric. From ancient times most samurai have been of eccentric spirit, strong willed, and courageous.
>
> Just as all artistic creations are born of a resistance to one's era, these teachings of Jōchō Yamamoto were recorded against a background of the extravagant, luxurious tastes of the Genroku and Hōei Eras [1688–1704; 1704–1709]. . . .

"I Found That the Way of the Samurai Is Death"

When Jōchō says, "I found that the Way of the Samurai is death," he is expressing his Utopianism, his principles of freedom and happiness. That is why we are able to read *Hagakure* today as the tale of an ideal country. I am almost certain that if such an ideal land were ever to materialize, its inhabitants would be far happier and freer than we are today. But what actually existed is merely Jōchō's dream.

The author of *Hagakure* devised a cure too potent for the modern malady. Presaging a splintering of the human spirit, he warned of the unhappiness of such a division, "It is wrong to set one's mind on two things at once." We must resurrect a faith in purity and its glorification. Jōchō, who could not help recognizing the validity of any kind of passion as long as it was genuine, well understood passion's laws. . . .

The Misfortune and the Happiness of the Man of Action

10 Whether to consider natural death, or as *Hagakure* does, death by the sword or disembowelment as the proper completion of a man's training to perfection, it seems to me makes little difference. The fact that one is expected to be a man of action does not alter or ease in any way the law that human beings must bear the passage of 'Time.' "In a fifty-fifty life or death situation, simply settle it by choosing immediate death." Jōchō is merely preaching the good common sense that whatever the situation, self-abandonment guarantees a minimum of virtue. And a truly fifty-fifty situation does not come along often. It is significant that while Jōchō chooses to emphasize the decision to die quickly, he obscures the criteria for judging when a situation is in fact "fifty-fifty." The evaluation that ultimately produces the decision to die trails behind it a long chain of evaluations and resultant decisions to live, and this ceaseless tempering of one's judgment toward the final decision suggests the long period of tension and concentration that the man of action must endure. To the man of action, life frequently appears as a circle to be completed by the addition of one last point. From instant to instant he continues to discard such circles, incomplete because of one missing point, and goes on to be confronted by a succession of similar circles. In contrast, the life of an artist or philosopher appears as an accumulation of gradually widening concentric circles around himself. But when death finally arrives, who will have the greater sense of fulfillment, the man of action, or the artist? I should think that a death which in an instant completes one's world by the addition of a single point would afford a more intense feeling of fulfillment by far.

The greatest calamity for the man of action is that he fail to die even after that last unmistakable point has been added.

Yoichi Nasu lived long after he shot his arrow neatly through the fan held up for a target. Jōchō's teachings on death emphasize the true happiness of the man of action rather than the external fact of the action itself. And Jōchō, who dreamed of attaining this happiness, wanted to commit suicide at the age of forty-two on the death of his lord, Mitsushige Nabeshima (second generation daimyo of the Nabeshima house), but was prevented from doing so by an interdiction against suicide in loyalty to the daimyo. Jōchō shaved his head, took

Buddhist vows, and died a natural death at the age of sixty-one, reluctantly leaving *Hagakure* to posterity. . . .

Times Have Changed

Hagakure is based on the principles of the samurai. The occupation of the samurai is death. No matter how peaceful the age, death is the samurai's supreme motivation, and if a samurai should fear or shun death, in that instant he would cease to be a samurai. It is for this reason that Jōchō Yamamoto puts such emphasis on death as his fundamental motivation to action. However, in present-day Japan under a constitution that outlaws war, people who consider death to be their occupational objective—and this includes the National Defense Force[1]—cannot exist, on principle. The premise of the democratic age is that it is best to live as long as possible.

Thus in evaluating the impact of *Hagakure,* it becomes an important question whether or not the readers are samurai. If one is able to read *Hagakure* transcending the fundamental difference in premise between Jōchō's era and our own, one will find there an astonishing understanding of human nature, a wisdom applicable to human relations even in the present day. One reads lightly and quickly through its pages (stimulating, vigorous, passionate, but extremely sharp and penetrating, paradoxical pages), letting one's body be refreshed as by a spring rain. But in the end one is forced to confront again the fundamental difference in premise.

The reader, temporarily surmounting this difference in premise, comes to resonate with the text; then at the conclusion he must give way once more before the unresolvable difference. That is what is interesting about *Hagakure.*

The Significance of *Hagakure* for the Present Day

But what exactly is this difference? Here we transcend occupation, class discrimination, and the conditions ascribed to any individual in a specific era, and we are brought back to the basic problem of life and death, a problem we too must face in this day and age. In modern society the meaning of death is constantly being forgotten. No, it is not forgotten; rather, the subject is avoided. Rainer Maria Rilke (poet, born in Prague, 1875–1926) has said that the death of man has become smaller. The death of a man is now nothing more than an individual dying grandly in a hard hospital bed, an item to be disposed of as quickly as possible. And all around us is the ceaseless "traffic war," which is reputed to have claimed more victims than the Sino-Japanese War, and the fragility of human life is now as it has ever been. We simply do not like to speak about death. We do not like to extract from death its beneficial elements and try to put them to work for us. We always try to direct our gaze toward the bright landmark, the forward-facing landmark, the landmark of life. And we

[1] National Defense Force: the Japanese armed forces.

try our best not to refer to the power by which death gradually eats away our lives. This outlook indicates a process by which our rational humanism, while constantly performing the function of turning the eyes of modern man toward the brightness of freedom and progress, wipes the problem of death from the level of consciousness, pushing it deeper and deeper into the subconscious, turning the death impulse by this repression to an ever more dangerous, explosive, ever more concentrated, inner-directed impulse. We are ignoring the fact that bringing death to the level of consciousness is an important element of mental health.

But death alone exists unchanged and regulates our lives now as in the era of *Hagakure*. In this sense, the death that Jōchō is talking about is nothing extraordinary. *Hagakure* insists that to ponder death daily is to concentrate daily on life. When we do our work thinking that we may die today, we cannot help feeling that our job suddenly becomes radiant with life and meaning.

It seems to me that *Hagakure* offers us a chance to reevaluate our views of life and death, after twenty years of peace since the Second World War. . . .

2. *Decision*

> I discovered that the Way of the Samurai is death. In a fifty-fifty life or death crisis, simply settle it by choosing immediate death. There is nothing complicated about it. Just brace yourself and proceed. Some say that to die without accomplishing one's mission is to die in vain, but this is the calculating, imitation samurai ethic of arrogant Osaka merchants. To make the correct choice in a fifty-fifty situation is nearly impossible. We would all prefer to live. And so it is quite natural in such a situation that one should find some excuse for living on. But one who chooses to go on living having failed in one's mission will be despised as a coward and a bungler. This is the precarious part. If one dies after having failed, it is a fanatic's death, death in vain. It is not, however, dishonorable. Such a death is in fact the Way of the Samurai. In order to be a perfect samurai, it is necessary to prepare oneself for death morning and evening day in and day out. When a samurai is constantly prepared for death, he has mastered the Way of the Samurai, and he may unerringly devote his life to the service of his lord. (Book One)

"When a samurai is constantly prepared for death, he has mastered the Way of the Samurai" is the new philosophy discovered by Jōchō. If a man holds death in his heart, thinking that whenever the time comes he will be ready to die, he cannot possibly take mistaken action. When a man takes mistaken action, Jōchō believes it must be in failing to die at the proper time. The proper time does not come along often, however. The choice between life and death may come only once in a lifetime. Think of Jōchō himself: With what feelings did he greet death when after so many years of daily resignation he realized it would overtake him undramatically in bed at the age of sixty-one?

But Jōchō is concerned with death as a decision, not with natural death. He spoke not of resignation to death from illness, but of resolution to self-destruction. Death from illness is the work of Nature, whereas self-destruction has to do with a man's free will. And if the extreme manifestation of man's free will is the free will to die, Jōchō asks, then what is free will? Here is the typical Japanese view that being cut down in battle and committing ritual suicide are equally honorable; the positive form of suicide called *hara-kiri* is not a sign of defeat, as it is in the West, but the ultimate expression of free will, in order to protect one's honor. What Jōchō means by "death" is the deliberate choice to die, and no matter how constrained the situation, when one breaks through the constricting forces by choosing to die, one is performing an act of freedom. This is, however, inevitably an idealized view of death, and Jōchō knows perfectly well that death does not often appear in such a pure and uncomplicated form. The formula death-equals-freedom is the ideal formula of the samurai. One must read between the lines to find Jōchō's deep-rooted nihilism: He knows that death is not necessarily like that.

3. "Delicacy" *[In English]*

A man's world is a world of consideration for others. A man's social ability is measured by his consideration. Though the era of the samurai may at a glance seem a rough-and-tumble world, it operated precisely on a delicate modulation of consideration for one's fellow man much finer than exists today. Even on the subject of criticizing others, Jōchō preaches at length the virtue of care and "delicacy." . . .

No Death Is in Vain

And what does it mean for a living being to confront death? According to *Hagakure,* what is important is purity of action. Jōchō affirms the height of passion and its power, and he also affirms any death thus arrived at. This is what he means when he says that calling a death in vain is the "calculating *bushidō* of arrogant Osaka merchants." Jōchō's most important pronouncement on death, "I have discovered that the Way of the Samurai is death," cuts through with one stroke of the sword the Gordian knot, the adversary relationship between life and death.

> Some say that to die without accomplishing one's mission is to die in vain, but this is the calculating *bushidō* (samurai ethic) of arrogant Osaka merchants. To make the correct choice in a fifty-fifty situation is nearly impossible.

Accomplishing one's mission, in modern terms, means to die righteously for a just cause, and *Hagakure* is saying that on the point of death one is by no means able to evaluate the justice of the cause.

"We would all prefer to live, and so it is quite natural in such a situation that one should find some excuse for living on." A human being can always find some excuse. And human beings, simply by virtue of their being alive, must invent some sort of theory. *Hagakure* is simply expressing the relativistic position that rather than to live on as a coward having failed in one's mission, having failed in one's mission it is better to die. *Hagakure* by no means maintains that in dying one cannot fail to accomplish one's mission. Here is the nihilism of Jōchō Yamamoto, and here, too, is the ultimate idealism, born of his nihilism.

We tend to suffer from the illusion that we are capable of dying for a belief or a theory. What *Hagakure* is insisting is that even a merciless death, a futile death that bears neither flower nor fruit, has dignity as the death of a human being. If we value so highly the dignity of life, how can we not also value the dignity of death? No death may be called futile.

LEARNING MORE

Additional resources for the study of Yukio Mishima and of Japanese history can be found on the *Ideas Across Time* website.

QUESTIONING THE TEXT

1. Mishima's explains his devotion to Jocho Yamamoto's *Hagakure* (c. 1700) in intentionally paradoxical and elusive terms. How is *Hagakure* a book of "peerless morality" (par. 3)? How can people living "under the restrictions of a rigid social morality" enjoy life with "exuberance and freedom" (par. 4)? What's good about fanaticism (par. 5)? The answer to these questions prepares the ground for Mishima's challenge to the values of his time.
2. How is the life of action preferable to the life of art? Why are these the essential contrasts for Mishima?
3. Why does it matter so much to Mishima that the times have changed?
4. How is the modern outlook on death unhealthy?
5. Explain what Jōchō and Mishima mean when they applaud the idea that "the Way of the Samurai is death" (par. 19). What is your response to their point of view?
6. Why is natural death undesirable?
7. Explain why Mishima believes that "No death can be called futile" (par. 27).

ANALYZING THE WRITER'S CRAFT

1. Who is Mishima's audience?
2. Mishima undertakes an enormous challenge: he wants to persuade his readers that the fundamental values of society—*their* values—are wrong and that there is a better way. What do you find most effective in Mishima's effort to persuade us to think differently? What do you find least persuasive? Explain.
3. What is the tone of this essay? Specify and explain.
4. Is Mishima's position logical? Why or why not?
5. Mishima observes that *Hagakure* was written for an audience of samurai—but that there are no samurai in twentieth-century Japan (par. 13). He considers the Way of the Samurai applicable by analogy. Do you think the analogy is appropriate? Effective?

6. Mishima's essay is an interpretation of *Hagakure*. In par. 19, Mishima provides us with a key paragraph from *Hagaksure* and proceeds to interpret it. Is Mishima's interpretation appropriately rooted in the original, or does Mishima use *Hagakure* for his own purposes?

MAKING CONNECTIONS

1. Three of the writers in this chapter committed suicide (Virginia Woolf, Anne Sexton, and Mishima), and one calmly accepted death (Socrates). How is Mishima's understanding of death different from those of the others? Are there similarities?
2. Like Jōchō, Marcus Aurelius (pp. 646–648) lived in a warrior culture and was himself a notable warrior. How do their views of the life of action affect their outlook on death?
3. Sherwin Nuland, a physician, says that suicide is almost always the wrong choice (see pp. 696–701). Imagine an exchange between Mishima and Nuland on the subject of ritual suicide.
4. Ralph Waldo Emerson was a prophet of art as the highest calling (see Chapter 7, pp. 581–585). Compare and contrast his view of art and the artist with Mishima's.
5. Paul Tillich (Chapter 2, pp. 123–130) argues that modern society has trivialized the age-old profound questions. Does Mishima's see things the same way? How much do these two thinkers have in common?

FORMULATING IDEAS FOR WRITING

1. Write an essay that amplifies and agrees with Mishima's view of ritual suicide or that takes exception to it. In either case, be sure to address the points Mishima himself raises before going on to taking a stance—assuming you do go on to take a stance—based on values or ideas that may derive from a quite different worldview.
2. Emily Dickinson, in "The Last Night That She Lived" (pp. 658–659), observes that in the face of death we struggle "Belief to regulate." *Hagakure* aims to prepare us at all times to die, to die on the spur of the moment. Even assuming we embrace Jōchō and Mishima's view of the matter, do you think that armed with this samurai ethic most of us would still find it a struggle, in the confrontation with death, to act as our preconceptions dictate? Does *Hagakure* contain as much (and as little) wishful thinking as every other prescription for how to die?
3. How has Mishima influenced your views of suicide—if at all?
4. Is Mishima right that modern society has made death "smaller" and that we can no longer "extract from death its beneficial elements" (par. 16)?

From a High Arid Plateau in New Mexico (1986)

Leslie Marmon Silko

Born in 1948 and raised on Laguna Pueblo, Leslie Marmon Silko is of mixed Anglo, Mexican, and Native American ancestry. She concentrates her writing on relations among cultures and between the human and natural worlds, as in this selection that first appeared in the magazine *Antaeus* in 1986. Considered by many the leading Native American writer, she draws on the depth of her heritage, in particular the stories of her grandmother Lilly and her Aunt Susie, who, Silko says, passed down to her "an entire culture by word of mouth." Her work aims to plumb the Laguna oral tradition for insights to illuminate contemporary life. For example, her best-known novel, *Ceremony* (1977), narrates the struggle of a veteran of World War II to reenter his New Mexico reservation after the war. Tayo, the novel's protagonist, after a dark period of disintegration, finally discovers in the teaching of his culture a path for his personal healing and ultimate growth.

Leslie Marmom Silko was educated on Laguna Pueblo and at a Catholic school in Albuquerque to which she commuted fifty miles daily. She received her B.A. from the University of New Mexico in 1969. In addition to *Ceremony,* her many works include *Laguna Woman: Poems* (1974), *Almanac of the Dead* (1991), *Yellow Woman and a Beauty of the Spirit: Essays on Native American Life Today* (1996), and *Garden in the Dunes* (1999). She is recipient of the Pushcart Prize for Poetry (1977) and a MacArthur Fellowship (1981).

You see that after a thing is dead, it dries up. It might take weeks or years, but eventually if you touch the thing, it crumbles under your fingers. It goes back to dust. The soul of the thing has long since departed. With the plants and wild game the soul may have already been borne back into bones and blood or thick green stalk and leaves. Nothing is wasted. What cannot be eaten by people or in some way used must then be left where other living creatures may benefit. What domestic animals or wild scavengers can't eat will be fed to the plants. The plants feed on the dust of these few remains.

The ancient Pueblo people buried the dead in vacant rooms or partially collapsed rooms adjacent to the main living quarters. Sand and clay used to construct the roof make layers many inches deep once the roof has collapsed. The layers of sand and clay make for easy gravedigging. The vacant room fills with cast-off objects and debris. When a vacant room has filled deep enough, a shallow but adequate grave can be scooped in a far corner. Archaeologists have remarked over formal burials complete with elaborate funerary objects excavated in trash middens of abandoned rooms. But the rocks and adobe mortar of collapsed walls were valued by the ancient people. Because each rock had been carefully selected for size and shape, then chiseled to an even face. Even the pink clay adobe melting with each rainstorm had to be prayed over, then dug and carried some distance. Corn cobs and husks, the rinds and stalks and animal bones were not regarded by the ancient people as filth or garbage. The remains were merely resting at a mid-point in their journey back to dust. Human remains are not so different. They should rest with the bones and rinds where they all may benefit living creatures—small rodents and insects—until their return is completed. The remains of things—animals and plants, the clay and the stones—were treated with respect. Because for the ancient people all these things had spirit and being. The antelope merely consents to return home with the hunter. All phases of the hunt are conducted with love. The love the hunter and the people have for the Antelope People. And the love of the antelope who agree to give up their meat and blood so that human beings will not starve. Waste of meat or even the thoughtless handling of bones cooked bare will offend the antelope spirits. Next year the hunters will vainly search the dry plains for antelope. Thus it is necessary to return carefully the bones and hair, and the stalks and leaves to the earth who first created them. The spirits remain close by. They do not leave us.

The dead become dust, and in this becoming they are once more joined with the Mother. The ancient Pueblo people called the earth the Mother Creator of all things in this world. Her sister, the Corn Mother, occasionally merges with her because all succulent green life rises out of the depths of the earth.

Rocks and clay are part of the Mother. They emerge in various forms, but at some time before, they were smaller particles or great boulders. At a later time they may again become what they once were. Dust.

5 A rock shares this fate with us and with animals and plants as well. A rock has being or spirit, although we may not understand it. The spirit may differ from the spirit we know in animals or plants or in ourselves. In the end we all originate from the depths of the earth. Perhaps this is how all beings share in the spirit of the Creator. We do not know.

LEARNING MORE

Additional information about the Pueblo people can be found on the *Ideas Across Time* website.

QUESTIONING THE TEXT

1. How does the essay's location (a high, arid plateau in New Mexico) contribute to its theme?

2. How is the Pueblo understanding of decay in death the same as and different from the traditional Judeo-Christian view?
3. How does the Pueblo practice of burying people in vacant rooms of their houses reflect their philosophy? What is your reaction to this practice? What can we learn about how American culture views death from our funerary practices?
4. How is the hunt for antelope analogous to Pueblo funerary practices?
5. How are we and rocks alike? Has Silko's explanation raised your valuation of rocks, or do you find the connection between rocks and humans far-fetched?

ANALYZING THE WRITER'S CRAFT

1. What is the thesis of this essay, and where is it found?
2. Cite two or three of the essay's illustrative examples, and show how they illuminate the main idea.
3. What is the tone of this essay? Specify and explain.
4. In places this essay seems ungrammatical. Is the departure from standard practice justified?
5. Does this essay develop from introduction to conclusion? Discuss.
6. Is the essay's conclusion effective?

MAKING CONNECTIONS

1. Compare and contrast Silko's account of traditional, oral culture with those of N. Scott Momaday (Chapter 7, pp. 612–616).
2. To what extent is the Pueblo understanding of the cycle of matter in accord with science (see Chapter 3)?
3. Is there a meaningful pattern in nature? Compare and contrast Silko's essay with those of Luther Standing Bear ("Nature," (Chapter 3, pp. 187–191) and Annie Dillard (Chapter 3, pp. 209–217).
4. Marcus Aurelius (pp. 646–648) also sees the universe as constantly in flux. Is the Pueblo view of things essentially the same as his, or are there more differences than similarities?

FORMULATING IDEAS FOR WRITING

1. Write an essay that explores the question of whether there is a meaningful pattern in nature. In addition to Silko, consider what Charles Darwin (Chapter 3, pp. 167–180) has to say, as well as perhaps Marcus Aurelius (pp. 646–648).
2. Compare and contrast the Judeo-Christian notion of "ashes to ashes and dust to dust" with that of the Pueblo.

3. How can a traditional worldview rooted in the experience of an ancient people struggling to survive on an arid plateau speak to a twenty-first-century urbanized, globalized society?
4. Silko ends her essay with the words "We do not know." Explore the relation between knowledge and knowing-we-don't-know in the human accounts of the universe. In addition to Silko's views, consider, for example, those of Socrates (pp. 640–644) and Richard Feynman (Chapter 3, pp. 201–207).

Suicide and Euthanasia (1993)

Sherwin B. Nuland

Sherwin B. Nuland, Clinical Professor of Surgery at the Yale School of Medicine, writes about health, illness, and death from the vantage point of a lifetime's practice of medicine. Addressing subjects that fascinate but also terrify or repel most readers, such as how we die, Nuland has established himself as an exceptionally lucid, sane, and ethically reflective cultural voice. His writing shows how intellectual rigor and moral acuity can shed light on the sensitive human questions. The present selection is taken from Nuland's highly praised *How We Die: Reflections on Life's Final Chapter,* which received the National Book Award in 1994.

Nuland studied at the Bronx High School of Science in New York and received his M.D. from the Yale School of Medicine in 1955. He has practiced and taught at the Yale–New Haven Hospital ever since. Among Nuland's other books are *The Mysteries Within: A Surgeon Explores Myth, Medicine, and the Human Body* (2000) and *The Doctor's Plague: Germs. Childbed Fever, and the Strange Story of Ignac Semmelweis* (2003). Nuland is a contributing editor to *The New Republic.*

Premature death by disease or unprovoked violence can be viewed dispassionately by only very few in the legions of those who care for the sick. But when the premature death is the result of self-destruction, it evokes a mood quite different from the aftermath of ordinary dying—that mood is not dispassion. In a book about the ways of death, the very word *suicide* appears as a discomfiting tangent. We seem to separate ourselves from the subject of self-murder in the same way that the suicide feels himself separated from the rest of us when he contemplates the fate he is about to choose. Alienated and alone, he is drawn to the grave because there seems no other place to go. For those left out and left behind, it is impossible to make sense of the thing.

I have seen my own attitude toward self-destruction reflected in the response of my eldest child. My wife and I had driven one hundred miles to the city where she was a college senior, because we both agreed that we should be with her when she heard the shocking news that one of her most admired friends had killed herself. As gently as we could, and at first without any of the few details available to us, we told our daughter what had happened. It was I who spoke, and I said it all in two or three short sentences. When I was finished, she stared at us unbelievingly for a moment as the tears began overflowing onto her suddenly flushed cheeks. And then, in an uncontrolled paroxysm of rage and loss, she burst out, "That stupid kid! How could she do such a thing?" And that was, after all, the point. How could she do it to her friends and to her family and to the rest of those who needed her? How could such a smart kid commit such a dumb act and be lost to us? There is no place for this kind of thing in an ordered world—it should never happen. Why, without asking any of us, would this beloved young woman just go ahead and take herself away?

Such things seem inexplicable to those who have known the suicide. But for the uninvolved medical personnel who first view the corpse, there is another factor to consider, which hinders compassion. Something about acute self-destruction is so puzzling to the vibrant mind of a man or woman whose life is devoted to fighting disease that it tends to diminish or even obliterate empathy. Medical bystanders, whether bewildered and frustrated by such an act, or angered by its futility, seem not to be much grieved at the corpse of a suicide. It has been my experience to see exceptions, but they are few. There may be emotional shock, even pity, but rarely the distress that comes with an unchosen death.

Taking one's own life is almost always the wrong thing to do. There are two circumstances, however, in which that may not be so. Those two are the unendurable infirmities of a crippling old age and the final devastations of terminal disease. The nouns are not important in that last sentence—it is the adjectives that cry out for attention, for they are the very crux of the issue and will tolerate no compromise or "well, almosts": *unendurable, crippling, final,* and *terminal.*

5 During his long lifetime, the great Roman orator Seneca [c. 3 BCE–65 CE] gave much thought to old age:

> I will not relinquish old age if it leaves my better part intact. But if it begins to shake my mind, if it destroys its faculties one by one, if it leaves me not life but breath, I will depart from the putrid or tottering edifice. I will not escape by death from disease so long as it may be healed, and leaves my mind unimpaired. I will not raise my hand against myself on account of pain, for so to die is to be conquered. But I know that if I must suffer without hope of relief, I will depart, not through fear of the pain itself, but because it prevents all for which I would live.

These words are so eminently sensible that few would disagree that suicide would appear to be among the options that the frail elderly should consider as the days grow more difficult, at least those among them who are not barred from doing so by their personal convictions. Perhaps the philosophy expressed by Seneca explains the fact that elderly white males take their own lives at a rate five times the national average. Is theirs not the "rational suicide" so strongly defended in journals of ethics and the op-ed pages of our daily newspapers?

Hardly so. The flaw in Seneca's proposition is a striking example of the error that permeates virtually every one of the publicized discussions of modern-day attitudes toward suicide—a very large proportion of the elderly men and women who kill themselves do it because they suffer from quite remediable depression. With proper medication and therapy, most of them would be relieved of the cloud of oppressive despair that colors all reason gray, would then realize that the edifice topples not quite so much as thought, and that hope of relief is less hopeless than it seemed. I have more than once seen a suicidal old person emerge from depression, and rediscovered thereby a vibrant friend. When such men or women return to a less despondent vision of reality, their loneliness seems to them less stark and their pain more bearable because life has become interesting again and they realize that there are people who need them.

All of this is not to say that there are no situations in which Seneca's words deserve heeding. But should this be so, the Roman's doctrine would then deserve consultation, counsel, and the leavening influence of a long period of mature thought. A decision to end life must be as defensible to those whose respect we seek as it is to ourselves. Only when that criterion has been satisfied should anyone consider the finality of death.

Against such a standard, the suicide of Percy Bridgman was close to being irreproachable. Bridgman was a Harvard professor whose studies in high-pressure physics won him a Nobel Prize in 1946. At the age of seventy-nine and in the final stages of cancer, he continued to work until he could no longer do so. Living at his summer home in Randolph, New Hampshire, he completed the index to a seven-volume collection of his scientific works, sent it off to the Harvard University Press, and then shot himself on August 20, 1961, leaving a suicide note in which he summed up a controversy that has since embroiled an entire world of medical ethics: "It is not decent for Society to make a man do this to himself. Probably, this is the last day I will be able to do it myself."

When he died, Bridgman seemed absolutely clear in his mind that he was making the right choice. He worked right up to the final day, tied up loose ends, and carried out his plan. I'm not certain how much consideration he gave to consulting others, but his decision had certainly not been kept a secret from friends and colleagues, because there is ample evidence of his having at least informed some of them in advance. He had become so sick that he felt it doubtful that he would much longer be capable of mustering up the strength to carry out his ironclad resolve.

10 In his final message, Bridgman deplored the necessity of performing his deed unaided. A colleague reported a conversation in which Bridgman said, "I would like to take advantage of the situation in which I find myself to establish a general principle; namely, that when the ultimate end is as inevitable as it now appears to be, the individual has a right to ask his doctor to end it for him." If a single sentence were needed to epitomize the battle in which we are all now joined, you have just read it.

No contemporary discussion of suicide, at least not one written by a physician, can skirt the issue of the doctor's role in assisting patients toward their mortality. The crucial word in this sentence is *patients*—not just people, but *patients,* specifically the patients of the doctor who contemplates the assisting. The guild of Hippocrates should not develop a new specialty of accoucheurs[1] to the grave so that conscience-stricken oncologists,[2] surgeons, and other physicians may refer to others those who wish to exit the planet. On the other hand, any degree of debate about physicians' participation should be welcomed if it will bring out into the open a muted practice that has existed since Aesculapius[3] was in swaddling clothes.

Suicide, especially this newly debated form, has become fashionable lately. In centuries long past, those who took their own lives were at best considered to have committed a felony against themselves; at worst, their crime was viewed as a mortal sin. Both attitudes are implicit in the words of Immanuel Kant.[4] "Suicide is not abominable because God forbids it; God forbids it because it is abominable."

But things are different today; we have a new wrinkle on suicide, aided and perhaps encouraged by self-styled consultants on the limits of human suffering. We read in our tabloids and glossy magazines that the actions of the deceased are, under certain sanctioned circumstances, celebrated with tributes such as are usually reserved for New Age heroes, which a few of them seem to have become. As for the pop cultural icons, medical and otherwise, who assist them—we are treated to the spectacle of those publicized peddlers of death willingly expounding their philosophies on TV talk shows. They extol their own selflessness even as the judicial system seeks to prosecute them.

In 1988, there appeared in the *Journal of the American Medical Association* an account by a young gynecologist-in-training who, in the wee hours of one night, murdered—*murder* is the only word for it—a cancer-ridden twenty-year-old woman because it pleased him to interpret her plea for relief as a plea for death that only he could grant. His method was to inject a dose of intravenous morphine of at least twice the recommended strength and then to stand by until her breathing "became irregular, then ceased." The fact that the self-appointed deliverer had never seen his victim before did not deter him from not only carrying out but actually publishing the details of his misconceived mission of mercy, saturated with the implicit fulsome certainty of his wisdom. Hippocrates winced, and his living heirs wept in spirit.

15 Though American doctors quickly reached a condemning consensus about the behavior of the young gynecologist, they responded very differently three years later in a case of quite another sort. Writing in the *New England Journal of Medicine,* an internist from Rochester, New York, described a patient he identified only as Diane, whose suicide he knowingly facilitated by prescribing the

[1] accoucheurs: male midwives.

[2] oncologists: physicians whose specialty is the treatment of cancer.

[3] Aesculapius: Greco-Roman god of medicine and healing.

[4] Kant: German Enlightenment philosopher, 1724–1804.

barbiturates she requested. Diane, the mother of a college-age son, had been Dr. Timothy Quill's patient for a long time. Three and a half years earlier, he had diagnosed a particularly severe form of leukemia, and her disease had progressed to the point where "bone pain, weakness, fatigue, and fevers began to dominate her life."

Rather than agree to chemotherapy that stood little chance of arresting the lethal assault of her cancer, Diane early in her course had made it clear to Dr. Quill and his several consultants that she feared the debilitation of treatment and the loss of control of her body far more than she feared death. Slowly, patiently, with rare compassion and the help of his colleagues, Quill came to accept Diane's decision and the validity of her grounds for making it. The process by which he gradually recognized that he should help speed her death is exemplary of the humane bond that can exist and be enhanced between a doctor and a competent terminally ill patient who rationally chooses and with consultation confirms that it is the right way to make her quietus. For those whose worldview allows them this option, Dr. Quill's way of dealing with the thorny issue of assent (since then elaborated in a wise and outspoken book published in 1993) may prove to be a reference point on the compass of medical ethics. Physicians like the young gynecologist, and the inventors of suicide machines, too, have a great deal to learn from the Dianes and the Timothy Quills.

Quill and the gynecologist represent the diametrically opposed approaches which dominate discussions of the physician's role in helping patients to die—they are the ideal and the feared. Debates have raged, and I hope will continue to rage, over the stance that should be taken by the medical community and others, and there are many shades of opinion.

In the Netherlands, euthanasia guidelines have been drawn up by common consensus, allowing competent and fully informed patients to have death administered in carefully regulated circumstances. The usual method is for the physician to induce deep sleep with barbiturates and then to inject a muscle-paralyzing drug to cause cessation of breathing. The Dutch Reformed Church has adopted a policy, described in its publication *Euthanasie en Pastoraat*—"Euthanasia and the Ministry"—that does not obstruct the voluntary ending of life when illness makes it intolerable. Their very choice of words signifies the churchmen's sensitivity to the difference between this and ordinary suicide, or *zelfmoord,* literally "self-murder." A new term has been introduced to refer to death under circumstances of euthanasia: *zelfdoding,* which might best be translated as "self-deathing."

Although the practice remains technically illegal in the Netherlands, it has not been prosecuted so long as the involved physician stays within the guidelines. These include repeated uncoerced requests to end the severe mental and physical suffering that is the result of incurable disease which has no other prospect for relief. It is required that all alternative options have been exhausted or refused. The number of patients undergoing euthanasia is approximately 2,300 per year in a nation of some 14.5 million people, representing about 1 percent of all deaths. Most frequently, the act is carried out in the patient's home. Interestingly, the great majority of requests are refused by doctors, because they do not meet the criteria.

20 *Involvement* is the essence of the thing. Family physicians who make house calls are the primary providers of medical care in the Netherlands. When a terminally ill person requests euthanasia or assistance with suicide, it is not a specialist to whom he is likely to go for counsel, or a death expert. The probability is that doctor and patient will have known each other for years, as did Timothy Quill and Diane, and even then consultation and verification by another physician is mandatory. The length and quality of Quill's relationship with Diane must have been major considerations in the decision of a Rochester grand jury in July 1991 not to indict him.

In the United States and democratic countries in general, the importance of airing differing viewpoints rests not in the probability that a stable consensus will ever be reached but in the recognition that it will not. It is by studying the shades of opinion expressed in such discussions that we become aware of considerations in decision-making that may never have weighed in our soul-searching. Unlike the debates, which certainly belong in the public arena, the decisions themselves will always properly be made in the tiny, impenetrable sphere of personal conscience. And that is exactly as it should be. . . .

LEARNING MORE

Useful resources to learn more about the debate concerning assisted suicide can be found on the *Ideas Across Time* website.

QUESTIONING THE TEXT

1. Why are physicians usually without sympathy for those who have taken their own lives?
2. On what grounds does Nuland say that "Taking one's own life is almost always the wrong thing to do" (par. 4)? What criteria does he establish as a precondition that a person needs to meet before contemplating suicide (see par. 7)? Do Nuland's points seem sufficient to explain his position?
3. What is the flaw in Seneca's position, according to Nuland? On the whole, does Nuland agree or disagree with Seneca?
4. What distinguishes the roles in assisted suicides of the gynecologist and Dr. Quill?
5. What aspect of medical practice in the Netherlands makes assisted suicide more likely to be ethically based than it might be in the United States?
6. What is Nuland's position on assisted suicide?

ANALYZING THE WRITER'S CRAFT

1. What is the tone of this essay? How does its tone express the writer's attitude toward his subject?
2. Does this essay present a balanced view of suicide and euthanasia? Support your answer by detailed evidence from the essay.

3. Offer three examples of especially effective transitions in this essay.
4. Nuland's points often depend on modifiers rather than nouns, as he himself stresses in par. 4. Consider the following sentence from par. 18 (emphasis added): "In the Netherlands, euthanasia guidelines have been drawn up by *common* consensus, allowing *competent and fully informed* patients to have death administered in *carefully regulated* circumstances." Do Nuland's modifiers (in italics) contribute to the balanced presentation of the essay, or are they a way to make the unpalatable palatable and hence to sway the audience? Support your answer by reference to other sentences in which Nuland similarly takes pains to qualify the bare nouns of a statement.
5. What evidence do we have in this essay that Nuland is a physician? Could this essay have been written more or less in the same way by an informed individual outside the medical profession? Explain.
6. Nuland builds his essay around key examples. Do you find these examples sufficient? Can they bear the burden of his argument? For the most part, Nuland has chosen specific illustrative examples rather than statistics to make his points. What is the effect of this rhetorical decision? Do you think Nuland needs more statistics in his essay? Why or why not?
7. Nuland concludes his essay by noting that it is "the shades of opinion" in discussions of suicide and euthanasia that raise our own awareness of our own assumptions and beliefs (par. 21). How does Nuland's essay reveal his own sensitivity to shades of opinion?

MAKING CONNECTIONS

1. Obviously, Nuland's views of suicide contrast with those of Anne Sexton (pp. 660–661) and (especially) Yukio Mishima (pp. 685–691). First, state the position on suicide of each of these writers in your own words. Then, discuss which of these writers you agree with most, and why.
2. Nuland also focuse on new dilemmas posed by contemporary science (in this case, medicine) for ethical behavior. What can guide us under these new circumstances? What guides Nuland? How are the holy books (see Chapter 2, pp. 68–96) helpful?
3. Richard Feynman (Chapter 3, pp. 201–207) says that scientists are no better than any of the rest of us at solving human problems. Does Nuland confirm or refute Feynman's point?

FORMULATING IDEAS FOR WRITING

1. Write an essay assessing the arguments for and against suicide presented by Yukio Mishima (pp. 685–691) and Sherwin B. Nuland.
2. Do you agree that there are two circumstances that may justify taking one's own life, as Nuland argues (par. 4 ff.)? Before writing on this topic, see the discussion of Argument in the Appendix (pp. 717–718).

3. Nuland quotes the great orator Seneca on old age, and then proceeds to expose what he thinks is the "flaw" in Seneca's position (pars. 4–7). But in par. 7, Nuland concedes that there may be "situations in which Seneca's words deserve heeding." What on balance is Nuland saying about Seneca's argument? Is he right that there is a "flaw" in Seneca's position? Would Seneca have qualified his position had he had the benefit of acquaintance with modern medicine?
4. Nuland offers a number of key examples to illustrate various approaches to suicide, assisted suicide, and euthanasia. Analyze these examples to see both how they form stepping stones in Nuland's overall argument and whether on closer examination Nuland's own analysis holds up. After reviewing Nuland's examples, do you agree or disagree with his conclusion?

The Conventions of Writing

The introduction to *Ideas Across Time* offered some preliminary observations on the discipline of reading in college. This appendix addresses key elements of college writing.

Writing is intricately bound up with conventions. With respect to written texts, a *convention* is a device, method, or rule that writers and readers agree upon, either explicitly or implicitly. Here, for example, is the opening paragraph of Adam Smith's *Wealth of Nations* (see Chapter 4, pp. 244–262):

> The greatest improvement in the productive powers of labour, and the greater part of the skill, dexterity, and judgment with which it is anywhere directed, or applied, seem to have been the effects of the division of labour.

Let's begin with something absolutely basic, the word "labour" in the first line. Why is it spelled with a "u"? Because "labour" was the agreed-upon spelling in Great Britain at the time Smith wrote (and remains the agreed-upon spelling in Great Britain today). In this sense, spelling is a convention. There is no intrinsically right or wrong way to spell "labor" or, for that matter, any word. The way a word is spelled depends on an implicit agreement, followed in everyday practice, among readers and writers. This kind of agreement applies to every aspect of language and its uses, from the most fundamental—such as why the word for labor is "labor" and not, say, "stone"—to the more sophisticated, such as the rules for the citation of sources (see p. 708). Moreover, Smith's opening paragraph embodies a great many other conventions that we are so accustomed to that, for the most part, we don't even notice them. Smith employs capital letters, commas, and a period. He writes in sentences. He opens his chapter by stating his thesis, and he expresses his thesis in a paragraph.

As Smith's opening makes clear, in the absence of these conventions, reading and writing would be impossible. These conventions have developed over centuries, have been generally adopted, and consequently carry the authority of the culture. In other words, there's no point in using "stone" when you mean "labor." The conventions of writing apply to everyone who uses the language.

But education invites you to take up membership in increasingly learned or specialized communities, and each of these communities depends on its own particular conventions. There are conventions about how to address a judge, for example, or how to lay out a legal argument that must be learned by all those who want to be part of the "legal community." In this sense, there is a community of college writers, ranging from senior scholars on the faculty to first-year students. As a member of this community, you are expected to become familiar with its conventions.

For our purposes, the conventions of writing can be grouped into five broad categories: conventions of address, conventions of generating ideas, conventions of integrating and citing sources, conventions of organization, and conventions of rhetoric.

CONVENTIONS OF ADDRESS

Conventions of address govern the relationship between the purpose of a piece of writing, its writer, and its audience. A formal research paper for psychology on the uses of aversion to alter behavior and a personal essay about how you gave up smoking will call for different conventions of address. When striving for formality, your writing should adopt an impersonal and objective tone. A personal essay, on the other hand, would likely involve the personal voice, the use of "I," and colloquial language. Just as you want to be careful to use the appropriate form of address as a writer, so too you want to be appropriately responsive to forms of address in your reading. It would show a misunderstanding of the conventions of address to protest that a formal report on methods used to help people give up smoking lacks personality, just as it would be inappropriate to object that the personal account of one person's experience with the nicotine patch is too subjective.

College writing often involves explicit assignments, and such assignments can provide you with a ready-made purpose and an explicit occasion for writing. But even when responding to an explicit assignment, you will often have to fashion a writing topic—and hence a purpose—on your own. And a great deal will depend on what kind of paper you decide to write. If you choose to write an analysis of the various methods available to help people give up smoking, you will probably use fairly formal and objective conventions of address. Such an essay, moreover, assumes a rational and curious audience interested in what you, an informed writer, have to say. But if you choose to write a more polemical essay, arguing that smoking should be banned and cigarette companies prosecuted for manslaughter, then naturally you will adopt a different *voice*, one that is impassioned and committed to a moral point of view. Such an essay needs to assess its audience carefully. What can you assume your audience knows? What can you assume your audience believes? In this way, then, the writer's purpose and audience determine which of the conventions of address are appropriate for any particular piece of writing.

In writing, as in life, conventions, crucial as they are for communication, should not obliterate individuality. The professional writer, a master of the conventions of writing, is always also recognizably an individual. The individuality of the writer is conveyed in particular through the writer's voice. Voice includes the words a writer uses, the grammatical constructions a writer employs, the evidence and argument a writer invokes, and the subjects a writer finds congenial. The point is that conventions followed rigidly and mechanically produce dull writing with an obviously false pretense to neutrality. Your writing should demonstrate not only respect for the conventions but also a personal stake in what is being said.

CONVENTIONS FOR GENERATING IDEAS

With your purpose for writing and audience clearly in mind, you are ready to begin generating ideas for writing. If your instructor hasn't assigned a topic and you aren't responding to one of the Ideas for Writing that follow the reading selections, you'll need to come up with your own essay topic. Finding an interesting topic to write about is an exploratory process that mirrors the active reading process described in this book's Introduction (see pp. 1–8). Sophisticated writers use certain conventions for generating ideas to engage more fully with a text and to begin crafting a meaningful response. These conventions include annotation, word searches, and directed questioning.

Annotation

As described in this book's Introduction, *annotation* involves the reader's active participation in a dialogue with the writer, a running commentary that includes underlining, summarizing, and questioning of the text at hand. Annotating a reading not only helps you understand it better but also initiates your process of responding to and analyzing the reading. As demonstrated by the sample annotation on p. 5, annotation is a key strategy in generating ideas for writing. For instance, the reader annotates the Gettysburg Address to highlight key words ("fathers"), repeated comparisons and contrasts ("Four score" and "Now"), central images (images of birth), and rhetorical moves (rising emphasis, repetition, and parallelism). From these annotations, the reader could develop the following essay topics:

- Lincoln's use of patrimonial language contrasted with his recurring images of conception, birth, and rebirth
- A comparison of the purposes, audiences, and rhetorical strategies of the Declaration of Independence and the Gettysburg Address

Intense engagement with a text through critical reading and annotating produces the raw material from which you will develop your essay.

Word Searches

Writing topics often emerge from a close look at the subtleties and nuances of writers's language. The complexity of writers's ideas, in fact, lurks in their words. *Word searches* in dictionaries and other reference materials can reveal the intricacy and interrelatedness of a reading's key terms and concepts. By examining a word's literal meaning (or denotation) and how it's used in particular contexts, critical readers often uncover the word's implicit meanings and associations (or connotation). In the sample annotation of the Gettysburg Address (see p. 5), for example, the reader underlines words that are especially important to Lincoln's address. Words such as "living," "dead," "dedicate," and "consecrate" appear again and again, emphasizing the central idea that all people of the United States, past and present, constitute "this nation, under God" and that Lincoln needs the participation of all Americans in the nation's "new birth of freedom." From these annotations, the reader could develop an essay on Lincoln's ability to urge his listeners to action.

Directed Questioning

With *directed questioning*, you poke and probe a text, asking specific questions that emerge from your purpose for reading and, ultimately, writing. Your questions about a text highlight your curiosity and confusion as you read with a particular goal in mind, such as wanting to explore the religious references in Lincoln's Gettysburg Address. These directed questions, in turn, point to the deeper layers of a text and provide material for possible essay topics. For instance, in the sample annotation of the Gettysburg Address, the reader asks several questions:

- "Why not 'eighty'?"
- "Is this true?"
- "Can the nation endure?"

The first question the reader asks ("Why not 'eighty'?") calls attention to Lincoln's elevated word choice, or diction, in his use of "Four score" as the first words of his address. This specific question leads to broader questions about the nature of Lincoln's language and his purpose for using such language:

- What other examples of elevated diction appear in the address?
- How do these examples reveal Lincoln's main ideas and his attitude toward his subject and audience?
- What is Lincoln trying to accomplish by using such language?

These questions, when explored fully, can lead to still more questions about Lincoln's language, his purpose, his audience, and his voice as a national leader.

Similarly, the reader's second and third questions ("Is this true?" and "Can the nation endure?") could stimulate essay topics about Lincoln's vision of a "government of the people, by the people, for the people." For instance, the reader examines the validity of the statement "all men are created equal," raising important questions about Lincoln's intended audience and exactly who (all men? both men and women?) the "people" of American democratic society are. The survival of American democracy depends on a clear definition of "equality" that accounts for the diversity of the American population. In this way, the reader's preliminary questions create more questions. This is the essence of directed questioning.

CONVENTIONS OF INTEGRATING AND CITING SOURCES

As an active participant in a community of learners, you build upon the foundation of knowledge established by scholars and by peers and colleagues. Engaging in a dialogue with a text involves conversing with other scholars and sources. College writing requires you to use the conventions of integrating and citing sources to recognize the contributions of other scholars to your academic work and to contribute your own voice to the ongoing conversation.

Summary, Paraphrase, Quotation, and Documentation

Summary, paraphrase, and quotation are key strategies for integrating sources into your writing.

- *Summarizing* involves distilling the essence of a source and recasting it in your own words.
- *Paraphrasing* requires you to reword important points a writer makes.
- *Quoting* involves selecting crucial passages from a source to illustrate a writer's use of language.

Summary and paraphrase are useful techniques for incorporating others' ideas into your writing when a source's original wording is not essential to the meaning of the passage. However, quoting a writer's exact words is necessary and beneficial when rewording is impossible or when you are making a point about the writer's actual language. For instance, if a writer were to develop the sample annotation of the Gettysburg Address on p. 00 into a full-length analysis, the writer might summarize the address as a pivotal speech in American history, comparing its language and rhetorical strategies (paraphrasing important points and quoting specific words and phrases) with the language and rhetoric of other important cultural documents, such as the Declaration of Independence and the U.S. Constitution.

Documentation is a formal way of acknowledging the sources of information that shape your thinking and writing. There are as many documentation styles as there are academic communities; many disciplines have their own conventions of citing sources that reflect their goals. The sciences, for example, emphasize a source's publication date over other citation elements since currency is crucial to the relevance and applicability of scientific research. Two of the most common documentation styles are those of the Modern Language Association (MLA), used in some of the humanities disciplines, and the American

Psychological Association (APA), used in the social sciences. Each documentation style requires you to acknowledge sources in two ways:

1. Cite your sources as they're used throughout your essay.
2. List complete source information at the end of your paper in a works-cited list for MLA style or a reference list for APA style.

Although your instructor may not require a works-cited or reference list if your paper cites only readings from *Ideas Across Time,* you should include in-text references to the selections from which you summarize, paraphrase, or quote information. Following are sample in-text citations and works-cited and reference list entries for a selection reprinted in *Ideas Across Time.* For more detailed information on documenting sources, refer to the Online Learning Center for this book.

	MLA	APA
In-text citation	Baldwin explores the "complex fate" of being an American as well as how the American writer abroad comes to realize this fate (29).	Baldwin (2008, p. 29) explores the "complex fate" of being an American as well as how the American writer abroad comes to realize this fate.
Works-cited/reference list entry	Baldwin, James. "The Discovery of What It Means to Be an American." *Ideas Across Time.* Ed. Igor Webb. New York: McGraw-Hill, 2008. 29–35.	Baldwin, J. (2008). The discovery of what it means to be an American. In I. Webb (Ed.), *Ideas across time* (pp. 29–35). New York: McGraw-Hill.

Avoiding Plagiarism

Academic communities thrive on the insights that emerge from spirited discussion. Articulating, probing, and rethinking ideas with others define our experience as perpetual learners. Across the disciplines, scholars are responsible for crediting other scholarly voices that influence their work. College writing requires a systematic and formal acknowledgment of the sources you use to construct an essay. Representing the words or ideas of others as your own, whether intentional or not, is known as *plagiarism.* Each time you use a writer's language or ideas in your writing, you must quote the source or rephrase the passage. Whether you summarize, paraphrase, or quote a writer's language or ideas, you must cite the source appropriately using the documentation style your instructor prefers. Various kinds of plagiarism occur when writers fail to distinguish between their words and ideas and those of others. For example, using a writer's exact terminology in your summary or paraphrase without quoting or citing the source constitutes plagiarism. Similarly, neglecting to enclose a writer's words in quotation marks, or quoting certain words but not all words you use from a source, is also a form of plagiarism. To avoid plagiarism, be sure accurately to summarize, paraphrase, quote, and document your sources, giving proper credit to the ideas that shape your own.

CONVENTIONS OF ORGANIZATION

The fourth major grouping of conventions pertains to organization. Conventions of organization have to do with the presentation of the material in an essay, with what it is useful to think about as the delineation and exposition of a writer's subject. *Delineation* (from the Latin *lineare,* meaning "to draw lines") refers to the process of drawing a line around a subject. In art, delineation is a detailed outlining or accurate portrayal. In writing, delineation draws a line around that part of a general subject that can be handled within the limits of any given piece of writing. For example, if you decide to write an essay about the auto industry—specifically, safety standards—"automobiles" might be the *general* subject, and "safety in automobile manufacturing" the *delineated* subject. *Exposition* refers to what a writer does with that particular (that is, well-delineated) subject; it is the process of unfolding the purpose and meaning of a piece of writing.

Thesis

Delineation results in a thesis and an introduction. The *thesis* is the controlling idea of a piece of writing. It balances the general and the specific guided by the writer's goal. A thesis such as "There is no possible other form of government for the post-industrial age than democracy" implies an essay of a certain length. If you are an independent scholar and decide to tackle the question of what government best suits the contemporary world, the thesis above may well do. Your study, however, will take a long time to complete and result in many pages of writing. A thesis as broad as this one cannot be handled in an essay of five or six pages. To revise the thesis to fit a five- to six-page essay, you might narrow the time period to something less encompassing than the "post-industrial age," or you might compare democracy to one other form of government.

Arriving at a thesis, then, is a process of selecting, narrowing, and focusing. In the thesis above, the writer offers both a topic and an assertion about the topic. The sentence asserts that only one form of government (democracy) is a good match for the post-industrial world. Again, this thesis implies a fairly lengthy piece of writing, but it provides both reader and writer with a focused subject and an assertion about that subject, the two essential ingredients of a thesis. It is important to note that often a writer may not be quite sure what assertion to make about the subject until well into the writing, or even until after several whole drafts. Often, delineation is a process of discovery. The process is successfully completed when the writer has settled on a focused subject taken from the vast number of possibilities that any general idea suggests, and has discovered what main assertion he or she wants to make about that subject.

Introduction

A thesis makes certain promises and raises certain expectations. The reader anticipates the fulfillment of the promises and expectations, and it is the writer's job to make sure that the reader is not disappointed. But readers are not always eager to hear everything you have to say. Readers are more like pedestrians hurrying to their destinations on a busy street. Before you can impress the reader with the importance of your subject and the incisiveness of your analysis, you have to attract the reader's attention and prepare the reader to heed what you have to say. This is the role of the *introduction.*

Here is the opening sentence of James Baldwin's essay "The Discovery of What It Means to Be an American" (Chapter 1, pp. 29–35):

> "It is a complex fate to be an American," Henry James observed, and the principal discovery an American writer makes in Europe is just how complex this fate is.

In one sentence, Baldwin achieves the main purposes of an introduction. He attracts the reader's attention, he efficiently delineates his subject, and he gives us a good idea of just what lies in store for us in the essay that follows. He promises discussion of the complex fate of being an American, as well as how this is discovered by the American writer abroad. Baldwin uses one of the standard tools of an introduction—the quotation. In this case, the quotation is succinct and comes from the pen of the emblematic American writer abroad, Henry James. The invocation of James adds a useful note of authority to the introduction's admirable focus and brevity.

A good technique for your opening, then, is use of an especially apt example, anecdote, or quotation. There are two obvious attractions to such an approach. Something concrete, especially if it's striking, is more immediately interesting than something vague and abstract. Moreover, using a quotation is efficient. You can't afford to waste time in the introduction, and you especially can't afford to lose the reader's interest.

Consider a different opening, this one taken from Meyer Schapiro's "The Introduction of Modern Art in America: The Armory Show" (Chapter 7, pp. 590–602):

> The great event, the turning-point in American art called the Armory Show, was briefly this. In December 1911 . . .

Schapiro takes a perfectly direct approach in his introduction. Clearly, the direct method often works best, although, of course, it helps when, as here, the topic under discussion is enticing in itself. Schapiro could safely assume that his potential readers would all want to learn about "the turning-point in American art." Not all subjects are of this intrinsic interest. A direct approach nonetheless has the advantage of avoiding broad but pointless generalizations, one of the main pitfalls of openings. Here is an example of an ineffective introduction:

> Throughout human history, people have debated what form of government is best. Some people have favored monarchy and some people have favored democracy. There are many arguments made to support each view.

Avoid this kind of introduction. It is nearly impossible to generalize about what has been thought "throughout human history." Since every reader obviously knows that there are varying opinions about government, nothing is gained by recounting such an empty piece of information. Better to get right to the point!

The examples of effective introductions quoted above don't go very far toward stating a thesis. In some cases, the thesis comes just a bit later in the introduction, but in others, it doesn't appear until much later, sometimes at the very end of the essay. Occasionally, a writer will not openly state a thesis at all, and the thesis remains implicit. For the purposes of college writing, however, it is always best to state your thesis as clearly as possible.

As you write, don't be surprised if your introduction and thesis change. Frequently, the introduction you first write, like the thesis you first write, will need revision. You may even find that you are not ready to write your introduction until your essay is complete. In this respect, the conventions of organization are significantly different for the writer and the reader. The writer arrives at a final draft through a process that may have false starts or require changing passages again and again. The reader arrives at the draft when it is already fully formed and, from that final draft, must figure out what the writer is trying to say. For this reason, a thesis is essential. A piece of writing that lacks a thesis will seem pointless, and even like a kind of betrayal, to the reader. A piece of writing that begins with a thesis statement that the writer later abandons is similarly a piece of writing that a reader will find frustrating and disappointing. The reader will experience writing of this sort as a broken promise, an exasperating violation of the conventions that bind writer and reader.

Exposition

At the core of the conventions of organization, then, is the promise that the writer makes to the reader through an essay's thesis. Fulfilling the promise of the thesis is the role of *exposition.* Whereas delineation is the process of settling on a focused subject and a pertinent statement regarding that subject, exposition is the process of taking the reader down the path that leads from your introduction to your conclusion, the path that persuades the reader of the validity of your thesis.

Exposition is an orderly process that includes explanation and interpretation. Writers usually convey their explanations and interpretations through a limited number of the conventions of rhetoric (discussed at length on pp. 714–718).

First, exposition is an orderly process. Successful writers, such as those featured in this book, seem to have a natural organizational sense. Their ideas seem to flow with ease, one thing smoothly leading to another. Usually, however, these ideas have been formed over time and have been honed over several drafts. For most writers, the writing process includes stumbling blocks and wrong turns. Many writers, for example, get stuck on what should come first and what should come second. If you find yourself struggling with problems of organization, bear in mind that there has to be a rationale for the organization of your writing. The reader should not feel that paragraph 8 could just as easily have been paragraph 2, for example. On the contrary, the reader must feel that there is a sound reason for the order of your paragraphs, and that your essay moves smoothly from beginning to end.

Second, exposition is a process of explanation and interpretation. The word "explain" derives from the Latin *planus*, meaning "flat." In its root sense, to explain is to make smooth or to take out the rough. So you can think of your thesis as a rough assertion that your exposition will smooth out for the reader. *Explanation* answers the question "What is it?" In trying to answer this question for the reader, your explanation should shed light on the logical implications, the development, and the relations of your ideas. (A few useful ways to do this are sketched on pp. 714–718 in the discussion of conventions of rhetoric.)

Interpretation, in contrast, answers the question "What does it mean?" Interpretation therefore adds to explanation the element of judgment. Although in clarifying your thesis or a passage in a text, explanation may well suffice, often your own understanding of a text will involve pointing the reader toward a conclusion that the reader might not have found without your guidance. Let's say you want to write about whether the wave of immigration into the United States over the last decade supports or refutes the idea of America as a melting pot. You plan to make reference to passages from Joel L. Swerdlow's article "Changing America" (see Chapter 1, pp. 11–19). Swerdlow writes about J. E. B. Stuart High School in Falls Church, Virginia, whose student population is composed of students born in over seventy nations. You are interested in statements Swerdlow quotes that seem to show that most of the immigrants, including those, like the Russians, whose skin is white, don't want to be identified as "white." Here is the conclusion of that section of Swerdlow's discussion:

> I end up wondering if these kids aren't just struggling with an age-old adolescent dilemma: wanting to achieve versus wanting to be "cool." If achievement—or at least too much achievement—is unfashionable and achievement, as they have defined it, is "white," then "white" is not cool.
>
> Whether they want to end up "white" or not, the kids here know they're in a blender: People of different colors and textures go in, and a mixture that appears homogenous comes out. Everyone has a backpack. Most boys wear jeans and T-shirts . . .

This passage can be invoked in relation to your topic in a number of ways, each requiring interpretation. Is the most important thing about the students in J. E. B. Stuart High School that they are adolescents wanting to fit in, and therefore is their use of the term "white" merely about fashion? In this respect, are these students an example of how the experience of America as a melting pot persists? Or is J. E. B. Stuart High School a good example of how people who come to the United States from all over the world remain on the outside looking in? Whatever the case, your reading of Swerdlow's article will require a detailed account of how you understand the passage you are quoting. That is interpretation. Your interpretation will rely on evidence, a critical aspect of any exposition. If you choose to argue that these students are "melting" into the American mainstream, you will support that view by stressing what all the students have in common, such as the way they dress. You will emphasize Swerdlow's observation that "the kids here know they're in a blender." If you choose to argue that the immigrant experience has done no more than throw these students together in one school, leaving them just as excluded from privilege and achievement as they were in their home countries, then you will rely on the words of the students themselves and their pejorative use of "white."

Conclusion

If your thesis can be understood as a promise to your reader, then a *conclusion* is a reminder to your reader that you have fulfilled your promise. But merely saying you have fulfilled the promise does not necessarily make it so. It might be a good idea to ban the phrase "In conclusion, I want to say . . ." from your writing. By saying "In conclusion," a student writer often assumes he or she is appropriately ending an essay regardless of what has preceded and what follows the words "in conclusion." But the invocation of the word "conclusion" is no guarantee that you are ending your essay well. Assuming that you *have* indeed fulfilled your promise, your conclusion does not have to waste words or wax eloquent. In particular, your conclusion should avoid making new promises by starting off on a new subject.

The conclusion should economically draw your essay to a close. This can be done by some kind of summary or brief restatement of the essay's thesis. This summary or restatement can take many forms, including an anecdote or quotation that nails the point and emphatically closes your argument. Another common way to close is to say something (brief) about what your essay implies. Here, for example, are the final two sentences of N. Scott Momaday's "The Arrowmaker" (Chapter 7, pp. 612–616):

> For the storyteller, for the arrowmaker, language does indeed represent the only chance for survival. It is appropriate that he survives in our time and that he has survived over a period of untold generations.

Momaday has been discussing the Kiowa parable of the arrowmaker, arguing that the parable is about language and survival. He repeats this point at the very end, succinctly, and then remarks, also succinctly, on the significance of what he has been saying, drawing his essay to an effective close.

CONVENTIONS OF RHETORIC

Especially important in exposition are the conventions of rhetoric (sometimes called patterns of exposition). Originally, in classical Greece, *rhetoric* was an essential feature of the education of aristocratic men whose lives were inevitably going to require some public, political service. Rhetoric at that time represented a useful set of skills for orators and aimed to help speakers be persuasive. Eventually, rhetoric was applied to writing. Misused and misunderstood, rhetoric can be artificial and empty. However, because the conventions of rhetoric govern how ideas are shaped, organized, and employed, you will find that these conventions are extremely useful resources in your effort to convey your own ideas in writing.

The most often-used conventions of rhetoric (or patterns of exposition) are narration, example, analysis, comparison and contrast, and argument.

Narration

A *narrative* tells about something that happened, usually over a period of time. In plain terms, it's a story. Stories are intrinsically interesting and are all around us. They can be a great help in conveying abstract information or making something dull appear lively. As such, narrative is an essential part of literature and of essay writing.

Two warnings about narrative writing are in order. First, most college writing assignments don't lend themselves to all-out narrative treatment. You may tell a story to get started, spark a discussion, or drive home a point. But making a point through a story is harder than it seems. Second, a story without a thesis will exasperate your reader; but how can a story argue a thesis? A master at exposition through narrative is James Baldwin (see "The Discovery of What It Means to Be an American" in Chapter 1, pp. 29–35). Baldwin uses the story of his own experience to illustrate the problem of the African-American writer. His thesis emerges from the story and is illuminated by the details of the story. It may seem that simply sitting down and telling a story is the easiest way to complete an assignment—but a glance at Baldwin's essay will show you how much skill the use of narrative for expository purposes requires. If you do choose to use narrative, here are some important questions to bear in mind:

- How much time are you going to cover?
- How much detail are you going to provide?
- Who is going to tell the story—and why?

Example

Like narrative, *examples* are something we use daily in every sort of human exchange. But unlike narrative, examples are almost unavoidable in most writing. A thesis requires proof and evidence to gain support; this support often comes in the form of specific and concrete examples. A reader wanting more support for a thesis might ask, "What does the writer mean?" These questions are best answered by example.

Because an example is expected to support a general statement directly and unequivocally, examples have to be chosen with care and attention. A good example should clarify the general point you are making and explain what the reader may not be sure about. A good example should not raise doubts in the reader's mind.

Although usually a thesis is best supported by several examples, one especially apt example can be used for an extended discussion. Adam Smith opens

The Wealth of Nations (Chapter 4, pp. 244–262) with the thesis that the division of labor has been the engine driving economic growth, and he supports his thesis by one famous example: the making of a pin. Smith's analysis of pin-making, though, is extensive and detailed, following the process point by point. Moreover, Smith then draws from this one example a lesson applicable to the economy as a whole: "In every other art and manufacture, the effects of the division of labour are similar to what they are in this very trifling one."

Analysis

Analysis involves taking something apart to see how it works. Learning is often analytical, and in examining ideas and propositions, it's important to analyze both how the parts of a whole relate and for what purpose. We take things apart not just to look at their elements individually, but to put them back together with an eye toward better understanding the nature of the whole. In the realm of ideas, then, the function of analysis is to explain how or why something is what it is.

Curiously, it is hard, and perhaps impossible, to do this by considering an idea all by itself; ideas and concepts only have meaning for us in context. An implement with two or more prongs becomes a fork only if we add that it is used, as the dictionary says, for "taking up," as in eating, and if we know that eating is governed by a whole array of conventions. Consequently, analysis usually proceeds by examining relationships—between one thing and another or between something specific and a general idea.

Comparison and Contrast

Comparison and contrast, or looking at likenesses and differences, is a powerful way of disclosing what and why something is what it is. It's not a method that's useful if the things we put side by side are so different or so similar that there's nothing to say. We only learn by zeroing in on likenesses and differences when the two ideas, events, or objects we are looking at fall within the same general category. It makes sense to compare the governments of France and Germany, but it doesn't make immediate sense to compare the government of France and the German national orchestra.

This same principle—compare like and like—applies as much to the details of comparison as to the objects of comparison. If two governments are being put side by side, distinguishing likenesses and differences between the heads of state in these two governments may be illuminating. But you know in advance that it won't be illuminating to compare the judicial system in one nation and the head of state in another.

It is especially important to consider why you're choosing to compare and contrast two things. What is there to be learned from discussing these two things in relation to one another that cannot be learned by pursuing a different method? Why does it make more sense, say, to discuss two poems on war together than to discuss one or the other alone?

Argument

If *argument* means getting the other person—the reader, the audience—to see things your way, then everything is argument, and all other rhetorical conventions serve argument. Without doubt, there's a lot to be said for this point of view. But for our purposes, it is more useful to narrow the meaning of argument to cover how people present their reasons for believing something, especially important matters that are generally seen as debatable. Since debate necessarily requires agreed-upon rules, argument—more than other conventions of rhetoric—depends on agreements between writer and reader.

In particular, argument appeals to reason. It presupposes that rationality is the highest form of thought, and it gives preference to thought over feeling. This accounts for the rigor of argument. In argument, not only must a claim or thesis be supported by evidence, but the process of validating the thesis has to be logical. In this way, argument is hemmed in by rules intended to ensure reliability, objectivity, and sound thinking. Reason, however, cannot be applied to all human problems or disagreements. The statement "I believe that eating X is immoral because God has so decreed" cannot be debated rationally. Reason does not apply and no argument can be made to support this claim. It is a matter of belief. We all hold beliefs of this sort—but it is important to recognize them as inhabiting a territory alien to reason. If, however, the person objecting to eating X adds, "Not only is eating X immoral, it is also unhealthy," then a debate can begin. The claim that eating X is unhealthy can be tested rationally—because it is subject to logical analysis and can be examined in the light of accessible and arguable evidence. In the first instance, only a change in belief (losing faith in God and no longer believing that eating X is immoral) can influence the author's claim. In the second instance, new evidence can change the mind of those arguing the issue. Argument, like science, is inevitably tentative. Even brilliant philosophers make mistakes in argument, and new evidence can always put matters into a wholly different light.

Argument, then, requires a focused thesis supported by an orderly presentation of credible evidence. Refuting reasons or evidence that may undermine the thesis is usually a part of a strong argument because it shows that the writer is aware of both sides of an issue. It also counters objections even before the reader has the chance to raise them. The foundations of argument are logic, testable propositions, and objective evidence.

One of the greatest masters of argument in human history was Socrates. Here he is addressing the jurors who have condemned him to death, still arguing and seeking to show that we have no cause to fear death (see Chapter 8, pp. 565–574):

> Death is one of two things. Either it is annihilation, and the dead have no consciousness of anything, or, as we are told, it is really a change—a migration of the soul from this place to another. Now if there is no consciousness but only a dreamless sleep, death must be a marvelous gain. . . . If on the other hand death is a removal from here to some other place, and if what we are told is true, that all the dead are there, what greater blessing could there be than this, gentlemen?

Socrates begins by stating a proposition: "Death is one of two things." He proceeds to tell us what those two things are and then to explore through logic what these things imply. Much of his argument reflects an "if . . . then" logical structure. If X is true, then Y must follow: "if there is no consciousness . . . [then] death must be a marvelous gain." To disagree with Socrates, you would have to show either that his original proposition is wrong—death is not either annihilation or migration of the soul—or, if you accept his original proposition, that there is a flaw in the logic of his analysis (it does not follow that *if* there is no consciousness *then* death must be a marvelous gain).

Socrates's evidence for his beliefs is mainly logical. His argument is not based on experience. But often argument does arise from evidence based on experience, especially when that experience is itself objective and reliable. This is especially true of scientific argument.

Description, Classification, and Definition

In addition to narration, example, analysis, comparison and contrast, and argument, there are other conventions of rhetoric used by writers in this book, or that you will want to use, including the chief conventions of description, classification, and definition.

Description is the visualization of physical qualities. Descriptive writing aims to capture qualities such as look, feel, and smell. Description answers questions such as "What does it do?" "What is it made of?" and "How does it work?" In writing description, look carefully at what you want to paint for the reader. Avoid clichés; make it fresh!

Classification involves sorting things into groups or categories as a way of understanding or highlighting a big idea. At its simplest, classification puts things that go together in one place and separates them from other things. In a supermarket, for example, all the soup is placed in one section, all the spices in another. At its more complex, classification sorts out all the things that go together into ever more limited and exclusive groups. The soup section is subdivided by maker and could be subdivided by kind (meat soups here, vegetable soups there, for example). For the purposes of writing, such subdivisions highlight networks of relations, and in this way clarify a larger idea.

Definition unpacks the full meaning of a word or concept. When you look up a word in the dictionary, you find a definition. But that definition is usually a fairly brief and limited account of a word's origin and meaning. Writers utilize extended definition when aiming to make a broader point about a word or a concept. What the dictionary says about the word "freedom," for example, may not include the kinds of connections and distinctions that a political scientist would find most illuminating, such as the connections and distinctions between freedom and equality that preoccupy many writers in Chapter 5, "Democratic Society." To fully explore the meaning of freedom, then, would require an extended definition in the form of an essay.

A FINAL WORD

Generations of writers have used and refined the main conventions governing writing discussed in this appendix. Critical reading, as you've been practicing with the selections in this book, involves careful analysis of how and why writers follow and break these conventions. You've annotated, defined, and questioned the rhetorical strategies and subjects of the selections in this book as a way of understanding the writers' ideas. College writing, writing with ideas, requires that you apply the practical skills and habits you employ as a critical reader. You've developed strategies for assessing your audience and purpose, generating ideas, refining your topic, integrating and citing sources, and organizing and shaping your ideas. The better you master the conventions of writing, the better you communicate with your readers. But you are more than simply a communicator; you are a writer and thinker using language as a tool to contribute complex ideas to an academic dialogue. The purpose of writing is not to display familiarity with conventions but to convey the writer's unique experience of the world. Understanding how to shape the rules of writing to fit your own developing style creates a vitality of individual voice and experience that is distinctly your own.

Credits

Text

Page 11: Swerdlow, John, "Changing America," *National Geographic*, September 2001. Copyright © 2001 John Swerdlow. Maps © NG Maps. Reprinted by permission of National Geographic, Inc.

29: Baldwin, James, "The Discovery of What it Means to be an American" was originally published in The New York Times Book Review. © 1959 by James Baldwin. Copyright renewed. Collected in *Nobody Knows My Name*, published by Vintage Books. Used by arrangement with the James Baldwin Estate.

37: Gordon, Mary, "The Ghosts of Ellis Island," *New York Times Magazine*. Copyright © 1985 Mary Gordon. Reprint with permission of Sll/Sterling Lord Literistic, Inc.

45: Cofer, Judith Ortiz, "Silent Dancing" from *Silent Dancing: A Partial Remembrance of a Puerto Rican Childhood*. Copyright © 1991 (Houston: Arte Publico Press—University of Houston, 1991). Used with permission.

64: Rodriguez, Gregory, "Catholic Confession." Copyright © Gregory Rodriguez. Used with permission.

68: Panikkar, Raimundo, *The Vedic Experience: Mantra Manjari*. Copyright © Raimundo Panikkar. Reprinted by permission of Motilal Banarsidass Publishers Ltd.

68: Beck, Sanderson, selections from *Upanishad*, trans. Sanderson Beck from *The Wisdom Bible*. Copyright © 2002 Sanderson Beck. Used with permission.

83: Waley, Arthur, excerpts reprinted with the permission of Scribner, an imprint of Simon & Schuster Adult Publishing Group from *The Analects of Confucius* translated by Arthur Waley. Copyright © 1938 by George Allen & Unwin Ltd. All rights reserved. Reprinted by permission of The Arthur Waley Estate.

109: Nietzsche, Frederick, "God is Dead" taken from *A Nietzsche Reader* selected and translated with an introduction by R. J. Hollingdale (Penguin Classics, 1977). Introduction, selection and translation copyright © R. J. Hollingdale, 1977. Used with permission.

123: Tillich, Paul, "The Lost Dimension in Religion," *Saturday Evening Post*, 6/14/58. Copyright © 1958 Saturday Evening Post. Used with permission.

132: Dalai Lama & Howard C. Cutler "Basic Spiritual Values" from *The Art of Happiness: A Handbook for the Living*. Copyright © 1998 by H.H. Dalai Lama and Howard C. Cutler. Used by permission of Riverhead Books, an imprint of Penguin Group (USA) Inc.

137: Armstrong, Karen, "History and Religion" from *A Short History of Islam*. Copyright © 2000 by Karen Armstrong. Used by permission of Modern Library, a division of Random House, Inc.

148: Mestel, Rosie, "Of Men and Mice: We're Quite Similar—Genetically," *Los Angeles Times*, 12/5/02. Copyright © 2002 Los Angeles Times. Used with permission.

182: Gould, Stephen Jay, "Introduction to Darwin" from *Ever Since Darwin: Reflections in Natural History*. Copyright © 1977 by Stephen Jay Gould. Copyright © 1973, 1974, 1975, 1976, 1977 by The American Museum of Natural History. Used by permission of W.W. Norton & Company, Inc.

187: Standing Bear, Luther, "Nature" from *Land of the Spotted Eagle*. Copyright © 1933 by Luther Standing Bear. Copyright renewed © 1960 by May Jones. Reprinted by permission of the University of Nebraska Press.

193: Einstein, Albert, "Scientific Proof" from *Essays in Science*. Copyright © Philosophical Library, NY. Used with permission.

193: Einstein, Albert, "Letters to Children" from *The Collected Papers of Albert Einstein*. © 1987–2006 Hebrew University and Princeton University Press. Reprinted by permission.

201: Feynman, Richard, "The Value of Science" from *"What Do You Care What Other People Think?": Further Adventures of a Curious Character*, as told to Ralph Leighton. Copyright © 1988 by Gweneth Feynman and Ralph Leighton. Used by permission of W.W. Norton & Company, Inc.

209: Dillard, Annie, "Life on the Rocks" from *Teaching a Stone to Talk*. Copyright © 1982 by Annie Dillard. Used with permission of HarperCollins, Inc.

220: Turkle, Sherry, "How Computers Change the Way We Think" *Chronicle of Higher Education*, January 30, 2004. Copyright © 2004 Sherry Turkle. Reprinted with permission.

232: Smith, Craig, S., "China Juggles the Conflicting Pressure of a Society in Transition," *New York Times*, 7/15/02. Copyright © 2002 New York Times Co. Inc. Used with permission.

288: Auden, W.H., "The Dyer's Hand" from *The Dyer's Hand and Other Essays*. Copyright © 1948, 1950, 1952, 1953, 1954, 1956, 1957, 1958, 1960, 1962 by W.H. Auden. Used by permission of Random House Inc.

288: Stein, Gertrude, from *The Saturday Evening Post*, August 22, 1936. Copyright © 1986 Estate of Gertrude Stein. Reprinted by permission of Stanford Gann, Jr., Literary Executive.

288: Gioia, Dana, "Money" from *The Gods of Winter*. Copyright © 1991 Dana Goia. Used with permission.

300: Terkel, Studs, "Mike LeFevre" from *Working*. Copyright © 1974 by Studs Turkel. Reprinted by permission of Donadio & Olson, Inc.

288: Singer, Peter, "The Singer Solution to World Poverty" Copyright © Peter Singer. Used with permission.

316: Ehrenreich, Barbara, excerpt from *Nickel and Dimed: On (Not) Getting By in America*. © 2001 by Barbara Ehrenreich. Reprinted by permission of Henry Holt and Company, LLC.

330: Zakaria, Fareed, "The Democratic Age" from *The Future of Freedom: Illiberal Democracy at Home and Abroad*. Copyright © 2003 by Fareed Zakaria. Used by permission of W.W. Norton & Company, Inc.

339: Machiavelli, Nicolo, "On the Exercise of Power" from *The Prince*, translated with an introduction by George Bull (Penguin Classics, 1961, Second revised edition.) Copyright © 1961, 1975, 1981 by George Bull. Reprinted with permission from Penguin UK.

390: Boorstin, Daniel J., "Technology and Democracy" from Democracy and Its Discontents. Copyright © 1974 Daniel J. Boorstin. Reprinted by permission of The Estate of Daniel Boorstin.

404: Havel, Vaclav, "The Power of the Powerless" from *Living in Truth*, translated by P. Wilson. Copyright © 1989. Rights administered by Aura Pont Agency.

414: Barber, Benjamin, "Jihad vs. McWorld" Copyright © 1992 Benjamin Barber. Originally published in The Atlantic Monthly, March 1992, as an introduction to the *Jihad vs. McWorld* (Ballantine paperback, 1996), a volume that discusses and extends the themes of the original article. Reprinted with permission from the author.

427: Jen, Gish, "In the American Society." Copyright © 1986 by Gish Jen. First published in *Southern Review*. From the collection *Who's Irish?* by Gish Jen, published in 1999 by Alfred A. Knopf. Reprinted by permission of the author.

446: Goodale, Gloria, "Black and White," *Christian Science Monitor*, March 3, 2006. Copyright © 2006 The Christian Science Monitor. Used with permission.

481: de Beauvoir, Simone, "What is a Woman?" from *The Second Sex*, translated by H.M. Parshley. Copyright 1952 and renewed © 1980 by Alfred A. Knopf, a division of Random House, Inc. Copyright © 1949 by Editions Gallimard. Used by permission of Alfred A. Knopf and Sanford J. Greenburger.

496: Friedan, Betty, "The Problem Without A That Has No Name" from *The Feminine Mystique*. Copyright © 1997, 1991, 1974, 1963 by Betty Friedan. Used with permission of Curtis Brown Ltd.

511: King, Martin Luther, "Letter from the Birmingham Jail" Copyright © 1963 Martin Luther King, Jr. Renewed © 1991 Coretta Scott King. Reprinted by arrangement with the Estate of Martin Luther King, Jr. c/o Writers House, as agent for the proprietor.

528: hooks, bell, "Feminism: A movement to end sexist oppression" from *Feminist Theory: From Margin to Center, 2/e*. Copyright © South End Press. Used with permission.

542: Rodriguez, Richard, "The Triad of Alexis de Tocqueville," and "Peter's Avocado," from *Brown: The Last Discovery of America*. Copyright © 2002 by Richard Rodriguez. Reprinted by permission Viking Penguin, a division of Penguin Group (USA) Inc. and Georges Borchardt, Inc., on behalf of the author.

552: Kincaid, Jamaica, "Girl" from *At the Bottom of the River*. Copyright © 1983 by Jamaica Kincaid. Reprinted by permission of Farrar, Straus & Giroux.

560: Barry, Dan and Carol Vogel, "Gulliani vows to cut subsidy over sick art," *New York Times*, 9/23/99. Copyright © 1999 New York Times Company, Inc. Used with permission.

590: Schapiro, Meyer, "The Introduction of Modern Art in America: The Armory Show" from *America in Crisis: Fourteen Crucial Episodes in American History*, edited by Daniel Aron. Copyright © 1952 Meyer Schapiro. Used with permission.

604: Sontag, Susan, "A Century of Cinema" *New York Times Magazine*, February 1996. Copyright © 1996 Susan Sontag. Reprinted by permission of The Wylie Agency, Inc.

612: Momaday, N. Scott, "The Arrow Maker" from *The Man Made of Words*. Copyright © 1997 by N. Scott Momaday. Reprinted by permission of St. Martin's Press.

618: Cisneros, Sandra, "Little Miracles/Kept Promises" from *Woman Hollering Creek*. Copyright © Sandra Cisneros. Reprinted by permission of Susan Bergholz Agency, on behalf of the author.

631: Terkel, Studs, "Will the Circle be Unbroken" from *Will the Circle Be Unbroken*. Copyright © 2001 Studs Terkel. Reprinted with permission from The New Press.

650: Woolf, Virginia, "The Death of a Moth" from *The Death of a Moth and Other Essays*. Copyright 1942 by Harcourt, Inc. and renewed © 1970 by Marjorie T. Parsons, Executrix. Reprinted by permission of Harcourt, Inc. and The Society of Authors.

655: Dickinson, Emily, "The last night that she lived" and "because I could not stop for death" reprinted by permission of publishers and the Trustees of Amherst College from *The Poems of Emily Dickinson*, edited by Thomas H. Johnson, Cambridge, Mass." The Belknap Press of Harvard University Press. Copyright © 1951, 1955, 1979, 1983 by the President and Fellows of Harvard College.

655: Thomas, Dylan, "Do not go gentle into that good night" from *The Poems of Dylan Thomas*. Copyright © 1952 by Dylan Thomas. Reprinted by permission of New Directions Publishing Corp.

655: Sexton, Anne, "Imitations of Drowning" from *Live or Die*. Copyright © 1966 by Anne Sexton. Reprinted by permission of SLL/Sterling Lord Literistic, Inc.

655: Rossi, Angelina, "Mothers and Sons" from *Will the Circle be Unbroken*. Copyright © 2001 Studs Terkel. Reprinted with permission from The New Press.

655: Rundle, Rick, "The Stranger" from *Will the Circle Be Unbroken*. Copyright © 2001 Studs Terkel. Reprinted with permission from The New Press.

655: Cortez, Carlos, "The Day of the Dead" from *Will the Circle be Unbroken*. Copyright © 2001 Studs Terkel. Reprinted with permission from The New Press.

677: Kubler Ross, Elizabeth, "On the Fear of Death" from *On Death and Dying*. Reprinted with permission of Scribner, an imprint of Simon & Schuster Adult Publishing Group. Copyright © 1969 by Elisabeth Kubler-Ross. Copyright renewed © 1997 by Elisabeth Kubler-Ross. All rights reserved.

685: Mishima, Yukio, from *The Way of the Samurai*, translated by Kathryn Sparling, Basic Books, 1977.

693: Silko, Leslie Marmon, "From a High, Arid Plateau in New Mexico: Death among the Pueblo People." First published in *Antaeus*, No. 57, Autumn 1986. Copyright © 1986 Leslie Marmon Silko. Used by permission of The Wylie Agency.

696: Nuland, Sherwin B., "Suicide and Euthanasia" from *How We Die*. Copyright © 1994 by Sherwin B. Nuland. Used by permission of Alfred A. Knopf, a division of Random House, Inc.

Photos

Page 12: © Karen Kasmauski/National Geographic Image Collection; **15**: © 2001 National Geographic Society. All rights reserved.; **16, 19**: Karen Kasmauski/National Geographic Image Collection; **41**: © Lewis W. Hine/Getty Images; **142**: S. Meltzer/PhotoLink/Getty Images; **143**: © Nikreates/Alamy; **144**: © Royalty-Free/CORBIS; **159**: Sadleir-Black Collection of Gothic Novels, Special Collections, University of Virginia Library; **228**: © Robert Clark/Aurora Photos; **234, 235, 236, 238, 239, 240**: © Ritz Sino/RS Photos/The New York Times; **324**: © American Century Proprietary Holdings, Inc., successor in interest to American Century Services Corporation; **326**: © Dan Nelken; **411**: © David Hume Kennerly/Getty Images; **442**: © David Hume Kennerly/Getty Images; **555**: © FIONA HANSON/EMPICS/Landov; **607**: © MGM/Photofest; **608**: © Zenith International/Photofest; **610**: © Impéria/Photofest

Index